# The Abbey of Paisley

# A Paisley Collection

1.Jubilee of the Paisley Provident Co-operative Society Limited
*David Rowat* ISBN 0-902664-73-5

2. Saint Mirin: An account of Old Houses, Old Families and Olden Times in Paisley
*David Semple* ISBN 0-902664-75-1

3.The Paisley Shawl
*Matthew Blair* ISBN 0-902664-80-8

4. The Paisley Thread Industry
*Matthew Blair* ISBN 0-902664-91-3

5. The Abbey of Paisley
*J. Cameron Lees* ISBN 0-902664-86-7

6. The Lordship of Paisley
*William M. Metcalfe* ISBN 0-902664-88-3

7. A History of Paisley
*William M. Metcalfe* ISBN 0-902664-89-1

8. Poems and Songs and Correspondence of Robert Tannahill
*David Semple* ISBN 0-902664-90-5

Paisley Abbey. The Nave, Looking West.

# The Abbey Of Paisley

From its Foundation to its Dissolution

*with*

Notices of the Subsequent History of the Church,

*and*

An Appendix of Illustrative Documents

*by*

J. Cameron Lees, D.D.

*Minister of St. Giles, Edinburgh,*

*late of the First Charge of the Abbey Parish of Paisley*

1878

Glasgow

The Grimsay Press

2004

The Grimsay Press
an imprint of
Zeticula
57 St Vincent Crescent
Glasgow
G3 8NQ

http://www.thegrimsaypress.co.uk
admin@thegrimsaypress.co.uk

Transferred to digital printing in 2004



First published in Great Britain by Alexander Gardner, Paisley, as part of the New Club Series in 1878.

**ISBN 0 902664 86 7**

Reproduced from the copy in the
Library of the University of Paisley, Scotland

TO

HER MAJESTY

The Queen,

REPRESENTATIVE OF THE ILLUSTRIOUS FAMILY BY WHOM

THE ABBEY OF PAISLEY

WAS FOUNDED,

THIS STORY OF ITS VARYING FORTUNES

IS, BY GRACIOUS PERMISSION,

Dedicated,

WITH THE DEEPEST FEELINGS OF LOYALTY AND DEVOTION.

# PREFACE.

THIS book is an attempt to throw into narrative form all that is known of the Abbey of Paisley—a building with many great associations. It has been well said that "it is impossible not to view with a reverential feeling the church which was founded by the first progenitor, and which contains the ashes of the earlier generations of that great family of the Stewarts, which, with all their failings, have furnished to Scotland and to England the most tragic elements of the history of the two Kingdoms, and through which the present royal family of England claim their inheritance of the Imperial Crown."* It will be seen by the reader that the author has had to traverse nearly the whole civil and ecclesiastical history of Scotland, and in going over so extensive a field, it is probable that errors have found their way into his book. It has not been from want of personal research if correctness in matters of fact has not been always attained.

Various sketches of the history of Paisley Abbey have from time to time been published, but nothing has been done in the way of rendering available to the general reader the facts contained in the Register of the Monastery, and the many side lights that volume casts upon the life and economy of a Scottish Abbey in the middle ages. There are many notices of the abbots of Paisley in the State Papers of the Record Office and the Vatican MSS. in the British Museum, which are here given for the first time. The author has been able to discover the names of abbots hitherto unknown, and though the list which he gives of the rulers of the

* The Dean of Westminster.

monastery is not perfect, it is more complete than any yet published. The life of the Paisley Saint, S. Mirin, has never been given fully before, and the episode of King Robert Bruce's absolution by the Abbot of Paisley, here narrated, is not without a certain interest. The Rental Book of the Abbey, which is printed for the first time from the original MS. in the Advocates' Library, Edinburgh, will give the reader a view of the management of the estates of the Church; and the ecclesiastical notices subsequent to the dissolution of the Monastery, drawn mainly from unpublished records, may help him in some measure to understand the curious alternations of Scottish Church history.

This work has been composed amid the many distractions and cares of a large parish, but the writer will be amply rewarded if the publication of this book, by shewing how closely the Abbey is associated with the history of Scotland, promotes in any way the restoration of the building. He wishes he could venture to hope that it might lead those to whom the care of the Abbey has been committed, to take a personal interest in it, as a most sacred trust.*

The author has to make grateful acknowledgments to many archæologists and others who have most kindly helped him with their counsel and advice. Among these he cannot but mention—David Laing, Esq., of the Signet Library, the friend of all students of Scottish Antiquities; the Very Rev. Dr. Reeves, Dean of Armagh; John Hill Burton, Esq., Historiographer of Scotland; the late lamented Dr. Stuart, Edinburgh; Thomas Dickson, Esq., of the Register Office there; M. Bruel, Archiviste Pub-

* The Abbey is in the keeping of the heritors or landed proprietors of the parish. They have almost entirely committed it to the care of what are called in Scotland factors, a class of persons who are not fit to have charge of a Gothic building. During my incumbency of eighteen years, I have rarely seen the larger heritors themselves present at any of their meetings. I regard it as a great misfortune that the Abbey, like the Cathedral of Glasgow, and some other Scottish ecclesiastical buildings, is not in the custody of the Crown. £14,000 would restore the whole building, but every obstacle to doing so has been thrown in the way, by the choir being allowed to be used as a common burying-ground, and by the erection of some hideous monuments.

lic of France; A. B. M'Grigor, Esq., LL.D., Dean of Faculty in the University Glasgow, to whose research the author is indebted for the interesting notes on the absolution of the Bruce; David Murray, Esq., Glasgow, who has furnished an account of the Black Book of Paisley; the Rev. Mr. Chisholm, C.C., Johnstone, an accomplished clergyman, whose knowledge of mediæval literature has always been available; David Semple, Esq., F.S.A., Paisley, and the Rev. J. S. Wilson, New Abbey, Dumfries. To the first of the two last-named gentlemen Paisley owes a great deal, for he has brought to light much of its ancient history; the other has long taken a tender care of the beautiful ruin of Sweetheart Abbey in his own parish, and is an enthusiastic student of monastic lore.

While the sheets of this book are passing through the press, the writer has received notice of his appointment to another charge.† He is not without hope that this work may be accepted as a token of his regard for many in Paisley of all classes and sects, with whom he has been long closely associated, and may perhaps lead his former neighbours to take a deeper interest than ever in the noble building which is the great glory of their town.

† St. Giles, Edinburgh.

# CONTENTS.


## CHAPTER I.

THE SCOTCH MONASTERIES. PAGES.

Paisley Abbey—One of the Great Monasteries of Scotland—Sketch of these—Their Architecture—Their Revenues—Their Position in the Country—Their Destruction. . . . . . . . . . . . 1— 6

## CHAPTER II.

MONASTIC LIFE.

Popular Idea of a Scotch Monk—The Inmates of a Monastery—The Abbot—The Prior—Other Officials—Religious Services—Fare of the Monks—Daily Life of a Convent. . . . . . . . . . . 7—17

## CHAPTER III.

CLUNAIC BENEDICTINES.

St. Benedict—His Rules for a Monastic Life—The Abbey of Clugny—Its Dependencies — Clunaic Monks — Their Rule — Their Discipline — Their Charity—Their Love of Literature and Study of Scripture. . . . . 18—24

## CHAPTER IV.

THE FOUNDING OF THE MONASTERY.

Paisley Abbey a Memorial of the Stewarts—The Origin of this Family—Walter, Son of Alan—The Shropshire Colonist—His Settlement in Renfrewshire—Founds a Monastery at Paisley—Brings Monks from Wenlock—Obtains the Sanction of the Abbot of Clugny—Endows the Convent with Lands and Churches—The Foundation Charters—Detail of Privileges—Paisley. . . . . . . . . . . . 25—35

## CHAPTER V.

ST. MIRIN AND THE PATRON SAINTS.

St. James—St. Milburga—St Mirinus—Legend of St. Milburga, the Shropshire Saint—Early Church in Paisley Dedicated to St. Mirin—His Life—Aberdeen Breviary—Mirin Leaves Ireland—A Companion of Columbanus, the Apostle of Gaul—Probably an Abbot—Notices of him throughout Scotland—Office for his day—Prayer and Lessons. . . . . . 36—44

## CHAPTER VI.

THE PRIORY—1164—1248.

Osbert First Prior of the Monastery—Benefactors of the House—Eschina of Molla—Gifts of Churches—Wealthy Men Assuming the Monastic Habit—Henry De St. Martin—Highland Benefactors—Reginald, the Son of Somerled, Lord of the Isles—The Followers of the Stewart—Their Generosity—State of the Country and its Inhabitants—Death of Walter, the Founder—His Burial in the Priory. . . . . . . . 45—53

## CHAPTER VII.

THE ABBEY—1200—1248.

The Monastery a Priory in the Beginning of Thirteenth Century—The Second Stewart—His Benefactions—Churches in Bute—St. Blane—Walter, the Third Stewart—His Gifts—Transference of the Lands and Property of the Monastery of Dalmulin to Paisley—Reservations of Privileges by the Stewarts—The Rights of the Chase—The Forest of Fereneze—Negotiations with Clugny for raising the Convent to an Abbey—Licence to Elect an Abbot given from Rome and Clugny—William, First Abbot of Paisley—His Defence of the Rights of the Convent—Goes to Rome—Dispute about Lands in Dumbartonshire—The Contumacious Rector of Kilpatrick—Defies Abbot William—Is Summoned before Papal Delegates and Obliged to Yield—Gilbert, Son of Samuel of Renfrew, a Despoiler of the Church—Is Excommunicated—Abbot William an Able Ruler. . . . . . 54—63

## CHAPTER VIII.

THE PROSPEROUS TIMES OF ALEXANDER III.—1248—1286.

Life of the Abbey in this Prosperous Period—Last Notice of Abbot William—His Enrichment of the Abbey—Curious Transaction in regard to Crosraguel—Attempt to Evade the Erection of a Cell at that place—The Abbot Compelled to Build a Monastery there by Earl Duncan of Carrick—Death and Burial of Walter the Stewart—His Son, Alexander—Encloses a Park for Deer—Goes on a Pilgrimage to St. James of Compestella—Comes to Paisley for the Benediction of the Abbot—His Valour at the Battle of Largs—Connection between the Abbey and Highland Proprietors—Incumbents of the Highland Parishes—Singular Payment by the Vicar of one of them—The Comfortable Estate of the Abbey at this Period—Money-lending—Boiamund of Vicci—Rental of Abbey in his Roll—The Great Bull of Pope Clement IV.—Confirms the Privileges of the House—Enumerates its Possessions—Defines its Rights—Excommunicates those who Infringe them—Death of Alexander the Stewart. . . . . . . . . . . . 64—77

## CHAPTER IX.

THE INTERREGNUM—JOHN BALIOL—1286—1292.

Death of Alexander III.—The Calamities which Followed that Event—The Abbey Shares in the Hardships of the Time—Few Gifts Bestowed—Privileges much Restricted—James, the Stewart, Prominent in all the Intrigues of the Time—Proposed Marriage of the Maid of Norway—Parliament at Brigham—The Abbot of Paisley Present—Subjugation of Scotland by the English King—Walter, Abbot of Paisley, Swears Fealty to him—Humiliation of the Abbot at Berwick—Obliged to Pay Certain Debts to Monastery of Sempringham—Other Troubles—Dispute regarding Lands in Kylpatrick—Robert Wishart, Bishop of Glasgow, takes part with the Abbot—Robert Reddihow and his Wife Attempt to Drag the latter before the Court of the Earl of Lennox—The Bishop Excommunicates them and All Aiding and Abetting them—Struggle Between the Secular and Spiritual Power—The Abbey Visited by a Ghost—Tale from the "Chronicle of Lanercost." . 78—88

## CHAPTER X.

WALLACE AND BRUCE—1297—1329.

Sir William Wallace—A Vassal of the Stewart—A Parishioner of the Abbey—Probably received his Education there—The Monks take the Patriotic Side—Disappearance of the English St. Milburga from the Records — The Stewart, their Patron, Involved in the Troubles of the Country—Sufferings of the Monks—The Abbey Burnt by the English—Abbot Roger Buys a House in Glasgow, to which the Monks probably Remove—The *Diram Gueram*—Murder of Comyn by Robert Bruce—Latter seeks Absolution from the Pope—Commission by the Pope's Penetentiary to the Abbot to Absolve Bruce and appoint him Penance—Death of James the Stewart—His Son, Walter, at Bannockburn—Marries Marjory, daughter of King Robert—Death of Marjory, and Burial in Abbey—Tradition regarding her Death—Walter bestows the Church of Largs on the Convent for her soul—He Dies at Bathgate, is carried to Paisley, and Interred there—Succeeded by Robert, his Son. . . . . . . . . . . . 88—100

## CHAPTER XI.

ACCESSION OF THE STEWARTS—1329—1370.

Abbot and Convent seek to repair their dilapidated fortunes—Gift of Three Churches by Brother Andrew, "Minister of Argyle"—Gift from John Lindsay, Bishop of Glasgow, towards Rebuilding the Church—Robert De Caral receives one of the Abbey Churches from the Pope—Barratry—Concession by Earl Malcolm of Lennox—Privilege of a Gallows—Regency of Randolph—Abbot John petitions the Pope for Right to Wear Mitre and Ring—Granted in Bull from Avignon—Abbey again in Difficulties—Edward Baliol keeps Christmas at Renfrew—Confirmation of Lands by Robert, the Stewart—Privileges of the Convent Invaded by the Bishop of Argyle—The Abbot appeals for Protection to the Conservators of the Privileges of the Clunaic Order—They deal summarily with the Bishop—His Contumacy—Settlement of the Dispute—Abbot at a Parliament at Perth—Robert, the Stewart, becomes King of Scotland—Abbey under Royal Patronage. . 101—109

## CHAPTER XII.

ROYAL PATRONAGE—1370—1405.

Abbey begins a new course of Prosperity—Reviving activity of the Community exemplified—The Abbot exercises Discipline, and holds a Visitation at Crosraguel—Cites Abbot Roger of that Monastery, and Relieves him of his Office—Enters upon a Contention with the Canons of Sempringham and their Procurators—Reginald and Sir W. More of Abercorn—The latter makes a Raid upon the Monastery—Abbot gives a pitiful account of it to the Conservators of the Privileges of his Order—King Robert II. and his Son, John, come to the Relief of the Monks—The King erects their Lands of Lennox into a Barony—Abbot John de Lithgw—Refuses to have his Election Confirmed by the Bishop of Glasgow, or to seek his Blessing—Constant Litigations, in which the Abbot was Involved—John of Auchinleck Severely Fined for Castrating a Monk—Death of King Robert II.—Accession of his Son John by the title of Robert III.—A Good Friend to the Abbey—Erects their Lands in Ayr, Peebles, and Roxburgh into a Barony—Falling-off of Benefactions—The Last of the Endowments—Sorrows of the King—His Death, and Burial in the Abbey—The Epitaph he desired for his Tomb—*Vanitas Vanitatum*. . . . . . . . . . . . 110—121

## CHAPTER XIII.

RESTORATION—1405—1459.

The Abbot and Convent Excommunicated, and Appeal to the Pope, who absolves them—William De Chishelme colleague to Abbot Lithgw—Thomas Morwe succeeds him—Receives Safe-Conducts to go to England—King James I. seeks to Reform the Church—His Letters to the Benedictine Monasteries—The Abbey of Paisley in need of his admonition—Relaxation of Discipline—Death of John De Lithgw—Abbot T. Morwe at a General Council—Richard De Bodwell Abbot—Is promoted to Dunfermline, and succeeded by Thomas De Tervas—Energy of the New Ruler—Revives Discipline—King James I. confers great privileges on the Abbot—Gives him exclusive jurisdiction over his tenants—Power of Repledging—Right to sell Wine and keep tavern within the Monastery—Abbot Tervas goes abroad, and brings home adornments for the Church—His Death and Character. . . 122—131

## CHAPTER XIV.

ABBOTS HENRY CRICHTON AND GEORGE SHAW—1459—1498.

Curious transaction at the death of Thomas Tervas—Henry Crichton made Commendator of Paisley on condition of paying a Pension to the Cardinal of St. Mark's, Venice—Fails to make Payment, and is Degraded from his Office—Patrick Grahame, Bishop of St. Andrews, made Commendator—Crichton makes his peace with the Roman authorities, and is made Abbot—His ability as a Statesman and Ecclesiastic—Curious Dispute with a Highland Chieftain—Crichton promoted to Dunfermline—Stir occasioned by the latter event—The King claims the appointment of all Abbots—Injury done to the Church by this exercise of Royal patronage—Decay of order and good Government—George Shaw made Abbot of Paisley—James II., his good friend, gives the Convent new privileges—Attempted Visitation of the Abbey by the Dean of Rutherglen—Scene at the Gate—Visit of the King to the Abbey and the shrine of St. Mirin—His Gifts to the Masons engaged in adding to the buildings—The works carried on by the Abbot—His kindness to the Monks—Is made Lord High Treasurer of Scotland—Becomes a Pensioner of the Abbey, and is succeeded by his nephew, Robert Shaw, vicar of Munkton—Character of Abbot George. . . . . . . , . 132—145

## CHAPTER XV.

THE BURGH.

Origin of Burghs—Their Privileges—The Village of Paisley—Jealousy of the Burgh of Renfrew—Exactions of the latter—Abbot Shaw seeks to have Paisley made a Burgh—Leave granted by the Pope and by King James IV.—New Burgh not viewed with much favour by neighbouring towns—Incursion of Renfrew Men—They throw down the Cross of the New Burgh—Abbot brings them into Court, and is Victorious—Charter of the Liberty of the Burgh of Paisley, and Erection of the same—Charter of the Abbot. . 146—158

## CHAPTER XVI.

MONASTIC ECONOMICS.

Management of the Abbey Lands—The Rental Book of the Abbots—The Monks as Landlords—Condition of their Tenantry—Their Revenues, whence derived—The Teinds of their Churches—"Kirklands"—Tacksmen of the Teinds—The Granges of the Abbey—Two Classes of Tenantry—*Steel bow*—Rents in kind—*Terra Dominice*—Revenues of the Kirklands—Licence to Marry given by the Abbot—No cases of Eviction—Thomas Hector, the Sculptor—Game Reservation—Revenue from *Annuals*—The Abbey Mills—Rate of Multure—Mill Dues—The *Angerem*—Fishings possessed by the Monks—The Orchard and Kale-yard—Fuel—Rules and Regulations laid down by the Abbot for his Tenants. . . . . . . 159—173

## CHAPTER XVII.

ABBOT ROBERT—1498—1525.

John, Earl of Ross, becomes a Monk of Paisley—His Troubled History and Unsuccessful Rebellion—Dies in the Abbey, and is Buried in the Choir—Benefactions to the Abbey by the Citizens of the New Burgh—Erection of Altars within the Abbey Church—Erection of Chapel to St. Mirin and St. Columba—James Crawford of Kilwynet, the Founder—The Endowment and Patrons of the Chapel—Dispute between the Abbot and the Bishop of Glasgow—Litigation with Sir John Ross of Halkhead—The King Visits the Abbey on a Pilgrimage to Whithorn—Is Entertained by the Abbot—Lord Sempil's Harper—Another Royal Visit—Gifts by the King and Queen—Flodden—Abbot Robert becomes a Politician—Reference to him by Dr.

Magnus, the English Ambassador—The Earls of Angus and Lennox threaten to keep Christmas at the Abbey—Letter to them by Dr. Magnus, Expostulating—The Invasion averted—Abbot wishes to be made Bishop of Moray—The Queen applies in his behalf to the Pope—Cardinal Wolsey supports his application successfully—Abbot Transferred to Moray—John Hamilton, son of the Earl of Arran, made Abbot of Paisley—Scandal of the Appointment. . . . . . . . . . . . . 174—185

## CHAPTER XVIII.

ABBOT HAMILTON—1525—1547.

The Youthful Abbot—Paisley a Place of Pilgrimage—Progress of the Reformed Doctrine—The Abbot leaves Scotland for France—Remains Abroad Three Years—His Home-coming watched with interest—Is expected to take part with the Reformers—Their Disappointment—The Abbot becomes the Champion of the Church—Sir Ralph Sadler's Notice of him—Receives high honour in Church and State—Made Bishop of Dunkeld—Often in Paisley at this period—Appoints the Master of Sempill Bailie of the Monastery—The Abbey Threatened by the Reformers—Immorality of the Abbot—Death of Cardinal Beaton—The Abbot made Archbishop of St. Andrews—Retains the Abbey along with his See. . . . . . . . . . 186—193

## CHAPTER XIX.

DISSOLUTION OF THE MONASTERY—1547—1571.

The Archbishop—His Endeavours to Reform Abuses and Encourage Learning among the Clergy—Resigns the Abbey to Claud Hamilton, his Nephew—The Pope Sanctions the Appointment—Curious Transaction—The Archbishop still holds the Government—In Conflict with the Reformers—Their First Visit to the Abbey—The Reformation Triumphant—Penalties imposed on the Catholics—Attitude of the Archbishop—His Letter to John Knox—Has his Livings taken from him—Flies to Paisley for Refuge—Overthrow and Burning of the Monastery—People of Paisley Loyal to the Old Faith—Preachers of the New Doctrine meet with a poor reception at Paisley—The Archbishop says Mass at Paisley—Is brought before the Court of Session—The Charge against him—Escapes Punishment through the Influence of Queen Mary—Baptises her Son at Holyrood—Is the leading spirit in the Faction of the Hamiltons—At the Battle of Langside—The Property of the Abbey given to Lord Sempill—The Archbishop comes back to Paisley and takes Possession of the Monastery—It is Besieged and taken by Lord Lennox—The Archbishop Retreats to Dumbarton Castle, which was Captured by the Regent—Trial of the Archbishop at Stirling—The Evidence against him—Black John—The Archbishop Condemned and Executed—Lines affixed to the Gallows—His probable Burial at Paisley—Monument in the Church there. . . . . . . . . . . . 194—205

## CHAPTER XX.

REMAINS.

More of the Abbey left standing than was the case with other Scotch Monasteries—The Buildings remaining—Their Extent—The Western Doorway—The Windows—The Nave—Triforium and Clerestory—Corbels—The Cloister Court—The Chapel of St. Mirin—Singular Sculptures, representing the History of the Saint—Burying-place of the Family of Abercorn—The *Sounding Aisle*—The Transept and Choir—Probable Arrangement of the Monastic Buildings—The Burying-Ground—Monuments in the Church—The Cathcart Pillar, and Tradition connected with it—Supposed Tomb of Marjory Bruce—John Morow, the Architect—Inscription in Melrose Abbey—Other Remains—The Seal of the Abbey—The Black Book of Paisley—The Rental Book—The Chartularies. . . . . . . . 206—226

## CHAPTER XXI.

THE COMMENDATOR.

The Causes which led to the Reformation—Illustrated by the History of the Abbey—The Character of the Old Church of Scotland—Usurpation of Patronage by the Crown—Decay of Discipline—The Bribe offered to poor Proprietors—Scandalous Gifts of Church Property—Revenues of Paisley at the Dissolution—Number of Monks at that time living in the Abbey—Hardships they endured—A small portion of the Revenues go to Erect a Grammar School in Paisley—Claud Hamilton's Conduct after the Death of his Uncle—Is Forfeited—Attacks Lord Sempill, who had Paisley *in Commendam*—The Treaty of Perth—Claud Hamilton put in Possession of Paisley—The Abbey Besieged by the Earl of Argyle—Lord Claud lives at Paisley—Marries Daughter of Lord Seton—Again Forfeited—Flies to England—Is again Restored to all his Ancestral Rights—Is made Lord Paisley, and his eldest son created Earl of Abercorn—Royal Visits to the Place of Paisley—Grand Reception of King James VI. by the Earl of Abercorn—Death of Lord Claud—The last link between us and the Monastery—Description of the Abbey in the days of its grandeur by the Bishop of Ross. . . . 227—238

## CHAPTER XXII.

THE NEW ORDER.

Paisley continues Hostile to Protestantism—Church doors *steyked* against Preachers—Remonstrance of the Kirk—The First Protestant Minister, Patrick Adamson—Unable to live at Paisley—Is Succeeded by Andrew Polwart—He gives up the place in despair—Stipends of the Ministers—The *Reader*—His Duties—Thomas Smeaton becomes Minister—His Character—Andrew Knox succeeds him—Severity of his Dealings with the Catholics—Old Lady Claud Hamilton is driven to despair, and Petitions the King—"Papistrie" put down with a strong hand—Efforts of the Minister supported by the Magistrates—He is appointed by the Presbytery to Watch the

Proceedings of Roman Catholics within their bounds—Arrests George Ker, who is Negotiating with Philip of Spain—Falls himself into the grasp of the law—Is Suspended by the Presbytery—Reproved after a very curious ceremony—Is appointed Bishop of the Isles—Paisley "a very nest of Papists." 239—247

CHAPTER XXIII.

DISCIPLINE.

Meetings of Presbytery in the Abbey—Curious Scenes at this Conclave—Manner in which their Business was Conducted—"Taking the Sacrament" insisted on—Hard times for the Catholics—A Paisley Parishioner cited for Non-attendance—Sentence of Excommunication—Excommunicated Persons Craving to be Restored—Points of Romish Doctrine required to be abjured—Penance inflicted upon Immoral Persons—Punishment for Profanation of the Sabbath—Sunday Sports—Keeping a Green—Pipers—Observance of Christmas—Charming—Sale of Quack Medicines—The people under an iron rule—Government by Ecclesiastics. . . . . . . . 248—261

CHAPTER XXIV.

THE ABERCORNS AND THE KIRK.

Claud Hamilton Succeeded by his Grandson—Dame Marion Boyd, Countess of Abercorn, his Mother, manages the Youth's affairs during his Minority—A Zealous Adherent of the Old Faith—Boyd of Trochrigg invited to become Minister of Paisley—Inducted notwithstanding the Opposition of the Countess—Receives Violent Treatment from her and her son, the Master of Paisley—Mr. Boyd Resigns the Charge—The Presbytery take up the Case of Lady Abercorn as a "suspected Papist"—She and her Servants dealt with—The Earl of Abercorn declares himself a Catholic—Process in the Presbytery against the Earl, his Mother, and Household—They are Excommunicated—The Earl Flies the Country—The Countess is cast into Prison in Edinburgh—After a long imprisonment obtains leave to go to Paisley—Dies there of *squalor carceris*—Odious Ecclesiastical Persecution. . . . . . 262—282

CHAPTER XXV.

THE SERVICE BOOK.

Early Scotch Episcopacy—Its Ritual—Book of Common Order—Mr. John Crichton, Minister of Paisley—Introduction of a New Liturgy—Curious "Supplication" Adopted by the Council regarding the Service Book—Commotion throughout Scotland—Mr. Crichton introduces Innovations into his Church—Is Complained against to the Presbytery—The Singular Charges brought against him—His case is Referred to the Assembly at Glasgow—Fasting and Prayer Meeting of the Assembly—Deposition of Mr. Crichton—The Covenant Confirmed. . . . . . . . . . 282—295

## CHAPTER XXVI.

THE COVENANT.

Paisley under the Rule of the Covenant—Founding of the Second Charge—Mr. Calvert and Mr. Dunlop, Ministers—"A Holy Groan"—Character of Mr. Dunlop—The Earl of Abercorn looked after—Ordered to Transport himself out of the Kingdom—Sells the Paisley Estates to Lord Dundonald—Strict Rule of the Covenanting Ministers—The Guidwife of Fergualie—Suspected as a Papist—Summoned—Admonished—Catechised—Dragged before the Presbytery—Is Ordered to Attend Church—Pleads Ill Health—Threatened with Excommunication—Carried to Church in her Bed—Part taken by the Presbytery in the Troubles of the Time—Battle of Philiphaugh—Covenanting Intolerance—Cromwell in Scotland—Puritan Officers at Paisley—The Presbytery Invaded—First Exhibition of Paisley Radicalism—Dispute between the Town and the Dundonalds—King Charles II. Proclaimed at Paisley—Joy of the Ministers—Induction of Mr. Stirling—Induction Supper paid from the "Mortcloth Money." . . . . . . . 296—309

## CHAPTER XXVII.

THE CURATES.

Intolerant Spirit of both Covenanters and Episcopalians—Episcopal Government Established—Abbey Ministers Resign—The Curate of Paisley—Hardships experienced by the Ministers—Fate of Mr. Dunlop and Mr. Stirling—A Presbytery Established in Paisley by order of the Archbishop—Minutes of this Court—Character of the Curates—Their Discipline—Refractory Elders—Delinquents proceeded against—Enquiry after "rebels"—Conventicles—The Indulgence—The Curate of Paisley paid to Retire—Mr. Ramsay—His Method of Rebuke—Visit of Archbishop Leighton to Paisley—Holds a Conference with the Non-Conforming Ministers—Speech of the Archbishop—Reply of Mr. Baird, the Second Minister—Failure of the Conference—Stricter Measures against the Covenanters—The Ministers of the Abbey Deprived—Ritual of the Episcopalians—Two Men Executed at Paisley—Landing of King William—Rabbling of the Curates. . . . . . 310—324

## CHAPTER XXVIII.

WITCHCRAFT.

Triumph of Presbytery—Difficulty in Filling Parishes—An Old Minister—Mr. Blackwell and Mr. Brown—Zeal of the former in Persecuting Witches—Indictment against a "Charmer"—Great "Manifestation of Satan's Power"—Sermon in the Abbey before Commissioners for Trying Witches—Diabolical Events at Kilmalcolm—Mr. Blackwell's Dealing with the Authorities—Deplorable Case of Christian Shaw—The Presbytery betake themselves to Fasting and Prayer—Three Confessants procured—Manifestoes by the Ministers—Utterances of Mr. Blackwell in the Abbey—Trial of the Witches—The Devil "a black grim man"—Seven Witches found Guilty—Waited on to the Fire by the Ministers—Mr. Blackwell goes to Aberdeen—Discipline of the Kirk Session—Extracts from their Minutes. . . . . . . 325—335

## CHAPTER XXIX.

CONCLUDING NOTICES.

**State of the Buildings—They fall into Disrepair—Abbey Gardens Feued—Walls and Buildings Sold—Lord Dundonald Sells the Property to the Earl of Abercorn—Disgraceful State of the Church—Brawling—Heritors' purpose to take down the building, and Erect a "commodious Kirk"—Abbey saved from Demolition by Dr. Boog—Restored to a state of decency—Allowed again to fall into disrepair by the Heritors—Restoration of 1862—Energy of Rev. Mr. Wilson—Successful Appeal to the Public—Present State of the Abbey—Hopes for the Future—Finis.** . . . . . . 336—340

---

## APPENDICES.

---

| | | PAGES. |
|---|---|---|
| A. | Priors, Abbots, and Commendators of the Monastery of Saint James and Saint Mirin of Paisley, . . . . . . . . . | i—iv. |
| B. | **St. Mirinus—September 15,** . . . . . . . . | iv—vi. |
| C. | **Extract from Breviarum Aberdonense,** . . . . . . | vi—vii. |
| D. | **Notices in Connection with Paisley Abbey of Members of the Wallace Family,** . . . . . . . . . . | vii—viii. |
| E. | **Notes on a Commission Professing to have been issued to Absolve Robert the Bruce,** . . . . . . . . . | viii—xx. |
| F. | **State Papers referring to the Abbey and Abbots of Paisley,** . . . | xx—xxxviii. |
| G. | **Bulls referring to the Abbey of Paisley, from the Vatican MSS. in British Museum,** . . . . . . . . . . . | xxxviii—xlvii. |
| H. | **Notes on Replegiation as Exercised in Scotland,** . . . . . | xlvii—xlix. |
| I. | **Notes referring to the Abbey from the Acts of Parliaments of Scotland,** . | xlix—liii. |
| J. | **Immorality of Abbot Hamilton,** . . . . . . . | liii—liv. |
| K. | **Assedation of Ye Kirks of Paslay and Loytwinzok to Mast Johne Steward for xix zeris,** . . . . . . . . . . | liv—lv. |
| L. | **Rental Book of The Abbey,** . . . . . . . . | lvi—clxxviii. |
| M. | **The Black Book of Paisley,** . . . . . . . . . | clxxix—clxxxii. |
| N. | **Bull of Pope Julius III. Conferring the Abbey *In Commendam* on Lord Claud Hamilton.—Dated 5th December, 1553,** . . . . . | clxxxiii—clxxxv. |

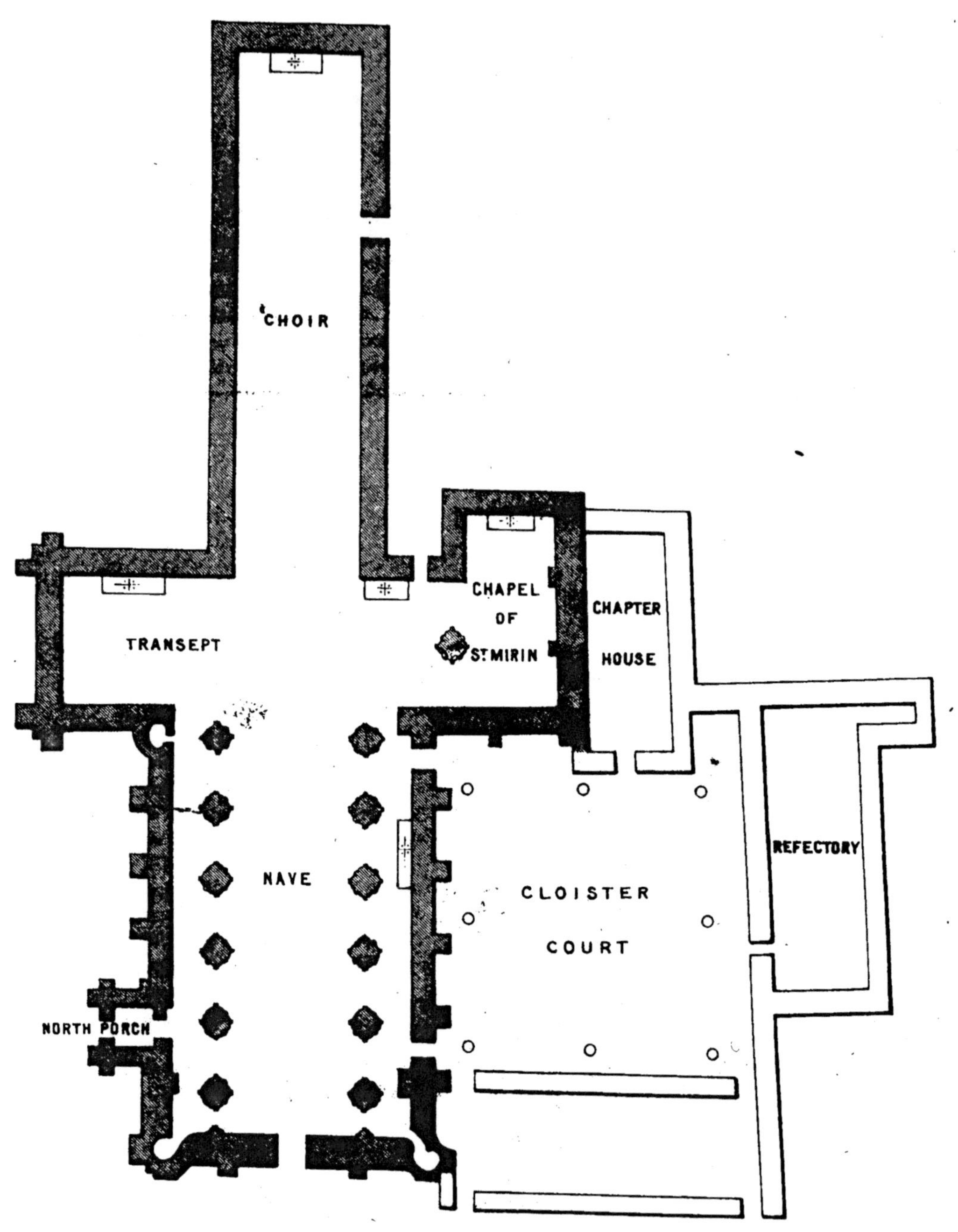


GROUND PLAN OF PAISLEY ABBEY.

*The part to the South of the Church not shaded has been destroyed.*

## CHAPTER I.

### The Scotch Monasteries.

I doe love these auncyent Abbayes.
We never tread within them but we set
Our foote upon some reverend historie.

IN the heart of the busy town of Paisley stands the Abbey, its venerable appearance contrasting most strangely with its surroundings. Many chimneys—so many that it seems impossible to count them—pour forth their smoke on every side of it; crowds of operatives jostle past it; heavily-laden carts cause its old walls to tremble; the whirr of machinery and the whistle of the railway engine break in upon its repose; while within a stone's throw of it flows the River Cart, the manifold defilements of which have passed into a proverb. But it is not difficult, even without being imaginative, to see how beautiful for situation was once the spot where the Abbey rose in all its unimpaired and stately grace. It stood on a fertile and perfectly level piece of ground, close by the Cart, then a pure mountain stream, which, after falling over some bold and picturesque rocks in the middle of its channel, moved quietly by the Abbey walls on its course to the Clyde. Divided from the Abbey by this stream, rose wooded slopes, undulating like waves of the sea till they reached the lofty ridge called the Braes of Gleniffer, from the summit of which the lay brother, as he herded his cattle or swine, could get views of the Argyleshire hills, the sharp peaks of Arran, and the huge form of Ben Lomond. To the north, on the other side of the Clyde, were the fertile glades of Kilpatrick, and, beyond, the Campsie range. Gardens and deer park girdled the Abbey round; few houses were near except the little village of dependants on the other side of the stream; and no sound beyond the precincts broke the solitude, save the wind as it roared through the beech forest, the bell of a distant chapel, or, on a calm evening, the chimes of the Cathedral of Saint Mungo, seven miles away. It was a well-chosen spot, answering in every way the requirements of the Benedictines, who, we are told, "preferred to build in an open position at the back of a wooded chain of hills." *

The Abbey of Paisley is one of those fragments of monastic architecture which are scattered throughout Scotland, and which, even in their most ruined state, are sufficient to carry the mind back to the splendours of an earlier day. The hand of time has been more gently laid on Paisley than on most of its sister abbeys,—but even the most ruined of these is full of suggestions of former grandeur, and within none of them can we "tread,"—so associated have they been with the public life of Scotland—

"but we set
Our foote upon some reverend historie."

None of them can, for extent and magnificence, compare with Fountains, or Glastonbury, or Saint Albans; but yet the line of Border Abbeys—Melrose, Dryburgh, Jedburgh, and Kelso, Arbroath—rearing its gaunt walls on the wild headland overlooking the German Ocean,—Lindores, on the lowlying shores of the Forth,—or the last founded of them all, lovely Sweetheart, embosomed in its wooded glen by the Solway, are certainly not without an interest and romance of their own, and for so poor a country as Scotland was in the olden time, were wonderfully great and powerful.

The Monastic system of Scotland in its last development was of foreign origin, reared upon the ruins of the ancient Celtic or Culdee Church. What that Church was, in doctrine and in ritual, it is impossible, with anything like certainty, to say. Every statement upon the

* Ecclesiastical Art in Germany during the Middle Ages, by W. Lübke.

subject has been eagerly questioned, either on the one hand by those who make out the early Church of Scotland to be Protestant in its creed, and even Presbyterian in its government, or, on the other hand, by those who hold that in no essential particular did it differ from the Church of Rome. In the time of Queen Margaret it had beyond all doubt, fallen into a state of decrepitude and disorder.* Its lands were in the possession of laymen, and its priesthood had become an hereditary caste, descending from father to son. It was the work of that Princess who brought to the Scottish throne the blood of the Anglo-Saxon kings, to plant among the people the seeds of a more energetic faith. The reformation which she began was earnestly carried on by her sons, and especially by her son David, who created in Scotland Bishopricks and Monasteries on English models, and filled them with English Churchmen. He founded himself no less than fifteen Monasteries, and so largely endowed them from the royal revenues, that it was not without reason one of his successors † termed him a "sair sanct for the crown." So great was his zeal as a Church reformer that a parallel has been drawn between him and John Knox. He wrought a change in ecclesiastical affairs, it has been said, "almost as great as that afterwards accomplished by Knox. He in effect built up that which, when it was in a state of decay, Knox pulled down. He drove out the now antiquated Culdees, and introduced prelates and priests. Knox cast out prelates and priests, and brought in Protestant preachers." ‡

The Monasteries of Scotland in their architecture closely resembled, in the first instance, those on the English side of the Border. They were built either in the Norman or first pointed styles; but after the War of Independence, many of them which had been destroyed were reconstructed upon French rather than English models. In their general plan there was little difference between them and houses of the same order in other parts of the world. The glory of the Monastery was its church, which was built in the form of a cross, and its erection was generally the work of many years—the choir or east end, where service was celebrated, being erected first—the transepts, or arms of the cross,

* *Quarterly Review*, Vol. 85—An article so valuable that it should certainly be reprinted.
† James I. ‡ Cunninghame's Ch. Hist., vol. I., p. 145.

and the nave or western portion, afterwards. At the extreme end of the church rose the high altar, resplendent in its decorations; but in different parts of the church other altars stood, where mass was said by priests specially allotted to them. Sometimes the church was used only by the inmates of the monastery, but often, as at Paisley, it was used as a parish church as well. The tithes of the parish went to its support; the parishioners were admitted at certain times, and had priests who specially ministered to them. To the south generally of the church were the monastic buildings, ranged round the four sides of a court having a plot of grass in the centre, and bordered by the arched-in cloisters. These various buildings were of various kinds, suited to the different wants and occupations of the inmates. There was the *refectory* or *dining-hall*—a long wainscotted apartment, with stone benches, an high table, and a desk on which lay a Bible, the Legends of the Saints, or some devotional work, from which one of the novices read during meals; it had an opening to the kitchen, through which the food was passed. The *chapter-house*,* an octagonal room, with a pillar in the centre supporting the roof, with rows of benches, one above another, a reading-desk, a seat for the Abbot higher than the others, and a crucifix to remind the monks during discipline that their sufferings were nothing compared with those of Christ. The *dormitory* or *dortor*, where the monks and novices slept. The *infirmary*, where the sick were tended. The *guest-hall*, having bed-rooms connected with it for strangers. *Parlours* or *locutories*, where the monks assembled at certain times for conversation when silence was enjoined in other places, and where the monastic schools were often held. A *scriptorium* or *writing-room*, where the students and transcribers sat silently at their work. The house of the Abbot stood apart. *Granges*, *granaries*, *kilns*, *dovecots*, and a *prison* were grouped round the main buildings, and a wall, often of great strength † for purposes of defence, and broken by only one gate, at which was the *porter's house*, surrounded the whole.

* A very fine specimen is at Glenluce, Wigtonshire.

† Some of these buildings in connection with Scotch monasteries are still standing. The Abbot's house is shown at Arbroath, and also at Crossraguel; and the convent wall, built of huge boulders of stone, still surrounds the ruined Abbey of Sweetheart, in Galloway.

The following pages will show how these great establishments were upheld, and from what sources their revenues were derived. The Scotch Monasteries were liberally endowed by the faithful up to the time of the War of Independence, after which gifts were bestowed with a less liberal hand, and the stream of benefactions was turned into other channels. Notwithstanding much that has been said it may be doubted whether they did not yield to the country, at least in their best days, a good return for the wealth bestowed on them. In Scotland they filled a position which no other known institution could have done. They furnished in the midst of distraction a refuge for many a quiet and studious spirit. While kings and nobles were fighting around them, their inmates fostered the arts of peace; they were the agriculturists and the schoolmasters of their time. In the scriptorium of the Monastery were written those chronicles without which most of the past history of Scotland would be a blank, and we would be as ignorant of our forefathers as we are of the progenitors of any African tribe. They provided for the poor and the helpless when no legal provision existed. The poverty-stricken wretch driven from the castle gate could find a sanctuary in the Abbey, and was certain to receive his dole of food from the almoner at the gate. In a wild country without inns they furnished a resting-place for the traveller—he was always sure of a welcome in the guest-hall, his supper and his bed. In Scotland the Abbots assisted largely in carrying on the affairs of the State. They and other churchmen were the only men who had the time and the ability. They sat in Parliament, and were treasurers, chamberlains, judges. Above all, the Monasteries were the great witnesses against feudal caste; "with them was neither high-born nor low-born, rich nor poor—the meanest serf entering there might become the lord of knights and vassals, the counsellors of kings and princes." This was especially true of those of Scotland—a country where feudalism reigned supreme.

The destruction of the Monasteries of Scotland was complete. Of the one hundred and twenty monasteries and twenty nunneries, not one is untouched—of some there is no trace remaining. In our time it has been the fashion to whitewash every historic evil-doer. Nero was a saint, Diocletian, a mild and merciful ruler. Judas himself was an earnest and too enthusiastic disciple. The excesses of the Scotch reformers have in like manner been palliated and explained away. It is said they merely purged the church of idolatrous images, but laid no hand upon the buildings themselves. These were ruined by others who came after them, and many of them fell to pieces through sheer decay.* There is much to be said on the other side, and there seems little occasion to excuse those for whom no excuse is necessary. The Reformers did the work given them to do; and if they did it roughly, it is, on many accounts not to be wondered at; but when, as at Paisley, they set fire to the buildings, it can hardly be maintained that their work was one of purification alone. Certainly others supplemented well the destruction they inaugurated. Melrose was turned into a prison, Arbroath and Sweetheart farmed out as a common quarry, Kelso became a jail.

In the story of the Paisley Abbey will be seen at work both the forces which raised the Scotch Monasteries to their height of prosperity, and those afterwards which wrought their terrible downfall. Whatever they in time became, they were worthy of all respect when in their prime. We may think of them with tenderness even when we see in their ruined cloisters the fruit of their inherent weakness.† Had they not been good at first, they would not have endured throughout centuries; and had they not had in them great elements of weakness they would not have come to so great a destruction; and if we are insensible to considerations like these, we may perhaps truly deserve the caustic words of Newman—"Not a man in Europe who talks bravely against the Church, but owes it to the Church that he can talk at all."‡

* Robertson in *Quarterly Review.* † See Kingsley's, The Roman and the Teuton, p. 263.
‡ Newman's Historical Sketches, p. 109.

# CHAPTER II.

## Monastic Life.

A life of prayer and fasting well may see
Deeper into the mysteries of heaven than thou, good brother.

*Tennyson's Harold.*

THE Scotch monk differed in no way from those anywhere else who belonged to the same order with himself, and a monk of Paisley, in his dress and the daily routine of his life, would resemble very closely, and in every particular of costume, one of Wenlock in England, or of La Charité in France. From the day of his entrance into the brotherhood to that of his death he went through the same unvarying round of duty and work, no matter in what part of the world his convent happened to be situated. We are therefore able to tell with considerable exactness what was the inner life of the Abbey to which these pages relate. We can in thought rebuild the ruined walls, and repeople the Monastery with the old figures, and even tell what they were doing on a particular day, and at a particular hour.

The popular idea of a monk in Scotland is derived from the satires and caricatures of the pre-Reformation times which still linger among the people. He is a jolly, burly man, with a jovial countenance and capacious stomach; bound, indeed, at times to pray, but more given to drinking heavy potations; a lover of strong ale and good wine, with a loud ringing laugh, oftener found in the buttery and cellar than on his knees and telling his beads. Sir Walter Scott has given us a truer idea of the brotherhood; but the typical monk with the multitude is Abbot Ambrose rather than Abbot Eustace. Perhaps the common Scotch people are not singular in their conception of the monastic life and of its duties. "Novelists," as it has been well said, "have given us many a good monk, and checkmated us with many a wicked one. In volume after volume we have had the murderous monk, the robber monk, the bibulous monk, the felonious monk, and the poisoning monk. We are apt to forget that the duties of the monastic life were very varied; that there was scope in the Abbey and in the Priory for intellects of all degrees, that there were as many sorts of employment within a monastery as there are in a modern factory, and that the monastic establishments were, as a rule, admirably governed and conducted in a business-like way."* The truth of this statement will be amply verified by any student of the annals of Paisley Abbey. He will see that there were within it many wise, skilful, and practical men, able to hold their own in all the conflicts and business of their time, but though I have enquired diligently, the only tradition I can find regarding them in the town they founded is that the Abbot, and occasionally the monks, used after dusk to cross the river Cart, and spend the evening in an humble pot-house with the bailies of the town,—the enticements of the pleasant society of these municipal dignitaries being sufficient to induce the holy Fathers to steal from the convent.†

First in the Monastery came the *Abbot*, wearing the dalmatic, representing the seamless coat of Christ;‡ on his head, the mitre, emblematic of Christ, the head of the Church; in his hand, the crozier or pastoral staff; on his finger, a ring, as Christ was the spouse of the Church; on his feet, sandals, because as the foot was neither covered nor naked so the Gospel should neither be altogether concealed nor rest altogether upon earthly benefits. His power was great. It extended over the whole convent, and according as he used it, the brotherhood was well regulated or out of "gud rewl." He was subject to none but the head of his order and to the Pope. His privileges were great also. He could confer the lesser orders—give the benediction in any of his churches—appoint and

* Fraser's Magazine, Dec. 1875, where there is a most admirable article on the daily life of a monk.

† This place of select conviviality stood at the foot of what is called St. Mirin's Street.

‡ For the facts referred to in this sketch I am indebted to Fosbroke's British Monachism, to Du Cange, Mabillon's Annales, and Foxe's English Monasteries, and to allusions to the monastic life scattered throughout tho Paisley Chartulary.

depose Priors of cells, and hold visitations once a year. Bells were rung in his honour as he passed by the churches belonging to his house; he rode on a mule sumptuously caparisoned with an immense retinue attending him. The noble children whom he educated served him as pages. He styled himself by "divine permission" or "the grace of God," and signed his christian name and the name of his house to all deeds. He had generally a seat in Parliament; visited persons of the highest distinction on terms of equality; and attended at the court of the sovereign, where he often held an office of State. If devoutly inclined he attended the services of the church, and when he did so, was received with great and imposing ceremonial. One instance will suffice. When he was pleased to sing vespers, the vestment and cope for his use, water in silver basin, towels, the comb, mitre, gloves, and staff were placed in the vestry. The Abbot then combed his hair and washed his hands, clothed himself with alb, robe, mitre, and gloves, and assumed the ring and crosier, his chaplains humbly attending. Upon his being robed, all the bells were rung, and entering the upper choir, preceded by the chanters and prior, robed for the occasion, he went to his stall. At the beginning of the first Psalm, a senior, kissing the Abbot's hand, took the crosier and laid it near him, and this ceremony of kissing his hand was always used on receiving anything from him, or delivering anything to him. When he was seated a chaplain was to place a towel across his bosom, and always when he was in pontificals. When the psalms were finished he rose and took the censer from a senior, and his chaplains attended him with the Gospel and the lantern; he then said the Gospel with his mitre, as was always the custom. If we rehabilitate the ruined choir, and place either Abbot William or Lithgow, of whom we shall hear anon, as the central figure in this description of ecclesiastical pomp, with chaplains, and chanters, and prostrate monks, we have brought before us a scene of the past which must often have occurred exactly as we have now described it.

In our pages we shall have to relate the story of abbots both good and bad, of abbots careless and abbots strict, of some who squandered property and some who carefully husbanded it. Of one it is especially said in the loving record of his death, that he was "ane richt gude man." What was the monkish idea of a good abbot we learn from the description of an Abbot Ralph, in the chronicle of another Abbey, which, in all probability, would have applied to Abbot Tervas, of whom the eulogy above mentioned was written, and to others of his brethren in the abbacy of Paisley: "Though he continually governed those who were under his authority, yet he himself was subservient to rules, and commanded no one as a master. He sustained the infirmities of others, and called them forth to strength. His acts corresponded with what he taught. His example preceded his doctrine. He inculcated a prompt attendance on divine service, and, supporting his aged limbs upon his staff, preceded his young men to it. Ever first in the choir, he was ever last to quit it. Thus he was a pattern of good works. A Martha and a Mary. A serpent and a dove. He was a Noah amidst the waters. While he never rejected the raven, he always received the dove. He governed the clean and the unclean. He knew how to bear with Ham, and how to bestow his blessing on Shem and Japheth. Like a prudent husbandman, he caused occupied lands to be promptly cultivated, and those that lay waste he added in, and by this means increased their value by the sum of twenty pounds. Meanwhile he overlooked not the spiritual husbandry, tilling hearts with the ploughshare of good doctrine in many books which he wrote, and, although his style was homely, it was rich in the beauty of morality. Neither his racking cough, nor his vomiting of blood, nor his advanced age, nor the attenuation of his flesh availed to daunt this man, or to turn him aside from any purpose of elevated piety; but, lo! after many agonies and bodily sufferings, when he was eighty-four years of age, and had been a monk sixty years and thirty-six days, the great Householder summoned him to the reward of his day's penny."* Doubtless there were abbots of Paisley, whom this description of the good ruler answers, and when we think of them we may be pardoned if we bear it in mind, rather than the picture drawn by prejudiced satirists, and enshrined in the vulgar ballads of a coarse age.

After the Abbot came the Prior, and he it was who bore the burden and heat of the day. He was the Abbot's depute, and had often to take his place when he was absent, as he frequently required to be. He performed all the offices pertaining to the Abbot, except making or deposing obedientiaries and consecrating novices. Whether the Abbot was present

* Chronicle of Battle Abbey, by M. A. Lowder, p. 65.

or absent he struck the cymbalum, beat the table as the signal for work and *monitum* in the dormitory, as well as corrected the faults of the readers in the church and chapter. So onerous were his duties that he had special assistants allotted to him; and in the chronicles of Paisley we read both of a sub-prior and claustral prior. The latter was the Prior's vicar, and remained always in the cloister. Like his superior, the Prior had special privileges which distinguished him from the other brethren. He could give permits to the monks to go beyond the monastery, and fix the time when they were bound to return. If any strangers dined in the refectory, he was allowed to remain with them and keep them company; and when he sat at table he could send his cup to the Cellarer to be filled once or twice, and that officer could not refuse him. It was always a great matter for the Abbot when his second in command was one on whom he could thoroughly rely. To his discretion he committed many matters to which he would otherwise have had to attend personally; and in the various transactions at Paisley, the name of the Prior appears again and again in the signing of leases and making of agreements.

A more important official in the estimation of such inmates of the Convent as loved good cheer—and if report be true, they were not few in number—was the Cellarer. He was the father of the whole society, and as their happiness must have depended greatly upon the quality of their fare, it was good for the brotherhood when he was a man who had a fine taste in viands, and who dealt them out with a generous hand. In many a monastic chronicle the name of the Cellarer is embalmed in the gratitude of those to whom he ministered, and not unfrequently his brethren elected him to the government of the Convent itself when the Abbot's chair happened to be vacant,—a substantial token of their gratitude for the manner in which he had ministered to their wants. He had the care of every thing relating to the food of the monks, and the vessels of the kitchen, the cellars, and the refectory. He was to be careful of the healthy, and especially of the sick, so that he must always have had his hands full. This was true literally as well as metaphorically. He was to weigh the bread himself daily, and to collect the spoons after dinner, carrying the Abbot's in his right hand and the others in his left. Great allowance was made for him in the discharge of his onerous duties. His work was esteemed so sacred that he was allowed absence from masses, complines, and all the hours except matins, vespers, and prime. The stranger entering the refectory soon heard the sweet music of his keys as they rattled at his belt, for it was his duty to wait on visitors : monks returning from their journeys were made welcome by his genial countenance, and when any one asked beer in reason he was to give it to him. A most admirable man was the Cellarer, and happy were they who sunned themselves in his good graces. The comfort of the whole brotherhood depended on him.

If the harmony of the Convent, out of church, rested with the judicious Cellarer, in that sacred edifice it depended upon the *Precentor*. He it was who ruled the choir, and who governed despotically in all musical services. His office could be filled only by one who had been brought up in the monastery from childhood, and who had been reared amid sweet sounds. He arranged all processions. He raised the solemn chant in the church. He taught the monks to sing and read,—first the Abbot, afterwards the Prior, and then all the others. If any one hesitated regarding an accent or pronunciation the *Chanter* was to rectify it. In his own department he was vested with great power. He could box the ears of the boys, pull their hair, and chastise with his hand the novices who told lies, or who were negligent in the choir. He had a sub-chanter who assisted him in maintaining order, collected the song books and put them away in their proper places.

From the solemn choir to the kitchen of the Convent is a great descent, but there was an individual who ruled that secular department as despotically as the Precentor ruled the other. The head cook or *Kitchener* was an official of no mean importance, and the office was never conferred on one who had not made the culinary art his study. The Abbot himself could not dare to interfere with him in certain duties of his calling. In some monasteries he was free from every weekly office except the Great Mass and that of the Virgin Mary; and the Herdsman was subject to him, in order, probably, that at his wish the larder might be suitably supplied from the flock. He was chosen by the Abbot and Chapter after deliberation, that their choice might fall upon a mild and merciful man, who, being himself sober and moderate, might the more willingly afford protection to all sick and needy persons. Among his pots and pans, in pastry and boiling house, directing his monks and lay assistants, he was the principal figure and the guiding spirit.

Over the household matters of the Convent the *Seneschal* presided, and in charters we catch glimpses of such an individual at his work in the Paisley cloisters. He was constantly in converse with the Prior and the Cellarer, and was often outside the Monastery on the business of his office. He held courts of his own in the manors of the Abbey, and travelled at the expense of the Convent. All manner of provender came through his hands, and cellar and storeroom had to be supplied by his industry. The care of the church furniture was committed to the *Sacrist*. He distributed candles for the offices, took care of burials, saw that everything was kept clean and decent, that the lamps were properly lighted, and that the bell was rung at the proper times. The *Almoner* distributed charity to the poor, who were the special charge of the Convent, and who gathered at the church doors for their weekly dole. He and his assistants brought forth broken bread and meat, and dispensed them to the waiting crowd. The *Master of the Novices* superintended their training, preparing them for their duties as monks. The *Infirmarer* was head of the Hospital, and tended the sick, going daily into the kitchen and receiving what was wanted for their use. The *Porter* lived at the gate. Great stress was laid upon his character and duties. He was to be a man of mature age and of unblameable life; he was to eye all strangers who sought admission, and carefully to exclude such as seemed to him in any way suspicious; he was to be able to give and to receive an answer. His temper must have been often tried, and when, as at Paisley, wine was sold and tavern kept within the gate, it must have taken all his discretion to preserve the sanctity of the precincts from being violated. A rough and uncivilised population were without, and monastic privacy needed a wise guardian. He was always to receive poor people and pilgrims with kindness and in the name of God,—not to let them abide long at his gate, but to send them away with refreshments, for which purpose he was supplied with sundry loaves of bread by the Cellarer. The *Refectioner* took charge of all the table furniture, saw that the noggins were washed at certain feasts, and supplied from his revenues cups, pots, table-cloths, candlesticks, towels, and salt-cellars. The *Chamberlain* provided all the furniture of the house, the monks' dresses, beds for the dormitory, straw ropes and stools, knives, razors, and cowls. It was his duty to see the skins of the deer killed in hunting by the Stewart in the Forest of Fereneze, converted into leathern girdles and other articles of clothing, and to give them out to the brethren when needed. The Chamberlain of Paisley was a great official, and Sir Henry Mous, who at one time filled the post, appears in its Chartulary in all the pomp and pride of office. Two other officials of a much lower grade may close this long list. The *Granetarius*, or as he was called at Paisley, the *Granter*, had work assigned to him that was very onerous. It was his duty to keep an account of all the barley and wheat supplied to the Monastery. Vast quantities of of these were received from outlying granges, and as tithes paid by proprietors of surrounding lands. The Granter took note of it as it came in, and saw it sent to the kiln to be turned into flour or malt. The *Porcarius* had charge of the swineherds and the pigs which they tended. The Abbey of Paisley had vast herds of these animals feeding upon the beech-nuts of the neighbouring forests, and they were under the guardianship of the last named official.

These, with their deputies, were the chief officials of the Abbey. After them came the great body of the monks, the novices, and the lay brothers and servants, or as they were called at Paisley, "men" *(homines)*. The number of monks varied in different monasteries. Paisley began with thirteen, but there is reason to believe this number was largely increased afterwards. The duty of the *Monk* is too well known to need any description. He was a man who had left the world behind him, and who had dedicated himself to the service of God, taking certain vows upon him, obeying those set over him in his Monastery, walking by its rules, and so training himself for the eternal crown, of which his shaven head was the symbol. The *Novices* were those who were preparing for the monastic life. They were often children who had been dedicated to this vocation from their infancy, and who received fitting education, learning the psalms by heart, and being instructed in all parts of the rule to which they intended to conform. The lay brothers wore the habit of the order; they were employed constantly at the granges and in manual labour, working under the charge of the bailiff when beyond the convent, and when within its walls under a master of their own.

The religious services of the church varied according to the season of the year, and on certain religious festivals there were devout observances held of a very intricate and imposing character, which broke the monotony of the daily round. Day and night there were seven special services —matins, prime, tierce, sext, nones, vespers, and compline or completorium. Matins began at midnight, prime at six a.m., tierce at nine a.m., sext at twelve o'clock, nones at two or three, vespers about four, compline at seven. This was the last service of the day, after which the monks retired to rest about eight o'clock. This programme was broken up into a great variety of ceremonials, and there were nights upon which none of the inmates went to bed at all, passing the hours in fasting and prayer.

Nor must we forget that amusement was not shut out altogether from the cloister;—there were scripture plays acted,—there was the "Feast of Fools" and the "Abbot of Misrule." Parties of jugglers exhibited their tricks; a bear was occasionally baited in the church yard; the minstrel was always welcome, and sung in the guest hall the ballads of the time; and pilgrims from other lands rehearsed the wonders of their travels.

The food of the monks was plain enough. It varied with the season of the year, and consisted chiefly of fish, with bread and vegetables, ale, and occasionally wine. With the Paisley monks beans were in great request, and from the Cart, from Lochwinnoch, and the "Crooket shot" on the Clyde, their table must have been plentifully supplied with fish. At Christmas and the great feasts there were many offices, some of them performed with great splendour. Between the various services the monks retired to Cloister, Dormitory, and Refectory, or the Chapter was held, when business was transacted, confessions were made, sermons were preached, and monks were punished for their offences. There were also intervals when the studious could retire to the library or the writing room, and others to their daily manual labour.

Even this slight sketch of the inner life of an Abbey may show that it was not one of laziness and repose. Many gifts and faculties were called into exercise. Outside altogether of the offices of devotion there was plenty for a man of energy to do. He could work in the garden or the field. He could assist the sacrist in the church, the cook in the kitchen, the cellarer in his pantry. He could peruse books in the library, write in the scriptorium, attend the sick in the infirmary, knead in the bakehouse, or, under the superintendence of the almoner, minister to the wants of the poor. There is a letter from the great abbot, Peter of Clugny,* to a monk in some distant monastery affiliated to that celebrated convent which illustrates what has been said regarding the opportunities afforded by the monastic life for activity both of brain and of hand. It is of special interest, as Paisley was likewise a cell of Clugny. After having spoken of prayer and meditation, he says, "But I know, my most dearly beloved, that these are difficult of attainment, and that it is not easy for any one to pass his life in these pursuits only. Let these things therefore be followed by manual labour; that when the mind is fatigued with spiritual things, and being cast down by the weight of flesh, falls from the highest to the lowest things—it be turned, not to the vain conversation of men, but to the exercise of the body. Trees cannot be planted, fields cannot be watered, and no agricultural work can be carried on consistently with perpetual seclusion; but, what is more useful, instead of the plough you may take in hand the pen, and instead of marking the fields with furrows, you may store page after page with sacred letters, and the word of God may be sown on the parchment, which, when the harvest is ripe, that is when the book is completed, may fill hungry readers with abundant fruits, and so heavenly bread may dispel the deadly famine of the soul. If, however, from injuring your sight, or from headache, or from its wearisome sameness, you cannot or will not be content with this one manual employment,—make a variety of other handy-works,—make combs for combing and cleaning the heads of the brethren; with skilful hand and well instructed foot turn needle cases, hollow out vessels for wine, or try to put them together,—and if there are any marshy places near weave mats, (an ancient monastic employment), on which you may always, or frequently sleep,—may bedew with daily or frequent tears and wear out with frequent genuflection before God, or, as Jerome says, 'Weave little baskets with flags or make them of wicker.' Filling up all the time of your blessed life with these and similar works of holy purpose you will leave no room for your adversaries to intrude into your heart or into your cell: but when God hath filled all with his virtues there shall be no room

* Maitland's Dark Ages, pages 451, 452.

for the devil, none for sloth, none for the other vices." These advices from the Archabbot of Clugny we may be sure found some to put them in practice in the subordinate Abbey of Paisley. Entering in at the stately gatehouse, after having satisfied the jealous porter, we find, not a scene of idleness and sloth, but of toil and bustle; or if an holy calm pervades all things the echo of the chanted Psalms tells us the reason. We see the lighted windows, the priest before the altar, the chanter at the head of the choir, the abbot with his mitre standing in his stall with his crozier in his hand. Then darkness falls upon all and we are back from the Middle Ages amid the prose of the nineteenth century.

# CHAPTER III.

## Clunaic Benedictines.

> "Esse niger monachus si forte velim Cluniaci
> Ova fabasque nigrascum sale saepe dabunt
> Surgere me facient media de nocte, volentem
> Amplius in calido membra fovere thoro
> Quodque magis noliens vellent me psallere sursum
> Et geminare meos in diapente tonos."
>
> *Brunellius.*

IN the Church of Rome there were various orders of monks, each governed by its own peculiar rule. Among these orders the most famous was that of the Benedictines. As the monks of Paisley belonged to this great brotherhood, it may not be out of place to give some account of its history and government. The order of Benedictines takes its name from St. Benedict of Nursia. This wonderful man was born about 480 A.D., at Nursia, in the diocese of Spoleto, in Italy. He received his early education at Rome, but when only fourteen years of age, betook himself to an ascetic life, and lived for years as a hermit in a cavern, receiving his food through a hole in the roof from the hands of a friend. The fame of his sanctity spread far and wide, and many put themselves under his spiritual direction, and in A.D. 529 he retired to Monte Casino, where he founded a monastery on the site of a heathen temple of Apollo,. and instituted that order which afterwards became celebrated throughout Europe. Here he drew up rules for a monastic life which became the pattern of all others. These are constructed with wonderful skill and knowledge of human nature, and bear the impress of a powerful and statesmanlike mind. He was the great prophet of his time—he was called the second Elias, and had a deep insight into human nature in its various phases. It has been well said by Sir James

Stephen that "the comprehensiveness of thought with which he exhausted the science of monastic polity, so that all subsequent rules have been nothing more than mere modifications of his own, the prescience with which he reconciled conventual franchises with abbatial dominion, the skill with which he at once concentrated and diffused power among the different members of his order, according as the objects were general or local, and the deep insight into the human heart by which he rendered myriads of men and women throughout successive generations the spontaneous instruments of his purposes: these all unite to prove that profound genius, extensive knowledge and earnest meditation had raised him to the very first rank of uninspired legislators." * It would be out of place to give a minute description of the spiritual polity of this great man. We can only glance at some of its features.

The rule of St. Benedict consists of a code of seventy-seven chapters, in which directions for a monastic life are laid down with great minuteness. The whole history of a monk, from the day that he entered the cloister to that on which his brethren said their office for the repose of his soul, may be clearly learnt from them. As an illustration of the severity of his rule it will be sufficient to cite the directions which St. Benedict gave for the admission of a new member: "For four days he was to stand at the gate and entreat the porter, who was to repel his advances to admission in the severest manner. If he persevered and obtained an entrance he was to be led into a chamber appointed for strangers, and there to be attended by one of the most ancient men of the monastery who was to make him acquainted at first with the severest rules of the order, and then, if he expressed no backwardness to submit, with the remainder. Having passed this preliminary examination, the candidate was to become a novice, and when he had completed six months of his novitiate he was again examined. If his answer proved satisfactory he was allowed to remain among the novices, and at the end of four months the examination was renewed. This was the last ordeal he was to endure, and if he passed it successfully he was numbered among the brethren. In the ceremony of his admission he had to take the most solemn vows that he would continue faithful to the obligations of the

* Sir James Stephen's Essays, vol. I., p. 365.

order; that he would never leave the boundaries of the monastery; and that whatever he possessed had been or was to be resigned to the establishment or the poor. The substance of this declaration was to be written down and signed by the new monk, after which he was to be admitted a member of the order."* The Benedictines wore a black gown with large wide sleeves, and on their heads a cowl ending in a point behind, and were styled *black monks* from the colour of their dress. "No monk had property of his own, but each was provided with two coats, two cowls, a knife, a needle, a handkerchief; and his cell was furnished with a mat, a blanket, a rug, and a pillow."† Their devotional offices were many, and their feasts frequent; but for us the most interesting features of their life were their constant study, and their practice of agriculture. When within their convent they devoted a great part of their time to reading and writing, and became famed throughout the world for their learning and culture; when abroad, they worked assiduously at the tillage of the soil, and gave an impulse to the practice of agriculture throughout Europe. "Idleness," said Benedict in his rule, "is the enemy of the soul. Therefore at certain times the brethren must be occupied in the labour of their hands, and again at certain hours in divine study. We think that both ends may be accomplished by this arrangement. From Easter till the kalends of October let them go out in the morning; and from the first hour till nearly the fourth let them labour for the procuring of that which is necessary. Again, from the fourth hour to about the sixth let them be at leisure for reading. Rising from the table after the sixth hour let them have an interval of rest upon their beds, or if any one should wish to read, let him so read that he may not disturb his neighbour. At the ninth hour let them again work till the evening if the necessity of the place or their poverty require it, and let them gather the fruits of the earth, seeing that these are true monks who live by the labour of their hands as our forefathers and the apostles did. But let all things be done moderately and in measure on account of those that are feeble. From the kalends of October till the beginning of Lent let them be at leisure for reading till

* Lardner's History of the Christian Church, vol. I. p. 321. † Encyclopaedia Britannica, Art. Benedictine.

the second hour, then from the third to the ninth hour let all labour at the work which is enjoined them. In the days of Lent let them be at leisure for their readings from the early morning to the third hour, from thence to the eleventh, let them do the work which is enjoined them."* This part of the rule brings prominently to view what was the great glory of the Benedictines, the union of study and manual labour.†

The most celebrated Benedictine Abbey after that of Monte Casino was the Abbey of Clugny, near Macon, in Burgundy. In this noble monastery, founded A.D. 940 by the Pious Duc Daquitane, Bernon, the abbot, and his successor, Odo, perfected the rule of St. Benedict, which had fallen into considerable decay. The discipline of this house became famed throughout Europe, so celebrated indeed that the fame of the Benedictines became eclipsed by that of the Clunaics. In the twelfth century nearly 2000 monasteries scattered throughout France, Germany, Spain, England, and even the East owned allegiance to the house of Clugny from which they originally sprung, and which continued still to exercise authority over them. It was the greatest of all abbatial churches, equal to Cologne in the splendour of its medieval architecture, vaster than St. Peter's in space and majesty. "Of its vast nave, of its four transepts, of its innumerable chapels, of its seven towers, there remain only three scanty fragments to indicate what had once been the glory of medieval France."‡ It was described by one who knew it well, and who was a competent judge, as the most beautiful monastery in Christendom.§ One Pope after another conferred special privileges on the house of Clugny and its numerous dependencies. It possessed a large territory over which it ruled supreme. Its abbots

* Quoted in "Learning and Working," by Maurice, p. 52.

† "Pope John the 22d, who died in 1334, found after inquiry that since the rise of the order it had produced 24 popes, nearly 200 cardinals, 7000 archbishops, 15,000 bishops, 15,000 abbots, and 4000 saints, besides founding upwards of 37,000 monasteries. There have been likewise of this order 20 emperors and 10 empresses, 47 kings and above 50 queens, 20 sons of emperors, and 48 sons of kings. The order has produced an immense number of eminent writers and learned men. Rabanus set up the school of Germany, Alcuinus founded the University of Paris, Guido invented the scale of music, Sylvester the organ; and they boast of having produced Anselm Ildephonsus, Venerable Bede, and many others of equal or superior name."—*Ency. Britannica, Art. Benedictine.*

‡ Dean Stanley in "Good Words."  § De Thou.

were directly subject to the Pope, and no bishop could intrude within the precincts of the monasteries of the order, or exercise any jurisdiction over them and the dependencies. Many of these dependencies were in England, and at one time the Abbot of Clugny received £2000 from the English houses of his order. Among these houses was the monastery of Wenlock in Shropshire, from which the monks of Paisley came. It was an offshoot of the Priory of La Charite in France, and was founded by Roger, Earl of Shrewsbury. But though the monks of Paisley came immediately from Wenlock, it was to the great Abbey of Clugny that they looked as their head. Thither their abbot had at regular intervals to go to make obeisance. The privileges conferred on Clugny by the different Popes were carefully treasured in their archives, and founded upon again and again in their various contentions with ecclesiastical and civil powers. From documents relating to Clugny in the Paisley Chartulary, the history of that great house might be written and not the smallest change in the discipline and government of its Scotch offshoot could be effected without the special authority of its French parent.

The rule by which the Clunaic monks were everywhere governed differed only from that of St. Benedict in certain ritual observances. A French writer on the religious orders considers worthy of special remark the manner in which they prepared the bread for the sacrifice of the altar. Read in the light of our time their practice may be called superstition; viewed in the light of theirs, it betokens deep reverence and earnest piety. "They first chose the wheat grain by grain and washed it with great care, putting it in a bag used only for it. A servant known to be a good man carried it to the mill. He washed the stones, covered them with curtains above and below, and, dressed in an alb, he hid his face in a veil, letting only his eyes be seen. The same care was taken with the flour. It was not passed into the sieve until it was well washed, and the guardian of the church, if he were a priest or deacon, finished the rest, being helped by two other monks who were of the same order, and by a novice chosen expressly for it; these four, at the end of matins, washed their hands and faces. The three first put on their albs. The first washed the flour with pure clean water, and the two others baked the paste on the iron. Such was the respect and reverence which the monks of Clugny had for the holy Eucharist."*

Their discipline was of the strictest kind. Silence was so strictly guarded amongst them that they would sooner have suffered death than have broken it before the hours of prime. Amusing stories are told of the inconveniences they suffered rather than break this rule. One allowed his horse to be stolen, and two suffered themselves to be carried off by the Norsemen when they might have been saved by crying out. During the hours of silence they used signs instead of words. After complines the monks were never given permission to eat. From the 12th September they had only one meal in the day, except on the feast of the twelve lessons and the octave of Christmas and Epiphany when they had two. The bread and wine remaining in the refectory they distributed to poor pilgrims. Mabillon states that they were required at the end of the meals to consume their crumbs. There was a disposition at first to evade this regulation, but when a dying monk exclaimed in horror that he saw the devil holding up in accusation against him a bag of crumbs which he had been unwilling to swallow, the brethren were terrified into obedience. At best their food was not of a very *recherchè* character, and a satirical poet, once himself a monk, thus speaks of their daily fare: "When you wish to sleep they wake you; when you wish to eat they make you fast. The night is passed in praying in the church, the day in working, and there is no repose but in the refectory: and what is to be found there? Rotten eggs, beans with their pods on, and liquor fit for oxen. For the wine is so poor that one might drink of it for a month without intoxication."† They were however charitable with what they had. Eighteen poor men were fed every day, and the charity during Lent was so profuse that in one year from the beginning of Lent there were at Clugny seven thousand poor to whom a great quantity of salt meat and similar alms were distributed. They loved to teach young children, and the youth whom they brought up were trained with the same care and received the same education bestowed on the children of princes, in the palaces of their fathers.†

* Mabillon, Dictionaire des Orders Religieuses, Tome II. p. 306. † Fosbrook, p. 107.

In 1122 Peter the Venerable was Abbot of Clugny, and in a controversy which he held with St. Bernard, Abbot of the rival house of Citeaux, he gives many particulars regarding the Clunaics and their mode of life; * but a more interesting account of the interior economy of the monastery is given in a letter to a friend by a Monk Ulric, who belonged to the convent, and who tells at length how he and his companions lived from day to day.† There is but one part of his most interesting narrative to which we may refer, namely, to the constant study of the Scriptures which occupied the time of the brethren. They read the Bible alternately with the writings of the fathers. The winter evenings at Clugny were spent in listening to large portions of the Word of God. The book of Genesis was read through in a week, Isaiah in six evenings, and the Epistle to the Romans at two sittings. The Acts of the Apostles in Easter week. "When one of the monks who portioned out the lessons," says Ulric, "had made them shorter, he was prohibited by our seniors in chapter." Every monk had the Psalms by heart and was able to say them from memory. This is a most pleasing picture in the life of the brethren, and there is little reason to doubt that the scene which Ulric describes in the Abbey of Clugny, was one which might constantly be witnessed in the humbler house of Paisley, the reader, seated in an elevated place, reading in the long winter night the Bible to his brethren on benches along the wall, while a monk went round with a wooden lantern, open on one side, to see if any were asleep. "Should he find any one asleep he must throw the light in his eyes three times, if on the third time he does not wake he must place the lantern before him, that when he is wakened he may take it up and carry it in like manner until he finds another sleeper like himself."

* Maitland's Dark Ages, p. 1.

† Ibid, p. 332.

# CHAPTER IV.

## The Founding of the Monastery.

In the antique age of bow and spear,
  And feudal rapine clothed with iron mail,
Came ministers of peace, intent to rear
  The Mother Church in yon sequestered vale.

*Wordsworth.*

PAISLEY ABBEY is a memorial of the coming to Scotland of the great house of Stewart, which has left so broad and deep a mark on Scottish history. The origin of this family has been and still is a great subject of controversy among genealogists and antiquaries. While some have with Shakespear traced its descent to Fleance, the son of Banquo, others, with probably greater likelihood, have sought for the house a less romantic ancestry, and have made out the first Stewart to be "a Norman of the Normans." Into this genealogical controversy there is no necessity for us to enter. It is sufficient to know that probably in the time of The Conqueror, certainly in that of King Henry I., his successor, there was a certain Alan, the son of Flaald,* a great magnate in the county of Salop,

* Those who wish to enter into the historic question of the origin of the Stewarts will find it ably discussed in "Stewartiana," by J. H. Riddel, Chalmers' "Caledonia," and by Mr. Eyton in the "Archæological Journal," Vol. XIII. The latter argues very ably in favour of the Stewarts' descent from Banquo. Mr. Cosmo Innes, in his "Scottish Surnames," page 4, and in his "Scotland in the Middle Ages," page 127, classes the Stewarts with other Norman nobles. In the stone of the western wall of the church of Dives, in Normandy, is carved a list of the alleged companions of William the Conqueror in his invasion, and among these occurs the name of "Alan le Roux." This may be the Alan, son of Flaald, who was the undoubted ancestor of the Stewarts. Beyond this Alan all is conjecture, and they have not with any certainty been traced beyond the county of Salop whence the first Stewart and his following came to found a colony in Renfrewshire. Some of his companions who obtained grants of lands in Scotland are shown by Riddel and Eyton to have had property in Shropshire, and to have been benefactors of the church in that county.

owner of the lordship of Oswestry, a large and noble estate which had belonged to a dispossessed Briton called Meridith ap Blechyn. On these lands Alan settled and became a man of great importance. He was frequently at court; and among the names of persons of high rank who witness the charters of King Henry, we often come upon the somewhat primitive designation, Alan the son of Flathald.* In course of time Alan married a lady in his own county of Shropshire. She was the daughter of a magnate, Warine, the Sheriff of the county. By this lady he had three sons,—William, Walter, and Simon.† With the first two only, however, are we now concerned. William succeeded his father in Shropshire, and improved his fortunes by marrying a lady of high rank and wealth, Isabel de Say, Lady, as she was called, of Clune; she was piously inclined, and liberally endowed the Monastery of Wenlock in her neighbourhood. Walter, like his father the Norman, was a soldier of fortune; and while his brother settled down as an English baron, he turned his face northward and got a holding in Scotland.‡ King David I. of Scotland was at the siege of Winchester in 1141, supporting the claims of his niece the Empress Maud in her severe contest with Stephen. William of Shropshire was also there in attendance on Maud, whose cause he warmly espoused; and his younger brother Walter was probably in his train. When David, overpowered by superior numbers, had to retreat, he was accompanied by Walter, who, a younger son with little property, was glad to attach himself to the court of the northern monarch in the natural hope of bettering his fortune. In this he was not disappointed. The king shewed him great favour; took him into his household and conferred on him the title of Lord High Stewart of Scotland.§ The successor of his patron was even more generous. He ratified the title to his favourite and his heirs, and bestowed on him a wide territory, chiefly in Renfrewshire. The

* Alanus Flaalde filius.

† Simon witnesses his brother's charter at Fodringhame, and probably accompanied him afterwards to Scotland.

‡ Mr. Riddel's "Stewartiana," and Mr. Eyton's "Archæological Journal," Vol. XIII., shew that he possessed property in his mother's county, but not probably to a great extent.

§ The *fes cheque* which the Stewart assumed as his armorial bearing was the counting board used in the duties of his office.

charter* containing this great benefaction still exists; it is addressed by Malcolm, king of Scots, to "the bishops, abbots, barons, justices, sheriffs, provosts, officers, and all other good men, clergy and laity, French† and English, Scots, and inhabitants of Galloway." The King confirms the grant which his grandfather David had made to Walter, of Renfrew and Passeleth, Pollok, Talahec, Kathkert, Le Drip, Le Mutrene, Eglisham, Lochinauche, and Inverwick, and again confers the office of the Stewartship on him and his heirs. Besides this he gives very liberally, in gratitude for service done both to King David and himself. He bestows as much of Preithe‡ as King David held in his own hand; also Inchinan, Steintum, Halestondene, Legardswode, and Birchinsyde. He gives in each of his burghs and regalities throughout his kingdom a full toft § for his entertainment therein, and with every toft twenty acres of land, and in return for all this Walter is to give the King and his heirs the service of five knights. The Stewart soon colonised, after the fashion of the time, the lands thus generously bestowed on him. He built a castle for himself in the neighbourhood of Renfrew, || and he gave holdings to his followers throughout his wide territory of Strathgryff, as his Renfrewshire property was called. On eminences here and there might be seen the strongholds of his retainers, and in their neighbourhood the settlements inhabited, and the lands cultivated by their followers. The same names which appear in the Doomsday Book as inhabiting Shropshire, are transferred to the neighbourhood of Paisley.

One thing, however, necessary, according to the ideas of the period, to complete the colonisation of Strathgryff, was the erection of a Monastery. It was the age of convent building. On the ruins of the ancient monastic system of Scotland, represented by the Culdees, religious houses after the Roman pattern were rising everywhere. Monks of many orders were coming across the border in the wake of

* The charter is given in the appendix to the Paisley Register.

† This indicates the number of Normans who had by this time crossed the Scottish border.

‡ Perth. § A plot for a house.

|| He is believed to have had a castle also in Neilston. A charter granted by James, High Stewart, who died in 1309, bears to have been executed "apud manerium nostrum de Renfrw." —*Ramsay's Views of Renfrewshire.*

the Norman settlers, drawn either from the convents in England, or from the parent houses in France. Cistercians from Rievaulx in Yorkshire were at Melrose, and Dundrennan in Galloway; Augustine friars from St. Quentin at Beauvais in France, were at Jedburgh; Tironensians, from Picardy, at Kelso; and Benedictines, from Canterbury, at Dunfermline.* These houses were mostly erected by royal munificence, but many nobles followed the example of the sovereign, and built and endowed monasteries on their possessions. Among these founders was Walter, the son of Alan.

In looking out for a monastic order to introduce into his newly-acquired northern territory, the Lord High Stewart was naturally influenced by his early associations. In his native county of Shropshire there was a convent of Clunaic Benedictines at Wenlock, with the order of which he was familiar. It had been founded by Montgomery, the Earl of Shrewsbury, a younger son of whom, Robert de Montgumbri, was among the Stewart's followers, and had obtained from him the manor of Eaglesham, in Renfrewshire. This monastery had also been greatly enriched by gifts from the Lady of Clune.† From Wenlock the Scottish colonist therefore sought to obtain his monastic contingent. Being in attendance on King Malcolm, his sovereign, at Fotheringay Castle, in Northamptonshire, in or about 1163‡ he entered into an agreement with

* Jedburgh was founded 1155.
Kelso ,, ,, 1128.
Melrose ,, ,, 1136.
Dryburgh was founded 1150.
Dundrennan ,, ,, 1142.

† Eyton's History of Shropshire. "Stewartiana," by J. H. Riddel.

‡ "The exact date of the foundation charter cannot perhaps be ascertained with certainty. From the phrase 'pro salute corporis et anime regis Malcolmi' occurring in the charter, it is evident that it was granted in King Malcolm's reign who succeeded in 1153. Of the witnesses, Ingleram, the chancellor, became Bishop of Glasgow in 1164, and was afterwards so styled in deeds; and Richard, the king's chaplain, was elected Bishop of St. Andrews in 1163. The period in which the charter must necessarily have been granted being thus narrowed, a reasonable conjecture is afforded of its exact date by the place at which it was granted. This is without doubt Fotheringay in Northamptonshire, a castle and manor inherited by King Malcolm, along with the Earldom of Huntingdon, and we know of no other occasion within the time limited which could bring together at this castle the chancellor and Stewart of Scotland, and the king's chaplain, persons usually in attendance on the king, with other Scotchmen, except Malcolm's visit to England in 1163, when he did homage to Henry II. on the first day of July, at Wodstoke, a place not distant from his own castle of Fotheringay."—*Introduction to Paisley Register.*

Humbaldus, who presided as Prior over the house of Wenlock. The agreement is carefully drawn out, and is witnessed by the chancellor and chaplain of the Scottish King, and the abbot of the great house of Rievaulx. On the one hand, Walter, the son of Alan, "for the soul of King David, and King Henry, and Earl Henry, and the souls of his parents and benefactors, and for the health of the body and soul of King Malcolm, to the honour of God," agrees to build an house of religion on his land of Passelay, "according to the order of the brotherhood of Wenlock, which is the order of the Clunaic monks." He is to have thirteen of the brethren to originate the Monastery, and is to have the right of choosing the Prior who is to rule over them, which right is to be vested in himself and his successors, and, except in the general recognition of the order, the proposed house at Paisley is to have no connection with Wenlock. On the other hand, Humbaldus is to procure for the new foundation the recognition of the Clunaic order, and especially of the Prior of La Charite* and the Abbot of Clugny, and in return for these services he is to receive from the Stewart certain properties in his Burgh of Renfrew, and rights of fishing in his waters,—among others, that of catching herring.† It took some time to procure the sanction of the project by Suaricius, the Prior of La Charite, and Stephen, the Abbot of Clugny,‡ and probably Humbaldus had to visit these foreign monasteries for this purpose. These dignitaries, however, readily gave their consent; and Stephen, in recognition of the generosity of Walter, received him into the brotherhood, and made him partaker of the prayers of the whole Order of Clugny, decreeing that, at his death (if he should not have become one of

* "The Monastery of La Charite Sur Loire," according to Martine, "was originally built half a league from the place where it now stands, near the ancient town of Seir, which no longer exists. Having been destroyed by the Vandals, it was re-established by King Pipin, who placed Benedictine monks there. It was soon after destroyed by the barbarians. Geoffrey of Nevers, Bishop of Auxerre, having rebuilt the church in honour of the Holy Virgin, gave it to Hughes, Abbot of Clugny, who made it a famous monastery, and gave the government of it to Givard, his prior, who is considered a saint at Clugny."—1 Voy. Lit., P. II., p. 214.

The Monastery of La Charite had many cells in England,—Wenlock was granted to it in 1087 by Earl Roger of Shrewsbury.

† Reg. de Pas., pp. 2, 3.

‡ Pope Innocent III. gave his sanction in 1209.

their monks before that time), the same prayers, and masses, and psalms, and other offices, should be said for him as for one of the order.*

Having now received the full concurrence of his superiors, Humbald set out with his thirteen monks for their future home. How they travelled, or by what road, we have no means of ascertaining. Such long journeys by members of religious houses were very common. The English monasteries were generally dependent on those of France, and nearly all the Scotch monasteries were cells or dependencies of others in England. As the mother house exercised a certain authority over its offshoot, it was necessary that there should be frequent communication between them; and, as all religious orders were dependent on the Pope, his authority had to be sought for all transactions of importance. Some of the monks were therefore great travellers. The difficulties of a journey like that undertaken by the Prior of Wenlock were not so great as might be supposed. The old Roman roads were clearly marked out and unbroken by the inroads of agriculture; and at short intervals there were convents where the travellers would always be sure of a hearty welcome. It was in the year 1169 that Humbald reached Renfrew,† where he and his monks were received by the High Stewart, and received lodgment on the island‡ near his castle, at a church dedicated to St. Mary and St. James,§ whilst their future home was being built. Osbert, one of their number, was chosen their Prior, and Humbald left them and returned home. Having formally inspected, in terms of the Stewart's charter, the

* Reg. de Pas., p. 3. † Chronicon de Mailros.

‡ The Inch called the King's Inch. This name was given to certain lands now belonging to Elderslie because of their insular situation, caused by the separation of the Clyde into two branches, the larger of which formed its present channel, while the other ran from the ford above Braehead house along the north side of the common, where the waters were united very near the place where the present ferry is. The course of the latter branch may still be traced."—*Ramsay's Views of Renfrewshire.*

§ *Reg. de Pas., p. 249.*—It has been supposed that the convent was first established at Renfrew, and afterwards moved to Paisley; we however agree with Ramsay ("Views of Renfrewshire") when he says—"Paisley Abbey was already founded, and we apprehend the only inference that can be drawn from the words of the Charter is that the monks who were destined for Paisley resided at Renfrew temporarily until the house at Paisley was ready for their reception. Nothing could be more natural than that they should in the interval dwell in the neighbourhood of the founder's mansion at Renfrew." It is possible that some of the brotherhood preceded Humbald.

fishings and property in Renfrew which the Stewart had given him and his house in return for their good offices with Stephen of Clugny, he came to the conclusion that they were of little value at so great a distance from their owners. Wenlock and Renfrew were three hundred miles apart. He accordingly resigned them to the donor, receiving from him instead a property nearer Wenlock, and likely to be more productive than the fishings on the River Clyde and the "toft" in the Burgh of Renfrew.* This property was called Menwede, or Manhood, a village giving name to an "hundred," in the south-west angle of Sussex, a county where Walter Fitz-Alan had other property.† Humbald then went back to Wenlock, doubtless carrying many stories of his travels in Scotland with which to entertain his brethren. He attests an English charter in 1170, and that is the last that we hear of him. In a chronicle of the time he is called "Holy Humbandus,"‡ but, as we shall see afterwards, he was not altogether worthy of that appellation, having, in his transaction with the Stewart, grossly deceived him, leading that nobleman to think he had given privileges to the house of Paisley, which he had no power to confer. Menwede, the gift he obtained from Walter for Wenlock, remained in its possession till the dissolution of the monasteries at the Reformation, perpetuating to the sixteenth century a memorial of Humbald's mission to Paisley in the twelfth. §

So soon as the buildings were sufficiently forward at Paisley the monks moved thither. The founder, accompanied by his son Alan and some honest men, || perambulated and measured off certain land in the neighbourhood for their use. He also drew up two charters ¶ in their favour, which, as they contain a statement of the nucleus of the wealth that they subsequently acquired, we venture to give in their entirety. The first is entitled "The Charter of Walter, the son of Alan, the founder, of various lands and churches as well on this side of the muirs as the other." It is as follows:—

* Reg. de Pas., pp. 2, 3. † Eyton's Shropshire. ‡ Chronicon de Mailros.

§ Eyton's Shropshire. || Probi homines. ¶ Reg. de Pas. p. 5.

"WALTER, the son of Alan, greeting, to all sons of Holy Mother Church, present and to come; Be it known to you that I have given and granted, and by this charter have confirmed, to God and Saint Mary, and the church of Saint James, and Saint Mirin, and Saint Myldburge de Passelet, and to the prior and monks serving God there according to the order of Clugny: for the soul of Henry, King of England, and for the soul of King David, and King Malcolm, and Earl Henry, and my departed forefathers, and for the spiritual welfare of my Lord King William, and David his brother, and of myself, and my wife, and my heirs, in perpetual alms, free from all temporal service, the Church of Ennyrwic, with all its possessions, and the mill of Ennyrwic, except a mark of silver in it which I have given Randolph of Kent; and the Church of Ledgerwode, with all its possessions, and the carucate of land in Hastendene which Walter the Chaplain held, by those boundaries by which he held it, and the Church of Kathkert, with all its possessions; and all the churches of Stragrif, with all their belongings, except the Church of Inchinan*; and that carucate of land which Grimketel held, with the boundaries by which he held it; and the Drep, with all its possessions by land and water according to the boundaries by which William held it; and the Church of Passelet, with all its possessions, and two carucates of land, measured and perambulated, about the river Kert, beside the church, and that land beyond Kert out of part of the wood which I and my son Alan perambulated, according to those boundaries which we perambulated with honest men, and that portion of land which is below the dormitory

* *Excepta Ecclesia de Inchinan.* Inchinan had been previously bestowed by David I. upon the Knights Templars. On their suppression in 1312 it passed into the hands of the Knights of St. John. Its church was dedicated to Saint Convallus, one of the disciples of St. Kentigern. Boece tells us that in his day the relics of the Saint, in a stately shrine at Inchinnan, were held in great reverence. The stone on which the Saint is said to have sailed up the channel from Ireland, called St. Conval's chariot, may still be seen in the wood at Blythswood, on the right bank of the Cart. It was supposed, down to a comparatively late date, to possess the virtue of working cures both in man and beast.—*See Semple's Lairds of Glen; Origines Parochiales, Art. Inchinan; Forbes' Scottish Saints, Art. Convallus.* In the Aberdeen Breviary, the life of this saint is given.

of the monks, and all the land which Scerlo held, according to its boundaries, with that house above the rock where my hall was built, and the whole Island near my town of Renfru, with the fishing between that Island and Perthec, and a full toft in Renfru, and half a mark of silver from the rent of that burgh for lighting the church, and a net for salmon and the mill of Renfru; and the land where the monks first dwelt; and that carucate of land which is between Kert and Grif; and the church of Prestwic, with all that land which Dovenald the son of Ywen perambulated for them between the land of Simon Loccard and the land of Prestwick as far as Pulprestwic; and along Prestwic as far as the sea; and from the sea by the torrent between the land of Arnold and the land of Prestwic, to the boundaries of Simon Loccard; and that church of my burgh of Prestwic, with all its possessions; and the salt pit in Kalentir which belonged to Herbert the chamberlain. I have given likewise and confirmed a full tenth of my hunting, with the skins; and all the skins of the deer which I slay in my forest of Fereneze; and four shillings from the mill of Passelet for the lighting of the church; and that they may grind there, without multure, next to him whom they may find grinding there, except when I myself am grinding the corn which comes from my own granary. And besides this, a full tenth of that mill of Passelet, and of all the mills which I have, or may have hereafter. I have given to them, and by this Charter have confirmed to them, a full tenth of all my waste lands, and of all lands in my forest which have been or will be reclaimed; and all the privileges of my forest of Passelet, and the same right of pasture in it for the cattle and swine of their house as belongs to me and my men. But if it should happen that I or any of my heirs wish to have our swine below the forest, part of the forest sufficient for their animals shall be provided for them; and in addition to this foresaid charity of mine, with their other honours, I grant and confirm to them these privileges, namely, right to fines and to hold courts; freedom from tolls and customs; to hold slaves and punish thieves.

"In presence of these witnesses:—Engelrame, Bishop of Glasgow; Richard, Bishop of St. Andrews; John, Abbot of Kelso; Osbert, Abbot of Jedburgh; Master Mark Salomon, deacon; Elia, clerk; Master John; Alan, my son; Robert de Montgumbri, Baldwin de Bigres, Robert de Costentin, Gaufred de Costentin, Robert, the son of Fulbert; Ewen the son of Donald; Walter de Costentin, Niel de Costentin, Alexander de Hesting, Hugh de Padinan, Richard Wal', Robert Croc, Roger de Nes, Richard, my clerk, and many others."

The second Charter is as follows—

"GIFT of the Churches of Ennyrwic and Legerdwode, and the carrucate of Hastenden, and all the churches in Stragrif."

"WALTER, the son of Alan, Stewart of the King of Scotland, to all the sons of Holy Mother Church, greeting. Know that I have given and conceded, and by this Charter have confirmed to God, and Holy Mary, and to the Church of St. James, and St. Mirin, and St. Milburg of Passelet, and to the prior and monks of that place, serving God according to the order of Clugny, for the soul of King David, and King Malcolm, and Earl Henry, and of my departed ancestors; and for the salvation of my Lord King William, and David his brother, and of myself, and my wife, and my heirs, in perpetual charity, and free from all temporal servitude, the Church of Ennyrwic with all its belongings, and the whole mill, except a mark of silver in it which I have given to Radulph of Kent, and a carucate of land between the sea and the Church of Ennyrwic assigned to them for their support; and the Church of Legerdwode, with all its belongings, and the carucate of land in Hastenden which Walter the chaplain held by these marches by which he held it, and the Church of Ketkert with all its belongings, and all the churches of Stragrif with all their belongings, except the Church of Inchinan. Besides this I give, and by this Charter confirm to them, a tenth penny of all the rents of my whole land excepting Kyle. I wish and command that the said monks should hold and possess the aforesaid as quietly, freely and peacefully as any abbey in the kingdom of Scotland holds and possesses the charities bestowed on it.

"In presence of these witnesses: Richard, Bishop of St. Andrews; Engelrame, Bishop of Glasgow; John, Abbot of Kelso; Osbert, Abbot of Jedburgh; Master Mark Salomon, deacon; Alan, my son; Baldwin de Bigres, Robert de Montgumbri, Robert de Costentin, Robert the son of Fulbert; Ewen the son of Dovenald, and many others.*

With these great endowments the Convent of Paisley began its career.

* The earliest forms of the name of the convent are Paslet, Passeleth, Passelay, Passelet, but in the records, as time ran on, occur many others, *e.g.* Paslowe, Passleke, Pateslo, Pasle, Paslewe, Paslay, and Paisley. The derivation of the name has been disputed. The following are some of the supposed derivations :—1. Paselet, Gaelic Pais-licht, brow of a rock, from a great ridge of rocks across the river Cart; 2. *Pas*, a crossing, ferry, and *let*, a house, in Strathclyde Welsh, the name given to some house at a ferry on the river; 3. Pasgel-laith, British, moist pasture ground; 4. *Bas*, Gaelic for death, *letum*, Latin for death. "On the Romans occupying this part of the country, and hearing the name *Bas*, referring to some place of execution, they added their own word for death, and called the place Pas-letum, afterwards Saxonised into Passeleth." There have been other conjectures still more fanciful than the last. The second which we have given is that of Mr. Jamieson, and seems the most likely.

## CHAPTER V.

### St. Mirin and the Patron Saints.

Faith is fresh of hue.

*Lyra Innocentium.*

WHEN the monks had founded their church at Paisley, they dedicated it to the Virgin Mary, to St. James, St. Milburga, and St. Mirinus. St. James was the patron saint of the Stewarts, and to him the church on the Inch of Renfrew, where the monks first took up their abode, was dedicated. St. Milburga was the patron saint of Wenloc. She was the grand-daughter of King Penda, the Saxon King of Mercia, and had presided over a nunnery at Wenloc, on the ruins of which, after its destruction by the Danes, the priory of that place had been erected. She had died in the odour of sanctity, and her memory was held in much reverence, but, when the church of Wenloc was to be built, the place of her burial had been forgotten * or lost sight of, though her remains were supposed to be within the precincts of the ancient building. A boy running over the floor of the proposed church trod upon the very tomb of the saint, and balsamic exhalations perfuming the sanctuary, at once revealed her resting-place. The discovery was hailed with enthusiasm by the devout, and crowds flocked to Wenloc. Miraculous cures were effected through the merits of the saint, and their fame spread everywhere. The chief cures were in cases of scrofulous diseases which had resisted all medical treatment.† People afflicted with these made pilgrimages to Wenloc in great numbers, and were said to obtain relief at the shrine of

* Eyton's Shropshire, and Introduction to Paisley Register. † Ibid.

the Saxon Princess. It was natural that the Shropshire monks should place their new home at Paisley under the patronage of a saint whom they must have held in great reverence. It was a link between them and the scenes of former days, of a strong and yet tender description.

As St. Milburga was the saint of the place whence they had come, St. Mirin or Mirinus was a saint of the country of their adoption. The one the Normans took from the Saxon Church, the other from that of the Celts. At Paisley they found a church with a parochial territory dedicated to his memory.* He was revered by the inhabitants as one of the early apostles of Christianity; and, like all the Celtic saints, his memory was regarded with the deepest affection by the natives. The new comers could not have taken a more judicious way of commending themselves to the people among whom they were to labour than by calling their new monastery after the name of this local and popular saint. They thus united themselves in sentiment with the old historic Church of Scotland. It was both a wise and a right thing for them to do.

As the name of Mirin is associated with the first preaching of Christianity at Paisley and in Strathgrif, it may not be out of place to state here what is now known of his life and labours. The materials for forming an estimate of these are but scanty. His name is found in both Irish and Scotch Kalendars, but there is little more than the mention of it,† and even this is given in so many forms that it is not easy at times to identify it as belonging to the same person. We are indebted for most of our knowledge of Mirin to the only complete and specially Scotch service book that has come down to us from the Roman Church, the Breviary, as it is called, of Aberdeen. This most interesting work was written by Bishop Elphinstone, and published in 1550. It contains the lives of the Scottish saints, and all the legends commonly received regarding them which floated about among the common people.‡ Neat little epitomes of these are inserted in the Breviary, and were read during service in the church. Among the lives of other saints, that of the patron saint of Paisley appears. We shall add at the end of this chapter the whole service for St. Mirin's day, taken from the book re-

* Glasgow Register, p. 60. † See Appendix.

‡ "Quae sparsim in incerto antea vagabantur."—*Title Page of Breviary.*

ferred to, as it brings before us an office which must have been particularly sacred to the monks of Paisley. Meantime we give in a more direct way, and apart from legend and miracle, what throws light on the history of Mirin.

Saint Mirin was a pupil of one of the most revered of the Irish saints, Saint Congal, Abbot of Bangor, who was famed for his piety, and who is described in an old Celtic book as a man who fostered and educated many saints, for he kindled and lighted up an unquenchable love of God in their hearts and minds.* He is especially said to have been the tutor of the blessed Mirinus.† Congal was born in A.D. 517, and in 558 founded the great Monastery of Bangor, in County Down, on Belfast Lough. This institution was famous for the learning and piety of its inmates. It seems to have resembled a town rather than a monastery of later times, and under the rule of Congal it contained no less than three thousand monks at one time.‡ Here Mirin was brought by his parents, and here, after having received his education, he joined the brotherhood, and in due time became their prior. The manner of life at Bangor resembled that of its sister institution at Iona, with which it was in constant correspondence. Its discipline was revered everywhere in Ireland and Scotland. The "rule" of its abbot, in Irish verse, has come down to our day, and was followed by many establishments of a similar kind to that of Bangor. An extract from this rule, as practised by one of its disciples, shews amid what surroundings and under what discipline our Paisley saint was reared :—

"Let the monk live under the discipline of one father and in the society of many, that from one he may learn humility, from the other penitence, from the one silence, from the other gentleness. Let him never gratify his own wishes. Let him eat whatever he is bidden. Let him possess only what he receives. Let him perform his allotted task with diligence; only when wearied let him retire to bed; let him be compelled to rise before he has slept sufficiently. When he is required, let him hold his peace. Let him fear the head of the monastery as a

* Mart Donegal.—Bp. Forbes's Kalendars, p. 309.

† Aberdeen Breviary.

‡ See Montalembert's Monks of the West.

master and love him as a father; let him believe that whatever he orders is for his good, and obey him without question, seeing that he is called to obedience and to fulfil all that is right. Let his fare be homely and sparing, sufficient to support life without weighing down the spirit; a little bread, vegetables, pulse or flour, mixed with water,—let this be his diet, as becometh one who professeth to seek in heaven an eternal crown."*

The whole mode of life at Bangor was simple in the extreme; studying and transcribing the Scriptures, with manual labour, formed the constant occupation of the brethren.

St. Mirin was a contemporary of St. Columba,† and must have been familiar with the great Scottish apostle. Mirin is mentioned as entertaining, when he was Prior of Bangor, St. Finian, of Moville or Maghbile, under whose teaching St. Columba had been reared, and who was the cause of his forsaking Ireland for Iona.‡ Congal was a frequent visitor at Iona, and on one occasion accompanied the saint of that place to Inverness, and it is not improbable, so constant was the intercourse between the Irish and Scottish monasteries, that Mirin as well as his abbot visited the sacred Island of the Hebrides. St. Columba was much attached to the house of Bangor; he remembered it in his prayers. In one of his sacred poems§ he says, "My visit to Congal was indeed delightful," and on one occasion, when he and his companions landed at Bangor, Congal washed their feet in token of his reverence for his holy visitors.

Bangor like Iona was a great missionary establishment. Its brethren went everywhere preaching Christianity, and many of them passed into the continent of Europe, founding societies and following a rule like that of the Irish Monasteries. Bernard speaks of these Irish monks overflowing the continent like an inundation,‖ and there are churches and localities that still bear their name, even as far south as Italy. Congal himself, possessed by the missionary fervour with which he inspired his disciples,

* M'Lear's Apostles of Medieval Europe, Art. *Columbanus.*

† St. Columba died 9th June, A.D. 597.

‡ The whole story is given in Reeves' Life of St. Columba.

§ See Preface to Reeves' Life of St. Columba. ‖ St. Bernard. Liber St. Malac, C 5.

crossed to Terra Heth or Tiree in the Hebrides, and in that lonely island founded a church. St. Mailrubha, in 671, left Bangor for Apercrossan (Apple-cross) in Ross-shire, where he reared a monastery which he governed for fifty-one years, until he was slain by the Danes.* It was in the same spirit that St. Mirin left his Irish home and came to Scotland. We cannot fix precisely the year of his departure, and can only give the proximate date as 580.† Nor can we state with certainty the place of his arrival in this country, though in all probability it was Dunbarton,‡ from whence he could easily come to Paisley. It was in that same year that Columbanus, an apostle of whom more is known than of St. Mirin, left Bangor. He had there been a companion of the Paisley saint, and we may form an idea of the life and spirit of the one of whom so little is known, from what is well known regarding the other. Columbanus, we are told, heard the voice which spoke to Abraham echoing in his ears, "Get thee out of thy country, and from thy kindred, and thy father's house, unto a land that I will shew thee." Obeying this command, he went first to Britain, thence he crossed to France, and in Burgundy attracted crowds of disciples, and founded a monastery that might rival that of Bangor, whence he came. He was famous throughout Gaul. After a time, meeting with difficulties, he moved further south into Switzerland. Traces of the Irish monk are still found there. Finally he crossed the Alps, and settled down between Genoa and Milan, where he founded a house after the pattern of that of his native land, at Bobbio, where he died. He carried with him the liturgy which is called the "Cursus Scotorum;" and the Antiphonal of Bangor is still preserved at Milan. § The life of his brother missionary who came to Paisley, though less varied in incident, was without doubt inspired by the same spirit which both had imbibed at the feet of the same master, Congal. "Who-

* Aberdeen Breviary, parsestiva.—Forbes' Kalendars, p. 383. † See Appendix.

‡ In the life of St. Kieran at March 5, in Colgan's Acta S.S. Hib. (p. 46) there is a notice of Medranus, who is mentioned in the lost Kalendar of Cashel, with a St. Tomanus in one church in Britain (Dunbarton) of Alcluid.

§ I am indebted for this notice of the Bangor saint to M'Lear's Apostles of Modern Europe, Montalembert's Monks of the West, and to M'Kenzie's Lives of Scottish Writers (Art. *Columbanus.*)

soever conquers the world," Columbanus was wont to say, "treads the world under his feet. No one who spares himself can really hate the world. If Christ be truly in us we cannot live to ourselves; if we have conquered ourselves we have conquered all things. If the Creator of all things died for us that He might redeem us from sin, ought not we to die to sin? Let us die to ourselves. Let us live to Christ, that Christ may live in us."

It is most likely that Mirin founded a church at Paisley. In an ancient litany, said to be used by the Culdees of Dunkeld,* his name is mentioned, with that of other Celtic saints, in a list of Abbots. Possibly he may have presided over a monastery at Paisley, similar in its rule to that of Bangor or Iona. The buildings of the Celtic monasteries invariably consisted of a number of huts constructed of wattles or twigs, and the appearance of their inmates must have been equally primitive. When they travelled it was in companies, their outfit was a pastoral staff, a leathern water bottle, a case of leather strung over their shoulders, containing their sacred books; and with the Irish tonsure high on their shaven head, and their long locks flowing behind, they must have presented a striking appearance.† These notices of them help us to realise Mirin as he lived at Paisley. Like his other brethren, he was a wanderer. He must have travelled over a great part of western and southern Scotland. His name lingers in the Stewartry of Kirkcudbright, and in the counties of Ayr and Dunbarton.‡ It is still an household word in Paisley, where, "full of miracles and holiness he slept in the Lord."§ Six hundred years after his death, the monks from Wenloc, when they came there, found his memory still green. In their charters, and in the bulls of Popes, he is called "the glorious confessor St. Mirin." His altar and tomb were in the church, and lights were kept always burning before them.|| A Fair was held on the day kept sacred in his honour, and his effigy was engraved on the seal of the Monastery in the vestments of a bishop, his right hand raised in benediction, and his left holding a crosier,

* Forbes' Kalendar—Preface.

† M'Lear's Apostles of Medieval Europe. Adamnan's Life of St. Columba, edited by Dr. Reeves. ‡ See Appendix. § Aberdeen Breviary.

|| Saint Mirin, by David Semple, F.S.A., p. 35. Various notices in Register.

while round the seal is written the prayer, which must often have been in use in Paisley, "O Mirin! pray to Christ for thy servants."

Of the legends regarding Mirin we need say little. We may, perhaps, smile at the story of the miracles and portents which cluster round him, in common with all the Irish saints; but, as it has well been said, "it matters little whether these legends are historically correct,—their value lies in the moral of them. The falsehood would not have been invented unless it had started in a truth, and in all these legends there is set forth the victory of a good and beneficent man over evil, whether it be of matter or of spirit."* Amid the traditions, and fables, if we like so to call them, associated with our local saint, we discern the form of one who is well worthy of reverence, and when the inhabitant of Paisley mentions the familiar name of Mirin it is well he should know that it is that of one of the apostles of primitive Christianity, the disciple of Congal, the friend of St. Columba, and the companion of Columbanus, the missionary of France and of Italy.

The following is the complete office in the Breviary of Aberdeen for St. Mirin's day:—

## PRAYER.

Oh God! who art merciful in Thy nature, and the ruler of our desires: graciously hear the prayers of Thy suppliants, that by the intercession of Thy blessed Pontiff Mirin we may be enabled to obtain the remission of our sins: through Jesus Christ our Lord.

## FIRST LESSON.

Mirin, the bishop, was entrusted by his parents, at an early age, through the Divine inspiration, to St. Congal, to be brought up in the Monastery of Bangor: not only that he might instruct him in all polite learning,† but that he might likewise carefully train him in all knowledge of holiness, humility, chastity, and other virtues. Mirin committed the precepts of eternal life and all pertaining to salvation to a retentive memory with all the ardour of his soul.

* Kingsley's The Roman and the Teuton, pp. 204-206.

† Literally, "that he might teach him in *the perfection of letters.*"

## SECOND LESSON.

With increasing years, deeming his ancestral halls, riches, landed possessions, and other earthly goods fleeting and delusive, he resolved to carry the yoke of the Lord from his youth, and asked and received the habit of Holy Religion from St. Congal in the Monastery of Bangor. Not long afterwards, the office of Prior of the Monastery having become vacant, he was elected Prior, against his will, by Congal and his brethren. Having entered upon the duties of his office, he reproved the Brethren more from a cordial love of charity than indiscreet zeal, and the one whom he outwardly chastised he inwardly loved.

## THIRD LESSON.

On a certain occasion, Finian, Bishop of Moville, a man of great sanctity, came on a friendly visit to the Monastery of Bangor during the absence of St. Congal, and was kindly received by blessed Mirin, the prior, of whom, on account of delicate health, he asked a drink of milk. Now, there was no milk in the Monastery, but the cellarer, by order of the blessed Mirin, going into the cellar, found a dish filled with the best of milk, which having brought, at a nod from him, he presented to blessed Finian. Thereafter, he kindly sent it round the company, sitting according to their rank.

## FOURTH LESSON.

Mirin afterwards proceeded to the camp of a certain king of Ireland, for the purpose of establishing the Catholic faith upon a firmer footing, where, the wife of the king at the time being near her confinement, was sorely distressed by various pains and sufferings. The king having heard of Mirin's arrival, would not permit him to enter his camp; but, [*on the contrary,*] treated him with utter contempt; which the blessed Mirin perceiving, he prayed God that that accursed king might feel the pains and pangs of the suffering wife, which immediately happened, as he had besought the Lord; so that for three days and as many nights he ceased not to shout* before all the chiefs of his kingdom. But the king seeing himself so ignominiously humbled by God, and that no remedy was of any avail, sought Mirin's lodging, and most willingly granted all that he had previously desired. Then blessed Mirin by his holy prayers freed the king entirely from his pains.

## FIFTH LESSON.

On a certain occasion the blessed Mirin remaining in his cell past the usual time, the brother who waited upon him went to ascertain the cause of the delay. On approaching the cell he instantly stood in rapt amazement, for through the chinks and

* With pain (to howl).

fissures he beheld a celestial splendour. That night the blessed Mirin did not join the brethren at the psalmody in the church according to their wont. But understanding by Divine inspiration that the brother had been witness to such stupendous wonders, he took him apart in the morning, and charged him to tell no one during his life what he had seen on the previous night, and that in the meantime he should not presume to approach his cell.

## SIXTH LESSON.

On another occasion likewise, whilst the brethren of St. Mirin were at work near the valley of Colpdasch, one of them quite overpowered by fatigue and thirst, falling down upon the ground, expired, and lay lifeless from noon till none.* But blessed Mirin was very much grieved that the Brother should have been removed by such an untoward and sudden death. He besought the Lord, and immediately the dead man was restored to his former life. At length, full of sanctity and miracles, he slept in the Lord at Paisley. The Church there is dedicated to God, under his invocation.†

* *i.e*, 12—3 P.M.

† The last sentence is literally, *in cujus honore*, &c., "in whose honour the said Church is dedicated to God," &c.

# CHAPTER VI.

## The Priory.

1164—1248.

> They gave their best. O tenfold shame
> On us, their fallen progeny,
> Who sacrifice the blind and lame,
> Who will not wake or fast with Thee.
>
> *Keble.*

THE first Prior of the newly-founded convent was Osbert, one of the thirteen monks who accompanied Humbald from Wenlock. He was succeeded by Roger, and they are the only two rulers of the Monastery whose names have come down to us until it attained the full dignity of an Abbey.* In their time the house increased in wealth; lands, churches, mills, and fishings were added to its possessions; while the original gift of the Stewarts was augmented by benefactions from himself and others of like mind, who sought by their donations to obtain for themselves and their families the favour and blessing of the Church. The wife of the founder, Eschina of Molla, in Roxburghshire, followed in the steps of her husband. She had a daughter who was buried in the chapter house of the Priory, the first of many of that noble race who lie within the sacred precincts; and the place had naturally for her the tenderest associations. Even in the dry, legal language of the charter in which her gift is set forth, there is a touch of pathos in the words, in which, after stating that her donation is "for the welfare of my Lord King William, and David his brother,

* They are the only two mentioned in any of the Chartularies of the religious houses of Scotland. Reg. de Pas., p. 19.

and my own soul, and those of our heirs, and for the soul of King Henry of England, and for the soul of King David, and King Malcolm, and King Henry," she adds, "and for the soul of Margaret, my daughter, who lies buried in the chapter house at Passlet."* Her gift was a carucate† of land, and pasture for fifty sheep. The land is described with great exactness, and the boundaries so clearly set forth that it would probably not be difficult even yet to identify them. "From where the Stelnburn falls into the Blakburne, and by the Blakburne upwards to the two stones lying by the bank of the Blakburne, and opposite the house of Ulfi the steward, and so upwards to a ditch, and to two standing stones in that ditch, and from these stones to another ditch filled with stones, and from that ditch to Heselensahe, and from that by the footpath to the shallow at the waterfall of Alernbarhe, and from thence to the ford of the Stelnburn, and so by the Stelnburn till it descends to the Blakburne."‡ The exactness and clearness with which such charters as this are drawn out is wonderful, and they exhibit an amount of legal skill and use of language which one would hardly have expected to find in those very early times.§ We find also from an examination of these charters the various sources of the wealth which flowed into the coffers of the newly founded convent. Gifts of churches to the Priory and its monks are frequent during those early years. The churches of Cathcart,‖ Carmunnoc,** Inverkip,†† and Mearns,‡‡ were bestowed on the Monastery with all their lands and tithes, their dues and privileges. The duties of these churches were discharged by a vicar, who collected their revenues

* Reg. de Pas.—The chapter house was probably among the first erections. The only other part of the buildings mentioned at this period is the dormitory.

† A *carucate* is the extent of land a pair of oxen could work in a year.

‡ Reg. de Pas., p. 75.

§ 1165. The influence of the Normans infused through the country by degrees the great feudal usages of the continent, in the structure of which they had taken an eminent part. It was their speciality that down to the minutest transaction, their operations should be articulated, and the articulation should be recorded for future use.—*Burton's History of Scotland*, Vol. I. p. 283.

‖ Reg. de Pas., p. 5. ** Ibid, p. 105. Cormunoc was given by Henry, the son of Anselm, who left his body and that of his wife, with the third part of their substance, to the Abbey. †† Ibid, p. 112, by Baldwin, Count of Lanark. ‡‡ Ibid, p. 98.

for the benefit of the house to which he belonged. The consequences of this system of endowment were little thought of, and yet they might have been foreseen. It was one of the chief causes which brought about the destruction of the Church, as we shall see. The tithes and property which the Church had obtained for the support of a resident clergy were in a great measure swallowed up by the monks. The parochial system of the country was destroyed, and though the monasteries became, and continued for some ages, the "home of religion and letters, the schools of civil life in a rough time, and the teachers of industry and the arts of peace among men whose sloth used only to bo roused by the sound of arms,"* even the advantages conferred by them were of small account in comparison with the mischief of degrading the parish clergy. "The little village church, preserving the memory of some early teacher of the faith, with its modest parsonage, where were wont to be found the consolations of religion, refuge and help for the needy, and encouragement for all on the road to heaven, was left in the hands of a stipendiary vicar, an underling of the monastery, ground down to the lowest stipend that would support life, whose little soul was buried in his cloister, or showed its living activity only in disputing about his needful support with his master in the Abbey, while his 'hungry sheep looked up and were not fed.' The Church which ignorantly, and for its own purpose, sanctioned that misappropriation, paid in time the full penalty."† The Clunaics were much given to holding churches as part of their endowments, and in a spirited controversy between Peter of Clugny, and Bernard of Clairvaux, on the merits of their different orders, the former defends very earnestly the use, or perhaps rather abuse, of this kind of ecclesiastical property. The incumbent of the Church of Mearns was a priest of the name of Helias,‡ and with the consent of his brother, Peter of Polloc, the patron, he bestowed the benefice on the convent, serving the cure as its vicar. Ruglen was given by King William,§ Innerkip by Baldwin, Count of Lanark,|| with all its possessions, except the house of Randulph, the chaplain of Renfrew, to be his as long as he

* Innes' Scotland in the Middle Ages shews this well.

† Innes' Sketches of Early Scotch History, p. 18. ‡ Reg. de Pas., p. 100.

§ Ibid, p. 106. || Ibid, p. 112.

lives, "unless he should change his life by putting on the religious habit," when, of course, his property would fall to the convent, as no monk could hold property of his own. Such a contingency was not unlikely. During those early years we have frequent notices of men who stripped themselves of their possessions and sought the quiet of the cloister, at that time the only home for either the studious or the devout. Henry De St. Martin, one of the followers of the Stewart, bestowed on the monks his land of Penauld, and, with the full consent of his lord, took his place among their number;* and the great Lord of the Isles,† the son of the mighty Somerled, bargains that he should be admitted a brother and his wife a sister of the monastic order, wishing to procure for themselves in life a quiet retreat, and in death a consecrated resting place.‡ It was in this way that a connection began between the Western Highlands and the Monastery, which in after years became very intimate. The account of the transaction between the Abbey and the Island Lord, as given in the charter, is very curious. There is in the story much that tells of the wild chieftain. Reginald was the son of Somerled, Lord, as he is termed, of Inchegal, who led an army of wild Islesmen on a plundering expedition to the mainland, and had been slain at Renfrew§ about the time that Humbald arrived there with his monks from Wenloc. Reginald became a great benefactor to the church. From an old Celtic record called the "Book of Clanranald, kept from time to time by the MacVurichs," we learn that he was the most distinguished of his day among the Gael "for prosperity, sway of generosity, and feats of arms." Three monasteries were founded by him, viz.:—A Monastery of Black Monks in Iona, in honour of God and Columkille;‖ a Monastery of Black Friars in the same place; and a Monastery of Grey Friars at Sagadale.¶ It may have been the circumstance of his father's death at Renfrew, in the neighbourhood of the newly-founded monastery, that led him to take an interest in the Paisley ecclesiastics, as well as those of far-away Iona. His "sway of generosity" was exercised to the full in favour of our Abbey. He be-

* Reg. de Pas., p. 48. † Dominus Inchegal. ‡ Reg. de Pas. p. 125.

§ 1166. ‖ Or St. Columba. ¶ Saddle in Kintyre.

stows on the convent, for the first year, eight cows, and two pennies from every house in his dominions from which smoke proceeds; and in every succeeding year, one penny; while his wife, Fonia, gives a tenth of all the goods which God has given her, "both those which she retains for her own use and those which she sends by sea or land for sale." Unless the tax is promptly paid by his heirs, he tells them they shall have his curse—a threat which to a highlander was of fearful import. He charges them to be always at peace with the brotherhood at Paisley; he beseeches his allies, and commands his men that wherever the monks or their men should go by land or sea they should hold them by the hand,* and aid them in all their transactions; if his heirs ill-treat them they are to have his malediction, if his men, they are to be punished with death. This he swears by the most sacred oath an Islesman could take,—by the patron saint of all highlanders, Saint Columba of Iona. For those good offices toward the Priory he is made a brother, and Fonia is made a sister of the house of Paisley and of the whole order of Clugny, sharing in their prayers and the "rites of the divine service." Reginald was buried at Iona. The Gælic chronicle, which we have already quoted, says, that, "having obtained a cross from Jerusalem and having received extreme unction, he died, and was buried at Reilic Oran, at Iona, in A.D. 1207." In the churchyard of the chapel in this sacred isle, there is a stone having on it a sword (which marks the grave of a warrior), a small cross, and below, a treasure-box, which is said to denote the founder of some church. This is probably the monument of Reginald, Lord of Inchegal, one of the first benefactors to the Abbey of Paisley. It has been supposed that about this time a colony of monks went from Paisley to Iona, and that this celebrated seat of learning and piety became a cell of Paisley, filled with Clunaic monks.† The Pope addresses a bull to Celestinus, Abbot of Iona, dated 9th December, 1203, and to the brethren, present and future, then professing a religious or monastic life, and takes under his protection the Monastery of St. Columba, in order that the monastic order instituted in that place,

* Manuteneant.

† Ancient Church of Scotland (by M'Kenzie Walcott); Lanagan, and others.

according to God and the rule of Saint Benedict, may be preserved inviolate in all time to come. It is evident, however, that this monastery could not have been an offshoot from Paisley. The superior is designated an abbot, and the house of Paisley itself was only ruled by a prior. This fact shews that the Iona monks must have belonged to another order of Benedictines than that of the Clunaics.*

The Stewarts held their land from the Crown on condition of their furnishing the service of a certain number of knights, and among the benefactors of the monastery we come on the names of many of these with their Norman and Seignorial titles. The names of De Croc, Radulph de Insula, Philip de Perthec, Alanus de Montgomery, Henricus de Nes, and others, occur frequently; while among them are occasionally seen those of their Saxon followers, such as Thor, Grymketel, Ulfus, and Swene. There are no names, or almost none, of the Celtic inhabitants, the natives of Strathgryfe, who appear to have sunk into entire serfdom, and became the hewers of wood and drawers of water to the Norman lords.† They were a Gælic people who scarcely knew the name of charters; and, living on their lands without them, they had no valid title to what they possessed in the opinion of English lawyers. The country was Celtic, governed by Celtic customs, and animated by Celtic principles.‡ We hear nothing of any rising of the people in opposition to the intruding Normans and their customs.§ Those of them who came, with the lands they inhabited, into the guardianship of the convent must have profited by the change. "For ages they had enjoyed no settled government; crushed by oppression, without security of life or property; knowing nothing of law but its heavy grip; alternately plundering and plundered; neglecting agri-

* Society of Scottish Antiquaries, April 14, 1873.—Paper by W. P. Skene.

† On May 12, 1348, a jury was empanelled in the church yard of Kettle, to try a question regarding the ownership of three serfs. The claimants were Alexander, Abbot of Dunfermline, and Duncan, Earl of Fife. The disputed property, consisting of a father and two sons, was found to belong to the Lord Abbot.

‡ David I., in the early part of his reign, granted to the Episcopal Church of Glasgow the tenth of his *can* in swine and other beasts from his county of *Strathgrive* (Chart. Glas. 17). *Can* was a *Celtic* duty payable to the king or the superior by the occupiers of the land.

§ Chalmers' Caledonia, vol. 3, p. 778.

culture, and suffering the penalty of famine and disease. They were transferred to kinder masters, who ruled them with a gentler hand, employing them in tilling the soil, and imparting to them a certain amount of culture and education."* It was part of the Benedictine rule, not only to cultivate learning in the cloister, but to impart it to the children of those beyond their walls, and from the very beginning of the Benedictine Order there were in their houses two kinds of schools—a greater or less, according to the size of their house—the greater open to all students, who were free to attend them. † The very existence of the Convent must have exercised a certain civilising influence on all classes, Normans and natives, throughout Strathgryfe. The skill and accuracy, and even literary power, with which the early deeds are drawn up show that men of culture had made the priory their home. Architects and masons, and skilled labourers of various kinds, must have been employed for years before the buildings of the Monastery appeared above the surrounding forests, and the mention which we have of mills, roads, carriages, measurements of land, and even gardens, in the early charters tells how agriculture must have made progress under the monastic rule. That rule, however beneficent and liberal in some respects, was very strict in others, and in nothing more than the manner in which it guarded the rights and privileges of the convent. A striking instance of this is given in the deeds of the house during the time of the Priory.‡ Two followers of the Stewart—Robert Croc and Henry de Nes—"special friends" of the house, "inspired by divine love," came to Roger the Prior and his chapter, asking leave to have churches in their castles,§ where religious service might be celebrated for themselves, ‖ their families, and their guests. The first of these knights who had founded an hospital for the sick,

* Sketches of Early Scottish History, by C. Innes, p. 114.

† Historical Sketches by Newman, p. 156.

‡ Reg. de Pas., p. 77.

§ His castle was at the place called after him, Crocston. Part of this castle, built in the twelfth century, is still standing. See "The Tree of Crocston," by David Semple, F.S.A., pp. 13 and 21.

‖ In clausis suis.

was particularly desirous that religious offices should be performed by a duly qualified person in the hospital for their benefit. Their requests were at once granted, but only on condition that the chaplains should belong to the Monastery, that they should swear fidelity to the Convent, and bring all the offerings made at their chapels to the Mother Church. No parishioners were allowed to hear mass in the chapels, and when any of the brethren at the hospital, or their servants should die, their bodies were to be brought at once to Paisley without celebration of mass at the chapel. The Monastery would allow no interference with its privileges, and Robert Croc and Henry de Nes had to swear that it would suffer no damage from their pious intentions.

Thus the early years of the Convent passed away under the government of its priors. Probably no part of the church buildings of that time remains unless it be the Norman doorway, at the south east of the nave, and the three adjacent windows. The first erections were probably of wood and twigs, and the masons' work followed in the course of years. We know more certainly the state of the surrounding country. Vast forests of oak or beech clothed it on every side, stretching away towards Ayrshire on the one hand, and the newly-formed burgh of Renfrew on the other, unbroken except by the clearings of some Norman lord or his follower, like Croc at Crooston, De Nes on Leveran side, or Grymketel on the ridge of Arkilston. In the lower reaches of the forest, herds of cattle and swine were tended. Among the upper glades of Fereneze, and where now stands the busy town of Barrhead, herds of deer wandered at will.* On the verge of the hunting grounds, at Blackhall, was the lodge of the Stewart. There the forest broke into brushwood till it reached, near what was called the Linn, the Mill of Paisley. On the other side of the river were two carucates of cleared ground, where stood the church of St. Mirin, and some adjoining land held by a man called Scerlo; but this was "cut out of the wood," which rose darkly on every side, and in the glades of which the monks were for many a day to ply their axes.

Walter, the generous founder of Paisley, died in 1178. In his old

* The ruins of the Tower of Rais (Roes) can still be seen.

age he became a monk of Melrose, a convent which had shared his benefactions. He died there, but was buried at Paisley.* He had been a princely benefactor to the church, and the monkish chronicler who records his death, not unnaturally adds, "*anima beata vixit in gloria*"—his blessed soul lives in glory.

* Chronicon de Mailros.

## CHAPTER VII.

### The Abbey.

1200-1248.

> All without is mean and small,
> All within is vast and tall,
> All without is harsh and shrill,
> All within is hushed and still.
>
> *C. Kingsley.*

THE beginning of the thirteenth century found the Convent still in the second rank of religious houses, and under the government of Roger the Prior. Its wealth was steadily on the increase. Various individuals of high and low degree contributed to the monastic revenues, but the chief support continued to come from the lordly house of the Stewart. Alan the son of Walter, the founder, followed in his father's footsteps, and gave with a liberal hand for the repose of his father's soul. Little is known regarding this second Stewart. He was a friend and counsellor of King William the Lion, and was helpful to him both as a soldier and adviser. He married a daughter of Swene, the son of Thor, of whom we know only through his benefactions to the Abbeys of Holyrood and Scone. He is said to have joined in the fifth Crusade proclaimed by Pope Innocent III. The Chartulary of Paisley bears strong testimony to his piety and munificence. Gifts from him of the most varied kind are chronicled in its pages. He gave to the Priory the Mill of Paisley,* and a piece of ground for the miller's house, charging

* Reg. de Pas., p. 13.

only four chalders of wheaten flour and four of grain as an annual rent. He transferred to the monks five marks of silver, which the convent of Melrose used to pay him for his lands of Maphelim.* He ordered three of his knights—Robert Croc, Henry de Nes, and William the son of Maidus,—with other honest men, to perambulate and designate for the Monastery the valuable lands of Moniabroc,† near the great boulder stone of Clochroderick.‡ He gave the monks rights of fishing in Lochwinnoch, and he bestowed on them the church of Kingarth and its chapels, in the Island of Bute.§ This Island had been granted to him in his father's lifetime. In the eyes of churchmen, it was a very sacred spot. Thither, in the beginning of the seventh century, had come St. Blane in a boat without oars. Here he had ruled as bishop and worked many miracles, and on the headland of Kingarth had placed his church, which was associated for centuries with his presence and regarded with the greatest reverence. The custody of this sanctuary, with all its revenues, Alan gave to the house of Paisley, for the soul of his father, and mother Eschina. "The Church of Kingaif, in the Island of Bute, with all the chapels, and the whole parish of that Island, together with the whole of those lands of which the boundaries, said to have been fixed by St. Blane, are still apparent from sea to sea." This was his last gift to the Church. In 1204 he died, and was buried before the high altar of the Priory. His son Walter, the third Stewart, was better known in public life than his father; but, like him, his gifts are the chief record of his life. He was appointed by Alexander II., in 1231, the Justiciary of Scotland; and in 1238 he was sent as an ambassador to negotiate for that King a marriage with Mary, the daughter of Engelram, Count de Coucy. This indicates the position he occupied in the transactions of the time, but most of the interest of his life centred in Paisley and its convent. Four years after his father's death he gave the Monastery all the land between the two small streams that still bear the names of the Altpatrick and the Espedair, "as the Altpatrick descends into Kert

* Reg. de Pas., p. 14. Now called Mauchline.

† Reg. de Pas., p. 13.

‡ This is the first notice we have of this curious rock.

§ Reg. de Pas., p. 15.

Lochwinnoch, and the Espedair descends to the land of the monks lying between *le Linne* and Kert." * He gave them wood for building and dead wood for fuel in his forest, and pasturage there for an hundred swine in time of mast. He gave them also all the land between Mach and Calder, and the portion of ground to the east of the Mill of Paisley, to the burn on the south of *The Cross of the Lord*, as that burn rises at the boundaries of the monks and falls into the Kert. He excambed with them the land they possessed in Ennerwick for the land of Hillington, which Radulphus the chaplain held, and thirty bolls of flour paid by Ada de Kent for his lands of Ingliston, and some other privileges which he possessed.† But all these donations sink into insignificance compared with the munificent gift of his later years. Imitating his grandfather, the first Stewart, Walter had founded a monastery on the north bank of the River Ayr, ‡ at a place called Dalmulin. It was dedicated to the Virgin Mary, and peopled by canons and nuns of the Order of Sempringham, from Sixile, in Yorkshire. He endowed this house with lands, mills, fishings, and with many churches and chapels in Ayrshire. The canons and nuns, however, did not stay long at Dalmulin. The northern air did not agree with them, and, pleading want of health, they returned to Yorkshire. The Stewart then with liberal hand transferred all their possessions, temporal and spiritual, to Paisley.§ Dalmulin became a cell of the Priory and was filled with Clunaics, and its great wealth passed into the hands of the Paisley chapter, subject only to a payment of forty merks annually to the Master of Sempringham, who waived his rights to all the property.

While thus generous in his benefactions, the Stewart was always particular in reserving to himself certain rights and privileges. The birds and beasts on the land transferred to the monks are always specially retained. "The preservation of game and the whole economy of the forest were necessarily of prominent importance in an age when the time of the free born was divided between war and the chase."||

* Reg. de Pas., p. 17.

† Reg. de Pas., p. 17, *et seg.*, where all Walter's gifts are chronicled.

‡ 1229. § 1238—Reg. de Pas., p. 24.

|| Sketches of Early Scottish History, p. 102.

The Stewarts were strict preservers of game. In their early grants to Melrose, they expressly reserve the rights of the chase. "Except only that neither the monks, nor lay brethren, nor any, by their authority, shall hunt, nor take hawks in that forest, for that suiteth not their order, and we think it not expedient for them." "Salva eadem foresta mea tantum in bestiis et avibus." * Walter, in his transactions with the Paisley monks is equally particular. His forest of Fereneze was to be free from all their encroachments, lest his deer should be disturbed. If any of their cattle should pass the boundaries below Fereneze in charge of a keeper, they should pay a fine of five cows, and if without a keeper, they should pay a fine of a penny for every five cows, a heavy penalty for trespass.

Notwithstanding all the wealth bestowed on the Convent, it had one drawback to its prosperity. It was in the second rank of religious houses, and was ruled only by a Prior. In position it was inferior to the other principal monasteries of Scotland. The Abbey of Clugny was very jealous of raising any of the houses over which it had jurisdiction to the rank of an abbey. It held them more firmly, and enforced its discipline over them more easily when they were in the subordinate position. It was, however, very inconvenient for the Monastery of Paisley to be in strict subjection to a superior so far away as the French Abbot. The distance rendered it a great hardship for the Paisley House to be constantly sending an account of its doings to Clugny; and there were other drawbacks of an ecclesiastical kind which rendered it desirable that the Monastery should be ruled by an Abbot of its own. In some cases not even a novice could be received without the consent of the Arch-Abbot, and those who were to be admitted as monks had to go to Clugny in order to make their profession. Accordingly, King Alexander, influenced doubtless by the Stewart his counsellor, applied to Pope Honorius III., setting forth in his petition the loss the Convent had sustained for want of an Abbot, how the monks had not been able to make regular profession "to the great danger of their souls, the dissolution of order and the loss of their property," and asking his authority for the creation of an

* Sketches of Early Scottish History, p. 103.

Abbot in the Monastery.* The Pope, by a bull dated at Reate, in 1219, the third year of his pontificate, issued a commission to the Bishop of Glasgow and the Abbots of Kelso and Melrose to enquire into the whole circumstances of the case, and if they thought proper to allow the monks to proceed to the canonical election of an Abbot. † The commissioners accordingly (with the exception of the Abbot of Melrose, who sent "sufficient excuse,") met at Jedburgh, and, by the advice of certain men "skilled in the law," summoned the Prior and Convent of Wenlock to appear before them and state whether they had any objections to the proposed change in the House of Paisley, as it was from their Monastery that the Convent of Paisley was planted. No one appeared at the proper time from Wenlock, but letters were received from the Shropshire House stating that they made no objections to the proposed change. The commissioners, therefore, with reservation of the rights of other parties, decreed that the monks of Paisley might proceed to the canonical election of an abbot, and the Patron of Paisley, the Lord High Stewart, also gave his permission.‡

Any connection that might have existed between Paisley and Wenloc was thus severed, but that between Paisley and the house of Clugny remained firm as before. In the Bull of Honorius, the rights of others were reserved, and not even the Pope ventured to erect the Paisley house finally into an Abbey, without the consent of the Abbot of Clugny. It was not until twenty-six years afterwards that this dignitary gave his permission.§ During that time the Cistercians, a religious order that had become powerful in Scotland, did all in their power to get the Paisley house transferred to them, by promising the Stewart those privileges for his monastery which Clugny refused to grant, and the monks themselves were subjected to considerable persecution to induce them to consent to this transference. In the year 1245, the Council of Lyons was held in furtherance of the Crusades. At this Council William the Bishop of Glasgow, and other Scottish Bishops, were present, and being in the neighbourhood of Clugny, took occasion to bring before Hugo the Abbot the condition of the Convent of Paisley. After the Council was over, the

* Reg. de Pas., p. 8. † Ibid. ‡ Ibid., p. 10. § Ibid., p. 15.

Abbot of Clugny entertained with munificent hospitality the Pope, the Emperor of Constantinople, the King of France, and many church dignitaries,—twelve cardinals, three archbishops, fifteen bishops, and an host of others, clerical and lay, without depriving the brethren of their chambers, their refectory, chapter house, and other ordinary apartments. It is probable that the Bishop of Glasgow and some of his brethren were among the guests, at any rate, they pleaded very earnestly the case of Paisley. They stated strongly that Humbaldus, the Prior of Wenloc, had cheated and deceived the founder of Paisley, concealing from him the fact that the head of his convent had no power to receive the profession of the monks, and it had thus happened that all the monks during the course of many years had died without making profession, on account of the want of an abbot, contrary to the intention of the founder, who might have provided an abbot for the said house from any order he chose to select. Hugo granted their request, and consented to the election of an abbot; and the bishops, in return for this favour, became bound, in behalf of Paisley, to pay two marks yearly to the Monastery of the Clunaic order at Pontefract in England, at the Feast of St. Peter ad Vincula. This subsidy the monks of Paisley seem to have forgotten to pay, and the license granted by Hugo was withdrawn by his successor, Stephen. The Bishop of Glasgow again pled the cause of the Paisley monks, and again obtained the requisite permission on his promising, in their name, prompt payment of the two marks for the future, and undertaking that the Abbot of Paisley should personally or by proxy, visit Clugny every seven years to make obeisance, and render an account to his superior.

William was probably the first abbot of Paisley, though it is possible that Roger may have assumed the title. The former is mentioned frequently in various deeds between 1225 and 1248. He seems to have been an ecclesiastic of no small energy, if we may judge from the zeal and determination which he showed in defending the privileges and possessions of his house. He had a notable controversy with his diocesan, Walter, Bishop of Glasgow, who, with the Bishop of St. Andrews, claimed right to tax the revenues of the churches belonging Paisley for proper payment of the vicars who served them, and to exact from them certain dues in name of "procurations."* This assumption, though backed by the decree of a Scotch ecclesiastical Council, William stoutly resisted. He made a journey himself from Paisley to Rome,† and pled his cause before the Pope, as the supreme protector of the order of Clugny and its privileges. Honorius III., who was at that time Pope, wisely refrained from pronouncing judgment upon a matter so intricate and of so local a character as the taxation of parish churches, and by a bull dated at Reate, in 1226,‡ referred the whole matter to the Bishop of Lismore and the Abbots of Kilwinning and Dercongal, giving full powers to any two of them to settle the dispute. These commissioners were successful in effecting a compromise between the contending parties. They met together in the church of Peebles, and drew up a scale of stipends for the vicars serving the churches belonging to the Abbey. These stipends were not very large, and consisted chiefly of the altar dues, eked out by a chalder or two of wheat, and supplemented occasionally by a few acres of ground in the neighbourhood of the church. The bulk of the revenues went to the Monastery. The question of procurations was settled at the same time; a scale of taxation for this purpose was agreed upon, and the church of Erskine was ceded to Glasgow. A firm peace was thus apparently concluded between the contending parties. It does not seem to have been so lasting as was expected, and even in William's time the controversy was revived. There was always a strong jealousy between the regular and the secular clergy, and their jurisdiction was perpetually clashing. As far as we can judge, the abbot on this occasion came off victorious.

A more serious dispute, because involving greater issues, was waged by Abbot William in connection with certain lands belonging to the Abbey on the other side of the Clyde, and in the Earldom of Lennox. The church of St. Patrick, built on the supposed birth-place of the saint, and regarded as a place of sanctity and pilgrimage, had been largely endowed with lands by the Earls of Lennox. These lands, with the church itself, were, in 1227, conveyed by Maldowen, the Earl of the time, to the Monastery of Paisley.§ Lying on the northern bank of the Clyde, and

* Reg. de Pas, p. 323, *et supra*. † Ibid., p. 314. ‡ Ibid., p. 320.

§ Ibid., pp. 158, 159, 160.

sloping to the sun, they formed a goodly possession, and probably on that account were difficult to retain. The wild Highlandmen who inhabited that part of the Lennox were continually seeking, by fair means and by foul, to obtain possession of them, and it took all the power of the Church to hold its own against their devices. The family of Lennox themselves seem no sooner to have parted with their fair lands than they sought to get them back. The eldest son of the Earl challenged the right of his father to bestow certain of the lands which he said belonged to him hereditarily, and the Abbot had to give him sixty merks to buy off his claim, or, as it is, put *pro bono pacis.** Duffgal, the brother of Earl Maldowen, made himself particularly obnoxious. He was at the time of his brother's gift rector of the church of Kilpatrick, and probably thought the Abbot an intruder in his domains. Being a churchman, and thus probably possessed of some skill in the drawing up of deeds, he forged some charters, making himself out proprietor of the lands of Cochmanach, Dalevanach, Bachan, Fimbalach, and others bearing similar Celtic names, and entrenching himself behind these titles defied Abbot William and his convent to meddle with him. The Abbot having found his former appeal to Rome successful, carried his grievance to Pope Gregory IX.,† who issued a commission to his "beloved sons" the Deans of Cunninghame and Carric, and the Master of the School of Ayr to try the case between Duffgal and the Abbot.‡ For a time the Kilpatrick rector kept to his own side of the river and refused to answer the citations of the papal judges or appear before them. At last, however, his courage gave way before the threat of excommunication, and being handed over to the secular arm, and in the parish church of Ayr, on the Sabbath following the Lord's day on which is sung *Quasi modo geniti,* he appeared before the deputies. The charge was brought against him of having forged charters in order to obtain possession of certain lands contrary to his own salvation, and the duty which he owed to the church. Duffgal made no answer to this grave accusation, but "smitten by his own conscience, and seeing the imminent danger to

* Reg. de Pas., p. 16.

† June, 1232. ‡ Reg. de Pas., p. 164, *et supra.*

his body and soul if the charges were proved against him, sought mercy instead of judgment" and placed himself in the hands of the Abbot and convent, who, on the advice of the judges, gave him the mercy he sought, and allowed him to hold his church and half a carucate of land at Cochmanach. Duffgal then made formal resignation of his lands, confessing in the most abject manner his wickedness in forging the charters, and betook himself to his church and diminished acres, probably thankful to have got off so well.

There were other lands in question before the judges besides those wrongly held by the Rector of Kilpatrick, and the name of one portion of them, that of Monachkeneran, appears constantly in the charters, inhibitions, and agreements of the time. These lands, lying to the east of the Church of Kilpatrick, had been tenanted in the end of the twelfth or beginning of the thirteenth century by a person named Beda Ferdan, who lived in a large house built of twigs, and who rendered for his holding the duty of receiving and feeding such pilgrims as came to the shrine of St. Patrick.* He had not been allowed to retain peaceful possession of his lands, and had been slain in defence of the right and liberty of the Church, and at the time of the Papal Commission which dispossessed the rector, Monachkeneran was held by a certain Gilbert the son of Samuel of Renfrew, probably a follower of the house of Lennox. With Gilbert, therefore, the Papal judges proceeded to deal, and summoned him to appear before them in the Parish Church of Irvine. Gilbert treated their citation very lightly, and merely sent them word that he would do what was right, taking no further notice of their summons. They proceeded, therefore, in his absence, to take proof, and to hear the witnesses brought forward by the convent. The evidence of these witnesses is taken in a manner that would do credit to any Court of Justice, and what they said is set down in a very terse and distinct way. Two diets of proof were held, and fourteen witnesses sworn and examined, all of whom testified to the lands in question having belonged to the Church of Kilpatrick.† Some of them having been born and brought up in the

* Habitantem in quaddam domo, magna fabricata de virgis—Reg. de Pas., p. 166.

† Reg. de Pas., pp. 166, 167, 168, 169, where a full account of this investigation is given, and from which we have drawn the narrative above. The following are the names of some of the witnesses :—Anekol, Gilbethoc, Ressin, Nemias, Rotheric Beg, and Gillekonel Manthac.

neighbourhood remembered Beda Ferdan well, and one stated that when he was a boy he and his father had been entertained as strangers by him, and one Anekol swore that when Earl David of Lennox, in the time of King William, sought to raise men from the lands of Kilpatrick as from the other lands of his barony, the Church interfered in defence of her tenants and proved their exemption from military service. The judges held that the Abbot and Convent had amply proved their right to the lands in dispute, according to their own judgment and that of men skilled both in canonical and civil law. They allowed them possession, and condemned Gilbert in expenses, namely, "in thirty pounds, to be sworn to and taxed." They then asked execution of their sentence of the Bishop of Glasgow. Gilbert was excommunicated for contumacy, and King Alexander II., at the request of the commissioners, put in force against him "the secular arm." This does not, however, appear to have been done with sufficient energy, for some time afterwards they again have recourse to His Majesty, wishing him "salvation in that which gives salvation to kings," and asking him not to relax the secular arm which had been extended against the excommunicated Gilbert until he had obeyed the sentence and satisfied his judges. Neither the secular arm nor the sacred arm of the Church appear to have been able, however, to dispossess him, and it was not until two years afterwards that his chief, the Earl, induced him to resign his charters and the claim to his lands, by agreeing to pay him sixty merks of silver, in three portions of twenty merks at a time. Other pendicles of land which had been alienated were one by one brought back, and peace reigned between the Monastery and the men of the Lennox.

William's incumbency as abbot lasted a long time. He thoroughly established and consolidated the prosperity of the Convent. Perhaps his visit to Rome may have helped him in his labours. Besides the commissions which he obtained from the Popes, and which we have noticed, he got in his time several Bulls conferring special privileges on the Monastery. As these privileges were extended by a subsequent Pope, we shall notice them hereafter. They were very extensive, and gave the Monastery power to hold its own against all who might seek to molest it.

## CHAPTER VIII.

### The Prosperous Times of Alexander III.

1248—1286.

Who loved the Church so well, and gave so largely to it,
They thought it should have canopied their bones
Till Doomsday;—but all things have an end.

DURING the early periods of the history of the Abbey, all we can learn regarding it is gleaned from the charters of endowments, the inhibitions and excommunications hurled against those who assailed its privileges, and the bulls of successive popes by whom those privileges were confirmed. The abbots seem to have taken no prominent part in the general history of the time, and appear to have been fully occupied with the extension and defence of the property and possessions of their house. It is not, however, difficult to form some idea of what the life of the Convent at that time was from the slight materials we possess. The monastic devotions were gone through with perfect regularity, varied by special services for the souls of those who had been benefactors of the house. In the scriptorium and chapter house were drawn up by skilled hands those wonderful charters which have come down to us, and for their terseness and accuracy, cannot be surpassed. Pilgrims to the shrine of St. Mirin would be received in the refectory; messengers would be despatched to the many outlying lands belonging to the Convent for the receipt of rents and making arrangements with tenants. From time to time the Abbot or his procurators would take a journey to Rome on special business, or to Clugny, to make obeisance to the head of the Order, bringing back to the brethren many a story of their travels. The Stewart and his knights were constantly their guests, if we may judge from the frequency with which they witness deeds in the chapter house, and were doubtless entertained with all the respect and hospitality due to their station. In the forest of Gleniffer the monks or their men might be seen herding their cattle, and in the low grounds busy with the operations of agriculture. It was a peaceful period in Scottish history—that period which all the old chroniclers speak of with rapture, when they contrast it with the stormy time which followed the death of Alexander III. The people were prosperous, and were glad to share their prosperity with the Church, as we learn from the gifts of many kinds which they poured into her treasury. The picture of life in an abbey of the Middle Ages, which has been so well drawn by a master hand, might be seen by any visitor to the banks of the Cart and to the Abbey of the Stewarts, in the happy days of King Alexander. "In black tunics, the mementoes of death, and in leathern girdles, the emblems of chastity, might then be seen carters silently yoking their bullocks to the team, and driving them in silence to the field, or shepherds interchanging some inevitable whispers while they watched their flocks, or wheelwrights, carpenters, and masons plying their trades like the inmates of some dumb asylum, and all pausing from their labours as the convent bell, sounding the hours of prime, nones, or vespers, summoned them to join in spirit where they could not repair in person, to those sacred offices. Around the monastic buildings might be seen the belt of cultivated land continually encroaching on the adjoining forest, and the passer-by might trace to the toils of these mute workmen the opening of roads, the draining of marshes, the herds grazing, and the harvests waving in security under the shelter of ecclesiastical privileges which even the Estergoth and Vandal regarded with respect." If we exchange for the "Estergoth and Vandal" the marauding baron and Highland chief, the picture is a true one of the surroundings of Paisley Abbey in those peaceful years.

The last we hear of Abbot William is witnessing a charter of the Earl of Lennox in 1248,* between which date and 1272 we have no mention

* See Lennox Papers.

of any abbot,* and are entirely ignorant who William's successor was, or when that able ruler gave place to another. He certainly left the Abbey in a prosperous state to his successor, whoever he was. He had increased its possessions to a great extent, adding to them in the Highlands and western coasts of Scotland, and even in Ireland. The churches of Rosneth † and of Kilfinan,‡ fishings on the Leven and on the Garloch; lands on Lochgilp and at Kilmun, and the land called "Tiberir at Dumals in Ireland,"§ became the property of the convent in his time.

In one of the many controversies which he waged in defence of the possessions of the Abbey, he was unsuccessful. Sometime before 1240, Duncan, the first Earl of Carrick, gifted certain lands, churches, and possessions to the Convent on condition that they should establish in his domains a monastery of their order. The Abbot and Convent were in no haste to do so. They built an oratory or chapel, which they served by monks of their own, and used the gifts of Earl Duncan for the benefit of the Abbey. The Earl, however, was determined to have his contract with them fulfilled to the very letter, and, after considerable controversy, he and the Abbot submitted the matter to the decision of the Bishop of Glasgow. The Bishop decided in favour of the layman. He ordained that a monastery should be erected at Crosragmol,‖ the monks of which should be drawn from Paisley, and who should have full power to elect an abbot for themselves. The abbot and monks of the new house should be free from all interference on the part of the Abbot of Paisley, except that he should visit them once

* An Abbot Henry is generally mentioned in the lists given of the Abbots on the authority of a Bull by Pope Clement, dated 1265. There is an Abbot Henry spoken of in the attestation of a notary who gives a transumpt of the Bull, but this is Henry Crichton, Abbot between 1460-70. Pope Clement IV. in 1265 issued a Bull to the Abbot of Paisley without specially mentioning his name. On 9th December, 1469, John Reston, notary, made a transumpt, or copy of that Bull (during the incumbency of Henry Crichton, Abbot of Paisley). In consequence of some confounding the *copy* of 1469 with the Bull of 1265, they have entered Abbot Henry under 1265 instead of 1469. See Reg. de Pas., p. 308.

† Reg. de Pas., p. 209. Rosneth was given by Amelec, the brother of Maldowen, Count of Lennox.

‡ Reg. de Pas., p. 132. Kilfinan, with the chapel of St. Mary and some land at Kilmun and Lochgilp, was given by Duncan, the son of Ferchar.

§ Reg. de Pas., p. 412. ‖ Now called Crosraguel.

every year. All the possessions which Paisley had in Carrick were to be made over to the use of Crosragmol. The parent house, however, was to receive ten merks sterling annually from its daughter, and the monks of the offshoot were to wear the habit and observe the rules of the order of Clugny. Very wrathful were the Paisley brotherhood at this decision of the Bishop. The ten merks annually, and privilege of an annual visitation, were poor compensation for the goodly possessions of Carrick. The Abbot appealed to the Pope in 1265, stating the "enormous lessening" of revenue his Abbey had sustained, and praying earnestly for redress. The Pope granted a commission of enquiry, which appears to have given them three churches,* but, beyond this, the gift of the Earl passed altogether away from Paisley.†

In 1246, Walter Stewart, who had been so generous a benefactor to the Abbey, died. He had stood well by the Abbots in their many contentions, and more than one agreement favourable to the Abbey was made at Blackhall, where he from time to time resided, probably effected by his influence and authority. The last time he appears in connection with the Abbey is giving an annual payment of two chalders of meal from the Mill of Paisley for the support of a monk to perform divine service for the soul of Robert de Brus. The Lord of Annandale, who bore this great name, died in 1245, a year before the friend who held his memory in so great reverence. It shews an early connection between the house of Stewart and that of Bruce, which became more close in after years. The Stewart, or Senechallus, as the monks delighted to call him, was, like his ancestors, buried in the Abbey he had loved so well.‡

He was succeeded by his son Alexander, a man of action and wisdom, like his ancestors, and distinguished also by their piety. Alexander lived in the closest relationship with the Convent, and added in some measure, though not on so munificent a scale as his predecessors, to their possessions. Shortly after his accession he finished the enclosing of a park for deer, which he had begun in his father's time, in the

* Turnberry, Stratton, Dalmakeran. † Reg. de Pas., p. 427 *et ante.*

‡ Chalmers' Caledonia, Vol. II., 779. Fordun and the Chronikil of Melrose give his death in 1241.

neighbourhood of his house, and to the east of the Rivulet Espedair. The wild deer which his father and grandfather had hunted in the forest of Fereneze had probably begun to disappear before the encroachments of agriculture, and he enclosed this space near his house that his larder might not want for venison. He took into the park some of the lands belonging to the monks, but honourably gave them acre for acre in land near their chapels of Innerkip and Lochwinnoch.* He also gave them permission still to draw water from the Espedair for their mill, and bestowed on them eight chalders of meal from the rents of Inchinnan. Like many of that time, he desired to make a pilgrimage to one or other of the holy places—Jerusalem, Rome, or Compestella in Spain. Of these he chose the last, which at that time was a favourite place of pilgrimage.† The shrine of Saint James, the patron saint of his house, was there. He was one of the saints to whom the Abbey of Paisley was dedicated, and his image in pilgrim garb, with staff in hand, gourd by his side, and cockle-shell in his hat, appeared on its seal. It was a long and dangerous journey between Paisley and the Spanish shrine, and before taking it the Stewart sought the blessing of the Abbot and Convent. On the second Sunday of Advent, 1252, he came to the Abbey‡ and received their benediction and permission to depart in peace on his sacred errand, "that in devotion and holy pilgrimage he should visit the bounds of the blessed Apostle James." We know well from the formularies of the Church the religious rite that was performed that day in the Abbey over the Stewart and his companions. After confessing their sins they lay prostrate before the altar. Special prayers and psalms were then said and sung; when these were over, the pilgrims arose from their prostrate position, and the Abbot consecrated their scrips and staves, saying, "The Lord be with you." He next sprinkled holy water upon their scrips and staves, and placed the scrip round the neck of each pilgrim, accompanying these acts with other religious services. Afterwards, he delivered to them the staff, with similar prayers.§ Before

* Reg. de Pas., pp. 87, 88. † See Fosbrook. ‡ Reg. de Pas., pp. 90, 91.
§ Fosbrook, p. 433.

leaving the Abbey the Stewart confirmed by charter all the gifts made by his ancestors, and added that if he should, "as might perhaps be the case," be cut off in this pilgrimage, his heirs were to fulfil his desires, at the peril of their souls if they failed. The departure of the Stewart was a day of great solemnity at the Abbey. All his household seem to have been gathered around him, for his brother, his chaplains, and his knights, with "many others," witness his deed.

The gleanings of the Chartulary—almost our only authority for the history of the Abbey at this early period—tell us nothing of the pilgrim's adventures, but we know that he was back in Scotland in 1255, when he was appointed one of the regents of the kingdom, and began to take a prominent part in public affairs. Eight years later, 2nd October, 1263, he distinguished himself at the battle of Largs, when he led the Scottish army in repulsing Haco, King of Norway, from the shores. It must have been an anxious time for the inmates of the Abbey. Before the invaders landed at Largs a detachment of their fleet had sailed up Loch Long, dragged their galleys across the Isthmus of Tarbert, and launched them on Loch Lomond. They had ravaged the lands of the Lennox, and their doings in this district, with which the monks of Paisley had so intimate a connection, must have been faithfully reported at the Abbey. Many of their lands and churches were in the fertile county of Ayr, where the Norsemen sought to effect a landing. The Danes were from earliest times the despoilers of monasteries, and the distance between Largs and Paisley is but short. Happily, fears of rapine were soon dissipated. In the accounts that have come down to us, both from Scottish and Norwegian sources, the Stewart is a prominent and gallant figure. In one of the most graphic pictures of the fray, that by Boece, he is called by the designation of "Pasley," and doubtless many of the men of Strathgrif, and perhaps even the tenants of the church, as a rule exempt from bearing arms, partook of the glory of the victory. "Incontinent," says the quaint old writer, "Alexander Stewart of Pasley came with ane bachment of fresche men to the middleward, quhair King Alexander wes fechtand aganis King Acho with uncertane victory. The Danis seand this Alexander cum gaif bakkis, on whome followit the Scottis, with gret cruelte, throu all

Cunninghame, and maide ithand slauchter on thaim, quhill the nicht put ane end to all their labor." No doubt the Abbey rejoiced in the victory of their protector, for had the result been different it would assuredly have gone hard with them.

The extension of the possessions of the Abbey in the Highlands, which had been fostered by Abbot William, continued steadily for several years after he disappears from view. The Argyleshire chieftains seem to have divided their gifts to the church between Iona and Paisley. Dovenald de Gilchrist, Lord of Tarbert,* gave the monks full liberty to cut timber in his woods along Loch Fyne for the building and repair of their monastery. Angus, son of Dovenald, one of the Lords of the Isles, gave them the church of St. Querani in Kentyr.† Dugald, the son of Syfyn,‡ in the same district, gave them the church of St. Colmanel, with the chapel of St. Columba, near his castle of Schyphinche,§ for the welfare of himself and his wives, Juliaine and Johanne, and desired that his body, when he died, should be interred at Paisley. These distant possessions appear to have been somewhat difficult to manage. The Abbot on several occasions had recourse to the good offices of the Bishop of Argyle to compel the incumbents of the Highland parishes belonging to the Monastery to render an account of their revenues and pay their dues with regularity, and one of these curates who had bound himself to make the curious annual payment of a "weight of iron commonly called rock (petra)" had to be dealt with very severely, and, in addition to his tribute of iron, was ordained to pay yearly to the monks, at the time of the Glasgow Fair, sixpence, or a pound of wax, an imposition which, even to the Highland pastor of our time, would not appear grievous.||

There is a source of revenue, appearing at this time to have been opened up, which is worth noticing, as it indicates the comfortable estate of the Abbey. The monks seem to have largely engaged in money lending, and we constantly find them taking lands and tenements in satisfaction of loans which they had made to people in their necessity.

* Reg. de Pas., p. 157. † Ibid, p. 127. ‡ Ibid, p. 120. § Now Skipness.

|| Reg. de Pas., p. 127 *et ante.*

"Adam (called the carpenter), compelled by the necessity of poverty, which knows no law," makes over to the Abbot and Convent, his lands of Haldingleston,* in consideration of a sum of money with which they, in his great need, paid his debts and relieved the poverty of himself and his family. Cecilia, widow of John de Perthec, conveys in like manner her property† in Rutherglen, because the Abbot and Convent, "filled with charity," had given her in her great necessity three chalders of oatmeal. Adam de Burne and Marjory, his wife, being "so borne down by their adversities that they could not rise above them," sold their lands in Newton of Ayr‡ to the Convent for five merks of silver, which the monks placed in their hands to pay their debts; and Adam, a burgess of Glasgow, called "of Cardelechan,"§ transferred his property, lying "in the street of the fishers below the bridge over Clyde," for a sum of money to enable him to discharge his obligations. Many instances of a similar kind are to be found among the charters of the Abbey, and shew how wealthy a corporation it must have become when it had thus added banking to its other sources of emolument. We form an idea of its wealth at this period from a well-known scheme of taxation of the Church which was drawn up for Scotland in 1275. In that year the Pope sent a certain Boiamund of Vicci to collect the tenth of the benefices of the kingdom for the relief of the Holy Land. The Church resisted the imposition of the subsidy on the ground that it should be imposed, not on the real value (*verus valor*) of the Church property, but according to an old valuation (*taxatio antiqua*), and they sent Boiamund back to Rome to state their case. They were not, however, successful in their resistance, and Boiamund returned to Scotland and completed his valuation according to a scheme which was long called "Boiamund or Bagimond's Roll," and which was the basis of all church taxation until the Reformation.‖ In this roll, which is probably correct in the form it has come down to us, the Abbey of Paisley is valued at £2666, and that of Crossraguel at £533 6s. 4d.

We perhaps get the best idea of the privileges and possessions of the Convent during the period immediately preceding King Alexander

* Reg. de Pas., p. 58. † Ibid, p. 376. ‡ Ibid, p. 71. § Ibid, p. 400.

‖ Burton's Hist., Vol. II., p. 38. Statuta Ecclesia Scot., p. 65 *et seq.*

III.'s death,—so disastrous an event for the Church as well as the country in general,—from the great Bull of Pope Clement IV.* (1265). As this document gives us a view of the Monastery in its most prosperous days, before the sorrows into which Scotland was plunged, and in which the Abbey fully shared, we give it entire:—

"CLEMENS Bishop, servant of the servants of God, to his beloved sons, the Abbot of the Monastery of Paisley, and St. Mirin, Confessor of Paisley; and to the brethren there and in all time coming, following the monastic life.

It is proper that the Apostolic protection be given to those choosing a religious life, lest, perchance, any indiscretion either draw them off from their purpose or—which heaven forbid—impair the strength of their sacred vows. Wherefore, beloved sons in the Lord, we mercifully assent to your just demands, and receive the Monastery of St. James the Apostle, and St. Mirin, the Confessor of Paisley, in the diocese of Glasgow, in which you are vowed to divine obedience, under the protection of St. Peter and our own, and fortify this ordinance by the present writing. In the first place, we ordain that the Monastic order which, it is known, was instituted in that Monastery according to God, the rule of St. Benedict, and of the Clunaic brethren, be observed there inviolably in all time coming. Moreover, let whatever property and whatever goods the said Monastery may at present justly and canonically possess, or can in future acquire by the concession of Popes, the bounty of kings or princes, the oblation of the faithful, or in other just methods, by the favour of God, remain sure and inalienable to you and to your successors: of which things we have reckoned the following worthy of express mention:—The place in which the said Monastery is situated, with all its pertinents, and the Chapel of Lochwynoc, with its

* Reg. de Pas., p. 308.

pertinents; the Churches of Innerwyc, of Lygadwod, of Katcart, of Rughglen, of Curmanoc, of Polloc, of Merness, of Neilston, of Kylberhan, of Hestwod, of Howston, of Kylhelan, of Harskyn, of Kylmacolm, of Innerkyp, of Largyss, of Prestwic burgh, of the other (in the monks) Prestwic, of Cragyn, of Turnebery, of Dundonald, of Schanher, of Haucynlec, of Kylpatrik, of Neyt (Rosneath), of Kyllynan, of Kylkeran, of St. Colmanel, of Scybinche, with chapels, lands, and pertinents; the Chapels of Kylmor, at Kenlochgilpe, with its pertinents; and the land which Duncan, son of Ferchard, and Lauman, his cousin, gave to the Monastery there; and that whole land lying on both sides of the Kert, as the late Walter Fitz-Alan Steward of the King of Scotland, founder of the Monastery, himself bestowed it; and the carucate of land which formerly Grimketil held, and which is now called Arkylliston, and the carucate of land which they possessed between the Kert and Grif, which is now called the Island; and the whole land of Drumloy and Swynschawis, and the Graynis, which is now called Drumgrane, and the whole land of Hakhyncog of Dalmulyn, and the land which they had in the manor of Polloc; and the whole land of Drepss, which the late William, son of Maduse, held at ferm of the Monastery; and a carucate of land at Hunteley, which the late King William of Scotland excambed, with lands which they had in the manor of Hastanisden; and the carucate of land which the late Eschena de Molla bestowed on them in that place, and the fishing which they had upon the Water of Clude between Perthec and the island which is commonly called the Island of Renfrw, and an annual of half a merk of silver from the ferm of the burgh of Renfrw and the Mill which they had in the tenement of that burgh, with the water courses and all its pertinents, and a plenary toft in the town of Renfrw, and one net for salmon in the River Clude at Renfrw, and the land which they possessed there near their mill, and the lands of Hyllington and Castelside; and the whole mill of Innerwyc, with the water courses and all the pertinents; and the whole land of Prestwic, which is now called Monkstoun, and the land of Moniabroc, and the land of Cnoc, and the Mill of Paisley, with its sequel which they held by the gift of their founder, and half the fishing at the issue of Lochwinoc, with that liberty of fishing in the lake itself, which Walter, their founder, granted; and the whole land of Penuld, which is called Fulton, as Henry de St. Martin, with the consent of his overlord, conferred it; and the land situated between the Mach and Caldouer, and that part of the land where the Mill of Paisley is situated, which Walter the Steward conceded by certain boundaries; and the land beyond Kert, between the Espedar and Aldpatrick, as the said Steward gave it; with all their liberties and easements in the forests of Paisley and of Seneschathir; and the land at Carnebro, which they had from the gift of the late Uctred, son of Paganus; and the land at Orde, which the late Walter, called Murdhac, bestowed on the Monastery; and the annual rent of a chalder of wheat which they received from the late Patrick, Earl of Dunbar; and the annual rent of a chalder of wheat and of half a mark of silver which they possessed at Cadiow by the gift of Robert de Loudoniis, brother of the late King of Scotland; and an annual mark of silver from Kilbride by the gift of the late Philip de Valoinis, and by the gift of the late Earl Maldoven of Lennox, and that fishing upon the water of Lewyn, which is called Linbren, with the land between it and the highway leading to Dunnberton; and the lands which they had in the county of Lennox, which are commonly called Coupmanach, Edinbernan, Bacchan, Finbelach, Cragbrectalach, Druncrene, Dallenneach, Drumtocher, Drumteyglunan, Drumdeynains, Cultbwy, and Reynfod; and the land which they had in the place called Monachkenran with its pertinents; and the land which Thomas the son of Tankard conferred at Moydirual; and the land called Garyn received from the late Rodulfus de Cler; and the whole land of Crosragmol and Sutheblan, by the gift of Duncan, Earl of Karric; and two chalders of meal received from Alexander, the patron of their Monastery, in exchange for the multure of the Rass; and an annual rent of two marks of silver for the Mill of Thornton, with lands, vineyards, woods, customs and pastures, thickets and open grounds, water, mills, roads, and pathways, and all other liberties and immunities. Let no one presume to demand or extort from you tithes of your newly-reclaimed lands which you cultivate with your own hands, or at your own charges, of which no one has hitherto received tithes, nor from your animals' food. It shall be lawful also for you to receive as converts, free and unfettered, clerical or lay, persons fleeing from the world, and to retain them without any contradiction. However, we forbid any of your brethren, after making his profession in your Monastery, to depart thence without leave of his abbot, unless he joins a stricter Order. But let no one dare to detain a person departing without authority of your common letters. It shall also be lawful for you, when a general interdict is laid on the land, provided that you yourselves do not give cause of interdict, to perform Divine services, with shut doors, and having excluded excommunicated and interdicted persons, but with suppressed voice and without ringing of bells. You will receive also chrism, holy oil, consecration of your altars and churches, the ordination of priests for administering rites, from the bishop of the diocese, if he is Catholic and has the favour and communion of the Holy Roman See, and is willing honestly to give them to you. We forbid anyone to dare to build chapel or oratory within the bounds of your parishes without your consent and that of the bishop of the diocese, reserving the privileges of the Roman Pontiffs. We prohibit entirely to be made against you all new and unjust exactions by archbishops, bishops, archdeacons, deans, and all ecclesiastical or secular persons. We decree also the burial ground of that place to be free: that no one resist the burial of those who, in their devotion or by their last will, have desired to be buried there, unless they are interdicted, or excommunicated, or publick usurers, saving the just rights of those churches by whom the bodies of the dead are claimed. You are also permitted by our authority to recall to the use of the churches to whom they belong the tythes and possessions pertaining to your churches, which are detained by laymen, and to redeem and lawfully to free them from their hands. And when you, Abbot of this place, or any of your successors go away, no one shall be placed there by cunning or by violence, except by consent of the majority of the brethren or wiser part, according as the election is provided by God and the rule of St. Benedict. We, wishing with paternal solicitude for the future to provide also for your peace and tranquility, prohibit by apostolic authority, within the enclosures of your places or granges, all rapine or theft, fire-raising, blood-shedding, rash seizure or slaying of men, or exercise of violence. Moreover, we confirm all the liberties and immunities made to your Monastery by our predecessors the Roman Pontiffs; also, liberties and exemptions from secular exactions granted you for good reason by kings or princes, or by others of the faithful, and we fortify this privilege by this writing. We therefore decree that it shall not be lawful for anyone soever rashly to disturb the said Monastery, or to take away any of its possessions, or to retain them when taken away, to diminish them, or to annoy it by any vexatious acts; but that all things which have been granted for any future purpose whatsoever shall be preserved entire for the discipline and maintenance of its inmates, reserving the authority of the Holy See and the bishop of the diocese. If, therefore, in future any secular or ecclesiastical person, knowing this writ of our constitution, shall attempt rashly to contravene it, let him, after being twice or thrice admonished (unless he shall atone for his fault by a suitable satisfaction), be deprived of the dignity of his power and honour, and let him know that he stands charged by Divine justice with the iniquity so committed, and let him be cut off from the most sacred Body and Blood of our God and Redeemer the Lord Jesus Christ, and let him lie under His severe vengeance at the last judgment. But on all who shall preserve for the said place its rights let the peace of our Lord Jesus Christ rest, so that here they may receive the fruit of their good deeds, and obtain at the hands of the Righteous Judge the rewards of eternal peace. Amen."

Pope Clement IV., who granted this Bull, gave the Monastery about the same time a few other privileges, in addition to those which the above contains: freedom from being brought before secular judges, freedom from sequestration for debt, and right to receive the dues of all their churches without being interfered with by any diocesan bishop. It was when thus prosperous and privileged that the trials of those days of sorrow, in which all Scotland shared, came upon the Monastery like a whirlwind.

Alexander the Stewart, who had been so good a friend to the Abbey, was gathered to his fathers before that time came. It is not known exactly when he died,* but before the death of Alexander III., and about the year 1282, James the Stewart, his son, gives the monks a right to "cross the river Kert Lochwinok between his yare and theirs," and promises to allow no one to put up any obstruction in the stream to injure their fishings. In all probability, Alexander was buried with his ancestors in the choir of the Abbey.

* Symson and Duncan Stewart say in 1283, and that he was buried in the Abbey. Fordun gives 1281 as the year of his death, and with him concurs the Stemma Senescalli.

## CHAPTER IX.

### The Interregnum—John Baliol.

1286-1292.

> "A storm shall roar this very hour
> From Ross hills to Solway sea,"
> "Ye lied, ye lied, ye warlock hoar,
> For the sun shines sweet on fauld and lea."
> He put his hand on Erlie's head,
> He shewed him a rock beside the sea,
> Where a King lay stiff beneath his steed,
> And steel-dight nobles wiped their ee'.
>
> *Scott.*

ALEXANDER III. was killed at Kinghorn on 12th March, 1286.* At his death a deep gloom settled down upon Scotland, and one of the saddest chapters in Scottish history began. During his reign, says an old writer, "the Church flourished, its ministers were treated with reverence, vice was openly discouraged, cunning and treachery were trampled under foot, injury ceased, and the reign of virtue, truth, and justice was maintained throughout the land."† All the accounts which we have of the time fully corroborate these words of Fordun, but nowhere do we get so true a conception of the changes which the death of the good King produced as in the words of the old Scotch poem, the oldest specimen of the kind which has come down to us:—

* Burton's Hist. of Scot., Vol. II., p. 43. † Fordun by Goodall, Vol. II., Book X., Chap. xii.

Quhen Alysander oure Kyng wes dede
That Scotland led in luive* and let†
Away wes sons of ale and brede
Of wyne and wax, of gamyn and gle.
Oure gold wes changyd into lede—
Christ born into virgynyte,
Succour Scotland and remede
That stad‡ is in perplexyte.§

Doubtless the clergy, both secular and regular, could most truly make this prayer their own. For the succeeding years brought to them the deepest sorrow, and their records are, like the roll of the prophet, inscribed within and without with "mourning, lamentation, and woe." The Abbey of Paisley shared in the hardships of the time. During the turbulence of these years there is scarcely a gift chronicled in the Chartulary, and the munificence towards the Church which marked the prosperous days of the country almost entirely ceased. The only exception is the confirmation by James the Stewart of the gifts of his ancestors, to which he adds a few of his own. Only one church,‖ and no land save what was obtained by purchase or the loan of money, came into the possession of the Abbey between the death of Alexander and that of Robert I. Even in the gift of the Stewart in 1294¶ there is a defining of rights, and marking of boundaries, and insertion of saving clauses, that is not found in connection with the lavish gifts of his ancestors. The charter of James the Stewart is a long one—lengthy because of the number of restrictions and reservations which are scattered through it. The boundaries of his parks and preserved forest are strictly defined, and heavy fines are to be imposed on the monks should any of their cattle be found trespassing. The part of the old forest of Fereneze still unencroached upon by the progress of agriculture comprehended a district of Neilston Parish, and a small part on the north of Paisley. Very carefully are the bounds of this sanctuary marked out, "as the Ruttanburn falls into Lauerane, and ascending by the Laueran to the Blakburn, and by the Blakburne ascending to a certain ditch between Lochleboksyd and the Wlplayss, and by that ditch going up to the Loch of Cochlebok, and by the said Loch

* Love. † Tranquility. ‡ Placed. § Wynton, Vol. I. p. 401.
‖ Largs in 1313. ¶ Reg. de Pas., p. 92.

westward to the marches of Caldwell, and by the marches of Caldwell northward, ascending by a certain ditch on the west of Carmelcolme between the Langesawe and Dungelesmore, and from that ditch across the moss to the head of the Haldpatryk, and descending that stream to the march of Stanley, and by the march of Stanley, descending between Stanley and the Cokplayss, to the Ruttanburn, and so by Ruttanburn to Laueran." This district stretches along the breezy heights of Gleniffer, and, though more circumscribed than the former forest, afforded full liberty for the deer to roam in. No sportsman of the present day could be more careful of his preserve than the Stewart was of this forest sanctuary; and, lest the deer should be disturbed in their retreat by any intruding stranger, roads lying in the low grounds, and away from their haunts, were marked out, by which alone the monks and their servants were allowed to travel.* The "roads of Arlaw, Conwaran, the Rass and Stokbryg, and the customary tracks of the husbandmen," were the passes to which they were bound to confine themselves. No monk, however great his love of sport might be, was allowed to strike a deer, or fly a hawk, or slip a greyhound within the sacred territory thus marked off. They were permitted to go armed with swords, bows and arrows, and other necessary weapons of defence, and even to lead with them greyhounds and other dogs, but when they came within the preserved forest they must unstring their bows and lead their greyhounds in a leash. It is to be hoped that their own lands afforded them the pleasures of the chase which were denied to them elsewhere. On these lands the Stewart graciously gave them leave to hunt and hawk, and he also allowed them to fish in the streams of the forest, and in "the rivers of Kert Paisley and Kert Lochwinoc below the yare of Achindonan;" but he reserved to himself birds of game, hawk, and falcon. None of his ancestors had dealt so strictly with the Convent. His gifts are very unlike their noble benefactions and seem very paltry in comparison with them. He gave the monks, however, power to quarry stone for building, and limestone for burning within his Barony of Renfrew. He allowed them to dig coal

* A Forest, in charter language, does not necessarily mean a wooded territory, but there is every reason to believe that the Stewart's Forest consisted of extensive woods of beech, and perhaps oak.

for the use of the Monastery—its granges, smithies, and brew houses,—to make charcoal of dead wood, and take green wood for their house and their granges within the Barony, and the operations of agriculture and fishing, and dead wood for fuel without restriction. He gave them also a right of carriage for all these necessaries, whether in wains, or on horses, or on oxen, except through his manors, orchards, gardens, corn ground, and preserved forest. He permitted them, also, a right of watercourse for their mills from the water of the Espedair, both within and without his park of Blackhall, but only on condition of being allowed the use of their mills for his own corn at his own expense.*

The Stewart was probably more taken up with his duties as a politician than with those which he owed to the Church. He was prominent in all the intrigues, the plots and counterplots of that troubled time. Within a month after the death of the King he was appointed by the Estates of Scotland one of the guardians of the kingdom under the Lady Margaret, the nominal Queen, the infant daughter of Eric, King of Norway.† He does not appear to have acted a loyal part towards his mistress, for his name appears among the signatures to the famous Turnberry bond,‡ which was drawn up by some of the most powerful barons of Scotland, who were anxious to support Robert Bruce's title to the crown. Probably they supposed the succession of the infant princess was not likely to take place, and sought to provide against that contingency by preparing in time for the elevation of their own friend. All ranks and classes in Scotland, however, were bent on the accomplishment of a project which seemed the most likely to afford a peaceful settlement of the distractions by which the country was already threatened. This was the marriage of the young Queen—the Maid of Norway—to the Prince

* This charter of James the Stewart with its mention of granges, gardens, and orchards, indicates the great progress of agriculture under the monastic rule. It gives us the first notice of coal. The common fuel in the country was wood and peats, and what was called a "peatry" was of great value. The monks were probably the first workers of coal in Scotland. Eneas Sylvius, afterwards Pope Pius II., tells us in an account of a visit he paid to Scotland in 1433, how he saw with wonder pieces of stones joyfully received as alms by the half-naked beggars who stood shivering at the church doors.—Stat. Ec. Scot., pp. 93, 44.

† Tytler, Vol. I., p. 24.

‡ Sept. 20, 1286. Documents Illustrative of the History of Scotland, Vol. I., p. 22.

of Wales, the son of King Edward I., who was beginning to take a very suspicious interest in the affairs of Scotland. The English King was strongly in favour of the marriage, and as the youthful pair were within the forbidden degrees, he procured a dispensation from the Pope in favour of the union. All the Estates of Scotland favoured his scheme—an assembly of the lords, barons, and dignified clergy, was held to take it into consideration, and among the latter we come on the name of the Abbot of Paisley,* or rather upon his title, for his christian name is not given. This assembly met at Brigham, a small village on the Tweed, near Roxburgh, in 1289, and was evidently composed of the chief men of the nation, both in Church and State. They agreed upon a letter to the King of England which stated that they were overjoyed to hear the good news now commonly spoken of, "that the Apostle had granted a dispensation for the marriage of Margaret, their dear lady and Queen, with Prince Edward," and they assured him of their hearty concurrence. They also directed a letter to King Eric of Norway, urging him to send over the young Queen to Scotland, at the latest, before the Feast of All Saints, and intimating to him that if this were not done, they would be obliged to follow the best counsel which God would give them for the good of the kingdom.† The Stewart was the fourth to sign these letters. The Abbot was naturally of the same mind with his patron, and would return from Brigham to his brethren at Paisley full of hope that a time of peace and quiet was about to dawn upon Scotland.

How this hope was disappointed is known to every reader of history. With the death of the Maid of Norway at Orkney, on her way to Scotland, all expectation of a peaceful settlement of the national troubles passed away. Then followed the wrangling and contention of the suitors for the Crown—the unpatriotic submission of their claims to the English King—and their still more unpatriotic obedience to his haughty demand, that, prior to his sitting in judgment on these, he should be acknowledged as Lord Paramount.‡ The Stewart was one of those who joined in this acquiescence, probably with the hope of favouring the claim of his friend the Bruce. He was one of the arbiters on the part of Bruce in the

* De Passelay. † Burton, Vol. II., p. 122. ‡ Tytler, Vol. I., pp. 28, 355.

presence of the King of England,* who had taken care to secure his interest by a gift of lands of the annual value of £100.† Judgment was given in favour of John Baliol, who was crowned King of Scotland, after having, as a vassal, performed homage to Edward. The newly-created Sovereign could not brook the indignities that were heaped upon himself and on the country by his haughty superior, and raised the standard of rebellion. Then came the terrible subjugation of Scotland by the English King, who, with an army of thirty thousand foot and five thousand horse, passed, in 1296, from Berwick to Elgin, crushing all opposition and devastating the land. Happily for our Abbey, his course both northwards, and on his return, was by the east rather than the west of Scotland, though he did not leave the country without letting both the Abbot and monks know that he must be acknowledged henceforth as their King. On the 28th of April he left Berwick, on the 26th July he was at Elgin, and Berwick was reached on his return on the 22nd August.‡ In that town, on the 28th of that month, he held a Parliament, to which he had summoned the heads of the clergy and laity of Scotland to swear fealty to him. Their names and their oaths of homage, filling thirty-five skins of parchment, are still preserved among the English archives.§ Great landowners and churchmen were summoned, and though the choice offered them was taking the oath or martyrdom, each of them is specially made to say that what he does is from a sense of duty and of his own free will.‖ In the sorrowful list is found the name of Walter, Abbot of Paisley, who, like others, swore on the Holy Gospels, that he would be "true and loyal, and keep faith and loyalty to the King of England and to his heirs, and that he would never bear arms for any one, or give advice or aid against him or against his heirs in any case which can happen. So may God help me and the saints." It probably cost many a Scotchman a sore heart to put his name and seal to a document like this, but in the

* Tytler, Vol. I., p. 38. † Rymer's Foedera, Vol. II., p. 556.

‡ Bannatyne Miscellany. Diary of the Expedition of Edward in 1290.

§ Tytler, Vol. I., p. 47. Ragman Rolls, Bannatyne Club.

‖ Burton's Hist. of Scot., Vol. II., 177.

case of Abbot Walter, the pang was exceeding bitter, for it was accompanied by an infliction from which others were free.

It will be remembered that when Walter the Stewart, in 1246, transferred the lands and churches belonging to the house of Dalmulin to Paisley, the Abbot was held bound to pay to the Master of Sempringham, who resigned Dalmulin and its possessions, the sum of forty merks annually.* This was to be paid every year at the Monastery of Dryburgh. The successors of Abbot William, who made the agreement, had apparently not been very faithful in making this payment. They probably did not like to send any Scotch money across the border, and as the jealousy of everything English extended to the clergy as well as to the laity, the Paisley monks could not brook any acknowledgement of obligation, pecuniary or otherwise, to an English house. Abbot Walter, when at Berwick, was sharply reminded of his liabilities. The Prior of Malton, who was of the order of Sempringham, brought up against him his defective payments. The Abbot was in the hands of the Philistines, and had to submit with the best grace that he could. Accordingly, there is given in the same document† that records his submission, a clear acknowledgement of his debts. The Abbot of Paseleke (as he is called), owns that he is indebted forty merks to the Master of the Order of Sempringham, of which he should pay him ten merks after the feast of the beheading of John the Baptist, and thirty next after the feast of St. Michael following, and unless he makes this payment, he agrees for himself and his Convent that the said money should be levied from their goods and chattels in the County of Lanark.‡ This acknowledgement is witnessed by the King, and it is added that Abbot Walter then paid ten merks, and he doubtless returned to Paisley with a wholesome dread of what would happen if the other thirty were not forthcoming at the proper time. He had looked on the face of Edward, and any one who saw the determined countenance of the "Hammer of Scotland" must have known that he was not a man to be trifled with. But the impost was felt to be a very disagreeable one by the Convent, and they waited for a fitting opportunity to get rid of it.

* Reg. de Pas., p. 27. † Rotuli Scotiae. ‡ This comprehended Renfrewshire.

Other troubles besides these pressed upon Abbot Walter and his brethren. Their title to the valuable lands in Kylpatrick, which had been disputed in the time of Abbot William, was again called in question. That energetic ruler had apparently brought all the matters in dispute to a satisfactory termination, but when his guiding hand was removed, the old difficulties began afresh. So early as 1272, three persons,—John de Wardroba, Bernard de Erth, and Norinus de Monnorgund, who had married grand-nieces and heiresses of Dugald, the contumacious rector whom Abbot William had so summarily silenced, renewed, in right of their wives, the claim that he had abandoned, and were apparently inclined to prosecute it with vigour. The Abbot did not, however, go to law with them. Possibly there may have been dealings with Dugald that it would not have been convenient to bring to light. The claim was hushed up, and the claimants were bought off by the payment on the part of the Abbot of an hundred and fifty merks, "*pro bono pacis*," after which he received from each of them a separate resignation of all their claims, and in 1273 the Earl of Lennox, "before he received knighthood," wishing to be at peace with the Church before undergoing that ceremony, confirmed to the Monastery all the lands which they held in his barony.* But in the time of Abbot Walter the old disputes broke out again. Taking advantage of the troubled state of Scotland, vigorous attempts were made in 1294 to strip the Abbey of its Dumbartonshire possessions. These might probably have succeeded had not Walter found a firm friend and ally in his diocesan, Robert Wishart, the Bishop of Glasgow. This patriotic Scotchman—the friend both of Wallace and of Bruce, and the determined foe of England—entered into the contest between the Abbey and its assailants with the vigour which history shows characterised all his actions, and he hurled against the latter the thunders of the Church. A certain Robert Reddehow, and Johanna his wife, claimants like those already noticed, brought the Abbot into the Court of the Earl of Lennox; and the Earl and his bailiff, under Royal authority, proceeded to try the case, as his predecessor had done with the claimants of his time.† The

* Innes's Parochiales, Vol. I., p. 31. Reg. de. Pas., pp. 158, 159, 204.

† Reg. de Pas., p. 261, *et seq.*

Abbot, instead of giving these claimants a sum of money, "*pro bono pacis*," refused to meet them in a secular Court or to acknowledge the right of the Earl and "those holding court with him" to interfere with the property of the Church, even under Royal authority. The Bishop, with whom the "Royal authority" of John Baliol did not probably count for much, at once took the same view, and stood on the high ground of "spiritual independence." He issued a mandate requiring the Earl wholly to cease from the cognition of such causes as by Royal authority he had caused to be dragged into his Court, and he ordered Reddehow and his wife to desist from their prosecution of the Abbot under pain of the greater excommunication. The Earl and his bailiff disregarded these fulminations, and proceeded in his Court, "against God and justice, and to the great prejudice of ecclesiastical liberty," to cognosce upon the lands in dispute. Robert Reddehow and his wife Johanna also persisted in litigation, fearless of the greater excommunication, "maintaining a protracted obduracy of mind, and irreverently contemning as sons of perdition the Keys of the Church." This was more than the Bishop could endure, and he laid injunctions on five of his clergy—the Vicars of Cathcart, Pollok, Carmunnoc, Kilbarchan, and Kilmalcolm—to go, on the day on which the Abbot was summoned to the Earl's Court, to the place of trial, and, taking with them "six or seven of their order, personally to advance to the said Earl," his bailies, and those holding court with them, and again warn them altogether to desist from the cognition of all such causes. He further enjoined them again to warn Reddehow and his wife by name, and any others who might prosecute the said religious men in regard to their lands before the said court, wholly to cease from their prosecution. Should all this fail, the guilty parties were to be held as excommunicated, and their lands and chapels interdicted. The vicars, clothed in white sacerdotal vestments, in full court, were further, if they thought expedient, publicly and by name to denounce, and cause to be denounced, the persons thus excommunicated in all the churches of the deanery of Lennox and archdeaconry of Glasgow, especially on each Lord's Day and festal day, with candles burning and bells ringing, after offering of masses. They were to warn all the faithful in Christ to avoid them, and to place the lands and chapels of such as refused to obey under special interdict. The inhibition expressly warns Sir Patrick de Graham, Duncan the son of Ameledy, Maurice of Ardcapell, and twenty-four others, not to presume to intercommune with the excommunicated persons, or any one of them, in court or out of court, by assistance, favour, or counsel, by supplying them with food, drink, or fire, by grinding corn, or buying and selling. This terrible document is dated from Casteltaris, 22d August, 1294. Whether it had altogether the desired effect is doubtful, for we find the Bishop two years afterwards returning to the contest, and commanding the Dean of the Christian Jurisdiction of the Lennox to take with him four or five of his Order, and admonish the Earl and his bailiffs not to presume to drag the Abbot and Convent of Paisley before his court in regard to the oft-disputed lands.* The whole controversy furnishes a striking illustration of the struggle between the spiritual, or rather ecclesiastical, and secular powers, which in some form or other is constantly emerging even in modern times.

We may note here, from one of our oldest chronicles,† an account of an event which must have caused as great a sensation among the inmates of the Abbey as the summons of the persecuting Earl or the English King. This was no less than the return from the other world of one of their brethren, or at least a ghost who wore the dress of their Order. The terror caused by this spiritual visitation was widespread, and tidings of the apparition were carried to the English monastery of Lanercost, where it was chronicled by the monks among the grave transactions of Church and State. The house which was chiefly visited by the apparition is that of the family of Lyle or De Insula, afterwards Lord Lyle. It was a strongly-fortified castle on the confluence of two streams, not far from the present village of Kilmalcolm. Little more than the site of the mansion is visible now. The "auld house" and the powerful family to whom it belonged have passed away. Alanus de Insula, Alexander de Insula, Radulph de Insula, and others of the family are frequently mentioned in the Paisley Chartulary. The story shows the great lord seated beside the hearth, with his family and domestics around him, after the

* Reg. de Pas., p. 204.* The abstract of this transaction is chiefly taken from the admirably edited Lennox Papers, by Mr. Fraser. † Chronicon de Lanercost. Bannatyne Club.

fashion of the time. We shall give it in the words of the chronicle, as nearly as they can be translated from the very crabbed monkish Latin in which the tale is told:—

AT this time,* in the west of Scotland, in the valley of the Clyde, about four miles from Paisley, there happened in the house of a knight, Duncan de Lyle,† an event at once dreadful and wonderful, which may fill the wicked with fear, and show the appearance of the damned on the day of the final resurrection. Under cover of our holy religion, a certain man had lived in wickedness and died in sin, with the ban of excommunication upon him for sacrilege committed in his monastery. Having long after his burial frightened several in the same monastery by appearing to them in the shades of night, this son of darkness went to the house of the said knight to try the faith of the simple and scare them by contending with them in daylight, or rather to indicate in this way, by a mysterious judgment of heaven, who were implicated in his crime. Assuming a bodily form, whether natural or ærial, is uncertain, but foul, gross, and palpable, he used to appear in broad daylight in the dress of a black monk, and to take up his position on the top of the houses or granaries.‡ If any one attacked him with arrows, or sought to transfix him with pitchforks, whatever pierced that accursed mass, was on the very instant reduced to ashes, and all that wrestled with him he shook and mauled as if he would break every bone in their bodies. In these contests the young squire, the knight's eldest son, was specially troublesome to him. One evening, as the head of the family § was sitting at the fireside with his domestics, the spectre appeared among the crowd and terrified them with missiles and with blows, and when the rest fled, the young squire alone stayed to fight; but, sad to tell, was found next day slain by the ghost. Now, if it is true that the dead receive power over none but those that live like swine, we may easily infer why that youth met with his death in such a manner.

* 1296. † Duncani de Insula. ‡ Thesauros bladii. § Paterfamilias.

## CHAPTER X.

### Wallace and Bruce.

1297—1329.

**They brent all in fire,**
**Baith kirk and quire.**

SIR WILLIAM WALLACE of Elderslie began his public career in 1297,—a career in which the inmates of the Abbey must have taken a deep interest. He was one of their parishioners. Their Church was a Parish Church,* had a wide parochial territory, and within that territory the House of Elderslie is situated. The Chartulary tells us that the family of Wallace was closely associated with the Monastery. A Richard Wals' attests a charter by the founder, Walter the son of Alan,† and the names of several of his descendants appear from time to time in connection with similar deeds.‡ This ancestor of the patriot, we may almost confidently assert, came to Scotland in the train of the Stewart, and was one of those colonists who, under his patronage, settled on his lands. These colonists were mainly drawn from Shropshire and the neighbourhood of Wenloc, which is but a little way from the borders of Wales. If Wallace means simply "Welsh," and Le Walays (as the hero is sometimes called) the Welshman, there is every probability that he accompanied Robert Croc and others when they cast in their lot with the fortunes of the Son of Alan. Blind Harry, the popular minstrel who celebrated the deeds of the hero, seems to take for granted his connection

* See charter of founder. † Reg. de Pas., p. 5. ‡ See appendix.

with the Stewarts and with Wales, and though he can in no sense be taken as an historic authority, yet we may look upon him as giving the popular tradition, which is in this case the more likely to be correct, as the Scots would not invent an English origin for their favourite patriot.

His forbears, who likes to understand,
Of whole lineage, and true line of Scotland,
Sir Ronald Crauford, right Sheriff of Ayr,
So in his time he had a daughter fair;
And young Sir Ronald, Sheriff of that toun,
His sister fair, of good fame and renown,
Malcolm Wallas her got in marriage
That Elderslie then had in heritage.
Auchenbothie and other sundry place
The Second O*, he was of good Wallace,
The which Wallace full worthily that wrought
When Walter, he of Wales, from Warine sought,
Who likes to have more knowledge in that part
Go read the right line of the first Stewart.

The inference from this rough ballad is that Malcolm Wallace, the father of the patriot, was the great-grandson of a good Wallace who bore himself worthily when Walter, son of Alan, the founder of the Abbey, sought from Warine "her of Wales." This refers to some forgotten incident in the life of the first Stewart, probably some love romance which was well known in the popular traditions of Scotland. "Walter's mother," as it has been well observed,* "was a Warine of Shropshire," and the conclusion certainly is that before the first High Stewart came to Scotland he wanted to marry some Welsh lady over whom his mother's family had control, and that on that occasion he received much help from an adherent "who afterwards accompanied him to Scotland, and whose name appears in his early charters as Richard Wallace—*i.e.*, the Welshman"—of Ricarton,—some lands in Ayrshire, which had been granted him, and which were called by his own name.

The connection between the family of Elderslie and the monks of Paisley would naturally be very close. The lands of Elderslie are

* "Second O," great grandson.

† The Early Days of Sir William Wallace, by John, Marquess of Bute, p. 18.—Paisley, 1876.

situated on the west side of the Altpatrick Burn or Rivulet, two and a half miles from the Monastery. They contained about five hundred acres of land, and their boundaries could be pointed out at the present day. The Abbey would be to the Elderslie people, as to the other dwellers on the lands of the Stewarts, the source of any literary and religious influences they enjoyed. The patriot had evidently received a good education for the time in which he lived. He could speak two languages, Latin and French, besides his own,* and as learning was almost entirely confined at that period to the cloister, he most probably had been trained at the school taught by the Paisley Clunaics. Such teaching was, as we have seen, part of their daily life, and was required by the Benedictine "rule." From them also Wallace would naturally learn that veneration for the Church, her services, and her ministers, by which he was distinguished. One of the few reliable documents which have come down to us concerning him tells of his kindness to two monks of Hexham, who had been insulted and had their church pillaged by his rude soldiers. "He venerated the Church," says Fordun, "he respected the clergy; his greatest abhorrence was for falsehood and lying, his uttermost loathing for treason, and therefore the Lord was with him, through whom he was a man whose every work prospered in his hand."† If this kindly picture of his character by the old chronicler be true, it is pleasant to think that it was the result of his upbringing in the Paisley cloisters. It is natural that we should thus seek to connect with them the presence of one whose name is dear to Scotsmen, and it adds another charm to the many associated with the old walls even to think it probable, which we certainly may, that "there Malcolm Wallace and Margaret his wife took their little boys on the great festivals to listen for hours to the solemn rise and fall of the Gregorian chant. At least three-fourths of the public worship of the period consisted in singing Psalms, and it may well have been as the sublime compositions of the Hebrew poets alternately thundered and wailed

* Early Days of Sir William Wallace, p. 45.

† "Super omnia falsitatem et mendacia prosequens, ac proditionem detestans; propter quod fuit Dominus cum eo, per quem erat in cunctis prospere agens; ecclesiam venerans, ecclesiasticos reverens."—Fordun by Goodal, Vol. II., p, 170.

through the Abbey Church of Paisley that William Wallace contracted that love for the Psalms, which lasted until he died, with a priest holding the Psalter open, at his request, before his darkening eyes."*

The monks of Paisley, in common with all other Scots ecclesiastics in those times, took the patriotic side. They were the good friends of Robert Wishart, the Bishop of Glasgow, who was so great a patriot that no oath could possibly bind him in allegiance to the English King, and who passed a great many years in an English prison. There is a singular indication of how thoroughly Scotch the Paisley ecclesiastics had become in the fact that they quietly dropped from their charters, after the War of Independence, the name of the English saint to whom the Abbey was dedicated. The Saxon Milburga disappears from their records, and the Scottish Mirin is elevated into prominence on all occasions as "the glorious confessor." The Stewart, their friend and patron, upheld in those troublous times, as a rule, the national cause, though, like other great men, he vaccilated considerably. At first, with some of the more powerful barons and the Bishop of Glasgow, he joined Wallace.† Soon after, along with the bishop, he made his submission to King Edward at Irvine, and entreated forgiveness for the robberies and slaughters they had committed.‡ At the battle of Stirling he was with the English army, but on its defeat he joined his countrymen, and turned upon his former friends.§ In letters issued soon after he is recognised as a friend to the English King, but in 1302 he is sent by the Scots to promote their interest at the French Court,‖ and in 1304 he is specially mentioned in an English proclamation as among those who were to be exempted in the general amnesty.¶ His political position must have entailed much hardship on his followers and vassals, and on the Abbey, with which his family were so very closely associated. The lands of the monks were ravaged continually, and "men," as they say themselves, "taking advantage of the lawlessness of the times, invented claims against them, and seized sometimes the monks themselves, sometimes their converts, and sometimes their animals and goods, detaining them until they received such satisfaction as would please themselves." The Convent appealed

* The Early Days of Sir William Wallace.

† Hailes, vol. p. 246. ‡ Tytler. § Ibid. ‖ Ibid. ¶ Ibid.

piteously to the Pope against these robbers, and in 1300 Pope Boniface VIII. issued a Bull from the Vatican at Rome strongly denouncing those who troubled them, and enjoining that no one should invade the possessions of the Monastery.*

The Bull of the Pope could not long shield them from the calamities in which every part of Scotland shared. Their parishioner, the Knight of Elderslie, was executed on August 22nd, 1305; and in 1306 Bruce, the friend and ally of their patron, the Stewart, began his contest for the independence of Scotland. The struggle that then ensued is well known to every reader of Scottish history, and there is no occasion to repeat it here. One line in that history tells the fate of the Abbey of Paisley—

"*Hoc in anno seiz 1307, Anglici combusserunt Monasterium de Pasleto.*"†

"In this year, 1307, the English burnt the Monastery of Paisley." There is no notice of this in any of the chronicles of the time except the one we have quoted, and we do not know by what army or party of English the deed was done. The destruction must have been complete, for the architecture of most of the present building belongs to a subsequent period. Nothing but blackened walls were left standing, and the monks had to carry on their services amid the ruins, if they attempted service in the church at all. They must have suffered very great hardships in common with many of their brethren at that time. The Church felt heavily the scourge of war. Wallace found two canons lurking amidst the ruins of the splendid Priory of Hexham, which had been destroyed by the Scots, and celebrating mass in the midst of the devastation. During the same wars which brought ruin to the Abbey of Paisley, the magnificent Benedictine Abbey of Kelso was also burnt, and the Bishop of St. Andrews, appealing to the benevolent for assistance, tells what was the sad condition of its inmates. "Through common war and the long depredation and spoiling of goods by fire and

* Reg. de Pas., p. 416.

† Fordun by Goodall, Vol. II., p. 238.—In the "Black Book of Paisley," of which an account will be given afterwards, a *hand* has been drawn on the margin of the manuscript, pointing to this entry.

rapine it is destroyed, and we speak it with grief; its monks and '*conversi*' wander over Scotland, begging food and clothing at the other religious houses."* It is not probable that the Abbot and monks of Paisley were reduced to such straits as these. About this time Abbot Roger bought a tenement in Glasgow, in "the street which is called the Rattonrow, between the land of Sir Maurice Starine, chaplain, on the west, and the King's highway which is called *le Weynde* on the east," and it is not improbable that the Convent removed thither when the locality of Paisley became dangerous, and took up their abode under the shadow of the Cathedral till better times should come.† The succession of abbots was regularly kept up during this period of depression,‡ but they probably suffered many privations, and it is not without reason that they speak of the war as the "*diram gueram.*" The death of King Edward I. took place at Burgh-on-Sands on 7th July, 1307, the same year in which his soldiers had burned the Abbey, and the year following an honour was conferred upon the Abbot by the Pope—not improbably as a solatium for the loss which he and his brethren had sustained.

All readers of Scottish history are familiar with the story of the murder of the Red Comyn by Robert Bruce before the high altar of the Franciscan Friars of Dumfries. It has been told with all its picturesqueness by all writers of our national annals. It is as weird an incident as any therein related, Bruce stabbing his rival with his dagger in the privacy of the church and going into the street defiled with blood—

> Kilpatrick's bloody dirk,
> Making sure of murder's work.

The deed lay heavy on the conscience of the King, and though it is said he was absolved by the patriotic Bishop of Glasgow before assuming the crown, he longed for the assurance of pardon from the Pope himself, and

* Sketches of Early Scottish History, p. 196.

† Reg. de Pas., p. 385.—The date of the purchase is not given. But a subsequent charter, p. 387, of date 1321, states that it was made by Abbot Roger.

‡ Roger is mentioned as Abbot in 1312, and John in 1327. There are also a few deeds in the Register belonging to this time.

sent messengers to obtain it from him.* Who these messengers were we are not told, but it is very probable the good offices of the Stewart were employed. He had been associated with Bruce in the closest manner, and was a very fit messenger on this occasion. The Pope (Clement V.) was at the time at Poictiers with Philip, the King of France, and the Stewart knew the latter well, having a few years previously (1307) been sent to him by the Scots to obtain his aid. In the Stewart the King had a powerful advocate, and he did not plead in vain. The Pope had at that time been taking considerable interest in the affairs of Scotland. He was angry at the imprisonment of the Bishop of Glasgow, and was disposed to lend a favourable ear to the petition of the Scottish King. It was, however, desirable that the boon sought should be bestowed in as quiet a manner as possible, that offence might not be given to the English sovereign. A commission was therefore issued to the Abbot of Paisley by Berengarius, the penitentiary of the Pope, to absolve the Bruce, and appoint him proper penance for his crime. Berengarius was a well-known cardinal, and was in attendance on the Pope at Poictiers. The commission would likely have been sent to the Bishop of Glasgow had not that prelate at the time been in an English prison. The name of the Abbot of Paisley might have been readily suggested by his friend the Stewart, and it may also have been thought that, as he had suffered so much from the English, he deserved to have the honour conferred upon him of restoring to the full favour of the Church their greatest foe. As the incident is interesting, we may here give the text of the commission :—

"BERENGARIUS, by the Divine mercy Cardinal Presbyter, by the title of Saint Nereus and Achilles, to the holy man the Abbot of the Monastery of Paisley, of the Order of Saint Benedict, in the diocese of Glasgow, salvation in the Lord. A petition presented to us by a certain noble, Robert de Bruce, layman of Carrik in the said diocese, stated That he lately, with certain accomplices, being inspired by the Devil, slew John and Robert Comyn, knights, who provoked him very much, in the church of

* I have given in full in the appendix my reasons for believing the correctness of this incident as given in Fordun by Goodall, Vol. II., p. 231.

> the Minorite brothers of Dumfries. But as he and his accomplices, on account of the great strifes and the perils of war, are not able to go to the Apostolic Seat, or even his own diocesan or his vicar, he humbly made supplication that he and his accomplices might be mercifully dealt with by that Seat. We, therefore, who rejoice to succour the faithful in Christ, by the authority of the Lord Pope, whose penitentiary we are, and, indeed, are the utterance of his living voice, commit the matter to your discretion, that, if it is as has been stated, you may, after the said Robert and his accomplices have made proper satisfaction to the aforesaid church, absolve him and them for this occasion from the excommunication which they have incurred for this thing, and from the charge of slaying that layman, according to the customary form of the Church, and after having heard with care their confession and considered their fault, you may appoint them, by the said authority, salutary penance and those other things which are commanded by law. Given at Picenum, tenth kalends of August, and the third year of the pontificate of Clement the Fifth."*

How the duty committed to him was discharged by the Abbot or what penance he enjoined we do not know. It may have been to fulfil the penance imposed at Paisley that Bruce desired so ardently to visit the Holy Sepulchre. He was excommunicated again soon afterwards, and years elapsed before he was finally restored to the favour of the Church; but his absolution at Paisley was a gleam of sunshine in the midst of his stormy life, and one of the most interesting pictures in the history of our Abbey is that of the monarch kneeling before its altar and amidst its fire-stained walls.

James the Stewart died on 16th July, 1309, and is believed to have been buried in the ruined Abbey.† He was succeeded by his son Walter, who, like his ancestors, took a leading part in the transactions of the time, but, unlike them, his accession is not marked by any gift to the Convent for the soul

* I have in the appendix given my grounds for supposing Picenum for being a misreading of Poictiers.—Goodall has shewn in his notes that the date is as given above.

† History of the Stewarts, by Andrew Stewart, M.P., p. 16.

of his father. It was not a time for giving and receiving gifts, and the monks must have found it hard enough to keep together what they had left them. Edward II., in 1310, penetrated with his army to Renfrew, burning and wasting the country.* This certainly would not improve their condition, and the only reference in the Chartulary to this period regards the settlement in 1313 of a dispute between them and a certain John Pride, a burgess of Renfrew, who had been giving them some trouble.† Hope came to them and the rest of Scotland with the decisive battle of Bannockburn, in 1314. Walter the Stewart, then only in his twenty-first year, was there with a large body of men, many of whom must have been from his lands of Strathgryfe. He commanded a division of the Scottish army, and Barbour, in his graphic way, makes mention of him :—

Walter Stewart of Scotland syne
That then was but a beardless hyne,
Came with a rout of noble men
That might by countenance be ken.

His bravery on this occasion obtained for him the close friendship of the King. In the end of that year he was appointed to receive Elizabeth, the wife of King Robert, and Marjory, his daughter, at their entrance into Scotland on their return from captivity in England, and the year after he married the latter, whose acquaintance he had thus made, and who may have been captivated by the gallant bearing of her escort. She did not come to him empty-handed, for he received from the King as her dowry the Barony of Bathgate and other valuable possessions. Their wedded life was short; it lasted only a year, and sometime in 1316‡ Abbot Roger had a grave to dig in the Abbey for Marjory.

The circumstances attending her death have been often told, and, though there may be in the story as it has come down to us little more

* Tytler, p. 108. Rotuli Scotiae, vol. I., p. 103.

† Reg. de Pas., p. 376.

‡ Stewart's History of the Stewarts:—"I have chosen this date as the most probable." Crawford says October, 1317, as also Balfour (Annals, Vol. I. p. 96). Chalmers (Caledonia, Vol. III., p. 824) gives the date 1315-16.

than tradition, it is impossible not to believe that there is in it a considerable substratum of truth.* Midway between the Abbey and the Castle of the Stewarts at Renfrew there is an eminence called "the Knock," a name which it has borne from earliest times.† This little elevation then rose in the midst of the wood which stretched between Paisley and the Clyde, and was probably a frequent hunting-ground of the Stewarts. Here, it is said, Marjory, while following the chase, to which the family of her husband were devoted, was thrown from her horse in its struggles through a marshy piece of ground long after shown as the scene of the accident.‡ The pangs of labour seized her, and she died on the field; but the Cæsarean operation was performed, and the life of the child was saved, though it was hurt in the eye by the operator. This child afterwards bore the name of "Blear-Eye," and his mother by tradition was called "Queen Blear-Eye," though she never was Queen. This is the story that has come down to us.§ Whether it was thus that one of our Scottish kings came into the world may perhaps be doubted, but that Marjory was killed in this way is not at all improbable. Down to modern times a stone pillar stood on the spot where the mother of the Royal house of Stewart was said to have met her death. It was an octagonal column ten feet high, inserted in a solid pedestal also eight-sided, and about six feet in diameter. It bore the name of "Queen Blearie's Cross." No vestige of it is now to be seen. When last observed it was being used as the lintel of a door in a neighbouring farm house,‖ and the materials of the pedestal were employed to repair fences. It was one of the memorials of the Stewart to the wife of his youth, and the mother of a line of kings, and

* The reader who wishes to see what may be said on the other side, may read Lord Hailes' Essay. I give the story as tradition has handed it down.

† See Reg. de Pas.

‡ See M'Farlane's description of the locality in 1842.—Stat. Acct. of Renfrew.

§ See appendix to Hamilton's Renfrewshire, where Lord Hailes' criticism on this story is, I think, successfully controverted; also p. 146, where the story as told by Dunlop is given.

‖ In the appendix to Hamilton's Renfrewshire, it is stated that the pedestal became loosened in the socket, and required a little repair. This was refused by the proprietor, and time did its work. It either fell, or to save it from breaking, it was removed and built into the barn a short time before the foundations of the pedestal were dug up. It is not too much to hope that the present public-spirited proprietor will replace that which his ancestor, in a time of indifference to archaeological study, allowed to be removed.

deserved better treatment. It was not the only token of affection which he displayed. In the Abbey he caused a "faire monument"* to be erected to her memory—the only monument of all the Stewarts that has escaped the destruction of after years. The Chartulary tells also how he had prayers said for the repose of her soul. He gave to the Abbey the Church of Largs, in Ayrshire, "inspired by love, and for the salvation of my soul and of Marjorie, formerly my wife, and for the salvation of my ancestors and of all the faithful departed."† The donation included all the tithes, and properties of every kind belonging to that Church, and though the Abbot and Convent were only to come into the possession of these revenues on the death or promotion of Sir William Lyndsay, the rector of the benefice, in the midst of their dilapidated fortunes the gift must have been received very gratefully. On the 3rd February, 1318, Sir William Lyndsay resigned the Church, and they entered on the full enjoyment of its emoluments, but institution to these was given them, not by their old friend Robert Wishart, the Bishop of Glasgow,—he had died about the same time as Marjory, with whom he had been a prisoner in England,—but by the Chapter of the Cathedral, the See of Glasgow being vacant.‡

After the death of Marjory we have frequent notices of Walter in the history of the time.§ He was a brave soldier and often distinguished himself in the field. When Berwick was taken in 1318 it was committed to his charge, and, assisted by his Renfrewshire vassals, he in the following year repulsed from that town Edward II. and his army.‖ The next year he signed the spirited letter of the Barons of Scotland to Pope John, in which, among other grievances, they state how much the Church had suffered at the hands of Edward I. Their prelates had been incarcerated, their monasteries burned, their religious robbed and murdered.¶ None could more truly confirm that statement than the Stewart, who had so lately buried his wife in the ruined Abbey of his ancestors. There he himself was laid after a few more years of active service and of chivalrous deeds, which earned him the title of the "noble

* Balfour's Annals, Vol. I., p. 9. † Reg. de Pas., p. 237. ‡ Reg. de Pas., p. 238.

§ Chalmers' Caledonia, Vol. III., p. 783. ‖ Ibid.

¶ Fordun by Goodall, Vol. II., p. 276.

warrior."* He died at Bathgate, a property which he had received as the dowry of his wife Marjory, on the 9th April, 1326, and the historian of the Bruce tells how he was honoured and sorrowed for at his death.

> When long time their dule had made,
> The corps to Paslay have they had,
> And there with great solemnity
> And with great dule eirded was he.†

Robert, the son of Walter and Marjory, was but a boy of ten or eleven at his father's death, but he was a boy with great expectations. Failing the death of the King's son without heirs, it had been solemnly agreed by Parliament that he should succeed to the throne of Scotland. This must have raised the hopes of the Convent, of whom he was the hereditary patron, and who might naturally look forward to benefit by his elevation. The good King Robert the Bruce died three years after his trusty friend Walter, and their hopes came thereby one step nearer fulfilment.

* "Nobilis bellator."—Fordun by Goodall, Vol. II., p. 288.

In 1322 he took part in the forced march to Biland Abbey, and pursued Edward II. to York with 500 men, and in the true spirit of chivalry expected that Edward, with a similar number, would renew the combat without the walls.—Chalmers' Caledonia, Vol. III., p. 782.

† Barbour, p. 386.

## CHAPTER XI.

### Accession of the Stewarts.

1329—1370.

Thou shalt get kings, though thou be none.
So, All hail! Macbeth and Banquo.

*Shakespeare.*

DURING the comparatively peaceful years that closed the reign of King Robert the Bruce, and the short interval of quiet which succeeded his death, the Abbot and Convent set themselves to repair their dilapidated fortunes and reinstate the Abbey in its former prosperity. Abbot John succeeded Abbot Roger shortly before the death of the King, and the first mention we have of his name is in connection with a deed of charity to the impoverished brethren. In 1327,* Brother Andrew, as he styles himself, "Minister of Argyle," compassionating the poverty of the common table of the monks, "which was not sufficient for their maintainance and to enable them to respond to the calls of hospitality, and the other onerous duties incumbent upon them, as the law of charity demands," with the consent of his chapter, gave the brethren, in answer to their earnest request, the rectorial tithes and dues of three churches in his diocese—Kilfinan, Kilkeran, and Kilcolmanel. This gift represented a considerable sum of money, and was burdened only by their liability to maintain a vicar in each of the churches. The vicars possibly were of their own number, and would be amply compensated by the altar offerings, and a small portion of land for the supply of their immediate needs.

* Reg. de Pas., p. 137.

This plan for replenishing the diminished exchequer of the Convent was resorted to also in the case of Largs, the church which had been bestowed on them by Walter, the sixth Stewart, in memory of his wife Marjory. About the same time * that Andrew thought with compassion on their scantily furnished table, their meagre fare, and generally sorrowful lot, living, it may be, as we have suggested, in some small tenement in the unsavoury precincts of the Rottenrow, his brother Bishop, John Lindsay of Glasgow, took into consideration the "great damage which the Monastery of Passelet had sustained by reason of the sad war so long waged between the kingdoms of England and Scotland," and for the rebuilding† of the fabric of the Abbey Church which had been burnt during this war, confirmed and conceded to them the church of Largs and chapel of Cumbraye, with all its dues, both great and small. When the chapter of Glasgow had formerly installed the Convent in possession of this church, it had bound them to place in it a vicar, and had fixed what his stipend was to be, namely, seventeen merks sterling, six acres of land, and four wains of hay, the Convent also paying the procurations of the bishop, and finding wax for the church lights.‡ The bishop was more generous, and relieved them from those charges, his own fees excepted, and allowed them to hold the church without presenting any vicar, provided they served it simply by priests placed and removable at their pleasure. One of their own number in priest's orders would, therefore, from time to time

* Reg. de Pas., p. 239. The date of the Bishop of Glasgow's concession is uncertain, but it must be between 1325 and 1335, during which time he occupied the see.

† *Juvamen.*

‡ Reg. de Pas., p. 237. Origines Parochiales, Vol. I., p. 89. This scheme for replenishing the conventual exchequer was a common enough one, as we learn from the other chartularies; thus in 1315 Bishop Robert Wischeart, on the ground that not only the movables of the monks of Melrose had been taken away during the late protracted war, but also that their places, far and near, had been destroyed, with consent of his chapter, gave them all the fruits of the vicarage of Hastenden for twenty years, to be wholly converted into a pittance for the convent at the discretion and sight of the Prior, so, however, that fitting service should be performed in the said church by a priest simply, and that it should not be defrauded of its other due services.—Lib. de Melrose, p. 393. Origines Par., Vol. I., p. 317.

cross the moors to Largs, and fulfil all the obligations of his house by performing service for the benefit of the parishioners.*

A curious decree from the Pope reached the Convent at this period (1329), which illustrates what the history of the time tells us regarding barratry or buying benefices at Rome, a practice which became very prevalent, to the great injury of the Church, and which furnished ground for the satire of Lindsay—

> It is schort tyme sen ony benefice
> Was sped in Rome except greit bischoprics,
> But now, for ane unworthie vicarage,
> Ane priest will rin to Rome in pilgrimage;
> Ane carell whilk was never at the schule
> Will rin to Rome and keep ane bischopis' mule,
> And syne cum hame, with mony-colorit crack,
> With ane burden of benefices on his back.

A certain Robert de Caral, one of the secular clergy of St. Andrews, obtained from the Pope a benefice of the value of twenty silver merks if accompanied with a cure of souls, and of ten if not so accompanied. This benefice was to be given him by the Abbey on the first vacancy occurring in one of their churches. The Abbot received strict injunctions to put no obstacle in the way of carrying out this decree under pain of excommunication, and a Papal commission was issued to certain ecclesiastics in the neighbourhood to see the arrangement carried into effect. It was not a pleasant missive for the impoverished Abbot to receive, and that, too, at a time when he needed to make the most of his resources.†

A charitable concession, which must have been gratifying to the Abbot and his brethren in their low estate, was made by Earl Malcolm of Lennox.‡ He gave them all their lands in his country of Dunbartonshire. The contested properties of Monackeneran, Backan, and others, appear in his charter for the last time, all their rights, churches, and fishings being for ever secured, so that no person, clerical or lay, should interfere

* This concession was ratified by Bishop John's successor, William Rae, and subsequently by Pope Clement VI.—Reg. de Pas., pp. 239, 241, 242.

† This curious document is in the Appendix.

‡ Reg. de Pas., p. 205. The date is 1330.

with them again. These properties had been an incessant cause of disquietude and litigation during nearly a century, and many of them amid the confusion of the War of Independence, had, in every likelihood, been lost altogether. The Earl now confirmed them inalienably to the Monastery "for the soul of the illustrious King Robert of Scotland," who had died two years previously. In order that the Convent might hold their lands with a firm hand, he gave them power to have "courts of life and members," and *escheat* at the death of a man, in all their lands. These powers would enable them to keep all the wild Celts on their Dunbartonshire lands thoroughly in order, without need, as formerly, to apply to the Bishop for spiritual excommunication. For the latter, the rude marauders of the Lennox, as we have seen, cared but little, and the Bishop thundered at them in vain; but the fear of summary execution and a short shrift, could not fail to instil into them wholesome respect for their monastic superiors. The Earl, however, provided that when any were condemned to death, they should pay the penalty at his own gallows of Lennox. Possibly he thought it might be necessary to have some check upon the clerical power in carrying out the last penalty of the law, or he may have felt it added to his dignity as a great feudal baron to have always a plentiful supply of offenders hanging, as a terror to evil doers, from his ancestral gibbet.*

During the short Regency of Randolph things looked brighter for the Church, and under his firm rule, aided by these donations from the benevolent, the Abbot and Convent would naturally begin to prepare for the rebuilding of their Monastery. The lawlessness which had caused them to suffer so much seemed passing away; and, if we believe the chronicler, "the traveller might tie his horse to the inn door, and the ploughman leave his ploughshare and harness in the field without fear.†" Inspirited by the hope of better days, and perhaps thinking that his house deserved some solatium from the head of the Church for all the privations they had undergone, Abbot John sent a petition to Pope Benedict XI.

* The privilege of a gallows was greatly esteemed in feudal times, and a day of hanging a source of great festivity to the tenants of a lordship. To this day, in Invernesshire, when any general rejoicing is afloat, the saying is often repeated as an incentive to jollity, "It's no every day that the M'Intosh has a hanging."

† Tytler,—Fordun by Goodall, Vol. II., Book 13th.

begging that the honour of wearing the mitre and ring might be conferred upon himself and his successors. The Pope, then residing at Avignon, granted his request.* He gave him and his successors in office, by a bull issued in August, 1334, leave to wear the coveted insignia, and to bestow the accustomed benediction after masses, vespers, and matins in his monastery, and in all priories, and other places belonging thereto, as well as in parochial and other churches under their jurisdiction, provided that no Bishop or Legate of the Apostolic See happened to be present. This was a great honour to the Abbot, who had hitherto been distinguished only by the crosier; but by the time the permission reached Paisley from Avignon, Scotland was again distracted by warfare, and the prospect of the restoration of the Abbey appeared indefinitely postponed. England had once more put forward its claim of sovereignty over Scotland. In 1332 Edward Baliol was crowned King, and the old strifes which seemed to have passed away under the government of King Robert began again. In these the Stewart, as yet a mere boy, took active part, with all the spirit and energy of his ancestors. Though only sixteen or seventeen years of age, he led a division of the Scottish army at the disastrous battle of Halidon Hill.† He was, says Fordun, a comely youth, tall and robust, affable and modest, liberal, gay and honest, and for the innate sweetness of his disposition, generally beloved by all true-hearted Scotchmen.‡ After the defeat at Halidon, the Stewart fled to Bute, and his lands in the Barony of Renfrew were confiscated and conveyed to David Hastings, Earl of Athol, who came down to Renfrew personally and received homage from all on his newly-acquired lands.§ The Stewart, with some of his friends, again recovered them, but only to lose them immediately; for about the time the newly-conferred honour of the Pope reached Abbot John on Christmas, 1334, Edward Baliol was holding high festival in the Stewart's castle at Renfrew, and with royal state conferring favours upon his guests,|| in which favours we may well believe Abbot John did not share.

* Reg. de Pas., p. 429. † Stewart's History of the Stewarts.

‡ Fordun by Goodall, Vol. II., p. 314. § Ibid. p. 317.

|| Chalmers' Caledonia, Vol. III., p. 734.—Genealogical History of the Stewarts.

For twenty-three years after this Scotland endured all the miseries and hardships of war. In almost every battle the name of the young Stewart appears as taking a gallant part. For a considerable time during the captivity of King David de Brus in England he acted as Regent of the kingdom, and "notwithstanding the national calamities, he supported the cause of his absent sovereign, and maintained a show of civil government in Scotland.* During this period there is not much to record in the annals of the Abbey. In 1346, the 17th year of King David's reign, the newly acquired mitre descended to James, who was then elected Abbot. In 1361, amid his many engagements, the Stewart found time to show his good will towards the Abbey. He gave no gifts after the manner of his ancestors,—the time for new endowments had passed,—but he fully confirmed those already given. The lands are all mentioned by name as lying within the Baronies of Kyle and Renfrew, but we miss from the catalogue several goodly portions which had probably been lost during the national troubles.† He did, however, what he could for his friends, and there is ample proof that though burdened by the care of State, he did not neglect to put forth his power for their protection whenever an opportunity was presented.‡ They needed all the friends they could get. In 1351 they became involved in a controversy with David Martin, Bishop of Argyle, who had succeeded Brother Andrew, the prelate who had been so kind to them in their necessity. They carried on the dispute with great vigour, and even our own day, so rife in ecclesiastical bickerings, could not furnish an instance of a more persistent fight. The highland Bishop, under the pretext that the churches of St. Queran, St. Finan, and St. Colmaneli, in his diocese, needed repair, seized upon the revenue which Bishop Andrew, his predecessor, had made over to the Convent for the supply of their table, and to help them in their necessity. Probably enough the Convent had not been so careful of the interests of these distant parishes as they should have been, but they were not willing to part with their property, and

* Balfour's Annals, Vol. II., p. 21.—Fordun, XIV., 6.

† Reg. de Pas., pp. 6, 7.—There is no mention of Prestwick and several other lands.

‡ Reg. de Pas., p. 31.

appealed piteously to certain conservators of the privileges of the Clunaic Monks whom the Pope had appointed to watch over the rights of the Order.* These were ecclesiastics residing in the east of Scotland,† who felt it was a hardship to bring the accused Bishop so far from his diocese, since the distance and "dangers of the way" were so great, and who wished to spare parties all the expenses they could. They therefore delegated their powers to four Canons of Glasgow, who were to adjudicate upon the matters in dispute.‡ The Canons, acting on these powers, cited all parties before them. The Bishop, however, paid no attention whatever to their summons. It was "a far cry to Lochawe," and the citation of four Glasgow Canons was likely to give him as little uneasiness in his Argyleshire castle of Lismore, as the scream of the sea-gulls of that island fastness. On one occasion on which he was cited to appear in the Glasgow Cathedral he happened to be residing in the city,§ and treated the command with contempt, and went back to Argyleshire perfectly indifferent as to what they might say or do. This at last roused the ire of the Canons, and they determined to bring the highland prelate to book. He might not have been able to come to them from Argyleshire, for the dangers of the way were great, but to be under the shadow of the Cathedral and to pay no attention to their summons was an open defiance of their authority which they could not and would not submit to. They accordingly took high ground—as in their persons representing the full authority of the Apostolic See—and issued a manifesto to all abbots, priors, deans, archdeacons, officials, rural deans, rectors, vicars, and chaplains, whether holding cures or not, throughout the whole diocese and townships of Argyle and Sodor, and also to the learned Sir Richard Daurog, Walter Rewl, and Thomas de Arthurly, rectors and vicars of Kirkmichael, Herskyn, and Dayel. They stated that they had cited the venerable father in Christ, Lord Martin, by the grace of God, Bishop of Argyle, at the instance and petition of the Abbot and Convent of Paisley, to appear

* Reg. de Pas., p. 143.

† The Abbots of Cupar, Dunfermlyn, and Newbattle.

‡ They were—John Penney, sub-dean, Neil Carrotherys, Malcolm Kenedy, and Henry de Mundavilla.

§ Reg. de Pas., p. 145.

before them on the 30th May, that he had not appeared though he was in the City of Glasgow on that day, and for many days previous, but had contumaciously absented himself, on account of which they adjudged him contumacious, and suspended him altogether from pontificals.* They commanded each of the aforesaid clergy, under pain of the greater excommunication, if they refused, within three days after they received the mandate, to take witnesses with them, to go personally into the presence of the said Lord Bishop of Argyle, and announce publicly that the prelate was suspended by the apostolic authority they possessed, from all pontificals on account of his contumacy. They were nevertheless to cite him to appear before them in the Cathedral Church of Glasgow, according to the form and tenor of the first citation, on the fourteenth day of the month of June, to answer to the Abbot and Convent of Paisley, or their procurators, for the loss and injury which was mentioned in the first summons. This fiery document apparently had a wholesome effect upon the contumacious bishop. He appears to have come in hot haste from his diocese to Glasgow five days before the court to which he had been cited was to meet.† Probably fearing to appear before the irate canons in judgment, he compromised the matters in dispute with the Abbot and his Convent. An agreement between them was drawn out, in which the Abbot seems to have got the better in the dispute, and the Bishop promised to have the agreement proclaimed and explained, in their mother tongue,‡ to the people belonging to the churches in question, who were to be specially convened for this purpose.

This compromise was made in 1361, in which year an Abbot John is mentioned as presiding over the Convent. § He was present at the Parliament held at Perth three years || afterwards to make arrangements for payment of the ransom of King David, and the establishing of a firm peace between England and Scotland. The Stewart was there also with his eldest son, John, Lord of Kyle, endeavouring to combat, with the ability of a great statesman, the fickleness and treachery of the King. King David

* Reg. de Pas., p. 145. † Ibid, p. 145. ‡ *In materna lingua.*

§ See Lennox Charters; also, Eglinton Charters, Vol. II., 2.

|| 13th June, 1364. See Tytler, Appendix HH.

seems to have hated him with a cordial hatred, and at one time he and his sons were imprisoned by his orders, * and remained in confinement for more than a year. The Stewart had led a chequered life from his very boyhood, and had suffered much in the cause of his country. His trials were now seemingly at an end. The King died on the 22nd February, 1370, and Robert the Stewart ascended the throne by the title of Robert II. The Abbey was now under royal patronage, and Walter the son of Alan, its founder—the Shropshire colonist—the progenitor of a race of kings.

* Fordun by Goodall, Vol. II., p. 380.

## CHAPTER XII.

### Royal Patronage.

1373-1405.

> "True son of our dear Mother,
> Nursed in her aisles to more than kingly thought."
>
> *Keble.*

UNDER royal favour and patronage the Abbey began a course of prosperity which remained unbroken till the time of the Reformation. No endowments like those that marked its early days flowed into its coffers, but the property it possessed was well husbanded, and its possessions firmly consolidated. The reviving activity of the community is marked by an incident which, even as detailed in the formal language of a notary public in the pages of the Chartulary, is not without a certain picturesqueness. When the lands which were given by Duncan, Earl of Carrick, to the Abbey for the erection of a monastery, were wrested from it after a prolonged process in the ecclesiastical courts,* and devoted to their original purpose, a monastery was built at Crosragmol, now called Crosraguel, in Ayrshire. This house was governed by an abbot, and was peopled from Paisley by brethren of the Order of Clugny. It was in no way subject to Paisley, except that the Abbot of Paisley was bound to visit it once a year, with a moderate following, and reasonable expenses. The discipline of Crosragmol had, during the

* Reg. de Pas., 422, 424, 425, 427. See ante.

distractions of the time, fallen into decay. Abbot John, on visiting it, took note of many faults and direlictions from the rules of the Order, which from various causes he was unable at the time to correct, being probably fully occupied with the misfortunes of his own house. Shortly after the accession of King Robert, however, the times having become quiet, he determined, if possible, to put things right at Crosragmol. He accordingly issued a mandate to the Abbot of that place, commanding him to "admonish his monks, whether within or without the Monastery, wherever they were to be found, to appear before him at Crosragmol on Wednesday next, the feast of St. Michael the Archangel, at the house of the chapter, to hear and perform those things which are known to pertain to our office." Accordingly, at the time appointed Abbot John, with his attendants, appeared in the chapter house at Crosragmol, and Abbot Roger, and the brethren of that place, were all convened in his presence. There had probably been some private inquiry previously, for the Abbot of Crosragmol saved the Court from the necessity of further proceedings. "At once," to quote the words of the notary, "the said Lord Roger, without violence, fraud, or circumvention, as it appeared to me, placed, in presence of his Convent, all the dignity and honour of the station of Abbot of the Monastery of Crosragmol, which he had until then governed, in the hands of the Lord Abbot of Paisley of his own free will, purely and simply, without the addition of any condition whatever." Abbot John then asked him what was the reason of this resignation, to which question poor Abbot Roger plaintively and touchingly replied, that "burdened by old age and debility, he was so constantly vexed by bodily infirmity, that he was not able to govern the flock committed to him by God, their lands and goods, and other possessions, to their benefit, as behoves the office of a good pastor; for," he said, "he would rather altogether give up the abbatic honour than under the name of pastor have the desolate flock be devoured by the greedy wolf." This high view of the pastoral office commended itself to Abbot John, for he accepted the resignation profered him, and released Roger altogether from the office of Abbot of Crosragmol, and commanded the monks to fix among themselves a certain day for the election of one who should be their pastor in the future, piously observing "that it was necessary that this should be done, that the church might not be long deprived of a pastor in spiritual things, or suffer damage in things temporal."*

In regard to the latter duty of the pastoral office, the guardianship of temporalities, Abbot John himself set no mean example to his brother of Crossragmol. He was exceedingly active in conserving the endowments which remained to his house, and in putting its finances on a good footing. Through his energy, the question of the pension of forty merks to the English house of Sempringham was finally adjusted. It had been a grievance for more than a century. It will be remembered how at Berwick Abbot Walter was forced to promise its regular payment, and to make acknowledgment of the debt. Succeeding Abbots had repudiated it, or at least had neglected to pay it, probably because they were not able. The canons of Sempringham then, for a consideration, transferred the pension to a Scotchman, who was better able to fight the battle† with the Paisley monks than they were. The fight over the forty merks then began in earnest. The representative of Sempringham was Reginald More, and subsequently his son, Sir William More, of Abercorne. The former began the battle with the Abbot and monks in 1328, by summoning them into the Bishop's court in Glasgow, and Andrew de Kelkow or Kelso, Prior of Paisley, appeared as their representative. He acknowledged that the Abbot owed the pension from the time when peace had been proclaimed between England and Scotland, but as Reginald was unable to produce a mandate from Sempringham authorising him to settle as to the arrears, the court did not proceed further at that time with the case, and Reginald and the Prior agreed upon certain arbiters—two appointed by each, with a fifth chosen as umpire by both parties—who were to meet on a certain day at Berwick-on-Tweed, and settle the whole dispute as to the arrears of the pension.‡ Nothing seems to have come from this carefully-adjusted scheme. The Abbot refused to pay the pension unless Reginald should produce

* Reg. de Pas., 425. † Reg. de Pas., p. 42.

‡ Reg. de Pas., p. 27. The arbiters were—For Reginald More, James, Bishop of St. Andrews, and Sir Robert de Lawdyr, Justiciar of Lothian; for the Abbot, Lord James of Duglas and Alexander de Meynes. Thomas Randolph, Earl of Moray, was chosen in case the four could not agree.

authority from Sempringham. This Reginald promised to do, and placed in the hands of Robert the Stewart the titles of all his lands in the Barony of Kyle, to be forfeited to the Abbot, unless he should by a certain time procure letters of perpetual security from the canons and nuns of Sempringham. He seems to have failed to do this, though he exacted payment, and accordingly in 1367, at the request of the Abbot, his lands were handed over to the Convent in lieu of the pension, which for some years they held had been unjustly extorted from them.* The Stewart did more than this; he issued a document,† in which he gave the history of the foundation of the Abbey by his ancestors, and its endowment by them, with many lands and churches; but as he puts it—" A certain Abbot of the Monastery, induced by we know not what spirit, without liberty, consent, or authority from any superior, secular or lay, presumptuously made, what by law he had no power to do, an immense bequest or alienation of forty merks sterling of an annual pension, for no use, and under no compulsion of necessity, to the canons and nuns of Sempringham in England, which, there is no doubt, has led to the lessening of divine worship, the detriment and loss of the Monastery, the peril of needy souls, and our own prejudice and injury." The Stewart then, as " special defender and patron of the Monastery," proceeds to pronounce the bequest null and void, and to forbid the Convent to pay the pension any more, and enjoins them to apply it, with the lands of Sir William More, which he has conveyed to them, to their own uses. The Abbot gladly obeyed the command of his patron not to pay the pension, but Sir William More of Abercorne, who had succeeded his father, was not disposed to yield ready acquiescence. He made a raid upon the churchmen. He plundered the lands of the Monastery, and lifted the cattle of the Monks. He even ventured wrathfully into the sacred precincts of the Abbey, and generally behaved himself in a very violent manner. He was clearly a dangerous man, and determined to get his rights by force if necessary. The Abbot in 1368 applied to the conservators of the privileges of his Order in Scotland for protection, and in his application he gives a pitiful account of the doings of

* The lands were those of Sankar, Camceskane, Dowlargis, Cowdane, Staffour, and Hormisdalle.—Reg. de Pas., p. 30. † Reg. de Pas., p. 32.

lawless Sir William of Abercorne. "He had injured them again and again,* entering their Monastery against their will, breaking their doors and windows, striking their men and servants who resisted him, wounding a man within the village † of Passley, going with his followers to their church lands in various places, beating their men, and spoiling and robbing them of their goods." ‡ He was duly summoned by the Church authorities to appear before them, and answer for his doings; but they do not seem to have been able to bring him into subjection. It was in the time of Abbot John, in 1373, that the whole matter was finally compromised. Robert the Stewart was now King, but his son, John, who took the title of Stewart, was as interested in the affairs of the Abbey as any of his family had been. He appears to have mediated between the determined Sir William and his refractory creditors at Paisley. He and William, Count of Douglas, Hugh of Eglynton, Sir Adam Stewart, John of Carric, Canon of Glasgow and Chancellor of Scotland, and William de Dalgarnoc, Canon of Dunkeld, Adam Forester, Alderman of Edinburgh, and Alan de Lawedre, met together at Edinburgh in the chapel of St. Katherine, in the Church of St. Giles,§ and there they settled for ever the vexed question of the forty merks. The agreement ‖ is a long one, and there is no need to give it in detail. The Convent were to pay the Lord of Abercorne three hundred merks sterling in three different instalments, and to restore him all his lands which they had received from Robert the Stewart; on the other hand, Sir William was to give them all the documents by which he claimed the pension, and become bound that the canons and nuns of Sempringham should never make any charge against the brethren of Paisley in all time coming. It must have taxed all the revenues of Abbot John to raise this large sum, especially with the work which he had in hand in the rebuilding of the Monastery; but he had many friends to help him, and it must have been with no small satisfaction that he saw this vexatious burden for ever re-

* Reg. de Pas., p. 40. † *Villam.*

‡ The valiant Lord of Abercorn, ancestor of the present family of Caldwell, was aided and abetted by his brother Gilchrist and a certain John, son of John, burgess of Linlithgow.—Reg. de Pas., p. 41.

§ Sancti Egidii de Edynburg.—Reg. de Pas., p. 46. ‖ Reg. de Pas., p. 43.

moved. In 1380, King Robert II.* gave him a token of his good will by erecting into a barony all the Abbey lands of Lennox, with all the privileges which a barony usually possessed, assigning as the reason for this favour, that the Monastery had been founded by Walter son of Alan, Stewart of Scotland, of beloved memory, and liberally endowed by him and other of his ancestors, as well as by various other faithful Christians. In return for his concessions, the King asks the offering of their earnest prayers, and the only condition which he attaches to it is that they should continue to pay, as hitherto, five chalders of oatmeal to the watchmen of the Castle of Dunbarton. He reserves also the "points" of the Crown.

We come upon the name of a new Abbot in 1384—John de Lithgw or Lithgow, so called probably, to distinguish him from his predecessor, who is always called John simply. He ruled the Monastery at least fifty years, and is the only Abbot whose name is to be found on any of the monastic buildings.† His accession to office was marked by an invasion of the privileges of the Monastery by Walter, Bishop of Glasgow. The relation between the Abbey and the Cathedral was of a varied character. At one time we find the Bishop, as in the case of Robert Wishart, interfering on behalf of the monks, at another meddling with their affairs in a way which provoked their resistance. It was only a phase of the strife which went on over all Europe between the regular and the secular clergy. It was certainly somewhat annoying to the Bishop to have a body of clergy in the heart of his diocese who were in most matters free from the exercise of his authority, while they drew the principal revenues of his churches, leaving only a miserable pittance to the

* Reg. de Pas., p. 208.

† On the porch, and on the tomb of Marjory Bruce.

My friend, Mr. David Semple, makes the following suggestion regarding him—"The sound of the Abbot's name brings to my recollection the name of John Lithgw, the stone engraver who was employed to make the stone lettering around the tomb erected in 1329 in the Abbey Church of Dunfermline to our Lord King Robert Bruce. The Abbot was probably the grandson of the engraver, and was probably taught the art of stone engraving and sculpture, memorials of which, particularly of the former, have remained, I presume, in Paisley Abbey for at least 438 years as sharp as when the chisel left them. The patron of the Abbey was the grandson of the King, and the Abbot may have been the grandson of the engraver of the King's tomb, and from that connection appointed Abbot of Paisley."—Saint Mirin, p. 25.

clergy who were subject to him, and who looked naturally to him as their protector. The Bishop was, therefore, constantly seeking to extend the very few rights which the privileges of the order of Clugny allowed him in connection with the Abbey, and the Abbots were equally determined to allow him to interfere no more than they possibly could. Upon Abbot Lithgow's election, the Bishop of Glasgow summoned him to have his election confirmed, and to receive his episcopal blessing. This demand the Abbot did not comply with, and went elsewhere for the benediction. The Bishop complained of him to the Patron of the Abbey, King Robert II.* That King, with whom were his two sons, John and Robert Earl of Fife, heard parties at Dunbarton on the second of June, 1384. The Bishop put forth his claim in the royal presence, and Abbot Lithgow, on the other hand, asserted that he and his convent were specially exempt from all episcopal jurisdiction, by virtue of certain special privileges conferred upon them and the whole order of Clugny, which had existed from time immemorial. No judgment was pronounced; it was stated that the Bishop of Glasgow "was appointed ambassador on business of the King and kingdom in distant parts," and, therefore, that no further proceedings could be taken at that time. The Bishop, Walter Wardlaw, was eminent as an ecclesiastic, a statesman, and a scholar. He became a cardinal of the Church, was frequently employed on embassies of importance, and taught philosophy with applause in the University of Paris.† The business that suspended the controversy between him and Abbot Lithgow was the negotiating in England of a truce between that country and Scotland.‡ In this he was successful,—more so than in any attempt to invade Abbot Lithgow's jurisdiction. That ecclesiastic had the support of the whole order of Clugny behind him, and no Bishop could tamper with its rights with much prospect of success.§

The records of the Abbey give abundant proof of the difficulty which they had in maintaining their privileges and possessions. They seem to have been constantly involved in litigation and strife. Sometimes they appeal to the secular arm for protection, and sometimes from the secular court to the court ecclesiastical, and at times we find them transferring the

* Reg. de Pas., p. 330. † Burton's Hist., Vol. II., p. 348. ‡ Tytler, Vol. II., p. 334.
§ Reg. de Pas., p. 328.

case from the court ecclesiastical to the Pope himself. At one time they are at war with the Bishop, at another with some powerful chieftain, like the Earl of Lennox, or lawless aggressor like Sir Reginald of Abercorne. In 1385 they punish severely John of Auchinlek, in Ayrshire, who had attacked and brutally injured one of their monks.* What provocation the Ayrshire laird received we know not, nor to what court, secular or sacred, the Abbot appealed; but the offender had to pay† heavily for his transgression. He was fined in twenty shillings sterling, an annual rent, payable half-yearly at Whitsunday and Martinmas. The deed drawn up for the purpose of making the payment binding is of the strictest character, and the son of the culprit, on entering into possession of his estate, is taken bound to pay the fine for his father's transgression.‡ In 1390, Abbot Lithgow lost his good friend and patron, King Robert. Like his ancestors, he did many a kind act to his friends at Paisley. He was always ready to defend them from their enemies, and one of the last acts of his life was to procure for them from the Pope a continuance of the liberty to use the revenues of the Church of Largs§ to help them in rebuilding their house. It is expressly mentioned that the Pope grants the permission in "consideration of his most dear son in Christ, Robert, the illustrious King of Scotland, whose predecessors had founded the Monastery." The King was a kind benefactor to the monks, who must have offered many prayers for the repose of his soul. He died at his Castle of Dundonald, in Ayrshire. For some reason he was not buried among his ancestors, but at Scone.‖ If this be true, he was the first of the Stewarts who were laid elsewhere than in the precincts of the Abbey, and the circumstance is all the more strange because Elizabeth More, the much-loved wife of his youth, and Euphan Ross, his Queen, are buried there.

* Reg. de Pas., p. 359.

† "Pro contemptu et violatione eis factis, occasione injurie cuidam monacho ipsius monasterii, vasa sua seminaria amputando, per me et complices meos."

‡ It continued to be paid till the Reformation.

§ Reg. de Pas., p. 242. In 1389, the year before his death, by order of the King £30 were paid from the Exchequer for glass for the Abbey of Paisley. Exchequer Rolls, No. 102.

‖ Fordun by Goodall, Vol. II., p. 418.

John, Earl of Carick, whose name has appeared more than once in the pages of this history, the eldest son of Robert II., succeeded his father as King of Scotland by the title of Robert III., the association of the name of John with the ill-fated Baliol being regarded with aversion by the nation. Very soon after his accession to the throne we find him manifesting his interest in the Abbey. For the safety of his soul and that of his ancestors, "Kings and Stewarts of Scotland," he erected all the lands of the Abbey in Ayrshire, Peebles,* and Roxburgh,† into a free barony of regality, asking nothing in return but their prayers.‡ He took all their lands, men, and possessions, and all their goods, movable and immovable, ecclesiastical and secular, under his special protection. He granted them exemption from capture for debt,§ and he confirmed all their endowments, ancient|| and modern—the latter were of no great importance—liberty to draw water to their Mill of Monkton¶ by an ancient lead through the land of Adamton, and forty silver pennies granted for the safety of his soul by a certain Adam Fullerton, Knight, Lord of Crosseby.** Any gift, however small, seems to have been thankfully received, and for half a stone of wax paid at the Feast of St. Mirin by Hugh Boyl,†† Lord of Rysholm, and John Kelsow, Lord of Kelsowland,‡‡ respectively, the monks consented to receive them and their wives into perpetual participation of the brotherhood and prayers of the whole Order of Clugny. This was a wonderful falling off from the time when this privilege was obtained by large gifts of land and other valuable donations. So far as giving was concerned, the times had become very evil. In 1403 we come to the last of many endowments.§§ Sir Hugh Walas, a descendant of the patriot, who was one of the esquires to the King, "for the safety of Robert, King of Scots, of good memory, deceased, and the souls of his ancestors, and for the safety of our Lord

* Their lands of Orde.

† Five marks of their lands from their lands of Molla and Huntlaw, in their land of Hastenden.

‡ Reg. de Pas., p. 91. § Ibid, p. 96. || Ibid, p. 97. ¶ Ibid, p. 363.

** Ibid, p. 364. †† Ibid, p. 368.

‡‡ Ibid. Kelso gives his donation for the soul of Christiana Lewinston, his wife.

§§ Reg. de Pas., p. 79.

the King, and of all his successors, and for the safety of the donator's own soul, and all his ancestors and successors, with consent and assent of William Walas, his brother, gave, for the glory of God, the Virgin, St. Mirin and St. James of Passelet, and for the monks there, the ten merk lands of Thornle, lying within the Barony of Renfru and Sheriffdom of Lanark." They are fair and fertile lands, yet unencroached upon by the fast-extending town of Paisley. They were the last gift of the faithful to the Convent,* and their confirmation by the King his last deed of kindness to the Abbey. He executed this confirmation three years before his death, at Rothesay, for the soul of his illustrious father and mother Elizabeth, and his charter is signed by Robert, Duke of Albany,† and James Douglas, his ally.‡ The former exercised a powerful influence over the King in his government of Scotland. He was a designing and unprincipled man, and two years before we find him in attendance on the King, he and the Douglas, who signs along with him, had caused or procured the murder in Falkland Palace, under most horrible circumstances, of the Duke of Rothesay, heir to the throne. The miserable King bitterly lamented the fate of his son, but dared not bring to justice the perpetrators of the crime. Accordingly, we find these ruffians in attendance upon him, and witnessing his charitable deed. There was but one life between Albany and the throne, that of the young Earl of Carick, and the King resolved on sending this son to France, avowedly for his education, but in reality to shield him from the intrigues of his unscrupulous uncle. On his way thither he was captured by an English vessel, and thereafter imprisoned in the Tower of London. There is good reason for believing that Albany and the Douglases had to do with this imprisonment of the Prince. They did everything to prevent his release. It was the last drop of bitterness in the cup of King Robert. When the sad news was brought him he was at supper

* There are one or two donations immediately prior to this. In 1403, on 5th January, John de Kelsow, son of the Lord of Kelsowland, bestows the land commonly called Langlebank, in the Parish of Largs—Reg. de Pas., p. 244. On May 10, 1399, Robert Portar, of Portarfield, gives an annual rent of sixteen pennies from himself, and confirms a donation by his father of twelve pennies from burgage property in the town of Renfrew.—Reg. de Pas., p. 374.

† Patre nostro germano. Reg. de Pas., p. 82.

‡ Domino de Dalkeith.

in his Castle of Rothesay. "Touched by grief," says the old chronicle, "his bodily strength vanished, his countenance paled, and, borne down by sorrow, he refused all food until at last he breathed forth his spirit to his Creator."* He was buried in the Abbey of Paisley,† before the great altar,‡ the last of the Stewarts who were laid there. The Abbot received six stones of wax for performing his obsequies.§ In his humility, the chronicle we have quoted tells us, the King deemed himself worthy of no such sacred resting-place. One day his Queen Anabella enquired of him wherefore, after the manner of his predecessors on the throne, he should not provide for himself a splendid monument, and fix on a laudatory epitaph to be inscribed upon it. The King, in his sorrow, is said to have thus made reply—"You speak as one of the foolish women, because if you consider well who and what I am; what in nature but a corrupt seed—what in person but food of worms—what in life but the most miserable of men, you would not care to erect any proud monument. Those men who desire the pleasures of high station in this world may have glittering tombs, but I would desire to be buried in the depths of a dunghill, that my spirit might be safe in the day of the Lord. Bury me, therefore, I pray you, in such a dunghill, and write for me this epitaph—'Here lies the worst king and most miserable man in the universe!'"|| It is, perhaps, as pathetic an utterance on the vanity of earthly greatness as history records. Curiously enough his desire has found almost literal fulfilment. Robert III. is perhaps the only one of the Scottish Kings who has no monument over his

* Fordun by Goodall, Vol. II., p. 440.

† Ibid. Fordun gives this curious monastic verse on the subject of the King's death—

Quadringentesimo quinto, mille sibi juncto
A dato Christi anno mortem subit iste
Tertius Robertus, Aprilis quarto Kalendas
In Botha leto cessit, pausat Passleto,
Qui Rex Scotorum vivat in aede polorum.

‡ In Pasleto ante magnum altare tumulatur. Fordun by Goodall, Vol. II., p. 440.

§ Chamberlain Rolls, Vol. III., p. 153.

|| Fordun by Goodall, Vol. II., p. 440.

grave. The only record of his place of burial is in the pages of the historian. The rank grass of the neglected and ill-kept churchyard waves over his resting-place, and the dust of the humblest mingles with his royal remains. *Vanitas vanitatum omnia vanitas.**

* The burying-place before the high altar has been appropriated by the parish gravedigger for the use of his family, by what authority I know not.

## CHAPTER XIII.

### Restoration.

1405-1459.

The darkened roof rose high aloof,
On pillars lofty, and light, and small;
The keystone that locked each ribbed aisle
Was a fleur-de-lys or a quatre feuille.
The corbels were carved, grotesque and grim,
And the pillars, with clustered shafts so trim,
With base and with capital flourished around,
Seemed bundles of lances which garlands had bound.

*Scott.*

WHEN ROBERT III. was laid in his last resting-place the Abbot and Convent were under the ban of excommunication. They had incurred the wrath of the Bishop, and had been formally excommunicated, interdicted, and suspended in their own Church of Rutherglen by a certain Walter de Roule, Rector of the Parish Church of Torbolton, acting for Matthew the Bishop.* The Abbot appealed directly to the Pope, who took under his special protection the Order of Clugny. It was, as he put it, the only remedy left them against the power of their oppressors. The language of the appeal is very strong, and states their grievance in a very unmistakeable way. Walter had caused to be fulminated against them the sentence of excommunication "to the great prejudice and injury of us and of the whole Order of Clugny, and in contempt and defiance of the privileges of our whole Order of Clugny, and

* Reg. de Pas., p. 332. This was in 1388.

the privileges of its members." These privileges exempted them from the jurisdiction of the ordinaries of their houses, and they could not allow them to be invaded; they therefore invoke "our Lord the Pope," and appeal to the most holy Apostolic See, and they commend to that See the preservation, the defence, and the protection of themselves and their goods, and especially the revenues of the Church of Rutherglen, which appear to have given rise to the contention. It was in 1388* they took their appeal, and it was twenty years afterwards before it was finally disposed of. The Archdeacon of Glasgow, Symon de Mundavilla, heard the case by Papal authority and freed them from their excommunication, and from the suspension of their Convent, and the interdict laid on their Monastery and their Church, and decreed, declared, and publicly pronounced them absolved. The chief agent on the part of the Abbot in carrying out this appeal to the Pope was a monk of the name of William Cheshelme, or, as he is called, De Cheshelme. Whether he occupied any office in the Monastery we do not know, but he acted often as procurator for Abbot Lithgow, and appears to have been well skilled in canon law. He probably became indispensable to his superior, who was now becoming an old man, and was appointed coadjutor abbot. Of the precise date of his elevation to this office we are ignorant, but in 1414 we find him entering into an agreement with the burgesses of Renfrew regarding the mill of that town, which belonged to the Abbey. He did not enjoy his honours long, for the venerable John de Lithgow soon after appears to have found another colleague. His name was Thomas Morwe. We know of him only from the fact that in 1420 he received from King Henry V. of England a safe conduct for himself and six companions,† which was to last from the 13th October to the 1st of January, 1421. On the 21st April in that year he receives a similar permit for himself and three attendants,‡ and, on the 9th of June, for himself and four attendants. It

* Reg. de Pas., p. 336.

† Rotuli Scotiae, p. 8. Hen. V.

‡ Safe-Conduct for Thomas Morwe, Abbot of Paisley. Rotuli Scotiae, 8, Hen. V., 1420, 13th October. It is in these terms—"The King of Britain, under his patents to last till the first day of January next, undertakes, for the safe and secure conduct and protection, security and defence of Thomas Morwe, Abbot of the Monastery of Paisley, with the three attendants accompanying

would be interesting to know the business which took the Abbot of Paisley across the border so frequently, but as to this we are simply left to conjecture.* Negotiations were going on at the time for the release of the King of Scotland from his captivity. They were conducted chiefly by ecclesiastics, and the Abbot of Paisley may have been among them.† These negotiations were finally concluded at the great Clunaic Monastery of Pontefract, and in 1424 King James I. returned to his own country, having learned many lessons during his captivity well calculated to help him in his administration. He addressed himself with great zeal to the pacification of his kingdom. "Let God but grant me life," he said, "and there shall not be one spot in my dominions where the key shall not keep the castle, and the furze bush the cow, though I myself should lead the life of a dog to accomplish it." He appears to have been true to his word. The only occasion on which his name appears in the Chartulary is in connection with the settlement of a dispute between the Convent and a certain Godfrey Nisbet,‡ regarding the lands of Achinhoss,§ in the Barony of Renfrew. The King heard both parties in his council in the December of the same year of his return, and decided in favour of the Abbot.|| He seems to have been earnestly desirous to promote the welfare of the Church. Heretical opinions were beginning to take root in the country, and the

him, and horses, goods, and baggage whatsoever, into the kingdom of the King of England, coming together or separately, staying or trading; returning thence as often as he pleases to his own home, separately or conjointly. Provided always as in similar cases.—This safe-conduct, granted at Westminster 13th October, in presence of the Council."

* In 1423 Thomas Morwe was in Rome, and on 20th September of that year paid certain dues into the Papal Treasury, 1333 golden florins. "The Episcopal Succession," by W. Maziere Brady, Vol. I., p. 204. Rome, 1876.

† On the 26th April, 1416, a Letter of Safe-Conduct is granted to the Abbot of Balmerino and others going to England as Commissioners to treat for the ransom of James I. of Scotland. On the 19th August, 1423, the same Abbot receives a commission to go to England on the same business. On the 16th September of the same year Henry grants another Safe-Conduct to him and others going to London on that embassy. See also Tytler, Vol. II., p. 48; Balmerino and its Abbey, p. 101.

‡ The Nisbets were proprietors of the lands of Johnstone, now called Milliken, in the Parish of Kilbarchan; and the heiress was married to Thomas Wallace, a younger son of Ellerslie.

§ Auchinhoss—Auchinhouse was situated in Houston Parish, on the banks of the river Gryfe.

|| Reg. de Pas., p. 70.

King felt that the only way of meeting them was by a revival of church discipline and vigour. He addressed a letter* to the Abbots of the Benedictine and Augustinian Monasteries,† exhorting them "in the bowels of the Lord Jesus Christ to shake off their torpor and sloth, and set themselves to work, to restore their fallen discipline, and rekindle their decaying fervour, so that they might save their houses from the ruin which menaced them." There is some ground for believing that the Abbey of Paisley was not without need of the royal warning it thus received, and there is a very suspicious circumstance recorded about this time, which shows that it was not keeping by the rules of its Order so strictly as it should have done. Before William de Cheshelme had been made Abbot he acted vigorously for the Convent, in defence of its rights, and especially in resisting the demands of the vicars who served its churches, when they plead for augmentation of their stipends. To some of these needy priests the Convent gave doles beyond what it owed them, and the brethren in chapter gave William de Cheshelme leave to try and induce them to be contented with their legal stipends, and to "keep to himself and for his own use," in consideration of his trouble, and the expense he had been at, all in excess of this. This was clearly an infraction of the rule which did not allow any monk to hold property of his own, and they boldly and shamefully mention in the record of their grant to Cheshelme ‡ that they do this, "notwithstanding any statutes and and customs of their order to the contrary." This was a very reprehensible transaction, and shows that Paisley, in common with other monasteries in Scotland, had allowed its discipline to fall into neglect. The renunciation of property, abstinence, and simplicity in food and clothing, and other virtues strictly enjoined by the monastic rules, were now but rarely practised. "Not only the Abbots and other superiors kept luxurious tables, dwelt in magnificent halls, wore costly garments, and were attended by youth of good families as pages in rich liveries, but the private monks also spurned the sober fare, homely garb and devout retirement of their predecessors. They kept horses, and on various pretences were continually going about in public; they lived

* In 1424. † Robertson's Statuta Eccles. Scot., Vol. I., p. lxxxix.

‡ Reg. de Pas., p. 336.

separately upon portions allowed them out of the common stock; they bought their own clothes; and the common dormitory in which they slept was partitioned off into separate chambers."* This was the case with the Cistercians of Melrose and Balmerino, and there is too much reason to think that much the same state of matters prevailed among the Clunaics of Paisley. Abbot Lithgow was a very old man, and could not hold the reins of government with a firm hand. William Cheshelme, his coadjutor, appears to have joined in the abuses of the house, and was often absent. The place became, in the words of the chronicler, "out of all gude rewle."†

The venerable John de Lithgow died on the 20th January, 1433. He was laid in the porch of the church, which he specially selected as his burying place, probably because it was that portion of the church which he had built during his incumbency, or because, in his humility, he deemed himself unworthy of a more sacred place of rest. He had governed the Monastery during the reigns of three Kings and twelve Popes, and he is the only Abbot of whom the monumental inscription is now to be seen. It is written on the inside of the porch of the church. It is in these words—

Iohn of Lithgow, Ab-
bot of this Monastery, 20th day of the
Month of Ianuary, yr. of our Ld. 14
33, selected to be made his sepulchre.

In 1440 Thomas Morwe is still Abbot,‡ and we find him assisting in that year at a general council at Stirling, held specially by King James II. to take into consideration the distracted state of the country. The times, both in Church and State, were terribly out of joint. "Many and innumerable complaints were given into the council, the like of which were never seen

* Balmerino and its Abbey, p. 108.

† Chronicle of Achinleck, p. 19.

‡ Scot. Acts of Par., Vol. II. Mr. D. Semple (Lairds of Glen, p. 13), plausibly infers that Thomas Tervas and Thomas Morwe may have been one and the same person. Mr. Brady, ("Episcopal Succession," Rome, 1876,) however, has discovered, in making his investigations in the Vatican, that they were different persons.

before. There were so many widows, bairns and infants, seeking redress for their husbands, kindred, and friends, that were cruelly slain by wicked, bloody murderers, sic like, many for herschip, theft, and reif, that there was no man but he would have ruth and pity to hear the same."* In 1444 Richard de Bodwell was elected Abbot. Of him we know only that he sent 590 florins to the Papal treasury on his appointment. His procurator, who made the payment, was Thomas de Tervas, a monk of Arbroath. In the year following this, Thomas appears himself as Abbot of Paisley, and pays the Pope's chamberlain a considerable sum of money on his own account. Richard had, in the meantime, been promoted to the Abbey of Dunfermline, and Thomas, his friend, being in Rome, procured the mitre of Paisley for himself. It was a happy appointment for Paisley, which the new Abbot governed for fourteen years with great ability. He had plenty to do on his accession in repressing disorder and restoring good government. The Convent was "in debt, and many of the churches in Lordis hands." He set himself most vigorously to reform all this. Walas of Craigy is made to acknowledge, with sorrow and penitence, that he had greatly injured the Lord Abbot, in regard to the lands of Thornle, and to promise better behaviour for the future.† A Bull was procured from the Pope revoking leases of property which had been granted during the easy reign of his predecessors.‡ All such property was to be restored to the use of the Convent, notwithstanding any documents to the contrary, even letters of former Popes were not to be regarded, and the protection of the Bishop and of the King was invoked against a Laird named Robert Boyd of Tynwald, who had held a lease of certain rents of Largs, and who was very irate at being interfered with.§ "Foralsmekill," says the King's admonition to the refractory Robert, "as we ar informit that yhe adres yhow tobe at the Kyrk of Largyss on Friday nextocum, with a multitude of our liegess in feyre of were, in hurtyn and scath of our devote oratours the Abbot and Convent of Passelay, brekyn of our crya and

* Pitscottie, Hist. of Scot., p. 24. † Reg. de Pas., p. 83.

‡ Reg. de Pas., p. 416. This Bull, dated 1446, is directed to William Turnbul, Canon of Glasgow.

§ Reg. de Pas., p. 245.

offens of our Maiestie, Our will is, and straitly we charge yhou gif it sua be that ye desist tharof and mak na syk gaderin, undyr all the hiest payne and charge ye may inryne agane our Maiestie, and gif ye haif ochut aganes our said oratours, folond* thame as law will."

The King was a good friend to the Abbot in his endeavours to put things right. He had enjoyed the support and advice of his clergy against the tyranny of his fierce nobility, and so, in gratitude, granted them for their aid some very important privileges which they had not hitherto possessed. On the Bishops he conferred the much-coveted privilege of making their testaments, of levying the fruits of vacant sees, and converting them to their own use.† In the same spirit he granted privileges to the monasteries. To Abbot Tervas he confirmed, in 1451, the regality into which Robert III. had erected the Abbey lands, granting even, in regard to their Dunbartonshire lands, the four points of the Crown which that King had reserved.‡ This concession gave the Abbot very wide criminal jurisdiction, and,—as the name regality implies,—the power of a king over his vassals. Besides this, he gave the Abbot power of repledging § all his tenants and husbandmen within the bounds of the church lands, who should be indicted, attached, or arrested for any crimes or transgressions, with the power of holding courts himself, by the King's chamberlain or his deputy, summoned by the Abbot or his bailies, for assisting them with his aid and council. Whenever, therefore, any dweller on the Abbot's lands was accused before the King's courts, the Abbot or his deputy had the power of rescuing him, bringing him into the court of the Monastery, and trying him there, and none of the royal judges could interfere with the Abbot or his officers in thus sitting in judgment on his own vassal. It was a curious privilege, and was often exercised to the great detriment of justice; but it gave the Abbot exclusive jurisdiction over all his tenants, and put him on an equality with the great nobles of Scotland. These privileges were given to Thomas Tervas, his Convent, and his successors,

* Summon. † Tytler, Vol. II., p. 150.

‡ Rape, rapine, murder, and fire-raising.—Reg. de Pas., p. 256.

§ Reg. de Pas., p. 267.—Repledging or claiming offenders from the royal courts to be judged by those of the regality. See "Notice of the early system of Replegation," by Dr. Stewart, in Appendix.

in "recognition of his virtues and the reformation he had effected in his Monastery." But a more singular concession is made to the Abbot than any of these, one which furnishes an illustration of the manner in which funds were raised for ecclesiastical purposes, and may even give a hint to the church extensionists of the present day. The King gave and conferred on all officers, deputies, and servants of the Abbot of Paisley, full power of holding tavern,* and of selling wines within the gates of the Monastery, at the will and pleasure of the Abbot, without any hinderance or disturbance from any of the lieges whatsoever. This extraordinary privilege was doubtless taken great advantage of by the thirsty souls of the neighbourhood, and the visitor who looks with admiration on the beautiful clerestory and triforium of the church may remember that it is, in great part, due to the tavern-keeping of Thomas Tervas.

This part of the building was erected under his superintendence. He finished the roof and built a great portion of the steeple, and also the gatehouse, which was of a stately character.† Having thus prepared the church for divine service, he went to Rome to get suitable furnishings for the worship of the sanctuary, which the poverty of Scotland could not supply. Probably the English soldiers had taken away everything that was of any value when they burned the Monastery. On 30th May, 1453, the Abbot received a safe-conduct from Henry VI.‡ "to visit the shrines (*liminia*) of the Apostles," along with George Falowe, Burgess of Edinburgh; Walter Steward of Dalswinton; James Inglis, Canon of Glasgow; and Sir Thomas Fersith, Vicar of Legardwoode—with seven persons in their company. The Vicar of Legardwood, who served that Church, which belonged to the Abbey, probably acted as chaplain to his venerable superior. They crossed the Straits of Dover at Calais, § whence they would find their way by easy stages to Rome, calling probably at the Monastery of Clugny to render obeisance to

* Reg. de Pas., p. 258.—Potestatem plenariam habernandi et vendendi vina infra portas dicti monasterii.

† Chronicle of Auchenleck.

‡ Rotuli Scotiae.—"Salvus conductus pro abate Pasletensi et aliis liminia apostolorum visitare volentibus," "venerabilem patrem Thomam Abbam de Pasle."

§ Rotuli Scotiæ.

the head of the Order. The Abbot did not return from his quest empty-handed, but carried back for the Abbey adornments of a very sumptuous character, with which he had been furnished by the faithful, or had bought for himself, at Rome. "He brocht hame," says the old chronicle,* "mony gud jowellis, and claithis of gold, silver, and silk, and mony good bukis, and the statliest tabernackle that was in al Skotland, and the maist costlie." The same historian tells also of the mitre which he wore —one of the best in Scotland—of chandeliers of silver, and a lectern of brass. All this was probably the cunning work of Italian artists,—work like that of the same period which may be still seen in the Duomo of Florence and the Cathedral of Milan; and the treasures of the Abbot, when he unfolded them, on his return, to the simple monks of his Convent at Paisley, must have produced upon them the most powerful impression.

We do not know how long Abbot Thomas remained abroad. He was present in the Parliament held in October, 1456, and on the 19th of that month was chosen to sit in "a committee of causes and complaints." He died three years afterwards, on the 29th June, 1459. He was the most energetic ruler the Convent had had since Abbot William, who did so much for it in its early days, and well deserved the character given him in the account of his death, "ane richt gude man." † Though we have drawn already on the Chronicle for our information regarding him, it may not be out of place in closing this chapter to quote what it says of this distinguished ecclesiastic in full:—

"The quhilk was ane richt gude man, and helplyk to the place of ony that ever was, for he did mony notable thingis, and held ane nobil hous, and wes ay well purvait. He fand the place al out of gude reule, and destitute of leving, and all the kirkis in lordis handis, and the kirk unbiggit. The bodie of the kirk frae the bricht‡ stair up he biggit, and put on the ruff, and theekit it with sclats, and riggit it with stane, and

* Chronicle of Auchenleck.

† Among other of his achievements, he obtained a perpetual lease of the third part of a famous fishing on the Clyde, opposite Dunbarton, called the Crooketshot.

‡ This was probably an outside stair. The word indicates, possibly, that a portion of the church remained unroofed.

biggit ane porcion of the steple, and ane statlie yet-hous; and brocht hame mony gude jowellis, and claithis of gold, silver, and silk, and mony gude bukis, and made statlie stallis, and glass yuit, mekle of al the kirk, and brocht hame the statliest tabernakle that was in al Skotland, and the maist costlie; and schortlie he brocht al the place to fredome and fra nocht till ane michty place, and left it out of al kind of det, and al fredome to dispone as them lykt, and left ane of the best myteris that wes in Skotland, and chandiliaris of silver, and ane lettren of brass, with mony uther gude jowellis." *

* Chronicle of Auchenleck, p. 19.

# CHAPTER XIV.

## Abbots Henry Crichton and George Shaw.

1459—1498.

Still in the minster mass was sung,
With small bells ringing and censers swung,
Still bow'd the priest before the pyx,
The altar high and crucifix;
And still the grand old psalm
Pealed through the pillared calm.

*W. C. Smith.*

A VERY curious transaction took place before the death of the good Thomas Tervas.* Pope Pius II. decreed, that at the decease of the Abbot the disposition of the office and of the whole revenues of the Monastery should fall to the Pope. Accordingly, when the demise of Tervas was reported to Rome, the Pope appointed Henry Crichton, a monk of Dunfermline, to be Commendator of the Abbey, and assigned a pension of 300 florins out of the revenues to Pietro Barlo, Cardinal of St. Marks in Venice, to be paid him by Henry and his successors at the Feast of St. John the Baptist, under pain of excommunication, in case of his failing to make payment within thirty days after the appointed term, and total deprivation if he persisted in his opposition six months after his excommunication. Crichton probably paid well for the Commendatorship, after the manner of too many ecclesiastics at that

* See Appendix where the papers from the Vatican MS.S are given.

time. He drew the revenues and held the abbacy, accounting for his intromissions to the Papal authorities. When he had got himself fairly installed in the Abbey, he declined to pay the stipulated pension to the Cardinal of St. Marks, making some legal quibble the ground of his neglect. The Pope then took severe measures with the defaulter. He instructed John, Cardinal of St. Laurence and Damascus, to deal with Henry, and to summon him to appear in Bruges or elsewhere. Henry, however, did not go to the Belgian town, and for more than three years continued to enjoy his revenues at Paisley in defiance of all citations. Pope Pius then ordered Cardinal John to proceed to the final stage of deposing Henry, but before this step could be taken Pope Pius died,* and was succeeded by Paul II. This Pope took up the case against Henry, and finding that Cardinal John was prevented by other duties, he commissioned Nicholas, Cardinal Priest of St. Cecilia, to bring the case to an end without delay. This was done, the Abbotship of Paisley was finally declared vacant; and the Abbot descended from his high dignity to the station of a monk in the house he had governed.† The Pope then claimed all the revenues of Paisley for the Roman See, and for their proper administration appointed Patrick, Bishop of St. Andrews, to exercise *in commendam* sole jurisdiction over the Abbey in things temporal and spiritual so long as he lived, ordaining him at the same time to see that the usual number of monks was maintained, and the requisite provision for the various wants of the Abbey sufficiently cared for. We have no record in any charter of the government of the Abbey by Patrick Grahame, Archbishop of St. Andrews, though he had charge of it for three years. His sad fate is well known to the readers of Scottish history.

By some means Crichton made his peace with the Roman authorities, and on the 27th February, 1469, he was raised to the full dignity of Abbot of Paisley; and all excommunications and other disqualifications were annulled by a special Bull of the Pope, who commanded all the monks and tenants of the Monastery to give him all due obedience as their superior. He proved an energetic ruler; many copies, or, as they were

* 15th August, 1464.

† In his subsequent appointment he is spoken of as such.

called, transumpts, of the charters of the house were made under his direction. Old parchments containing grants of lands and other bequests, bulls of Popes, agreements with Bishops, and concessions by the Stewarts and by the Kings of Scotland were carefully transcribed, and certified as new copies by a notary public at the instance of Abbot Henry. It was in his time that the admirably kept rental-book was begun, which gives us so clear an idea of the management of the Abbey lands. His familiarity with charters appears to have enabled him to settle in a happy way a dispute into which the Convent had fallen with an Highland chieftain, Lawmund of Lawmund, regarding the patronage of the church of Kilfinan in 1466.* The Celt had been very pugnacious, and had claimed very determinedly the right of appointing his own parish priest, and had even gone to law in the ecclesiastical courts in defence of what appeared to him his just privilege. He was probably one of those "lordis" who in the days of easy-going Lithgow and Cheshelme had managed to get into his hands a portion of the Abbey patrimony, and was loth to give it up. Abbot Henry induced this Argyleshire warrior to pay him a visit at Paisley, which he did, accompanied by his brother and his shield-bearer, a clansman. There the Abbot, as one who was "a true lover of peace,"† treated him kindly. Doubtless he regaled him with the best that his refectory and wine-cellar afforded~~, but~~, in addition, he took the chieftain to the chapter-house, and showed him "all the letters, charters, monuments, donations, concessions, and confirmations made by his ancestors and progenitors of revered memory, to the Abbot or Convent, to the praise of God, and the increase of divine worship." This formidable array of documents seems to have quite overcome the Highlander, for having "fully pondered"‡ them, he acknowledged that he had no such right as he claimed to the patronage of his parish church, and "piously and healthfully acknowledging, and mentally revolving" the matter, that it would be "wicked to annoy the servants of God by putting them to trouble or expense," he resigned all his rights in connection with Kilfinan church, and confirmed all the donations of his pious ancestors. Two notaries record the transaction

* Reg. de Pas., pp. 149, 150, 151. † Vere pacis amator.

‡ Plenarie prependebat.

between the Abbot and the chieftain, and as several of the surrounding lairds were witnesses,* the occasion was probably accompanied by conviviality, and the laird would return to his castle by the Kyles of Bute, feeling more kindly towards the Church than when he left home.

Abbot Henry was a statesman as well as an ecclesiastic, and a person of importance at the Court of the young King James III. When commissioners were engaged in negotiating a truce with England at Newcastle the Court was at Berwick. Abbot Henry was there also, empowered by Parliament to give advice as to the matter under consideration. He was in Parliament in 1464, and also in 1469,† where he saw, and it is to be feared took part in, the accomplishment of one of those tragedies so common in that turbulent age. The Abbot was in Parliament on the 21st of November, and on the 22nd Sir Alexander Boyd, who had been the tutor of the King, was sacrificed by Parliament to the jealousy of his enemies, and executed on the Castle-hill of Edinburgh.‡ Abbot Henry was in Parliament again in 1471, and also the year following. The Abbey probably benefited by the position its lord held at Court. One mark of royal favour has come down to us in the gift to Abbot Henry of a quantity of lead in the Castle of Bute,§ which the King gave him for the roofing of the church, which Abbot Tervas had only "theekit ‖ with sclate." A better gift than this came to him from the same source; this was his promotion to the Benedictine Abbey of Dunfermline, which took place in 1473.

Abbot Crichton's life at Paisley had been comparatively uneventful and quiet, but his removal occasioned no small stir throughout Scotland.

* James Hammylton of Torrens, George Wales of Elyrisle, John Knok of Knok.

† Index to Scottish Acts of Parliament.

‡ Tytler, Vol. II., p. 203.

§ The following is the deed of gift:—"28th Jan., 1470.—James, be the grace of God King of Scottis till our lowite cousing John Lord Dernle capitane of our castell of Bute, greeting. We charge you that ye deliver till a venerable fader in God, Henry, Abbot of our Abbaye of Paslay, or his assignais the lede that ye have in keeping in our said castel of Bute, indenting with him quhat that ye deliver, keep, and the ta part of the indenture with zou, and deliver, the tother parte of it to the said Abbot haldand thir our letteris for your warrand. Given under oure signet at Strivelyne, the 28th day of Januar of oure regne, the 11th year.—Lennox Papers, Vol II.

‖ Thatched.

It was an act of royal favouritism which has occasioned much comment, not of a very favourable kind, and has been referred to by a well-known historian of the Church of Rome * as the beginning of those abuses which led to the downfall of that Church in Scotland. Hitherto the Abbot had been elected to his high position by the monks of his Monastery, and it may be presumed they exercised their right with considerable discrimination, if we may judge from the position which the dignified ecclesiastics occupied among the leading men of their time. Sometimes the monks chose some brother who had occupied an inferior position—the sub-prior or the cellarer—and sometimes one of themselves, who had shown aptitude for business and the management of secular transactions; generally those whom they selected were well able to hold their own in Court or in Parliament, and again and again filled the high position of ambassadors and officers of State. This mode of election was very jealously guarded, and in the reign of James III. Parliament passed an act declaring any nomination to an abbey or a cathedral, even by the Pope invalid, and asserting the right of the clergy to the election of their own dignitaries.† The King who sanctioned this law was the first to violate it. The monks of Dunfermline, on a vacancy occurring in their Abbey, elected in the usual way one of their own number, Alexander Thomson, to be their Abbot, but the King interfered, annulled the election, and promoted Henry Crichton to Dunfermline. It is supposed that the transaction was effected by a bribe, which is not unlikely. The Pope, at the request of the King, confirmed the appointment, and thus inaugurated a system which was most disastrous in every way to the Church. Men were appointed to abbacies who knew nothing of monastic discipline, and who were totally unfit to govern the Convent over which they were placed. When an abbacy became vacant it was sold for money, or given to reward services often of a very doubtful character. Many of the abbots were the bastard sons of nobles. Nothing could have been more hurtful to the Church than this system of appointment. It led to the decay of order

* Bishop Leslie.

† Cunninghame's Ch. Hist. Vol. I., p. 200, cap. 12. Thomson's Acts, Vol. II., p. 83.

and good government. Abbots were found oftener at Court than in their convent; some of them never made any pretence to piety at all, many led lives of a shameless character,* and even the monasteries under their charge became nurseries of vice.

The monks of Paisley were denied their old right of election as well as their brethren of Dunfermline, and, instead of one of their own brethren, they had placed over them by the King a parish priest, George Shaw, Rector of the Church of Mynto, in Roxburgh. He, indeed, did honour to his nomination, for he was a man of learning and good sense, and he set himself heartily to discharge the duties of his new position as an abbot of the Order of Clugny. Had all those elected under the new system been as worthy of their elevation as the parson of Mynto no great harm would have been done.

George Shaw owed his promotion to Paisley to his family connections. He was a son of the Laird of Sauchie, in Stirlingshire, and his family were hereditary keepers of Stirling Castle, and prominent among the aristocracy of the time. Like his predecessor, he was in favour at Court, for King James III. entrusted him with the education and upbringing of his second son, the Duke of Ross, wishing to place him in the quiet Convent of Paisley beyond the reach of those turbulent nobles who made his

* Lest this should be thought exaggerated, we may give the following account of the promotion of Crichton from the Catholic Bishop of Ross:—"The Abbacye of Dumfermlinge, vacand, the Convent chusit ane of thair awne monks callit Alexander Thomsoune, and the King promovit Henry Creightoune, Abbot of Paslaye there to, quha wes preferit be the Paip through the King's supplications to the said Abbacye, and sic like Mister George Shawe, Persoun of Mynto, wes promovit be the King to the Abbacye of Paslaye, and sua there first began sic manner of promotioun of secularis to Abbacyies be the Kingis' supplications, and the godly erections were frustrate and destroyed becaus that the Court of Rome admittit the Princes' supplications the rather that they gat gret soumes of money thairby, wherefore the bischoppis durst not confirm thame that wes chosen be the Convent, nor thay quha were electit durst not maintain thair awne right, and sua abbayes cam to secular abussis, the Abbotis and Pryouris being promovit forth of the Court wha livit courtlyke, secularlye, and voluptouslye, and than cessit all religious and godlyke mynds and dedis whair withe the secularis and temporal men beand sklandirit with thair evil example fell fra all devocioun and godlyness to the warkis of wickedness whairof daily meikle evil did increase."—Lesley's de Reb. gest. Scot., 1574.

reign one of terror and strife.* He devoted himself with great assiduity to this duty, and it is not improbable that the familiarity of the Prince with the ecclesiastics of Paisley led him afterwards to choose the Church as his profession, in which he rose to the high dignity of Archbishop of St. Andrews.† Abbot Shaw was present in the Parliament of 11th January, 1487, which precipitated the collision between the King and a great body of his subjects, and led to the unnatural rebellion of his son. In this rebellion the Abbot's brother, James Shaw of Sauchie,‡ took a leading part. He was Governor of Stirling, and guardian of the Prince, and held the Castle in his name.§ The result is well known. The battle of Sauchieburn was fought on the lands belonging to the family of Abbot Shaw, and, by the base assassination of the King while fleeing from the field, the rebellious Prince succeeded to the throne, to the great advantage of those who had sympathised with him and his faction, and, in particular, to the advantage of the family of Shaw.

Very soon after his accession, the new King began to shew an interest in the Abbey over which his friend and the tutor of his brother presided. In the first year of his reign he confirmed to the Abbot all the privileges which the Stewarts and Kings of Scotland had bestowed on Paisley, alleging as his reason the great favour and love which he bears to Abbot George Shaw, "our chief counsellor," || for the faithful service which he had rendered to them in byegone years, especially in the education of his brother, the Duke of Ross, in his tender age. He also erected the town of Paisley into a burgh, a royal concession of which we

* Abbot Shaw was regular in his Parliamentary duties—

1476, 10th July, he was chosen, among others, to negotiate as to the royal marriage.

| | | | | | |
|---|---|---|---|---|---|
| 1478, | 6th April, | he was in Parliament. | 1482, | 2nd Dec., | he was in Parliament. |
| 1478-9, | 1st March, | do., | 1484, | 17th May, | do., |
| 1479, | 4th Oct., | do., | 1484-5, | 21st March, | do., |
| 1481, | 11th April, | do., | 1487, | 11th Jan., | do., |
| 1481-2, | 18th March, | do., | 1487, | 6th Oct., | do., |

† The Duke of Ross was appointed Archbishop of St. Andrews in 1497, and died in Jan., 1504, aged 28.

‡ He visited his brother in 1485, on 28th August, for a charter of that date is witnessed—"Jacobo Schaw de Sawquhy."

§ Burton's Hist., Vol. III., p. 33.

|| The date of this charter is 19th August, 1488, at Stirling.—Reg. de Pas., p. 84.

shall take notice more fully in another chapter. The Regality of James IV. is the fullest of all those granted to the Abbey. It gave the Abbot full power of trying his tenants for all offences, and "repledging" them from the royal courts for this purpose. The four points of the Crown, "rapine, rape, murder, and fire-raising," are specially granted to his jurisdiction, and there is power given, not only for the trial of stealers of green wood, but also of those who catch or kill salmon, called "reidfisch," which shews that even at that early date poaching was not unknown in the neighbourhood of Paisley. The Abbot had thus full despotic power within his bounds—he could imprison or execute offenders. In the immediate neighbourhood of Paisley, there is still a mound bearing the ominous name of Gallowhill, and in the charters there is mention of the "Blackhoil,"* or Blackhole, probably the prison of the Monastery. According to the Clunaic statutes, the prison was "a place accessible only by a ladder, without window or door;"† the prison of the Abbey was thus a dismal enough place of confinement, and well deserving the name it commonly received.

Abbot Shaw, like most of his predecessors, had to guard the possessions of his Monastery against encroachments of various kinds. A certain Hugh Fleming,‡ of Kynmunchayr, gave him trouble about certain lands called Dunnotyr, and pasture lying between Bachan in Kilpatrick, and his own property. The Dean of Lennox was instructed by apostolic authority § to assume with him chaplains and clerks, and going personally to the place ‖ of the King at Dunbarton, once, twice and thrice, solemnly to warn Hugh, on the part of the Pope and the Bishops of the Scottish Church, that he was not, under pain of excommunication, to draw the Abbot and Convent before any lay tribunal, and to cite him to appear before apostolic delegates for the trial of his case. After this, we hear no more of Hugh Fleming, who likely thought he would gain little by an appearance against the clergy before an ecclesiastical tribunal.

There is also given in the Chartulary¶ a very graphic account of how the Abbot withstood any intrusion on his privileges by those of his own

* Saint Mirin, by Semple, pp. 69, 70, 72. † Fosbrook's Brit. Mon., p. 355.

‡ Hugo Flandrenses.—Reg. de. Pas., p. 176.

§ Vested in the Dean and Archdeacon of Dunblane. ‖ *Placita.* ¶ Reg. de Pas., p. 351.

Order; and, in the minute and formal document of a notary public, we get a glimpse of the convent life. On the last day of January, 1489, at three o'clock in the afternoon, as it was getting dark, the Rural Dean of Rutherglen, going on his regular visitation, came riding to the gate of the Abbey with a retinue of servants, and sought admittance for himself and his followers. The door was, however, closed firmly against him, lest his unchallenged admission should be taken as a submission to his authority, or imply that he possessed any jurisdiction over the monks of the Order of Clugny. Meantime, notice of his arrival was sent to Abbot Shaw, who arranged how the Dean, who was kept waiting outside, was to be received. The Chamberlain of the Monastery, Sir John Mouss, came to the gate in all the pomp of office, accompanied by Robert Quhytford, the Cellarer, Alexander Clugston, a notary-public, and many other inmates of the house, clerical and lay, a Mr. Henry Newton, a Sir Cuthebert Mulykyn, and John Makquhen, a layman, being prominent. At the gate a little ceremony took place. The Chamberlain, meeting the Dean, informed him that by order of the Abbot he could not be admitted by right in his capacity of *visitor*, the Convent being exempt and privileged from the visitation of all ordinaries, as were also the places and churches belonging to them. The Dean then at once gave up any idea he may have had of an official visitation, and sought only the rights of hospitality. "Seeing he could not be received for the purpose of visitation, he was content to be received into the Monastery by the grace of the Abbot and Convent." Before the company, however, left the gate, Alexander Clugston was called on to take note of what had happened, and he drew up afterwards, in the form of a public instrument, his account of the interview at the gate, writing with his own hand "those things which he had seen and heard."

A visitor came to the Abbey in the summer of the same year who would not be kept so long in waiting as the intrusive Dean. This was the young King, who on the 11th May paid the Abbot a visit, the first of many with which he honoured the Abbey. He was again in the neighbourhood in July of the same year, engaged in quelling the insurrection of Lennox and Lord Lyle.* The castle of the one, at Crookston,

* Tytler, Vol. II., p. 250.

SEAL OF ABBOT GEORGE SHAW.

THE SEAL OF THE MONASTERY OF PAISLEY.

SEAL OF ABBOT ROBERT SHAW.

and of the other, at Duchal, was soon taken by his energy; and a reminiscence of their siege is found in the Chamberlain's Books, where we have the following item:—"The Laird of Hillhouse to ga to Paslay to get workmen, with spades and shools,* July 22, 1489."

The great families represented by the above-mentioned lords were good friends to the Abbey; but Abbot Shaw had a greater friend in the King, with whom it was better worth his while to keep on good terms. There is little doubt that he sent the King both the workmen and "shools."

Abbot Shaw was one of the three churchmen† commissioned by Pope Innocent the VIII. to absolve all those concerned in the insurrection against the late King, and to restore them to the communion of the faithful after prescribing them salutary penance. King James IV. bitterly repented the share he had in his father's death. He inflicted severe penances on himself and made many pilgrimages to sacred shrines to atone for his guilt. The Bull of the Pope directed to Abbot Shaw was dated in July, 1491, and in the month of November in that year the King presented himself at the Abbey. He had been on a pilgrimage to the shrine of St. Ninian at Whithorn, and now he came to the Abbot to receive the absolution that father was commissioned to bestow.‡

The Abbot had a grievance, which was doubtless related in due form to the Royal visitor. The old contentions as to the Argyleshire churches belonging to the Convent were revived. Robert, the Bishop of Lismore, sequestered the revenues of three of these churches,—Colmanell, Kylkeran, and Killelan.§ The Abbot appealed to the curators of the privileges of Clugny appointed by the Pope, and they put into operation the full powers of the law against the rapacious prelate. Alexander Clugston, the notary public belonging to the Abbey, first warned the bishop, whom he found in the town of Dunbarton, of their orders, and finally, on their authority, pronounced sentence of excommunication against him in the cathedral of Glasgow. The Highland Bishop, however, still kept firm hold of the churches, defying even the decision of the Pope. All this

* Shovels.

† See Bull appended to Thomas Innes' Scotland. The other two to whom the Bull was addressed were the Abbot of Jedburgh and the Chancellor of Glasgow.

‡ Chamberlain Accounts. § Reg. de Pas., p. 154.

would be doubtless told to the King, and not without good result, for shortly after he put the Bishop's successor above the temptation to attack the churches appropriated to Paisley, by bestowing some more churches on the bishopric, assigning as a reason for his bounty the poverty of the See, "situated among wild and untameable tribes."*

When the King visited Paisley, he found a scene of bustle and activity around the Convent. The Abbot was engaged in adding to the buildings, and the King visited the works, and gave drink money to the men. In the treasurer's book appears this notice,—"*Item*, 21 Novembris, to the Masonis of Pasla . . xs."† Abbot Shaw, in his time, improved greatly the surroundings of the Abbey. He built a refectory and other conventual buildings, and reared a lofty tower over the principal gate; he also enclosed the church, the precincts of the convent, the gardens, and a little park for deer, within a wall about a mile in circuit.‡ The wall is spoken of with admiration by those who were privileged to see it. Bishop Lesley grows eloquent as he describes its magnificence, its four-sided beautiful stones, and the lofty statues by which it was adorned. On the middle of the wall, to the north side, he caused place three different shields,—the royal arms in the middle, the arms of the founder, the great Stewart of Scotland, *a fess cheque*, on the right side, and his own on the left. There are niches at the angles of the wall of most curious graved work, in one of them there was a statue of St. James the apostle, the patron of the Abbacy; in another, an image of the blessed Virgin, with this distich near it, but somewhat more inward :—

Hac ne vade via nisi dixeris Ave Maria,
Sit semper sine via, qui non tibi dicet Ave.§

Of this wall, that called forth such rapturous description, but very few fragments indeed remain.|| The statues that adorned it have all disap-

* Historical Accounts of the Priory of Beauly, by P. C. Batten, p. 152.

† Chamberlain Accounts.

‡ I give these particulars on the authority of Crawfurd, in his "Officers of State." He wrote in 1726, and so probably saw something of the splendour of which he speaks.

§ "Go not this way unless you have said Ave Maria. Let him be always a wanderer who will not say Ave to thee."

|| Part of the wall can be seen on the east and west sides of the north end of the Abbey Bridge.

peared, but there are still two tablets that belonged to it. The one is the Royal Arms of Scotland, mentioned in the description we have quoted, and the other is an inscription by the pious builder himself.*

> Ya callit ye abbot Georg of Schaw,
> About yis abbay gart make yis waw;
> A thousande four hundereth ȝheyr,
> Auchty ande fywe, the date but weir.
> [Pray for his saulis salvacioun.]
> That made thus nobil fundacioun. †

Many an inmate of the Monastery would obey the wish which the pious Abbot thus expressed. He was "a true father" to his monks, and they had every cause to think of him with gratitude. For their comfort he assigned them certain rents within the new-formed burgh, to be paid yearly, at Whitsunday and Martinmas, and to be shared by all the monks in common. The whole amounted to £2 2s 8$\frac{1}{12}$d, but as the monks could have nothing but what was allowed them by the rule of their Order, liberty had to be asked from the authorities of Clugny to receive even this sum. A supplication was therefore addressed to them at the Mother Abbey, and the monks received from these dignitaries‡ leave to enjoy their pittances. A copy of the license is still in existence,* and it states how, "For the augmentation of the pittance, and recreation of his Convent, the Abbot gave and granted to the said Convent for ever, *trigenta scuta auri* of annual and perpetual rent for the foundation and support of a solemn anniversary, and of some other suffrages in the said Monastery of Paisley, to be made and celebrated by the said Convent and their successors according to the intention of the said Lord Abbot in each year for ever." The monks of Paisley had good reason to think kindly of their Abbot.

* The first tablet was built in the wall of a house in Incle Street, and the second in a house in Lawn Street. They are to be placed for preservation in a more suitable situation.

† The fifth line of this inscription has been chiselled off.

‡ The pittance rental is given in the "History of the Paisley Grammar School," by Robert Brown. The license to hold the pittances is in the charter chest of the town. It is dated at the Monastery of Clugny, 13th May, 1492, and is issued by the "definitors," persons appointed by the superior to determine all difficulties that might arise regarding the rules and statutes of the Order. Among them is mentioned the Bishop of Lepanto.

The King, with whom he seems to have been a great favourite, made him, in 1495, Lord High Treasurer of Scotland. His chief interest seems to have centered in his Monastery, for two years after his appointment he resigned the white staff of office which he bore as treasurer into the hands of another, and retired to Paisley to spend the evening of life in the midst of the good works he had done. He erected a manor-house at Blackston, in the neighbourhood—one of the Abbey Granges—and there he passed much of his time. It was a pleasant, shady spot, by the banks of the Kert Lochwinnoch, and memories of the old Abbot's sojourn there still linger around it. It is a saying in Renfrewshire when any special authority is required in confirmation of a statement, that "a line must be brought from Blackston for it,"—an unconscious reference to the time when the good Abbot Shaw resided there.

As the Abbot grew old he felt himself becoming unable to fulfil his duties, and looked about for one who should succeed him in the Abbacy. His choice fell upon his own nephew, Robert Shaw, Vicar of Munkton, a son of the Governor of Stirling who had been so good a friend to the King in his youth. He was canonically elected, and his election was approved by the Crown. The Pope also gave his consent, on condition that Robert Shaw should take the monastic habit within six months, and decreed that the old Abbot should enjoy as his pension a third part of the fruits of the Monastery,* and might return to his former position when he thought proper. Robert Shaw took possession of the Abbot's stall in March, 1498. His uncle lived some years afterwards. He is called in charters "the pensioner of the Abbey." † He was living seven years after his resignation of office, and is supposed to have died in 1505. He filled his place well, and the visitor to Paisley who sees his shield of three covered cups with the pastoral crook behind them upon the wall of one of the outhouses, which has been ruthlessly transformed by modern iconoclasts, or reads the defaced inscription which tells of the "nobil fundacioun" he reared, will do well to remem-

* A full account of the transaction is given from the Vatican Archives, by Mr. Brady in his "Episcopal Succession," Vol. II., p. 206.

† Reg. de Pas., p. 354.

ber that they are the memorials of a good man, one of the best of his time, to whose wisdom and benevolence the town of Paisley itself owes its existence.*

* The memorials of Abbot Shaw should be carefully treasured by the sons of Paisley. Hitherto, the very reverse has been the case.

# CHAPTER XV.

## The Burgh.

Yet more, around these Abbeys gathered towns,
Safe from the feudal castle's haughty frowns;
Peaceful abodes where Justice might uphold
Her scales with even hand; and Culture mould
Her heart of pity, train the mind in care
For rules of life sound as time could bear.

*Wordsworth.*

WHEREVER throughout Scotland there rose the towers of a castle or the spires of a cathedral or abbey, there were to be found the humble houses of a hamlet or village, built under the shadow of the greater pile. These, when adjacent to a castle, were inhabited by the vassals of the baron who owned it; when near a cathedral or abbey, by artisans and labourers. Their inhabitants were bound by feudal ties to their over-lord, to whom also—whether baron, bishop, or abbot—the profits of their industry belonged, so that when there were amongst them a number of successful traders, or clever artisans, the revenues of their feudal superior greatly increased.* As wealth accumulated, the inhabitants of these villages bought their liberty from their over-lords, and formed themselves into communities, to which the Sovereign granted peculiar privileges. They had power of self-government, and were able to carry on with spirit commercial and industrial operations. These privileged communities were called Burghs. The earliest description of Burghs

* For the general statements in this chapter I am indebted chiefly to "Scotland in the Middle Ages," by Cosmo Innes.—Tytler's Hist. of Scot., Vol. I., "Lindores and its Abbey," and Robertson's "Early Kings of Scotland."

are the Royal Burghs, so called because they were directly constituted by the Sovereign, and had special privileges bestowed on them by him; but the great lords of the Church, anxious to share in the advantages of trade which attended these new erections, obtained privileges of the same nature for the villages which sprang up around their cathedrals and abbeys. Thus the Burghs of St. Andrews, Brechin, and Glasgow were created by the special favour of the Bishops of these Sees; Selkirk, by the Abbot of Kelso; Newburgh, by the Abbot of Lindores; and Paisley, by the Abbot of its Convent.

The privileges of a Burgh depended on the charter of its erection; but in all cases the inhabitant of the Burgh was thereby raised in his status both socially and politically. He was no longer in the condition of a serf or slave, who could be transferred from one master to another, and he escaped from all the severities and exactions of the feudal system. The Burgh in the early period of its existence was a place of freedom, a sanctuary to the slave. "Gif oney maunis thryll barounis or knychtis cummys to burgh and byis a borrowage, and duellis in his borrowage a twelfmoneth and a day foroutyn challange of his lorde or of his bailye, he shall evir mare be free as a burges within that Kingis burgh, and joyse the fredoume of that burgh,"* so runs one of the earliest laws for burghal government. The burgess, besides, was subject only to municipal government. The baron or abbot's "baylie" could not lay hold of him, and the dungeon of the castle or convent thereby lost its terror. He was amenable only to the community and its officials, and if attacked and carried before another court, he could claim "hys awen cross and market,"—could demand to be tried before the court of his own burgh, by his fellow burgesses.† Each burgh had the privilege bestowed on it of holding one or more fairs during the year. Institutions of this kind were peculiarly serviceable in the earlier stages of society. The number of shops, and the commodities in them, must have been comparatively limited, and but little sought after by dealers. It was, therefore, for the advantage of all that fairs should be established, and merchants induced to attend them. For this pur-

* Leges Burgorum, No. 15.—Robertson's Early Kings.

† Lindores and its Abbey, p. 147.

pose various privileges were annexed to fairs, and numerous facilities afforded for the disposal of property at them. To give them a greater degree of solemnity they were associated with religious festivals. In most places they are even yet held on the same day, as the feast of the saint to whom the church of the place is dedicated, and till the practice was prohibited in England, it was the custom to hold them in the churchyards.* The fair was a day of perfect liberty. Though the owner of a bondman met him at the fair, he dared neither "chace nor tak him." On the day of the fair the humblest trader from a distance could exhibit his wares as freely as if he were a burgess of the town. Every facility was given to induce merchants to bring their goods for sale, and on Saint Mirin's Day—the day of the great Paisley fair—the "*mercator extraneus*," as he is called, would be welcomed within the Burgh.

When George Shaw became Abbot, a considerable village had gathered in the neighbourhood of the Abbey, and especially on the opposite bank of the river. Its inhabitants were chiefly artisans and labourers, with one or two priests or chaplains who officiated at altars in the Abbey.† The tenants of the Abbey formed a community large enough to excite the jealousy of the Burgh of Renfrew. That burgh monopolised all the trade of the neighbourhood, and levied tolls and customs up to the very gates of the Monastery. Its exactions were very vexatious, and in 1487 the inhabitants of the Abbey lands made a fierce attack upon their oppressors, for which they were fined at the circuit court, or "justice aire" of Renfrew. Abbot Shaw had interest to obtain remission of the penalties inflicted on his vassals. James III., in the last year of his reign, and his son, in the first of his, granted them a free pardon.‡ "For asmeikle," says the latter, "as umquhile oure fader quham God assolye, in honor of God and of the glorious Confessor, Sanct Meryne, and for the special devotioun he had to the said Confessor, patrone of oure Abbay of Paslay, remittit and forgaife to venerable fader in God, and our well-belovit orator, George, Abbot of our said Abbay, all the amerciamentes

* M'Culloch's Dictionary of Commerce.—Chitty on Commercial Law, Vol. II.

† A plan of the village of Paisley is given in Semple's "Saint Mirin."

‡ Reg. de Pas., pp. 272, 273.

and unlawis in the quhilk the said venerable faderis tennandis, servandis, and all personis inhabitants of his regalite and landis pertenyn to our said Abbay was adjugit in the last justice aire of Renfrew, and gaif alsua his free remissoun to thaim for the actioun of forthocht felone done be thaim in the cummyn apone our leigis of our Burgh of Renfrew. We geive by these our letteres oure free remission to all persons, for the said actions of forthochte felone."

In order to save his tenants further molestation from their neighbours at Renfrew, and following the example of other Scots Abbots, Abbot Shaw took steps to erect his village into a burgh, with its own cross and market, and all the privileges belonging to a town. He applied first to the Pope for liberty to feu certain ground in the Village of Paisley, alleging that it would be for the benefit of the Monastery, all the lands hitherto yielding only a rent of twenty-five ducats. The Pope, in 1483,* referred the matter to two commissioners—John Crichton, Precentor of the Cathedral of Glasgow, and Walter Abernethy, Provost of the Collegiate Church of Dunbarton. These, having made inquiry, and consulted men able to advise them and skilled in the law, were of opinion that it would be for the advantage of the Monastery that the Abbot's request should be granted, and gave him, accordingly, the requisite permission.† Having now got the sanction of the Church, Abbot George sought the sanction of the State, which was bestowed with equal readiness—the King, James IV., willingly granting the privilege to one to whom his family had been so much indebted.‡ He mentions in the charter erecting the village into a burgh his gratitude to the Abbot for the virtuous education and upbringing of the Duke of Ross, the King's brother, in his tender estate, and dwells on the singular devotion he had to the glorious Confessor, St. Mirin, and the Monastery founded by his progenitors, where many of their bodies were "buried, and lie sleeping."§ His charter gave the inhabitants the right and privilege of buying and selling within the burgh all kinds of goods and merchandise, and having all kinds of tradesmen and artisans; also, the right of having a market cross

* Reg. de Pas., p. 260. † Reg. de Pas., p. 261. This was in 1488.
‡ See *Ante*. § Reg. de Pas., p. 264.

and holding a weekly market on Monday, and two fairs yearly, one on Saint Mirin's day and the other on Saint Marnock's day. It conferred, also, on the Abbot and his successors the power of electing annually a provost, bailies, and other officers for the burgh, and of removing them and electing others when necessary, without any election of the burgesses. It gave the Abbot right to hold with a firm hand his authority over the town he created. The Abbot having thus obtained the sanction of the necessary authorities, spiritual and temporal, granted a charter,* which was for long the palladium of the burgh. It defines its boundaries, its privileges, and its government,† and thus, by the favour and goodwill of the Abbot, the village of Paisley began its career as one of the towns of Scotland.

The new burgh was not viewed with much favour by the group of similar towns in the neighbourhood. Its older sisters regarded it with a jealous eye as an intruder on their privileges. Immediately after its erection, the King addressed a letter to the Burghs of Air, Irwine, Renfrew, Ruglen, Dumbarton, and Glasgow, charging them that none of their burgesses should take upon hand to vex, trouble, or inquiet the "venerable fader in the peaceable broiking and jousing of the said Burgh of Paslay, and the privileges of the same, as ye and ilk of you will answer to us thereupon."‡ One of these burghs, that of Renfrew, thought fit to disregard the royal admonition. Its burgesses could not view with equanimity another burgh in their neighbourhood, possessing equal privileges with their own. Its regular fairs and market cross were very offensive. Possibly the burgesses of Paisley, in their youthful zeal, prosecuted their trade in a way that seriously injured the resources of the sleepy old town by the Clyde. The Renfrew men stole up to Paisley by night and cast down with contumely the cross of which the Paisley people were so proud.§ The Abbot was very indignant, and the King coming soon after to the Abbey, he made to him a complaint of how his burgesses were treated by their neighbours, and the King wrote letters to the Earl of

* Reg. de Pas., p. 265. † See end of chapter for the King and Abbot's charters.

‡ Reg. de Pas., p. 274.

§ The cross was ordered by the Town Council in 1693 to be taken down, and the place where it stood to be "calsayed." Its removal was probably due to Protestant zeal.

Lennox, and his son, Matthew Stewart, "charging them to make proclamation at the market cross of Renfrew of his Majesty's displeasure with the communite and burgess of Renfrew, for having, under silence of night, gone to Paisley and destroyed the hewn work of the new market cross of the said town, which had recently been erected by the King into a free Burgh of Barony, charging them to apprehend, if possible, and punish with rigour of law, the persons who had committed the said offence." The letter is dated from the Abbey, two years after the erection of the Burgh.*

The letter of the King does not appear to have had much effect upon the irate burgesses of Renfrew, for a few years afterwards they made another raid upon Paisley, seizing, in the market place, upon certain things in payment of their customs,—"a quarter of beef for a penney of custome, a cabok of cheese for an halfpenney of custom, and a wynd of white claith for a penney of custom." The Bailies of the Abbot, Alan Stewart and John of Quhiteforde, were equal to the occasion, and valiantly resisted the Renfrew invaders, recovering from them the beef, the cheese, and the white claith, and sending them back empty-handed. The Renfrew community raised an action before the Lord Auditors against the Abbot's bailies for interference with them in levying their customs. The Abbot himself defended his servants, and the case was decided by the judges in his favour, confining the aggressive citizens of Renfrew within their own bounds, beyond which their privileges did not extend.† Abbot Shaw, elated by this victory over his troublesome neighbours, raised an action against them in turn,‡ prosecuting them for illegally levying dues in Paisley for an hundred years to which they were not entitled, for demolishing the cross, interfering with the fishings and pasture of the Convent, casting down a house in the town of Arkylstone, and other misdeeds, for each of which he demanded a certain compensation. It is probable that this only meant a threat of what would happen if the Renfrew people did not behave themselves. Nothing more apparently came of it, and the Paisley people were allowed hence-

* The letter is in the Lennox Papers, and is dated 23rd December, 1490.

† Reg. de Pas., p. 403. ‡ Reg. de Pas., p. 404.

forth to enjoy their privileges in peace, with no fear of their beef, cheese, or white claith being taken from them. It was in recognition of all that the Convent had done in bestowing upon them burghal privileges and maintaining their rights, that several of the chief townsmen endowed altarages in the church of the Abbey. Though all connection of a formal kind between the Abbey and town has long since been severed, the people of Paisley are still proud of the venerable church which represents the source whence all their prosperity has come. It is to be hoped, they will always be ready to do everything in their power to maintain it in a condition worthy of its history and of their own.

We subjoin in full the two charters, in virtue of which Paisley became a burgh :—

*Charter of the Liberty of the Burgh of Paisley, and Erection of the same.*

"JAMES, by the grace of God, King of Scots, to all honest men of his whole country, both clergy and laity, greeting: Be it known that for the singular respect We have for the glorious Confessor, Saint Mirin, and our Monastery of Paisley, founded by our most illustrious progenitors, where very many of the bodies of our ancestors are buried, and are at rest, and for the singular favour and love which We bear to the venerable Father in Christ, George Shaw, present Abbot of the said Monastery, our very dear counsellor, and for the faithful service rendered to us in a variety of ways by the said venerable father in times past, and in a particular manner for the virtuous education and upbringing of our dearest brother James, Duke of Ross, in his tender age, We have made, constituted, erected and created, and by the tenor of our present Charter make, feu, erect, and create the Village of Paisley, lying within the Sheriffdom of Renfrew, a free Burgh of Barony; We have granted also to the present and future inhabitants of said burgh the full and free liberty of buying and selling in said burgh wine, wax, and woollen and linen cloths, wholesale and retail, and all other goods and wares coming to it, with power and liberty of having and holding in the same place bakers, brewers, butchers, and sellers both of flesh and fish, and workmen in their several crafts, tending in any respect to the liberty of the burgh in barony. We have granted likewise to the burgesses and inhabitants of the said burgh of Paisley, therein to have and possess a cross and market place for ever, every week on Monday, and two public fairs yearly for ever,—one, namely, on the day of St. Mirin, and the other on the day of Saint Marnock, with tolls and other liberties pertaining to fairs of this kind; of holding and having for the future the said village of Paslay a real and free burgh in barony with the foresaid privileges, grants, and all other liberties, as freely, quietly, fully, entirely, honourably, and well, in peace, in every time, circumstance, and condition, as the burgh of Dunfermline, Newburgh, and Aberbrothwick,* or any other burgh or barony in our Kingdom in any time past is freely endowed or held: and we have granted, besides, to the said venerable father and to his successors, the Abbots of Paisley, the right and power of choosing annually the provost, bailies, and other officers of the said burgh, and of removing the same as need shall be, and of choosing and installing others anew in their room as shall seem most expedient to the said Abbot and his successors, and without any other election of the burgesses and community of the said burgh, and without any revocation or contradiction to be made by us or by our successors on the above premises: Wherefore we command all and sundry who have, or may have interest, that they presume not in any way to contravene this, our concession, under pain of incurring our royal displeasure. In testimony whereof, we have commanded our great seal to be affixed to this our charter. These reverend fathers in Christ being witnesses—Robert Bishop of Glasgow; George, Bishop of Dunkeld: and our beloved cousins—Colin, Earl of Argyle; Lord Campbell, our Chancellor; Archibald, Earl of Angus; Lord of Douglasse; Patrick, Lord Hailes, Master of our Household; Robert, Lord Lyle, our Justiciary; Andrew, Lord Gray; Laurence, Lord Oliphant; John,

* These burghs, like Paisley, were founded by the Abbots of their monasteries.

Lord Drummond; the venerable Father in Christ, John, Prior of our Monastery of St. Andrews, Keeper of our Secret Seal; Sir William Knollys, Preceptor of Torfichin, our Treasurer; Master Alexander Inglis, Archdeacon of St. Andrews; and Archibald Quhitelaw, Sub-Deacon of Glasgow, our Secretary.—At Stirling, the 19th of August, 1488, and in the first year of our reign ——.

The Abbot's Charter was as follows:—

To all and sundry who may see or hear this indented Charter, George Shaw, Abbot of the Monastery of Paisley, and Convent of the same place, of the Order of Clugny, and diocese of Glasgow, wisheth salvation in the eternal God. Be it known to your university, that forasmuch as we have the village of Paisley made and erected by our most excellent Lord the King into a free burgh, to us and to our successors, as is fully contained in a Charter granted thereupon, under his Majesty's great seal, therefore we, having diligently considered the premises, always providing for, and wishing the utility of, our said Monastery, with advice and consent of our whole chapter, chapterly convened, to have given, granted, set, and in feu farm let, and by this our present Charter to have confirmed, and hereby grant, and in feu farm let, and by our present charter to have confirmed to our lovites, the Provost, Bailies, Burgesses, and community of Paisley, All and Whole our said burgh in barony, with the pertinents lying in our regality of Paisley, within the Sheriffdom of Renfrew, within the bounds and limits underwritten, namely—Beginning at the end of the Bridge of Paisley, upon the water of Kert, and extending by the King's highway towards the west to the vennel opposite to the Welmedow, and from thence equally ascending towards the north by the dyke of the lands of Oxschawside to the wood of Oxschawe, betwixt the said wood, as also the passage to the common of the said burgh, and the broom dyke which extends by the lands of Snawdon, from the common of the said burgh to the water of Kert on the north, and the said water of Kert; as also the torrent of Espedair on the east part, and the mustard yard and way extending on the south part of the house of John Murray, and so by the hedge extending above the west end of the Whitefauld on the south part, and the said Whitefauld; as also a part of the common of the said burgh; and said Wellmeadow and ditch of the said lands of Oxschawside on the west part upon the one side, and the other for erecting and building tenements, mansions, and yards, to said Provost, Bailies, Burgesses, and Community, as is specially assigned, or hereafter shall be assigned to every one of them by us and our said Convent, by our charter of feu farm, together with certain acres of the nearest lands lying within the limits and bounds aforesaid, assigned or to be assigned to every tenement, mansion, and yard, according to the terms of our said charter, made or to be made thereupon: moreover, we annex and incorporate the toft, house, building, mansions, yards, and land of Seedhill to the liberty and privilege of our said burgh in barony of Paisley, to be possessed perpetually in all times hereafter: as also we have given, granted, set, and in feu farm let, and such like given, granted, and set, and in feu farm let, to the said provosts, bailies, burgesses, and community of our said Burgh of Paisley and their successors, for the time being, our lands underwritten: whereof, one part of the lands lies at the west end of our said burgh towards the south, betwixt the lands of Calsaysid and the lands of Thomas Leich, called *le bank*, on the east part, and the lands of Castlehed; also, the lands of Sir Henry Mous, John Whiteford, and *le Stobis* of Ricardsbar, on the south parts, and end of the ward called *the bodum of the ward*, on the west part, and the tail of the Brumlandis, as also Welmedow, and the croft of the Prior on the north part; and the other part of the said lands lies on the north part of the said burgh, between the lands of Oxschawhead and the wood of Oxschawe, as also the croft of Robert Cavers, called *le Sclattbank*, on the south part; and the lands of Snawdon and water of Kert, as also *le holmine* of Wardmedow, on the east part; and the marchdyke of Inch and the common moss of Paisley on the north part; and the said moss on the west part upon the one side and the other, for the convenience of the said burgh for ever, to be possessed for the common pasturage of the cattle of the said provost, bailies, burgesses, and community. And also we have given and conceded free license and power to the said provost, bailies, burgesses, and community, and their successors for ever, for gaining and taking their fuel from any of our peatries of Paisley, for sustaining the said provost, bailies, burgesses, and community, and for gaining and taking stones from our quarries for the construction and building of the said burgh as often as it will please them, provided we have what is necessary for ourselves in these peatries and quarries when we please. And if the said provost, bailies, burgesses, or community, shall find or gain a coal pit or coal pits in their said common of the said burgh, we will and order that we and our successors shall thence have our necessaries, making payment of our part of the expenses of gaining the said coal pit, or coal pits, as the said provost, bailies, and community of the said burgh pay for their part thereof, or are willing to pay. Further, we give and grant to the said provost, bailies, burgesses, and community of the said burgh, a common passage of the breadth of twelve ells on the north side of Saint Ninian's Cross, extending from the said part of the foresaid common lands even to the other part thereof. Having and holding, all and whole, the foresaid burgh of Paisley in a barony, with the tenements, mansions, gardens, acres of land, bounds and limits thereof, assigned by us to them, or to be assigned, with the common pasturage of their animals upon our moss of Paisley, and license in our peatry and quarry aforesaid, as the same lie in length and breadth, to the said provost, bailies, burgesses, and community of the said burgh, and their successors, in feu farm, heritable for ever, by rights hereof used and divided, limited, or to be limited, by us to them, with power of buying and selling in the said burgh, wine, wax, cloth, woollen and linen, crafts or arts, and whatever other goods or merchandise may come thither, with the little customs and tolls, and with all and sundry other liberties, commodities, profits, and easments, and just pertinents whatsoever, belonging, or which may justly be understood hereafter to belong to the said burgh in barony, with power of choosing and of making burgesses and stallingers according to the customs, laws, and statutes of burghs made thereanent, which burgesses and stallingers, and every one of them, shall, at their entry, swear that they will keep faith to our supreme lord the King, and his successors, the Kings of Scotland; as also to the Stewart of Scotland, his heirs and successors, and to us the Abbot and Convent, and our successors, and to the said bailies and community and common utility of the said burgh, in the same manner as burgesses in other burghs do or have been in use to do. Moreover, we give and grant to the provost and bailies of the said burgh chosen by us, and their successors for the time being, full power of holding, convening, and fencing burgh courts of the said burgh, and of continuing the same as often as shall be needful, of levying the issues and amerciaments of the said courts, of fining absentees, of punishing transgressors and delinquents according to the statutes and laws of the burgh, and of choosing sergeants, officers, ministers, tasters of ale and wine, and appreciators of flesh, and other servants whomsoever necessary for a burgh, as is statute and ordained in other burghs, according to the strength, form, and tenor so far as concerns the extension of the foresaid liberties, as is at length contained in the charter of the said burgh in barony and privileges thereof, granted by our sovereign lord the King to us and our successors. Further, we give and grant to the bailies of the said burgh, to be chosen by us and our successors, full power and faculty of taking and receiving resignations of all and sundry lands, acres, and tenements lying within the burgh, and to give and deliver heritable state and seisin as is the use in burghs, to the wives of the possessors, or their true heirs, provided they give seisin to no other person, neither receive resignations without our consent and assent obtained thereto. We will also that the said provost and bailies of the said burgh be annually chosen by advice of us and our successors at the term and court limited by law within burghs, and that they shall be deprived as oft and often as need be, without any hindrance whatsoever. And further, we will and grant that the said provost, bailies, burgesses, and community of the said burgh, shall for ever have for the sustaining the common purse and good of the said burgh the fines of all the burgesses and stallingers of the said burgh, to be made in all time coming with the little customs and tolls of the said burgh, as is the custom in other burghs. Rendering yearly the said provost, bailies, burgesses, and community of the said burgh, to us and our successors furth of the said tenements, mansions, gardens, and acres of land within the limits of the burgh before written, the burghal farm and service of court used and wont, with the yearly rents then owing according to the tenor of our rental and register, and is at more length contained in our Charters of the feu farm tacks of the same tenements, mansions, gardens, and acres; and that the said provost, bailies, burgesses, and community of the said burgh and their successors shall come with their grain, whatsoever quality they may grind to our miln of Paisley, and to no other mill whatever, paying to us multure to the thirty-one dish, as men abiding forth of our lands; also, for all other burden, exaction, demand, or secular service which can justly be demanded or required from the said burgh in barony, tenements, mansions, gardens, and acres lying within the said burgh, with all their pertinents whatsoever. In witness whereof the common seal of the chapter of the said Monastery is appended to this indented charter, remaining with the said provost, bailies, burgesses, and community of the said burgh, and the common seal of the said burgh of Paisley is appended to the said indented charter, remaining with the said Abbot and Convent. At the Monastery, and for said burgh, the second day of June, 1490. Before these witnesses, namely:—James Schaw de Sawchy, David Schaw, his son; Thomas Stewart of Craginfeoch, Robert Sympill, John Ralston of that Ilk, John Schaw, Sir Alexander Clugston and James Young, notaries public, with many others.

## CHAPTER XVI.

### Monastic Economics.

Who with the ploughshare clove the barren moors,
And to green meadows changed the swampy shores?
Thinned the rank woods; and for the cheerful grange
Made room where wolf and boars were used to range?
Who taught and showed by deeds that gentler chains
Should bind the vassal to his lord's domains?
The thoughtful monks, intent their God to please
For Christ's dear sake, by human sympathies.
—*Wordsworth.*

THIS is perhaps the best place—before we have to tell the sad story of decrepitude and decay—to give some account of the management by the monks of their revenues, the great landed property possessed by the Convent, and the tenants or vassals dwelling on their farms. We are fortunately able to do so with much certainty. Not only are there many notices of their management scattered throughout the Chartulary, but their Rental-book, which we append to the present volume, enables us to take a just estimate of the relations subsisting between them and their vassals, and throws much light on their management of their estates. This Rental-book, or perhaps rather book of leases, was begun in the time of Abbot Crichton, and was continued by his successors. It is beautifully written and neatly kept, and, perhaps more than any other manuscript of this same kind that has been published, gives us an idea of the conduct of the monks in their capacity of landlords. The view one takes of their government, after a study of this volume, is a very kindly one, and corroborates all that historians tell us regarding the lands of those ecclesiastics being the best cultivated and the best managed in Scotland. There were good reasons why they should be so. The monks were not needy landlords, grinding out of their tenants every penny they were able to pay. They were proprietors whose own wants were few, and who had education enabling them to adopt the best methods of agriculture, and sense to encourage improvements. Their tenants were exempt from military service. The husbandman on their lands was never called away like the retainer of the neighbouring baron to follow his master's banner, and leave his field unploughed, or his harvest unreaped. He remained quietly cultivating the land of which he knew neither himself nor his children after him had any likelihood of being dispossessed so long as they paid their moderate rent to the bailiff or steward of the Monastery. The neighbourhood of a convent was always recognisable by the well-cultivated land and the happy tenantry which surrounded it, and those of the Abbey of Paisley were no exception to the general rule prevailing throughout the rest of Scotland.

The revenues of the monks were derived from the tiends of their churches, the produce of the lands which they held in their own hands, the dues of their mills, their feu-duties, and the rents of their fishings and such farms as they thought proper to let.

The tiends were the rectorial tithes of the churches belonging to them, and of these we have had occasion to speak often in the preceding pages. The collection of these dues involved them in many disputes, both with their needy and ill-paid vicars and with the bishop of the diocese, who took the part of these stipendiaries. The tithes were payable at the various churches, and occasionally, as we learn from the Rental-book, were gathered by a person residing at the church, who received, for his trouble in collecting them and bringing them to Paisley, a piece of land at a very moderate rent. Of this, we have the following among other notices :—

> "The forty-shilling land beside the Kirk of Largs is let to James Crafurd, and Margaret Kelsoland, wife of the said James, for two pounds annually, with horses and carts for collecting the tithes at the said land, and keeping the same."

"The Kyrkland of Kylmacolm is let to George Fleming for twelve shillings annually, with the reception of the tithes of the congregation when it happens, and *custody of the same, and riding to us with them when required.*"

The collection of these dues either by the monks or their deputy must have been very troublesome. They often, therefore, farmed them out, receiving from their lessee a single sum, and leaving him to make the most of what he could gather. In the Appendix we give a lease by an abbot of the vicarage and altarage of the Kirks of Paisley and Lochwinnoch, and there are many other similar instances. These "tacksmen of the tiends" would be able to exact more from the farmers than the easy-going monks were likely to collect for themselves.

The lands of the Abbey were in Renfrew, Dumbarton, Ayrshire, Peebles, and Roxburgh. How they managed their Peebleshire land of Orde we have almost nothing to tell us, but on their other properties they had granges—large farm-houses under the care of a person called a granger, probably a lay brother, where were gathered the cattle, implements, and stores needed for the cultivation of their lands. The chief grange of the Abbey was at Blackston, a few miles from the church, on the river Gryfe, which is often mentioned as "being in the Lord Abbot's hands for grange." The "barns" of Kilpatrick are also noticed as the head steading of the Abbey on the other side of the Clyde, and the "Place" of Muncton was the centre of management for their Ayrshire estates. At Huntlaw,* near Hassendean in Roxburgh, there is a ruin still called the "Monk's tower," the only approach to a grange possible in that wild border land. The tenantry of the Abbey consisted of two classes—the cottars, who paid a small rent, from ten to forty shillings, and laboured on the monks' lands, and the farmers, who paid their rent chiefly in grain, and who cultivated their land with oxen and implements furnished by the Abbot. The latter description of holding is termed *steel bow*, and all the large farms of the Abbey appear to

* There is only one notice of Huntlaw in the Rental. It is let to John Hamilton of Stirkfield, and the place called "ane dogleche."

W

have been let on leases of this kind. Thus the lands of Candren were let to two parties, and it is specially noted that

"Those tenants have of goods of the Abbey forty-eight bolls of oats, six bolls two firlots of second bere, ten acres of medo *wyn and stakyt*, one chalder of horse corn, four oxen, twenty-four tidy kye."

The crops grown were wheat, oats, and barley, and as an instance of a farm paying rent in those kinds of grain, we may give that of Barns in Kilpatrick :—

"It is let to Thomas Hasty and Thomas Knock, paying annually four chalders flour, eight bolls corn, and eight bolls barley."

The notices of holdings whose tenants paid small rents, and gave various services at the Abbey granges, swell the pages of the rental book. Most of the rents are payable in kind, but there is also mention of "le bon silvuer," a money payment also exigible from them. The items of the rental payable in kind are varied—stirks, calves, poultry, capons, chickens, geese, stones of cheese, wedders, and loads of coal. It is impossible for us to give the exact value of these products, which must have kept the Abbey larder and coal cellar well supplied; but in a late rental we find a valuation which helps us to form some idea of the amount brought in by those rentals in kind :—*

"Memorandum of the statute of the *do service*. That each capon is 8d. ; each poultry, 4d. ; each chicken, 2d. ; the load of coals, 4d. ; the plough, 2s. ; the day shearing, 3d. Also two poultry for a capon, two chickens for a poultry ; also each laid of coals, three creels of *huch*, to be laid in the Abbot's place betwixt Whitsonday and Michaelmas, or else the price of the laid, 6d. The entry of the fowls begins at Pasch, capons and chickens at Michaelmas, and from Michaelmas, poultry till Fasterns Eve. The penny mail

* It is at p. 177 original MS.

to be paid at Whitsonday and Martinmass. The *do service*, as carriages, plowing, harrowing, and shearing, to be paid at Martinmass, with the rest of the coals and fowls, and the sergeant to answer therefor as he does for the penny mail of them that are unspecified; also, after each plough, 6d, for harrowing each merk land, three capons, each long carriage, 10s."

The personal service referred to in this valuation was of a very varied kind. It consisted chiefly in work done on the monks' lands, with ploughs, harrows, and carts, tillage in spring, shearing in harvest, and grass-cutting in summer. Sometimes, also, the tenant was bound to give a riding man, and at others a bed when required. There was a duty also called long-carriage, which probably refers to the transportation of necessaries between the Monastery and their granges. The Ayrshire tenants were almost all liable to this service. We give a few instances, taken at random from the rental-book, of the duties payable by the tenantry to their superiors:—

"It is ordained that each tenant in the town of Foulton shall pay annually four *bonys*† in autumn: two carriages, one in summer and one in winter; one day with harrows, one day in summer, *ad fenum, anglice*, a day's work of mowing."

"Achinch is let to James Tat, paying annually fifty-three shillings and fourpence, with twelve poultry, four days in autumn, and a day with harrows and a day cutting grass, and with service and carriage use and wont."

"Monktonehill five pound eighteen shilling land.—One part is let to Patrick Rese for fifteen shillings and fourpence, two capons, two poultry, two chickens, two loads of coals, half a bed, half a plough, a long carriage, and five days' shearing.—Another part is let to John Osborn at thirty-six shillings, four capons, four poultry, eight chickens, four loads of coals, a riding man, a long carriage, a bed, a plough, and eight days' shearing."

There was a species of property which is noticed occasionally as the

* Bonsilver? or perhaps bondagers.

Kirklands or *Terra Dominie.* They pertained to the churches belonging to the Abbey in various counties. We read of the Kirklands of Largs, Roseneath, Kilpatrick, Achinleck, Legardwood, and others. These were let at a small rent, and are often noticed. The parson of Achinleck enjoyed his own Kirklands, as the following shows :—*

"Us, Robert, be the permission of God, Abbot of Paslay, grants us to have rentalled our servant, Sir William Hume, curat of our Kirk of Achinleck, in the whole Kirkland of the same, upon paying therefore yearly as it was wont to do; and, also, we ordain and make the said William our curat of our said Kirk for all the time of his life, and when the said Sir William may not make service in the parish he shall cause another to make service for him, that shall be sufficient."

Occasionally the proceeds of the Kirklands went to maintain service either in the church to which they belonged, or in the Abbey. This was the case with those of Eastwood and Neilston, which were appropriated to pious uses.

—"Oswald Maxwell † rentalled in the chantor's land at the Kirkstyle of the Eastwood, paying, therefor, yearly to the said chantors forty shillings at two terms usual in the year. The Kirkland of Neilstown is assigned to James Young for forty shillings, paying to the chantors of the choir singing to the glory of God in the chapel of the blessed Mary, within the chapter of the Monastery of Paisley." ‡

There were two chapels belonging to the Abbey, the lands of which were let on similar conditions :—

"The land of the chapel of West Cochny or Warthill § is let to William Anderson paying annually thirteen shillings and fourpence, and

* Page 54 original MS. † Ibid, page 19.
‡ Ibid, page 149. This is the only notice we have of this chapel.
§ Ibid, page 109.

the said William shall maintain a bed at all times for the use of the poor, and shall keep the chapel in good repair."

"The chapel land of Boquhanran,* let to Will Atkin, paying, therefor, yearly, thirteen shillings and fourpence, with one bed to travellers for God's sake and our founder's, with all freedoms usit of before." †

The tenants of the monks were not allowed to marry without express permission from the Abbot, and paid him a fine even when the permission was granted. Several licenses to contracting parties are to be found in the rental book, similar to the following :—

"The land which she now occupies in Drumgrane is let to Elizabeth Edmonston, and we give leave to the said Elizabeth our license to contract marriage with James Hamilton, notwithstanding all acts and rules of our court to the contrary."

The monks were kind masters. No cases of eviction or deprivation are recorded. The same lands descended without rise of rent from father to son. Children are held bound to maintain their parents in their old age, and widows are especially cared for, and are occasionally provided with another husband!

"Part of Snawdoun is let to Allan Sunderland, paying annually twenty shillings, but the widow is not to be removed. Langyard to Richard Thomson, on which he will keep Janet Logan, widow by the will of God. The twenty land of Braidfield is let to Findlay M'Gregor, for Temple, widow of Robert Brison, and we give our consent to the said widow to contract matrimony with the said Findlay."

Among the many tenants whose names are recorded in the rental book, there is one who attracts special attention, and who rendered for his

* Buchanan in Dumbartonshire, where there was probably a chapel dedicated to St. Mirin, by whose name one of the islands on Loch Lomond is called.

† Page 113 original MS.

land service more valuable than the days' harrowing or ploughing exacted from his neighbours. This was a sculptor of the name of Thomas Hector, to whom Abbot Henry Crichton let, at a moderate rent, the lands of Nether Crossflat, lying to the east of Paisley, and not far from the Monastery where he was called to exercise his art, and where specimens of his workmanship may still be seen. The notice of this craftsman is as follows :—

> "Memorandum—That the place which is called Nether Crossflat is let to Thomas Hector, sculptor, for twenty shillings, and all use and wont as the place was formerly held by Robert Slater, with the subjoined condition, that the said Thomas will hold himself ready and prepared to the said Abbot and Convent in all that concerns his art as a sculptor, and shall receive no other work pertaining to his art without obtaining leave of the Abbot and Convent, and while he is required by the Abbot and Convent to perform the work of a sculptor at the Monastery, he shall entirely lay aside whatever he has in hand and come back within a month to the work at the Monastery, under pain of forfeiting this, his lease, and, beside, penalty of a hundred shillings.*

It was in 1460 that the Abbot let Nether Crossflat to the sculptor, and he lived there for many years, the last notice of him is forty-two years after the preceding entry. He is called familiarly "Ald," or old Hector. In 1502 his land was let to another :—

> "Crossflat, that ald Hector brukyt, the twenty shilling land of the same, on the east side of the common beyond the dyke, set to George Houston."

In all the leases given, it is worthy of note, there is but one reservation of game, namely, of hares and rabbits :—

* Page 6 original MS.

"One part of the Nether Ward, namely, the five acres called Brown Holm, with two acres lying opposite Brown's acre, is let to Peter Algeo, paying annually five bolls of barley, reserving to ourselves hares and rabbits found in the said land.—28 July, 1554."

The Abbey derived considerable revenue from annuals in payments that were made them, either in commutation of certain dues, or in the way of pension or fine. They received a pension from the Monastery of Crossraguel, in payment of expenses incurred by the Abbot of Paisley in his visitation, and the fine of 20 shillings imposed on the laird of Achinleck, for his brutal usage of one of the monks,* continued to be paid regularly by his successors until the dissolution of the Monastery. They had also property in Glasgow, from which they drew small sums, and a house called *domus monachorum*, or house of the monks, probably the tenement which Abbot Roger purchased for them in the Rotten Row of Glasgow, after the English had burned the Abbey. The following is a list of their annuals in various parts :—

Houston, 6s. 8d.

RENFREW.

Porterfield, 6s. 8d.
The Monkdyk in Renfrew, 5s.
Berlymo Montgomery, 8s.
John Cunnock, 12s.
Wilzram Snap, 8s.
The Mill of Renfrew, 13s. 4d.

The Annual of Ruglen, 10s. 1d.

GLASGOW.

Master Thomas, lease of the Stockwell, 5s.
Maryon Scott, 5s.
Thom. Walcar and Wilzam Baxter, 2s. 6d.
The house at the Wynd head.
The Inn before the Blackfriars, 13s. 4d.

KYLE IN AYRSHIRE.

Adamton, 40s.
Corsbe, 8s. 4d.
Auchinleck, 20s.
Corseraguel, £6 13s. 4d.

Glebe of Killenan in Argyle, 40s.
Stralachlau in Argyle, 40s.

The mills belonging to the Abbey were very valuable property. They had one connected with each portion of their lands—at Muncton, Dalmul-

* See *ante*.

ing, Duntocher, Drumgrane, Glen, and Paisley. At these mills all their tenants were bound to grind. These tenants were called "sukeners," and were spoken of as "thirled" to the mill. Most readers of Sir Walter Scott will remember Hob, the miller of "The Monastery," and the sharp outlook he kept for his dues—the *dry multures*, the *lock* and the *gowpen*, the *knaveship*, and the *sequels*—which were the constant subject of his talk.* All these dues were received at the Abbot's mills, to his great profit. Most of the mills were let with all their perquisites, and the amount received for them is given in the rental-book. The Mill of Paisley the Convent kept in its own hand until the later years of its history, when the Abbot let it, "with all sukoms, profits, casualties, and pertinents pertaining thereto," on a lease of nine years; though he specially bargained that our "corns for us and our successors to be ground at our said myll free from multure and casualties, free as use and wont as before."† The Abbey Mill stood in the Seedhill, near the Falls on the River Cart. It was an object of great care on the part of the monks, and many charters regarding it are to be found in the Register. When the town of Paisley was feued by Abbot Shaw the burgesses were still held bound to grind their corn at the Abbey Mill. The whole growing oats, seed, and horse-corn excepted, were thirled to it. Any one grinding corn elsewhere was fined in 100s. The rate of multure was each twenty first peck, besides the dues of the miller and his servants, namely:—"three fills of meal of a dish called the *angerem*, containing six pounds of Dutch weight, for fifteen bolls, two fills for ten bolls, and one fill for five bolls; and one streaked dish full of meal of the said dish for every boll of sheling." These dues were very formidable, and it is supposed that the wrath of the tenants at seeing the miller appropriate the large dishful of their meal led to that vessel getting the curious but suggestive name of the "angerem."‡

* The *dry multures* were money payments for not grinding at the mill. The *multures* were the grain paid the miller; the *knaveship* the portion claimed by his servant. The *lock*—a small quantity) and the *gowpen* (a handful) were additional perquisites demanded by the miller. All these and other petty dues were called *sequels*. See Notes to "Monastery," by Sir W. Scott.

† See charter of Abbot Hamilton in Appendix.

‡ These dues were shown in an action of declarator raised in the Court of Session by the Earl of Abercorn in 1796. See Semple's "Lairds of Glen."

The last source of revenue which we shall notice as belonging to the Abbey were the fishings. A large portion of the food of the monks was fish, and they needed a constant supply. In many Scotch monasteries they possessed fish-ponds in the neighbourhood of their convents,* which were plentifully stocked with perch. We find no trace of such preserves having belonged to the Abbey of Paisley. Probably they were not needed, as the brethren must have been amply supplied with the best of salmon and trout from the many fishings that belonged to them. Many notices of fishings abound in the Chartulary. The chief of these was upon the river Leven, in Dunbartonshire, called Lynbren.† It was bestowed on the Monastery in 1225 by a priest named Robert Hertford when on the point of death,‡ and continued in the possession of the Monastery during the rest of its history. It was fished by means of a *yare* or cruive. The Lords of Lennox gave them liberty to take stone and wood from their land for its repair.§ One of them forbade the erection of any other yare between that of the monks and Loch Lomond, and another added to these privileges the right of fishing on the lake and of drying their nets, and of erecting houses for their fishermen on any of the islands. An Earl of Lennox also gave them liberty to draw nets along the whole Gareloch on the Clyde for the capture of salmon or other fish.|| After the fishing on the river Leven, that on the Clyde was most important. At one time they had a fishing between the Isle of Renfrew and Partick, but latterly they seem to have possessed only on the river the fishing, or a third part of the fishing, of the Cruiketshot. This was purchased by Abbot Thomas Tervas in 1452 from Lord Lyle. That peer was in great need of money for certain expenses he had incurred,¶ and parted with the fishings to the Abbot for a moderate sum.** They were connected with the lands of Auchintorly and Dunnerbouk, and were worked with nets. Besides these two famous fishings, the Abbey possessed others at Paisley, at Muncton, on Lochwinnoch, and on the Gryffe. The

* The fish-pond of New Abbey is still to be seen.

† Reg. de Pas., p. 211.

‡ Reg. de Pas., p. 212, "Dum laboraret in extremis."

§ Reg. de Pas., p. 215, *et seq.*

|| Reg. de Pas., p. 211.

¶ Videlicet ad exponendum in prosecutione fienda terrarum de le Garriach mihi jure hereditaris pertinentium.

** Reg. de Pas., p. 251.

latter river was fished by *cruives* at a place called Auchindonan, and latterly they were at Blaxton, near the Abbot's grange. During the period to which the rental-book refers most of the fishings appear to have been let, and each paid so many fish annually to the Convent. The following are some of the notices of these sources of monastic revenue. Several others are scattered throughout the rental-book.*

> The fyschyng of Linbrane, set to my Lord of Ergill for five years, paying thirty-six salmon.—Surety, Donald Campbell of . . .
> The fyschyng of Crukitshot, set to George Brownside for . . .
> The fyschin of the water of Paisley . . .
> The fyschyn of the water of Blaxton, with the crewis.
> The fyschin of the loch of Lochtwynnoch with one boat, set to James Glen of the Bar during our will alanerly, payand . . .

The rental of some of these fishings is not given, from which we may probably infer that the Abbot retained them in his own hands, sending for his fish at such times as he needed them.

The Abbey possessed an orchard, a kale yard, and a columbarium. The orchard consisted of six acres and one perch of land,† and lay on the opposite side of the river from the Abbey. The dovecote was near the orchard, and the cabbage or kail yard opposite the Abbey mill, on the other side of the river.

For fuel the monks, in the early days of the Convent, used wood, which the Stewart had given them the right to take from his forests. In later times they burned peats, and had a right of peatry which they retained when they feued the lands on which Paisley was built. It was situated in a moss to the north of the town, and bore the name of "the monks' rooms." They got abundance of coal from their Ayrshire estates, the tenants of which were charged to lay down so many loads at the Abbot's "Place."

* Page 175 original MS.

† It extended from what is now 12 Causeyside to what is called Gordon's Loan. Abbot Shaw feued it in 1490, but excepted the columbarium. For the latter the ministers of the Abbey Parish draw stipend at the present day. There is a very fine specimen of a columbarium at Crossraguel.

We may conclude this sketch of monastic economics, by giving the rules which one of the Abbots drew up for the government of his tenantry. They give us a very good idea of that potentate in his character of landlord. We have somewhat softened the rough Scottish dialect in which they are given, but any reader who wishes to see them in their original form will find them in the Rental-book, from the pages of which they are extracted :—

"First, that no man taking land, or tenant within the Abbot's land, make tenant, or set, or make interchange of land under him without leave of the Abbot, asked and obtained, under the penalty of one hundred shillings, and forfeiture of his holding, and removal from it without mercy.

"Also, that he purchase no lordship to speak or to plead against his Lord the Abbot, nor against his neighbours, under the penalty aforesaid.

"Also, whosoever he be that receives not the Abbot's servants when on his service shall be fined in forty shillings, and unforgiven for his default.

"Also, that he shall be no man's man, but only the Abbot's, and that he take service with no man without special leave of the Abbot, or whom the Abbot deputes, or gives him liberty to serve with—under the penalty aforesaid.

"Also, that he shall set no crop land to anyone without leave of the Abbot, under the penalty of forfeiting his holding.

"Also, that no man purchase lordship against the Abbot in any way to his hurt or that of the common profit of the house, or slander him or his monks in word or deed, under penalty of one hundred shillings, and forfeiture of his holding, and removal from it without mercy, as it is before written.

"Also, he that dirties his land with guld and does not clean it by Lammas shall pay a merk without mercy, and if the land be afterwards found dirty all his goods shall be escheated.

"Also, whoever he be that makes wrongous landmers, or consels them, or suffers men to occupy them, shall certify the Abbot and the

Convent within sufficient time—that is to say, within the space of six months following from the time that he has knowledge thereof—under the penalty before written.

"Also, whosoever has goods to be sold,—whether marts, wedders, or fed swine,—shall offer their goods at usual and compatable price to the Abbot's officers before they go to any market, under the penalty aforesaid.

"Also, that no man be found by an inquest a common brawler, or an unlawful neighbour; but each tenant act towards the other neighbourly, under pain of law.

"Also, that each tenant be ready, without obstacle or debate, to compear at Court, or at Whitsunday, when they are warned by the sergeant on the day before, to come on the morrow, as lawful day and lawful warning, under pain of fine by the Court.

"Also, that no man go with their corn or their multure from the Abbot's mill, under the penalty of forfeiting his holding, and a punishment of an hundred shillings.

"Also, whatsoever tenant belonging to the sukin of the Mill of Dalmulin, or to the sukin of any other mill of the Abbot and Convent, wherever it be within the Abbot's land, who upholds not his part of the dam sufficiently, or does not come when he is warned by the farmer to mend and repair, if anything be in need, for the first fault he shall pay five shillings, and the second ten shillings, and the third time shall suffer forfeiture of his holding without mercy.

"Also, that no man be found by an inquest a common destroyer of the Abbot's wood, under the pain of forfeiting his holding and the fine, namely, . . .

"Also, that no tenant, man or woman, be found an adulterer by an inquest of their neighbours, under pain of forfeiting their holding without mercy.

"Also, whatever tenant or farmer that pays not his rent and farm with service forfeits his holding, and shall not presume to occupy it in time to come.

"Also, that whenever they are charged with their *bwnys* in harvest and other times of the year in the service which they owe, if they come not on the day on which they chance to be summoned, the sergeant shall take from each defaultour a *wedder*, and the second time two wedders, and the third time an ox or a cow, for the Abbot's behoof, without remission.

"Also, that no one be found an unlawful neighbour, or brawler with the Abbot's servants of his house, or of his retinue, nor strike them or any of his tenants, under penalty of five pounds and forfeiture of his holding.

"Also, that any tenant on the Abbot's land, in the lands of Kilpatrick in the Lennox, who, without the Abbot's leave specially asked and obtained, shall *haldin nychburis* and plow to his neighbour after the old *stent*, as use and custom requires, shall forfeit his holding.

"Also, the other payments of the defaulters of the aforesaid points, is one hundred shillings to the Abbot, unrecoverable, to be raised, and the holdings of the defaulters to be in the Abbot's—*(sic)*

"Also, in addition to these, all other statutes and styles, use and wont, anent greenwood, guld and swine, and other matters of neighbourship, shall be held binding as required by law.

"Also, it is ordered that each tenant dwelling within the Abbot's lands of the Lennox, or any other lands of the Abbot's, shall help and assist each other to *pound* strange cattle and goods that intrude to destroy or occupy the Abbot's land, and he that does not come to help his neighbour when he is warned, and does not assist him to pound strange cattle, his holding shall be in the Abbot's hand.

It will be seen from these regulations that the tenants of the Monastery were strictly looked after.

## CHAPTER XVII.

### Abbot Robert.

1498—1525.

> The monarch joy'd in banquet bower;
> But 'mid his mirth, 'twas often strange
> How suddenly his cheer would change,
> His look o'ercast and lower,
> If in a sudden turn he felt
> The pressure of his iron belt
> That bound his breast in penance pain
> In memory of his father slain.
>
> —*Scott.*

IN the same year in which Abbot George transferred the mitre to his nephew, there died within the Abbey precincts one who had been famous enough in his time, and who in the world had led a troubled and stormy life, under the name of John, Earl of Ross, Lord of the Isles. When the King visited the Monastery he saw the old warrior in the black Benedictine dress, and must have looked upon him with interest, for he had given the reigning family much trouble in his day. The island lord was born a conspirator. In the time of the King's grandfather, when but a boy, he had entered into an alliance with certain seditious nobles,* and had broken into open rebellion, seizing the Royal castle of Urquhart, Inverness-shire, and burning the stronghold of Ruthven in Badenoch,—the ruins of which the traveller sees as he speeds along the Northern railway, near the village of Kingussie. Later on, the chief sent

* The Earls of Douglas and Crawford, 1449.

from his island territories a fleet of a hundred galleys, manned by five thousand of his vassals, which made a raid along the western coast of Scotland, reaching the Firth of Clyde, levying black mail in Bute, and wasting the islands of Cumbrae and Arran with fire and sword.* After a period of strife he laid down his arms and sought the Royal mercy, which was extended to him, and to prove his gratitude he attended at the siege of Roxburgh with a contingent of wild highlanders to support the King.† Two years later he again girded on his armour against his Sovereign. He proclaimed himself King of the Hebrides; and as an independent potentate, entered into alliance with the English King Edward, sending his Ambassadors to Westminster, and making an agreement with the English monarch for a joint invasion of Scotland, after the conquest of which he was to be rewarded with a gift of the northern part of the kingdom, "to the Scots water or Frith of Forth."‡ This attempt ended in failure, and the insurgent chieftain appeared a second time before his Sovereign at Edinburgh in 1476, and a second time received the Royal pardon, though he was deprived of the Earldom of Ross and the territories of Knapdale and Cantire. Six years afterwards he again renewed secret negotiations with England,§ and forfeiture was denounced against him in the vigorous reign of James the Fourth. His lordship of the Isles was taken from him, and his wild territories reduced to order. A third time he petitioned for and obtained the Royal pardon,|| but this time he was forbidden to return again to the regions which he had troubled. The tourist who, in the bright summer time is carried pleasantly through the Sound of Mull, sees the ruined walls of his castle of Ardtornish upon a rock overhanging the sea. It had long been the abode of this proud island lord and of his forefathers, where he had ruled like a prince, and maintained a barbaric sovereignty. Thither he was never to come back. One of his old friends, with whom he had entered into more than one conspiracy, the Earl of Douglas, had been condemned to pass the evening of his life in the convent of Lindores,¶ and the Lord of the Isles was

* Tytler, Vol. II., p. 166. † Tytler, A.D. 1460, Vol. II., p. 185.

‡ Burton's Hist. of Scot., Vol. III., p. 3.

§ Scott's Hist. of Scot. || 1494, Tytler.

¶ Lindores Abbey, by Mr. Laing, p. 113.

sent in like manner to Paisley.* "He that can do no better," said the aged Earl in the bitterness of his soul, as he heard his sentence, "must needs be a monk." His old ally, John of the Isles, would feel the same as he laid aside for ever his coat of mail, and assumed the monkish cowl. In the Paisley cloister he perhaps found the peace and rest to which he had been long a stranger. He did not survive his confinement many years. In 1498 he died† and was buried, not like his forefathers in St. Oran's aisle in Iona, but in the choir of Paisley, and, at his own request, beside the tomb of King Robert the Third, one who, like himself, had tasted the bitterness of disappointment, and had closed life amid deepening shadows.

Abbot Robert, like his uncle, carried on the extension of the newly founded Burgh of Paisley, and reaped his reward in various important benefactions to the Monastery from the citizens. Altars were erected by several burgesses in the nave of the Abbey, which, like that of other abbey churches, was set apart for the use of parishioners, the monks retaining the choir for their own use.‡ There were altars to Our Lady, St. Peter, St. James, and St. Nicholas, St. Katherine, St. Ninian, St. Anne, and St. Rocques.§ These altars were well endowed, || and special priests were appointed to officiate at them. One burgess, however, outdid all his fellow townsmen by erecting not only an altar but a chapel to the patron Saint of the Abbey, with whom he joined in his dedication the Saint of Iona, St. Columba. This generous benefactor was James Crawfurd of Kylwynet, a burgess of Paisley, and friend of Abbot George. The townsman, with his wife, Elizabeth Galbraith, devoted his savings to this pious purpose.¶ The charter states that they were "moved by a desire of pious devotion, and for the increase of divine worship." The new chapel was "built by the granters from their own industry in praise and honour of Almighty God, and Son, and Holy Spirit, the glorious Virgin and Mother

* Donald Gregory's History of the Western Highlands and Islands, Edinburgh, 1863, p. 58.

† Reg. de Pas., Introduction. ‡ Lindores Abbey, p. 188.

§ There was a chapel to this Saint in the west of the town, in the Broomlands, which had "twa aikes of ground." || The endowment charters are in the town chest of Paisley.

¶ An admirable paper on St. Mirin's Chapel, read before the Glasgow Archaeological Society, has been published by David Semple, F.S.A., to which I have been indebted for my facts.

Mary and the blessed Peter and Paul the Apostles, and in honour of all saints; also, for the souls of that excellent deceased Prince James, King of Scots, and likewise for our illustrious Prince, King James the Fourth, and their predecessors and successors; and for the souls of them, the said James and Elizabeth, and Master Archibald Crawfurd, vicar of Erskeyne, and for the souls of all their friends, benefactors, ancestors, and successors, and the salvation of all the faithful dead." For the endowment of the Chapel, altar, and chaplain, they grant all their lands of Seedhill, "near the mill of the Lord Abbot," the outfield land of Seidhill, and the lands of Welmedow, with pertinents. The bailies of the town were made patrons of the chapel, with right to present a chaplain on the death of the founders; and unless they made a presentation within twenty days after a vacancy, the right to do so devolved on the Prior and Convent. If such a person could be found qualified, the chaplain was to be a Paisley man. He was to reside at the chapel and give daily attendance to perform masses for the welfare of the souls of those mentioned in the narrative of the mortification, and if he absented himself for fifteen days without leave, the patrons could dismiss him. The handing over of the mortification to the patrons took place on the 21st July, 1499, in the Council Chambers of the town house. It was a great day in the new formed burgh. All the inhabitants were present, and the two bailies,—the first dignitaries of that name in Paisley,—with the town clerk,* were present in all the pomp of civic dignity. James Crawford was the first of Paisley's many sons who have endowed the town of their adoption with the savings of their industry. The choice of a native to be chaplain indicates his love for the burgh; and when he died, in the same year as that in which he made his bequest, many of the citizens would comply with the request which is still inscribed on his tombstone in the nave of the Abbey, "*orate pro anima ejus.*"

The chapel appears to have been finished before James Crawford drew up his charter of endowment, for in the year following that on which it is dated we find Abbot Robert taking, by notary public, an appeal to the

* The names of these worthies were Alan Stewart and Stephen Ness, bailies, and William Stewart, town-clerk.

Pope in the chapel of St. Mirin against his namesake Robert, the Archbishop of Glasgow. The Archbishop, like his predecessors, was at war with the Abbot, for the Cathedral and the Abbey were seldom at peace. The prelate had sequestered the fruits of the Abbey churches, he had denied the monks "letters of justice" against detainers of their tithes, he had interfered with them and their monks, notwithstanding their acknowledged exemption from his jurisdiction. He had thus injured them greatly, and had contemned the Apostolic See. Abbot Robert therefore appealed against him to the Pope, though with what measure of success we are not told. The Abbot was in conflict with another neighbouring magnate besides his ordinary. This was Sir John Ross of Halkhead, a well-known knight in his day, and ancestor of a family who have done well by their country.* He came into violent collision with the Church. With three of his followers,† he "unjustly occupied and laboured the lands of Thornle, lying in the parish of Paisley, and withheld from the Abbey its tiends—sixteen bolls of meal from the lands of Halkhead, and twelve bolls of meal and two of flour from Thornle.‡ The day was when the thunders of the Church would have been launched at the recusant knight, but these thunders were beginning to be somewhat lightly esteemed—the Abbot therefore applied to the "secular arm," and raised an action against Sir John, and, as we hear nothing further of the matter, it is probable the knight of Halkhead made peace with his neighbour the Abbot. A few years after his dispute with the Abbot he lay with many another brave man among the heaped up slain on Flodden Field.

The King again made a pilgrimage to Whithorn in 1504, and was entertained by the Abbot on his return. No Scotch King ever travelled more through his dominions. Through the mountains of Perthshire, among the Western Islands, from Berwick-on-Tweed to Tain in Ross-shire he was well-known; and wherever he went he was generously received. He often visited the monasteries, and generally dedicated part of Lent to strict retreat from the world, when constant

* The family of the Earls of Glasgow.

† William Glenny, John Dunlop, and John Whiteford.

‡ The meal is valued at six shillings and eightpence per boll—the flour at eight shillings. This was in 1503.

prayer, fasting, and acts of penance were unsparingly employed to expiate the crime which afflicted his conscience. He was often at the shrine of St. Ninian. He made a pilgrimage to that of St. Duthac in Ross-shire,* and with the same object came to that of St. Mirin at Paisley. After the fashion of pilgrims of that time, he mingled a certain amount of dissipation with his devotion. The records of his treasurer are full of payments to "harpers, fithelaris, and lutaris." At one time, we have nine shillings given to "the brokin-backit fitular of Sanct Androis;" at another payments are made "to the maddins of Forres that dansit to the King."† Abbot Robert was able to offer him some entertainment on his visit to Paisley. Lord Sempill, the Sheriff of the County, was there to meet him, and brought with him John Haislet,‡ his famous minstrel. His performances pleased the King, for he was honoured with a gratuity which is duly recorded in the treasurer's books. "1504. *Item* the last day of King in Paysley, to Lord Sempille's harper, xiiijs."

Two years after this, in 1507, the King was back again at the Abbey, this time accompanied by his Queen, Margaret, daughter of Henry VII. She had borne him a son on the 21st February, and being dangerously ill after her delivery, the King, in performance of a vow which he had made during her illness, went on foot to St. Ninian's Church at Whithorn.§ On this occasion he does not appear to have come to Paisley; but in July of the same year both he and his Queen together made a pilgrimage to the Galloway shrine, to offer thanks for her recovery.|| On his way going and coming he tarried at Paisley, as we learn from the faithful treasurer's books. Buildings were in progress at the Monastery, and the King inspected them and gave a gratuity to the masons—"1507, Item, IX day of July, to ane man to pass fra Paslay to Dumbartane with ane letter to Andro Bertoun, ijs.—Item, to the masonis in drink-silver, xxiijs."¶

On their return, the Royal pair stayed in the Monastery for eight days, and attended the religious services of the church. One of the days of

* This was in 1505. † Chamberlain Accounts.

‡ Second Supplement to Saint Mirin, by David Semple, F.S.A.

§ Balfour's Annals, Vol. I., p. 228. || Ibid.

¶ Sup. to Saint Mirin, by D. Semple, F.S.A.

their visit was the festival of St. Anne. They accordingly visited the altar newly founded in her honour, and gave an offering to the priest, a Sir Andrew Makbrek, to give to the poor. Nearly all the entries in the treasurer's book during this visit relate to religious observances.

| | | |
|---|---|---|
| 1507. | Item, the 21st day of Julij in Pasley to the offerand to the reliques, | xiiijs |
| | Item, that day to the Kingis offerand to ane priest's first mes in Pasley, | xxiiijs |
| | Item, to the Kingis offerand at the hie mes, | xiiijs |
| | Item, xxiiij day of Julij to the workmen in Pasley in drink silver, | xiiijs |
| | Item, the xxvi day of Julij in Pasley to Schir Andro Makbrek, to dispone, | iijs |
| | Item, that day, Saint Anne's day, to the Kingis offerand at the mes, | xiiijs |
| | Item, to the Kingis offerand on the bred to Sanct Anne's lycht, | xiiijs |

Abbot Robert seems to have remained pretty closely at Paisley, looking after the affairs of his Abbey, during the first part of his tenure of office. His name appears in various business documents. He feus ground in the Burgh of Paisley, executes various deeds regarding the Abbey property,* and, among other things, takes possession (whether by purchase or by gift is not stated) of three houses in Glasgow,—two lying on the west, and one on the east of the highway leading from the Cathedral to the Cross.† But a short time after the calamity at Flodden we get glimpses of him as a politician, and a leader in all the political intrigues of that troubled time.‡ The Abbot is no longer the "father of his monks," and the Prior has to look after them and their duties.

Renfrewshire, like the rest of Scotland, suffered heavily at Flodden Field, and many of her nobles found a grave by the banks of the Till,

> "When shivered was fair Scotland's spear,
> And broken was her shield.—*Marmion.*

The gloom which overspread the land would be intensely felt by the inmates of the Abbey where the chivalrous King was well known, and where his presence and that of his courtiers had so often brightened the life of the cloister. In October of the year of Flodden a Parliament was called to consider what was to be done. Few of the nobility were there,

* Saint Mirin, by D. Semple, F.S.A. Reg. de Pas., p. 430-431.

† Reg. de Pas., p. 394.

‡ May 15, 1515, he witnesses a treaty of James V.

for most of them had been slain, and the gathering consisted chiefly of the clergy. Abbot Robert was among them.* Then there followed that incessant warfare between contending factions which desolated Scotland. In 1524 we get a view of the sad state of the country from the letters of English ambassadors and English spies, and when the curtain is lifted, we find Abbot Robert a prominent figure at Court, one of the "most venerable and saddest" counsellers. He was evidently a man of mark, and Norfolk writes to the English Ambassador, Dr. Magnus, to make the most of him. "In anywise," he writes, "falle in famyliarte with the Abbot of Paslaye, by whom ye shall know most of the secrets; but in anywise speak nothing to him of the Bishop of St. Andrews, for he doth not love him."† Magnus obeys his orders, and was in close relations with the Abbot, who supported the English interest. We get glimpses in the State papers of a certain George Shaw, "a near kindsman of the Abbot," whose duty it was to win him over, and who received payment for his services. Won over he was, and he is constantly mentioned as a man whose influence could be calculated on for the English interests. Magnus speaks of him in a letter as one of those Scots who was "a right good Englishman," and a spy, writes his master, that "The Abbot of Pasley beryth very good mynd unto your grace, by whom I have knolege partely what is done dayly in the Council." He seems to have occupied a good position at court, and to have been tutor to the young King. He and his close friend, the Abbot of Holyrood, write a joint letter to Lord Norfolk giving an account of the Prince to the English Earl, "our maister is in gude heill and prosperity, and grows ane fair Prince, loving to God, not doubting that he is inspired by grace to all virtue and honour that should pertain to ane noble Prince, and, as we trust, shall be intending to nourish and authorise *pece* and justice in his realm. We shall await and attend contynuallie upon his service, for we give little estimation to ony uther things." They then offer to do anything they are able for their correspondent, "to the utmost of our power. Beseeching almychti God and our blessed Lady to conserve you at your noble

* Acts of Parliament, Index.

† Cot. MSS., Caligula 8 VII., fo. 85, Norfolk to Magnus. The whole of the State Papers referring to Abbot Shaw are in the Appendix.

heartis desire."* So wrote Abbot Robert, like many another man at that sad court, where bribery and corruption held sway, involved in the toils of intrigue and deceit which were spread around. He made enemies, politic though he was. In the December of 1524, while hanging on at Court, he received ominous notice that the two powerful Earls —Angus and Lennox—intended to keep their Christmas in his Monastery at Paisley. Their proposed visit was certainly a strain upon the hospitality of the Convent, as they were to be accompanied by two hundred men. In his distress at this threatened invasion of the Abbey, he betook himself for help to his friend, Dr. Magnus, the English Ambassador. "The good Abbot of Pasley," † Magnus wrote to Cardinal Wolsey, then in the height of his power, "of late shewed unto me he was likely to sustyne gret hurte and damage, both to himself and his Monastery, by the said two earls, if remedy were not founden in tyme convenient, for as he shewed to me the said two earls intended to keep their Christmas in his house, and to use everything there at their liberty and pleasure, both for horse and man, to the number of two hundred persons, and, therefore, desired me to write for him to the said Earl of Angwisch, and so I did." The letter of Magnus to the earl has been found among the repositories of the State Paper office.‡ "Mine own good lorde," he says, "full heartely I recommend me unto your lordship, and where, among other things, it is reported here that ye and my Lord Lennox, with your company and servants attending upon you, do use the house and Monastery of Pasley, as if the same were your own, and intend so to continue, and to use it for a season to the great hurt and hynderance of the said Monastery, so that the monks and brethren of that house, with good and convenient hospitality, cannot nor may be maintained as to the same it doth of right appertain. I, your assured friend and good lover, do marvell thereof, considering, as I know of truth, how well and how lovingly the Abbot of that Monastery beareth his special and singular good mind and person to your good lordship, and to my said Lord of Lennox. Insomuch as his lordship hath sustained no little blame for

* State Papers, Scot., Henry VIII., Vol. II., No. 69, Oct. 5, 1624.

† Ibid., No. 138.

‡ State papers, Scotland, Henry VIII., Vol. II., No. 86.

both your causes, and is, and will be content that both your lordships shall have your pleasure in his Monastery as any lords in all Scotland, ye both shall be welcome to that house, using it as his friends and loving lordis in good and reasonable manner." The invasion that threatened the Abbey never took place, and the monks, it would appear, escaped all intrusion from the stalwart troopers of the two earls, for Angus wrote the English Ambassador in reply to his remonstrance, that he intended to spend his Christmas with the Earl of Lennox, and would do nothing to the displeasure of "my Lord of Paisley," and that nothing but what he might wish would be done either to his place or himself.* The brethren thus enjoyed their Christmas festivities in peace.

Abbot Robert desired, like most other Scotch courtiers, some reward for his services; and Hals, the English spy, writes to Norfolk, "The Abbot of Paisley hath made meanings unto me, not by his own speech, but by others, to write unto your grace to be good lord unto him." What the Abbot sought by his hints through friends was the office which his uncle had held, that of treasurer, but better promotion was in store for him. The Bishopric of Moray became vacant, and those in power arranged that he should be promoted to it.

A good deal of "wire-pulling" was needed before this arrangement could be carried into effect. The Earl of Arran had a natural son, John Hamilton, who had entered the Church as a monk of Kilwinning,† and whom Magnus speaks of with contempt as "a yonge thing." The Earl, then in high favour with the Queen,—who really had at the time the disposal of the Church benefices,—wished the Bishopric for this son. The Queen could not pass over old Abbot Robert, and got him appointed to the See of Moray, and Hamilton to the Abbey of Paisley. The Pope's approval had to be obtained to both these appointments, and there seemed some likelihood that Hamilton's at least would come to nothing, as the ratification did not arrive at once from the Pope. Abbot Robert got alarmed at the delay, and wrote to Cardinal Wolsey on 8th May, 1524, a very humble letter, beseeching him to do the best he

* State Papers, Scotland, Henry VIII., Vol. II., No. 87.

† See King James V.'s letter in Appendix.

could for him.* He says that the King of England's ambassadors at the Court of Rome had solicited the Pope's Holiness for his promotion to the Bishopric of Moray according to his humble prayer, "not the less because that the Kingis Hienes, my master, hes writen for the promotion of a son of the Earl of Arran to my Abbasy of Paslay. He being of tender age and bastard, our holy fader the Pope deferris to promise me to the said bishoprick. Howbeit the impediments rising on the part of the said Erle's son ouch not to be reason to differ my cause." The anxious Abbot then asks the Cardinal's interest with the Pope for "expeditione of his mater." Apparently this appeal produced no effect, and the summer passed away and the new year opened and Robert was still Abbot of Paisley. Those interested got alarmed,—King James V. himself wrote a letter to the Pope, in which, with very limping latinity, he states how he had ventured to nominate to the See of Moray one "of mature years, exemplary life, and integrity of manners, Robert Schawe, for many years Abbot in the Monastery of Paisley, of the Order of Clugny," and also "John Hamylton, monk of the Order of the blessed Benedict in the Monastery of Kylwinning, natural son of our dearest cousin, James, Earl of Arran, to the Abbacy of Paisley," and asks the sanction of these appointments from his Holiness. He also wrote Henry VII., a few days afterwards, a long letter on the same subject, asking him to write to the Pope,† and use his influence to further the appointments, which the King immediately did.‡ Perhaps the best friend the Abbot had was Dr. Magnus, who, at the same time, wrote to Cardinal Wolsey. Of the promotion of Hamilton he says nothing, but he pleads very earnestly the cause of Abbot Robert. "In my most humble and lowly manner," he says, "I beseech your grace to be good and gracious towards the advancement of the said Abbot's causes: At my repairing into these parts, my Lord of Norfolk advised me to lean to his counsail, and so I have done ever since my coming hither, and have found not only gret comfort of him at all times, but also he hath been the most forward of any man to follow the King's high pleasure, and joins in such

* Cot. MSS., Caligula B 1, p. 82. Robert, Abbot of Paisley, to Wolsey, dated 8th May, 1524.

† See Appendix. ‡ See King Henry's letter in Appendix.

causes as have concerned the weal and safety of the young King; wherefore I account myself bound to declare and shew unto your grace the goodness of the said Abbot." This letter was probably the "best spoke" in the Abbot's wheel. John Clerk, an agent of Wolsey at Rome, acknowledges the King's letters regarding the Bishopric of Moray and the Abbey of Paisley,* and the appointments were soon after ratified by the Pope. That of Hamilton was most scandalous, and it is no wonder his Holiness hesitated before giving his approval; but the interest of two Kings and his faithful Cardinal prevailed, the evil was done, and it bore terrible fruit to the Church that allowed it. Abbot Robert was received in the cathedral of his northern diocese on the 19th October, 1525, accompanied by Robert Mortoun, a monk of Paisley,† and the mitre of our Abbey was placed on the head of the "yonge thing"—as Magnus calls him—a scandal almost sufficient to have brought from the dead the pious Abbots of former days. It was only one of many similar deeds of shame that were being enacted in the Scottish Church.

* See Appendix.

† Registrum Moraviensis.—Bannatyne Club.

## CHAPTER XVIII.

### Abbot John Hamilton.

1525—1547.

> Ebbed, far away from prior and priest,
> The life that day by day increased ;
> From kirk and choir ebbed far away
> The thought that gathered day by day ;
> And round the altars drew
> A weak, unlettered crew.
>
> *W. C. Smith.*

THE youthful Monk of Kilwinning, whose appointment to the Abbacy of Paisley scandalised Magnus, the English Ambassador, seems to have had nothing against him but his tender age. He was a lad of virtue and of learning, and even John Knox allows him to have had in his youth a reputation for piety and purity of life which was not always associated with ecclesiastics of that period.* At the time when he assumed the mitre, Paisley was famed throughout the kingdom as a place of pilgrimage and devotion. It was then one of the four great places of pilgrimage in Scotland, and shared that honour with Melrose, Scone, and Dundee.† The shrine of St. Mirin and Our Ladye of Paisley were held in high esteem by the devout, and in the Chamberlain's Accounts of James V. there is a disbursement to "thirteen chaplains to say mess afor oure Ladye of Paislay."‡ The youthful head of the Abbey seems at this time to have

* John Knox, Hist., Vol. I., Wodrow Society, page 106.

† Chambers' Domestic Annals, Vol. I., p. 27.

‡ Chamberlain's Accounts in Pitcairn's Criminal Trials.

taken little interest in its affairs. In October, 1525, Alexander Walcar, claustral prior of the Monastery, acts as his depute in letting the Abbey lands.* Four years after his appointment, the Abbot constituted certain noblemen and others his procurators, giving them full power for holding courts, levying rents, inflicting fines, and carrying on the management of the temporalities.† The names of these commissioners are not given in the deed of appointment, but the transference of authority to them indicates that the Abbot himself hardly pretended to rule. In 1535 his name appears in the Parliament which prohibited the works of the great heretic Luther from being introduced into Scotland, and forbade all discussion of the new opinions except with a view to prove their falsehood. In 1540 he was again in Parliament. The new doctrines were beginning to spread. Several heretics had been burned. The English Court was doing everything possible to promulgate the Reformed opinions in Scotland, and it took all the power of King and Parliament to repress them.‡ They seemed, however, for a time to be successful in staying the growth of heresy. The Church was seemingly as powerful as ever; and it was with little idea of any impending change that the Abbot left Scotland for France—it is said to study at the University of Paris,§ leaving the Abbey under the government of the Prior.

The Abbot remained abroad for three years, during which great changes took place in Scotland. When he returned James V. was dead. The Earl of Arran, the brother of the Abbot, was Governor of the Kingdom. The principles of Protestantism were in the ascendant. The Governor was favourable to the new views, and entertained in his house two Protestant preachers. Cardinal Beaton was in disgrace. The Bible in the vulgar tongue was permitted by Parliament to be read by the common people, and the way to obtain favour at Court was to profess reformed opinions. The coming home of the Abbot of Paisley was watched by the Church party and their opponents with the greatest interest. There was much speculation as to the part he would take. Henry VIII. received him graciously at his Court as he passed through England, and bestowed on

* On 21st April, 1535, he signs leases at Paisley as Abbot.

† Reg. de Pas., p. 435, dated 20th Jan., 1529. See Rental, in Appendix.

‡ Pitcairn's Criminal Trials, p. 278. § Crawford's "Officers of State."

him many presents,* seeking to bind him to his interest and that of the Reformation party. It was the custom of that Monarch to attach men to him by bribes, and much of the spoil of the English monasteries went in that way. The Abbot was accompanied by David Panter, a distinguished ecclesiastic, afterwards Bishop of Ross; and John Knox tells what deep interest they excited on their return.† "The brut‡ of the learning of the two, and their honest lyff, and of thare fervency and uprightness in religion, was such that great esperance thare was that their presence should have been comfortable to the Kirk of God. For it was constantly affirmed of them that without delay the one and the other of thame wold occupye the pulpit and trewly preach Jesus Christ."§ These hopes were disappointed. The Abbot, with great energy, threw himself into the opposite interest, and became the great champion of the Church. His presence was soon felt at his brother's Court. The two Protestant preachers were dismissed. The Governor recanted his heretical opinions, and became reconciled to the Cardinal. The French party, which was the party of the Church, became triumphant, and what seemed to be a failing cause appeared to have new vigour suddenly infused into it. The famous historian whom we have quoted uses very strong language in speaking of the Abbot's influence. He calls him a hypocrite. He and his friends are represented as actuated by the lowest motives, "hastening to their prey like ravens to carrion." "He led his brother so far from God that he falsified his promise, and dipt his hands in the blood of the sancts of God, and these were the first fruits of the Abbot of Paslaye, his godliness and learning." It is questionable whether this vituperation by Knox is deserved. Hamilton was a staunch Catholic, brought up in all the traditions of the Church, and his residence in France naturally strengthened his attachments. He appears from the first never to have had any sympathy with the Reformers, and there seems no reason to believe that

* 1543.—"Johne Hamiltone, Abbot of Paisley, the Regent's brother, who had been long in France following his studies, returns home through England, and is made very welcome by King Henry, and is dismissed with rich propyns."—Balfour, Vol. I., p. 278.

† Hamilton returned between the 2d and 15th April, 1543. ‡ Report.

§ Knox Hist., Wod. Ed., Vol. I., p. 106.

in the course he pursued he was actuated by any sordid motive such as is attributed to him by his opponents. He was certainly no hypocrite.

All the historians of the time speak of the Abbot, and the prominent position he occupied at Court. Sir Ralph Sadler, the English Ambassador, notices him in his letters again and again as the leading spirit of the French party, and the trusted counsellor of the Regent. "Ever since his brother the Abbot of Paisley came home he hath been chiefly ruled and counselled by him, who, they assure me, is altogether at the cast of France, and the Cardinal's great friend, and whatsoever they do mind with the Governor to-day the Abbot of Paisley changeth him in the same on to-morrow."* So wrote Sadler in the year of the Abbot's return. When not at Court, the Abbot resided in his Abbey at Paisley, where on more than one occasion he entertained his brother the Governor, several of whose letters and commissions are dated from the Monastery.† The Abbot, like many of his predecessors, did something for the architecture of the church. He was passionately fond of building,‡ but his attempt at Paisley was not so successful as his subsequent efforts of a similar kind. He built a tower to the church at immense expense, but the foundations not being secure, the structure, when hardly finished, fell by its own weight.§ Its fall was an omen of coming troubles, and it is doubtful whether it was ever built up again.

The Abbot was made, by his brother, Keeper of the Privy Seal in the year of his return from abroad, and was soon after promoted to the office of Lord High Treasurer for Scotland, in room of Kirkcaldy of Grange, a distinguished friend of the Reformation. High honour was in store for him in Church as well as State. The Bishopric of Dunkeld became vacant in 1543-4,‖ and the Abbot was appointed to it by his brother, acting for the young Queen. He continued to be styled by his old title of Abbot of Paisley. Notwithstanding his elevation he retained his Abbey; and it is doubtful whether he ever was

* Sadler's State Papers, p. 145.

† Report on Historical Manuscripts. Argyle MSS., 4th Report, p. 489.

‡ A catalogue of his erections in Fifeshire is given in M'Farlane's Genealogical Collections MSS., Vol. I., Advocates Library.

§ Lesley's History of Scotland, see Chap. XX.

‖ Keith.

installed in his northern diocese. In 1546 he is styled Abbot of Paisley in the Acts of Parliament. A certain Robert Crichton, Provost of St. Giles, claimed the Bishopric in virtue of a decree of the Pope, and the Abbot entered into litigation with him, and successfully vindicated his own appointment.* About this time he was often at Paisley. The Reformation principles were taking firm hold in the west, and the presence of the champion of the Church was greatly needed there. An English army was threatening the borders. The Earl of Glencairn was using his powerful influence in Ayrshire on the side of the reformers, and the head of the house of Lennox,—the family which had in old days befriended the Abbey,—had gone over to the enemy.† The monks and their possessions were in great peril : at any moment their lands might be invaded, and their Church and Monastery given to the flames. They were actually threatened by their enemies, and would have suffered but for the aid of the Master of Sempill who interfered for their protection. The young noble was in consequence appointed in 1545 bailie and justiciary over the whole lands of the Abbey.‡ The Charter of his appointment begins by a reference to the troubles of the time, which is somewhat striking. "In these days," it says, "the wickedness of men so increases that nothing gives them greater delight than to invade the possessions of the monks, and to overturn their monasteries, nor had

* Index to Acts of Parliament—" John, the Abbot of Paisley, having been nominated by Queen Mary to the Bishopric of Dunkeld, according to the privilege belonging to the Queen and her predecessors to nominate to vacant Sees, and sent her nomination to the Pope, who, in virtue thereof, granted him the Bishopric, and having been opposed by Robert Crichton, Provost of St. Giles, who produced an alleged decree from the Pope, that the promotion of John was conditional upon his being appointed Bishop of Ross, failing which, he himself was Bishop of Dunkeld, and since the Queen had promoted her secretary, David Panter, to the Bishopric of Ross, this decree declared contrary to the Royal privilege." The Abbot raised an action against his opponent in the Court of Session accusing him of barratry at Rome ; and the defender pled that he was a Churchman, and the Lords only temporal judges. The Abbot, however, was victorious. The dispute was also carried to Rome, and on 8th June, 1546, the Pope, in consistory, referred the cause to the adjudication of certain Cardinals. The decree is given from the Barberini MSS. in Brady's Episcopal Succession, Vol. I., p. 131.

† October 23, 1547, Glencairn writes the Earl of Lennox, that he has managed his affairs so well that nothing is wanting but his presence. All the Barony of Renfrew is his own, except the Sempills. He requests him to come immediately, when they will be ready to pass with him to Glasgow or Paisley.—Papers in State Paper Office.—See Appendix.

‡ Reg. de Pas., Appendix, p. 2.

we ourselves been saved from that disaster but by the aid and assistance of that noble man, Robert Sempill, master of the same, son and apparent heir to Lord William Sempill. The same master bravely defended us, not only from the madness of heretics, but also from the insults of most powerful tyrants, and unless he continues to defend us by his arms, friends, counsel, and assistance, without doubt nothing will soon be saved to us. But so far as we are concerned, nothing must be omitted which tends to our greatest safety, for, according to the old proverb, it is not less a virtue to preserve what we have than to acquire what we have not." The deed goes on to appoint Robert and his heirs bailies of the Abbey at a stipend of three chalders of oatmeal yearly, paid from "our granary," and forty-three shillings and fourpence from our lands of Glen, called *Lie Lochied.* It gave Sempill great power over all the possessions of the Abbey, and he and his family became bound to defend the monks against all their foes, and to see that all the tenants of the Monastery paid their rents and dues regularly to the "chamberlain, grainter, and cellarer." The father of the Master of Sempill also entered into an agreement* to bring the whole power of his family to their aid in time of need, and to see that all the lands and revenues of the Abbey were conserved to their proper owners.

The connection between the Abbot and the family of Sempill was not merely that indicated in the deed of protection. Hamilton, in common with many of the ecclesiastics of the time, had, it is to be feared, given way to profligate habits, and there is little doubt that he kept openly as his concubine the daughter of this Master of Sempill, widow of James Hamilton of Stanehouse, Provost of Edinburgh, who was killed in an affray, by whom he had three sons, who were afterwards legitimised.† The immoral lives of men in his position gave great scandal to many who wished, if possible, to preserve the Church, and furnished too much ground for the satires which were launched by Lindsay and others against the clergy, and for the mocking ballads which were circulated among the common people.

*Reg. de Pas., Appendix, p. 6, "Ane Obligatioun of the Lord Sympill and Robert Sympille, maister of the samyn."

† See Appendix. Gordon's Monasticon, Vol. II., p. 289.

There were other causes besides the evil lives of the priesthood bringing on a great national crisis. On 29th May, 1546, Cardinal Beaton was murdered at St. Andrews, and most important results followed. The struggle between the Church and the Reformers became pronounced, and it became evident that the issue must be the entire subversion of one or the other. In this struggle two men took the lead,—one on either side,—John Knox and John Hamilton, Abbot of Paisley. They become henceforth the great figures in the religious warfare. The one the bold champion of the Reformed opinions, the other bravely, but unsuccessfully, endeavouring to support a failing cause. On the death of his friend the Cardinal, the Abbot at once came to the front. Stewart of Cardonald,* living near Paisley and a friend of the Reformation, seems to have been deputed by the English Government to keep watch on the movements of the Abbot, his neighbour, and his letters are to be seen in the State Paper Office, shewing how well the spy performed the work assigned to him. "The Abbot," he writes on one occasion from Cardonald, "is to go secretlie to France to get the King's consent to the Governor's desire to have the Princess, and to get the red hat to himself to be Cardinal, and the Bishopric of Mirypois in God. He goes immediately and passes at Dunbartane in ane James Howmes' ship, which is lately come in with two English prizes."† The Bishopric of Mirypois in France, to which the laird of Cardonald alludes as the object of the Abbot's ambition, was one of the preferments held by the late Cardinal Beaton. Whether the Abbot made the voyage to France we do not know, but higher dignity was in store for him than the mitre of the French See, and on the 28th November of the year in which his neighbour at Cardonald took so keen an interest in his movements, the Pope, through the influence of the governor, had him appointed Archbishop of St. Andrews, and Primate of Scotland.‡ He still retained the Abbey

* Cardonald is about two miles from the Abbey.

† State Papers, Scotland, Edward VI.—Vol. I., No. 13.

‡ The following is the consistorial decree of his appointment to St. Andrews, with Paisley *in commendam*;—"John Hamilton, Die 28, Nov. 1547, S.D.N, absolvit R.P.D. Johannem Hamiltonum, Episcopum Dunkelden, a vinculo quo ecclesiae Dunkelden, cui tunc prae erat, tenebatur, et ad ecclesiam St. Andreae tunc per obitum bonae memoriae Davidis Beton, St.

along with his See, but henceforth he is known by the title of Archbishop, and he probably never came to Paisley until, in the adversities of his later years, he sought refuge there among the friends of his youth.*

Stephani in Coelio Monte, dum viveret, presbyteri Card. St. Andreae nuncupati extra R.C. defuncti, vacantem transtulit, ipsumque eidem ecclesiae St. Andreae in archiepiscopum praefecit et Pastorem, curam de committendo, cum retentione monasterii de Pasleto Cluniacen. ordinis. Glasguen. dio. cui ex dispensatione apostolica praesse dinoscitur, et cum dispensationibus etiam super defectu natalium, quem de soluto nobili et illustri genere procreato genitus et soluta, aut alias patitur; necnon derogationibus et clausilis opportunis et consuetis. Absolvens, &c. Fructus 3,000 Marcharum. Taxa 600 flor. Barberini."—Brady's Epis. Success. Rome, 1876.

* In 1550 he let the Abbey lands. See Rental, where he is called both Archbishop of St. Andrews, and Abbot of Paisley.

# CHAPTER XIX.

## Dissolution of the Monastery.

1547—1571.

The ruffian band
Came to reform where ne'er they came to pray.

*Keble.*

THE Abbot of Paisley was now Primate of Scotland, and we need only follow his career in so far as it was connected with the Abbey, of which he was superior, and whose revenues he retained. All readers of Scottish history know with what determination he fought the battle of the Church; and though many of the deeds of his life are to be condemned, we cannot but admire the bravery of the man. His primacy, like that of his predecessor, was marked by the persecution of those who held the new opinions. Toleration was then a virtue unknown. Two heretics were with his sanction condemned to be burnt,* one a decrepit priest of the name of Mill, eighty-two years of age. The Archbishop attempted most energetically a reformation of abuses in the Church, and presided at more than one council of the clergy in which strict measures were passed for making the priesthood more zealous and learned, and in which their immoralities were censured and denounced in the strongest terms. He sanctioned the publication of a Catechism, and is even supposed to have compiled it himself. It is written in the Scottish vernacular, setting

* Adam Wallace was burned on the Castlehill of Edinburgh in 1551, shortly after the Abbot's elevation. Walter Mill in 1552.

forth the doctrines of the Church, for the instruction of the common people, and was to be read to them before High Mass, when there was no sermon, and the clergy were enjoined to exercise themselves daily in reading it, lest their stammering or breaking down might excite the jeers of the people. The Archbishop felt that the only hope for the Church lay in a revival of learning and energy among the clergy. He completed St. Mary's College at St. Andrews, and endowed it largely from the revenues of his See, and he ordained that each of the monasteries should send at least one of their members to the University, setting apart some of their churches for the students' maintenance. The Abbey sent a student to Glasgow, and the tithes of Kilmalcolm were assigned for his support.* All the endeavours of the Primate failed to turn the tide that was setting in. The new opinions were spreading everywhere. The clergy continued as immoral as before. The Archbishop himself set them a bad example, and many of them, it is asserted, finding the new regulations disagreeable, especially those that enjoined the putting away of harlots, abandoned the Church, and went over, in name at least, to the party of the reformers.† In 1553, the Archbishop resigned the Abbacy of Paisley to his nephew, Claud Hamilton, a child of ten.‡ This deed was sanctioned by a Bull of the Pope, Julius III., in which the boy's age is said to be fourteen.§ After deducting a fourth of the revenues of the Abbey, if he had a separate establishment, and a third if he lived in the Monastery, for the upholding of the fabric, the purchase of ornaments, or for charity to the poor, the fortunate youth was to be at liberty to dispose of the surplus. The Archbishop was to administer the temporal and spiritual concerns of the Abbey until his nephew reached his twenty-third year. If the Prelate died before that time, the Claustral Prior was to take charge of these. The whole revenues are valued at 600 golden florins in the Roman

* See Robertson's "Statuta" (Ban. Club) for a full account of the Archbishop's endeavours to stay the progress of heresy.

† Leslie, Bishop of Ross.

‡ He retained the title of Abbot, for in a charter of 1558 he is still called Abbas de Pasleto.—See Gordon's Monasticon, Vol. II., pr 286.

§ Introduction to the Chartulary. The Bull of the Pope, which we give in the Appendix, is dated 9th December, 1553.

Camera. All these were made over to the Commendator, who was warned to be careful that neither the splendour of the divine worship, nor the number of the monks should suffer any diminution. The boy is addressed as "clerico," and must have been in some of the minor orders. All the good things are bestowed on him on the petition of "our beloved son, the Duke of Chastellerault, Regent of the Kingdom, and guardian of our beloved daughter in Christ, that illustrious minor, Mary Queen of Scots, by whom your moral life and other qualifications have been highly extolled to us." It was a curious transaction. The Archbishop probably foresaw that the evil day might not be far off, and that, by the Abbey being in lay hands, something might be saved from the general ruin.* Whether he did so or not, he shewed no trace of fear, though the storm soon began to rage wildly around him. His Abbey of Paisley was attacked by men of Lennox,† a district which had become Protestant; Knox was thundering against the Church; monasteries were being burned; the Lords of the Congregation were in arms; but Hamilton maintained a determined front. When Knox threatened to preach in St. Andrews, the Archbishop sent him word, by Robert Colville of Cleish, "that in case he presented himself at the preaching place in his town and principal church, he should gar him be saluted by a dosane of culverings, quherof the most part should light upon his nose."‡ The Reformer persisted despite this threat, and the Archbishop had to give way. This was in 1559. In the same year the reformers appear to have again visited the Abbey. Sadler, the English Ambassador, writes that he had been told by one Whitelaw that "they had suppressed the Abbeys of Paslowe, Kilwinning, and Dunfermling, and burnt all the ymages and ydolls and popish stuff in the same."§ What this meant we know well. It has been described by Sir Walter

* See Tytler, Vol. II., p. 159. This practice of saving something from the wreck became afterwards very general.

† On the 26th July, 1555, Mat. Stewart, Barscube, and others, twelve persons in all, came to the Monastery of Paslay, by way of *hames suken*, and there invaded John Hamilton, son of John Hamilton of Ferguslie, grainter of Paslay, for his slaughter, and mutilating his arms, and sundry other crimes.—Pitcairn's Criminal Trials, Vol. I., p. 382.

‡ Knox Hist., Wodrow Society, Vol. I., p. 348.

§ Sadler, Vol. I., p. 468. The date of this letter is 29th September, 1559.

Scott with his wonderful power.* "They fumigated the church with burnt wool and feathers instead of incense, put foul water into the holy water basins; they sung ludicrous and indecent parodies to the tunes of church hymns; they violated whatever vestments belonging to the Abbey they could lay their hands upon; and playing every freak which the whim of the moment could suggest to their wild caprice. At length they fell to more lasting deeds of demolition, pulled down and destroyed carved woodwork, dashed out the painted windows, and in their vigorous search after sculpture dedicated to idolatry, began to destroy what ornaments yet remained entire upon the tombs and around the cornices of the pillars." So the great master brings the scene on that autumn day at Paisley before us. The adornments of the church were broken down; the treasures of Thomas Tervas despoiled; the tombs of kings broken, and destroyed as idols, and the peaceful brotherhood scattered. Who the invaders were we do not know. They were probably from Ayrshire or the Lennox. The people of Paisley, who clung tenaciously to the old faith, must have seen the devastation with sorrow. The Sempills do not appear to have come to the rescue. They soon after went over to the successful party, hoping, like too many of their order, to get their reward in the spoil of the Church lands.

On 17th August, 1560, Parliament adopted the Confession of Knox as expressing the religion of the land, and on the 24th of the same month, the Pope's jurisdiction was abolished. To say or hear mass was made a criminal offence,—on the first occasion, to be punished with confiscation of goods, on the second with banishment, and on the third with death. Toleration was no part of the reformed doctrine any more than of the Catholic. The reformers then proceeded to draw up a scheme for the constitution and government of the Church, to be set up on the ruins of the old. It is embodied in the First Book of Discipline, and an ecclesiastical system more unlike that which preceded it could scarcely be imagined. The Archbishop was present in the Parliament which accepted the Confession, but seeing, probably, that opposition was useless, he said little. There was an overwhelming majority

* "Abbot," chap. xiv.

arrayed against him, who were prepared to adopt the most violent measures to obtain success. The Archbishop had been, it is supposed, threatened with death if he offered opposition. Silence was therefore the only policy that was safe.* When he saw how complete was the destruction of the old ecclesiastical system proposed by the reformers, he ventured to remonstrate. He had endeavoured in his own way to reform the Church, and was by no means insensible to its faults; but the utter destruction of the ecclesiastical polity filled him with horror. He actually condescended to send a friendly message to John Knox himself on the subject. His messenger was John Brand, a monk of Holyrood, who afterwards became minister of the Canongate of Edinburgh. "He willed him to say" to the Reformer, "that albeit he had innovated many things, and made a reformation in the doctrine of the Church, whereof he could not deny but there was some reason, yet he would do wisely to retain the old polity which had been the work of ages, or then put a better in place thereof before he did shake off the other. Our Hielandmen," he said, "have a custom when they break young colts to fasten them by the head with two strong tethers, one of which they keep ever fast till the beast be thoroughly made. The multitude, the beast with many heads, should just be so dealt with. Maister Knox, I know, esteemeth me an enemy, but tell him from me he shall find it true that I speak."†

The time for compromises was past, and nothing but extreme measures were likely to prevail. The Archbishop had his livings taken from him by a decree of Parliament.‡ His Cathedral of St. Andrews was sacked,§ and, finding things too hot for him in the east, he retreated to the Abbey of Paisley for refuge. Here he was surrounded by staunch friends, who adhered to the old religion, and to whom his presence was welcome. His enemies soon followed him to his retirement, and he had

* Throckmorton (quoted by Burton) says that when the Confession was proposed for ratification, "the Bishop of St. Andrews said it was a matter that he had not been accustomed with, and had no sufficient time to consider or confer with his friends, howbeit, as he would not utterly condemn it, so was he loath to give his consent thereunto." According to Keith, the Duke of Chatlerhault had threatened the Archbishop with death if he dared to exert himself against it.—Pp. 150, 487.

† Spottiswood, Vol. II., pp. 372.

‡ Tytler, p. 132, Vol. II.

§ June 11th, 1561.

to fly for his life. The final overthrow of the Monastery is thus chronicled by John Knox, and having followed its fortunes through so many vicissitudes, we may be pardoned if we cannot read of its fate without a pang of sorrow :—" The Lords of the Secret Council made an act that all places and monuments of idolatry should be destroyed, and for that purpose were directed to the west, the Earl of Arran having joined with him the Earl of Glencairne, together with the Protestants of the west who burnt Paisley. The Bishop of St. Andrews, who was Abbot thereof, narrowly escaped."* This account of the final overthrow of the Abbey, from the pen of the great Reformer, is the only one that has come down to us. Crosraguel was destroyed at the same time.

The people of Paisley still continued firm in their adherence to the old faith, and their Abbot was soon back among them again. John Knox preached in the neighbourhood, but there is no trace of his ever coming to Paisley. In the same year that Paisley and its cell of Crosraguel were overthrown, he disputed with the able and learned Quintin Kenedy,† Abbot of the latter house, but he never confronted the Superior of the Mother Abbey. Bold preachers of the new doctrine came to Paisley, but they met with a poor reception. They were refused admission to the church; and the General Assembly denounces those who "steyked" the doors against them "when they presented themselves to have preached the Word," and demanded their punishment.‡ The Archbishop himself was the great offender. He treated the denunciations of Parliament against those who said mass with contempt,§ and at last he was summoned before the Supreme Court to answer for his offences. He appeared accordingly before the Court of Session, under the presidency of Argyll, the Justice-General, on 21st March, 1563, accompanied by a number of priests, probably monks of the Abbey who still lingered around their ruined Convent. Little of the reverence he was accustomed in old

* 1561. Knox's History, Wodrow Soc. Vol. I., p. 238.

† A full account of his dispute is given in the Wodrow Society's publications. The discussion took place at Maybole, 28th September, 1561.

‡ Book of the Universal Kirke, Vol. I., p. 53.—Bannatyne Edition.

§ "The Bishop of St. Andrews and Abbot of Crosraguel kept secret convention that same tyme in Paislay, to whom resorted diverse Papists."—John Knox, Vol. I., p. 87.

days to receive was shown him. He was compelled to stand at the bar as a common criminal, and his great opponent, John Knox, seems to have taken a somewhat unworthy delight in noticing the indignity offered to his fallen enemy. "A meary man," he says, who now sleeps in the Lord, "Robert Boswell, instead of the Bischoppis croce, bair before him a steyl hammer, whereat the Bishop and his band were not a little offended." He and his friends* were accused "in the toun of Paslay, kirkyard and Abbey place thereof, openlie, publicklie, and plainlie taking auricular confession in the said kirk, toune, kirkyaird, chalmeris, barns, middens, and killogies thereof, and thus makand an alteration and innovation in the state of religion, which our Soverane Lady found publicklie standing and professit within this realm, ministrand, and alswa irreverently and indecentlie the Sacramentis of Haly Kirk, namely, the Sacramentis of the Body and Blood of our Lord Jesus Christ." It was a serious charge, and, if proven, was punishable by death. The Archbishop had a powerful friend in Queen Mary, who interfered in his behalf. He and his companions were committed to ward; and, if we believe Knox, his imprisonment was but a very slight hardship, for he had a fair custodian to watch over him. "The Lady Erskine (a sweet morsel for the Devil's mouth) gat the Bischoppis for her pairt."†

The young Queen, through whose intervention he thus escaped severe punishment, did all in her power to reinstate him, in his former dignity and position. In 1566 he baptised her son, in the Chapel of Holyrood, with all the pomp of the old ritual,‡ to the great scandal of the reformers. After the murder of Darnley, of which he was accused as having been an accomplice, he was in close attendance upon her. She restored to him the consistorial rights he had possessed as Archbishop, and one of the first acts of his court§ was to divorce Bothwell from Lady Jane Gordon, in order

* A full account of the Archbishop's trial is in Pitcairn's Criminal Trials, Vol. I., p. 429. The names of those tried with him were—Maister John M'Quheyne, elder; Maister Andro Davidsone, Dene William Lepar, Friar James Johnstone, Alexander Somerville, Mr. John M'Quheyne, younger; Schir Johne Hamilton, curat of Paslay; Schir Johne Craig, Schir Johne Elder, Schir Johne Wry, Schir Johne Browne, Schir Johne Dunlop, Dene David Brance. Will. Sempill of Thirdpart and Michael Naysmith of Posso were cautioners for the Abbot. See also "Diurnal of Occurrents," Bannatyne Club, p. 65. Keith, p. 239.

† John Knox. ‡ Tytler, Vol. II., p. 248.

§ Diurnal of Occurrents. Keith. Tytler, Vol. II., p. 231.

that he might be free to marry the Queen. He was the leading spirit in what was called the faction of the Hamiltons, who were her strongest supporters. He took part in planning the Queen's escape from Lochleven, joined her immediately afterwards, and was at the battle of Langside, which decided her fate. It is said he accompanied her to Dundrennan, and earnestly endeavoured to dissuade her from venturing into England, wading knee-deep into the water, and catching with both hands the boat that bore the ill-fated Mary away.*

After the battle of Langside, things grew very sad for the old Prelate. He was shut out from Paisley. The Regent Murray gifted all the church property to Lord Sempill,† who had become his supporter, and who fought on his side. The Archbishop was proscribed, and his former bailie reigned in his stead at Paisley. The outlawed Prelate still, however, maintained an undaunted front to his enemies, and when the Regent was assassinated by Hamilton of Bothwell-haugh, he is said to have been among those who received the murderer with congratulations.‡ In the confusion that occurred, the Archbishop came back to Paisley, and took possession of the Abbey House, which the Sempills had probably restored. They made no resistance, and it was supposed that they were in league with their former master.§ The Archbishop himself, in a letter which he wrote during his last hours to the English Queen,|| describes the place as deserted. He speaks touchingly of his loyalty and "treu service done to my Prince and realme." The place he was accused of violating was "his own, and he had it these forty-five years, and as my said place of Paisley was standing waste,¶ and no man

* I have seen this again and again stated, though I have been unable to find the authority on which the assertion is made. Tytler, Vol. II., p. 270, makes the almost inconceivable statement that in 1567 the Archbishop wished to put the Queen to death, in order to open up the succession to the throne to his family. Burton, Vol. V., p. 305, shews how the charge against the honour of the prelate was probably exaggerated.

† Privy Seal, Reg. xxxvii., 84.

‡ Tytler, Vol. II., 320. 17th Jan., 1570. Diurnal of Occurrents.

§ State Papers, Foreign, Elizabeth, Vol. CXVI., Sir W. Drury to Cecil, dated 25th January, 1577—*i.e.* 1570-71.

|| This letter is given in the Appendix. I was fortunate enough to find it in the State Paper Office.

¶ Empty.

in it but only a boy that had the key of the yeit,* and my servants did no violence to any man, but entered into my own place without any trouble; and when it is said that I was in Paslay and held courts in our Soverain's name, that is manifest fals, for I was not there these three years and mair." It would appear, however, notwithstanding this disclaimer, that not only did the attendants of the Archbishop take possession of the Abbey, but that they seized Lord Sempill himself and kept him a prisoner.† It was even suspected that they endeavoured to poison him. The Regent Lennox came against the Abbey with a considerable force and besieged it, and the defenders surrendered on the condition that their lives should be spared. This condition, though granted by the victorious party, was not fulfilled. Whether the Regent found that his prisoners had been all implicated in the murder of the King's father or not, he certainly shewed them no mercy. Thirty of them were taken on the 7th March to the Easter Borough Muir of Glasgow and there hanged, and one or two others imprisoned.‡ There was an intense hatred cherished by the Regent against the Hamiltons, and he certainly gratified it to the utmost.

He soon afterwards had an opportunity of taking still more dire vengeance upon his enemies. On the 1st April, 1571, the castle of Dum-

* Gate.

† Drury to Cecil, State Papers, Foreign, Eliz., Vol. cxvi., No. 1062, Appendix. The following is from the records of the third report of the Commission on Historical MSS. "Letter by King James VI., with consent of Mat. Earl of Lennax, Regent, to his Sheriffs, to charge the keepers of the Abbey and Place of Paisley to surrender the saide Abbey, with their own persons, into the hands of Thomas Crawfurd, or else to put into the hands of the said Erle of Lennax, Regent of the Kingdom, Robert, Lord Sempill, together with the said Place, before ten o'clock on the following day, under an assurance that all the persons therein would be set at liberty excepting those who were suspected of the murder of Henry, Lord Darnley, his Majesty's father, 15th February, 1570."

‡ The Archbishop complains bitterly of the treatment his followers received (see letter in Appendix). The following are the names of some of those captured at the "taking of Paisley":—John Hamilton, junior, Paris Hamilton, William Schirlaw, William Donaldsone, John Arbuckle, George Naismith, John Hastie, Thomas Toucht, Donald Schirar, Sir Thomas Dickson, granter of Paisley; Michael Hamilton, and John Walker. The last two being convicted were taken to the gallows and got their lives. The sons of Andrew Hamilton of the Cochnacht (Cochno) were put in ward. Diurnal of Occurrents, p. 201. The latter attempted to escape (Ibid. 217), and were afterwards beheaded (Ibid. 223).

barton was captured by the gallantry of a Captain Crawfurd of Jordan-hill, and among other prisoners was the Archbishop himself, clad in a shirt of mail, and with a steel cap on his head. He had little mercy to expect from his captors, but he wrote a letter in his own defence to the English Queen in the hope, probably, that she might interfere in his behalf. There was no time given for any such intervention, even if it had been likely. The Archbishop was taken to Stirling, and there hurriedly brought to trial. George Buchanan, the historian, was one of his accusers, and narrates his trial,* and we have also the narrative of another who was present, and graphically describes the scene. The prisoner was accused by Lord Ruthven, the Justice-Clerk, and Mr. George Buchanan. He was charged with the murder of King Henry, with conspiring against the King, with lying in wait in the woods of Callandar for the slaughter of Lord Lennox, and with participating in the murder of the Regent Murray. He denied all the charges. The evidence against him was somewhat strange, and not very convincing, but it was deemed sufficient. The master of the school of Paisley, a Sir Thomas Robeson, gave evidence that a follower of the Archbishop's had made auricular confession to him of the murder of the King at Kirk of Field. The name of this follower was John Hamilton, commonly called Black John. He and eight vassals of the Archbishop had received from him the keys of the house where the King slept: they strangled their victim, and drew him into the garden. The deed weighed heavily on the mind of Black John. "He was troubled in his soul by day and night, his conscience tormenting him. Endeavouring to find ease, he remembered a schoolmaster in Paisley, a Papist, who comforted him, reminding him of the mercy of God. Soon after he died."† This schoolmaster was now brought from Paisley to Stirling to tell his story against his former Abbot. The Archbishop

* Buchanan's History of Scotland, p. 266. There is an uncertainty about the date of the capture of Dumbarton, and the Archbishop's execution. I have followed the narrative in the "Diurnal of Occurrents," as the writer was evidently present himself at the latter event. The letter to the English Queen is noticed doubtfully in some of the accounts. I have given it in the Appendix.

† Buchanan, p. 266.

answered nothing to his tale, but, eyeing him, said, "You are not ignorant of the punishment due to those who reveal the secrets of Confession?"* The prisoner was condemned to death, and on the scaffold is said to have confessed that he knew of the Regent's murder and might have stopped it, for which he asked God's mercy. † "As touching his religion," says the writer we have followed, "I reasoned with him, and could find naething bot he was ane Papist, and exhorted such as were near him on the scaffold to abide in the Catholic faith (so he termed the Papistrie), and in the castel he desired some Papist priest to whom he might confess him, and of whom he might receive consolation (absolution?) of his sins according to the order of the Kirk (so he spak), and so he continued to the death in his Papistrie as he lived. As the bell struck at six hours at even he was hangit at the mercat cross of Stirling upon the jebat."‡

So died the last Archbishop of the old Church of Scotland, and the last Abbot of Paisley. He was a man of great ability, and, if he had faults, he was not worse than most men of his station and of his time. Upon the gallows his enemies affixed the lines:—

Cresce diu felix arbor, semper que vireto,
Frondibus ut nobis talia poma feras.§

But there were some in Stirling who sorrowed at his fate, and at the dead of night these other lines were nailed to the door of the church of the town.

Infelix pereas arbor, si forte virebis,
Imprimis utinam carminis authoreas.

* Buchanan. He says that fifteen months afterwards this schoolmaster suffered for saying mass, and that he still adhered at his death to the evidence he had given at Stirling.

† Diurnal of Occurrents.

‡ Gallows. Ibid. I can find no authority for the statement that he was hanged over the Bridge of Stirling in full canonicals.

§ Grow long happy tree, and ever let thy leaves be green,
That thou mayest bear such fruit for us.

The wretched latinity of the second verse has been thus skilfully translated by a friend:—

Perish thou wretched gallows tree,
Or if perchance thou flourish should,
That rhymster vile, I pray to good,
May quickly find his way to thee.

After his execution, his body was quartered,* but those friends who had so curiously expressed their regret, probably carried his mangled remains to Paisley. There is in the church a tablet, which looks as it had marked his grave. It has upon it the Archbishop's coat of arms, the letters J. H., the initials of his name, and the motto he assumed, and which contrasts strangely with his troubled life and tragic end—"Misericordia et Pax." †

* Tytler, Vol. II., p. 337.

† This tablet was taken at the last restoration of the church from the outside of the west gable, where it had been carelessly built in, and placed for safety in its present position at the west end of the north aisle.—See Chap. XX.

## CHAPTER XX.

### Remains.

> They dreamt not of a perishable home
> Who thus could build. Be mine, in hours of fear
> Or grovelling thought, to seek a refuge here.

MORE of the Abbey of Paisley was left untouched at the Reformation than was the case with the other Scotch Monasteries. The nave is almost as perfect as when it was built. The chapel of St. Mirin is also entire. The northern gable of the transept, with its beautiful window, is untouched; but the choir has only part of its walls remaining. Both it and ~~the~~ transept are unroofed, and are used as part of the parish burying-ground. The church, taken as a whole, is perhaps as beautiful a specimen of pre-reformation architecture as there is in Scotland. Of the conventual buildings none remain. They were almost all converted after the Reformation into dwelling-houses, and though fragments of the old houses, such as an occasional pillar or arch, are to be found, there is little to remind one of dormitory, parlour, or refectory. The shape of the cloister court has, however, been partially retained, and the cloisters themselves can still to some extent be traced. We give below* the measurements of the

* The Nave is 96 feet in length by 29 feet 3 inches within the piers. The North Aisle 11½ feet, and the South 10 feet 10 inches. The Piers are each 4 feet, thus making the whole Nave and Aisles 59 feet 7 inches in width—*i.e.*, 96 feet by 59 feet 7 inches.

The Transept is 90 feet 9 inches in length from north to south, by 32 feet within—*i.e.*, 90 feet 9 inches by 32 feet.

The Choir is 123 feet 9 inches in length from east to west, by 32 feet within—*i.e.*, 123 feet 9 inches by 32 feet.

various parts of the church buildings, which we shall now briefly notice in detail, making free use of the various descriptions of them which have been given by those conversant with the details and technicalities of Gothic architecture. "The first feature that demands attention is the western doorway. It is broad and deep, with large bold mouldings, exhibiting, though the style in general is early English, some remnants of the toothed decorations of the Norman period. On either side of the pointed arch of the doorway there is a narrower archway of the same character, faced with stone. Above the doorway there are three windows, generally speaking of the same period of architecture; but while the single window in the highest department is of a more decorated character, the two others, occupying the compartment between

Saint Mirin's Aisle is 48 feet 8 inches by 22 feet 6 inches.

| | Feet. | Inches. | |
|---|---|---|---|
| East Gable, | 5 | 6 | Total length over 270 feet. |
| Choir, | 119 | 9 | |
| Screen, | 4 | 0 | |
| Transept, | 32 | 0 | |
| Screen, | 4 | 0 | |
| Nave, | 96 | 0 | |
| West Gable, | 5 | 6 | |
| Buttresses outside of West Gable, | 3 | 3 | |

The site of the Tower is 40 feet square.

The length of West Front over the Flank Towers is 77 feet 6½ inches.

| | Feet. | Inches. |
|---|---|---|
| The greatest extent across the Transept, | 127 | 9 |
| North Buttresses, | 4 | 2 |
| Or, | 131 | 11 |

| | Feet. | Inches. |
|---|---|---|
| South Wall, | 4 | 0 |
| St. Mirin's Aisle within, | 22 | 3 |
| Screen Wall there, | 5 | 0 |
| Transept within, | 90 | 9 |
| North Gable, | 5 | 9 |
| | 127 | 9 |
| North Buttresses, | 4 | 2 |
| | 131 | 11 |

The total length 270, by the greatest breadth 132 feet.

The above actual measurements were taken in 1829, by the late Mr. James Russell, architect, whose friends have courteously given me a copy of them.

it and the door, are somewhat remarkable for the breadth and simplicity of the mullions."* The window in the highest department to which the above description refers, goes by the name of the "crown window." Its tracery forms the figure of a crown, and it is not improbable that it may have been designed to commemorate the connection between the Kings of Scotland and the Abbey, and especially the Royal favour shown to Thomas Tervas in enabling him to complete his restoration of the church.† The four turrets at each angle of the nave are staircases; the two at the west front are in as good condition in the interior as when erected. The two buttresses in the west front are also staircases from where the turret stair ends, for ascending to the top of the building. The porch of the church is to the north of the building. It has a small room above it, and has a stone bench on each side of the interior.

Entering at the porch, we cannot fail to be struck with the beauty of the nave. It has a north and south aisle. Ten massive columns, seventeen feet in height, with simple but elegantly moulded capitals, divide these aisles from the body of the fabric. Of these columns, the circumference of each of the two nearest the west is more than double that of any of the others, plainly indicating that they were intended by the architect, along with the front wall, to support two western towers. "From the imposts of the columns spring pointed arches, with antique and graceful mouldings. From a floor formed above the first tier of arches, spring those of the triforium; they are large and semi-circular, springing from clustered columns, and are enriched with a variety of mouldings. Within these finely-sweeping arches are included two pointed ones, cinque-foiled in the head, and separated from each other by a short but delicately-clustered column, with an ornamental capital. The space between the heads of these minor arches and that of the principal arch above them is open to the body of the structure, and beautifully cusped. From the summit of the spandrils, between each pair of arches, a semi-

* The Baronial and Ecclesiastical Antiquities of Scotland, illustrated, by Robert William Billings, architect—part, Abbey of Paisley.

† See *ante*.

hexagonal projection juts out three and a-half feet, supported by two ranges of blocked corbels, receding downwards. These projections or platforms are each supported by a sculptured grotesque figure, which seems groaning under the weight."* One of these figures near the west gable is somewhat singular, and represents a man clothed in a kilt, telling of the antiquity of the garb of old Gaul. The employment of these grotesque figures was very much affected by the monks of Clugny, and drew forth a severe rebuke from St. Bernard. "What business," he said, "had these devils and monstrosities in Christian churches, taking off the attention of the monks from their prayers." Many worshippers in the Abbey in more modern times have, in the midst of long sermons, found relief in the contemplation of those curious carvings which the

Saint thus vigorously denounced. They were mostly the work of Thomas Hector, a sculptor, who lived at Crossflat, and whom the Abbot retained for his skill in his art.†

* New Statistical Account of Scotland (Renfrewshire), from which, and Mr Billings' book, the technical details above are taken.

† See chapter on "Monastic Economics," and the "Rental-Book" in the Appendix.

Above the triforium rises the clerestory, the arches of which, opening also to the interior of the edifice, are simple, pointed, and narrow, with clustered piers and plain mouldings. In the space occupied by each broad arch of the triforium there are two clerestory windows. A gallery passes along the clerestory, and in the division between each window, which is above the keystone of the arch below, it passes through the department, while in passing each alternate division, above the pillars and the separations of the triforium arches, the gallery passes round the exterior, and is supported by the corbels. The object of these peculiarities is clearly to give the roof the full support of solid masonry above each pillar without its being weakened by a perforation. The clerestory windows have pointed arches, each divided into two departments, with trifoliate tops, and a quatrefoil between them in the enclosing arch. These windows are twelve in number.

The aisles are lighted by pointed windows, in the decorated style, divided by mullions into two, three, and in some cases four lights, the arched heads filled with flowing tracery of diversified character. Of the four in the north aisle, the first and second from the transept seem to have undergone less change than the others, as their style has an appearance of greater antiquity, or, at least, bears fewer marks of alteration or renovation than that of the others. This remark applies also to the three windows next the transept in the south aisle, which belong to the same period as the Norman doorway leading to the cloister court, and which may possibly date from the time of the Priory.*

Three sides of the cloister court are standing:—the north, formed by the south wall of the church; the east, by the Chapel of Saint Mirin; and the south, by the old residence of the Abercorn family. The cloister wall, which formed the west boundary, was twenty-four feet from the west front of the Abbey. About the end of the fifteenth century, another wall was erected, nine feet beyond the west front of the Abbey, and extended eighty-two feet southwards. A roof was erected on this wall and the cloister wall, and the inside fitted up for monastic purposes. The south front wall

* See *ante*. The foundations of the south wall were lately examined. The portion corresponding to the Norman doorway and windows was of different material from that of the rest of the building, being broken stones, the rest being rubble work.

of the Abbey was made a gable to the building. That building was sold in 1874 to the Town Council, by the present Duke of Abercorn, for the purpose of widening the street from twenty-two feet to fifty feet in breadth.* The arms of Abbot Shaw, which were upon the interior wall, were taken down, and inserted in the west gable of a house on the south side of the court.

The only building in the court worthy of notice is the Chapel of St. Mirin and St. Columba, of the founding of which in 1499 we have given a full account. This chapel formed part of the south transept of the Abbey. It is entered from the court by a doorway which seems modern. The Chapel has a fine window divided into three mullions, but it is built up, and its beauty completely destroyed. The ceiling is beautifully groined. Two arches dividing the Chapel from the transept are built up. The eastmost part of the Chapel rises, with four steps, two feet higher than the other portion. The altar stood on this elevated platform. Immediately below the eastern window there is a frieze of one foot eight inches deep, between two cornices of eight inches deep, which were intended for sculpture.† Three compartments, measuring four feet, at the north or right side, and seven compartments, measuring ten feet, at the south or left side, have been carved and filled with sculptures of a very striking character. Various conjectures have from time to time been made as to what these sculptures represent. Most writers have given it as their opinion that they stand for the Seven Sacraments of the Roman Church.‡ Any person, however, who will read the legends of St. Mirin, which we have given in the fifth chapter of this work, will have no difficulty in recognising them in the antique work of these curious carvings. The reference of them to Mirin is clear beyond all doubt.

* A full account of the taking down of these buildings is given by David Semple, F.S.A., in his "Second Supplement to Saint Mirin." The sale of these houses occasioned considerable controversy as to their antiquity.

† For this description of the Chapel I am much indebted to an admirable paper by Mr. Semple, read to the Glasgow Archæological Society.

‡ Mr. Billings says—"The ingenuity of antiquaries has failed to discover the subjects they represent."

In the one on the extreme left we see Mirin's mother bringing him to St. Congal. In the next, St. Congal putting the religious habit on Mirin. In the next, Mirin taking oversight of the Monastery of Banchor. There is after this a blank, and then we have certain sculptures relating to Mirin's encounter with the Irish King, who wears a crown on his head. In the first, we have the servant of the King driving Mirin away from the door of the palace. In the next, the King roaring with pain and held by his servants. In the next, the Queen lying in bed with a picture of the Virgin on the wall, it being the custom to hang such before women during confinement. Then we have the King on his knees before Mirin, and afterwards Mirin received by him with joy. The next two sculptures represent the last two acts of the Saint—the brother looking through the keyhole and seeing Mirin illuminated by a celestial light, and the Saint restoring to life the dead man in the Valley of Colpdasch. The full account of these miracles we have already given from the Aberdeen Breviary. As they are evidently earlier than the date of the erection of the chapel they have probably been transferred with the relics of the Saint from an older shrine. They look like twelfth century work, but it is possible they may be even earlier.

There is a dormitory above the chapel, arched by stone, of twelve feet in breadth by ten feet high to the keystone of the arch. The entrance is by a doorway in the middle of the south side of the arch, and the apartment is lighted by two windows—one in the east gable, and the other in the west. In the west gable there is a private stair leading from the dormitory to the chapel. The priest, who was bound by the charter to live at the chapel, doubtless occupied the sleeping place above it.

The chapel at the Reformation was converted into a family burying-place by Claud Hamilton, the Commendator. Its endowment, as we have seen, was applied to the support of a grammar school. There is a memorial of the old Commendator in a tablet erected on the north side of the chapel by him to three of his children, with the following Latin inscription :—

D. O. M.

PIÆ . INFANTVM . MARGARETÆ .
HENRICI . ET . ALEXANDRI . HAMIL
TONIORIVM . MEMORIÆ . CLAVDI
VS . HAMILTONIVS . PASLETI DO .
MINVS . ET . MARGARETA . SETON .
EIVS . VXOR . PROLI CHARISSIME .
CVM . LACHR : POSS : OBIERE .
MARGARETA : AN : SAL : 1577 . X.
KALEN : IAN : NATA . MENSES TR
ES . DIES . XXII . HENRICVS . 1585
ID : MAR . NATVS . MENSES .
TRES . DIES . DVOS . ALEXAND
ER . 1587 . XI. KAL : DECEMB . NA
TVS . MENSES . OCTO . DIES TRES.

FELICES . ANIME . VOBIS . SVPR
EMA . PARENTES
SOLVVNT . VOS . ILLIS SOLVERE
QVÆ . DECVIT ♣ *

[Abercorn Arms.]

Various members of the Abercorn family lie buried in the vault below, and the chapel belongs to the present Duke, and is under his control.†

* Translation :—*To God the Greatest and Best.*—Erected by Claud Hamilton, Lord Paisley, and Margaret Seton, his wife, with tears, to the pious memory of the infants Margaret, Henry, and Alexander Hamilton, their beloved children, who died—Margaret, on the 23d December, in the year of grace 1577, aged three months twenty-two days ; Henry, on the 15th March, 1585, aged three months two days ; Alexander, on the 21st November, 1587, aged eight months three days. Happy souls ! to you your parents pay the last rites, which ye should have paid to them.

† I have thought it right to say this, as during my incumbency I have received many complaints from visitors as to the state in which this chapel is kept. It is coated with common, rough whitewash. The splendid window is bricked up ; the wonderful sculptures whitewashed over. The tomb of Marjory Bruce is dirty and ill-kept and scribbled upon. A smith's-shop has been built against the east end of the chapel, and a shed against the south side for keeping whiskey barrels. When so much has been done by the public to restore the other

The supposed tomb of Marjory Bruce, which will be noticed further on, is in the centre of the chapel. The chapel is famed for an echo, which has been noticed by every writer in succession who has described the Abbey. As early as 1774, Pennant, in his "Tour Through Scotland," says*:—"The Earl of Abercorn's burial place is by much the greatest curiosity in Paisley. It is an old Gothic chapel, without pulpit or pew, or any ornament whatever; but it has the finest echo, perhaps, in the world. When the end door (the only one it has) is shut, the noise is equal to a loud and not very distant clap of thunder; if you strike a single note of music you hear the sound gradually ascending, till it dies away as at immense distance, and all the while diffusing itself through the circumambient air; if a good voice sings, or a musical instrument is well played upon, the effect is inexpressibly agreeable." This description of the echo by the famous traveller is either much exaggerated, or the strength of the echo has become diminished since his time. When any number of persons are within the building, an echo is scarcely audible at all. It is amusing sometimes to see a group of people expending the strength of their lungs in vain by attempting to evoke it.

The transept of the Abbey, and the choir, which had no aisles, are roofless. Two piers of the central tower remain. Whether the tower was built again after its fall in the time of Archbishop Hamilton† is uncertain. It is said, in an account of Renfrewshire, supposed to be written previous to 1653, to have "fallen by its own weight, and with it the quire of the church."‡ It is probable that this refers to the fall in Hamilton's time, to which we have referred, and that the Reformation found the monks worshipping in the nave. The massive wall dividing the nave from the choir seems, from its workmanship, to belong to the pre-reformation

parts of the Abbey, it is a pity that this chapel should not be kept in common decency. It has been well said by the present Dean of Westminster, who visited the chapel in 1876, that "It ought to be impossible for any member of that great branch of the House of Hamilton to view with indifference the cradle of their family, from which their fortunes and their titles were derived, and in which for two centuries their ancestors resided, and found their last resting-place."

* Tour Through Scotland, by Thomas Pennant, p. 168.

† See *ante*.

‡ Hamilton's Renfrewshire, p. 147.

period. A large bell is said to have hung in the tower, and to have been carried by the English soldiers, in the time of Cromwell, to Durham, and placed in the Cathedral of that city. There is no trace of it to be found there now.* The four sedilia at the south-eastern extremity of the choir, and the altar drain and credence niche, mark the spot where the high altar stood, before which, King Robert the III. was buried, and where his remains might probably still be found.

We are only able to conjecture what was the position of the conventual buildings. But after comparing the plan of Wenlock, from which the monks originally came, with that of Crosraguel, which they afterwards erected, we think it is probable that the chapter house,† with Saint Mirin's chapel, occupied the east side of the cloister court, the refectory the south side, and the dormitory the west. The Abbot's house probably stood at the south end of what is called Cotton Street. There were buildings also between the Abbey and the river Cart attached to the Monastery, portions of the foundation of which are occasionally uncovered.

The present burying-ground has been used only since the Reformation. The churchyard of the Monastery probably was near Seedhill, where there was an old graveyard some time after the Reformation.‡

Crosses seem to have been placed at intervals on the roads leading to the church. There is mention in the Abbey charters of two of these erections. The Cross of the Lord, on the other side of the Cart, near the *Saucel*, and the Cross of St. Mirin on the lands belonging to the Burgh. The names of Corsebar and Corseflat in the neighbourhood seem to indicate that crosses also stood at these places.

There are several monuments and inscriptions of an ancient date in the

* I have made enquiries, in which I have been assisted by one of the Cathedral clergy. All the Cathedral bells were recast under Dean Comber in 1693, having been previously recast in the same century. None of the present bells have any inscription referring to Paisley.

† The supports of the groining of the Chapter House are still visible on the outside of the south wall of St. Mirin's Chapel.

‡ On the 2d April, 1620, "The laich house in the Seedhill, with an auld graveyaird attached thereto, was set for a year to John Greenlees, son natural of Thomas Greenlees, in Blackland Mill, for four pounds (6s. 8d.). Entry to the yaird at once, and to the house at Whitsunday."

church. In the porch is the tablet to Abbot Lithgow which we have already noticed.

iohes . d . lychtgw . ab
bas . huius . monastij . xx . die .
mesis . Januarij . ano . dni . m° . cccc°
xxxiij . Elegit . fieri . sua . sepultura*

In the north aisle is one bearing the following inscription in relief :—

HEIR LYIS THOMAS INGLIS
BAILZE OF PASLAY. QVHA
DECESSIT YE 1502. AND DAVID
INGLIS HIS SONE 1533. IOH
NNE INGLIS SONE TO DAVID
1559 THOMAS INGLIS
SONE TO JOHNE
BALLIIS OF YE BVR
GH FOR YE TYME.
AND ISSABELL
MVIR SPOVSE TO
YE SAID THOM
AS

The family of Inglis was well-known at one time in Paisley, and several of them were bailies of the town. Near the window at the east end of the north aisle is a large tablet inserted in the wall, bearing the following inscription executed in relief :—

* John of Lychtgow abbot of this monastery made choice of his burial place the xx day of January MCCCCXXXIII.

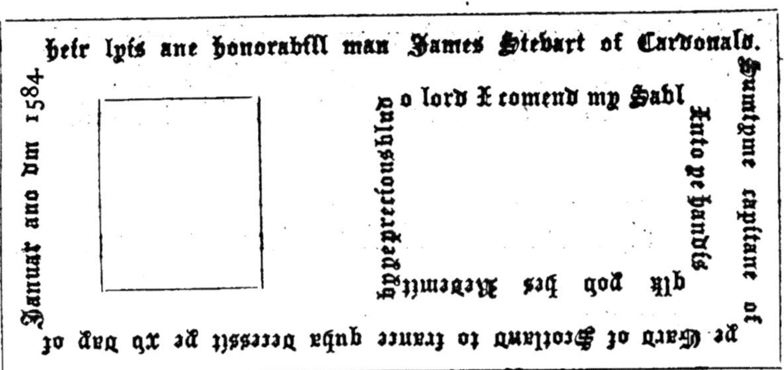


The Stewarts of Cardonald were a family in the neighbourhood of Paisley, and are often mentioned in the Abbey Charters. They became Protestants at a very early period, and the soldier to whom the above is erected, though born a Catholic, seems from the inscription to have died a Protestant. He was an ancestor of the family of Blantyre.* Below the window which fills the east end of the north aisle is the tablet which we have noticed as probably having formed part of the tomb of Archbishop Hamilton. It was inserted in its present position at the last renovation of the Abbey in 1861. The upper part contains the ecclesiastical heraldic arms of the Archbishop. The first and fourth quarters of the shield, a ship with its sails furled for Arran; and second and third quarters, three cinque ports for Hamilton; the cross for a crest, and two angels for supporters, with the initials of his name.†

In the east gable there is a tablet bearing the following inscription:—

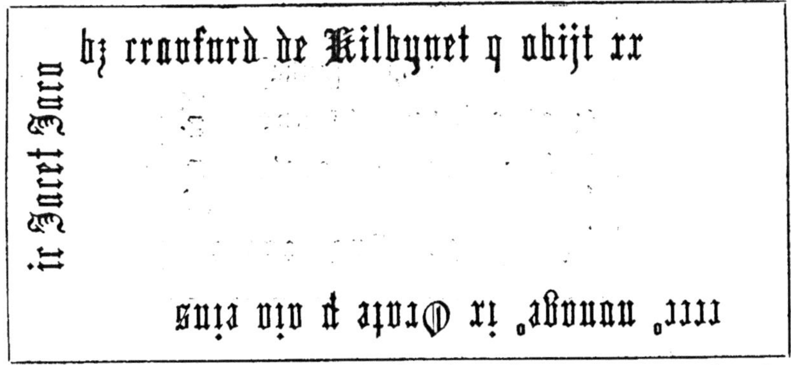


* He was a generous man. † An engraving of the tomb is given at the end of the previous chapter.

This is the tomb of the generous burgess of Paisley who, with Elizabeth Galbraith, his spouse, founded the Chapel of Saint Mirin.

In the east gable is also another tablet inserted in the wall.

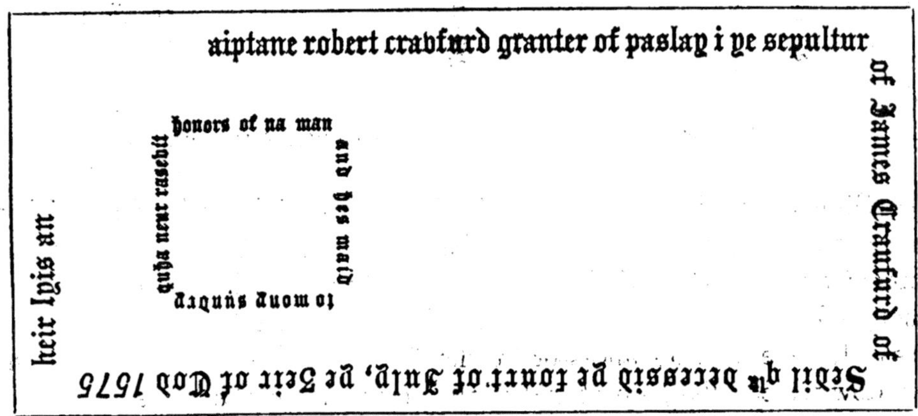


This Captain Robert Crawfurd was a great-grandnephew of James Crawfurd of Kilwynet and Seedhill, and held the appointment of grainter, or granary keeper, to the Monastery.

In the south aisle there is a small tablet inserted in the wall bearing the following inscription, executed in relief:—

William · Pyrre [quha]
of god · mᵒ vᶜ and
ix · zers · orate

died on ye
first day of Junij
ye zeir.

These Pyrries were an opulent family in Paisley for a century.

On the west buttress of the transept, twenty-one feet above the base, there is a shield containing the cheque of the Stewarts, with the top of a pastoral staff for a crest in bold relief, and the engraved word:—

One of the south pillars of the nave is called the Cathcart Pillar, and bears upon it the shield of that family, beautifully carved in stone. The Cathcart family were long closely connected with the Abbey,* and the tradition attaching to this pillar is worthy of notice. Sir Alan Cathcart was an intimate companion of King Robert Bruce, and on many occasions fought by his side. Barbour gives a striking description of this stalwart and courteous knight, in words which are applicable to many of his descendants, who have often occupied a prominent place in the military annals of the country:—

A knycht, that there wis in hys rout,
Worthy and wycht, stalwart and stout,
Curtaiss and fayr, and off gud fame,
Schyr Allane of Catkert by name.

King Robert the Bruce died in 1329, and Sir Alan of Cathcart and his old companion in arms, the good Sir James of Douglass, sailed in the following year for the Holy Land with the King's heart. Sir James was killed in Spain in conflict with the Moors, as every reader of Scottish history knows. Sir Alan came back with the heart of the

* The family have a burying-place in the transept. I am much indebted to the present Earl of Cathcart for the interest he has taken in this work, and for an elaborate paper which he has sent me, shewing the connection between his family and the Abbey.

King,* and the pillar in the Abbey—then being restored after its destruction by the English—commemorates his safe return. The cross crosslets above the crescents on the shield may have some reference to the conflict with the Moors in which the Douglass fell. Thus this pillar carries us away in thought to the plains of Andalusia and to this most romantic episode in Scottish story. The arms are undoubtedly those of the Cathcarts, and there is nothing improbable in the tradition, which we have thought right to give.

In the centre of the Chapel of St. Mirin stands the supposed tomb of Marjory, the daughter of King Robert the Bruce, through whom the Stewarts came to the throne of Scotland. It is of beautiful workmanship, and is in every way worthy of inspection. It was reconstructed by Dr. Boag, one of the ministers of the Parish, from fragments which he

* The band of knights who accompanied Douglas is supposed to have been composed of the following persons:—

Sir William Keith—Not in action; suffering from a broken arm.
Sir William Saint Clair of Rosslyn, }
Sir Robert Logan, } Killed in action.
Sir Walter Logan, }
Sir Alan of Cathcart—Probably returned to Scotland with Keith.
Sir Symon Locard of Lee—Went on to the Holy Land.

The centre pillar is what is sometimes called a founder's pillar. For example, amongst many others, Bishop Cameron's arms are on the spire, which he constructed, of Glasgow Cathedral. It is said by Nesbit that of old the Cathcarts carried only crescents, and that afterwards they added the cross-crosslets. It is highly probable that at an earlier period a Cathcart assumed the well-known Moslem badge, the crescent, in consequence of some distinguished achievement in the Holy Land, and that, in addition, Sir Alan the VI. assumed the cross-crosslets fitché on his return from his pilgrimage with the heart of Bruce. In regard to the date of the Cathcart pillar, there can be but little doubt; the shape of the shield, the architecture generally, and one minute but suggestive circumstance, the lion supporters of the shield, all point to the time of Sir Alan of Cathcart the VII. The idea, in all probability, was that of the pilgrim father, Sir Alan VI., carried out by his son.—*MS. of Lord Cathcart.*

found lying about in the neighbourhood of the Abbey,* and placed by him in its present position. The tomb is an altar tomb with the recumbent figure of a woman resting on a pillow; over her head is an ornamental canopy, with a sculpture of the crucifixion. Round the tomb is a series of compartments filled with boldly sculptured figures of ecclesiastics, and shields with armorial bearings. On a scroll is written the name of Robert Wyschard, and under another figure, that of an abbot celebrating at an altar, is inscribed the name, *Johes d Lychtgw*, which is repeated below another kneeling figure. The stone at the head of the monument is divided into three compartments, each containing a shield. The shield on the right bears the fess cheque between three roses,—that on the left the fess cheque surmounted by a lion rampant, and the one in the middle two keys en saltire between two croziers en pale.

There has been considerable controversy as to the credibility of the tradition which assigns this tomb to Marjory Bruce.† It has been locally called "Queen Blearie's" tomb, the name "Blearie" which was given to Robert II. her son, having, it is supposed, in the lapse of years, been transferred to his mother. We see no reason to set aside the ancient tradition which assigns this tomb to Marjory Bruce. Though she was never a Queen, she was the daughter of one King, and the mother of another. "Time," as it has been said, "produces many changes in early records, and it was a very natural one that the people should, in the course of ages, when speaking of the accident of King Robert's birth, designate his mother as Queen." The figure on the tomb is obviously that of a female of rank connected with the family of Stewart. The Abbey was the place where Marjory would naturally be buried, and the Stewart is said to have caused a "fair monument" to be erected to his wife.‡ Robert Wyschard, whose name is on

* See Transactions of the Society of the Antiquaries of Scotland, Vol. II., p. 456, where there is a Paper by Dr. Boag upon this tomb. See also "Saint Mirin," p. 22-23, and Ramsay's "Views of Renfrewshire."

† See Scot. Anti. Trans., Vol. II., part 2, pp. 456-461; also Appendix 3d Vol. of Maitland Club for 1831. The subject has also been discussed at great length in *Notes and Queries* and Hamilton's Renfrewshire, Appendix III.

‡ Sir James Balfour's Annals, Vol. I., p. 96.

the tomb, was Bishop of Glasgow, and was a captive in England with Marjory. He returned in her company to Scotland and was Bishop of the diocese at the time of her death. John Lithgow was Abbot during a great part of the reign of her son, and the monument was probably erected during his term of office, which accounts for his name being found upon it. We may add, also, that the features of the statue are said, on good authority, strikingly to resemble those of Robert the Bruce, the father of Marjory.*

The only name of any of the architects or builders of the Abbey that has come down to us is that of John Morow, or Murdo, a master mason, and Frenchman by descent. A Thomas Morwe was Abbot between 1420-23, and it is possible that they were related. We are indebted for our knowledge of the mason to two inscriptions on the wall of the south transept of Melrose Abbey.† Over a door in this transept there is a sunk panel, inclosing a shield, which displays two mason's compasses, partially opened, laid across one another, so as to form a figure somewhat like a saltire, and on each side, and in base, what has been described as a *fleur de lis*, forming probably a combined masonic and heraldic emblem. The compass is the badge of a master mason, and the three lilies may be those of the shield of France, his native country. On each side of this panel there are the remains of a black-letter inscription in relief. It is as follows :—

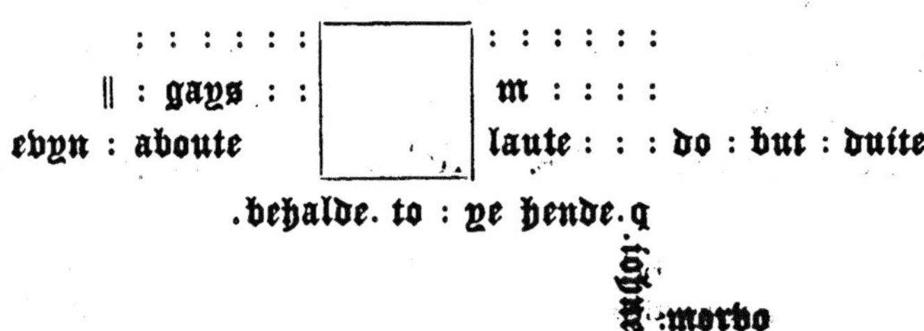


* I have been assured of this on the authority of a very eminent numismatist.

† Trans. of Society of Antiquaries—Notes on Melrose Abbey, by John Alexander Smith, M.D. F.S.A. Scot., from which I have taken the description above.

This is commonly taken to be—

> Sa gayes the compass even about,<br>
> Sa trouth and laute do but doubt.<br>
> Behald to the hend, quoth John Morvo.

The sentiment of this inscription may be rendered thus :—As the compass goes round about without deviating from the circumference, so doubtless truth and loyalty never deviate. Look well to the end, or see to the work, quoth John Morvo. This Morow, we learn from another inscription, was the architect employed in the building, or, at least, in the maintenance of Paisley :—

> John : morow : sum : tym : callyt :<br>
> w : : : s : : : : d : born : in parysse<br>
> certainly : and : had : in : keping :<br>
> al : mason : werk : of : santan<br>
> drays : ye : hye : kirk : of : glas<br>
> gw : melros : and : paslay : of<br>
> nyddysdall : : : d : of : galway :<br>
> i : pray : to : god : : : d : : : y : bath<br>
> : : : : : : : : : : : : : : : : : : : : : : : : : :<br>
> : : : : : : : : : : :

This inscription runs thus :—

> John : Morow : sum : tyme callet<br>
> was : i : and : born : in : Parysse :<br>
> certainly : and : had : in keping :<br>
> al : mason : werk : of Santan<br>
> drays : ye : hye : kirk : of : Glas<br>
> gw : Melros : and : Paslay : of<br>
> Nyddysdayll : and : of Galway :<br>
> I : pray : to : God : and : Mary : bath<br>
> and : sweet : St : John : keep : this : haly : kirk :<br>
> frae : skaith :

For what portion of our Abbey we are indebted to the skill of Morow we do not know. His name has been rescued from oblivion only by the inscriptions we have given.

We may perhaps fitly notice in this chapter one or two other relics of the olden time, besides those architectural remains which we have described. The first is the seal of the Abbey. This has been lost, but its form is well known from the impression attached to the charters still in existence. On one side of the seal is a figure of St. James with pilgrim's staff and scrip. At each side of the Saint is a shield,—that on his right bearing the fess cheque of the Stewarts, that on his left a saltire cantoned with four roses, the armorial bearings of the family of Lennox, who, with the Stewarts, were great benefactors of the Monastery; above the right shield is a saltire, a crescent, and a star, above the left a saltire and a star. The background is ornamented with foliage, interspersed with crosses, *fleury* and *fleur de lis.** On the other side of the seal is a figure of St. Mirin as a vested Bishop, his right hand raised in benediction, and his left holding a crozier. The shields on each side of the Saint are the same as those on the other side of the seal; above the right shield is a saltire and a crescent, above the left a saltire and a star. On the one side of the seal is the following inscription:—

S : Capitbli : Sci : Jacobi : et : Sci : Mirini : De : Passeleto.

The seal of the Chapter of Saint James and St. Mirin of Passelet.

On the other side of the seal is engraved the following prayer:—

Xristbm : Pro : Famulis : Posce : Mirine : Tbis

O Mirin! Pray to Christ for thy servants.

The last notice that we have of the common seal of the Abbey is in 1574, in which year Claud Hamilton, the Commendator, brought an action against Lord Sempill,† alleging that the latter, during his occupancy of

* See Gordon's Monasticon, p. 556.

† Suit by Claud Hamilton, Commendator of Paisley, against Robert Lord Semple, narrating that in the late troubles the said Lord Semple got into his hands the common seal of the said Abbey, with the "buke callit the blak buik of Paslay," and that he would not return the same. Lord Semple denied that he ever had the said articles, but the Lords held that the pursuer had proved his point, and granted letters against Lord Semple for the recovery of the seal and book. —Register of Acts and Decreets, Vol. 54, fol. 220, 29th March, 1574.

aurrelat in firmitate ita q in grabato vehebatur quam
eum contingeret removeri. De hac ligna dicitur. cum semel
et ter et septem in hijs supradictis. Natalicii die ps an
glica vitta putor. De Sleuath redijt. treugas de
rege petunt. Quas rex concessit clementer et inde reces
sit. Petrum intrepidus ibi pstitit octo diebus. Anno pre
dicto circa finem anni capitur dominus Symon fra
sar dominus Walterus logan milites et plures valentes
armigeri et mediocres capti fuerunt per quosdam Scotos
regi anglie adherentes. Qui Symon ductus est
londoniis et duris penis interemptus. Eodem Johelina
in pena cadit de carnarvan filij regis anglie tunc
princeps wallie suspendi iussit. Post tunc regis anglie
precis et potenciores scoti fuerunt domini Johannes comyn
comes de buchanne Willelmus comyn et Johannes de moubre
milites. Qui in admictis [illegible] anglis post hunc regem R.
acriter invaserunt et in maximo periculo ubi obitum

de cadit conquestu regis

regis anglie construxerunt. Qui anno domini M CCC vij
In [illegible] Johis baptiste De lanrost ubi tactus
fuit infirmitate in expedicione sua ad humiliandum regem
[illegible] et regnum scocie ut finaliter proposuit sub
iugandum illius holme cultory tendens [illegible] pu
riore caritate consequenti pridie [illegible] translacionis
sancti thome martiris in medio suo regibus apud Burgum
Sabuli sinistra pene [illegible] expiravit. In eadem
venerande infirmitatis [illegible] miles anglice
nacionis Willelmus lanel nomine. Qui in eadem nocte qua rex obiit
in extasi raptus vidit dominum suum regem in spiritu [illegible]
catum a magna multitudine demonum [illegible]
[illegible] in [illegible] et [illegible]. Eu rex
edwarde celacius ut leopardus. [illegible]
[illegible] male [illegible]. [illegible] comes ibis [illegible]

[illegible]
[illegible]
15

[illegible] [illegible] et demonibus [illegible] et sequi
[illegible] tempore remoto. [illegible] flagellis et
scorpionibus [illegible] eum [illegible]. [illegible]
aliquantulum inquit hunc [illegible] debitum mortis
[illegible] filia est mortis et [illegible]
[illegible] tenebrarum [illegible] luas. dicentes. Eu rex
edwarde. Ecce [illegible] que elegisti. [illegible]
[illegible] sine. [illegible] dilectione [illegible]
emula [illegible] non [illegible]
nos letaris. Ubi nunc est vanitas tua. ubi vana leti
cia quid [illegible] gloria. brevis leticia mundi
potencia. [illegible] voluptas. false diuicie [illegible]
magna familia et mala [illegible] ubi iocus ubi risus
ubi iactancia ubi arrogancia. de tanta leticia
[illegible]. post tantam voluptatem. tam [illegible]
et post tanta [illegible]. tam magna [illegible]
post tantas victorias. tam [illegible] tormenta. [illegible]
[illegible] sit [illegible]. Cumque huiusmodi exprobraci
onibus et [illegible] maligni [illegible]
[illegible] et ad me [illegible] miles tremente et [illegible]
[illegible] me [illegible]
[illegible] extra. [illegible] neque [illegible]
[illegible] in [illegible] est me

ita ut dum mecum et illius recordacio [illegible] leta
[illegible] absorptus est in momento [illegible] puteo voce lugu
bri [illegible] et exclamans. Heu [illegible] fallor. [illegible] no
bis [illegible]. Heu [illegible] perit [illegible] amavi. Heu
[illegible] video [illegible]
[illegible] tormenta [illegible]. Ad se [illegible] miles de extasi [illegible]
[illegible] regis [illegible] cognito [illegible]
ab eo [illegible] se habuit rex [illegible]
qualiter [illegible] ne [illegible]
[illegible] veritatem [illegible]
suo in [illegible]. Non sic [illegible] miles. [illegible] mortuus est.
[illegible] morte [illegible] et non est [illegible]
ex [illegible] Qualiter Willelmus banelt [illegible]
ne regis [illegible] cxiiij.

Willelmus est pro regis filio principe tunc wallie.
Anno primo [illegible] regis [illegible] sepulto
[illegible] londoniis [illegible] ubi [illegible]
regebat [illegible] et in [illegible] holmo
[illegible] in principio [illegible] bella mo
nens anglicos [illegible] flagellis [illegible] et
[illegible] totum [illegible] et [illegible]
[illegible] sancte [illegible] dolo [illegible]

[illegible] et scotos [illegible] regno [illegible]
[illegible] Johannem de balliolo regem [illegible] filio
[illegible] platos [illegible]
[illegible] quosdam [illegible]
[illegible] et alia [illegible] mala [illegible]. Hunc successit
filius eius de carnarvan [illegible] post [illegible]
[illegible] de morte [illegible] semel et [illegible]
[illegible] in orbe [illegible]
[illegible] in burgo sabuli [illegible] marchia regni.
Edwardus [illegible] scotos male [illegible]
[illegible] in holmo [illegible] bella
[illegible] anglis [illegible] flagella. [illegible]
[illegible]
[illegible]
[illegible] platos [illegible]
[illegible]
[illegible] anglia [illegible]
de [illegible] regis [illegible]
rege [illegible]. [illegible] ubi [illegible]
eius in orbe [illegible] deus [illegible] ... anno ... vij anglia [illegible] de palleto

anno vij [illegible] de pall

Dictus dominus Willelmus lancelot de infirmitate qualiscumque
[illegible] actus militares [illegible]
tanto in [illegible]
[illegible] attendebat. [illegible]
in [illegible] horrifica [illegible] demonum. [illegible]
[illegible] et flagellacionibus in dominum suum regem
[illegible] et [illegible] flore [illegible]
[illegible] et ad [illegible]
[illegible] ut dicitur [illegible]
[illegible] et [illegible]
rex [illegible] ab illo [illegible] egame [illegible]
[illegible]

currebat in infirmitate ita quod in grabato vehebatur quousque
eum contingeret removeri. De hac biga dicitur. cum semel
et ter C. septem cum hiis superadde. In talique die prius anglica victa pudoris. De Llewelyn redyt. treugas de
rege petiunt. Quas rex concessit clementer et inde recessit. Ipse tamen intrepidus ibi prestitit octo diebus. Anno pre-
cedenti circa finem autumni comes uterque dicte. dominus Symon Fraser dominus Walterus logan milites et plures valentes
armigeri et mediocres capti fuerunt per quosdam Scotos
regi anglie adherentes. Qui Symon ductus est
london et diris penis interemptus. Certi in dolicuna
in prima Eadwardi de Carnarvan filii regis anglie tunc
principis Wallie suspendi iam. Pro timore regis anglie
proceres et potenciores Scocie fuerunt dominus Johannes comyn
comes de buchane Willelmus comyn et Johannes de mowbray
milites. Qui in adventus eius anglis post hiis regem R-
acri in valescunt et in marcio predicto usque obitum
De morte Eadwardi primi post conquestum anglie regis
regis anglie constituerunt. Qui anno domini M° ccc° vij°
In vigilia sancti Johannis baptiste De lanercost ubi tactus
fuit infirmitate in expeditione sua ad humiliandum regem
nostrum Robertum et regnum Scocie ut finaliter proposuit sub-
iugandum illius dolue castrum tenens pro futura puriore sanitate consequenda predie cum sui translacionis
sancti Thome martyris in vectore suo regibus apud Burgum
sabulum super nota prima invocabit expiravit. In eadem
venerante infirmabatur senex quidam miles anglice
nacionis Willelmus lamb nomine. Qui in eadem nocte qua rex obiit

in extasi raptus. vidit dominum suum regem in spiritu cir-
cumdatum a magna multitudine demonum circumseptum
eidem cum maximo cachinno in subsannacionem et derisionem. Ecce rex
edwardus delicatus ut leopardus. Olim dum viveret
primo dominum male duxit. Nobis nec talis [amices?] ibis carcerali. quo contempneris ut demonibus socieris. Te sequi
voto pro[positi?] tempore remoto. cum hoc flagellis et
scorpionibus cedentes eum abigebant. Cantemus
aliquantulum inquiunt huic misere anime debitum mortis
canticum. quia filia est mortis et cibus ignis inextinguibilis
amica tenebrarum et inimica lucis. dicentes. Eu rex
edwardus. Ecce misera proles quem elegisti. cum quibus ar-
sura es sine fine. mater scandali. amatrix discordie pro-
emula caritatis invidia. quare nunc non superbis quare
non letaris. Ubi nunc est vanitas tua. ubi vana leticia quid profuit tibi inanis gloria. brevis leticia mundi
potencia. carnis voluptas. false divicie congreste terre.
magna familia et mala concupiscencia. ubi iocus ubi risus
ubi iactancia ubi arrogancia. de tanta leticia
quanta tristicia. post tantam voluptatem tam gravis miseri-
a post tantam exaltacionem. tam magna ruina.
post tantas victorias. tam inmania tormenta. atque
ignominia sit tibi gloria. Cumque huiusmodi exprobraci-
onibus et verbis [illegible] spiritus malignus insultaciter [illegible]
[illegible] suorum ad me misit miles tremente et exsanguem dixerit [illegible] ut correcturum me velle sicut
solito in bello opem ferre. Sed quia meam neque vox neque
sensus remansit. [illegible] oculis in tenebris est me.

Ule rex tirannus a demonibus cruciatus

uo ar credas

ita ut diu miro et illius recordatio. nunquam letari
potest. cum hic absorptus est in morituro infernali puteo voce lugubri
eiulans et exclamans. Heu michi peccatum fallax quod non
bis carni. Heu quod peccatum perit et ille est quod amavi. Heu
michi peccatum video quod lites amavi. cum audire gemitum in
met tormenta premi. Ad se igitur miles de certa sui reditus
misit per regis cubiculario suo caro cognato petens
ab eo quem secum habuit rex. benedicant viventes. ma[ter] pa
qualescumque. Hic sed precatus ut simulans ne si sibi in firma
ta veritate annunciaret. nimis etiam amicis
suo inferret. Non sic insulti miles. quod mortuus est.
diu heu morte preventus et non est qui ei opem ferret
ex omnibus cunctis eius. Qualiter W. Banestus fratris uxorio
ne regis despexit mundum                                        c. xiiij.

Missus est per regis filio principe tunc Wallie.
Quo primo veniente cum regis patris sepulture
dispositis londoniis corpus perducitur. ubi nunc humatum
requiescit. ex tales tamen et in testamento sua in holmo
sublevantur. Hic in principio multa e sua bella mo
vens Anglicos diris flagellis verberavit. et
suis nequiis totum orbem perturbavit et undique
commovit. Passagium terre sancte suo dolo impedivit sco
ciam invasit et Scotos a regno fraudulenter ... egit
Walliam conflixit Johannem de Balliolo regem cum filio
carceri mancipavit. ecclesias destruxit prelatos vincula
vit et carcerali squalore quosdam extinxit. papam ... occi
dit. et alia infinita mala perpetravit. Hunc successit
filius eius de Carnarvan Edwardus ii post conquestum
nem. alias quintus. Vero de morte patris ... semel et ...

r septem mirabilis in orbe. Apparuit translato. Thomas sine
fine beato. In burgo sabuli quo sunt marchia regni.
Edwardus cecidit, qui scotos male cecidit. Vulsa cum cerebro cum tumulant in holmo. Iste monens bella
cedit anglis dira flagella. Colla superborum per te
conculcavit eorum. Orbem corrupit tirannum strauit qui
fefellit. Scotos invasit regnum cum fraude liberavit
Gestias strauit prelatos carcere clausit. Decedit post
Christi decem tulit annum. Cuius pena toto sit orbe notata
Anglia deflebit qui vastata iacebit. Scotia plan-
de manum per finem regis avari. Grates redde deo vobis
rege necato. Nunc vi virtutis castigat virga salutis
Cuius in orbe statum faciet deus esse beatum. Hoc anno S.
iiij etc vij anglia combusserunt monasterium de palleto.
Dictus dominus Willelmus lancastrie de infirmitate convalescens
quanto prius ferventius circa actus militares estuabat
tanto in vim altiori mutatus vehementius animi ex
desidio militie spiritualis ipse attendebat. Contigit enim
in cur sunt horrifica visione demonum. calamitose
excruciacionibus et flagellacionibus in domum suam regem
frementium. que ruinosum mundum cum flore eius omnia dele-
perit. et ad emendacionis consolacionis solacium
mentem se contulit. quod ut de cauce prophetia tentura
prodiret et pluribus absencia anima manir prima h
rex. Edwardus dicitur xiij ab illo comite andegavense qui
desponsavit quandam diabolam humana carne velatam.

Hoc ano.
vij ag
sent
de pall

the Abbey, had obtained possession of the seal, and refused to give it up. The judges commanded Lord Sempill, who denied that he ever had the seal, to return it to Claud Hamilton. Whether the Commendator ever received it, we do not know.*

Along with the seal, Lord Sempill is said, in the record of the suit in the Court of Session, to have "got into his hands the buke callit the Black Buik of Paslay." This the lords ordered him to return with the seal of the Abbey, though he denied ever having had it any more than the other missing article. The "Black Book of Paisley" has been often referred to as one of the most important of Scottish chronicles. It was written in the last days of the Monastery, and was the property of the Abbey. Fortunately, it has been preserved, and may be seen in the manuscript department of the British Museum. We append to this book a more detailed description of this interesting volume,† and we give a fac-simile of one of its pages. It is a beautiful manuscript, with coloured initial letters, and is written in double columns, on thick vellum, in a large folio. It is one of the most interesting relics of our Abbey, and when we turn over its pages, on some of which the words, "*Iste liber est sancte Jacobi et sancte Mirini de Pasleto*" are written, a weird feeling comes over us, and we are carried away in thought to the silent figures working in the scriptorium of the Convent. The manuscript is almost entirely a transcript of John of Fordun's Scotichronicon, with the continuation of Walter Bower.

Three other books connected with the Abbey have come down to us from the olden time. The one is the Rental Book, commenced in the time of Abbot Henry Crichton; and the other two Chartularies of the Abbey. The former is a folio manuscript of common paper, the entries in which are carefully made, and we append a copy of it in full at the end of this volume. The latter are also manuscripts of folio size, written in a uniform character, apparently of the earlier part of the fifteenth century. The contents of one are given in the "Registrum

* On the new iron gates of the Abbey there are large, well-executed representations of the seal.

† See Appendix.

Monasterii De Passelet," from which we have so largely quoted in this work, and without which we could have known but little of the history of the Abbey of Paisley. Both the Rental Book and the first volume of the Chartulary are in the Advocates' Library, Edinburgh, and the second Chartulary volume is among the archives of the Burgh of Paisley.

## CHAPTER XXI.

### The Commendator.

> "Stern Claud replied with dark'ning face,
> Grey Paisley's haughty Lord was he."
>
> *Scott.*

IN tracing the history of the Abbey of Paisley from its foundation to its dissolution as a religious establishment, some of the main causes which led to the downfall of the old ecclesiastical polity of Scotland have come into view. One cause was the almost entire destruction of what is called in our day "the parochial system." The Church in Scotland was monastic, and, with but few exceptions, all the churches belonged to the great Abbeys. We have seen how almost all the cures in Renfrewshire, and some in other counties, were gifted to Paisley. They were served by Paisley monks, and when, as in some cases, vicars were placed in them, these were men who were paid with the lowest stipend they could be induced to take, and at times they could hardly extort even that from their superiors. The Chartulary of Paisley supplies constant evidence of the manner in which the parishes belonging to the Monastery were cared for. The Bishops of Glasgow and Argyle had often to enter into litigation with the monks to induce them to give up a moiety of their revenues to their parish clergy. The fabrics of the churches were again and again suffered to fall into utter disrepair, because the Monastery would not supply the funds to keep them even in a state of decency. A Church so governed could have but little hold on the people. The pastoral tie between them and the hireling of the

Monastery, or the monk who rode his sheltie across the moor on Sundays and Feast-days to say mass in the wretched chapel, was of the very slenderest kind, and when the time of trial came it was easily broken. In later days, also, the Monasteries, which were the centres of ecclesiastical power in the districts where they were situated, became very much broken down in discipline, and, it must be remembered, through no fault of their own. So long as the election of the Abbot was vested in the Chapter, the government of the house was well maintained; but, as we have seen, the King usurped the power of appointment, and the result was most disastrous. Instead of the monk of pure and blameless life, who had been trained from his infancy in the rule of his order, and who was elected on account of his well-known virtues by his own brethren, a man of very different character, some royal sycophant or profligate courtier, had the mitre given him, and was suddenly placed over the brotherhood. For a time the royal patronage, as in the case of Abbot Shaw, seems to have been exercised with some discretion; but latterly appointments of the most shameless character were made. Abbeys were gifted to bastard boys like Hamilton, and five illegitimate sons of the King were at the head of five of the richest Abbeys in Scotland. Nor is there any reason to believe that the authorities of the Church resisted this scandalous system as they should have done. Appointments like that of Hamilton received the sanction of the Pope; and Cardinals took bribes from men like Crichton to make their promotion easy. The whole ecclesiastical framework was worm-eaten and decayed, and it did not require a heavy stroke to break it up altogether. The blow came, not from the people, but from the aristocracy. The idea that the common people had become so instructed in the truths of Scripture as to abhor the doctrines of the Papacy, is far from being historically correct. They were too ignorant to read Scripture, far less to understand abstruse theological disquisitions; but they had little respect for their clergy, and were more ready to follow their laird than their priest. The laird had everything to gain by favouring the new doctrines—the Abbey lands, so much richer than his own, afforded too tempting a bribe, and poor proprietors like Sempill saw an easy way to fortune by an appropriation of the Church revenues. The manner in which the Church property was gifted away forms a scandalous episode in the history of Scotland. Men like Claud Hamilton, who never had done anything for their country, became enriched and ennobled through the spoliation. It is vain to picture regretfully what might have been; but anyone can see how much better it would have been for Scotland if the whole community, instead of a few unworthy individuals, had got the benefit of the Church's wealth. Those who did get it have in too many instances made a very miserable use of their ill-gotten gain.

The revenues of Paisley at the final dissolution of the Monastery were very large, and we have a very exact account of them. In 1561 the Privy Council decreed that all holders of ecclesiastical benefices should give up one-third of their revenues for the Crown and the maintenance of the Protestant clergy. The thirds were lifted by collectors specially appointed, and a certain Michael Chisholm discharged this duty for Paisley. At the assumption of the thirds, the rental of the whole Abbacy* was as follows:—Money, £2467 19s; the meal, 72 ch. 3 b. $3\frac{2}{3}$ f.; the bear, 40 ch. 11 b.; the horse corne, 43 ch. 1 b. 1 f., 1 p. great mete; the cheese, five hundred, five score and six stones. Among the items deducted are seven chalders of meal yearly for the almoners' weekly doles to the poor; for the maintenance of the Convent in kitchen expenses and clothes yearly, according to the accounts of the cellarer and grainter, £473 8s. 4d.; for the fees of the grainter and cellarer, and their under servants, £38; for the Archbishop's claim for procurations now converted into money, £13 6s. 8d.; for the contribution to the Lords of Session and pensions settled on the Abbey, £550 2s 8d. There were twenty-nine churches in possession of the Monastery at the dissolution,† eleven of which were in Renfrewshire.

It is uncertain how many monks belonged to the Abbey when its overthrow took place. The Archbishop-Abbot's name and those of fifteen

* Origines Parochiales, Vol. I., p. 70.

† These churches were:—

| | | |
|---|---|---|
| Cathcart. | Killellan. | Neilston. |
| Eastwood. | Kilbarchan. | Paisley. |
| Erskine. | Lochwinnoch. | |
| Inverkip. | Mearns. | |

monks are subscribed to a Tack in 1539,* and the Archbishop's name and those of fifteen monks to a charter in 1559.† Nor do we know what became of them in their day of adversity. In 1571 the Archbishop found the Monastery "standing waist," and no one in it but a boy who had the key of the gate. By that time the convent was entirely broken up. Some of the brotherhood lingered, as we have seen,‡ about Paisley, where they had many supporters; and there is reason to believe that, so long as they refrained from openly performing the offices of religion, they were permitted to retain certain pittances for their support.§ Their case was a hard one—perhaps less hard at Paisley than in other parts of Scotland, as they had the sympathy of the people; but all of them must have experienced suffering, and one of them, at least, suffered death for saying mass.||

The revenues were secularised, and were successively gifted, as we shall

* An Assedation of the kirks of Paisley and Lochwinnoch is signed in 1539 by the following members of the Convent:—

| | |
|---|---|
| Johne, Abbot of Paslay. | Johne Hamilton. |
| David Cant. | Wilza Litchen. |
| Wilza Sclatr. | David Mossman. |
| Richard Watsoun. | Johne Alexr., sen. |
| Wilza Leper. | Johne Fork. |
| John Pade. | Johne Sandilandis. |
| James Taynne. | Robert Ker. |
| Robert Morton. | David Brante. |

† A Charter of the Lands of Over Gallowhill, dated 18th July, 1559, was signed by—

| | |
|---|---|
| John, Bishop of St. Andrews. | Edward Logan. |
| Alex. Tait, prior. | Augustine Pegaw. |
| William Leper, dean. | Thomas Lochheid. |
| John Padine. | John Alexander. |
| David Branche. | Archibald Hammiltoun. |
| Robert Morton. | John Hammiltoun. |
| John Hammiltoun. | Alex. Bern. |
| William Letham. | John Hammiltoun. |

‡ See account of the trial of the Archbishop for saying mass.

§ Lindores Abbey, p. 31. In the Grammar School Charter the rights of the occupiers of the altars, &c., are reserved.

|| Buchanan's Hist. of Scot., p. 266.

see, to more than one individual.* One moiety of the possessions of the Abbey was rescued from the spoiler and applied to a noble purpose. The altarages of St. Mirin, St. Columba, St. Ninian, St. Mary the Virgin, St. Nicholas, St. Peter, St. Catherine, St. Anne, the chapel of St. Rocques and the seven roods of land or thereby belonging and adjacent to the said chapel, with the pittances of money, obit silver, and commons formerly possessed and lifted by the monks of the Monastery of Paisley, were gifted by King James VI. to the Burgh for the erection and support of a Grammar School and its teacher.† The charter setting forth the benefaction thus expresses its worthy object—"that the youth may be instructed in good morals, and the knowledge of letters and virtue, and may be qualified not only for serving God in the ministry of the Word, but also for being able and useful members of the community." This was the origin of the Grammar School of Paisley, which has been so serviceable to successive generations. Its endowment is the only feature which is in any way pleasant in the story of the spoliation and overthrow of the Monastery. Everything else connected with it is cruel and unjust.

When the last Abbot, on his promotion to a Bishopric, made over the Abbey to his nephew, Claud Hamilton, *in commendam*, it was probably his intention that the youth, when he came of age, should take orders, and become Abbot in reality. This had been the case with himself, and he intended it should be so with his nephew. The circumstances of the time prevented this, and Claud Hamilton probably lived and died a layman, or at least was only in some of the minor orders. But though he never wore the mitre of the Abbey, he was styled its Abbot, and had a very firm hold of its revenues, which he regarded as his own.‡ During the troublous times that preceded his uncle's death, "stern Claud" took a leading part on the side of Queen Mary; and after the battle of Lang-

* In 1567, Beatrice Livingstone complains to the Privy Council that her pension of 40 marks yerlie, out of the thirds of Paslay, had not been regularly paid her by Michael Chisholm, the collector.—Reg. Priv. Council Act, 1567.

† This charter is given at length by Mr. Brown, in his "History of the Paisley Grammar School," a very interesting and accurate work. Mr. Brown supposes, I think with reason, that the town was indebted for this gift to the good offices of Mr. Adamson, the first Protestant minister in Paisley.

‡ He was infeft in the temporalities on 29th July, 1567.

syde, his estates were forfeited, and he himself declared a traitor.* The Abbey and its possessions were then given to Lord Sempill,† who had fought on the side of the Regent, and whose great ambition seems to have been to become proprietor of the estates of which his family were hereditary bailies. After the execution of the Archbishop, Claud led a wandering life. He was one of the leaders in the surprise of Stirling.‡ He and his followers rushed through the streets of the town "crying this slogane, Ane Hamilton, God, and the Queen! think on the Bishop of St. Androis."§ The object seems to have been instigated by a desire to revenge the death of the prelate, to whom Claud was much attached. This object was so far attained: the Regent, in the confusion, was foully murdered, being shot through the back by a Captain Calder, who afterwards confessed that he had received his orders from the Lord of Paisley.|| Scotland was now divided into factions, and the name of Claud Hamilton appears among the leading spirits of the time. Vowing vengeance against Sempill, he came to the neighbourhood of Paisley¶ to dispossess, if possible, the usurper of his rights; and "as Lord Sempill was, upon the 10th July, 1572, passing forth to berreft some puir tenants, Lord Claud set upon him, chasit him back, slew forty-twa of his soldiers, tuik fyfteen of them prisoners, and than after layd men about the house sa lang till a greter power was come furth of another part to rescue Lord Sempill."**

Claud was unexpectedly put in possession of what he could not obtain by force. A gleam of peace came to Scotland by the Treaty of Perth. The forfeiture of the Lord of Paisley was recalled, and Sempill was ordered to give him possession of his lands. That nobleman was not inclined to part with them,†† and refused to do so. The Abbey was besieged and

* Acts of Par., 18th Aug., 1568.

† Privy Seal Reg., xxxvii., 84.

‡ 4th Sept., 1571.

§ Bannatyne Memorials.

|| Sir J. Melville's Memoirs, p. 242.

¶ Hist. of King James VI., p. 113, 1572.

** Ibid.

†† Appendix to "Fourth Report on Historical Records," p. 488, June 10, 1573. Commission under the Great Seal by King James VI., with advice, &c. The Commission narrates that by pacification concluded at Perth, and ratified by Parliament on 23rd Feb. last, it was declared that Lord

taken by the Earl of Argyle in the name of the King, and Lord Sempill got "six days to transport himself and his gear." Lord Claud now settled down at Paisley, and on the 1st August, 1574, married a daughter of Lord Seyton, "at Niddrie, with great triumph." Children were born to him at the Abbey, or, as it then began to be called, the "Place of Paisley," and his days of fighting were apparently over. He would not, however, rest contented, and again embarked in the intrigues of the time. The Regent Morton was his bitter enemy, and by his influence Claud was again forfeited,* and his posterity disinherited. The Earl of Morton and others were commissioned "to search for and administer justice to him," and accordingly Paisley was again besieged.† This time no resistance was made. The Abbey was surrendered to the Master of Glencairn in 1579, but "the Abbot," as he is called in a journal of the time, was not "in his strength, but conveyed himself quietly to sic pairt as no man knowis.‡

The Lordship of Paisley after this seems to have been rapidly conveyed from one proprietor to another. Alan, Lord Cathcart,§ Master of the King's Household, received a lease of the temporalities immediately on Lord Claud's forfeiture; then they seem to have been gifted to John, Earl of Mar, in the same year, ‖ and subsequently we find them in the posses-

Claud Hamilton, Commendator of Paisley, should be restored to that benefice to possess the same as freely as if no tumults had ever happened, which pacification was approved by the Regent: that the Regent had dealt favourably with Robert, Lord Sempill, and that the King's order had been sent forth against the latter, commanding restitution of the said benefice to be made to the said Lord Claud Hamilton, but that as yet no obedience had been rendered to the same. For these causes the said Earl of Argyle is appointed Lieutenant and General within these parts, Lanark, Clydesdale, &c., with the usual powers, and specially with authority to assemble the lieges within the bounds, at Glasgow, on the 27th of June; and also, "our standing army," and to procure warlike necessaries for the siege of the House and Monastery of Paisley, and for the subjection of the rebels and disobedient within the same, and their accomplices, for which end he was to display the King's Standard, to plant an army before the said Monastery, and to use fire and sword for its recovery under lawful authority." The Commission was to last till the recovery of the said Monastery. Dated at Holyrood House, 10th June, 1573.

* Acts of Par., Vol. III., pp. 125, 129, 137, 159.

† Moyse's Memoirs, p. 22. ‡ Ibid.

§ In the Cathcart Papers there is a tack or letter of the Chamberlain, dated October, 1579, in favour of Alan Lord Cathcart, the King's Master of the Household, of the Abbacy of Paisley, in the King's hand, by the forfeiture of Alan Hamilton, Commendator thereof.

‖ Moyse's Memoirs, p. 26.

sion of a nephew of that nobleman, William Erskine of Balgownie, Parson, as he was named, of Campsay. He is called "Commendator of Paisley," and resided at the Abbey.* Lord Claud was now a fugitive. For a time he hid himself in various parts of Scotland, but at length was compelled to fly to England, where he received kind treatment from Queen Elizabeth, and remained at her Court waiting for better times.† They were long in coming, but they arrived at last. After fourteen years of exile, Claud was again restored to his ancestral rights. The Parson of Campsay was forfeited in 1584,‡ and in the following year Claud was back at the Place of Paisley.§

The remaining years of his life were comparatively peaceful. He rose high in Royal favour, and several Acts of Parliament were passed consolidating his possessions and securing them to himself and his descendants. In 1587 he was made Lord Paisley, and his eldest son was created Earl of Abercorn in 1606. Lord Claud took an active part in the government of the neighbouring burgh, and exercised the old right of the Abbot in appointing one of the bailies. As he grew older, however, he seems to have retired from public life, and in 1598 he granted a commission to his eldest son to act for him. In the summer of 1597, Anne of Denmark, the Queen of James VI., came to visit the old lord,‖ and the King himself was there on the 24th July, 1617. Lord Claud was then too old a man to take part in gaiety, but his son, the Earl, did the honours of the Abbey. The nobility and gentlemen of the county were present, and the monarch was most hospitably entertained.

* During his residence he caused a well to be sunk at the Abbey Place, which is still yielding a plentiful supply of excellent spring water, and bears the name of "Balgownie Well."—Semple, p. 27.

† Hist. of King James VI., p. 175.

‡ Act of Par., Vol. III., pp. 332-336-344.

§ Ibid, p. 383.

‖ Town Council Records, 8th July, 1597—"The quhilk day the bailies and counsall, understanding perfytly that the Queen's Majesty is to be shortlie in the Place of Paislay, and in respect thereof for decoration of the Kirk and Portis of the said burgh, in sic sort as may be gudlie done for the present, they haf concluded that there be ane pyntour sent for to Glasgow, for drawing of some drauchts in the Kirk, as shall be thocht maist necessar for the present."

It was no new thing for the King of Scotland to visit the Abbey of Paisley, but this King was the last who did so. His reception recalls that of his ancestor, James IV., in the days of Abbot Shaw, but the circumstances were changed. The altars where that monarch paid his devotions and offered his gifts had been swept away. The Abbey had become the Kirk of Paisley; the Monastery was called "The Place." Protestant ministers took the place of priests, and psalm-singing that of the old ritual. Still there was entertainment, such as it was. The King was received in the "great hall" of Abercorn, and a "pretty boy"* delivered a bombastic

* The pretty boy was a son of Sir James Sempill of Beltrees. As the address presented to the King is curious, we give it in full :—

"A GRAVER ORATOR (Sir) would better become so great an action as to welcome our great and most gratious Soveraine ; and a bashfull silence were a boyes best eloquence. But seeing wee read that in the salutations of that Romane *Cæsar*, á sillie Pye amongst the rest cryed *Ave Cæsar* to : Pardon mee (Sir) your M. owne old Parret, to put furth a few words, as witnesses of the fervent affections, of your most faithfull subjects in these parts ; who all by my tongue, as birds of one Cage, crye with me, *Ave Cæsar, VVelcome most gratious King.*

"Welcome then is the word, and welcome the work wee all aime at. A verball welcome were base, trivial and for everie body ; and à Real or Royal welcome answering either our harts desires, or your H. deservings, *Ad hæc quis sufficiens?* Actions can never æquall affections. Saying then is nothing ; shall I swear your M. welcome ? I dare ; but it becommeth not a boy to touch the Bible ; and yet, because an oath taken by nothing, is but nothing, *J sweare by the Black Book of* PAISLEY *your M. is most dearlie VVelcome.*

*Thus have J said* (Sir) *and thus have I sworne.*
*Performance tak from Noble* ABERCORNE.

Welcome then (SIR) every where, but welcomer here, than any where. This seemeth a Paradox, but if I prove it, your M. I hope will approve it. Three pillars of my proof I find in our old Poet, *Phœbus*, his *Clytia;* and his *Leucothoe* ; whose fabulous Allegorie if I can applie to our selves by true historie, all is well.

"*Phœbus* (SIR) you knowe is knowne to all, because seene of all : that Sunne, that Eye, by which the world seeth, shining alike both on good and bad. And are not you (SIR) our royall *Phœbus ?* are not you, as ane eye of world, seeing vpon you are the Eyes of the world, some for good, others for evill according to their minds. And as that Sunne in his course, compasseth and passeth by the whole world ; so hath your M. since you beganne to shine in your royall Sphære, inhanced a good part of the world; but passed by, and buried all the Princes, as well of the Heathen as Christiane world. O shine still then our royall *Phœbus*.

"Now that your M. is the peculiar *Phœbus* of our westerne world, if any did doubt, then, *Ex ore duorum aut trium,* your three Kingdomes ar three witnesses. Still shine then our royall *Phœbus*. Now (SIR) *Clytia* and *Leucothoe* were *Phœbus'* Mistresses ; *Clytia* the daughter of the *Ocean*, *Phœbus'* first Love. Hence did the Poets faine, that the Sunne rising in the East, holdeth his course westward, for visiting his love, and according to their long or short embracements, aryes

address, in which he compared himself to "the King's parrot," and the King, with perhaps less truth, to "Royal Phœbus." It is certainly a wonderful production, and perhaps charmed the ears of the King as much as the strains of Lord Sempill's harper charmed those of his ancestors.

our long or short dayes and nights. And are not wee then (Sir) of Scotland, your M. owne old kindlie *Clytia?* are not you (Sir) our *Phœbus*, comming from the East, with glorious displayed beames, to embrace vs in the mouth of the *Ocean?* and is not this verie place now (Sir) your vestermost period? Ergo (Sir) your kindliest *Clytia*.

"Your *Clytia* (Sir) is of many goodlie members. Your M. hath past alreddie her head, neck, and armes, your greater Townes & Cities; but till now came you never to her hart. Why? because in this verie parish is that auncient seat of William Wallas, that worthie Warrier, to whome (vnder GOD) wee owe that you ar ours, and *Britanne* yours. In this very parish is that Noble house of *Dairnley-Lennox*, whence sprung your M. most famous progenitors. In the Citie you came from, the bed that bred you: In the next you go to, That noble Race of *Hamilton*, wherein your H. most royall Stémme distilled some droppes of their dearest Blood: and in this very house, is, your M. owne noble *Abercorne*, a cheefe sprigge of the same roote, removed only á litle by tyme, but nothing by Nature. And therefore are you in the verie hart of your *Clytia*, and so welcomer to her hart, than to any other part. And so I hope your M. Parret hath proved his Paradox.

"Now (Sir) *Leucothoe*, that fairest Ladye, *Phœbus* second love, shee is even your M. owne glorious *England* most worthy of all love. When that *Phœbus*, first wowed that *Leucothoe*, hee was faine to transforme him selfe in the shape of her Mother, and so to chift her hand-maids for a more privat accesse. But when your M. went first to your English *Leucothoe*, you went lik your selfe, busked with your owne beames, and backed with the best of your *Clytia*: So were both you and wee welcome, and embraced of your *Leucothoe*. And retourning now to your *Clytia*, you bring with you againe, the verie lyfe (as it were) of your *Leucothoe*, these Nobles and Gentrie which accompanie you; and should not both bee; nay; are not both most dearlie welcome to your *Clytia*.

"That *Phœbus* in his love to his *Leucothoe* forgot his *Clytia;* he came no more at her; her nightes grewe long, her winters tedious, whereupon *Clytia* both revealed and reviled their loves; and so *Leucothoe* was buried quick by her owne furious father, and *Clytia* cast out for ever of *Phœbus*' favour. But your M. in your most inward embracements of your *Leucothoe*, thén were you most mindfull of your old *Clytia*, Jndeed our nights have beene long, a fourtein yeeres winter, if wee weigh but your persone; but yet the beames of your Royall hart (the onlie lyfe of Love) were ever awarming vs. The onely remedie were, that these two Ladyes, as their loves are both fixed on one, so themselves become both one; and what will not true love vnite? As they have alreadie taken on one Name for their deare *Phœbus* sake, let them put on also one Nature for the same sake. So shall our *Phœbus* shine alike on both; be still present with both: our nights shal be turned in day, and our winter in ane endlesse Sommer; and one beame shall launce alike on both sides of our bound-rod, and our *Phœbus* no more need to streach out his armes on both sides of it, devyding as it were his Royall body for embracing at once two divided Ladyes. Hee that conspireth not to this Union, let never *Phœbus* shine more on him.

"Lastly (Sir) that poore *Clytia*, thogh shee lost her *Phœbus* favour, yet left shee never of to love him, but still whether his Chariot went, thether followed her eyes, till in end by her endlesse

Lord Claud, the Commendator, could take but little part in the festivities, and they were given in the name of his son, the Earl. He died in 1621, aged 78, having survived his son, who died in 1618. He had seen many changes during his most eventful life. Whether he ever became a Protestant is doubtful. Generally he is spoken of as a Catholic* or "Papist." In a chronicle of his time,† we are told of his attending sermon in Edinburgh, and going out before the prayer. He certainly gave as little encouragement as he could to Protestantism in Paisley during his first residence there. Probably after his visit to the Court of Queen Elizabeth he thought it wise to render outward conformity to the "new opinions," and we give in the Appendix a letter from him to Lord Burleigh, treasurer to Queen Elizabeth, in which he expresses great indignation at a rumour that he had "changed his religion." But he does not say which religion he means, and probably his expressions are designedly ambiguous. On the whole, we incline to the opinion that he died in the faith in which he was born,‡ and at the altars of which it was at one time intended he should minister.

With the death of the old "Commendator," the last link between us and the Monastery of Paisley is severed. When in his boyhood, he was

observance shee was turned in that floure called *Heliotropion* or *Solsequium*. And how much more (SIR) shuld wee who grow daylie in your grace and favour; be all turned in a Βασιλιοτροπιον with a faithfull *Obsequium*, Our eyes shull ever be fixed on your Royall Chariot: and our harts on your Sacred Person.

"*O Royal* Phœbus *keepe this course for ever,*
*And from thy deare* Britannia *never sever,*
*But if the Fates will rather frame it so*
*That* Phœbus *now must come, and then must goe,*
*Long may thy selfe*; *Thy race mot ever ring,*
*Thus, without end; vvee end.* GOD SAVE OUR KING.
"Amen."

* Bannatyne Memorials, where there are many notices of Lord Claud.

† Colville Memoirs (Bannatyne Club).

‡ In 1588 he was reported as "a receiver of Jesuits, and since his last comming to Scotland refuseth to subscribe and communicate. Those that resort to him are the Laird of Fintry, Mr. Robert Bruce, and Mr. Gilbert Browne."—Calderwood, Vol. IV., p. 662. Well on to the end of the Commendator's life his deeds are witnessed by a Robert Rer, or Ker, as "servitor to my Lord of Paisley." A person of the same name was among the last monks of the Abbey, and probably continued in the service of Lord Claud as Almoner.

made "Abbot," the Church seemed firm and almost beyond the reach of change. He had known the Abbey in its splendour, had assisted at its services, and had probably received his education within its walls. He had lived to see all its glory vanished, its walls defaced, its shrines despoiled, its brethren scattered and proscribed. With the notice of his death, we take our last look at "the things that were." In doing so, we may give the description of the Abbey as it stood in its latter days, by one who was the last surviving Bishop of the old Church of Scotland,* and who grows eloquent as he writes of its departed glories.

"Two miles from Renfrew is the town of Paisley, situated on the bank of the Cart, in a pleasant situation, amid hills, woods, and gardens. Thence there is a passage to a certainly magnificent and wealthy Monastery of the same name, built for the district, surrounded by a very splendid wall of dressed stone, with beautiful statues on the summit, for more than a mile on all sides. The beauty of the buildings of this temple, the splendour of the church furniture, and the beauty of the gardens, may rival many churches which are to-day considered more magnificent among foreign nations, a remark that might be made with perfect truth about all our monasteries without exception. Moreover, John, the last Bishop of St. Andrews, erected for the church of Paisley a tower second to none in our own country, at immense expense, which, from the first, resting on an insecure foundation, when hardly finished, fell by its own weight.

Probably the "Commendator" was among the last who remembered the Abbey as the Bishop describes it.

* Leslie, Bishop of Ross.

## CHAPTER XXII.

### The New Order.

"The old order changeth, yielding place to new."
*Tennyson.*

WITH many of our readers all interest in the subject of our story ceases with the dissolution of the Convent. There are, however, some more modern associations connected with the Church and Place of Paisley which are of an interesting character, and which are perhaps worthy of notice. To some of these we will now refer. Up to the death of the Archbishop no preachers of the new opinions "obtained a settlement in Paisley." The doors were "steyked" against them; and as we have seen, the Assembly of the Kirk vehemently denounced those who turned away the ministers "when they presented themselves to have preached the Word." In the year after the Archbishop's death, 1572, Paisley continued hostile to Protestantism. Mass was still said there, and the Kirk called on all the neighbouring professors of religion to assist in putting down and finally stopping what they felt to be a great scandal and sin.* It was probably in consequence of the measures taken in pursuance of this order that the first Protestant minister obtained an entrance into the Church. His name was Patrick Adamson or Constant, and he afterwards rose, through his interest with Lord Morton, to eminence, as Archbishop of St. Andrews,—one of the *tulchan* prelates, as they were called derisively, who were appointed to the different Scot-

* Book of the Universal Kirk, p. 319.

tish Sees.* He was a man of great ability and eloquence; but does not appear to have been much appreciated in Paisley. He resided in Glasgow, not being able to obtain a lodging in his parish, and was sharply rebuked by the Assembly for not "waiting on his cure." He seems to have been connected with Paisley for three years, during part of which time Lord Claud and his wife resided at the Abbey, and they were not likely to shew much kindness to the Protestant divine. On Mr. Adamson leaving Paisley, Mr. Andro Polwart was appointed minister. He also was unable to make any way among his parishioners. Like his predecessor, he was found fault with by the Assembly for not waiting on his cure,† and indeed he had but little inducement to do so. He was hindered in the discharge of his duties in every possible way, and his life was threatened if he remained. The Assembly itself seemed to give the place up in despair, and, on his supplication, they released the minister from his charge, after he had been there for two years, "that he might serve other where it pleases God to call him." The stipends of Mr. Adamson and his successor were not very large. Each of them had £200 5s., Scots money, per annum.‡ They were assisted by a reader of the name of William Makfingoun, who received £20. As the term "Maister" § is prefixed to his name in the list of ministers, it is probable he was one of the old clergy who had conformed. Such were frequently employed as "readers" throughout the country, though they were not allowed to preach or administer the sacraments. It was the duty of the reader to conduct a service preliminary to that of the minister. "He took his place at the lectern, read the

* Melville's Diary, Ban. Club, p. 42, 1575.—"There was then resident in Glasgow Mr. Patrick Adamson *alias* Constant, minister of Paisley, a man of notable ingyne, letters, and eloquence. After he had craftilie insinuat himself in Mr. Andros' favour, and the Ministrie of Edinburgh, he began to step in forwart to the first degree of a Bishop, and leaving Paisley, past to Court, and became minister to the Regent."

† Book of the Universal Kirk, Ban. Club, Vol. III., pp. 324, 342.

1577.—"Andro Polwart was decernit to be frie and at liberty fra the Kirk at Paisley that he may serve uther quhair it pleases God to call him, because of the contempt of discipline, thair manifest vices, minacing and boasting of doing his deutie, his labours cannot be profitable to them." He became sub-Dean of Glasgow.

‡ Regist. of Ministers. Miscellany of the Wodrow Society, Vol. I., p. 382. § M.A.

Common Prayers, and, in some churches, the Decalogue and the Creed. He then gave out large portions of the Psalter, the singing of which was concluded with the *Gloria Patri*, and next read chapters of Scripture from the Old and New Testaments, going through in order any book that was begun, as required by the First Book of Discipline. After an hour thus spent, the bell rang, and the minister entered the pulpit."* We hope the "reader" met with a better reception than his superiors in the parish.

In 1578 a remarkable man, Thomas Smeaton, was induced, after much persuasion, to come as minister to Paisley. He was famous for his learning, had travelled much, and was respected for his many private virtues. He was more successful than his predecessors. Lord Claud had been obliged to fly for his life, and the new Commendator was favourable to Protestantism. Smeaton was gentle and kindly in his manner, and these qualities, conjoined with his earnestness, possibly won for him a certain amount of respect. He was held in high esteem throughout the Church, and was more than once made Moderator of the General Assembly. "Mr. Thomas," says his biographer, "was verie wacriff and painful, and skarslie tuk tym to refresh nature. I haiff seen him oft find fault with lang dinners and suppers at General Assemblies, and, when uthers were thereat, he would abstain, and be about the penning of things (wherein he excellit, bathe in language and form of letter), and yet he was nocht rustic, nor austere, but sweet and affable in companie, with a modest and naive gravitie. Very frugale in food and reyment, and walked maist on foot; whom I was verie glad to accompanie whiles to Stirling, and now and then to his kirk for my instruction and comfort. He lovit me exceeding well, and wald at parting thrust my head into his bosom and kiss me."† Smeaton remained only two years in Paisley, and in 1580 was made Principal of the University of Glasgow.

The next minister of whom we have any notice is one of much more energy and determination than his predecessors. Mr. Andrew Knox

* Introduction to "Book of Common Order," by Messrs. Leishman and Sprott, a book that should be read by all interested in the history of public worship in Scotland.

† Melville's Diary, p. 58, where a very full account of Smeaton is given.

came from Lochwinnoch to Paisley in 1585, about the time of Lord Claud's return from banishment.* Lord Abercorn, the son of this nobleman, sat frequently in the General Assembly as an elder,† and as the old lord probably wished to spend the evening of his days in peace, Mr. Andro Knox had it all his own way.‡ He put down with a strong hand any opposition to the Church established by law, and any "Papist" must have found Paisley a disagreeable place of residence during his incumbency. He produced outward conformity by the measures he adopted, though it is probable that many clung in secret to the old faith. No parishioner was allowed to absent himself from the Abbey Church in time of sermon, and especially from the Sacrament of the Lord's Supper. The parishes of Renfrewshire were erected into a presbytery in 1590, and after that the Catholics of Paisley got little rest—certainly no mercy. They were excommunicated, fined, imprisoned, or compelled on their knees publicly to acknowledge their sin. Many ladies of rank in Renfrewshire, whose husbands had conformed, remained attached to the old faith; but they were treated with little deference.§ Old Lady Claud Hamilton, driven to despair by the persecution to which she was subjected by Mr. Knox and his coadjutors, wrote a letter to King James, imploring him to interfere in her behalf.|| "These four years past," she says, "I have been subject to a vehement payne, arising from distillations and humours in my head, with a continual toothache, giving me sic torment as scarce I have half-an-hour's release by night or by day, and notwithstanding, to aggravate my payne, I am summoned by the Church to confer and attend on the Presbyteries and other dyets, upon what suspects I know not, for I have never been proved repyning nor disobedient to the least of his Majesty's laws. I hope his Majesty, who hath always had a

* Andrew Knox was the second son of John Knox of Ranfurlie, in the parish of Kilbarchan.

† Book of Universal Kirk.

‡ As superior of Paisley, Lord Claud allowed Knox to build a house for himself in the High Street of Paisley, but the minister got into trouble and litigation with his neighbour in building it.

§ Lady Glencairne, Lady Duchal, and others, who were terribly badgered.

|| Letters to James VI., Ban. Club, date 1st Sept., 1610.

gracious regard to me and mine, will not think me unworthy in my extreme of sickness." The records of the Presbytery shew with how strong a hand any one who ventured on non-conformity was put down. The usual rule was for the Presbytery to instruct the minister of the parish to summon him for the first time; then, if contumacious, for the second; and, if he still continued so, for the third time. The minister was then directed to proceed to the first admonition, then to the second, and afterwards to the third. If the offender still remained obstinate, he was to be prayed for for the first time, then the minister was afterwards to proceed to the second and third prayer. If the person continued still impenitent, excommunication followed, and he was delivered over to Satan for the destruction of his body, that his soul might be saved in the day of the Lord. Many of those so delivered over would have taken it very lightly if civil consequences had not followed, and imprisonment, banishment, and other penalties been inflicted.* Andro Knox was very faithful in Paisley in looking after suspected persons and subjecting them to discipline, and the Council of Paisley seconded his efforts. They passed an Act† "anent sic persons that willfulie remains fra the kirk in tyme of Sermount on the Sonday." They were to be apprehended, fined twenty shillings for each offence, and, if unable to pay this fine, were to be "put and halden in the stocks be the space of xxiii. hours." The inhabitants were also ordered to give regular attention to morning and evening prayers,‡ which were read from the Book of Common Order in the Chapel of St. Mirin by the "reader;"§ and as there was a service in the Abbey every Tuesday, all merchants were required to shut their doors during prayers, and to attend the kirk for hearing of the Word, under pain of eight shillings.|| All "disobedient to the kirk were to be put in ward till they find caution to compear before the session of the kirk." Under this "iron rule," Mr. Andro Knox bade fair to stamp out all "Papistrie" in his parish.

* Town Council Records, Jan. 24, 1622, "Enacted, that nae houses be let to persons excommunicate, and that none entertain them in their houses, under the pain of ten punds."

† Town Council Records, 1546, Jan. 27th.

‡ Town Council Records, 1602, Jan. 28. § See Brown's History of the Grammar School.

|| Ibid, Nov. 22, 1603. Ibid, March 3, 1668.

In consequence of his energy in this work he was appointed by the Presbytery to watch the proceedings of all Roman Catholics within their bounds, to collect information from his brethren, and to report to a central committee in Edinburgh. This was very congenial employment for Mr. Andro, and he achieved in it great success. The Roman Catholics, goaded to despair by the fierce persecution to which they were subjected, began to intrigue for the overthrow of the Government that sanctioned the system under which they were so terribly oppressed. Their leaders entered into negotiations with Philip the Second of Spain, in the hope that foreign assistance might enable them to obtain some relief from their tormentors. Suspicions of this were very general, and Presbyteries were on the watch for conspirators. Mr. Andro was especially active, and having heard that a certain George Ker, a doctor of laws, and brother to the Abbot of Newbattle, who had been excommunicated for Popery by the Presbytery of Haddington, was in the neighbourhood of Paisley, he at once proceeded to enquire after him. Setting off with a body of armed men, furnished by his parishioner Lord Ross of Halkhead,* the minister traced Ker to Glasgow, and thence to one of the islands of the Cumbrae, where he apprehended him during the night on board the vessel by which he was about to proceed to the continent. Suspicious papers were found on him, and the minister bore him off in triumph to Edinburgh. It was on a Sabbath toward the end of December that he reached the capital. The ministers hearing of the approach of the prisoner shortened their sermons, and the populace, under the influence of their exhortations, went out to meet the captive with every expression of insult.† His captor received the thanks of the council for his diligence, and went back to Paisley a happy man. A few years ‡ after he performed another exploit similar to the capture of Ker. A catholic laird, Barclay of Ladyland, seized Ailsa Craig, in the Frith of Clyde, with the intention of fortifying it and then delivering it to the Spaniards, who had promised to make a descent upon Scotland. Andro Knox discovered the plot, and with a few daring assistants sailed to the rock, attacked the desper-

* Tytler, Vol. II., p. 316. Other accounts say he was accompanied by students of Glasgow University. I have followed the account of Tytler as most probable.

† Cunninghame, Vol. II., p. 313. ‡ 1597.

ado, and "reduced him to such extremity that, rather than be taken alive, he rushed into the sea, and in one moment chocked both himself and his treason."*

It is somewhat amusing to find this disciplinarian minister falling himself into the grasp of the law. He seems to have been on bad terms with a certain Gavin Stewart, minister in Paisley, who probably resented his high-handed proceedings, and who was bound over by the Magistrates† not to molest the minister directly or indirectly. The peace was not long kept between them, for before they left the "town house of the Tolbuith the minister made an attack upon Gavin in presence of Lord Abercorne and the bailies, and struck him on the head with a key to the effusion of his blood, upon the occasion of certain words which fell furth rapidly between them." The Presbytery four days afterwards suspended him from all the functions of the ministry. Very soon after the offender sent them a petition, with which they were not satisfied, especially as he had not submitted to their edict of suspension. They ordered his suspension, therefore, to be proclaimed in the church of Paisley, and "ordained Mr. John Hay and Patrick Hamilton to travell for taking up of the variance betwixt him and Gavin Stewart, and to report their diligence." The minister again approached them, and this time they were satisfied with his penitence, and resolved to restore him to his office, and instructed one of their brethren from the pulpit of the church to "warne all gentlemen and elders within the parochin of Paisley to be present on the 16th inst. with the brethren to advise upon the forme of his repossession." These worthies accordingly met together, and resolved that the erring Mr. Andro should be reponed in the following manner:—"The said Mr. Andro shall sit in the maist patent place of the Kirk of Paislay upon Sunday next to come, before noon, being the 19th day of November, and thereafter that Mr. John Hay, appointed by the brethren to supply the place, has delated the fault and offence of the said Mr. Andro to the people, the said Mr. Andro, in all humiliation, shall confess his offence to God, the brethren, and the party offendit, and shall get down upon his knees, and ask

* Tytler, Vol. II., p. 260.

† 1st Oct., 1604. Council Records.

God's mercie for the same—the same being done, the bailies and sum honest men of the parochin shall receive him by the hand." Let us hope his own experience of discipline made him more tender in administering it to others.*

Mr. Knox was appointed in 1605 to the Bishopric of the Isles. He came to the Presbytery and asked leave of absence for four or five weeks that he might visit his new diocese, promising on his return to demit either the bishopric or the parish of Paisley. He continued absent for many months, and when he came back shewed no inclination to fulfil his promise. The Bailies of Paisley, and James, Earl of Abercorn, accordingly complained to the Presbytery of the minister's absence, and the desolate state of the church for want of service. The Presbytery had many interviews with the minister, who shewed every intention of remaining a pluralist as long as he was able. He offered to provide for a second minister as a coadjutor, but this offer was not accepted. After much negotiation, however, he was induced to demit his charge, and Mr. Patrick Hamilton, who was minister of Lochwinnoch, was chosen, and inducted to the Abbey in December, 1607. The Bishop then retired to the diocese of the Isles, where he maintained his warlike character.† He was afterwards translated to the See of Raphoe, in Ireland.

We know but little of what happened at Paisley for some time after the demission of the Bishop. On his removal the strict repressive measures which he enforced were relaxed, for when we come upon the history of Paisley again we find Roman Catholicism once more shewing itself. The next minister of whom we know anything had as troublous a time there as any of his predecessors. The Abercorn family seem always to have had a warm side to the old faith, and the traditions of the Monastery, and stories of the kindness and hospitality of its inmates, between whom and the people of Paisley there had always existed the closest intimacy, would be handed down from father to son. At anyrate, nearly

* He had previously made an humble apology to the bailies.

† In 1614 he invaded Islay with 70 men to attack the Highland robber "Coll Kittoch."—See Pitcairn's Criminal Trials.

one hundred years after the Reformation, and notwithstanding all the persecutions of the Presbytery, we find Paisley described, in the words of a most reliable writer, as a "very nest of Papists." It is a curious circumstance that it continued Catholic so long after other parts of Scotland.

## CHAPTER XXIII.

### Discipline.

What are their orders, constitutions,
Church-censures, curses, absolutions,
But sev'ral mystic chains they make
To tie poor Christians to the stake.

—*Hudibras.*

PAISLEY was the seat of a Presbytery, and that court held its meetings within the Abbey Church. It met at least once a month, and sometimes more frequently. Here the poor "Papists" were cited to appear, and were dealt with at different stages of the process against them. Here offenders against morals were brought, clothed in haircloth and bare legged, to receive their sentence; and here fulminations were hurled against all contraveners of the rules laid down by the stern Churchmen. Of the many scenes which the Abbey has witnessed, none are more strange than some of those which were enacted before this conclave, and which are recorded in their minutes. We are not wandering far from the line of our story in making a few extracts from these, illustrating as they do the civil and ecclesiastical history of the time. The business of the Presbytery was opened by prayer and "handling a portion of the Word" by one of the ministers. A Latin thesis was occasionally delivered on some point of controversy, such as "*Dum possit ecclesia errare?*" "*An sit ecclesia infallibilis?*" or some other debated question in theology. The ministers then gave in reports as to the state of their parishes, and especially as to those of their parishioners who absented themselves from church, and who did not come regularly to the Holy Communion.

"Taking the Sacrament" was rigidly insisted on, and all persons of full age were bound to partake, or give a reason satisfactory to their "ordinary," the minister of the parish. If not able to do so, a process against them was commenced before the Presbytery, ending, if they continued obstinate, in their excommunication. Attachment to the Church of Rome was generally suspected when a parishioner did not appear at his parish church, and he was very strictly inquired after. The Presbytery minutes begin on the 16th September, 1602, with the citing of a Paisley parishioner, the Laird of Stanelie, for non-attendance. He was complained of by that zealous champion of Protestantism, Mr. Andro Knox.

> "The Presbytre of Paslay halden within the Kirk of the same the 16 day of Sep., 1602.
>
> "Because of the sklander arysing upon Johne Maxwell of Stanelie, his refusale to communicat the Holy Supper of our Lord Jesus Christ with the remanent his parishioners, within the Paroche Kirk of Pasley, alleging himself, albeit he came thare to that same effect the day of the celebration of the said Holy Supper, he had been stayit by the sicht of some of his unfriends present at the said holy actioun, which the brethren estimit no relevant excuse, and thairfore they have ordainit his ordinaire, Mr. Andro Knox, to summon the laird to compear before them the last of this instant, for receiving injunctions to remove the said sklander."

On the 14th October, the Laird appeared, and gave account of himself:—

> "The Laird of Stanelie compearand, and confessing himself penitent for the giving of the occasion of sklander, etc. The brethren has ordainit that in respect the said Johne Maxwell allegit that he might not conveniently resort to his paroche Kirk of Pasley for sundrie occasions of deadly feud, he find cautione of 500 merks money that he and his family shall keep ordinarlie paroche Kirk of Renfrew, and subject himself to the discipline of the Kirk thereof, and shall compear personally in the Kirk of

Pasley upon Sonday next, in tyme of sermon, and confess himself penitent for not communicating with his brethren and neighbours and that his abstinence thairfrom proceeded of no scrupill in religion, but of lack of due preparation, the which he shall be obliged under the penalty aforesaid to amend by communicating upon the first occasion at the holie table of the Lord that the same sall be publickly ministrat within ony kirke of ye Presbyterie of Paslay, due intimation thereof being made to him by Mr. John Hay, for observing of quilk promisses Thomas Inglis, burges of Paslay, became caution and securitie, under the pain above written.

In our next chapter we give an example of the manner in which the Kirk proceeded against such as were "suspected of Papistrie." Many instances similar to that which we shall adduce are to be found in the records of the Presbytery; but, as the process was the same in all cases, we need not repeat them. In very few cases did the offenders "satisfy the Kirk." Sometimes they desired conference with the ministers for "satisfying of their doubts," but this was evidently only to gain time; they very seldom showed signs of repentance, and were almost always after some delay excommunicated. At one time, the power of excommunication lay entirely with the Presbytery, and was very freely used. It was afterwards decreed that the consent of the Bishop should be obtained before sentence could be pronounced. The words of this sentence were very solemn. It "shut them out from the communion of the faithful, debared them from their privileges, and delivered them to Satan for the destruction of their flesh, that their spirits might be saved in the day of the Lord." The Records of the Presbytery contain many instances of excommunicated persons craving to be restored.

"October, 1606.—The which day compeared Mr. Alex. Maxwell of Kilmalcome, and produced judicially before the Presbytery ane supplicatioun in name of his brother germane, John Maxwell of Barefill, containing an earnest and humble desire of the said John to be relaxit by the brethren fra the fearful sentence of excommunicatioun, and that because the said John protested he is resolved in the grounds of true religion, and from his heart renounces Papistrie. The Moderator, enquiring at Mr. Daniel Cunninghame quhat assurance he had of the trew and unfeinit conversioun of the said John, answered that he could perceive no external sign in him, but that, in his judgment, he dealt sincerely with the Kirk; and thairfore the brethren, advising upon the manner of absolving the said John from the said fearful sentence, they ordain that Mr. Daniel Cunninghame, Mr. W. Brisbane, and Mr. Andro Hamilton, confer with him upon the several points of religion controvertit, before he be absolved, to the end he may be moved to renounce his Papistrie and embrace the true religion with the greater sinceritie, as also that before his absolutioun the said brethren shall receive of him these bonds following of his good behaviour in tyme coming:—First, that he shall publicklie, in the Kirk of Kilmacolme, in presence of the congregatioun, subscryve the Confession of Faith, sware by halding up his hand in the presence of the people that fra his heart he willingly renounces, and shall renounce hereafter, Papistrie, and shall walk according to the truth of God for the present publickly preached in Scotland. Also, that he shall find sufficient caution, under the pain of five hundred merks, that he shall communicate at the table of the Lord betwixt the date hereof and Whitsunday, and produce a testimonial under the hands of the pastor of the church where he communicates before that time; that he shall be a diligent hearer of the Word and maintainer of trew religion; and that he shall noways, directly or indirectly, privatly or publickly, speak or reason against the same, but defend the same to his live's end, and shall have no traffick with the enemies of the land: the which having been subscribed in manner aforesaid, the brethren ordains the saids Mr. Daniel and Mr. Andro to relax the said John from the sentence of excommunicatioun on the Sabbath thereafter."

The following is a very curious entry bearing upon the same subject. The excommunicated asks *leave to attend church.*

"October 25, 1626.—The which day Hew Steward, excommunicate, gave in a supplication entreating humblie that the brethren would be pleased to grant unto him some reasonable and convenient tyme to resolve such important business which touched his salvation, as likewise that he might have liberty to frequent the Kirk and hear sermons, whereunto the brethren agreed this—That, for frequenting the Kirk and hearing sermons, they thought it lawful he should do so, *providing he came in after the first prayer and went out before the last;* and as for delay of tyme which he sought for, they thought he had gotten great favour already, and that they were willing to continue the same, if he would at the next synod give obedience and satisfaction."

Before the restoration of any excommunicated Papist, he was bound by the Presbytery to give a very full recantation of his errors. The following were some of the points of Romish doctrine he was called on to abjure:—

"The point of transubstantiation wherein he confessed the body and blood of Christ is not eaten and drunken corporalie, and that the bread and wine in the sacrament is not changed into the body and blood of Christ. 2, That he should abjure the point of justification by works, and that he acknowledged that he and all the faithful were justified by faith in the merits of Jesus Christ. 3, That he should abjure the invocation of saints and prayer to them. 4, That he abjured and should abjure the point of praying in an unknown tongue. And, 5, The said Robert promised to use all means of instruction anent whatsoever doubt he conceived, and shall labour to give satisfaction, as likewise without any tergiversation to communicate at the first occasion."

The Presbytery, though greatly occupied in enforcing unity of faith, exercised also very strict supervision over the morals of the people and their manner of life. Certain cases of immorality were dealt with by the sessions of the various parishes, but more flagrant ones were brought before the Presbytery, and were very severely treated, as these extracts, taken from among many similar notices, shew :—

"November 16, 1626.—The which day compeared John Robesoune, and in all humilitie confessed his guiltiness of the sinne of adulterie. Tho brethren therefore ordained that he shuld remove the said slander so farre as laye in him in this manner, namely, that the said John, being not only convict but confessing his guilt, shuld, according to the acts and lawes of the Kirk, stand and abyde six Sabbaths barefooted and barelegged at the Kirk door of Pasley between the second and third bell ringing, and thereafter to goe to the place of public repentance during the said space of six Sabbaths, and further, ay and until it shuld evidentlie be kythed by tokens of unfeened repentance that he was truelie penitent."

"December 24, 1626.—The quilk day compeared William Steward in Woodsyde, and in presence of the moderator and remanent brethren, in hairclothe, barefooted and barelegged, in all humilitie, with signes and tokens of unfeigned repentance, confessed his guiltiness, &c., wherefore the saids brethren ordained the said William to extract his injunctions, namely, that he shuld stand six Sabbaths in the said hairclothes upon the place of publick repentance within the Kirk of Pasley."

This offender seems to have returned again to his evil courses, and is more severely dealt with accordingly :—

"March 3, 1642.—Which day compeared William Steward in Woodsyde, and confessed his guiltiness, &c., who, for removing the scandal of the said offence committed, was ordained to make his repentance in sackcloth in all the churches within the Presbyterie, beginning at Paslay, and to report the testificat of every one of the saids ministers of his obedience, and that during said space the said William present himself every presbyterie day in the said habit, that the brethren after exercises may confer with him."

"January 14.—The which day compeared William Wallace of Ellerslie,* confessing, &c., whose offence the brethren considering great, and he of the rank of a gentleman, ordained him, for the removing of the slander of the offence, to stand in his own desk in the Kirk of Pasley, and confess as he should be inquired by his pastor, and to pay to the Session of Pasley the sum of twentie pounds money."

Various persons are summoned for the profanation of the Sabbath, and severely punished. The custom that prevailed in Scotland during the Roman Catholic period of having sports on Sunday and dancing on the village green seems in some parishes to have continued. It was, however, put down with a strong hand. Markets which appear occasionally to have been held on the Lord's Day were forbidden.

"October 14, 1602.—Because the mercat called the Fair of the Hill halden in Lochwinnoch yeirlie, the 6th day of November this yeir falls upon the Lord's Day, whairfore for eschewing the abuse of the Sabbath to the said mercat, the Presbyterie has ordained every brother to give admonition to his parochiners to keep the said mercat upon Saterday the fyfth day of the month."

"December 19, 1602.—John Knox of Ranfurly, accused of profaning the Sabbath and Kirk of the Lord by evil words to the vicar of Kilbarchan and his elders, whereon followed ane tumult within the said Kirk, &c., ordained, after sermon made by Mr. William Brisbane, to come out of his own seat, and thereafter upon his knees confess his offence to God for profanation of the Sabbath and oversight of his duties to the vicar and the session."

* The descendant of the patriot.

"19th June, 1606.—The brethren being informed be Mr. Andro Law, minister at Neilston, of the great profanation of the Sabbath by the great resorting of the common people of sundry parochins about, to the green of Little Caldwall, whairupon they profane the Sabbath day by pyping and dancing. Therefore ordains the ministers of the aforesaid parochins to inhibit and forbid openly, out of the pulpit, their own several parochiners to make any resort to the said green in any tyme hereafter, with certification that whosoever shall be found to contravene the said instruction shall be proceeded against be the censures of the Kirk. Also ordains Hew Erston, pyper, for keeping of a green to be summoned, *pro primo.*"

"August 21, 1606.—Gavin Maxwell reportit to the brethren that John Paterson, piper, in Mernis, was found guiltie of profaning the Sabbath, for keeping of the green of Over Pollok, and that he had summoned the said John, *apud acta*, before the Session of Merns, to compear before the Presbyterie. The said John being callit, and not compearing, was ordanit to be summoned, *pro secundo.*"

"2nd July, 1607.—Mr. Andro Hamilton delated John Hall, parochiner of Kilbarchan,* for profanation of the Sabbath day by keeping of a green every Sabbath, at afternoon, with piping and dancing, and had summond the said John . . . not compearing, he is summond, *pro secundo.*"

Paterson, Hall, and Robert Fisher, pyper, were cited, admonished and prayed for at various dates.

"September 3, 1607.—The which day Mr. Andro Hamilton reportit that according to the ordinance of Presbyterie, the 13th of August last, he had proceedit be admonitions against John Hall,

* It was in this village that the famous piper, Habbie Simson, lived, who is immortalised in the song of "Maggie Lauder," and celebrated by Francis Semple of Beltrees.

pyper, who was to compear this instant day. John compeared, and being accusit of profaning the Sabbath, by keeping his grein for the convening of the common people thereon on the Sabbath. Quhilk he confessit, and therefore was ordainit to find caution to the Session of Kilbarchan, under the pain of twenty pounds money, that he shall abstain, in all time coming, from the keeping of the said grein, which he promissed faithfullie in presence of the Presbyterie to do."

"4th May, 1635.—The brethren were informed that there was very great profanation of the Sabbath at Douecot Hall by pyping, whereby multitudes of people were convened, preaching, vilipended, and misesteemed; and that John Dunlop receives the said pypers, and entertained drinkers in his house in time of sermon. The brethren ordained the said John to be cited.

"18th May, compeired John Dunlop, and confessed he had sold drink in tyme of sermon, and had received pypers, and promised reformation faithfullie. The brethren interdicted him all such enormities in tyme coming, under the pain of church censures."

The Presbytery seem to have been greatly opposed to sports and amusements of all kinds at Christmas. The festivities of that joyous time were very sternly forbidden as savouring of "Papistrie," and the people who, under the old clergy, were permitted freely to enjoy themselves, saw the season pass altogether unnoticed. They attempted in some places to keep up the old games, but without much success. Their jollity was very severely repressed.

"19th January, 1604.—The Presbyterie being informed by thair brother, Mr. Patrick Hamilton, that Robert Arthur and Robert Miller, parochiners of Lochquinoche, superstitiously behaved themselves by ringing of girdles, the day of January; as also that Hendrie Paslay, Robert Paslay, Robert Paton, and James King in Muirdykes, after ane profane and godless manner behavit thaimselves, in disagyissing (disguising) themselves, quhilk is naething less than abomination in the eyes of the Lord, as also being informit by their brother, Gavin Hamilton, vicar of Kilbarchan, that James Andro, Robert Henderson, John Hutcheson, &c., usit superstitious plays a lytle before Yuile; also on the day callet Yuill-evening, came throu the clachan of Kilbarchan, making open proclamation and giving open liberty to all men to take pastime for the space of aucht days, as also usit superstitious playis upon the 26th December at the Corsefurd, and gave themselves to strolling and drinking,—the brethren ordainit all tho foresaids persons to be summoned to the next Presbytery day by their brothers, Patrick Hamilton and Gavan Hamilton, vicar of Kilbarchan."

"February 2, 1604.—The persons, proclaimers of Yuille within the parochin of Kilbarchan, upon the day callit Yuill Evening, and passing throu the clachan of Kilbarchan to that effect, and many of them afterwart upon the Monday callit St. Steven's Day passing to the Corsfurd, carrying ane *brechan*, strolling and drinking, and using sundry other godless and profane behaviour, whose names follows, viz., James Andro, &c., superstitiously using themselves at the said two places and dayes foresaid, compearing as they were summoned, and being accusit of ye godless and profane misbehaviours foresaid, and pairt of them denying and pairt of them confessing that they were proclaimers of Yuile ye foresaid tyme, as all admit, are ordainit to compear before ye civil magistrat ye Laird of Craigends, maister to a great number of ye foresaids persons, whom ye brethren requestis to punish thame civilly in body or gear, or both, as he thinks fit, and before ye session of Kilbarbarchan, and in the meantime direct our loving brethren, Mrs. Andro Knox and Patrick Hamilton, commissioners to continue at the said session and try the foresaid offenders, and thereafter to shew their diligence to the Presbyterie, that injunctions may be given unto them according to the worthiness of the offence they shall happen to be convicted of."

The girdle-ringers and the disagysit persons are to be summoned *pro secundo*.

"20th April, 1604.—The which day compeared William Atken, in Lochquinoch parochin, and being accused of using superstitious pastyme by disguising himself upon the last of December, confessit that upon the said nicht he put his cloke about his waist in form of women's clothing, that he put his sark above his doublet, and his napkin upon his face, and thairfore the brethren ordainet the said William to remove the said sclander by making his repentance two days in sackcloth, and that in the publick place of repentance; and found David Henderson, burgess of Pasley, caution under the payne of xx. pounds for abstinence in time to come.

"May 10, 1604.—The which day compeared William Dougall, and being accusit for going superstitiouslie at Yuille in dancing, and, in greater contempt to God and his Kirke, that he came throu the Kirk yard with a drawn quhinger in his hand, confessit that he was in company with the pypers and dancers, and therefore the said Presbyterie ordeint him to remove the said sclander by making his repentance in his lynin (linen) clothes two Sabbath days for abusing himself in the superstitious tyme of Yuille, and for his blasphemous aiths and injurious language given to the session of Kilbarchan and commissioners of the Presbyterie, as also that he find burgess of Paisley, caution, under the payn of six pounds, for obedience to the said injunction and abstinente in time to come."

"August 21, 1606.—The which day George Maxwell, minister at Mearns, delatit to the Presbyterie these persons following, namely, John Miller, David Pollock, John Gilmour in Hillhead, John Gilmour in Malletsheuch, and that for the offence following, to wit, that the said persons abovenamed upon Sunday at even, the day of being disagysit in the nicht, came to Robert Watson's house in Kirkhill, and for some malicious purpose invadit the said Robert, his sonne, and hurt his servant, intending also to bring sclander upon his house and bairnes, of the which the brethren taking due consideration, and finding the said persons guilty of *nichtwaking*, which is a common offence in that parochin, brewing manifold sclanders and contentions, they ordained George Maxwell to summond, *pro primo*, the said persons to appear before the brethren the 4th September next to answer for the saime."

These lively persons, however, unlike the girdle-ringers of Kilbarchan, escaped punishment.

"October 9, 1606.—The which day, in respect there was suspicion of plague within the parochin of Merns, so that the parochiners cited were hinderit to compear before the Presbyterie, therefore the brethren thocht it expedient to desiset any further process against the said parochiners, while it should please God to relieve them of that suspition."

The Presbytery had no cases of witchcraft before them at this early period. These appear considerably later on; but charming, and other deeds of darkness, particularly when accompanied by the sale of quack medicines, are strongly denounced.

"Sep. 16, 1602.—Anent the sclander givin by Gavin Stewart, burges of Paslay, in prostrating himself before Martha Pinkertoun upon his knees, craving the health of Gavan Ralstoun, younger of that Ilk, fra her as was allegit, the said Gavan compearing, as he was lawfully summond, to answer for the sclander aforesaid, conffessit that he gaed to the said Martha, and said to her (it is said thou hast taken the health of this man Gavin Ralstoun fra him, the which if thou hast done I pray thee, for God's sake, give him again), but he denyit any humiliation to have been made upon his knees, or lifting of his bonnet. Therefore, and in respect of the said Martha's affirmation, the brethren has summond the said

Gavan, and ordained also the said Martha to be summond before them in the Kirk of Paslay the last day of this instant, for puttin tryall taken in the said cause.

"Nov. 27, 1620.—Mr. Andro Hamiltoun, minister at Lochwinzeoche, informed the Moderator and brethren of the Presbyterie of Paslay of a heinous sclander of Andro Robesoune, suspected of charming, making and applying of sawes [salves] to diverse diseases, he being altogether unlearned, seducing thereby the common people; and in respect of his ignorance endangering the lives of thaim to whom they were applyed, the brethren ordained Mr. Alex. Hamiltoun to cause summond the said Andro Robesoune to compear before them the next Presbyterie day."

"Dec. 11.—Compeared Andro Robesoune, parochiner of Lochwinzeoche, against whom the brethren had allegit sundry accusations of charming, and making and applying sawes for blasting, and ill winds, for the which as for grounds the said Mr. Alex. had onelie common report, and no evidence of his charming. Notwithstanding, the said Andro confessit he made sawes and gave them to sick persons, whereby the brethren alledged the people might be seduced and deceived, as also in respect of his ignorance he endangered their lives, they therefore prohibited and interdicted the said Andro, as likewise he of his ain accord submitted himself to the interdiction, that in no tyme comeing he should make or give these kind of sawes under the pane of fourtie pounds, *toties quoties.*"

"Ap. 25, 1629.—The brethren, resenting that Andro Robesoune had yet continued to give sawes, and was suspect of charming, notwithstanding his interdiction, ordain Mr. John Lawe to cause him to appear before them this day 15 dayes."

"20th June.—Compeared Andro Robesoune, who yet denyed that he had contravened the Act of Presbytery. The Moderator charged

> the brethren to give a proof of their dilligence for tryall against him the next Presbyterie day, and ordain the baillies to cause the said Andro to find sufficient caution, under the payne of five hundred merks, to compear the said day."

Robesoune, when called, did not compear. He seems to have fled the country, and the case was stopped.

These extracts might be largely extended, but those we have given are sufficient to shew what was the discipline of the Kirk in the years succeeding the Reformation, and how strict was the surveillance the clergy exercised over all within their jurisdiction. The people lived under an iron rule. If the Priests chastised them with whips, the Presbyters used scorpions. The days for such a rule, it may perhaps be thought, are past for ever; but it is the tendency of all ecclesiastical bodies to descend from the sphere of the spiritual to that of the secular, and were a powerful and united Church set up in Scotland again, as some seem anxious to see, scenes not unlike some of those to which we have referred would probably be re-enacted. Men would have to submit to the tyranny of ecclesiastics, or give up public profession of religion altogether. A powerful Church becomes, almost in the nature of things, antagonistic to civil liberty.

## CHAPTER XXIV.

### The Abercorns and the Kirk.

> "New Presbyter is but Old Priest writ large."
>
> *Milton.*

AFTER Mr. Andro Knox had been induced to leave Paisley, and retire to his island diocese, three ministers of the name of Hamilton* appear to have, one after the other, succeeded him. Of these we know little : the Presbytery records for this period are awanting, and they are almost our only source of information regarding the Parish at this time. In 1626 the Presbyterial minutes are resumed, and the curtain, when lifted, reveals to us a somewhat stormy scene.

The family of Abercorn continued to live in the Abbey buildings, or, as these were called, the "Place of Paisley." Claud Hamilton, the Commendator, was succeeded by his grandson, the second Earl of Abercorn—his own son, who had borne that title, having died before his father. The youthful Earl seems to have resided principally in England and France, probably among the friends who had received his grandfather in his period of banishment. During his minority and while absent, the affairs of the family were managed by his mother, Dame Marion Boyd, first Countess of Abercorn—a woman of great determination and energy.† The

* Patrick Hamilton is mentioned in the Presbytery records as Mr. Knox's successor ; Archibald Hamilton in those of the Town Council as paying a sum of money to the burgh on January 4, 1617 ; and Wodrow mentions Boyd of Trochrigg as succeeding Mr. Alexander Hamilton on his resignation.

† She is mentioned in the Town Council records as electing a Bailie for Paisley in her son's absence.

family had outwardly conformed to Protestantism, and any desire they may have had to support the old faith with which they had been so closely connected, was repressed by the stern discipline exercised by the Kirk, and, in particular, by Mr. Andro Knox, who had a keen eye for marking a heretic, and who would have made it especially disagreeable for them had they shewn any inclination towards "Papacy." They cherished, therefore, their religious convictions in secret, waiting for a time when they might venture to profess them openly. Such a time seemed to be at hand. Only some fifty years had elapsed since the Archbishop's death, and the Protestants began to fight among themselves. The great questions agitated were not whether the Pope was Antichrist, and the Mass idolatry, but whether Bishops were lawful in a Christian commonwealth, and whether the sacrament should be taken kneeling at an altar or sitting at a table. There was a lull in the persecution of the Papists, and the persecuted ventured to assert themselves. "All this summer season, 1626 (says Wodrow), many persons, both men and women, south, west, east, and north, kythed themselves, by proud speeches, yea, and sometimes by deeds, declared themselves Papists." Among these "persons" was Marion Boyd, Countess of Abercorn, who resided sometimes in Paisley and sometimes at Blackston, the pleasant residence and grange of the Abbots, which, with the other possessions of the convent, had passed to her family. She and her household, and many in Paisley, began openly to avow themselves followers of the old religion, and found to their cost that the persecuting spirit of Presbytery was still as fierce and vigorous as it had ever been. Mr. Alexander Hamilton, who appears to have been minister of Paisley towards the close of 1625, resigned his charge, and Mr. Boyd of Trochrigg was invited by Lord Ross of Halkhead and other parishioners of Paisley, in the absence of the Earl of Abercorn, to take his place. This distinguished divine was well known, not only in Scotland, but also abroad. He was a man of great erudition, and had filled many situations of eminence at home and in France. He had been professor at Montauban, minister at Anteuil, Principal of the Universities of Samur, Glasgow, and Edinburgh, and had the reputation of being one of the most learned men of his time. His last appointment he had lost through his opposition to some new developments of Episcopacy; but as he now seemed ready to conform, it was thought the Parish of Paisley would be fortunate in obtaining his services. It was supposed, also, that his appointment would be acceptable to the Abercorn family, as he was related to the Countess.* But it did not suit the purpose of that bold lady that any preacher should be "planted" in Paisley. The letter from the parishioners to Mr. Boyd was very pressing :—

> "Reverend Sir,—Having been long destitute of a minister, to every one of our particular griefs, and to the general regret of every true professor, according to God's Providence and the desire of our hearts, ye was called to us by every kind of consent requisite; and finding some private impediments, as ye wrote to us, we meaned ourselves to Lord Ross, as present chief of our parish, and having the chiefest desire of our design, whereupon his Lordship, being sensibly touched, went into Glasgow on Wednesday last, accompanied with some gentlemen of the parish, who, for his Lordship's special interest, and for the whole parishioners in general, took occasion to deal earnestly with the Bishop of Glasgow; that by his Lordship's worthy, zealous, and careful endeavours, we are not only in hope, but confident that immediately after your return to us, the Bishop will remove all whatsoever impediments as may hinder you from using that talent which in itself is so precious and so necessary to be applied to us, presently destitute of the sweet comfort of the gospel."

The letter finishes with many fervent expressions of attachment to Mr. Boyd, and desires that he and they "might perfect the marriage made in heaven for the advancement of God's glory." The divine, however, did not shew any great desire to form this tie: there were difficulties as to his being admitted to the enjoyment of the temporalities of the cure, to which he was far from being indifferent, and he feared that his induction during the absence of the Earl would be displeasing to his Lordship,

* "He was of noble descent, being related by his father, James Boyd, to the noble families of Boyd and Cassilis, and by his mother, Margaret Chalmers, daughter of James Chalmers, Baron of Gadgirth, to the families of Glencairn and Loudon."

"notwithstanding of the pains of that worthy nobleman Lord Ross." His scruples were overcome, and he was inducted by the Presbytery in the Abbey Church on the 1st January, 1626. He left Paisley immediately afterwards for three months, until he should see how the Abercorns would receive his appointment, leaving a letter for the Earl, in which he tells how he had been pressed to come, and "begs, as the house which he should have cannot be soon repaired, he might be allowed the use of some chamber in the Abbey. He had requested it of his mother, but had been referred to him." In his absence, a certain David Alexander writes him* "that a person had been engaged to collect his stipend; that they long after him, because they sometimes want sermon, and because of Mr. Robert Park's sickness, no prayers have been read these fourteen days;† that they hear my Lord the Earl of Abercorn sent his servant from Paris to London, and his servant writes to his own wife that my Lord will be in Scotland before Pasch. As to the making patent of your house, there is no word of it, since it cannot be known in whose hands the keys are." The Earl did not return so soon as expected, and Mr. Boyd came back to his cure. He was kindly received by many of his people, but "the potent dame," Lady Abercorn, gave him no welcome. "I do not design," he writes, "to continue long here. I am just now come from Blackstoun, where I found Lady Abercorn. She is so coldly disposed toward me that I expect no friendship or courtesy on her part. She denies me that she has received any letter or news from her son relating to me; and when she gets anything from him, I believe she will rather suppress it than put it in my hand. It is believed here that the Earl is to receive a *(coup de pied)* disaster as to his Abbey.‡ Pray to the Lord not only to vouchsafe me courage and strength for accomplishing this charge, and sustain me under the burden of it, but also patience to bear me up when at a distance from my family." He had need of all the courage he could get. The treatment he received was very violent, and has been described by

* 1st February, 1626.

† Mr. Park was teacher of the Grammar School and reader in the church. The prayers to which Mr. Alexander refers were those in "The Book of Common Order," which were read in the Abbey daily.

‡ This refers to a threatened resumption by the Crown of all the property of the Church.

Wodrow. "He was ordained to have his manse in the forehouse of the Abbey, as the most convenient place for that use; * and having put his books and a bed thereintill, he being preaching in the afternoon, the Master of Paisley, being the Earl of Abercorn's brother, with some others, came to the minister's house, none being therein, and cast all his books to the ground, and thereafter locked the doors, whereby the minister should have no entry thereafter thereunto. And afterward the matter being complained of to the Lords of the Secret Council, and the Master of Paisley compearing, and the Bailies of Paisley with him, the Lords would have warded the said Master for some short space. The Master confessed with sorrow that he had done this wrong, and therefore the said Mr. Robert declared to the Council that he desired not the Master to be warded; but, in hope that things would be done better thereafter, he passed from the complaint. This the Master promised to do, and the Council ordained him to be repossessed, and so the matter passed over. Thereafter, the Bailies of Paisley, according to the Lords' ordinance, intending in outward appearance to put Mr. Robert again into possession of the house,† they found the locks stopped with stones and other things, that they could have no entry, and they would not break up the doors; and Mr. Boyd being going away, the rascally women of the town coming to see the matter (for the men purposely absented themselves), not only upbraided Mr. Robert with opprobrious speeches and shouted and hoyed him, but likewise cast dirt and stones at him, so that he was forced to leave the town, and went to Glasgow, not far off,‡ and from thence went to Carrick, his own dwelling-place; and miskent all and would not complain, so that the Bishop of Glasgow,

* This was because he could not get possession of the regular manse of the parish.

† This was the manse of the parish. Presb. Record, Sept. 28, 1628, "The mans of the parochin of Paslay."

‡ The names of these viragoes, as we learn from the Presbytery Records, April 27, 1628, were Isabell Greenlees, spous to James Smithe or Smith in Smithhills of Paslay, Jean Kibbil, spous to Malcolm Parke there, John Foreman, smith there, and Janet Greenlees, sister to the said Issobel. They were accused of "boasting and threatning to stane Mr. Robert Boyd of Trochrigge, the King his messenger and others who accompanied him for giving him possession of the said mans, according to the laws of the kingdom." The tradition in Paisley is that these irate females escorted the unfortunate minister as far as Williamsburgh on the road to Glasgow.

for his own credit, complained that justice should be done to the minister, and caused summon the said Master of Paisley and his mother, the Ladye thereof, who was thought to have the wyte of all, to compear before the Council to hear and see order taken for the contempt done to the minister. Likeas the Lady and the Earl, her eldest son, and the Master, her second son, in great pomp, with her eldest son's gilded carosche (he being lately come from his travels), accompanied with many gentlemen and friends, came to Edinburgh to the Council day; and there, the matter being handled in Council and reasoned where the Bishop of Glasgow was and five or six other bishops were, all that was resolved upon by the Council was, that it was promised by the Earl and his brother and their friends that the minister, Mr. Robert Boyd, should be repossessed, and no more impediments made to him, and no order taken with the delinquents and contempt done him by the rascally women; and this was one of the fruits of Papistry in the west."* Mr. Boyd had quite enough of these. Nothing would induce him to go back to Paisley. The Presbytery besought him to " continue in his charge, but the said Mr. Robert absolutely refused, and requested it to be planted with some qualified person."† This was done, and Mr. John Hay became minister of Paisley.

The Presbytery now took up the case of Lady Abercorn as a "suspected Papist" with great zeal, and she and her household—one of whom, Thomas Algeo, there is reason to believe, was a disguised priest—were persecuted with the utmost rigour. The following extracts from the records of Presbytery, though somewhat lengthy, best tell the story, and shew

* Dr. Sibbald writes Boyd, 22d Sept., 1628, "Yesterday, and no sooner, your purpose was handled in the Council and decided. They have ordained the Earl of Abercorn (who used his power here and all his friends and credit against you), his brother, family, and bailies, in peaceable, amicable, and honourable way to repossess you, under pain of all highest penalties; yea, he hath promised *(nec ultro)* to do the samein, otherwise presently he had been sickerly fined. Yea, it was told him in Council *(asserte)* that, had it not been your intercession, they could not have deserved less than a year's ward to his bailie, and the highest punishment to his brother."

† Of the many eminent men who have been ministers of Paisley, Robert Boyd is probably the most noteworthy. He died at Edinburgh, 5th January, 1627. He published several works, the most celebrated of which is his "Commentary on the Epistle to the Ephesians," which had formed his lectures at Samur. He wrote some beautiful Latin hymns; one on "The Holy Spirit" has been admirably translated by the Rev. Dr. M'Gill.

how admirably the clergy acted the part of inquisitors. Had they been members of the "Holy Office," they could scarcely have done better.

"April 20, 1626.—Apud Passlay,—The which day the Moderator and brethren being credibly informed that Thomas Algeo and John Naismith, servitours to the Countess of Abercorne, did neither frequent the house of God for the hearing of the Word preached, neither did communicate with others of the congregation at occasions offered, whereby they gave just occasion of suspicion of their apostacie and defection from the true religion, grounded on God's sacred Word, publickly professed within this kingdom, and authorised by His Majesty's laws: Therefore, they ordained the said Thomas Algeo and John Naismith to be summoned *literatorie* to appear before them in the Kirk of Paslay the next Presbyterie day to answer to the saids brethren anent the points aforesaid—*pro primo.*

"May 4, 1626.—The which day Mr. Robert Boyd of Trochrege, minister of Pasley, appointed commissioner with Mr. Robert Wilkie, one of the ministers of the citie of Glasgow, and Mr. William Blase, minister at Dumbarton, by act and ordinance of a synod and assemblie holden at Glasgow the fourth day of April, 1626, did intimate to the Countess of Abercorne that because she neither resorted to the public preaching of God's Word and participation of the sacraments, thereby declaring that she was not of that religion and profession grounded on God's sacred Word, publickly professed, and authorised by His Majesty's laws, that therefore the Presbyterie of Paslay would enter on a processe against her (according to the ordinance of the said synod) in case she gave not satisfaction to the said Presbyterie of Paslay by *swearing* and subscribing the Confession of Faith (embraced publickly by the Kirk of Scotland), resort to the hearing of God's Word preached, and to the participation of the holy sacraments, notwithstanding the intimation of the commissioners aforesaid, Mr. Robert Boyd, in name of the rest, reported to the Presbyterie that the said Countess shews herself obstinate against all the points aforesaid. Therefore the saids brethren ordained her to be summoned *literatorie* to appear before them in the Kirk of Paslay the next Presbyterie day for the causes above written, with certification—*pro primo*.

"May 4, 1626.—Thos. Algeo and John Naismith cited, called, and not compearing, to be summoned *pro secundo*. The Moderator and remanent brethren, being credibly informed that Claud Algeo had made apostacie and defection from the true religion grounded on God's sacred word, and professed within this kingdom, and authorised by her Majesty's laws, ordained the said Claud Algeo to be summoned *literatorie* to compear before them in the Kirk of Passley by the next Presbyterie day, to give account and reason of his religion, with certification—*pro primo*."

"May 18, 1626.—The Countess of Abercorn, having been summoned by affixing a copy upon the yett of her dwelling at Blackstoun, and being called, compears not, to be summoned to next diet —*pro secundo*."

"The which day compeared Thomas Algeo, who declared that he had some doubts concerning which he desired the means of resolution, that so he might labour and endeavour to give the Presbyterie satisfaction. The brethren therefore thought good to give him the Confession of Faith, that therewith he might advise and be resolved, which Confession the said Thomas embraced willingly, to whome also the brethren assigned a month, and immediately following the said 18 May above to give satisfaction according to the said Confession, and summoned him *apud acta* to appear the 15 June to that effect."

John Naismith excuses his absence by letter, and promises obedience. His case is continued, and he is summoned *pro secundo*.

"The which day the brethren, being informed that Claud Algeo is fugitive to Ireland, caused the process to cease till newe occassion."

"June 1, 1626.—The Countess of Abercorne, being called, and not compearing, to be cited—*pro tertio.*

"The same as to John Naismith."

"June 15, 1626.—Dame Marion Boyd, Countess of Abercorne's case continued till a minister be settled for the Kirk of Passlay. John Naismith, summoned, and not compearing, to be publickly admonished—*pro primo.*

"Thomas Algeo's case, at his own desire, continued till next day."

"June 29, 1626.—John Naismith had not been admonished, as there was no actual preaching these Sabbaths intervening. Whosoever shall be appointed to preach in the Kirk of Passlay shall admonish John Naismith as before.

"Thomas Algeo, called, and not compearing according to his promise, is ordained to be publickly admonished by Mr. Andro Hamilton, minister of Kilbarchan (the said Thomas then remaining with the Countess of Abercorne in Blackstoun, within the said parochin), unless he give assurance of obedience to the Presbyterie."

"Aug. 17, 1626.—The which day Thomas Algeo compeared, in whose presence Mr. Andro Hamilton declared the said Thomas had come to him, and had shewn that heretofore his business had witholden him, so that in respect thereof he could not give that satisfaction to the brethren which otherwise he would strive to do, willing likewise the whole brethren to continue all admonition till the next Presbyterie day, at which time he promised to give contentment and satisfaction, which the brethren granting, summoned the said Thomas to the effect foresaid, *apud acta,* to appear.

"The which day the brethren ordained Mr. Andro Hamilton, minister at Kilbarchan, to proceed by public admonition against the Countess of Abercorn, her ladyship now dwelling in Blackstoun, within the said parochin."

"August 31, 1626.—The which day compeared Thomas Algeo, and confessed he had some doubts anent the religion publickly professed within this kingdom, and desired to be resolved. The brethren therefore, for his better resolution, demanded if he would advise and diligently weigh and consider the Confession of Faith and the articles thereof which the Kirk of Scotland professeth. Whereunto the said Thomas condescended, and therefore the brethren ordained the said Confession to be extracted out of the buiks of the Presbyterie, and given to the said Thomas, and assign to him the sixteenth day of November next following to give satisfaction anent his doubts, certifying, if he fail to compear on the said sixteenth day of November, he would be proceeded against by the censures of the Kirk."

Thomas Algeo, seems to have fenced a good deal with the members of Presbytery, giving them hopes of his conversion, and thus gaining time. The Countess, his mistress, fled for protection to the Archbishop of Glasgow, who had more respect for her rank than his clergy. They seem to have acted impartially, and taken up cases without reference to the position in life of the persons they cited before them. The record thus proceeds :—

"The which day Mr. Andro Hamilton, minister at Kilbarchan, presented a letter sent unto him by my Lord Archbishop of Glasgow, willing him thereby not to make any public mention by public admonition of the said Countess of Abercorne's name until they heard from him, for which causes the said Mr. Andro desisted, and produced the said letter for his warrant. Wherefore the brethren acquiesced until they heard from the Bishop, or that he communed with them face to face."

"November 16, 1626.—The which day being assigned to Thomas Algeo to give satisfaction anent his doubts in religion, yet appeared not to that effect, therefore the brethren ordained to summond the said Thomas Algeo to compear the next Presbyterie day to give satisfaction, with certification if he fail they would proceed by public admonition."

"Dec. 28, 1626.—The which day it was declared by Mr. John Hay that John Naismith had excused his absence the last Presbyterie day by reason of his necessive employment in my Lady Abercorne's business, as likewise promised to appear the next day ensuing, was continued to be proceeded against by public admonition, who, being called, and not appearing, was ordained to be proceeded against *ut prius.*"

The Earl of Abercorn having now returned home, followed his mother's example, and declared himself a Catholic. This gave such scandal that the Archbishop was obliged to allow the Presbyters to have their own way.

"Ap. 19, 1627.—The which day the moderator and remanent brethren of the Presbyterie of Paslay, understanding that ane noble Lord, James Erle of Abercorne, had made apostasie and defection from the true religion, . . . . and that he doth openly avowe himself a papist, and verie contemptuously despiseth the word of God, preached publickly or read privately, and all other public religious exercises used in the Kirk and Kingdome, to the great dishonour and offense of God and of all truely religious hearted Christians. Therefore the said brethren ordained the said James, Erle of Abercorne, should be summoned personally if he could be apprehended, or at his dwelling house in Pasley, to appear before them, in the Kirk thereof, the third day of May next, to come to hear and see himself deserned *excommunicate* for the said apostasie and defection from the true religion; or else to give satisfaction to them anent the premises, with certification if he failed they would proceed against him by the censures of the Kirk to the sentence of excommunication."

"May 3d, 1627.—The which day the brethren, understanding the mind and will of my Lord Archbishop of Glasgowe that the process should be prosecute against the Countesse of Abercorne, therefore ordain Mr. John Hay to proceed by public admonitions against her in the Kirk of Paisley, her Ladyship having returned out of Blackstoun.

"The Erle of Abercorn, summoned, called, and not compearing, to be summoned—*pro secundo.*"

"May 18, 1627.—Thomas Algeo to be proceeded against by the third publick admonition, if he give not satisfaction by next presbyterie day.

"John Naismith to be proceeded against by the third prayer if he give not satisfaction.

"The which day Mr. John Hay reported he had superceded to admonish the said Countess publickly, her Ladyship having promised that, so soon as it should please God to give her habilities and strength of body, she should resort to the hearing of God's Word preached, and in the meantyme desired conference with one or two of the brethren anent these doubts which heretofore she had pretended, and therefore the said Mr. John Hay and Mr. John Maxwell were ordained to confer with her Ladyship, and to report the next day.

"The Erle called, and not compearing, to be summoned—*pro tertio.*"

"May 31, 1627.—Mr. John Hay has continued Thomas Algeo's third public admonition, as he promises obedience and solicits conference.

"He has also continued the third prayer for Naismith, who, compearing, is rebuked for his intolerable disobedience. He solicits the Confession of Faith, to resolve his doubts, which is given him.

"He reports he had not had opportunity to confer with the Countess. Her case is continued.

"The Erle summoned, but not compearing, Mr. Hay is to proceed by the first public admonition."

"June 14, 1627.—Mr. John Hay being absent, Thomas Algeo's case not reported on, and continued.

"Naismith does not compear to give answer to his doubts. To be proceeded against by prayer—*pro tertio.*

"The which day the saids brethren, appointed commissioners for a reference, reported they had conferred with the said Countess, and that her Ladyship had craved continuance therein, hoping thereby she might be profited, which the brethren granting, ordained the said commissioners to continue in conference with her.

"The which day Mr. John Hay reported he had superseeded to admonish the said noble Erle publickly, upon his earnest request and desire of conference for his satisfaction and resolution anent those doubts which his Lordship pretended why he could not come to the hearing of God's word publickly preached. The saids brethren therefore ordains Mr. John Maxwell and Mr. John Hay to confer with his Lordship anent the said doubts, and to report their dilligence the next presbyterie day."

"June 24, 1627.—Mr. John Hay reports Thos. Algeo promised to satisfy this day. He fails to do this, and is to be publickly admonished—*pro tertio, ut prius.*

"Naismith proceeded against by prayer, *pro tertio,* but remains obstinate, his process to be extracted, that warrant may be got from the Archbishop for his excommunication."

"The which day the brethren appointed commissioners for conference reported they had conferred with the said Countess, and that they had profited little by the same. And therefore the whole brethren ordained Mr. Daniel Cunninghame and Mr. John Hay to go to my Lady, and to intimate to her that, if she gives not obedience, the process will be prosecuted. The commissioners appointed to confer with the said noble Erle reported they had conferred with his Lordship, and that he had craved continuance therein, hoping thereby he might be profited, which the brethren granting, the said commissioners to continue conference with him."

"July 5, 1627.—The moderator and brethren understanding that Isobel Mouatt, servitor to the Countess of Abercorne, is not only an enemy to the true religion, but also openly avoweth her idolatry and papistrie, submitting thereby that she adhereth to anti-Christian doctrine . . . she is ordered to be summoned to appear in the Kirk of Paslay before the Presbyterie, 19th of July, and to answer to them anent the premises aforesaid."

"July 19, 1627.—Algeo proceeded against.

"The which day the saids brethren intimate, as was ordained, anent the Countess, who answered she hoped they would deal more favourably with her than to exercise any rigour. And therefore the brethren, to make her more inexcusable, ordain *de novo* Mr. J. Hay and Mr. Andro Hamilton to go to her Ladyship and confer with her till the next Presbyterie day.

"Isobel Mouatt to be cited—*pro secundo.*

"August 2, 1627.—Algeo proceeded against.

"The commissioners report they had profited nothing with the Countess, and therefore the brethren ordain Mr. J. Hay and Mr. Andro Hamilton to proceed by publick admonitions against her.

"A similar report and order made regarding the Erle.

"Mowat to be summoned—*pro tertio.*

"The brethren understanding Claud Algeo had returned from Ireland, ordain him to be summoned—*pro tertio.*

Aug. 16, 1627.—Mr. Hay reported he had proceeded by prayer *pro tertio*, for Thomas Algeo, according to the ordinance, and seeing the said Thomas Algeo hath obstinately and contumaciously disregarded all good order of the Kirk, and wilfully contumilts and adhereth unto his former grosse and damnable errors of the Kirk of Rome, notwithstanding any information given him by conference, whereby he manifesteth himself ane open enemy to the gospel and religion founded thereupon; therefore the said Moderator and brethren ordained that the process should be extracted and forwarded to my Lord Archbishop of Glasgow, that a warrand may be obtained for his excommunication. Mr. John Hay reports he had proceeded against the Countess by the first publick admonition. Mr. Andro being absent, and not having proceeded according to the ordinance, the brethren ordained Mr. John to proceed *pro secundo*, and Mr. Andro to proceed *primo* and *secundo*."

"The Erle to be similarly dealt with."

"Mouat to be proceeded against by first public admonition."

"Aug. 30, 1627.—The Countess to be proceeded against by third public admonition and first prayer."

"The Erle to be similarly dealt with."

"Mouat to be admonished—*pro secundo*."

"Claud Algeo to be summoned—*pro tertio*."

"The process against Thomas Algeo produced, and the deduction thereof approved and allowed by the Archbishop, likewise a warrant given by him to excommunicate the said Thomas, if he give not satisfaction within twenty days next thereafter."

"Sept. 13, 1627.—Mr. J. Hay and Mr. Andro Hamilton reported they had proceeded against the Countess by the third public admonition. They had, at her earnest request and promise of obedience, desisted to proceed by prayer, which promise if her ladyship perform, the brethren ordain them to continue, if not, to proceed by prayer."

They report similarly regarding the Earl.

"Which day also compeared Mr. Thomas Boyd, commissionar for continuation of prosecuting the process against the said noble Earl for a certain space, hoping that by their favourable dealing his

Lordship might be the more easily moved to obedience and satisfaction in all points. The brethren answered they could not intermit without great scandal, unless his Lordship would condescend and faithfully promise to come and hear God's word publickly preached, and to this effect they ordain Mr. J. Hay and Mr. John Maxwell to go and confer with his Lordship, and if he assenteth to the will of the Presbyterie, to continue, if not, to certify his Lordship that he would be proceeded against by prayer."

"Isobel Mouat has been proceeded against by the second public admonition. To get the third."

"James Crawford, servitor to the Countess, certified as a Papist, and summoned to appear before the Presbytery."

"Sep. 28, 1627.—Mr. Hay reported, that according to the Archbishop's warrand, he had pronounced the sentence of excommunication against Thomas Algeo."

"The warrant of the Archbishop for the excommunication of John Naismith produced.

"Mr. Hay and Mr. Andro Hamilton report that the Countess had not performed as she had promised. They had therefore proceeded to the first prayer. They were ordained to proceed to the second prayer.

"Isabel Mouat to be proceeded against by prayer, *pro primo.*

"The which day Mr. James Craufurd produced a confession of his faith, which the brethren thereof not accepting as sufficient for their satisfaction, he was ordained to be cited—*pro secundo.*"

"Oct., 1627.—The Countess to be proceeded against by the third prayer.

"Mr. John Hay and Mr. Hamilton report they had proceeded by prayer *pro secundo* against the Earl. Ordained to proceed by the third prayer. Notwithstanding of which ordinance, compeared William Hamilton, brother german to the Earl, as commissionar sent from him, who shewed that his Lordship would willingly have compeared himself if his absence had not been occasioned by some important business, and therefore most humbly entreated the brethren that they would supersede any further proceedings till his Lordship's return, at which time he hoped he would give satisfaction.

"The brethren were pleased, therefore, to continue his Lordship till the next presbyterie.

"Isabel Mouat to be proceeded against by prayer—*pro secundo.*"

"Mr. John Hay reported he had delayed to pronounce the sentence of excommunication against John Naismith publickly because of a verbal warrant he had obtained of the Bishop, and because of his earnest entreaty and promise to appear this day, who compearing, was demanded upon sundry points of religion, and being urged, the said John said he was not resolved at that time, and therefore craving time to the effect he might be resolved, ordain him to give in his doubts to Mr. John Hay upon Sunday next following, and him to confer with the said John anent the same, and if he give satisfaction, to continue; if not, to proceed on Sunday come eight days by the sentence of excommunication."

"November 19, 1627.—Mr. John Hay reported he had desisted to proceed against the Countess by the third prayer, upon some hopes of obedience, as her Lady's son, William, commissioner from her Ladyship, had shown unto him.—Which day the act of the Synodal Assemblie was produced, ordering the process against the Countess to be concluded, except her Ladyship promised by her writt, subscribed under her hand, and sent to the Presbyterie, that, upon her conscience and honour, she shall resort ordinarlie to the hearing of the Word when she may for her health, which act the brethren ordained Mr. John Hay and Mr. Andrew Hamilton to intimate to her, and if she promise not to give obedience thereunto, the said brethren ordain them to proceed by the third prayer, and to conclude the process.

"An act of General Assembly also produced regarding the Earl, importing that if his Lordship would resolve whether he would come to the church or not for hearing God's word betwixt and the 1st Dec., and to confer with Mr. Hay and Mr. Maxwell, that then the Assembly would grant him a suspension till the said day. Otherwise he is to be proceeded against by the third prayer.

"Mouat to be proceeded against by third prayer.

"Mr. Hay reported he had not proceeded against Naismith as he promised to confess his disobedience before the congregation, and to come to the hearing of the word.

"The brethren were ordained to make intimation of the excommunication of Thomas Algeo in their several kirks upon Sunday next, after sermon, to the intent no one should have familiar conversation or conference with him, under the pain and penaltie contained in the acts of the Kirk."

"Nov. 29, 1627.—Mr. John Hay reported that the Countess shewed she could not be resolved to give obedience to the act of the Synod, and therefore that he had proceeded by the third prayer.

"Same entry as to the Earl.

"Isabel Mouat's process to be sent to the Archbishop for her excommunication.

"Mr. Hay to continue with Naismith as before.

"The process against the Countess to be laid before the Archbishop, that warrant may be obtained for her excommunication."

"Jan. 10, 1628.—The warrant from the Archbishop being obtained, Mr. John Hay was ordained to excommunicate the Countess betwixt and next Presbyterie day.

"Same for John Naismith."

"Jan. 31.—Mr. John Hay reported that according to instructions he had pronounced the sentence of excommunication against the Countess the 20th day of January, 1628. He also reported that because the said noble Erle had taken journey to Court for his necessarie and lawful busness, he had consulted the Archbishop, who advised him to delay to pronounce the said sentence till his Lordship return, whereunto the brethren assented."

"April 27, 1628.—Mr. John Hay reported he could profit nothing anent John Naismith. He was therefore ordered to pronounce sentence of excommunication of him and betwixt and the next Presbyterie day."

"May 8, 1628.—Isabel Mouat ordered to be excommunicated by Mr. Andro Hamilton, minister of Kilbarchan, and as he had refrained to excommunicate the Countess, he is ordained, under pain of suspension, to come to the Kirk of Pasley on the 11th May to preach there, and after sermon publickly to confess his oversight and negligence in not excommunicating the said Countess as he was ordained.

"Mr. Hay reported he had hopes of John Naismith's obedience. He is therefore ordained to continue in reference to the said John."

"May 22, 1628.—Mr. Andro Hamilton not having excommunicated Isabel Mouat, four members of Presbyterie ordered to go to the Archbishop and complain thereof."

"June 5, 1628.—The brethren sent to the Bishop report that it is his will that Mr. Andro should be suspended if he did not excommunicate Isabel Mouat betwixt and next Presbyterie day."

"July 20, 1628.—Mr. Andro Hamilton reported he had excommunicated Isabel Mouat."

"Nov. 22, 1628.—Mr. John Hay produced a writting subscribed by John Naismith, testyfying his satisfaction to the Kirk, the tenor whereof followeth:—It obliges him to attend the parish church, receive the sacrament, and "attend such conferences as the Presbyterie may appoint for his better instruction in the grounds of true religion." The Presbyterie accept of it as sufficient to stop the proceedings."

The protracted dealings of the Presbytery were now closed. All the accused had at length been excommunicated with the exception of John

Naismith. The Earl fled the country, and so escaped being sentenced. Thomas Algeo appeared in the neighbourhood some time after, in the service of the Duke of Lennox, giving "great scandal and offence," and the Presbytery ordained he was "to have no liberty until he should first give satisfaction to the Kirk." The sequel as regards the poor Countess is more sad. This unfortunate woman, broken down in health, sought refuge in Edinburgh. She was there apprehended and cast into the Tolbooth,* a loathsome prison. Here her confinement produced "many heavy diseases, so as this whole winter she was almost tied to her bed, and she now found a daily decay and weakness in her person. Her miserable state was at last represented to the King (Charles I.) as "being oppressed with sickness and disease of body, and requiring the benefit of a watering-place." The King, not wishing on the one hand to slight the authority of the Church, or on the other "that the lady should be brought to the extremity of losing her life for the want of the ordinary remedies," ordered (July 9, 1629) that she should have a license to go to the baths of Bristol, but only on condition that she should not attempt to appear at Court, and, after her recovery, return and put herself at the disposal of the Council. Her Ladyship did not go to the baths of Bristol, being probably too weak for so long a journey, and after six months more imprisonment in the Cannongate Jail—probably an equally wretched prison with the Tolbooth—she was allowed to reside in the house of Duntarvie on condition that "she sall contain herself so warily and respectfully as she sall not fall under the break of any of his Majesty's laws, also, that she would, while living there, have conference with the ministry, but allow none to Jesuits or mass priests." In March, 1631, having been under restraint some three years, she was formally licensed to go "to Pasley for the outred of some weighty affairs," but only on condition that she should not, while there, "reset Thomas Algeo nor no Jesuits, and return by a certain day, under penalty of five thousand merks." The miserable lady, however, never returned. She reached Paisley worn out and broken down, suffering from *squalor carceris,* and died there shortly after her arrival. Her body lies in St. Mirin's Chapel, and a leaden tablet on the

* Records of Privy Council, quoted in Chambers' "Domestic Annals," Vol. II., p. 25.

wall of the vault records the year of her death. She was the victim of odious ecclesiastical persecution, and any who read her history may find in it another illustration of the saying of Milton which we have prefixed to this chapter, "new Presbyter is but old Priest writ large."

## CHAPTER XXV.

### The Service Book.

> Synods are whelps of th' inquisition,
> A mongrel breed of like pernicion ;
> Sure 'tis an orthodox opinion,
> That grace is founded in dominion.
>
> —*Hudibras.*

THE events related in the last two chapters took place under a system of Episcopal Church government. This may seem strange to those whose notions of Episcopal rule are taken from the Roman Church or the Anglican Establishment, but it will not be so to any who are acquainted with Scottish ecclesiastical history, especially in the period that succeeded the Reformation. The only Church that took any hold in Paisley after that time was Episcopal, but it was very different in many respects from what is now called by that name. A Presbytery met regularly in the Abbey, and carried on its business much as the business of a Presbytery is carried on now. The congregations were ruled by "sessions," composed of elders chosen from among the people. The discipline exercised was according to the form laid down by the General Assembly. The Archbishop of Glasgow presided over all, but kept in the background, and seldom interfered with his clergy. He was represented in the Presbytery by a moderator whom he appointed. He exercised supervision over the manner in which the power of excommunication was used, he conferred orders, and he gave collation to benefices. Nor was the worship of the Church very similar to that which is now associated with Episcopacy. It was essentially Scotch. It was partially liturgical, but the ritual was very simple. The character of the service was that which prevails now. The prayers read were those of the book of "Common Order," or, as it was called from being bound up with the Psalms, "The Psalm Book;" but extemporary prayer was constantly used also, and the sermon was the chief feature of the service. Under this Episcopal Church a generation had grown up. With few exceptions, the leading divines of Scotland conformed to it. Even one like Boyd of Trochrig, who had been so long on the Continent, and who had officiated in the continental churches, which were formed after the model of Geneva, came to Paisley with the consent of the Archbishop, and took "collation" to the Abbey Parish from that dignitary. There was no reason why this system of church government, with many of its obvious advantages, should not have continued to the present day, and it probably would have done so had it been left alone. Attempts were made to *Anglicanise* it, which roused the whole *amour propre* of the Scotch people, and precipitated a conflict, the results of which have not yet passed away. It would be foreign to our purpose to enter on the history of that conflict. We shall only notice some of those aspects, which belong to the subject of our story.

Mr. Hay, who succeeded the laird of Trochrig, was translated in 1628 to Renfrew, and the Earl of Abercorn presented to the Archbishop, for induction to Paisley, Mr. John Crighton, parson of Campsie. The Archbishop directed him to preach on two Sundays in the Abbey, that he might know what the parishioners thought of his doctrine. After he had done so, the leading men of the parish* held a meeting, and "all in one voice gave applause and approbation to the said Mr. John and his doctrine, and sent a deputation to the Archbishop earnestly to entreat his Lordship to give him admission as soon as possible may be, according to the order and constitution of the Kirk." The Archbishop granted

*** These were "James Lord Ross, Sir Robert Montgomery of Skelmorlie, Wil. Ross of Muirestoune, Robert Semple of Beltrees, Brice Semple of Cathcart, Alex. Cochrane of that Ilk, Malcolm Crauford of Newtoune, Allane Lockhart, Claud Hamiltoune, and James Alex., Bailies, with many others, the elders and honest men of the toun and parochein of Paislay, solemnly convened in the kirke thereof, to the effect they might advise and deliberate upon the fittest course to be taken for settling a minister in the said kirk."**

their request, and shortly afterwards Mr. Crighton was inducted, "being accompanied with the noblemen, gentlemen, and bailies of the burgh of Paislay," and subsequently was admitted to the "peaceable possession of the manse, barne, barne-yard, and glebe" enjoyed by his predecessors.* Mr. Crighton was a man of peculiar character, and having taken part with those who were anxious for the introduction of the new service-book and other innovations, he soon found himself in a very unpleasant position. The Presbytery deemed it their duty to take up a strong position against the new liturgy. They drew up a supplication against it to the Council, and appointed one of their number to support their petition, and "to advise and consult with the rest of the brethren, or other good christians that shall happen to be present in Edinburgh or elsewhere, concerning such a wise and fair course as shall be thought fit and expedient to be taken concerning the service-book presently urged." The "supplication" is in many ways interesting. It has been ignorantly supposed that the Church of Scotland has always been opposed to forms of prayer, whereas forms of prayer were in constant use for nearly a century after the Reformation, and their lawfulness was never doubted.† This supplication from Paisley is one of the many proofs that might be adduced to show that the Church was not opposed to any liturgy, but only to the particular liturgy that was forced upon it, and which was strenuously resisted chiefly on account of what were believed to be

* This was on 24th Feb., 1631. The subjects are described as "the ground of the house yard, barn, and barn yard, and four acres land on the east end of the burgh of Pasley." The Presbytery passed "To the ground of the house and yard at the kirk style of Paisley, and also to the barn and barn yard in the crofts, called little croft or neweyard, betwixt the barn of umquhile Thomas Inglis on the south, and the house and yard now possessed by Andro Boyd on the north parts, and siclyke, to the four acres land in the croft called the meikle croft of Paislay, and which house, &c., were all possessed by his predecessors, ministers of Paislay of before." They designed these subjects "to be the manse and glebe of the said Mr. John and his successors at Paisley, in the name of the Presbytery, at the desire of a letter direct to them by the Right Reverend father in God James, by the mercie of God Archbishop of Glasgow, within whose diocese the said Presbytery lies."

† A very prevalent feeling exists in the Church of Scotland for a "Book of Common Order" similar to that used so long after the Reformation, and a book has been published by the "Church Service Society" bearing that name. Those who desire such an aid to public worship are really "standing in the old paths," and walking in the ways of the fathers of the Church.

its doctrinal errors, and what was known to be its origin. We give the supplication to the Council in full:—

"Unto your Lordships, &c.—We, the brethren of the presbyterie of Paislay, notwithstanding that hitherto, partlie in respect of our vacation in tyme of harvest, partlie in respect we did not apprehend or suspect that the charge given to us to buy the service-book did stretch further than our own private perusing of it for our better information, that we may give our judgements touching the fitness thereof to be received and embraced in our Kirk, we have been too negligent in supplicating your Lordships, with the rest of the clergy and other well affected christians. Yet perceiving now, partlie by the proclamations made in December, 1636, partlie by his Majesty's declaration of his pleasure thereanent, it is his Majesty's will that the said book of service shall be presently embraced and perused throughout this whole Kirk and kingdome, we cannot but think ourselves bound in conscience to joyne with the rest of our brethren and other good christians in supplicating your Lordships most humblie to deal with his Majesty that he would be graciously pleased not to urge upon his good and loyal subjects the said service-book after such a fashion, in our judgement contrary to the practice of this Kirk and kingdom, wherein, so far as we know, nothing of this kind hath been established without the consent of the General Assembly and Parliament. *And, seeing we have had a liturgie established by authority, wherewith we have been bred and educated ever since the Reformation, and the same not abolished, and the liturgie now urged seemeth to us in sundrie particulars to be different from that we have embraced and professed*, it would please his Gracious Majesty to use such a fair course, without impeachment to the good and peace of the Church, and without grief and offence to the consciences of his Majesty's most loving and loyal subjects."

Things had gone too far to be stayed by any such supplication. The bishops drew upon them the wrath of the Church as supporters of the new liturgy, and the Church declared them no longer necessary in a christian commonwealth. The question of the lawfulness of the service-book, wearing a surplice, and kneeling at the holy communion became merged in the higher one of the lawfulness of Episcopacy. The Covenant was drawn up as the basis of the ecclesiastical polity of Scotland, and Presbytery declared supreme. The agitations of the time were strongly felt in Paisley. A solemn fast was kept upon a Sunday* throughout the Presbytery† for "removing the sins of the land, especially the contempt of the gospel, which hath provoked God to permit innovations to creep in upon the Church, and that it would please him to save this Kirk of Scotland from all innovations of religion, and that peace with the profession of the present religion may with liberty be entertained." All business was paralysed by the controversy, and the Town Council ceased to meet on account of the disturbed state of the country‡. But if the bailies on the one side of the Cart were afraid to convene, the Presbytery on the other were less timid. They met, not so frequently as before, but always to express their sympathy with the popular side. They ordered the moderator to lay down his office as the representative of the Archbishop.§ He answered "that he had his office of the Archbishop of Glasgow, with consent of the brethren of the Assemblie, and therefore could not, unless his office was discharged by them of whom he had received the same." His brethren paid little attention to this, and concluded that the moderator should be changed every six months. They had now become thorough-going Presbyterians, and in their records the Archbishop disappears from view. The minister of the Abbey, Mr. Crighton, in whose church they met, was not, however, in accord with his brethren. He protested against their supplication regarding "that most corrupt liturgy" the service-book, and he introduced into the Abbey those innovations against which they were fasting and praying. He accordingly drew down upon himself their wrath and

* A most unusual day for a fast.

† Ordered by the Presbytery on 24th May, 1638.

‡ There are no minutes of Council between 1631 and 1645 for this reason.

§ 22d June, 1638.

condemnation, and when some of his parishioners presented a complaint* against him, they were not slow to take it up. The probability is that it was inspired by themselves. Only one part of the complaint refers to a matter of character. It seems to have been recklessly made, and there was little evidence adduced in support of it. It was afterwards added to by the Presbytery themselves taking up, in a very unfair way, the gossip of the town. The charges are very singular, and as they illustrate the state of matters at that critical time, we give them as they were made :—

"He taught that Christ descended locally into hell.

"That Christ in his own person was the first that entered into heaven, and none before him, and that none of the fathers went to heaven, but were in *atrio coeli*.

"That Christ is really in the sacrament, but all the world cannot tell after what manner.

"That the Turk is the very and only Anti-Christ, and no other.

"Speaking anent the number of the sacraments, he affirmed that, if men were peaceably set, the Protestants and the Romish doctors might be easily reconciled, for the Romish doctors teach (saith he) that there are only two principal sacraments, and the Protestants say that there be only two properly sacraments, and so no difference if men were peaceably set.

"He taught that it was possible for us to fulfil the law, otherwise that sentence might be rased out of Scripture, 'By the grace of Christ which strengtheneth me I am able to do all things.' The same point he delivered again at greater length, preaching upon the words, Luc xviii., 22, 'All these have I kept from my youth up.' He sayeth, here we may see that the commandments are keepable, for if it had not been true that the young man had kept them, as he professed he had done, Christ would have checked him for it. Again, saith he, if the commandments were not keep-

* The complainers were Alexr. Cochrane of that Ilk, the Laird of Elderslie, Crawford of Cartsburn, and James Alexander, Bailie of Paisley. Those whom the Presbytery are fond of calling the "noblemen and gentlemen of the parish" took nothing to do with it.

able, God having commanded us to keep them, God were the cause of our sins, and not ourselves, for we are not guilty of the thing which we are not able to do; as for example, saith he, if God commanded me to leap up into the moon, not being able to do it, God would be in fault, and not I.

"Whosoever dare say (said he) that God ever elected or rejected any man without respect to works, I say that it is a fable, not worthy to be heard in the chair of veritie.

"Several times he hath mentioned universal grace and universal redemption, and affirmed that Christ died alike for all—for Judas and Peter.

"He taught that the difference betwixt Papists and Protestants, Calvinists and Lutherans, Arminians and Gonnarians, Conformists and Nonconformists, is but a mouthful of moonshine, and if churchmen were peaceably set, they might be easily reconciled.

"He hath several times affirmed that justifying faith might be absolutely lost.

"That there is no way for a sinner to go to heaven unless he make confession of his sins to the minister, alledging that he hath as great power to forgive sins as the apostles had.

"Being preaching on these words, Luc xviii., where children were brought unto Christ to be touched by Him, this, said he, was confirmation and bishopery, regretting withall that through iniquitie of time that laudable custom, which Christ himself practised, was forgotten. Yea, when Christ laid his hands upon these children, said he, He was the first author of confirmation Himself, and it continued successively in the Church from Him to His apostles, and from them to their successors for a long time, while through the iniquity of time it was neglected. At the same time he called it a sacrament, for, said he, the touching was an outward sign of an inward and invisible grace.

"Preaching upon Luke xxi. 6, Christ, sayeth he, left the linen clothes in the sepulchre to be His successors the ministers' apparel; and upon the fourth verse preceding, where it is said, 'Two men stood by them in shining garments,' he said, that seeing the angels ap-

2 O

peared in white, why should not the ministers imitate them in their apparell, and whereas some said he called the white surplice the w—h—'s smoake,* black apparell may as well be called the devil's coate.

"Whoever mentions, said he, election or reprobation before the foundation of the world, mentions a damnable doctrine.

"That it were better for us to communicate with Papists in case of necessity than want it altogether, for, said he, a man had better eat bread albeit it were mouldie nor die for hunger.

"Preaching upon Christ appearing to the two disciples as they were going to Emaus, upon these words 'He made as though He would have gone further': he taught that Jesus there dissembled with His disciples, and concluded in the end that it was lawful to dissemble. Also, in that same sermon he said that, albeit Christ made all things that were made, and that He was able by His word to undo and confirm all things, yet He could not make an ill man good, for, said he, notwithstanding all that these disciples heard Christ do and say, they remained still in their hardness of heart and unbelief.

"He taught that both Cain and Judas might have been saved if they had pleased: for (his reason was), if Cain do well, shall not he be accepted; and if he do evil, sin lyeth at the door,—so it was in his own will to be saved or not saved.

"Speaking of predestination, he fell out in these words, Predestination! predestination! what call ye predestination? This is a doctrine rashly devised, and hath been hatched in hell, and worthy to be delete out of God's Word.

"He taught that both Papists and Protestants went to heaven, but the one went by the string, the other by the bow, even as you go to Edinburgh, some by the muir gate† and some by the meall gate.

"He taught us from sundry opinions anent Christ's descension into hell, but for his own opinion he said Christ went where Abraham

* Shirt. † Way.

was, call it *Limbus Patrum* or Abraham's bosom, which of them you will.

"Being catechising, Feb. 18, he asked a young boy what he received when he came to the Lord's table. The boy answered bread and wine. What more got ye? saith he. The body and blood of Christ. What is that bread and wine? saith he. Is it not in effect the real body and blood of Christ? Yes. Which answer he approving, said—It is a sufficient reason for us to believe this because Christ hath said it. After which manner should we receive it? said he. Whether sitting, standing, or kneeling? We should receive it (said the boy) kneeling—being so previously taught by him. To this answer Mr. John replied—Yes, it is indeed so, for to sit at the receiving of the sacrament were to go to the Lord's table as we were going to a *landward brydal*,* and sit with God cheek by joule, and therefore, said he, they that sit at the sacrament communicate rather at the devil's table than at God's.

"At table in the Abbey of Paisley, before my Lord Abercorne's lady and sisters, with sundry others, similarly affected, he mentioned very hotely and stiflie against Sir William Cunninghame of Caprington, knight (who, being there by accident, did oppose him), that it was lawful to invocate the holy angels, using this for an argument, because God hath appointed a good angel to attend and wait upon every one of us for our protection.

"Dec. 11, 1637.—In Robert Robeson's house, publickly at table, before Patrick Bell, late Provost of Glasgow, James Hamilton, late Bailie there, Robert Wallace, a Bailie of Pasley, and others; he mentioned that prayer for the dead was a laudable and commendable custom in the Church for the space of 1200 years, and affirmed that it was in all the liturgies of the Church since that tyme.

"He affirmed publickly in the pulpit that the liturgie of the Kirk of England was so excellent and perfect that neither man nor angel

* A country wedding.

could make a better; saying further, that we were happy if we had such a perfect liturgy instead of our Psalm Book,* which was no ways to be compared therewith, shewing what great desire he had of that most corrupt liturgy obtruded upon our Church by our bishops, which every honest heart abhoreth as popish and superstitious. When a commission was sent from the Presbytery to supplicate against the Service Book,† he not only protested against their supplicating and sending of a commissioner at the Presbytery table, but also at dinner with the brethren, he said that if the Presbytery would accept of the said book, he would go to Edinburgh with good will to testify the same, albeit he should be stoned; and when it was replied to him by Mr. Brisbane, who was chosen by the Presbytery to be commissioner, 'he hoped they should come ill speed that were so willing to run upon an ill cause,' he answered in great spite, 'God send you ill speed, and God gar ye break your neck be the gate, that is going on that errand.'

"He likewise taught that it was never a good world since we had so much preaching; while, as he was commending the Service Book, and affirmed that men nor angels could make a better than the Service Book, he taught, mentioning free will, that notwithstanding Christ said to Peter, 'Before the cock crow twice, thou shalt deny me thrice,' Peter might have contained his tongue within his teeth, and not denied Christ. He taught that the world might have been saved, and Christ need not to have suffered.

"That the day the Covenant was subscribed he enquired at Patrick Baird, his nurse's husband, if he had subscribed the Covenant, who answered he had. 'Then,' replied Mr. John, 'when you subscribed the petition you subscribed to the devil, now you subscribed to his dame.'

"He said in his own house that he wont‡ to have good parochiners,

* The Book of Common Order, the Liturgy in use after the Reformation. † See *ante*.

‡ Was accustomed.

but now he had a pack of devils, and said 'the devil make me quit of them.'

"He said at my Lord of Abercorn's table that if he were king he should cut off the heads of one half and the hands off the other half of them that withstood the Service Book.

"He being drinking one night with Sir William Ross, Harry Stirling, and some others, in Robert Robeson's house, when they left him so beastly drunk that the Laird of Beltrees,* coming in by chance and seeing him in such a pitiful estate, was forced to help his man, Hugh Paterson, to carry him home with great difficulty.

"He sware before above fourscore of the best of his parochiners that he never gave the communion in Paisley sitting, whereas the contrar was presently proven in his face. Let it be judged whether he be mansworn or no, being at the session table, and whether after he ought to be believed or no.

"He taught that those who would not keep the five holy days would not be saved."

These curious charges were brought against Mr. Crighton, who, for some reason, did not appear to meet them. Seven witnesses were brought against him, who proved to the satisfaction of the Presbytery that most of the utterances of the minister were spoken out of the pulpit. The case of drunkenness was proved by Beltrees and his servant. The chief charges held proven were two that did not appear in the libel. He was said to have performed some cases of baptism without prayer or exhortation, and "to have profaned the sacrament of the Lord's supper by casting away the long table, and placing a short table altarwise, with a fixed rail about it, within which he stood himself, and reached the elements unto the people kneeling without about the rail." To this was added a curious story of his striking a beggar,† on his way to church for sermon, "to the effusion of his blood in great plenty." This was proved on the evidence of a certain Claud Hamilton and his servant. To the

* No great character himself.

† A similar story was brought against another minister deposed by the Assembly at Glasgow. Baillie's Letters, Vol I.

impartial reader, the evidence against the poor minister in regard to character appears to have been of the slenderest description. He was evidently a very eccentric man, and seems not to have deemed all important the matters which were to his brethren of vital moment. He was a cousin of the historian Baillie, who, in his letters, mentions him more than once, and always with kindness, though he failed, he tells us, to convince him of what he deemed his errors. The Presbytery itself did not venture to pronounce sentence against him, but referred his case to the ensuing Assembly. This great convention was to meet, not in Edinburgh, but in Glasgow, and all true-blue Presbyterians were preparing for it. It was expected to overthrow for ever all Episcopal power in Scotland. In the Abbey the Presbytery met, and elected their commissioners* to this Assembly, and there the members present solemnly swore, with uplifted hands, "that they were neither dealt with, nor would suffer themselves to be dealt with, to be perverted against the covenant, *nec prece, pretio, nec minis.*" They appointed "a solemn fast through all their churches these two Sabbaths following in the beginning of November the fourth, and Sunday, the eleventh of November, for a happy meeting, a prosperous proceeding, and a gracious success unto the General Assembly ensuing." They deemed their prayers well answered, for in their minutes they record their approval of all that the Assembly had done, and they endorse its famous declaration at length. It met within the Cathedral of Glasgow, and, as it has been well remarked, must have resembled one of the great Œcumenical Councils of the East, still so greatly revered, which settled some of the highest mysteries of the faith amid tumult and uproar.† It was a curious gathering—noblemen, barons, elders, clergy, jostled one another in the grand old church, to the scandal of the grave historian, who has given the fullest account of the meeting.‡ "Our vassals," he

* These were Mr. William Brisbane, Mr. Mathew Brisbane, and Mr. John Hamilton, together with Sir Ludovick Houston of that Ilk, the Laird of Bishopton, and the Goodman of Duchal, commissioners to attend the General Assembly to be holden in Glasgow the twenty-ane day of November next, 1638.

† Cunninghame's Hist. of the Ch. of Scot., Vol. II., p. 100.

‡ Baillie's Letters and Journals, Vol. I., p. 123.

says, " without shame, in great numbers, make such din and clamours in the house of the true God, that, if they were minded to use the like behaviour in my chamber, I would not be content till they were downstairs. So many bishops were deposed that he almost forgets to note the fate of his cousin from Paisley, who " was sent to give them convoy" and "hold up their train." He was the first minister deposed. He had gone to the court at London, and sought the King's interference, when he saw the Presbytery set against him. In this he was disappointed, and returned much dejected. According to Baillie, he was " willing to clear himself of many things laid to his charge, and to confess his errors if he might remain at Paisley." There was no prospect of this. He did not appear at the bar when called, and sentence went against him in his absence. " Mr. John Crichtone, minister at Paisley, being found by witnesses that he was ane professed arminiane and popish champion, him the Assemblie all in one voice deposed,"* and the Abbey knew that innovator, his Service Book, and railed-off table, no more.

* Balfour's Annals, Vol. II., p. 308.

## CHAPTER XXVI.

### The Covenant.

Because you have thrown off your Prelate Lord,
  And with stiff vows renounced his Liturgy,
Dare ye for this abjure the civil sword,
  To force our consciences whom Christ set free,
  And ride us with a classic hierarchy.

—*Milton.*

PAISLEY was now under the rule of the Covenant. Mr. Henry Calvert,* the minister of the Abbey who succeeded Mr. Crighton, was a very different man from his latitudinarian predecessor. He was a stern and unbending disciplinarian—a man of weak health but unflagging zeal, who put down with the strong hand everything that did not square with his own ideas. He did a generous thing at his entry in 1641. He assigned five chalders of his grain stipend to a second minister, who was to be "his colleague and helper, promising another chalder providing he should be a man agreeable to himself. After several disappointments in calling a minister, the session of the parish, which at this time appeared to have acted as patron, presented Mr. Alexander Dunlop to the newly-instituted second charge, and he was accordingly associated with Mr. Calvert in the care of the parish. Shortly after, Mr. Calvert's health broke down, and the parishioners secured for him an assistant—a Mr. Dryfesdale, who had left Ireland on account of persecution—giving him a stipend of seven

* He was an Englishman, and incumbent of Oldstane in Ireland, where he was deposed by Henry Bishop of Down in 1636 for refusing to subscribe the Canons. He was presented to Paisley by James Earl of Abercorn, 27th May, 1641.

hundred merks. These three gentlemen between them made Paisley a very uncomfortable residence for anyone who did not heartily accept the Covenant. Mr. Dunlop was an exceedingly able man, and was much respected for his great learning and powers as a preacher; and, according to Wodrow, "did wonderfully improve himself after coming to Paisley," a remark which perhaps may be made with truth regarding some of his successors.* "He had also great grace; great learning and a great gift of disputing and arguing; and a great painfulness in reading and studying, and in all his ministerial work. In the whole week he lay but three whole nights in his bed. This, and to all these great gifts, he also added as a great ornament to them all—that he was clothed with great humility, so that he thought highly of his honest brethren that were far inferior to him. He had but few words: he had but just so much as seemed to express his matter that he was to deliver. He had a strange gift and faculty in making very difficult things plain even to the common people's capacities." Many other excellent things are recorded by the historian regarding this minister of Paisley, and to his pages we refer the reader who desires to be better acquainted with the life of Mr. Dunlop. One remark regarding him is, however, worthy of notice. He "used in the pulpit" a kind of groan at the end of some sentences. Mr. Peebles called it a "holy groan," and one John Knox, a worthy and great Christian, who was related to the Laird of Ranfurly, in Kilbarchan, said of Mr. Dunlop, when he had been hearing him at Paisley, "Many a happy word he groaned over my head this day."† He was evidently a man deeply imbued with the spirit of the time. He had the best of all courage, that of his opinions. When he acted in some of the troubles as an army chaplain, he was distinguished for his bravery, and made an excellent soldier, and he was ready to go to prison and to death as a champion of the Covenant. He and his co-presbyters had much to do in standing up for this famous bond. "He said of some who were very troublesome to him in Paisley that he would never be quit of them till he prayed them

* Wodrow's Analecta, Vol. III., p. 21, where there is a life of Mr. Dunlop and of several other ministers of the time.

† Those acquainted with the preaching of many of the Highland clergy will recognise at once "the holy groan" as a great feature in their excellent performances.

out of the place"; but the Presbytery Records tell us that he and his colleagues used other methods for this purpose besides that of Prayer. The Earl of Abercorn was especially obnoxious as a suspected Papist, and from the days of Mr. Boyd of Trochrig he had been carefully looked after by his neighbours the ministers of the Abbey. Very soon after the famous Assembly at Glasgow, the Presbytery ordered Mr. Henry Calvert and another minister to go to him and "speak to his Lordship anent the subscription of the Covenant and anent his coming to the church, and anent the bringing back of his eldest son, according to the act of the Provincial Assembly."* The Earl answered to their demands that "he was entered in conference with the brethren at Edinburgh, and that he was going east again, and was to continue in conference with them; and anent his son, the ministers reported his Lordship shews he had recommended him to a very religious friend and Protestant for his education, namely, a cousin-german of his late wife's." This soft answer on the part of the Earl does not seem to have turned away the wrath of the Presbytery. Again they ordered Mr. Calvert "to go to him and intimate to him the act of the General Assembly both anent his religion and transportation of his children, and to report this day fifteen days." The Earl did not satisfy the church on these points, and had to suffer as his mother had done before him. After some more vexatious interference with himself and his family by the Presbytery, the General Assembly took up the case, and in 1649 he was excommunicated by that court, and ordered to transport himself out of the kingdom.† This sentence of banishment was put in force, and the Earl, in consequence of the persecutions to which he was subjected, was compelled to part with his estates, and to leave Scotland altogether. In 1652 he sold the lordship of Paisley to the Earl of Angus, who, in the following year, sold it to Lord Cochrane, afterwards created Earl of Dundonald, and the Abbey passed away for a time from the descendants of Lord Claud.

Mr. Calvert and his colleagues carried matters with a very high hand, and seem to have had it all their own way. In 1649, the Town Council

* 19th May, 1642.

† This Earl of Abercorn seems to have presented to the Abbey the communion cups now in use.

ordered the market day to be held on Friday, and sermon to be preached on the forenoon, during which "no business to be done under pain of five pounds, and every person to go to the kirk." Later on, they ordained that on the Sabbath day any horse kept on the common land should be *tethered*, so that the Lord's day be not profaned by persons abiding out of church in time of sermon, and in gathering together and using profaneness after sermon. "Penny brydals" were forbidden by the Presbytery, and all pyping and dancing at weddings, as "leading to blasphemy and profanity." The people were under very rigid government.

One instance of the rule of the covenanting clergy we may briefly relate, though the case to which we refer bulks very largely in the Records of the Presbytery. In the east end of Paisley, at Ferguslie, there lived a respectable family of the name of Wallace, the head of which was termed the granter of Paisley, as possibly enjoying some of the privileges of the old monastic official who bore that title. His wife, Margaret Hamilton, went by the name of the "Guidwife of Ferguslie," and whether from upbringing or from conviction, had leanings towards Romanism, and did not attend the Abbey to hear Mr. Calvert or his colleague as often as they thought she should. Mr. Calvert reported her to the Presbytery, and for several years between 1643 and 1647 that reverend court was greatly exercised regarding the opinions of the good wife and her family. The full report of the case of this unfortunate woman would occupy many pages. In vain her husband pleaded her inability to attend church on account of her health. The ministers of the Abbey were appointed to confer with her, and to examine her on oath whether it was inability or scruples of conscience that prevented her attendance on their ministrations. She was cited, and monished, and prayed for. On one occasion Mr. Calvert reports to the Presbytery* that "he went to Margaret Hamilton, and there did both read God's Word and raise observations thereupon, did sing psalms, her daughter and youngest son being present, but that he catechised none, unto all which exercises the said Margaret gave attendance." "The brethren did again ordain Mr. Calvert to go to the said Margaret, and

* June 8, 1643.

put her upon oath whether it were inability of her body onlie that restrains her from coming to God's house for hearing His Word, or if she have scruples of conscience anent the religion professed in the Kirk and Kingdom. Likewise he is ordained to catechise the said Margaret and the rest of her family." On another occasion the poor woman dragged herself to the Presbytery to beseech mercy from her reverend tormentors, "desiring supersedur from further processe, alleging she was taken up with a continual flux," and protesting, "so soon as it should please the Lord to grant her any respite on earth she should give all contentment to their demands. Hereunto the brethren consenting, ordained her to come to the minister of Paslay for conference whensoever, she being able for travel, he should call her." Many times after this she was dealt with. Her two sisters, Janet and Bessie, who shared her opinions, and who seemed to care very little for the citations and admonitions of the Kirk, were excommunicated, and that dread sentence was ordered to be pronounced against the "good wife of Ferguslie." She still protested that she was "infirm, and altogether unable in consequence of disease to come to church; and for the matter of the Covenant, she asked a covenant to be given to her, and read over and over again, and to be informed anent the meaning thereof." The minister was again ordered to confer with her. This he did, and left a copy of the Covenant with her, and the Presbytery "gave her to their next meeting-day, out of courtesy, when, if she do not obey, she will be proceeded against." The poor woman did not obey, and the church officer, George Ramsay, was directed to summon her. Being now hard-pressed, she promised the minister before next presbytery day "to abjure Popery, and subscribe the Covenant." The minister was appointed to return to her, "with some of the elders of his paroche, and there to receive her renunciation of Popery, first of one point, then on another point, and so on all the rest. This, after some further delay, was done in presence of the ministers." Mr. Dunlop now appears on the scene, and reports that in presence of John Vaux, Hugh Blair, and Robert Park she sware and subscribed the Confession of Faith and National Covenant, and renounced poperie, first on one point, then on another, and so all the points of poperie. And in the end renounced and abjured all poperie with an oath." This important fact is specially certified by Mr. R. Alexander, clerk to the Presbytery. The clergy seemed now to have triumphed, but the good wife still shewed signs of resistance. A month or two after she took the oath, the minister came again to the Presbytery to complain of his refractory parishioner. Notwithstanding the oath, "pretending inabilitie of bodie by reason of many diseases, now dwelling at Blakston, she does not come to the kirk at all." Mr. Dunlop and Mr. Glendinning were accordingly sent to her to desire her either to come to kirk or "to produce before the presbyterie a testimonial under the hand of James Fleming, physician, that she is unable to come to the kirk." For a time this certificate was not forthcoming, to the wrath of the Presbytery, who issued more citations; but at last a testimonial was produced, signed by James Fleming, "Testifying on his conscience that she is unable to travel either on foot or horse, for disease and several reasons contained in his testimonial." The Presbytery found this to satisfy the act, and appointed "the minister of Paisley to deal with John Wallace of Ferguslie to provide ane chamber in the toun of Paisley for his wife, that she may reside there for her more easy coming to the kirk." After a time they summon John Wallace, who assures them of his wife's ill health, and that she was not able to be removed at all. They desire him to bring her to Paisley, and "if she be not able to come to the kirk, that the ministers may have occasion of daylie or frequent conference with her, or to bring the testimonial of James Fleming, physician, that she is not able to be removed at all." Some time elapses, and her husband appears to say that he "cannot find opportunity for James Fleming to visit his wife, albeit he sent for him several times." The Presbytery thought this was merely trifling with them, for they order him to bring "her to Paisley by next Presbytery day, either by land or by water, or they will process her." A few more citations were now issued, and as they produced no effect, Mr. Calvert and Mr. Hamilton were appointed to "deal with Margaret Hamilton, and try her health and abilitie, inasmuch as she professes inabilitie and great infirmity of body, so that she is not able to travel anywhere." This conference did not produce any result, and she "was directed to be publickly admonished." She was also reported to the Synod. That exalted body now took up the case with more success than the Presbytery. Mr. Calvert and Mr. John Hamilton were ordered to go and see the "good wife." They report that "they had gone and seen her infirm, and so still pleading inhabilitie. They have gotten her promise to come to the Kirk of Paisley within twentie days to give content and satisfaction in that point, albeit she should be carried in her bed." The triumph of these grave seniors was now near: the poor woman was lifted on a bed, resting on a frame-work of wattles, and solemnly borne along, as if to her burial, from Blackstone to the Abbey, a distance of four miles. Surely a more singular procession never entered that edifice than this poor invalid on her couch with her bearers and attendants. Justice was now satisfied, and the covenanting fathers amply rewarded for their great labour in the conversion of this poor "Papist." They record solemnly the end of their toil, "2nd June, 1647. Mr. Henrie Calvert, minister at Paislay, reports that on last Lord's-day Margaret Hamilton, spouse to John Wallace of Ferguslie, came to the Kirk of Paisley *carried on ane wand bed.*"

The spirit they displayed in persecution of this poor woman was soon to be turned upon themselves. Traces of the conflict that ended in the proscription of the Covenant and the establishment, for a time, of Anglican Episcopacy, occur continually in all the local records of the period of which we are treating. When the covenanting army encamped at Dunsehill, the Presbytery sent one of their members to act as chaplain.

> "11 Ap., 1639.—The which day the brethren thought it most expedient and necessar that Mr. Math. Brisbane should go with the Colonel Montgomerie, and the company with him, to the Duncehill, for their comfort be preaching and other exercises."

When the Scotch Covenanters crossed the Tweed under Leslie, the Paisley ministers followed them with their prayers.

> "Ap. 1, 1641.—The which day the brethren declared that they had kept a solemn fast with the Church of Scotland for the preservation of the Scottish army, the keeping of the union and bond of

peace among ourselves, the advancing of the Reformation in all neighbouring countries, with the disappointing of the practices of our adversaries, and the getting of religion and solid peace."

Apparently their prayers were answered. Within a short time after their supplications, the form of religion they detested was overthrown in England as well as among themselves. The army of the Covenant, by their invasion of England, had abolished Episcopacy, and achieved the supremacy of Parliament. Accordingly, solemn thanks were offered for this success.

"9 Dec., 1641.—Which day the brethren were acquainted that the 9th day of Jany. next to come is appointed to be kept for solemn thanks giving to God for establishing peace within the kingdom of Scotland."

This peace was not of very long continuance. In 1643 the Puritans in England sought the assistance of the Scotch to aid them in their religious struggles. This was readily given. The idea filled the mind of the covenanters that a church on the pattern of their own might be established on the other side of the border, and a Scotch army, numbering three thousand men, under Leslie, entered England "to seek for conformity of religion amid the horrors of civic warfare." This expedition was exceedingly popular, and the Paisley brethren gave it both their spiritual and temporal aid,—the former by sending ministers to preach to the soldiers, the latter by raising contributions.

"23rd Sept., 1643.—Anent a letter of the estates requiring that the brethren would be pleased, every one, to put out a man, with other presbyteries, with the expedition to England. The brethren declared their willingness so to do."

"May 25.—Compeared Sir Ludovick Houston, Knight, and the Laird of Bishopton, Commissioners from the Council of Scotland, and

* Cunninghame's Hist. of the Ch. of Scot., Vol. II., p. 136.

presented their letter, together with an Act of Council craving the advice of the Presbytery for borrowing money for the supply of the Scottish army in England. The brethren agreed that they thought it a matter very advisable and expedient to be done."

"May 16, 1444.—The brethren ordained Mr. Ninian Campbell to go to the army now in England and supply there as minister till he were liberated, and that in my Lord Loudon's regiment, and ordained Mr. John Hay to write his Lordship to that effect."

"The which day the brethren having received letters, as they did before, from the Earl of Eglinton and Mr. Robert Douglas for relief of Mr. Robert Wise, now at the armie in England, and that the regiment might be supplied by one of their number, did then as now answer that they were few in number. Some kirks implanted, and many men, old and weak, and unable to undergo the charge, and have presently appointed one of their number to be preacher to my Lord Chancellor's regiment, and could not spare any more at this time, which answer Mr. John Hamilton undertook to deliver to his Lordship."

While the clergy were thus following with their goodwill the army in England, Montrose with fire and sword burst down like a torrent from the northern wilds, and filled the land with the terror of his name. Leslie, returning across the Border, met and defeated the devoted Royalist at Philiphaugh.* The latter gallant champion of a failing cause seems not to have been without supporters in the neighbourhood of Paisley, although he had been formally excommunicated from all the pulpits of the Presbytery for "his unnatural rebellion, and invading in a hostile manner the south of Scotland." One of his sympathisers was the son of the "good wife of Ferguslie," who had no goodwill towards the persecutors of his mother, and was only too glad to help their enemies. He thus came in himself for a taste of their discipline.

* The scene of this famous battle by the banks of the classic Yarrow is still pointed out, and various relics of the conflict are preserved in the house of Philiphaugh. There is no Scotch battle-ground more beautiful and more deserving of a visit.

"21 May, 1646.—The which day the ministers at Paislay required powers from the Presbytery for judicial tryall and examination of such persons as are suspected to have had compliance with James Grahame or Alexander MacDonald, or receivet protection from them, which was granted."

"7th Jan., 1647.—The which day compeared Andro Semple, town clerk of Renfrew, and grantit he was at the meeting of the gentlemen of the shyre of Renfrew when there was an act made for the outputing of a troup of horse for James Grahame. The Presbytery has warned him *apud acta* to this day twentie days to give up ane roll of the gentlemen that were there."

"14 Jan., 1647.—The which day compeared Allan Wallace, son to John Wallace of Ferguslie, and challenged for compliance with the enemy, confest he went to Bothwell, and that he received orders from the gentlemen at Renfrew to have horses, and it is further proven before the Session of Paisley against him that he threatened the people to raise the said horses for James Grahame's use. He is ordained to confess his fault *on his knees before the Presbytery*, which he did; and is also ordained to confess the fault *on his knees* in the kirk floor of Paisley, before the publick congregation in a place before the pulpit."

All the efforts of Grahame and his followers could not serve the King and his cause. The rigid Covenanters opposed all compromise with the unfortunate monarch as sinful; and when the Scotch Estates entered into an engagement with him of a moderate character, the Church denounced it as wicked, its supporters as malignant, and "threatened with the highest censure ministers who should not speak out against the acts of the legislature." The King was left to the mercy of the English sectaries, and on the 30th January, 1649, was beheaded. Nothing could exceed at this time the intolerance of the Covenanters; and nothing in the history of Ultramontanism could surpass the claims which they put forth to civil supremacy. They insisted on all men subscribing the

Covenant. They ordered the army to be purged of malignants; and after the defeat and execution of Montrose, who made a gallant attempt to place King Charles II. on the throne, intolerance know no bounds. The Records of the Paisley Presbytery at this period are filled with the inquisition after malignants, and their excommunication. Nothing would satisfy the Church but the reception of the Covenant in its most rigid and binding form.

"27th December, 1648.—Reported by the brethren that the Covenant was renewed with solemn fasting and humiliation on Sabbath last."

"12th April, 1649.—Compeared John Wallace of Ferguslie, Allan Wallace, his son, Robert Fork, elder, and Robert Alexander, late bailies of Paisley, who, for their accession to the late sinful engagement, are referred to the General Assembly."

"16th May, 1656.—Solemn thanksgiving for the overthrow given by the Majesty of God to James Grahame, appointed to be kept on Wednesday come eight days."

Their rejoicing was of short duration. Two years after this Charles II. came to Scotland and was recognised as King by the Covenanters, they having induced him to sign the Covenant, and "to humble himself in the sight of God for his father's opposition to the Solemn League and the idolatry of his mother." Charles had no sooner landed in Scotland than Cromwell with his Ironsides marched across the Border, and the Covenanters opposed him with an army which they had previously purged by dismissing from its ranks every soldier suspected of malignancy, and who had not subscribed the Covenant. They were met by a set of fanatics who were better soldiers if not so orthodox as themselves, and at Dunbar their ranks were scattered and broken. The defeat of the Scotch army at Worcester by Cromwell a year afterwards completed their discomfiture, and for nine years Scotland was more truly a province of England than it had been in the time of Edward the First. The Puritans had a strong detachment at Paisley. They taxed the inhabitants severely, levied from them considerable sums of money, forbade the usual courts, took possession of the Town-house and Tolbooth, and even compelled the Council to furnish them with the luxury of feather beds.* They exercised a wholesome influence over the tyrannical ecclesiastics who had hitherto had it their own way. Probably, as in other parts of Scotland, they abolished the stool of public repentance, which they regarded as a relic of the Roman sacrament of penance, and perhaps some of them even exercised their gift as preachers in the parish pulpit, as they did in other places to the great disgust of the ministry. They certainly ventured to interfere with that high court of inquisition the Presbytery, and we have the strange picture given of a Puritan officer bursting in upon this conclave as they were solemnly seated in the Abbey. It is amusing to think of these grim sons of the Covenant domineered over by a set of fanatics even grimmer than themselves. In only one point did the new fanaticism differ from and excel the old—the sectaries had some idea of religious liberty, whilst the Covenanting Presbyterians had none. The following extracts relate to this time of Puritan rule:—

"Sept., 1640.—In respect of our army in the fields against the sectaries is scattered at Dunbar, and that the gentlemen and ministers of the western shires are to meet at Kilmarnock, the presbytery appoints Mess. Alexander Dunlop and John Mauld to repair thither, and to concur with them in any good and necessary course for safety of the cause and kingdom."

"10th Aug., 1653.—This day unexpectedly, Captain Greene, one of the English army, with ane partie of soldiers, invadit the Presbyterie, and by violence interrupted their sitting, carried them out to a house in the town, and detained them there as prisoners, alleging that all presbyteries were discharged and had no power to sit. Thereafter, they being dismissed, did again convene, and considering the great distraction of the times, and the uncertainty of the

* Very curious entries are in the Town Council Records relating to the occupation of the English. Their first appearance is in 1651. In letters from "The Roundhead Officers," (Bannatyne Club), there is one given dated Paisley, Feb. 15, 1657.

continuation of their liberties, appointed the ordination of Mr. William Thomson to the ministrie at Merns, to be at Merns to-morrow, and the day to be observed as ane day of humiliation."

"1st Sept., 1653.—Compeared Captain John Green, one of the English officers, who, declairing that he was come to sit with the Presbytery, exhibited ane warrant from Collonell Lillbure for that purpose. The Presbytery did declare their great dissatisfaction therewith, and that with their consent he should not sit with them. Whereupon he did forbear for the tyme."

During the troubles to which this chapter refers the Dundonald family had resided at the Abbey House. They do not appear to have been very popular with the townspeople, and though they conformed to the kirk, and occupied their "loft" in it regularly, they were suspected of leanings towards Prelacy. One little dispute between them and their neighbours is amusing. A green sloped down from the "Place of Paisley" to the river Cart. It is the strip of land so often referred to in the early charters of the Monastery, as lying below the dormitory of the monks. It had come to be used as a public bleaching-green, and the washerwomen of the town might often have been seen there tramping their clothes in tubs and carrying on bleaching operations. Lady Cochrane and her son did not regard their industry with approval, and "declared that none should have liberty to bleach on the green under the chambers." They also threw down a "knocking stone" which had been set up by one of the bleachers. This gave great offence to the Magistrates of the town. "Without a contrary voice they concluded to go to the bleaching-green betwixt the Abbey Chambers and the water, and where the town's knocking stones are cast down, and to set the same up again." They accordingly marched thither in procession for this purpose, and the result of their opposition was that they discomfited the Dundonalds, and retained for the use of the burgesses the coveted washing-green. It was the first exhibition of that radical spirit for which Paisley has in later days been so famous.

Whatever disputes arose between the townspeople and the Cochranes, as the Dundonald family were called, there happened shortly after this an event in which they rejoiced heartily together. One day in June, 1660, there came "into Lord Cochrane's hands an act and ordinance, issued by the Parliament of England, ordaining King Charles the Second to be proclaimed righteous heir to the crown of these nations,* who intends to have the said proclamation read the morne upon the Cross, and desires of the Bailies and Council their concurrence thereto." This concurrence was heartily given—the King was proclaimed with rejoicing. No more English Sectaries would levy their contributions on the citizens, and even the ministers shared in the joy, for was not Charles a covenanted King? Mr. Alexander Dunlop and Mr. James Stirling offered publick thanksgivings in the Abbey, and the people were not restrained, even by covenanting severity, from exhibiting their hilarity in the manner for which Scotland has been always famous. This Mr. Stirling was minister of the second charge, Mr. Dunlop having been promoted to the first charge in 1653. Mr. Stirling was ordained to Paisley when only twenty three years of age, but was reckoned by all who knew him "a very considerable man." So says Wodrow,† and adds that "he was very acute, learned, and pious, and had a very polite and accurate way of preaching. He was mighty familiar and well acquaint with our great noblemen, such as the Marquis of Argyle and others, for he was well bred and well behaved. He was to have been settled at Erskine, but Mr. Dunlop enticed him to Paisley." The coming to the Abbey of so bright a light was an occasion of great rejoicing. The Town Council paid twelve pounds "from the mortcloth money" in giving a supper to the ministers of the Presbytery and their followers at his induction.‡ Had he and they known what was to be the end of his ministry at Paisley, their festivity would have been greatly modified.

* Town Council Records.

† Analecta, Vol. III., p. 23.

‡ Town Council Records, Nov., 1655. Mr. Stirling was inducted on 26th June, 1654.

## CHAPTER XXVII.

### The Curates.

> "Leighton stood
> Alone 'mong men of wrath and blood
> In the dim twilight of the day
> That dawned, uncertain, on his way;
> Nor might he comprehend
> Whither its strifes would end.
> He comprehended not; but tried
> To quiet now the wrath and pride,
> To heal when there was hope, to pray
> When hope of healing died away.
>
> —*W. C. Smith.*

WE have now come to a period in our story which it is not pleasant to contemplate. The spirit of the Covenanters, as we have seen, was essentially a persecuting spirit. With them, every one must be a Presbyterian or a Covenanter, and no one had a right to be anything else. The spirit of the Episcopalians, who succeeded them in the Establishment, was equally a persecuting spirit, but as they had the arm of the secular power more under their control than their predecessors, that spirit manifested itself in a more open and in a more repulsive form. The Covenanters fulminated excommunications, and would have proceeded to more serious measures if they had possessed the power. The Episcopalians had the power—the whole civil power of the kingdom—and they used it. Neither party could suffer a rival. Both were equally intolerant. But the one was on the popular, the other on the unpopular side; and while those belonging to the one party have come down to us glorified as martyrs and the champions of religious liberty, those of the other have been held up to execration, as if they monopolised all the intolerance, bigotry, and fierceness of the age. The latter, certainly, had a considerable share of these; but they had by no means an exclusive possession of them. This is perhaps the most that can be said in their favour. For their opponents, it must be pleaded, that they exhibited in their sufferings nobler qualities than they exhibited in their prosperity, and the trials through which they passed enlist our sympathy in a way the men themselves never could have done.

Soon after the accession to the throne of Charles II., it was clearly seen that he had not taken kindly to the Covenanting lessons that had been forced upon him when in Scotland in the time of his adversity. One measure after another was passed re-establishing Episcopal government, the Covenant was declared treasonable, and all in offices of trust who had ever taken it were required solemnly to abjure it. Bishops were consecrated for the Scottish Sees. All who had been admitted to livings during the Presbyterian period were required to seek institution to them from the Bishop; and as many in the west delayed to do so, a Privy Council, held in Glasgow, declared their livings forfeited, and ordered the ministers to be removed from them by a certain date.

The two ministers of the Abbey shared in the consequences of this decree. Both Mr. Dunlop and Mr. Stirling had to resign their charge, and a Mr. William Pierson took their place as curate of Paisley. The outed ministers continued for a time to hold conventicles in the neighbourhood of the town, to which their old parishioners flocked, leaving the Abbey deserted. Such meetings were soon interdicted, and those who attended them severely fined. As these gatherings were popular throughout Renfrewshire at this period, the fines received by Government were considerable.* The trials of the time fell very heavily upon the ministers of whom we have had glimpses in the course of our story, while they sat in the plenitude of their power as a Presbytery in the Abbey, a terror to all offenders.

* In the course of a very few years, the fines paid by twelve gentlemen in the county, accord-to Wodrow, amounted to £368,000. Sir George Maxwell of Newark was fined £94,000; the Laird of Duchal, £84,000; Cunninghame of Camcuran, £15,833; Maxwell of Dargavel, £18,900; Sir George Maxwell of Nether Pollok, £93,600.—*Ch. Hist. of Scotland by Cunninghame, Vol. II., p. 200.*

They were faithful to their convictions. Of the sixteen who composed the Presbytery, only two conformed to the new order of things.* They went through many hardships. "They were not only deprived of their livings in time to come, but of the last year's stipend for which they served, and in the winter season (Dec., 1663) obliged, with sorrowful hearts and empty pockets, to wander, I know not how many miles with their numerous and small families, many of them scarce knew whither. But the Lord wonderfully provided for them and theirs, to their own confirmation and wonder." So writes Wodrow regarding the dispossessed Covenanters, and it is probable his statement is not exaggerated. Of the fate of the ministers of the Abbey, we have ample information. On 6th January, 1663, Mr. Alexander Dunlop, after having been previously "silenced from preaching," was summoned before the Council for refusing to take the usual oaths. He was ordained "to be banished forth of his Majesty's dominions, the Lords reserving to themselves to fix the time of his removal, and in the meantime ordained him to confine himself within the bounds of the dioceses of Aberdeen, Brechin, Caithness, Dunkeld, and allow him the space of ten days to go home to order his business and affairs." His sentence would have been heavier if the King's physician,† Sir Robert Cunninghame, had not interfered on his behalf. He was to have been sent to Holland with seven other Nonconformists, but Sir Robert "told the Chancellor that they might as well execute him on a scaffold as send him to the sea, for he could not be twenty-four or forty-eight hours upon the sea but it would be his death, for by his extraordinary study and labour at Paisley he had brought his very strong body so low that he could not live upon the sea for a very short time." He seems to have lived in retirement at Culross, and after the hopes of the Covenanters were disappointed by the defeat of the in-

* The two conforming ministers were Mr. Taylor of Greenock, and Mr. John Hamilton of Innerkip. Those who gave up all were Mr. Alexander Dunlop, Mr. John Drysdale, and Mr. Jas. Stirling, all of Paisley; Mr. John Stirling, Kilbarchan; Mr. Patrick Simpson of Renfrew; Mr. Hugh Smith of Eastwood; Mr. William Thomson of Mearns; Mr. William Thomson of Houston; Mr. James Hutcheson of Killalan; Mr. James Alexander of Kilmalcolm; Mr. Hugh Peebles of Lochwinnoch; Mr. James Wallace of Inchinnan, and Mr. Hugh Wallace of Neilston.

† Wodrow's Analecta, Vol. IV., p. 19.

surgents at Pentland, he died, his biographer tells us, of a broken heart.* His colleague, Mr. Stirling, went, after he was driven from the Abbey, to the East Indies, where he died in 1671 or 1672 from the effects of a fall from a horse at Bombay.†

In 1662 a Presbytery was established in Paisley by virtue of an order of the Archbishop and Synod "to act as a presbytery in all matters that concern the discipline of the Church, and particularly to do all things incumbent on them for planting vacant churches." The minutes of this court have been preserved, and they are very curious. Like their predecessors, the curates met generally in the Abbey, but the matters that occupied their attention were very different from those that engrossed the Covenanters. The discipline they exercised was not so much over offenders against morals and "suspected Papists" as over those who refused to take the oaths, or ventured to decline the office of the eldership; and instead of the imposition of the Covenant, we have the enforcing of the test and the denouncing of conventicles. The whole character of the men as exhibited in their records is of a lower type than that of their predecessors. Compelled to act the part of common informers, to hand those who opposed them to the Magistrates, often detested by their parishioners, and looked upon by them as intruders into the ministry, it was no wonder that their tone was not so high asit should have been. We give a few extracts from the minutes of Presbytery as throwing light upon the history of the time. One difficulty the curates felt was getting men of respectability to act as elders and to form

* "He was about forty-seven years when he died at Borrowstouness in 1667. He was so concerned and troubled about the fall of that worthy company at Pentland that his deep concern for that terrible disaster did truly kill him and hasten on his end. For whenever he heard of their being broken he sat down and wept most bitterly; and when Mr. Hasty would after that have come in to see Mr. Dunlop, he would have seen him sitting with his gown among the ashes, in a most forlorn and dejected like condition, and he would have said to him, 'You look not like yourself! What makes you carry so?' He would have answered, 'What's the matter of me, Saunders, how I sit when I see the work and people of God sit so low? I never thought that the pulse of this nation would have beat so feverish as now I find it does.'"—Wodrow's Analecta, Vol. III., p. 19.

† "There, riding upon a great Indian horse, the horse cast him, and he took a fever and died. There was a soldier told my brother that afterwards riding upon the same horse he had almost broke his neck upon him."—Wodrow's Analecta, Vol. III., p. 26.

kirk-sessions. It was at last held to be criminal to refuse, and there are many cases in the records of the Sheriff Court* where heavy fines were imposed upon those who declined the office of the eldership. Many of them in doing so pretended they were addicted to drunkenness and other sins, in which case they were at once ordered to stand in sackcloth before the congregation.

"Oct. 27, 1664.—The names of the elders the minister (of Kilbarchan) did nominate being cited and called by the officer at the church door, those non-compearing are ordained by the Presbytery to accept the said office, and in case they obstinately refuse, the minister is appointed to give up their names to the Archbishop, in order to their being summoned before the High Commission. Only one, Robert Semple, is represented as unfit for the office because of his being overtaken twice with drink of late: therefore the Presbytery exclude him from the office, and ordain him to make his public repentance for his drunkenness two Lord's days, and to pay forty shillings Scots for his penalties."

"Nov. 23, 1664.—Ordains again the settling of sessions, and to all those who refuse to join with the minister in the exercise of discipline, and if they contemn their authority, to delate them to the Archbishop, to be summoned before the High Commission."

"Feb. 19th, 1665.—Ane Robert Pollok of Lilburne, refusing to be an elder in Renfrew, being summoned, &c., gave his reason of refusal because he had made a vow long ago that he would never be an elder, which ground the Presbytery finding irrelevant (a rash and unlawful oath not being obligatory), and therefore ordains him to accept of that office, and appoints the minister to give up his name, in order to his being summoned before the High Commission in case of his further refusal."

* See a very interesting volume on the "Records of the Sheriff Court of Renfrewshire," ably edited by Mr. Hector, Sheriff-Clerk of the County.

"Aug. 9, 1665.—John Shaw, parishioner in Kilbarchan, refusing to concur with his minister in the exercise of discipline, and being able to give no reason for refusing, his minister to get him summoned to the High Commission if he continue therein."

"May 25, 1668.—As for certain persons whom he (the minister of Greenock), sayd refuse to join with him in the exercise of discipline, he is required to use his prudentials, and see if by *fair means* he can gain their concurrence, the magistrates at present* being very slow and also unwilling to exercise their compulsory power against such recusants who refuse to embrace the office of an elder."

Those who, in the various parishes, refused to attend the services conducted in the church, were termed "delinquents," and were proceeded against with a severity that seemed to increase as time went on, and penal measures proved ineffectual. We give some instances in which the non-conformers were dealt with. Many more might be adduced of a similar kind. Very often when hard pressed they made their escape to Ireland.

"Nov. 29, 1664.—The Moderator, according to the acts of the Commission, required the brethren to have in to the Archbishop against the first of Jan., 1665, the names of the delinquents within their several parishes."

"Sep. 6, 1666.—Janet Cochrane, for her obstinacy and disobedience to the discipline of the Session and the present Church government, to be excommunicated."

"Nov. 8, 1666.—Renfrew delinquents for not communicating when that sacrament was last celebrated there, ordained to be summoned to next diet."

* During the indulgence when the severity against the Presbyterians was considerably relaxed.

When the Covenanters rose in insurrection in 1665, there was strict enquiry made by the Presbytery after any of their people who had taken part in the rising.

"Dec. 6, 1666.—The Archbishop his letter to the Presbytery requiring their diligence in searching out who, within their bounds, were engaged in the late rebellious insurrection, and to give up a list of the names of such, being read, strict obedience thereunto was enjoined to use all means for the finding out of such delinquents, and to report their names at the next meeting."

"Dec. 20, 1666.—His Majesty's proclamations against the harbouring of rebels were given in by the moderator, and are appointed to be publickly read the next Lord's Day in their respective churches,"

"Anent those within the Presbytery who were in arms in the late rebellious insurrection, the brethren report that none within the Presbytery were, to their knowledge, actually joined with the body who were in arms, only the young goodman of Caldwell, in the parish of Neilston, who was in arms with the Laird of Caldwell, going to these rebels, as also William Porterfield of Quarrellton, in the parish of Paisley, as also Alex. Porterfield, the said William, his brother, in the parish of Killelan, and their names well known and published in the printed papers. Two also were given up as suspected persons, who had fled their houses when searched, forby the soldiers in the parish of Eastwood, who also are already made known to His Majestie's forces, who are endeavouring to apprehend them."

Conventicles, as the congregations of the Covenanters were called, were very earnestly searched after, and a strict watch kept on all the movements of the "outed" and nonconformist ministers.

"Dec. 21, 1665.—The proclamation made against the nonconformist ministers was produced and delivered to the brethren, who are appointed with all diligence to get them intimated in their several churches."

"May 3, 1666.—Christopher Morison compeared, and being instructed to declare who married him, desired time to advise till next Presbytery, at which time he promised to give satisfaction both as to that and his oath of allegiance which he was required to take, with certification that in case he declared not who married him, or brought a testimonial to that effect from that minister, signed by two witnesses, he should be proceeded against."*

"July 26, 1666.—It is appointed that Mr. Adam Getlie be delated to the Archbishop for living so near his former church without a licence, and in that there is a presumption for his keeping of conventicles."†

"May 9, 1667.—As for ministers outed by the law and now residing in the Presbytery, the brethren declare that there are none but such as were given up formerly to the Archbishop, and such as frequent publick ordinances."

Dec. 20, 1666.—Mr. Alexander Leslie, minister of Inverkip, reported that there was some surmise in the country of a conventicle that should have been in the parish of Kilmalcolm about five weeks ago, upon which the Presbytery ordains Mr. Irving, minister in that parish, to use diligence for trying the truth of the same, and to search how it may be legally instructed."

"Feb. 27, 1667.—Anent the conventicle, minister can get no proof; further diligence enjoined to him."

"Feb. 28, 1667.—As to the conventicle, after all diligence can find no way so that the truth of it can be legally instructed."

The severities of this period were succeeded by an act of grace. An

* Morison escaped to Ireland.

† To preach at a conventicle was punishable by death and confiscation of goods ; to be present was to run the risk of a heavy fine.

indulgence was given to certain Presbyterian ministers who were permitted to occupy vacant pulpits upon specific conditions, and the persecutions to which the people were subjected were much lightened. No sooner was this done than the people in great numbers left the ministers they had been compelled to attend.

> "May 13, 1670.—Mr. Geo. Birnie declares that the ordinances were generally disdained by his people since September last, and that none brought children to be baptised by him since; that the people did not attend diets of examination, and that his session had deserted him."

> "Aug. 23, 1671.—Minister of Houston declares the kirk to be very ill-kept and baptism to be withdrawn from, and that he cannot very well visit families in regard they absent themselves."

Mr. Pearson, the first of the Episcopal ministers who came to Paisley, left for Dunfermline February 6, 1666, and was succeeded soon after by Mr. James Chambers, who filled the charge at the time the indulgence was granted. A sum of money was immediately offered him by the town of Paisley to demit his living, that they might get a preacher after their own mind. He accepted two hundred merks, resigned his parish, and "went his way."* Mr. Matthew Ramsay, who had once been at Kilpatrick, but had been deposed for nonconformity, succeeded him with the approval of Lord Dundonald, the consent of the Secret Council, and the concurrence of the parishioners. He was much esteemed in Paisley, according to Wodrow,† who gives a very minute notice of him, "and was much helped in public to be very free in reproving the sins of great men and rulers; and he did it in such a manner as they could be no means win‡ at him, for he always brought in most suitable and pertinent Scriptures for confirming all that he said about the sins of the times. He would have said, 'Ye need not say Mr. Matthew Ramsay says this, but

* Town Council Records, 26th August, 1669, where there is a full account of the transaction.

† Analecta, Vol. III., p. 63.

* Get.

its the prophets Isaiah and Jeremiah sayes this.' He was one day most free and faithful when a great number of nobles were present in my Lord Dundonald's loft; and when he had ended his sermon they were all forced to say, 'This is a very odd and strange man; for he has been all this day on the very borders of treason, but we could never get him uttering that which we could prove to be treason': he so confirmed all that he said by the plain word of God."

It was during Mr. Ramsay's incumbency that the saintly Leighton became Archbishop of Glasgow.* It was the earnest wish of this revered prelate that some compromise might be come to with the Presbyterians and peace restored to the Church. A conference between him and the non-conforming and indulged ministers took place at Paisley,† and one of the most interesting associations connected with the Abbey is the presence there of Leighton speaking words of conciliation and peace. A full account of the conference is given by Wodrow,‡ and by Burnet, who accompanied the Bishop, and who describes the meeting in his "History of His Time."§ It is amusing to read the two narratives of the meeting side by side, and to compare the account given by the Presbyterian with that given by the Episcopal historian; but they agree in this, that there was very little of a conciliatory spirit manifested on the side of the Covenanters, who were all resolute in their determination to have nothing to do with Prelacy in any shape or form. Leighton might as well have spoken to the winds as to the uncompromising men who confronted him. The conference began with prayer. "Who shall begin our conference with prayer?" said the Bishop. "Who should pray here," said Mr. Ramsay, boldly, "but the minister of Paisley?"‖ It was in the same unyielding spirit that his friends who spoke expressed themselves. Mr. John Baird, who had become Mr. Ramsay's colleague, replied to the Bishop,¶ who had opened the conference with a speech of

* 1670. † December 14, 1670.

‡ Wodrow's Hist., Vol. II., p. 130. § Vol. I., p. 51.

‖ Wodrow's Analecta, Vol. III., p. 65.

¶ "Mr. John Baird came to Paisley in 1659. He died in 1684, or beginning of 1685. He left a Manuscript de Magistratu, several sermons, a Treatise on Hearing the Curates. He wrote 'Balm for Gilead' and 'Violaut the Review."—Wodrow's Analecta, Vol. I., p. 170.

nearly an hour's length, which even the Presbyterian historian allows was "eloquent and elaborate." Mr. Baird shewed that the eloquence of the prelate had produced no impression on him. "They could not," he said, "without quitting their principles and wronging their consciences sit in judicature with a bishop, under whatsoever name he is chosen." One minister after another spoke in the same strain, and Burnet replied. His account of the proceedings is the most trustworthy, as he was present. "Leighton," he says, "laid out before them the obligation that lay on them to seek peace at all times, but more especially when we saw the dismal effects of our contentions. There could be no agreement unless on both sides there was some disposition to make some abatements and some step towards one another. It appeared that we were willing to make even unreasonable ones on our side, and would they abate nothing on their's? Was their opinion so mathematically certain that they could not dispense with any part of it for the peace of the Church and the saving of souls? Many poor things were said on their side which would have made a less mild man than he was lose all patience. But he bore with all their trifling impertinences, and urged this question upon them—'Would they have held communion with the Church of God at the time of the Council of Nice or not?' If they would say nay, he would be less desirous of entering into communion with them. He must say of the Church of that time, 'Let my soul be with theirs.' If they said they would, then he was sure they would not regret the offers now made them, which brought Episcopacy much lower than it was at that time. One of the most learned among them had prepared a speech to give the difference between Primitive Episcopacy and ours at present. I was then full of these matters, and replied." Burnet says he was not answered by his opponents. The Bishop was to put his proposals in writing, and the interview came to a close. It was with a sorrowful heart, though Wodrow quotes his words in ridicule, that Leighton exclaimed, "Is there no hope of peace? Are you for war? Is all this in vain?"* It was

* I must refer the reader to the historians I have named for a fuller account of this curious meeting. Wodrow says, "Mr. Alexander Jamieson reasoned so closely with the Bishop anent the prelate's power over Presbyters that the Bishop turned a little uneasy. His nose fell a bleed-

certainly in vain, but while we honour those stern men, who were so true to their conviction, that "they endured the loss of all things," we will not fail to pay a tribute of admiration to the man who, in that age of strife and conflict, gave his voice for peace rather than war, and who moved serene and tranquil, breathing the atmosphere of heaven across a scene of passion, turmoil, and bloodshed.

After the failure of this attempt at conciliation, Leighton retired into privacy. Stricter measures were resorted to by the Government against the Covenanters. Fines, torture, imprisonment, and banishment were employed to break their spirit and compel their submission; and Claverhouse and his dragoons were the terror of the frequenters of conventicles. Traces of this renewed severity appear in the records of the clergy, part of whose regular duty it had become to act as spies and informers. Mr. Ramsay, the minister of the Abbey, who had insisted on opening Leighton's conference with prayer, died shortly afterwards,* and was succeeded in his charge by his colleague, Mr. Baird, with whom Mr. Eccles was associated as minister of the Second Charge.† Both these ministers were regarded with great disfavour by the Episcopal Presbytery, who constantly found fault with them, and their licence to preach was at last taken from them.‡ Two new ministers, Mr. John Fullerton

ing, whether from this or not I shall not determine, but he was forced to retire a while!" Wodrow says that 26, Burnet that 30 Presbyterians were present. The Bishop was accompanied by the Provost of Glasgow, Sir John Harper of Cambusnethan, Mr. James Ramsay, dean of Glasgow, and Dr. Gilbert Burnet, then Professor of Divinity in the University.

* "When he came to die he lamented that he had not been free enough against the sins of that woeful time, and cried out, 'Oh that I had but one day in the pulpit of Paisley, I should be more free and faithful than ever I have been!' for he lived but a short time in Paisley. I know not certainly if he was there above three years, and when he died worthy Mr. Baird did much lament his death, and preached most particularly upon these words, Job xxiii. 8—'My stroke is heavier than my groaning.'"—Wodrow's Analecta, Vol. III., p. 66.

† "He was a godly man, and was very wise and prudent. His gift of preaching was not so popular or taking as Mr. Ramsay's was, but he had a great talent for moderating in a Presbytery or a Synod."—Ibid.

‡ Mr. Eccles was deprived of his licence by the Council on 30th Jan., 1683.—Wodrow, Vol. IV., p. 38. 11th April, 1784.—"Mr. John Baird, Paisley, being cited for breaking the indulgence given him by the Council, is deprived from the exercise of his ministry in all time coming, and in regard that his wife is sick, give him until 1st May to live regularly, otherwise to undertake banishment, and he and his family to remove out of the kingdom."—Fountainhall, Vol. II., p. 532.

and Mr. James Taylor* came to Paisley in their place. They were Episcopalians, and continued until the Revolution. The following notice indicates the increased severity of the measures against the Presbyterians :—

Aug. 19, 1674.—Mr. Robert Fleming is appointed to write to the Sheriff, in name of the Presbytery, anent the persons within their bounds, that because of their obstinacy were referred to him, and that in order to his interposing his authority for causing them give obedience."

"Dec. 2, 1674.—The brethren who were appointed to speak to the Sheriff report that he has done nothing as yet in what was recommended to him by the Presbytery, and therefore the moderator and Mr. Douglas are appointed to speak to the Archbishop thereanent, as also anent Mr. Cunningham's conventicling at Greenock and Innerkip, and to report their diligence at next diet. Likewise the said brothers are appointed to acquaint the Archbishop with Mr. James Wallace his conventicling in the house of Barochan.

"Jan. 6, 1675.—Mr. Douglas has spoke to the Archbishop and got a letter from him to the Sheriff, which the Moderator and Mr. Houston are to deliver."

"March 3, 1673.—Letter delivered to the Sheriff, who promises to obey the contents, whereupon several of the brethren gave in the names of the recusants, which were appointed to be given up in a list by the Moderator to the Sheriff."

"Dec. 27, 1682.—The Moderator shewing to the brethren that they were obliged to give in without any further delay the lists of schismatical separatists in their parishes enjoined by law, and

* Formerly minister of Mearns.

therefore required the brethren present to give them unto him that he might transmit them to the ordinary, whereupon all the brethren present, except Mr. Stewart, gave in lists of the schismatical withdrawers in their respective parishes.

The ritual of the Episcopalians did not differ very widely from that of the outed ministers. They never attempted to use the Service Book, and the only liturgical service they ventured upon was the saying the Lord's Prayer, the creed, and doxology; but even these forms were not in favour with the people.

"Ap. 25, 1667.—Enquiry was made by the Moderator if all the brethren observed the singing of the doxologies in all their churches every Lord's day. All of them answered that they did sing it, but some that they did not always, and that because the people would not join with them, none singing but the minister and his clerk. However, the Moderator enjoined such to be careful to sing it for the future, albeit they should do it alone."

"Sep. 6, 1682.—The Moderator enquiring of the brethren severally what obedience they had given to the Acts of Synod requiring them to celebrate the Lord's Supper, to read Scripture before sermon, to say the Lord's Prayer, to require the belief of parents at baptism, to say the doxology, all of them answered that they had obeyed all these acts, except only that of celebrating the Lord's Supper, and that none has observed except the Moderator, because of the paucity of their hearers."

"Sep. 16, 1685.—All have agreed concerning uniformity of worship, except some three or four of the brethren, who did acknowledge they omitted the repeating of the Lord's Prayer and the doxology several days for want of harmony, for which they were reproved.

On 3rd February, 1685, two plain countrymen were brought before the Earl of Glencairn, Lord Ross, the Laird of Cobistown, and John Shaw, at Paisley, and asked whether they would take the Abjuration Oath and the test. "If to save our lives," they replied, "we must take the test, and the abjuration will not save us, we will take no oath at all." They were immediately condemned to death, and at two o'clock the same afternoon were hanged at the Cross of Paisley, the soldiers being ordered to sound their trumpets and beat their drums to drown the psalm-singing of the victims. Many scenes like this took place over the country, and the spirit of the people was broken. But the time of deliverance was at hand. On 5th November, 1688, William of Orange landed at Torbay, and with his subsequent success hope came to the Presbyterians. The curates were rabbled, their prayer-books burned, and by the Revolution Settlement, Presbyterianism became the established religion of Scotland. Whether the ministers of the Abbey suffered much at their ejection, we do not know. Mr. Fullerton was taken under the protection of Lord Dundonald, and probably fared better than some of the other curates, who were subjected to all manner of indignities. He lingered in the neighbourhood of his church, and acted as a chaplain for a time to Lord Dundonald.* Afterwards he rose to dignity among the non-jurors, and became Bishop of Edinburgh in 1720.

* See Wodrow's Analecta, where there are several notices of Mr. Fullerton after his ejection.

## CHAPTER XXVIII.

### Witchcraft.

"The earth hath bubbles as the water has,
And these are of them."

—*Shakespeare.*

PRESBYTERY was now triumphant. The reign of the curates had come to an end, and a new set of men met in conclave beneath the arches of the Abbey, who gave solemn thanksgiving to God for their deliverance from "Popery and slaverie." Great difficulty seems to have been experienced in filling up the charges from which the Episcopal clergymen had been ejected. The curates had drawn their chief supply of preachers from Aberdeenshire and the Highlands, their successors procured their men principally from Ireland. An occasional "old minister," as those who had been deprived by the Privy Council when Episcopacy was established were called, was occasionally found and inducted into a vacant parish. One of these "old ministers" fell to the lot of Paisley. His name was Anthony Murray. He was of good family, and had occupied a leading position among the Covenanters. He was a relation of the Duchess of Lauderdale, and in 1677 had been asked by the Presbyterian ministers to use his interest with the Duke on their behalf. He did so, and pressed particularly the release of the persecuted ministers from the Bass, but with no success.* This "true-blue" Presbyterian was inducted

* Wodrow, Vol. II., p. 348. The other facts in this chapter are drawn from the records of the Presbytery of Paisley, to which the reader is referred. It is to be hoped these most interesting journals may yet be published in full.

to Paisley on 2d April, 1688. He was received with all honour, and the brethren gave him the right hand of fellowship, having been "ane old actual minister." He must have been well advanced in years when he came to the Abbey. He died soon afterwards, and a certain William Leggat from Ireland succeeded him. He "accepted the call from Paisley *(salve jure ecclesiae Hiberniae)*," and received the right hand of fellowship on the 22d August, 1690. Various attempts were made to fill up the Second Charge, but without success. A Mr. William Dunlop, a Mr. Veitch from Peebles, and a Mr. Young from Eaglesham were one after another invited to come to Paisley, but in vain. Mr. Leggat returned to Ireland in the end of 1691, and for nearly three years the parish remained without a pastor. The parishioners at length "called" Mr. Thos. Blackwell, a preacher in the Presbytery of Edinburgh, and after many delays he was inducted on the 28th August, 1694,* becoming bound at his entrance to concur in a call to a second minister.† A Mr. Thomas Brown, a probationer from Glasgow, was ordained to this charge 4th May, 1698.

Mr. Blackwell was an exceedingly able man, and had a great reputation for learning. He acquired a singular celebrity in Paisley as a zealous inquisitor of witches, and an earnest advocate for their prosecution by the civil power. After the Presbytery had got the various vacant parishes at the Revolution supplied, they entered upon the subject of witches with great vigour, and were as zealous in the prosecution of these unhappy creatures as any of their predecessors had been in stamping out Papists or indicting schismatics. The Episcopalians had taken up the matter of witchcraft in a feeble way, their time being fully occupied with the suppression of conventicles and the prosecution of refractory elders. They contented themselves with enjoining "any of the brethren that have any presumption of witchcraft in their parishes to give them unto the Bishop, to be by him preferred to the Council."‡ The Presbyterians,

* He seems to have had a libel before the Council hanging over his head for having written lines on a Lady Cramond. The Presbytery had great difficulty about admitting him. See Records, which are curious on this subject.

† The "concurrence" of the first minister to a call to his colleague was always required in those times.

‡ May 22, 1672.

on their advent after the Revolution, attacked the "powers of darkness" in a more vigorous fashion. One of their earliest indictments was against a "charmer" at Inverkip, who, among other diabolical practices, was said to have "taught John Hunter how to make his own corn grow and his neighbour's go back by sowing sour milk among it on Beltane day." "For curing convulsion fits, he had prescribed the pairing of the nails and the pulling of the eyebrows and of some hairs from the crown of the head, appointing them to be bound in a clout with a halfpenney, and laid down in such a place, alledging that whoever found this would take the disease. For curing John Hunter's beast of the sturdy, he taught to cut off a stirk's head, and boil it and burn the bones to ashes, and bury the ashes, which would be effectual to cure the rest. He also offered to teach, 'for a 14,' a man how to get a part of his neighbour's fishing by taking the sailing pin out of his neighbour's boat, when he would get fish enough." This impostor was summarily dealt with. He was ordered to be rebuked before the congregation of his parish, and declared "a scandalous person."

A more fearful "manifestation of Satan's power" than that exhibited by the wizard of Inverkip soon called forth all the energies of the Presbytery, who held many a consultation on the subject within the Abbey walls.

On the 13th April, 1697, a large congregation assembled in the old building to hear a sermon from one of the members of Presbytery specially appointed to discharge the office of preacher. It was a solemn occasion. Commissioners appointed by the Privy Council to try certain witches, who had been carrying on their evil practices in Renfrewshire, were about to proceed to their arduous duties. The accused were waiting in the Tolbooth. Before constituting the court, the judges desired to "hear sermon." A Mr. Hutcheson was the preacher for the day, and though no record of his sermon remains, his text, which is chronicled, is sufficient to indicate its tendency. It is taken from Exodus xx., 11-18—"Thou shalt not suffer a witch to live." The judicial proceedings which were thus prefaced had been brought about entirely by clerical influence, and especially at the earnest solicitation of Mr. Blackwell. It is a somewhat long story, but is not without interest; and as it illustrates the ecclesiastical life of the time, we shall relate it. On the 5th February, 1696, a tale of horror reached the Presbytery from the upland and secluded parish of Kilmalcolm. This retired region the Devil seemed specially to have chosen for his own delectation. Several persons had been delated there by a confessing witch. One of them had been apprehended and searched, and an insensible mark had been found upon her, yet she was still at liberty. These diabolical manifestations had extended to other parishes. In Inchinnan "a woman of bad fame" had threatened her own son, and thereafter the house had fallen and killed him. Various rumours of the work of the great enemy came also from the parish of Erskine. The powers of darkness were clearly laying siege to the Presbytery.

The ministers, led by Mr. Blackwell, at once girded on their armour, and not only went forth to meet their spiritual foes with spiritual weapons, but, lest these should not be sufficient, they also called to their aid the sword of the civil magistrate. The sheriff-depute and constables were invoked, and the Privy Council in Edinburgh besought to put forth its supreme power. "The sheriff-depute being present, and these things being laid before him, the Presbytery earnestly desired him that he would take the supposed witch into custody, and that he would apply to the Lords of her Majesty's Privie Council for a commission to put her and others suspected within the bounds to a tryall." The sheriff lent a ready ear to the request of the ministers: he promised to commit the suspected woman, and he advised the ministers to join with him in an application to the Privy Council for a trial of all suspected persons. This the Presbytery did. A letter was specially written to the Lord Justice-Clerk, and Mr. Blackwell and another minister were sent to Edinburgh to induce the authorities to send down a commission for the trial of all suspected of "trafficking with the devil." The Privy Council granted the commission for the trial of the witch Janet Wodrow. That evil-doer, however, became a confessant, and informed upon a number of accomplices. It was necessary, therefore, that the commission should be extended. The Presbytery sent again to Edinburgh, and their messengers returned with the hopeful intelligence that "the sheriff-depute and several gentlemen within the bounds had been selected by the head authorities for putting all delated for and suspected of witchcraft to a tryal." Having now the support of the civil powers guaranteed them, the Presbytery, to make their onslaught upon their foes certain of success, betook themselves to prayer and fasting, and "appointed a special day of humiliation throughout these bounds." Their adversary, however, nothing daunted by these preparations for the invasion of his territory, made an assault of a fiercer nature than he had hitherto ventured on, and the minister of Erskine told his assembled brethren a more terrible story than had hitherto reached them. So ghostly a tale had not been heard in the Abbey since the return of the excommunicated monk from purgatory in the days of Abbot Walter. We will give the minister's account of the cantrips of the infernal powers as he told it himself.

> "Mr. Turner represented the deplorable case of Christine Shaw, daughter to the Laird of Bargarren, in the paroch of Erskine, who, since the beginning of September last, hath been under a sore and unnatural-like distemper, frequently seized with strange fits, sometimes blind, sometimes deaf and dumb, the several parts of her body violently extended, and other times violently contracted, and ordinarily much tormented in various parts of her body, which is attended with ane unaccountable palpitation in those parts that are pained, and that these several weeks by past she hath disgorged a considerable quantity of hair, folded up straw, unclean hay, wild foule feathers, with divers kinds of bones of fowls and others, together with a number of coal cinders, burning hot candle grease, gravel stones, etc., all which she puts forth during the forementioned fits, and in the intervals of them is in perfect health, wherein she gives ane account of several persons, both men and women, that appears to her in her fits, tormenting her, all which began upon the back of one Katherine Campbell, her cursing of her. And though her father had called physicians of the best note to her during trouble, yet their application of medicine to her hath proven ineffectual, either to better or worse, and that they are ready to declare that they look upon the distemper as *toto genere preter-natural*, all which is attested by the

> ministers who had visited her in her trouble, upon all which Mr. Turner desired that the Presbytery would do what they judged convenient in such a juncture."

The Presbytery were stimulated by this fresh outbreak to greater exertions. They appointed "the exercise of fasting and prayer to be continued as it is already set up by Mr. Turner in that family every Tuesday." They appointed two of their number to go to Erskine and draw up a narrative of all the circumstances of the case, and they despatched two others to Edinburgh to lay the whole affair before the Lords of His Majesty's Privy Council. A commission, consisting of Lord Blantyre and others, was, by the authority of that body, ordered to take precognitions of these diabolical manifestations. The Presbytery volunteered to give them all assistance, and they appointed another day of public humiliation and fasting. Certainly the Devil was not to be allowed to have things all his own way.

The result of the joint labours of the Presbytery and Commissions was the procuring of three confessants—Elizabeth Anderson, James and Thomas Lindsay—and the incarceration of a number of suspected persons. Mr. Blackwell then made another journey to Edinburgh to procure their trial, and to represent to those in power "the lamentable condition of this part of the country, upon the account of the great number that are delated by some that have confessed, and of the many murders and other malifices that, in all probability, are perpetrated by them, and to entreat their compassion in granting a Commission for putting these persons to a trial, and for bringing the same to an effectual and speedy issue." The three confessants were well taken care of until the coming of the judges. They were "kept by turns in the houses of the ministers of the Presbytery, that they may have opportunity to instruct and deal with their consciences."

The judges came down to Renfrewshire in due time, armed with full power to try, acquit, or condemn those brought before them charged with the sin of witchcraft. The Presbytery appointed certain of their number to "wait upon their Lordships," and issued the following manifesto to all within their bounds:—

"The Presbytery, considering the great rage of Satan in this corner of the land, and particularly in the continued trouble of Bargarren's daughter, which is a great evidence of the Lord's displeasure, being provoked by the sins of the land (exprest as the causes of our former public fasts) so to let Satan loose amongst us. Therefore the Presbytery judge it very necessary to set apart a day of solemn humiliation and fasting, that we may humble ourselves under God's hand, and wrestle with God in prayer, that he may restrain Satan's rage, and relieve that poor afflicted damsel and that family from their present distress, and that the Lord would break in upon the hearts of these poor obdured that are indicted for witchcraft, that they may freely confess to the glory of God and the rescuing of their own souls out of the hands of Satan, and that the Lord would conduct and clear their way that are to be upon their trial, in order to the giving of Satan's kingdom an effectual stroke. Therefore the Presbytery appoints Thursday come eight days to be religiously and solemnly observed upon the accounts foresaid in all the congregations within their bounds, and the same to be intimate the Sabbath preceding."

Mr. Blackwell, who was the leading spirit in this conflict with "Satan's Kingdom," duly gave intimation of the fast in the Abbey, according to the above injunction. Being full of the subject, he added to the announcement certain utterances of his own, which were deemed so weighty and important that they were published, and so have come down to us. He was evidently full of the idea that a great struggle was going on between the Church and the Devil.

"My friends," he said, "we have been preaching of Christ to you, we are now about to speak of the Devil to you—the greatest enemy that our Lord and his kingdom hath in the world. The thing I am about to intimate to you is this,—the members of the Presbytery having taken into consideration how much Satan doth rage in these bounds, and which is indeed very lamentable in our bounds, and in ours only, they have thought to appoint a day of

> fasting and humiliation, that so He who is the lion of the tribe of Judah may appear with power against him who is the angel of the bottomless pit, and throw him down who is now come out in great wrath. O! that it may be because his time is short."

After this fervent aspiration, Mr. Blackwell went on to "hint" a few things as to the causes of the fast, the chief being "the mysteriousness and difficulty of the process of witchcraft, requiring much of the presence of God to guide the judges, that the truth may be found out and judgment execute," and he concluded his exhortation with the alarming suggestion, "Who knows but in this congregation there be many who have these many years hence been under vows to Satan, so it is the ministers' and the people of God's duty and interest to pray not only that God would find out the guilty among those that are apprehended, but that God would discover all others that are guilty and who are not apprehended, that the kingdom of Christ may run and be glorified, and the kingdom of Satan destroyed."

It is to be hoped the suggestion that any of his congregation were under vows to Satan was but an "arrow shot at a venture." If any such were in the Abbey that day, they must have been filled with fear as they listened to the exhortation of the minister. He was clearly one who would keep a sharp eye on their practices. His efforts in the trial of the tormentors of Bargarren's daughter were crowned with success. The judges proceeded to the trial with the text they had heard from the pulpit of the Abbey, "Thou shalt not suffer a witch to live," ringing in their ears. The confessants, after their residence in the manses of the ministers, were most pertinent in their evidence.* Meetings with the devil, a "black, grim man," whose hand was "very cold," whom they called their lord; their contrivances with that person for the destruction and torment of Christian Shaw, some being for "stabbing her with a touch, others for hanging her with a cord, a third sort for choking;" their receiving from Satan a piece of an unchristened child's liver to eat; their being carried through the air by the devil; their murdering of children,

* A full report of the trial is given in the interesting volume, "The Witches of Renfrewshire." Paisley, 1877.

and many other wonderful things were all sworn to. The accused had no chance of escape when it was found that they had on them the "insensible marks." The advocate for the prosecution loudly declared to the jury that, if they should acquit the prisoners, "they would be accessory to all the blasphemies, apostacies, murders, listures, and seductions whereof these enemies of heaven and earth should hereafter be guilty." The jury had no intention of running any such risks. Seven of these miserable creatures were found guilty as libelled, and condemned to the flames.

During the whole trial the Presbytery met constantly, waiting on the commissioners, and giving them "their thoughts of the affair," and when sentence was passed, they appointed some of their number to converse with the seven persons that were condemned to die. Two of them were appointed to preach to the miserable wretches in the tolbooth on the day previous to their execution. During their last night the whole of the members of Presbytery were instructed to spend some time with the condemned persons, and did allot to each one of the sentenced persons to be dealt with by them and *waited on to the fire.*

The minutes of Presbytery after this for some time continue to be filled with notices of their inquisition for witches, and when they were ordered by the Assembly to send ministers to preach in the north of Scotland, which continued to adhere to Episcopacy, they excused themselves on account of the sad condition of the country through "diabolical molestations." It has been our duty in the course of this history to shew the persecuting spirit of the different sections of clergy, Episcopal and Presbyterian alike, who succeeded the monks in the possession of the Abbey; but the story we have just narrated exceeds every other as an exhibition of ignorance, superstition, and cruelty.

Mr. Blackwell, who distinguished himself so mightily in the suppression of these "diabolical manifestations," was translated to Aberdeen on the 9th October, 1700. His brethren were opposed to his removal, as "the condition of the Parish of Paisley is of such consideration and importance as requires the greatest talents of the most accomplished ministers." Aberdeen, however, secured Mr. Blackwell. In that city he filled successively the situations of Professor of Divinity and Principal of the University. With his departure the "raging of Satan within the bounds" appears to have greatly calmed down, and the great adversary confined himself to those ordinary methods of operation which he employs in modern times. Presbyterial and Parochial ecclesiastical life moved along more smoothly than before. Mr. Thomas Brown was promoted from the second charge to fill the place vacated by Mr. Blackwell. No one appears to have been placed in the second charge for nearly twenty-two years.

We may close this chapter by an extract from the Minutes of the Kirk Session which show how the spiritual concerns of the Abbey Parish were looked after in the days of Mr. Thomas Blackwell and Mr. Thomas Brown.

"Nov. 2, 1699.—After prayers,

"This day the Session taking under consideration how great need there is, in this dead and declining day, of singular faithfulness and diligence, both in ministers and elders, for the suppressing of abounding sins and profanity, and reviving the power and practice of godliness in this congregation, they unanimously do conclude upon the following rules and directions, as so many acts to be observed by them in time coming, and appoints each elder to have a copy thereof so that none may pretend ignorance.

"1st. That every elder visit their respective proportion twice in the year, viz., once in July and once in January.

"2d. That in their visiting their respective proportion two of them always join together.

3d. That in their visiting of the families of their bounds they particularly, seriously, and gravely, inquire—firstly, if the worship of God be observed morning and evening, secondly, if all the family seek God in secret; thirdly, if all in the family can read the Holy Scriptures; fourthly, if all in the family attend the public ordinances; and, lastly, if all the family be sober and blameless, not given to lying, swearing, obscene discourses, mocking at God and godliness, or any other piece of profanity.

"4th. That the Session meet for prayer and privie censures twice in the year, viz., once upon the last Tuesday of July, and again upon the last Tuesday of January.

"5th. That the Session meet the last Monday of every month together with the ministers, and spend some hours thereof in prayer.

"6th. That the elders notice vagers and idlers after services upon Sabbath, and acquaint the ministers with the names of the persons observed by them.

"7th. That elders particularly inquire for testimonials from all that come to live within their bounds, and if not produced within a fortnight after, they are required, or some convincing reason why they are not, that in that case they give up the persons named unto the first Session.

"8th. That no elder delate any scandal to the Session till once he acquaint the ministers with it."

The Presbytery had previously ordered all ministers to have a magistrate in each of their Sessions, to commit to prison all contumacious persons. Between the zeal of the eldership and the terrors of the magistrate, evildoers must have had a hard time in Paisley. It is worth while noticing here, especially when we recollect the tenacity with which the people of the place clung for long to the old faith, that in 1704 the Presbytery reported only one "Papist" in Paisley—Joan Scougall, spouse to Robert Sempill, sheriff-depute of Renfrewshire.

# CHAPTER XXIX.

## Concluding Notices.

"I will now say,
Peace be within thee."
*Psalm CXXII.*

THOUGH our story of the religious associations of the Abbey is now told, there is something still to be said regarding the building itself. During the occupation by the Dundonalds of the Paisley property, the church was suffered to fall into great disrepair, but its surroundings remained the same as they were at the Reformation. The fair garden of the Monastery and a park with fallow deer figure in any sketches of the old buildings that have come down to us.* They stand with a back ground of hills, and enbosomed in wood; and the "Place of Paisley" was reputed one of the most beautiful residences in Scotland. Even in the present altered state of the mansion house, the remains of a great and stately dwelling, in every way worthy of a nobleman, can be traced. In 1757 all this was changed. The Lord Dundonald of the time, pressed for money, began to feu the Abbey grounds to the burgesses of Paisley and others. An advertisement from a Glasgow paper tells us that upon the "22nd day of January," in the same year, "there will be sold or feued, by public roup, at the Abbey of Paisley, various parcels of the Abbey gardens of Paisley, belonging to the Earl of Dundonald. The ground proposed to be feued consists of about four

* See Slezer's Theatrum Scotiae, 1693,—also Blacus' Atlas, 1654.

acres, very advantageously situated upon the River Cart, a little above the Old Bridge of Paisley. It is subdivided, and planned out for the steading of house and bleaching greens, now stacked off conform to a regular plan, whereby the situation of the houses is such that there will be a most commodious bleaching green from each house towards the river. Excellent materials for building will be supplied from the houses and garden walls of Paisley, where there is a vast quantity of hewn stones, which Lord Dundonald is to become bound to sell to the purchasers at a reasonable rate, to be specified in the articles of roup." This was the beginning of demolition. Any remains of the conventual buildings still standing were pulled down, the wall of Abbot Shaw destroyed, and Lord Dundonald was about to level the transept and the choir of the church when he was stopped by the heritors, who claimed them as church property.

Lord Dundonald sold the property of Paisley in 1764 to James, Eighth Earl of Abercorn, who came to live at Paisley, and who was buried in 1787 in the vault beneath St. Mirin's Chapel. Previous to his death he feued out any of the Abbey grounds that then remained unoccupied, and the New Town of Paisley was built on them. This was in 1781. The mansion house was at the same time dismantled, and let out to small tenants of the class who still inhabit it.

The church was in a dreadful condition. The roof was full of holes, through which the birds obtained free access, "distracting the attention of the worshippers in time of sermon."* They built their nests and reared their young under the arches of the clerestory. A few of the gentry had "lofts," or galleries, but the bulk of the worshippers brought their seats to church with them, the poorest sitting upon stones on the earthen floor. Contests occasionally arose for the best place, and the Session Records frequently notice "brawls and flyting in the kirk." In 1722 a case of this kind was brought before the Sheriff. The melee as described must have been of a very lively kind.

* A lamentable description of the state of the church is given in Douglas's "Description of the East Coast," published in 1782.

2 U

"Agnes Young being in the Kirk of Paisley after the Sacrament, ordering or setting in ane chair or stool where for several years byegone she used to sit, the said defender, coming upon her when she was sitting upon the said seat, bade her begone, therewith violently dragging the seat from under her, occasioning thereby a violent fall to her; and, not satisfied therewith, when the complainer getting up and getting hold of ane post, he did then rugg and ryve her, driving her head and other pairts violently against the said post, whereby she hath been so indisposed and bruised that she is not capable for any exercise, and thereby not able to earn her daily bread, which her circumstances doth not allow her but labouring with her own hands."*

The accommodation for the people was of the most wretched description, but it was in keeping with the state of the building. The noble doorway at the west end was filled up with a dunghill, and the roof was so rotten as to be incapable of repair. The heritors thought of pulling down the Abbey and building "a commodious kirk" with the stones! Happily this terrible calamity was averted by the energetic exertions of one whose name is well worthy, on this as on many other grounds, of being held by Paisley in "perpetual remembrance." This was the Reverend Doctor Boog, who was inducted into the First Charge in 1782. This excellent man is remembered by some who yet survive as an eloquent preacher and a remarkably able man of business.† The visitor to the Abbey will call gratefully to mind that to his intervention we owe all of it that now remains. He received much assistance from the Dowager Countess of Glasgow, who resided at Hawkhead, and through their joint exertions the Abbey was not only saved from destruction, but was repaired in a way which, considering the ignorance at that time on the subject of restoration, was highly creditable.

* "Judicial Records of Renfrewshire," a very interesting local history, by William Hector.

† The sermons of Dr. Boog were published after his death. To him Paisley owes its Infirmary. He was a great musician, and the musical service in the Abbey under the leadership of R. A. Smith was famed throughout Scotland.

In 1859, the writer of these memorials was inducted into the Second Charge of the Abbey as colleague to the Rev. Andrew Wilson, and he well remembers the dreadful condition of the building. The church was in a most disreputable state; the heritors, with their usual indifference, had done little since the time of Dr. Boog towards its maintenance. The burial-ground outside the building covered up the whole basement of the church up to the windows. The interior was like a vault in a graveyard. Water ran down the walls, and an unwholesome smell pervaded every part of the church. Heavy galleries round the place cut the pillars in two. The clerestory windows were blocked up, and whitewash was freely used. The whole of the moulding at the base of the pillars was hidden out of sight in the soil. The transept windows were destitute of tracery, and the wall of that part not having been pointed for many years, had in many places fallen down. A few more years would have seen it all in ruin. The pulpit was placed against the centre pillar of the north aisle, and round the floor of the church was a wide circular passage, with huge iron stoves placed in it at intervals. This passage formed a favourite promenade for stragglers during the time of service, who perambulated from one stove to another, occasionally lighting their pipes at them before going out, which they did whenever they were tired of listening, a frequent enough occurrence. A more dreary place of worship could scarcely be conceived. The porch was in a deplorable condition. The stone seats were all broken down, and people who entered the church had to creep in through a narrow doorway. A street of disreputable pawn-shops and public-houses abutted on the church, which was entirely hidden by the squalid buildings around it. People might pass within a few yards of it, and not know it was there.

A committee was organised in 1862, chiefly through the energy of the Rev. Mr. Wilson,* who set themselves vigorously to the work of restoration. The unsightly galleries were taken down, the floor cleared of

* It is impossible for me to do justice to the ability and zeal of my late revered colleague. He threw himself into the work of restoration with that energy which characterised him in all he did. I feel happy to be able to pay a tribute of affection to one with whom for seven years as minister of the same church I lived in the closest harmony and unbroken friendship.

the accumulated rubbish of centuries, the body of the church re-seated, the clerestory windows opened up, the transept walls and windows restored, and the turrets rebuilt. Men of all creeds contributed to the work,* and when the Abbey, on the 27th April, 1862, was re-opened for public worship, it could scarcely be recognised, so changed was it from its former condition. Since that time much has been done by the public in the way of improvement. The houses of the street which abutted upon the Abbey were one by one acquired by the Restoration Committee, and finally transferred to the Town Council of Paisley, who pulled them down. A neat railing has been placed round the churchyard, and the venerable building opened up to view. Many of the windows of the interior have also been filled with stained glass, and a costly organ has been erected by the congregation against the unsightly east wall.

Much still remains to be done to put this grand old church in a state befitting its great history. To accomplish this work is an object well worthy of the generosity of Paisley's sons. We trust the time is not far distant when the Abbey of the first Stewart will stand forth again in all its pristine beauty—with transept, and choir, and tower, as in the days of the founder. It is in this hope that the writer brings these memorials to a close. It is in this hope that he leaves the scene of eighteen years' labour, and parts from a church of which he can most truly say that its very stones are dear to him.

* The architect in the restoration was James Salmon, Glasgow. Nothing was more striking than the feeling of "proprietorship" which the Paisley people seemed to have in the old Abbey.

# APPENDICES.

## A.

### THE PRIORS, ABBOTS, AND COMMENDATORS OF THE MONASTERY OF SAINT JAMES AND SAINT MIRIN OF PAISLEY.

| | | | |
|---|---|---|---|
| 1172, | Osbert, | Prior, . . . . | Reg. de Pas., p. 408; Illus. of Scot. Hist., p. 33 (Maitland Club). |
| 1180, | Roger, | ,, . . . . | ,, pp. 77, 78. |
| 1225-1248, | William, | Abbot, . . . . | ,, pp. 170, 372; notices in Lennox and Melrose Charters. |
| 1272, | Stephen, | ,, . . . . | ,, p. 51. |
| 1296, | Walter, | ,, . . . . | Ragman Rolls. |
| 1312-1321, | Roger, | ,, . . . . | Reg. de Pas., pp. 204, 387. |
| 1327-1334, | John, | ,, . . . . | ,, pp. 137, 429. |
| 1346, | James, | ,, . . . . | Mag. Sig., elected 17th year of David II. |
| 1361-1370, | John,* | ,, . . . . | Reg. de Pas., 426, Lennox Charters. |
| 1384-1433, | John de Lithgow, Abbot, . . | | ,, p. 330, and many other pages; Inscription on tablet in north porch. |
| 1414, | William de Chishelme, Abbot, (coadjutor) . . . . | | ,, p. 247. |
| 1420-1423, | Thomas Morwe, Abbot (coadjutor), | | Scotiæ Rotuli, pp. 226, 229, 230, Camerarii Mandati. |
| 1444, | Richard de Bothwell, Abbot (elect), | | Vatican MSS., Obligazioni. |
| 1445-1459, | Thomas de Tervas, ,, . . | | ,, ,, Reg., p. 250, and many other notices; Rotuli Scotiæ; Chronicle of Auchinleck. |
| 1459-1466, | Henry Crichton, Abbot (deposed), . | | Vatican MSS., Brit. Mus., No. 15,383, fo. 570. |
| 1466, | Patrick Graham, Archbishop of St. Andrews, Commendator, . . | | ,, ,, No. 15,385, fo. 27. |
| 1469-1472, | Henry Crichton, Abbot (reponed), | | ,, ,, ,, fo. 196. |
| 1498-1525, | Robert Shaw, Abbot (made Bishop of Moray), . . . . | | ,, Reg. de Pas., p. 218; Regist. of Moray, (Ban. Club). |
| 1472-1498, | George Shaw, Abbot (pensioned), . | | ,, Quietanse; Reg. de Pas., p. 60, and many other pages; Mural Inscription. |

* There is some doubt whether this Abbot is not the same with John de Lithgow. On the whole, we think not.

| | | |
|---|---|---|
| 1525-1544, | John Hamilton or Burnet, Abbot, (made Bishop of Dunkeld, and afterwards Archbishop of St. Andrews,*) . - - - | Vatican MSS., Obligazioni; Reg. de Pas. p. 435. |
| 1553, | Claud Hamilton, Commendator, . | Bull of Pope Julius III., Abercorn MSS. |

In 1587 he obtained a grant from the Crown of all the property of the Abbey. He was created Lord Paisley in 1594, and died 1621.

Lord Sempil, Lord Mar, Mr. Erskine (Parson of Campsie), and Lord Cathcart were Commendators at different times after the Reformation. (See Text.)

---

## THE MINISTERS OF THE ABBEY PARISH OF PAISLEY.

| | |
|---|---|
| 1572, Patrick Adamson—Regist. of Minrs. (Mait. Club), p. 35, | Archbishop of St. Andrews, 1576. |
| 1576, Andrew Polwart—MSS. of Wodrow Society, p. 282; Book of Universal Kirk, . . . . . . | Made Sub-dean of Glasgow. |
| 1578, Thomas Smeaton—Melville's Diary, p. 58, . . . | Made Principal of Glasgow, 1580. |
| 1585, *(circa)* Andrew Knox—Presbytery Records, &c., . | Made Bishop of the Isles, 1606. |
| 1607, Patrick Hamilton— ,, . . . | ——— |
| 1610, Archibald Hamilton—Town Council Records, Jan. 4, 1617; Row's History, . . . . . . . | Bishop of Killaloe, 1623. |
| 1625, Alexander Hamilton—Wodrow's Life of Boyd of Trochrigg, . . . . . . . . . . | Resigned. |
| 1626, 1st Jan., Robert Boyd of Trochigg, Presby. Records, | Resigned. |
| 1627, 21st May, John Hay, from Killelan, ,, | Translated to Renfrew, 1628. |
| 1629, 1st Sept., John Crichton, from Campsie, ,, | Deposed Gen. As., 21st Nov., 1638. |

---

## MINISTERS OF THE FIRST CHARGE.

| | |
|---|---|
| 1641, 1st July, Henry Calvert—Presbytery Records, . . | Died 1653. |
| 1653, 28th Dec., Alexander Dunlop,† from Second Charge, Presbytery Records, . . . . . . . | Ordered to be banished, Jan. 1663. |
| 1663, William Pierson, Episcopal—From Kinaird, . . | Left for Dunfermline, Feb. 6, 1666, |
| 1667, James Chalmers, Episcopal—Town Council Records, . | Resigned, Aug. 26, 1669. |
| 1667, *(circa)* Matthew Ramsay, Indulged — Wodrow, Vol. I., 247, . . . . . . . | Died *post* 1670. |
| 1671, *(circa)* John Baird, Indulged, from Second Charge, Fountain Hall, Vol. II., p. 532; Wodrow's Analectic, Vol. II., p. 66. . . . . . | Deprived 11th April, 1684. |
| 1684, John Fullerton, Episcopal—Presbytery Records, . | Ejected at the Revolution; afterwards Bishop of Edinburgh. |
| 1688, April 2, Anthony Murray, ,, . | Translated to Culter, 1689. |
| 1689, Aug. 22, William Leggat—From Ireland, Pres. Records, | Returned to Ireland, 1691. |

* John Hamilton retained all his life the title of Abbot.

† In some lists a John Drysdale is mentioned in 1650. He was, however, only an assistant.

1664, Aug. 28, Thomas Blackwell—Presbytery Records, . . Tr'nsltd. to Aberdeen, 9th Oct. 1700.
1700, Thomas Brown—From Second Charge, ,, . Died at Paisley, 1708.
1709, Dec. 28, Robert Millar,* D.D., ,, . . Died at Paisley, 16th Dec., 1752.
1753, June 9, James Hamilton, D.D.—From Second Charge,†
—Presbytery Records, . . . . . . Died at Paisley, 14th March, 1782.
1782, Aug. 29, Robert Boog, D.D.—From Second Charge,
—Presbytery Records, . . . . . . Died 29th July, 1823.
1824, April 9, Robert M'Nair, D.D.—From Ballantrae, Presbytery Records, . . . . . . . . Died 22d July, 1851.
1852, Andrew Wilson—From Falkland, . . . . Died 5th March, 1865.
1865, James Cameron Lees, D.D.—From Second Charge, . Present incumbent.

## MINISTERS OF THE SECOND CHARGE (INSTITUTED 1641).‡

1644, Alexander Dunlop, A.M., . . . . . . . Translated to First Charge.
1654, 12th June, James Stirling, A.M.—Presbytery and Town Council Records, . . . . . . Ejected for Nonconformity.
1670, *(circa)* John Baird—Indulged, Wodrow, . . . Translated to First Charge.
1671, *(circa)* William Eccles, ,, ,, Vol. IV., p. 38, Deprived by the Council, 30th Jan., 1684.
1685, John Taylor, Episcopal—Presbytery Records, . . Deprived at the Revolution.
1698, May 4th, Thomas Brown, Presbyterian—Presbytery Records, . . . . . . . . . Translated to First Charge.
1722, Sept. 22, Robert Mitchell, A.M.—Presbytery Records, Translated to Low Church, Burgh of Paisley, Mar. 21st, 1739.
1740, June 26, William Fleming—From Kirkintilloch, Presbytery Records, . . . . . . . . Died Jan. 2, 1747.
1751, April 24, James Hamilton, . . . . . . Translated to First Charge.
1751, Jan. 24, John Rae, . . . . . . . . . Died 4th Sept., 1757.
1758, Sept. 7, Archibald Davidson, . . . . . . Translated to Inchinnan, 7th Sept. 1758.
1762, June 10, Alexander Kennedy, . . . . . . Died July 12, 1773.
1774, April 21, Robert Boog, . . . . . . . Translated to First Charge.
1783, March 27, James Mylne, . . . . . . . Elected Professor of Moral Philosophy in Glasgow, 4th Oct., 1797.
1798, Jan. 26, James Smith, . . . . . . . Died Jan. 27, 1817.

* An epitaph upon Mr. Millar's tomb is given in Crawfurd's Renfrewshire. He was author of the "History of the Propagation of Christianity," and other works.

† Mr. Francis Douglas gives in the *Scots Magazine* of 1783 a long epitaph on this minister. A marble monument was erected to him in the choir, of which no trace remains. The epitaph tells how, "unnoticed by the crowd, he chose to walk with virtue in the shade. Confiding in the Supreme Being, and animated by the hope of immortality, he bore a long decline of health with uninterrupted tranquility, and died in perfect peace. Gentle shade!" it continues, "congenial spirits gather round thee: Farewell."

‡ Established by an Act of the Scottish Parliament of March, 1645.

| | |
|---|---|
| 1828, April 10, Patrick Brewster,* . . . . . . | Died 26th March, 1859. |
| 1859, Sept. 1st, James Cameron Lees—From Carnoch, Ross-shire, . . . . . . . . . . | Translated to First Charge. |
| 1865, Dec. 2, James Dodds—From St. Stephen's, Glasgow, . | Translated to St. George's, Glasgow. |
| 1875, Sept. 16, James Mitford Mitchell, B.A., Cantab.—From Kirkmichael, Dumfries, - . . . | Present incumbent. |

---

## B.

### ST. MIRINUS,† SEPT. 15.

Merinus (Mart. Aberd. ; Brev. Aberd. ; Calend. Brev. Aberd.)
Mirinus (Dempster ; Mart. Aberd.)
Mirine (King.)
Mirenus (Fordun, ii., 59, Vol. I., p. 95, ed. Goodall.)
Murrin (In *Inch-Murrin*, New Stat. Acct., Vol. VIII., pt. 2, p. 90; Orig. Par. I. p. 35.)
Mirren (In *Kirk-Mirren*, Old Stat. Acct., Vol. VIII., p. 297.)
Wirrin (In *Wirrin's Hill* in Forfar, New Stat. Acct., XI., p. 688.
Morenus (In Camerarius, p. 143.)
Murdacus (Kal. Missal. Arbuthnot, Sept. 15.)
Murdach (Innes' Eccles. Hist., p. 161, at Sept. 1.)

Camerarius (a very chamberer in the wantonness of hagiological laxity and temerity !) gives a St. Mirinus at Sept. 17, and a St. Merinus at Jan. 28; and refers to the Breviarum Aberdonensis at 12th May, for Merenus. The legend in the Breviary of Aberdeen is fuller, more circumstantial, and more satisfactory than the generality of such notices in that compilation. It is to this effect :—An Irishman, committed by his parents in early youth to the care of St. Congall, Abbot of Bangor, in the present county of Down, who taught, trained, and perfected him. His father was rich, and noble, and had a *castrum*. The young man took the monastic habit under St. Congall, the Abbot ; and soon after, the office of Prior falling vacant, he was elected Prior by Congall and the brethren. On one occasion, in the absence of Congall, St. Finian of Moville arrived at the Monastery of Bangor, and was received by Merinus. Subsequently he visited the *castrum* of a King of Hybernia, who treated him with indignity, and had to pay for it by sustaining the pains of parturition. He had a *tugurium* of his own, and a brother who ministered to him. The brethren were working one day near *Vallem Colpdasch*, which was somewhere in Ireland, but has not been identified—(the name was probably in Irish, something like ᵹleann Colpṫach). *Plenus miraculis, et sanctitate apud Paslay obdormivit in Domino.*

* An handsome monument has been erected in Paisley to this minister by his many admirers. He was a great controversialist, but a man of striking ability, of an independent spirit, and an advocate for political reforms which since his death have been effected. Though he came under the censure of the Church, and was suspended for a time from his office for his political opinions, he was held in great esteem by the bulk of his parishioners.

† I am indebted to Dr. Reeves for these notes on St. Mirinus.

This is a very sudden and abrupt jump in the narrative, from the Abbey of Bangor to Paisley. I wish we had the MSS. from which this legend is meagrely taken, and we would make better use of it than Bishop Elphinstone did.

Now, what is the Irish or true form? No such name is in the Irish Calendar. We have an unbroken list of Abbots of Bangor for some centuries, but no Prior: so here we have no help. Neither is there anything to correspond to the name in the Irish Calendars at the 15th of September. The name Medhran, which occurs in the Martyrology of Donegal at June 6 and June 8, is easily susceptible of the phonetic form Mirrin. Colgan quotes the Calendar of Cashel at the 8th June, in these words: "Item, St. Medranus et Tovianus in una ecclesia in Britannica Alcluidensi." Also, "St. Medran and Toirran, (are commemorated) in one church in Britain of Alcluid." Now this brings a Medhran to the neighbourhood of Paisley.—Act. S.S., 465 *a*, note 31. We have an Ainmire of Clonfad in the Calendar at 15th of September; but this name could hardly become Mirinus.—(See Colgan, Trias Thaumaturga, p. 479 *a*, n. 16.) Innes speaks of St. Murdach, Bishop, as commemorated at the first of September; and this suggests the thought that the Irish Muireḋach might have been corrupted to Mirinus. There is an instance where the Irish Muiredhach is latinized *Marianus*. And, what is very remarkable, one of the Scotch Calendars has, at September 15, instead of Mirinus, *Murdaci episcopi et confessoris*, which looks as if that document regarded Murdach or Muiredhach, as the equivalent for Mirinus. The authority I refer to is the Calendar prefixed to the "Arbuthnot Missal," which is reprinted in Bp. Forbes' Kalendars, p. 104. It is very hard sometimes to identify the names of well known Irish saints under the Scottish transformation. For instance, who would suppose that the Arbroath *Vigean* is the famous Irish *Fechin*.

If the story of Mirinus' discipleship under Congall at Bangor, and his receiving St. Finian at Bangor on the occasion of a visit be accepted as a true or likely occurrence, then we are able to make an approximation to the date of the Paisley saint. For Congall founded the Church of Bangor in 558, and died May 10th, 601. Again, St. Finian of Magh-bile (Molville, in the county Down, not far from Bangor), died in 578, so that St. Mirinus must have held the office of Prior of Bangor between the years 558 and 578. Thus his function of secnab or Prior there commenced at some period during those twenty years. When, or under what circumstances he came to Paisley, is not recorded either in Irish or Scottish records; but as Bangor was a great missionary institution, I suppose his going forth was something like that of St. Malrubha of Applecross, in Ross-shire, whose date and mission are well ascertained. We might, I think, safely take 580 as an appropriate date for St. Mirinus' pilgrimage to Scotland, and regard his services as among the many benefits which this noble institution of Bangor conferred upon Ireland and North Britain.

His Scotch commemorations, as I noted them down many years ago, are—

1. Paisley, *ubi*, St. Mirren's Chapel,* St. Mirren's Aile,† St. Mirren's Mill.‡
2. Inchmurrin, in Loch Lomond, parish of Kilmaronach, "A chapel still known as St. Mirren's Chapel, marking by the name of its patron saint, some old connection with the Abbey of Paisley, stands now in ruins upon Inchmuryn, the largest island of Loch Lomond." —Orig. Paroch., Vol. I., p. 35; New Stat. Acct., Vol. VIII., Pt., II., p. 90.
3. In the Parish of Kilsyth is a remarkable spring on the south of Woodend, called *St. Mirren's Well*.—Orig. Paroch., Vol. I., p. 43; New Stat. Acct., Vol. VIII., Pt. II., p. 147.

* Orig. Paroch., Vol. I., pp. 63, 506.; New Stat. Account, Vol. VII., Pt. I. p. 212.

† New Stat. Acct. *ut supra.* p. 217. ‡ Ibid. p. 274.

4. Kirkmirren, an ancient chapel in the Parish of Kelton, County of Kirkcudbright, near its south-east boundary.—Old Stat. Acct., Vol. VIII., p. 297.
5. Knockmurren, a farm in the Parish of Coylton, Ayrshire.—New Stat. Acct., Vol. V. Pt. I., p. 656.

The choice of the original name of this saint lies between Medhran and Muireḋach, and I am unable to make a selection as at present informed.

---

## C.

### From "BREVIARUM ABERDONENSE, (Maitland Club, Londini, 1854,) Pars Estivalis, Fol. 106.

[September 17 Kal. = 15th day of the Month]. The folio is headed "Sancti Merini Episcopi et Confessoris."

---

*Sancti Merini Episcopi et Confessoris qui in Monasterio de Pasleto magno honore veneratur. Oracio.*

Deus qui es natura misericors et affectuum moderator; preces petencium benignus exaudi : ut interveniente beato Merino pontifice tuo peccatorum veniam impetrare valeamus, Per Dominum.

*Lectio prima.*—Merinus episcopus divina inspirante gratia sancto Congallo a parentibus in primeva etate in Monasterio de Bangour committebatur nutriendus, qui illuc non solummodo litterarum perfectione erudiret sed eciam in omni morum scientia humilitatis et castitatis ceterarumque virtutum diligenter informaret : qui documenta salutis eterne et quicquid ad anime salutem pertinebat toto mentis desiderio tenaci memoria commendabat.

*Lectio secunda.*—Crescenti itaque etate castra paterna res opulentas terrarum possessiones et cetera mundana vana et transitoria reputans: jugum Domini portare elegit ab infancia et in monasterio de Bangour a sancto Congallo sancte religiones habitum peciit et suscepit. Non multum post temporis vacante prioratu ejusdem monasterii per Congallum et confratres suos in priorem licet invitus eligitur cujus officii regimine suscepto fratres pocius et interiari caritatis amore quam iracundie fervore arguebat, et quem foris castigabat intrinsecus diligebat.

*Lectio tertia.*—Quodam autem tempore vir magne sanctitatis Fynianus Malbilensis episcopus ad monasterium Bangorii: sancto Congallo absenti hospitandi gratia veniebat : et a beato Merino priore benigne susceptus est. A quo potum lactis propter molliorem sui corpis qualitatem peciit. In monasterio vero nequaquam lac habitant, sed cellerarius jassu beati Merini in cellerarium intrans vas lacte optimo repletum nutu ejusdem delatum invenit et beato Fyniano presentavit. Deinde omnibus per ordinem discumbentibus benigne distribuit. Tu autem.

*Lectio quarta.*—Postmodum Merinus ad castrum cujusdam Hybernie regis: fidei catholice confirmandi causa accessit. Ubi eo tempore dicti regis uxor pregnans et partui vicina angustiis et doloribus fatigata diversis. Audiente rege dicti Merini adventum castrum suum illum intrare non permisit: nec aliquem honorem Merino tribuit sed penitus ipsum contempsit : quo percepto beatus Merinus Deum rogavit ut rex ille maledictus pressuras et angustias uxoris sue parientis pateretur. Quas ut Dominum rogavit more passus est ita quod tribus diebus et totidem noctibus coram omnibus regni sui hominibus clamitare non cessavit. Videns autem rex se a Deo ignominiose confusum nec aliquod remedium sibi esse perfuturum : ad habitaculum sancti Merine perrexit et omnia ante petita sibi libertissime accessit. Tunc sanctus Merinus suis sanctis precibus regem a pressuris omnino liberavit.—Tu.

*Lectio quinta.*—Quodam tempore beatus Merinus ultra tempus solitum moram in suo tugurio faciens : frater quidam qui ministrabat ei ad illum visitandum perrexit : qui dum ad tuguriolum suum accessit statim stupefactus stetit. Vidit enim perrimas et foramina fulgorem celitus emissum. Sanctus vero Merinus ea nocte ad fratres suos in ecclesia psallentes more solito non accessit. Sed cum divinitus agnovisset fratrem suum tot miranda vidisse miracula : mane seorsum illum assumpsit et dixit ei ut ea, nocti elapsa viderat : nemini in vita sua indicaret : et ne interim ad tuguriolum suum appropinquare presumaret.

*Lectio sexta.*—Alia itidem die fratribus sancti Merini juxta vallem Colpdasch operantibus unus earum labore et siti supra modum gravatus. Concidens in terram ipsum exaltavit ; et a meridie usque ad nonam jacuit exanimis. Sanctus autem Merinus vehementissime fratri suo condolens eo quod tam subitanea et imatura morte moveretur. Oravit ad Dominum atque continuo defunctus suis sanctis precibus prestine vite fuit restitutus et tandem plenus miraculis et sanctitate apud Paslay obdormivit in Domino. In cujus honore dicta ecclesia Deo dedicata est. *Cetera omnia de communi unius confessoris et pontificis cum expositione evangelii ejusdem.*

---

## D

## NOTICES IN CONNECTION WITH PAISLEY ABBEY OF MEMBERS OF THE WALLACE FAMILY.

About A.D. 1163, Richard Wallace witnesses a Charter of the High Steward, Walter Fitzalan, granting certain Churches, &c., to Paisley Abbey (pp. 5, 6).

Between 1207-1214, Henry Wallace is spoken of as having formerly held *(quondam tenuit)* certain lands. The High Steward, Walter II., refers to the matter in Two Deeds (pp. 19, 401), and the actual holder in another (pp. 401, 402).

About the same time, Richard Wallace (possibly another) witnesses a Charter of the High Steward, Walter II., giving Property in the Mearns to Paisley Abbey. In this Deed, Auchencruive is spoken of as the property of Richard Wallace (pp. 21, 22).

About the same time, Richard Wallace witnesses another Charter by the same High Steward, further endowing Paisley Abbey (pp. 23, 24).

A.D. 1239, Adam Wallace witnesses a Charter of Walter Fitzalan, High Steward, confirming to Paisley Abbey the Churches of Dundonald, Sanquhar, and Auchenleck (p. 19).

A.D. 1246, Adam Wallace witnesses a Charter of Walter II. transferring certain Alms from Sempringham to Paisley Abbey (p. 24).

A.D. 1253, Alan Wallace (intituled "Dominus") witnesses a Gift of the Church of St. Finnan to Paisley Abbey by Stephen, Bishop of Sodor (pp. 135, 136).

About 1260, Richard Wallace (intituled "Dominus") witnesses a Confirmation Charter by the High Steward, Alexander (pp. 59, 60).

About 1272, Richard Wallace (described as "Miles") witnesses the confirmation of Craigie Church to Paisley Abbey, by Walter Lindsay and Mathilda Hose (p. 233). Robert Wallace is the name of another of the witnesses.

A.D. 1363, 27th August, Sir Duncan Wallays, Knight, Sheriff of Ayr, witnesses with John, Abbot of Paisley, a Charter by Marjory de Montgomery to John Kennedy of the Lands of Cassilis. —Appendix to Fifth Report by Historical MSS. Commission.

---

## E.

### NOTES ON A COMMISSION PROFESSING TO HAVE BEEN ISSUED BY CARDINAL BERENGARIUS, BY AUTHORITY OF THE POPE, TO THE ABBOT OF PAISLEY TO ABSOLVE ROBERT THE BRUCE FOR THE MURDER OF COMYN.

The Deed will be found in Goodall's edition of Fordun's Scotichronicon, XII, 10, Vol. II., p. 231-2. The chapter in which it occurs being omitted in the Edition of Fordun edited by Skene (Historians of Scotland, I., p. 341), may be taken as part of the additions made by Bower or others to the original text. The only direct reference to it which I find in recent writers is in Kerr's "History of Scotland During the Reign of Robert the Bruce" (Vol. I., p. 313), who thinks the "Commission may have been a pious fraud, concocted between Robert and the Abbot, for quieting the weak consciences of the Scots; and that the English, having come to a knowledge of the deception, may have destroyed the Abbey for revenge." Hints, however, of some absolution of the kind are found in the Chronicle of Pluscarden, where (Book IX., cap. 7) it is stated that Bruce was unwilling to be crowned until he "deserved to receive the benefit of absolution from sacrilege," a later hand adding in the margin, "by the Abbot of Paisley, authority for this being given him by Clement III."; in Boece, who writes (xiv. 8, Tome II., p. 381, as translated by Bellenden), "Robert Bruce, after the slauchter of the Cuming, send to the Paip for absolution," and in George Buchanan's History, who (Cap. 8) says "Bruce stayed so long till he had obtained pardon from the Pope for killing a man in Holy Church, and then, in April following, he went to Scone and was crowned King."*

The history of Bruce, as it bears on his relations with the Pope, is of peculiar interest, and must be specially kept in view in judging of the authenticity of this Commission. I subjoin a brief digest of that history :—

*1305-6, 10th February.—Comyn slain at Dumfries.*

On the 4th Ides of February, Fordun Annales, 117. Liber Pluscardensis, 9, 6. Hemingburgh II., 245. On the feast of St. Scholastica (*i.e.*, February 10). Chron. Lanercost, p. 203. Trivet, in his Annals, makes it the 4th Kalends of February, *i.e.*, 29th January, and Matthew of Westminster (Cap. 27), followed by Rapin (I., p. 384), and Echard (I., p. 321), the 29th January. With the exception of Crawfurd, who (Hist. of Renfrewshire, p. 146) makes it the 9th, all modern writers make it the 10th February. Barbour and Wyntoun do not specify the date.

*1305-6.—Bruce comes to Glasgow on his way to Scone.*

Barbour I., p. 40.—The Bishop of Glasgow was accused by Edward of having given him "plenary absolution" within eight days of the murder, (Palgrave, Documents and Records, clxxx,

* Ruddiman, commenting on this, says it is manifestly an error, and suggests that the Bishop of Moray (whom Edward, writing to the King of Norway [Rymer II., p. 1045], speaks of as under the wrath of the Pope for having countenanced the murder) may have absolved Bruce, and that posterity may have assumed he did so by authority of the Pope. But he makes no reference to the Letter of Berengarius.

346-7; Reg. Epis. Glas. Introd. xxxv.) and also of preparing in his own wardrobe the Coronation Robes, and sending them, with a banner of the kingdom which had lain concealed in the Treasury, to Scone. (Palgrave *ut supra*—Tytler I., 216, Caledonia I., 673; III., 617-8.) Burton attributes this to the Bishop of St. Andrews, (II., 352). Tytler says he also sent him a coronet of gold, and refers to Rymer (II., p. 1048), where, however, there is only a pardon granted to a certain Golfridus de Coigners for making the coronet with which Bruce was crowned. Burns (Scottish War of Independence) II., p. 190.

Cunninghame, in his Church History, says the Bishop "absolved him in his Cathedral at Glasgow" (I., 173), but gives no authority. Gordon, in his Scotichronicon (II., p. 486), says that the Bishop of Glasgow assoilzied Bruce, and prepared the Robes and Royal Banner for his Coronation; and writing of Glasgow Cathedral (II., 439, and quoting from the *Quarterly Review*, (Vol. 85, p. 135, but which he wrongly cites as Vol. 84, p. 134), says, "It witnessed the absolution of Bruce while the Red Comyn's blood was scarce yet dry upon his dagger."

Guthrie, in his History of England (I., 952), writes that Edward prevailed on the Pope "to thunder out a sentence of excommunication against Bruce, who, despising it as trumpery, got himself absolved by a private prelate of his own, and thereby satisfied his subjects."

The author of "The Greatest of the Plantagenets" and "The Life and Reign of Edward the First" says (p. 309 of the latter work) that "on the 24th or the 25th of March, Bruce rode to Glasgow, and from thence, on the 27th, to Scone," but gives no authority.

*1306—27th-29th March.—Bruce Crowned at Scone.*

Bruce was crowned on the 27th, and again by Lady Buchan on the 29th. These dates seem pretty certain, though there is considerable divergence of statement.

Fordun (Annales, 118) gives the sixth kalends of April—*i.e.*, 27th March; Liber Pluscardensis, the Sixth ides of April—*i.e.*, 8th April.

The Chronicle of Lanercost (p. 203) gives "in annunciatione beatæ Virginis"—*i.e.*, 25th March.

Matthew of Westminster states (Cap. 27) that he was crowned on the day of the Annunciation, and again by Lady Buchan on the following Sunday (which would be 27th March)—the Bishop of Glasgow being present.

Hemingburgh (II., 247) states that he was crowned by *Lady Buchan* on the day of the Annunciation; and so says Trivet (Annales, p. 407), and a MS. in the Cottonian Library (Vitell., A. xx.), quoted by Tytler.

Crowned on 27th March.—Boece (Bellenden's Trans., XIV., 8).

Crowned in April.—George Buchanan (Cap. 8).

Of more modern writers, Rapin makes the first crowning 2nd February, and the second 25th March. Echard says he was crowned on Lady-day; Duncan Stewart (Account of Royal Family of Scotland, p. 37), on the 27th March, being Palm Sunday (which it was); Hailes (II., 1-2), the 27th and 29th; Kerr (I., 203, 206), and Tytler (I., 215), the 27th and 29th; but both of these make the 27th a Friday, whereas it was a Sunday. Burton (II., 352-3) makes Lady Buchan crown him on the 27th; and so says Cosmo Innes in his Introduction to Barbour (Spalding Club, p. 14), yet in a note to the same work (p. 32) he puts the Coronation as "a certain date" on 29th March; and Burns gives the 27th and 29th (II., 190).

*1306.—Edward applies to the Pope to have Bruce Excommunicated.*

Hailes, II., 4; Kerr, I., 212; Burton, II., 355; Burns, II., 192.—They refer to Rymer and Trivet, but I can find no passage in either to this effect. On 4th October, however, he did apply to have the Bishops of Glasgow and Edinburgh deposed for their share in the rebellion, though no reply seems to have been given to the application.—Rymer, II., 1028; Kerr, I., 252.

*b*

*1306—18th May.—A Bull issued from Bordeaux by Pope Clement the Fifth, addressed to the Archbishop of York and Bishop of Carlisle, authorising them, on examination of the facts, to excommunicate Bruce.*

The Bull, with this date (15 kal. Jan.), is given by Rymer (II., 997). Burton (II., 336) makes it to have been issued on 16th May; but in the notes to Hemingburgh (II., 253), the date is given as 18th May. It is a curious fact that there is no copy of it either in the Bullarium Magnum nor the continuation of that work (Vols. I. and IX.), and no reference to it in Raynaldius, though he speaks of the murder of Comyn by Bruce (IV., 411).

*1306-7—20th March.—Cardinal Peter S. Sabinus, at Carlisle, formally excommunicates Bruce.*

The Chron. Lanercost (p. 206) gives the date as on the Monday after Passion Sunday—*i.e.*, March 20th. Hemingburgh refers to the fact (II., 253), but gives no date. Hailes says (II., 21) "about February." Tytler (I., 231-2) says "in the end of February." Kerr (I., 267) "20th February." Burton makes no mention of the fact. Burns (II., 21) says "about February."

*1307—Paisley Abbey Burned.*

Fordun (not in Skene's Ed.), XII., 14. (Goodall's Ed., II. p. 238). This seems the only authority. The event is referred to by Hailes (II., 26). Gordon (Monasticon, p. 559), and Chalmers' Caledonia (III., 824), and in the New Statist. Account (VII., 206). Neither Tytler, Burton, Burns, Crawford, nor the Editor of the Registrum Monasterii de Passelet allude to it.

*1307—7th July.—King Edward I. Dies.*

*1308—12th February.—Philip of France and the Pope unite in urging Edward II. to consent to a Truce with the Scots, and Nuncios are sent by the Pope to both Kings proposing that during the Truce each should retain what they possessed, as on 25th July, 1308, and that Truce should last to November 1, 1309.*

Chron. Lanercost, p. 213. Kerr, I., 360. The Safe Conduct of the French Ambassador to Scotland is dated 4th March. Rymer, III., 127.

Neither Hailes (II. 38), Tytler (I., 255), nor Burton (II., 371) refer to the co-operation of the Pope.

Duncan Stewart, in his Account of the Royal Family of Scotland and of the Surname of the Stewarts (p. 17), says that, in 1309, Bruce "was favoured by Philip the Fair, King of France: he was absolved by the Pope, and solicited to a peace," and refers to Rymer, II., 997, which, however, is the page on which occurs Clement's Bull of Excommunication of 18th May, 1306, above referred to.

*1309.—24th Feb.—A Declaration by the Scotch Bishops, Abbots, Priors, and other Clerics, issued from Dundee, in favour of Bruce's Right to the Crown.*

Acts of the Parliament of Scotland, I., 460.

*1309—May 21.—A Mandate, issued on this date by Clement V. to the Bishops of London and Carlisle, in which the Pope states that the Bishop of London having, as guardian of the Minorites, excommunicated Bruce, and his obstinacy having continued for three years he should be denounced as excommunicated.*

Historical Papers from North Registers, p. 189. Hadden and Stubbs' Councils and Ecclesiastical Documents, II., p. 61.

*1309—30th July.—The Truce agreed to. Edward accuses Bruce of breaking it, and summons his Barons to meet to attack him.*

Rymer, III., 147. Hailes, *ut supra.* Kerr, I., 364.

*1309—August, November.—Edward again renews Negotiations with Bruce.*

Two deeds, in identical terms, are given in Rymer (III., 150, 163), authorising the Earl of Ulster to renew the Treaty, dated respectively 2nd and 21st August ; and one (III., 192) to the Earl of Angus and others.

See Hailes, II., 38 ; Kerr, I., 367 ; and Tytler, II., 56.

*1309—October 12.—The Bishops of Durham and Candida Casa directed to publish the Mandate of 21st May.*

Hadden and Stubbs, *ut supra.*

*1309.—Some time prior to November in this year a "new" sentence of Excommunication pronounced against Bruce and his Followers.*

"Nova Sententia Excommunicationis," Chron. Lanercost, p. 213. This probably refers to the Mandate of May 21.

*1309-10—16th February.—Edward renews Negotiations for Peace.*

Rymer, III., 201 ; Hailes, II., 39-40 ; Kerr, I., 369-70.

*1309-10—24th February.—The Scottish Clergy at Dundee issue a Declaration recognising Bruce as King.*

The Latin text is given by Anderson (Indep. of Scotland, Appendix No. 10) with a translation (App. No. 14). Hailes, II., 40 ; Kerr, I., 371 ; Tytler, I., 257 ; Caledonia, I., 818, Note C ; Cunninghame, I., 173 ; Burton, II., 372 ; Burns, II., 276.

*1310—7th July.—Edward complains of breach of Truce.*

Rymer II., 266.

*1311-12—8th January.—Seige of Perth.*

*1311-12—26th January.—Edward again endeavours to negotiate a Truce.*

Rymer, III., 200 ; Hailes, II., 47 ; Tytler, I., 262.

*1312-13—13th March.—Seige of Edinburgh.*

*1313—17th May.—Edward, at the instigation of the King of France, tries again to negotiate a Truce.*

Rymer, III., 411 ; Hailes, II., 50 ; Tytler, I., 269.

*1314—20th April.—Death of Pope Clement the Fifth.*

*1314—24th June.—Battle of Bannockburn. The Abbot of Inchaffray celebrates Mass for the Scotch army.*

Fordun (not in Skene) XII., 21 (Goodall, II., p. 250); Boece (by Bellenden) XIV., 11. These seem the only authorities for the Abbot's co-operation. Barbour does not mention it. See Hailes, II., 60 ; Tytler, I., 284 ; Cunninghame, I., 173 ; Kerr, I., 471.

*1314—September.—Bruce sends Messengers to Edward to propose a Truce.*

Rymer, III., 495 ; Hailes, II., 69 ; Tytler, II., 97 ; Burton, II., 389 ; Burns, II., 398.

*1314—Nov. 6.—Parliament held at Cambuskenneth Abbey, where Act passed against Bruce's enemies, sealed* inter alia *by six Bishops, fourteen Abbots, and five Priors.*

Chart. of Cambuskenneth, XXXIX. Acts of Par. of Scot., I., 104, and Tabula, pp. 13-14.

*1315—27th April.—Clergy and Laity meet in Parliament at Ayr, and unanimously resolve to bear true allegiance to Bruce against all men.*

The Declaration is given by Anderson (Indep. of Scotland, App. No. 24), and is dated on the Sunday next before the feast of St. James—*i.e.*, 20th July.

Acts of Parliament of Scotland, I., 464.

Fordun (not in Skene) refers to the Parliament (XII., 24 ; Goodall, II., p. 257) as meeting on the Sunday before the feast of St. Philip and St. James, which is the 27th April, and this is confirmed by the words of the Declaration itself, as given in the Acts *ut supra*, where, however, the heading given is 26th instead of 27th April. Buchanan (Cap. 8) gives no date. Hailes (II., 70) gives the date of meeting as April 26th, referring to Fordun, and adds, "Mr. Ruddiman, (*not.ad Buchanan*) mistakes the feast of St. Philip and St. James for the feast of the other St. James, hence he places this event in July, 1315. The mistake is not trivial, for it throws that part of our history into irretrievable confusion." Not only, however, might Ruddiman be excused by the text of the Declaration itself as given in Anderson ; but his Lordship is still wrong in the day of the week, the Sunday before the feast of St. Philip and James in 1315 being not the 26th, but the *27th* April.

Chalmers following Hailes (Caled., I., 818) makes the date 26th April, and so does Tytler (I., 299). Burton (II., 390) makes the Parliament meet on 1st May ; Burns (II., 348) in April.

*1316.—Pope John XXII. Elected Pope 7th August, and Crowned 5th September.*

*1316-17—1st January.—Bull issued by Pope John XXII. commanding a Truce for Two years between England and Scotland, and threatening with excommunication all who Disobey.*

Rymer, III., 594. He styles Bruce *dilectum filiun nobilem virum Robertum de Brus gerentem se pro Rege Scotiæ.*

The Chronicle of Lanercost (p. 234) says, under the date 1317, that the Pope sent this Bull to England after the feast of St. Michael (29th September), and that the Scotch being unwilling to agree, "nor caring anything about it," miserably fell under the sentence of excommunication declared in the Bull. And then the chronicler goes on to state that in the middle of the said truce *(tempore medio dictae treugæ)*, Clement died and was succeeded by John. There is clearly some great confusion of dates here. See Hailes, II., 92 ; Kerr, II., 121 ; Tytler, II., 310 ; Burton, II., 394 : Cunninghame, I., 174 ; Burns, II., 360.

*1317, 16th April.—Pope issues three Bulls,—one to Edward urging peace, and intimating that he had sent Cardinals to enforce his demand; a second to the Cardinals authorising them to excommunicate any opponents; and the third, to the Cardinals of same date specially authorising them to excommunicate Bruce as a rebel and burner of Churches,* "non obstantibus quibusvis privilegiis indulgentiis et litteris apostolicis, eisdem Roberto, vel quibusvis aliis, sub quacunque verborum forma concessa." *There is no reference to the murder of Comyn.*

Rymer, III., 612, 614. From a note to the Chronicle of Lanercost, (page 419, 20,) it would appear that the Pope, of the same date, wrote to Bruce apologising for not styling him King in the letters sent by the Cardinals. Kerr dates the three Bulls 17th March.

*1317, 28th April.—Two other Bulls issued, one specially authorising Excommunication of Bruce, his brother Edward, and their adherents, in respect of their invasion of England, Wales, and Ireland, destruction of Monasteries, &c.,* "non obstante si eis, vel eorum aliquibus, a sede Apostolica sit indultum, sub quacunque forma vel conceptione verborum, quod interdici, suspendi, vel excommunicare quavis auctoritate non possint et qualibet alia dicta sedis indulgentia, generali vel speciali, cujuscunque tenoris existat, per quam, presentibus non expressam, vel totaliter non incertam, effectus earum impediri valeret quomodolibet vel diferri;" *and one authorising Excommunication of Edward's enemies, with a clause nearly identical.*

Rymer, III., 627-30; Kerr (II., 123,) seems to date these Bulls in the early part of April; Tytler (II., 310,) dates them 4th April; Burns, II., 360.

*1317—1st May.—Another Bull issued authorising Excommunication of all who do not agree to the two years' Truce.*

Rymer, III., 636.

*1317—7th September.—Cardinals write the Pope that Bruce, while desirous of peace, will not receive his letters because not addressed to him as King.*

Rymer, III., 616: Kerr, II., 125; Tytler, II., 312; Burton, II., 395; Cunninghame, I., 174; Burns, II., 361.

*1317-18—18th March.—Commissioners appointed by Edward to conclude Truce with Bruce in conformity with the Pope's wishes.*

Rymer, III., 698.

*1318—23rd May.—Berwick taken.*

*1318—29th May.—Bull issued authorising Cardinals to Excommunicate Bruce for breach of Truce, and tearing Pope's letters,* "non obstante si eis, &c.," *as in Bull of 28th April, 1317. No mention of Comyn's murder.*

Rymer, III., 1317. The date is 4 Kal. July, but from the position of the Bull in the work it would seem that for July we should read June. Kerr (II., 136,) makes the date June; Burton, II., 396.

*1318—5th June.—Letter from the Pope to Edward intimating that Pope had written Cardinals to excommunicate Bruce.*

Rymer III., 711. Kerr (II. 136) dates this letter 6th June. See Hailes II., 92-7, 100. But the only Bulls or Letters to which his Lordship refers are those of January 1, 1316-7, and June 8, 1318. His reference to Rymer III., 713, is inaccurate.

*1318—5th July.—The Bishop of St. Andrews, in presence of Bruce, consecrates new Catholic Church of that See.*

Wynton, VIII., 21; Kerr, II., 156, but he makes the date 5th May.

*1318.—About the end of this year the Cardinals pronounce the sentence of Excommunication.*

Rymer, III., 752; Hailes, II., 108; Kerr, II., 194; Buchanan, Cap. 8. Tytler, II., 320; Burns, II., 368.

*1318—3rd Dec.—The Scotch Clergy and Laity, met at Scone in Parliament, declare their adherence to Bruce against all mortals, "however eminent they may be in power, authority, or dignity."*

The Statute, dated the Sunday next after the Feast of St. Andrews, is given in the Acts of the

Parliaments of Scotland, I., 465 ; in Anderson (Indep. of Scotland, app. 25) ; and in Fordun (not in Skene's ed.) XIII. 13 ; (Goodall's, II., 290) ; see Hailes, II., 103 ; Kerr, II., 181 ; Tytler, II., 320.

*1318-19—Jan. 9.—Edward writes the Cardinals that he hears messengers have been sent to the Pope by the Scots to procure reversal of sentence of Excommunication.*

Rymer, III., 752 ; Hailes, II., 108 ; Kerr, II., 195 ; Burns, II., 368.

*1318-19—Early in the year the Pope, in accordance with desire of Edward, orders the Scots at Avignon, and those that had corresponded with Scotland, into custody.*

Rymer, III., 761 ; Hailes, II., 108 ; Kerr, II., 196 ; Burns, II., 368.

*1319—20th September.—Defeat of English in Yorkshire.*

Tytler, II., 328.

*1319—24th October.—Edward again negotiates for Peace.*

Rymer, III., 791 ; Hailes, II., 114.

*1319—17th November.—Bull issued ordering sentence of Excommunication against Bruce and his followers for their rebellion against the Church, in violating the Truce, &c., to be pronounced.*

Rymer, III., 797 ; Hailes, II., 114 ; Tytler, II., 332. It should be noted that although, as Tytler says, this Bull is one of unexampled rancour, and though it extends to a much greater length than its fellows, narrating the incidents of Bruce at length, no mention is made in it of the murder of Comyn.

*1319—1st December.—Edward pursues his negotiations for Truce.*

Rymer, III., 803 ; Hailes, *ut supra.*

*1319—29th December.—Truce concluded between England and Scotland from 29th Dec., 1319, to 25th Dec., 1320.*

Rymer, III., 814. It began from the Feast of St. Thomas (29th Dec.) ; but Hailes (II., 115) dates it on 21st Dec. Tytler, II., 331. Burns, II., 380 ; but he makes it for two years, from Christmas, 1319.

*1319-20—8th January.—Bull issued by Pope to the Archbishops of York and London, and Bishop of Carlisle, instructing them to make a sentence of Excommunication (in conformity with the privileges of the Minorite Brethren) which Bruce had incurred in consequence of his murder of Comyn, final, and to declare it each Sunday and Fast-day with bell and candle.*

Rymer, III., 8-10.—The Bull proceeds on the narrative that Edward has signified to the Pope how, long ago (*dudum*), the murder was committed, and how, on account of it, Bruce is said to have incurred sentence of excommunication (not, be it remarked, by a Bull of Clement V., but) in virtue of the privileges given by the Apostolic See to the order of the Minorites in whose church the murder was committed. That the Archbishop of London had, as far as he could, made that sentence public ; and that the King begged—inasmuch as Bruce has proved incorrigible, and had sustained the sentence, damnably despising it, for three years and more, and up to this time remained with obdurate mind in contempt of the keys, nor sought to return to the Unity of the Church, to the peril of his soul and scandal of most—that the said sentence should now by the Pope be made "*firmitatis robur debitum obtinere.*"

Hailes *ut supra*, who states that the Pope ordered the ancient sentence of Clement to be published, though there is no mention of Clement in the Bull. Tytler, II., 332; Cunninghame, I., 175; Burns II., 381.

*1320, 6th April.—The "Barons, Freeholders, and whole Community of the Kingdom of Scotland" address from the Monastery of Aberbrothock a letter to the Pope, calling on him to justify their cause.*

The text of this remarkable document is given, along with a fac-simile, in the Acts of the Parliament of Scotland, I., p. 474, and by Anderson (Indep. of Scotland, App. No. 13). There is no reference in it to any excommunication either existing or impending. Nor is there any mention in it of the clergy. The language, as Hailes states (II., 118), was probably such as could hardly "be avowed by ecclesiastics, especially in an address to the head of their Church." The Latin text is given in Goodall's edition of Fordun. (XIII., 2-3. Vol. II., p. 275-9.) Note that the reference in Hailes is a misprint of 23 for 2-3.

See also Caledonia I., 819; Kerr II., 237; Stewart, p. 39; Tytler II., 332; Cunninghame I., 175-6; Burton II., 403; Burns II., 381.

*1320, 10th August.—Bull issued by Pope to Edward, advising him to make peace with Scotland,*

Rymer III., 846; Hailes II., 121; Kerr II., 249; Burton II., 407; but he makes the date the end of July. Burns II., 382.

*1320—August.—Ambassadors from Bruce go to Rome asking for repeal of Excommunication, and the Pope, holding they have not sufficient instructions, yet allows Bruce to appear by himself or his Procurator up to 1st May, 1321.*

Rymer III., 848, where, in a letter dated 18th August, 1320, the Pope informs Edward of these circumstances; Hailes II., 122; Burton II., 408; Burns II., 381-2; Kerr II., 250.

*1320—15th September.—Negotiations for a Treaty renewed by Edward.*

Rymer III., 857; Hailes II., 122; Burton II., 408; Kerr II., 251.

*1320—29th September.—A mandate arrives from the Pope to Excommunicate Bruce and his associates.*

Chron. Lanercost, p. 240-1. The Bull is said to have arrived about the feast of St. Michael. The Chronicler adds, "*Hoc autem non fuerat additum in sententia prius lata; ipse autem nihil de hoc curans, stetit in pertinacia, sicut prius.*"

*1321—May.—Pope sends Bishop of Winchester with letters to Bruce, but Edward will not let him pass.*

Rymer, III., 884. Edward excuses himself on the ground that there were some things in the letters which it did not seem wise that Bruce should see. Hailes, II., 123. Kerr, II., 253.

*1322—4th August.—Edward begs the Pope to enforce his sentence and processes against the Scots.*

Rymer, III., 967. He talks of the various sentences as "inchoatos." Hailes, II., 126; Kerr, II., 253.

*1322-3—14th March.—Edward proposes a Truce, but Bruce refuses.*

Rymer, III., 1001-4; Hailes, II., 134; Kerr, II., 296; Tytler, II., 345; Burton, II., 414; Burns, II., 393-4.

*1323—12th June.—Truce agreed on for thirteen years.*

Rymer, II., 1022, 1031. In the treaty it was provided that Bruce might procure absolution from the Pope; but if no peace concluded before expiration of truce, then the sentence of excommunication should revive. See Rymer, III., 1024 ; Hailes, II., 136 ; Tytler, I., 345 ; Burton, II., 414 ; Burns, II., 494 ; Kerr, II., 305.

*1323-24—13th January.—Randolph, going from Bruce as an envoy to the Pope, prevails on the latter to issue a Bull calling Bruce "King," and to agree to receive ambassadors from him to treat for reconciliation to the Church.*

Rymer, IV., 28 ; Hailes, II., 137-142 ; Kerr, II., 323-9 ; Tytler, I., 345-6 ; Burton, II., 415-17 ; Burns, II., 396.

*1323—1st April.—Edward writes the Pope protesting against his styling Bruce King.*

Rymer, IV., 46 ; Kerr, II., 329-30 ; Tytler, I., 346.

*1323—10th July.—Edward again writes the Pope remonstrating against his yielding to the Scots Ambassadors.*

Rymer, IV., 68 ; Kerr, II., 332.

*1326—15th July.—A Parliament held at Cambuskenneth, when the Succession entailed on David, son of Robert Bruce, and his heirs ; and clergy and laity swear homage.*

Chart. of Cambuskenneth, XL., XLI. See, as to the date, Acts of Par. of Scotland, VI., II., 627-8, 664.

*1327—24th January.—Edward II. deposed.*

Rymer, IV., 243.

*1328—1st March.—Peace concluded, and Edward III. recognises Bruce as King of Scotland.*

Kerr, II., 445, 525, where the document is given in English and Latin. See Hailes, II., 157-8 ; Rymer, IV., *passim.*

*1328-9—13th January.—The Pope issued a Bull in which, addressing Bruce as "a most devoted son of the Church," he grants, in answer to the request of his Ambassadors, authority to the Bishop of St. Andrews, whom failing the Bishop of Glasgow, to Crown and Anoint him and his Successors in the Kingdom.*

Gordon's Scotichronicon, I., 191, where a translation is given of the Bull. The original Bull is preserved in the Advocates' Library. Kerr (II., 472,) refers to it as dated 13th June, 1329.

*1329—7th June.—Bruce Dies.*

*1329—23rd August.—Pope condoles with David Bruce on his father's death, styling David King of the Scots.*

Notes to Chron. Lanercost, p. 427.

*1333—6th August.—Pope grants remission by Bull for the crime of taking Bruce's heart out of his body.*

Notes to Chron. Lanercost, p. 428.

Such is the curious and troubled record of the relation of Bruce to the See of Rome, as I have been able to give it from existing records. Let us now consider whether in that history the Commission of Berengarius may find a reliable place.

And, first, it is clear that there is an error in the date, which is given as follows :—

"Dat Piceni decimo Kalend Augusti pontificatus domini Clementis tertii anno quinto."

For the fifth year of Clement the Third, we must read the third year of Clement the Fifth. Clement the Third became Pope in 1178, and died in 1191. Clement the Fifth was elected 5th June, 1305, and crowned 11th November, (St. Martin's Day.—Robertson, IV., 8), or 14th November (Sir H. Nicolas' Chronology of History, p. 202) in the same year, and lived to 1314.

Goodall, or whoever wrote the notes to his edition of Fordun, points out the error, and adds, "*quisquid sit, satis aliande constat falli eos omnes, qui Robertum prius veniam pro caede in ecclesia a Papa impetrasse scribunt quam regni diademati se insigniori procuraverit.*" It will be noticed, however, that the writer in the text he is annotating is not necessarily one of those false writers, as he expressly guards himself by saying that "the King thus absolved, *or, in the interim, sending for absolution,* assumed in the following April, as has been stated (he means the sixth Kalends of April, *i.e.*, 27th March), the royal insignia."

The date must be taken as being the tenth Kalends of August, in the third year of the pontificate of Clement the *Fifth,* and as that Pope dated all his Bulls from his coronation, not his election, (Sir H. Nicolas, p. 202 ; see, for example, the Bulls in Rymer, II., 1059, III., 5,) this is equivalent to *23rd July, 1308.*

There is every probability that at this very time Berengarius was in personal communication with Clement at Bordeaux. He was evidently high in the confidence of the Pope. His name was Berenger de Fridole. He was made Bishop of Bezieres in 1298, had been one of those whom Pope Boniface had employed in the compilation of "du Sexte des Decretals," (Fleury, xc., 54), and was one of three deputies sent to King Philip of France by the Council summoned in October, 1299, at Bezieres, by the Archbishop of Narbonne (Fleury, xc. 1) in reference to the dispute with the Viscount of that town, which was one of the preludes to the memorable struggle between Benedict VIII. and the French King (Milman, xi. 9 ; Vol. V., p. 221). On the 15th December, 1305, he was made Cardinal Presbyter by Clement V. in his first nomination of Cardinals, and took his title from the Church of St. Nereus and Achilles (Fleury, xc. 54), which title he retained till he was raised to the rank of Cardinal Bishop of Jerusalem (Fleury, *ut supra*), which was sometime between the early part of 1309 and the latter part of 1311,* and by which title he is therefore correctly described in our Commission.

In 1308, and sometime after the 25th May, the French King having gone to Poictiers, the question as to his right to judge the Templars was discussed "a loisir devant les Cardinaux," and, as some of the Knights Templars had not been able to go as far as Poictiers, having taken ill at Chinon, in Touraine (Robinson Eccl. Hist., IV., 19), the Pope, who was then at Pictavis(see the following Bulls dated from thence :—

"Pictavis," 22d Dec., 1307. Rymer, III., 30.
"Pictavii," 22d Dec., 1307. Bullarium Magnum. Suppl., Tom. IX.

* I find him styled as "Cardinal Presbyter titulo St. Nereé et Achilles" in a list of Cardinals given in Rymer (II., 1031) between the months of November and December, 1306 ; and in a letter of date 12th December, 1307, as to the canonization of St. Thomas of Canterbury (Rymer, III., 31) ; and in two Bulls from the Pope to Edward and Philip respectively, dated 12th August, 1308 (Bull Magn. Suppl., IX., 137, Rymer, III., 101, and Bull Magn., I., 186), he is referred to by his title of St. Nereus et Achilles. In a letter commending the English King's Ambassadors, of date 4th March, 1309, I find the following address :—"Domino *T.* tituli Sanctissimi Nerei et Achillei Presbytero Cardinali" (Rymer, III., 129), where the "T" must, I take it, be a misprint for "B," as there was no nomination of Cardinals by Clement after 1305 till Dec. 1310 (Fleury, xci., Sec. 46). Even then no Cardinal was appointed by the title formerly taken by Berengarius. His nephew, however, of the same name, was made Cardinal Presbyter on 23rd Dec., 1312, by the same title of St. Nerei et Achillei. (Fleury, xcii., Sec. 4 ; Reynaldi, 121, Sec. 54—Tome IV., 594).

He gets his title as Cardinal Bishop of Jerusalem in letters in Rymer of date 13th Nov., 1311, 14th July, 1312 ; 1st April, 1312 ; 14th Sept., 1312 ; 23d Jan., 1313 (III., 190, 306, 312, 346, 377.) In a letter of date 15th Dec., 1316 (Rymer, III., 585), there is a misprint similar to what I have noticed above ;—"G" being put as the initial of the Bishop of Jerusalem instead of "B." We have not only the correct initial, but even the full name in many subsequent letters in the same volume. He died, according to Migue (Dict. des Cardenaux), at Avignon in June, 1323.

"Pictavis," 10th Dec., 1307. Bullarium Magnum. Suppl., Tom IX.
"Pictavis," 12th Dec., 1307. Rymer, III., 42.
"Pictavis," 9th April, 1308. Rymer, III., 73.
"Pictavii," 9th April, 1308. Bull. Mag. Suppl., Tom. IX.
"Pictavis," 9th April, 1308. Rymer, III., 76.
"Pictavis," 11th August, 1308. Rymer, III., 99.
"Pictavii," 12th August, 1308. Bull. Mag. Supp., Tom. IX.
"Pictavis," 12th August, 1308. Do. Do., Tom. IX.
"Pictavis," 12th August, 1308. Do. do. do., page 137, and Rymer, III., 104.
"Pictavis," 12th August, 1308. Bull. Magn., Tom. I., p. 185.)

sent three Cardinals to examine them, of whom Berengarius was one; and on the 17th August they are reported as being at their work. (Fleury, xci., Sec. 25; Bullarium Romanum, I., 185, IX., 137; Rymer, III., 102.)

As Bishop of Jerusalem, Berengarius was, in 1310, sent by Clement with two other Cardinals to examine into a dispute with the Freres Mineurs (Fleury xci., Sec. 42), and again in the same year with two other Cardinals to examine into the charges against the late Pope Boniface. (Ibid, xci., Sec. 44).

These gleanings seem to shew that on the 23d July, 1308, the date we have assigned to our Commission to the Abbot of Paisley, Berengarius was still a Cardinal Presbyter, that he was a likely person to be employed by the Pope in a matter of consequence, and that he was actually in residence with the Pope at Poictiers.

But what of the date "Piceni"?

The date of the Bulls issued by Clement from Poictiers in the month of August is, as we have seen, "Pictavis" or "Pictavii." The only Picenum of which I am aware is the *Italian province* of that name, between Umbria and the Adriatic. (Smith's Dict. of Geog.; Suppl. to Brunet's Manuel du Libraire; Notitia Dignitatum, Boëking, Pars Occident, 10, *et notæ*.) If the Commission were a forgery, it is inconceivable that the forgers would be so clumsy as to date it from an Italian province, and that province quite unconnected with Berengarius, at a time when, as must have been known to all the world, the Pope was resident in France. Had it been "Picenis," I should have been inclined to read it as a clerical error for "Pictonis," as this, equally with "Pictavis," would describe either Poictiers itself, or the district around it; but the tense is against me, as well as the name itself. Yet an error in the copyist of "Piceni" for "Pictavii" seems almost more likely than such a blunder as the intentionally dating from Picenum in Italy.

Passing from this, and reverting to the digest of dates given above, we find that the date we have assigned to the Commission places it a year after the death of Edward the First, and six months prior to the joint attempt of the Pope and the King of France, in February, 1308-9, to induce a truce between the English and the Scotch; and it is rather a curious coincidence that in the Chronicle of Lanercost we are told that it was proposed by the Pope and French King that each of the belligerents should retain the territory they held on the preceding Feast of St. James, being the first feast and only the second day after the date of the Commission by which it is proposed to free Bruce from the pains of excommunication.

Further, it is clear that, just before the date of this Commission, Clement had been taking an active interest in the affairs of Scotland. In a Bull addressed to Edward, of date the 9th April, 1308, (Rymer, III., 73), sent by the hands of Sicardus de Vauro, Archdeacon of Carbaria, "*in Ecclesia Narbonensi, Capillanum nostrum*," (we have seen the connection between Berengarius and the Archbishop of Narbonne,) he complains that whereas his father, Edward the First, had given orders to have the Bishops of Glasgow and St. Andrews delivered up to Cardinal Peter S. Sabinus for the purpose of being brought to Rome, he, Edward the Second, after his father's death, had refused to implement this order, and still kept them in captivity; and with most effusive and pretty strong language, insists on their being sent to be judged by the Roman See. Of the same date, he writes (Rymer, III., 76) to the Bishop of Winchester, to lend his aid to that effect. In consequence of this appeal, the imprisonment of these bishops was first made less irksome (see letter by the King to the Pope—Rymer, III., 96), and afterwards, on a renewed demand from Clement on 4th October (Rymer, III., 109), the Bishop of Glasgow was on 1st December, 1308 (Rymer, III., 118), released and handed over to *the Bishop of Poictiers*, who had been sent as a Nuncio by the Pope,—the Bishop of St. Andrews having been already released on swearing fealty to the King of England. (Rymer III., 95, 121.)

In the Record Edition of the Acts of the Parliaments of Scotland (I., p. 460) a writ is printed as though dated from Dundee, 24th July, 1309, in which a number of the Scottish Bishops, and among these the Bishops of St. Andrews and Glasgow acknowledge the right of Bruce to the Crown; yet it seems clear that the Bishop of Glasgow did sometime about this time go to Rome, and from a letter of the King to the Pope of date 1st February, 1311, (Rymer, III., 245,) protesting against the impending return of the Bishop of Glasgow from Rome to resume the duties of his See, (Edward had in vain asked the Pope to appoint another in his place, Rymer, III., 122,) it would appear as though his reception by Clement had not been unfavourable.* If this be so, and supposing a request to have been made by Bruce at the same time for pardon for the murder of Comyn, it is not improbable that a response may have been made by the Pope in the shape of such a commission as that which we are considering, and to which, at the time, it may not have been deemed advisable to give all the publicity which would attach to a formal Bull.

And this probability gains strength as we trace down the record given above of the doings between Bruce and the Papal See. If the excommunication of 18th May, 1309, was still unrecalled, what was the necessity for the mandate of 21st May, 1333; and unless Bruce had, in some way or other, been set free at one time from the burden of excommunication, it is hard to understand how Pope John XXII., in his Bulls of April and May, 1317, should have ordered a fresh sentence of excommunication to be passed on him, "*non obstantibus quibusvis, privilegiis indulgentiis, et literis apostolicis*," and "*non obstante si eis* (*i.e.* Bruce and his adherents) *vel eorum aliquibus a sede Apostolica sit indultum, sub quacunque forma vel conceptione verborum, quod interdici suspendi vel excommunicare non possint, et qualibet alia dictæ sedis, indulgentia generali vel speciali, cujuscunque tenoris existat.*"

These words, in one shape or other, occur in all the four Bulls specially relating to Bruce in April, 1317, and May, 1318, and almost seem to imply that there did exist some letter from the Apostolic See, which, though not a formal Bull, yet did purport to give absolution to Bruce.

On the whole, then, I am inclined to think that the balance of probability inclines in favour of the genuineness of the Commission by Berengarius.

But why was it addressed to the Abbot of Paisley?

Kerr suggests, as we have seen, that his participation in the forgery (as he deems it) may have been the cause of the burning of his Abbey. The fact was—the Abbey was burned the year

* Clement, however, seems afterwards to have changed his mind, for the Prelate was ultimately sent back to Edward, as appears from a letter by Edward giving directions as to his safe keeping, dated 20th November, 1313, (Rymer, III., 450). From a sentence in Tytler, II., 262, we might gather that the Bishop had been relieved for a time and sent to Rome; but, excepting Kerr, (I., 386,) I find no other writer who expressly refers to this: not even the editor of the Reg. Epis. Glasguensis.

before ; and if there be any connection between this outrage and the document in question, I would rather suggest whether, as they were the soldiers of Edward that perpetrated the former, there may not have been a delicate "*solatium*" implied in making this particular Abbot the medium of the absolution of Edward's greatest foe.

As the known and steady ally of the Scottish King, the Bishop of Glasgow would probably have been the natural party to have been chosen, and, failing him, the Bishop of St. Andrews ; but they were both in prison at the time. And we know that a close and intimate friendship existed between the Bishop of Glasgow and the Abbot of Paisley.

But further, the Abbey of Paisley had been from the beginning the special object of the munificence of the Stuart family (Caledonia, III., 822). James the Steward had been associated with the Bishop of Glasgow, both in the oath of fealty to Edward in 1291, and in the insurrection under Wallace in 1297. In 1302 he was sent to Philip of France to solicit his aid for the Scots, and in March, 1309, he was one of those who wrote to Philip acknowledging the right of Bruce to the Crown. His son Walter, who succeeded him in the latter year, married in 1315 the daughter of Bruce, who died in the following year, and was buried in the family burying-place in this very Abbey (Caledonia, III., 780). Thus we have the Abbot of Paisley and Bruce brought into close association with James the Steward, and he into close association with Philip of France, who at this very time was with the Pope at Poictiers. Is it too much to think that, if Ambassadors were sent by Bruce to Poictiers in 1308 to intercede with the Pope, they might, if they did not again include James the Steward himself, yet be of his kith and kin ; and if so, and if they had any voice in the suggestion or nomination of the recipient of Berengarius' letter, that they would, *under the circumstances*, and almost as a matter of course, suggest the Abbot of Paisley ?

ALEX. B. M'GRIGOR.

---

## F.

### STATE PAPERS REFERRING TO THE ABBEY AND ABBOTS OF PAISLEY.

*Cottonian MSS., Caligula, B. I., fo. 82. Ro. Abbot of Paisley to Wolsey, dated 8th May, 1524.*

"My lord in my maist humill maner I recommend my Rycht Lawly service To your grace, certifying ye samyn y$^{t}$ ye Kinges Hienes (your souerans) ambassadowrs being in ye court of Rome (hes at ye Instance and requeiste of your grace solisht ye papis holines for my promotione To ye bishoprik of murray according To my humill prayer maid. To your grace befor) no$^{t}$ ye les because y$^{t}$ ye Kinges Hienes my master hes virtyne for ye promotione of a sone of ye Erll of arrane To my abbasy of Paslay he being of Tender age and bastard our Holy fader ye pape in consideratione of ye premiss deferris To promoiss me To ye said bischoprik quhobeyt yai Impediments Rising one ye part of ye said Erll sone awcht no$^{t}$ be ressone To differ my cause. Heirfor It will pleise your grace dedene To writ To ye said ambassado . . . bein wyt our said Haly fader for expeditione of my mater Lattying y$^{t}$ vyer promotio . . . stand suspense quhil efterwart y$^{t}$ better ways be laborit. And faryer T[o] gyf saufconduct To my seruitours for avating apon my said besines, and gyf neid beys To pas in flandres To y$^{t}$ effect (assuring your grace y$^{t}$ in safer as my pur powar may extend I sall no$^{t}$ faill To be ane fay$^{t}$full & Trew servand To ye Kinges Hienes, your souerane & your grace abune all vyeris [others], nixt my souerane & master as of Just cause I am greit[ly] dettit To do, lik as master magnus your traist servitour can schew at le . . . [? length]. prayng God to conserff your grace in prosperite. At Edinburgh ye viij of maij be your graces humyll servitour & oratour at his extreme powar.

"RO. ABBOT OF PASLAY.

[Addressed] "To my lord cardinalis gud grace."

---

*Cottonian MSS., Caligula, B. I., fo. 256. Queen Margaret to Hamilton, dated 5th August, 1524.*

"In ye fyft paynt ye sal say to my lod of norfolke that as to my lod of paslay I vol [will] not that he knav [know] ony secret vay betwyxt Ingland ad me, bot tauschyng the pece ad as to my lod of angus that he gyff hy . . . [BLOT] ne credens to ye abot of paslay, as farthar mastar tomas Hanylton [Hamilton] vol schow you on my name.

"MARGARET R."

*Ibid., fo. 121.**—"Of this we be advertissed by the Abbots of Holy Roode Hous and Pasalewe (twoe good and honourable men)."

---

*Cottonian MSS., Caligula, B. III., fo. 96. From Hals to Norfolk, dated 1st Sept., 1524.*

"Please it your grace to be aduertised whereas I wrate in my letters dated on tewsdaye the xxiij$^{t}$ daye of Auguste by the enformacion of th abbot of Pasley that th erle of Argyle th erle of Murray & the Lord Maxwell shold haue seased all the goodes & catalles of the Byshopp of Seynt Andrews, as yet it is not don, wherof I suppose daunger maye ensue onles Kennedy maye be provided ryght shortely yn that behalf, for as I am enformed the seid byshopp hath Rewarded dyuers of the lordes & others and also promysed great Sommes of money to be at libertie as to the quene xx$^{mli}$ Crownys. To George Shawe seruaunt to the quene & kynnysman to th abbot of Pasley to th entent he sholde turne the seid abbott to favour his partie as mych money as sholde paye for the purchace of londes to the valewe of xx$^{li}$ yerely of this money. And he geoyth wekely to th erle of Argyle duryng the tyme of his abode her to helpe yn his Causes C$^{li}$ of this money. And I do suppose th erle of Murray is not vnrewarded, which ij Erlys favour his partie couertely as mych as they can. I haue don as mych as lyeth yn me aswell to the quene as to dyuers lordes of the Councell for the seasyr to be made, which is not don nor lyke to be onles the Kynges highnes or your grace wryte to the quene substancially for the same. And if it sholde chaunce the seid byshopp to atteyne libertie of his person and goodes together The pouerty and unstabulness of the people of this londe consideryd, he beyng a man of great wisedom, maye & vndoubtedly woll do mych hurte yn derogacion & hynderans of maters purposed for the welth of both Realmys of Englond & Scotlond.

* * * * * * * * *

"Item, the abbot of Pasley who beryth very good mynd vnto your grace by whom I have knolege partely what is don dayly yn the Councell hath made meanys vnto me, not by his owne spech but by others, to wryte vnto your grace to be good lord vnto him & that it wold please you to make Requeste to the quene by your letters that the seid abbot myght have th office of Treasourer her, which, with dyuers other great offices as chaunceler, priuat Seale, secretary, & others, Remayne yet nott disponyd."

---

*Cottonian MSS., Caligula, B. III., fo. 80. Wm. Hals to Norfolk, dated 12th Sept., 1524.*

"Please it your grace to be aduertised that uppon fridaye laste paste, about ·x· of the clok yn the mornyng, I Receyuyd from your grace by davy fawkoner's seruaunt, a letter to the quene, a Copy of a long letter from my lord Cardynall, with a letter yn french, sent to your grace by the Duke of Burbon. And Incontynent as I had red the seid letters & perceyuyd the Contents I

* Magnus of Ratcliff to Wolsey, dated 26th November, 1524.

went to the quene and delyueryd vnto her grace your letter, & also the seid copy & the Duke of burbon's letter, And dyd Sollicite the contents of the same the beste I cowde, openyng vnto her grace the consideracions conteigned yn my lord cardynall's letter as well concernyng the sendyng of the seid ij byshoppys to berwyk, as for restitucion of the englyshe shyppys & goods yn them conteigned, late taken by scottyshemen comyng out of Irelond. And for because my lord Cardynall's letter was very long, and at that tyme the quene had no leyser to rede the same, her grace commaunded me to resorte to her the nexte daye for aunswer. And accordyng to her sayd Commaundement I went to the Courte yn the mornyng and first spake with th erle of Arran & the Abbot of Pasley, and desyred theym to be fauorable concernyng the seid restitucion, which they promysed. And Incontynent the said Erle went to the quene & mocioned her grace of the same," &c.

* * * * * * * * * *

"And whereas the quene by th advise and consent of all the lordes had appoynted th abbot of Holyrood Howse to be president of the Councell, and the abbot of Pasley & others to hym associat to her & determyne causes uppone complayntes by bylles put upp to the Kyng & to her grace, as well for wrongs commytted by scottismen withyn the lond as uppone the borders of England yn peas tyme, to th entent that the offendours myght be punyshed and redresse made to the partiez greved, accordyng to the order of Justice and custumes before tyme vsed. Wheruppone all such bylles as were put upp to the Kyng and quene duryng the parliament and sythens were delyueryd to the seid abbot of the Holy rood & his associates & to the same entent. Neuertheles the Erle of Arran who bereth moste Reule about the Kyng and quene, beyng a man ryght Inconstant, enclyned to auarice & parcialite, at the labour & request of Dan Carr lard of Cesseford & Mark Carr, which with their adherents haue commytted many wrongs uppone the seid borders, caused the quene to send to the seid abbot of the Holy rood, not only commaundyng hym to send agayn to her grace all such billes of complaynt as were to hym delyueryd but also Revoked his auctorite of th office of president of the Councell (without other cause as I am enformed), wheruppone the seid abbot redelyueryd the seid bylles to her grace accordyng to her seid Commaundement, not willyng to take lyke charge therafter. And thus the admynystracion of Justice is sequestryd (w<sup>t</sup>out which no realme maye prosper), to the great hynderauns & enpoueryshement & danger of th ynhabitants of th. And onles remedy maye be shortely prouyded yn that behalf, the people, as well lordes as Comons, begyn to murmur and grudge that the quene taketh uppone her the Rewle of the Realme hoolly w<sup>t</sup>out councell of others sauyng of the seid Erle of Arran, who hath neyther great wisedom, constancye, experiens nor fauour of lordes nor Comons of this londe (but by many of the lordes had yn great hayne), and onles for fere of ayde of the kynges highnes neyther the quene nor yet the seid Erle (as it is spoken here ryght playnly shold contynewe any long tyme yn the seid high Rule & auctorite, but by the lordes & chiefly such as do fauour th erle of Anguyshe to be shortely deposed. And it is to be feared leste the same shall yn brief tyme be put yn execucion onles the seid quene, by th advice of the Kynges highnes, take such Councellours about her that will mynyster Justice Indifferently."

*Cottonian MSS., Caligula, B. VI., fo. 345. Wolsey to Norfolk, dated 15th September, 1524.**

*Ibid., fo. 364.—Magnus and Ratcliff to Norfolk, dated 8th November, 1524.*

"Your grace writeth that ye wold that by the meanes of Adam Otterburn we shuld assaye to wyn the busshop of saint Andrewes after suche a waye as your grace moved vs at our departing

* Acknowledges receipt of letter, in which, among other things, was contained "the sayings of master Adam Oterbourne and th' abbot of Paslay."

from you. We have not pretermytted the same, but thereunto have added some deale more, trusting he wolbe a good man, making well by all aperance to our purpoos (the circumstances your grace shall perceive in the commyng vnto yow of our next lre.) We can write nothing of the Abbot of Paslaye, bicause he hath not been here sethens our commyng, nor we have no knowlege of his commyng hither. Adam Otterbourne, Patrik Synclere, and master John Chesom be very favourable and forward in our causes."

*Cottonian MSS., Caligula, B. VII., fo. 17.—Norfolk to Queen Margaret, dated 14th September, 1524.**

"And as touching th erle of Lennox, aftir my poore opinion, your grace shuld doo asmooche as ye goodly might, your honour saved, to reconsile hym, wherein I think no man maye do more than th abbot of Pasley. And, madame, if I were able to gif your grace counsell, I wold aduyse you to doo asmooche as ye conuenyently might doo, to have the good will of all the noble men and the favour of the commynaltie."

*Cottonian MSS., Caligula, B. I., fo. 47.—Gonzolles to [Albany], dated 16th September, 1524.—In French.*

Only mentions that the signatures of the abbots of "†" (Holyrood ?) and "Paseles" (Paisley) were among those of them who, as partizans of the King and Queen Mother (in opposition to the Chancellor), signed, and consented to break the truce and discharge Albany.

*Cottonian MSS., Caligula, Book VI., fo. 361.—Norfolk to Wolsey, dated 19th September, 1524.*

*(In the Postscript.)*—"Also Hals hath shewed me that the quene shewed hym that the bushop of saint Andrews had offred to laye in pledgis in england that he wold be a true subiect to the King his souerain lord. And one george Shawe who is nere kinysman to th abbot of paslaye and seruaunt to the yong King, by whom I have had dyuers knoelegis, whiche had been w$^t$ the said bushop of late, shewed Hals that he wold laye in pledgis in the King's handes to be true to his souerain lord, and that he woll fynd meanes to take suche direccion that the Duke of albany shuld no more comme in the land. And th abbot of paslaye and patrik Synkclere in likewise shewed Hals that the seid bushop w$^t$ good will wold laye in pledgis in england for his dutie to be obeisaunt to the King his souerain lord."

*Norfolk to [Wolsey], dated 10th October, 1524, according to the Calendar, which refers to Cottonian MSS., Caligula, B. I., fo. 113. The reference, however, is incorrect.† There is nothing of the kind at that place.*

"P.S.—Last night, Carlisle appeared with the enclosed letters. As the Queen and Arran declare that, if Angus come to Scotland, they will hinder the coming of the ambassadors, and the safe-conduct for Magnus and Radcliffe is deferred, has detained Wolsey's letter to the Queen, with the articles. As she seems to have some confidence in Norfolk, has determined to send Hals to her to-morrow, with a letter to her, and one to Arran. (Copies enclosed.) If no good effect comes of this, despairs of any other mode of reconciling her and Angus. If Hals find they are both determined to hinder the coming of the ambassadors, he will practise with Cassilis, the bishop of Dunkeld, and the abbots of Paisley and Holyrood House, to promote it."

* Date supplied in the Calendar of State Papers.

† The above extract is taken from the Calendar which speaks of the document as a fragment of a letter, with a postscript. From the extract it does not appear that the notice of Paisley is important.

*State Papers, Scotland—Henry VIII., Vol. II., No. 69.—October 5, 1524—Abbots of Holyrood and Paisley to Norfolk.*

"My Lord, we commend ws to your Lordschip In our maist hartly manere, certifying yow yat ye Kingis grace our maister Is in gude heill and prosperite, and growis ane fair prince loving to god. Nocht dowting but he is Inspirit be grace till all vertew and honour yat suld perteine to ane noble prince. And as we traist salbe Inclynit to nuris and auctorise pece and Justice in yis his Realme.

"We sall await and attend contynualie apon his seruice, ffor he being weill, we gif litill estimatioun to ony vthir thingis. And quhen ye qweny's grace pleis to charge ws with ony seruice, we sall be reddy yairto. Praying god to send her ane good counsell, and gif hir grace to vse ye samyn.

"My Lord, we think ws mekill addettit to your L. for ye gude part, counsell, and mynde ye beir to our Soueraine.

"Gif yair be steid, plesour, or seruice we may do for your L. or ony yat pertenys to yow, we salbe reddy yairto at ye vtermast of our power.

"Beseking almychti god and our blissit Lady to conserue your L. at your noble hartis desire. At Edinburgh ye fyft day of October. Be your huil seruitours and chaplains with lefull seruice.

"GEORG ABBOT OF HALLERHUTH.*
"ROBERT ABBOT OF PASLEY.

[Addressed] "To my Lord Duke of Northfolk, greit admirall
& Thesaurare of Ingland, and Lieutenent of
ye North parts of ye samyn," &c.

---

*British Museum, Cottonian MSS., Caligula, B. VII., fo. 85.—Norfolk to Magnus and Ratcliff, dated 5th Nov., 1524.*

"Also it shalbe well doon that by the meanes of master Adam Ottirburn ye assaye to wyn the busshop of saint Andrewes (aftir suche wayes as I shewed to you) before your departure from me. And in any wise falle in famyliaritie w[t] th abbot of paslaye, by whome y[e] shall knowe moost of the Secrets, but in anywise speke nothing to hym of the said busshop of saint Andrewes, for he doth not love hy[m]. And thus hertely fare ye well. Written at Newcastell the v[th] daye of Nouembr."

---

*State Papers, Scotland—Henry VIII., Vol. II., No. 86, Dec. 14, 1544.—Magnus to Earl of Angus.*

"Copye.—Myn oune good lorde, full hartely I recommaunde me vnto your lordeship. And where amongg other thinggs it is reapoorted here that ye and my lorde of Leneux, w[t] your company and seruaunts attending vpon youe, doe vse the hous and monastery of Pasley as if the same where your oune, and intende soe to contynue and to vseh it for a season, to the grete hurte and hynderaunce of the said monestary, soe that the monks and breder of that house, w[t] good and convenient hospitalite, canne not nor may be maynntayned, as to the same it dooth of right apperteine, I your poor frende and assured good lover doe marveill therof, conscidering, as I knowe of trouth, how well and howe lovingly the Abbot of the saide monastery bereth his speciall and singuler good mynde and favour to your said lordeship and to my saide lorde of leneux, In somych as for your booth causes his lordeship haith susteyned noe litle lakke nor blame, wherunto I haue bene and am priued, and is and wolbe aswell content that booth your lordeshippes shall haue your pleasures in the same his monastery as any lordes in all Scotlande, and asmyche hit is his mynde ye booth shalbe welcom to that hous, vsing it as his frendes and loving lordes in good and resounable maner. And albe it I write thus vnto your saide lordeship, yet knowing your good gentilnes and honour I doute not but ye woll haue consideracion to theffecte of these premisses, sondery causes remembred further thenne nowe I write vnto youe. Right glad I am, my lorde, that your said lordeship dooth so well and so soburly vse your selff and your seruaunts in every thing that may be to the contentacon of your soveraine lorde and maister, and to the obeisaunce of his precepts and commaundements, making noe transgressions to the same. Not doubting but your lordeship, soe doing, it shall not be long but by the meanes and mediacon of the Kingg's Highnes, my soveraine lorde and maister, a mych better way shalbe taken for your reconsiliacon to the quene's favour, and redubbing of your estate thenne canne be by any violence or other attemptate by youe to be enterprised at your owne hande. And assuredly your lordeship may put your truste and confidence in the Kingg's Highnes, my maister, and in my lorde legate's* grace, as in thoos whiche in due and convenient tyme woll not faill to see every-thing ordoured as shalbe to your honour, profite, and contentement. And as a poor man may, I shall at all tymes be a meane to and for the same purpoos. Letting youe wete [know] that yester-day I received sondery letters and writinggs from oute of Einglande. Amonggis other oon conteynnyng newes of suche expedicion as the ffrench King haithe by his sodayn arivall and repar-ing into Italy. (Copy wherof w^t^ this I sende vnto your saide lordeship, whoom almighty god haue in his preseruacon. At Edinburgh, the xiiij^th^ day of December.

[Addressed] "To my lord of Angwise, to my lord's grace."

---

*State Papers, Scotland—Henry VIII., Vol. II., No. 87—Dec. 15, 1524.—Angus to Magnus.*

"Maister Magnus, in my maist hairtlie maner I commend me tho yow, quhame pleis to vyt I haif resauyt your writting yis last thursday, datyt at Eddinburgh, xiiij day of December, w^t^ ye copy of ane byll of tytbandis [tidings] quhar of I thank yeo hairtly. And I am rycht glad of yesamyn. And quhar yo wreit tho me yat it is reportit my lord of lenox, and I w^t^ our company and serwauntts, purpossis till vse ye hous And monestery of Paslaye has our awne, veralie ye sall knaw yat I am cumyt in yis countre tho speik with^t^ my lord of lenox. And he & I to be to-gyddir at yis tyme of cristymmis knawand na thing bot [th]at my lord of Paslay wald haif beyne weill contentyt of ye samyn. And belief weill we will do na thing to ye displesur of my lord of Paslay, prayand his L. tho cum hayme; and I taik on me yair salbe na thing done till his place nor till hymself bot to his plesur. Prayand you gif yer be ony thing yat I may do to your plesur yat yo will charge me, quhome yo sall fynd redy at ye vtermest of my powar. And yo so doand yo do me singler plesur. And addetts me tho do for yow ye residew of my lyf, & foryer, god haif yow in his keping. At Kylmaw^r^ ye xv day of December.

"Yours at command,

"Erl of Angus.

[Addressed] "Till gie the rycht honorable & his traist
frend, maistir magnus, [A]mbaxator
tho ye King's grais [of I]ngland," &c.

---

*Ibid., fo. 138, dated 22d December, 1524.—Magnus to Wolsey.*

"The good Abbot of Pasley of late shewed vnto me he was likly to susteyne gret hurt and damage booth to hym self and his monastery by the saide two Erles,* if remedy were not founden in tyme convenient, for, as he shewed vnto me, the saide twoe Erles intended to kepe thair

* ? Wolsey's.

Cristenmas in his saide house, and to vse every thing there at their libertye and pleasur, both for hors and man, to the noumber of ij$^{x}$. persons, and therfore desired me to write for hym to the Erle of Angwisshe, and soe I did, and besides that matier gave vnto the saide erle of Angwische my poor aduertisment according to the contynue of your saide gracious letters. Copy of my letter, w$^{t}$ his ansuer therunto (pretermitting a gret parte of the effectuall matier, wherynne I shulde have knowen his mynde), I sende also vnto your said grace."

---

*British Museum, Additional MSS., No. 15,387 (? Transcripts of Documents in the Papal Archives at Rome), pencil fo. 155.—James V. to Clement VI., dated 11th Jan., 1525.*

"Ann. 1524.

"Ex autographis litteris Jacobi Scotorum Regis.

"Epist. Princ., Tom. I., pag. 132.

"Beatissime Pater, humillimam prostrationem ad pedum oscula beatorum. Cum jam dudum vigilans admodum Moraviensis Ecclesie Episcopus cognomine Hepburne hac mortali vita ad ultimum usque functus est, ut ejusdem Ecclesie status non inferior videretur. De novo atque idoneo pastore Vestre Sanctitati nominando curam gessimus non minimam, ut eidem Vestre Sanctitati illum commendaremus, quem de rei ecclesiastice cura quam optime mereri putamus. In illum tandem qui annorum maturitate, vite exemplo, ac morum integritate alios longe antecedit, et quem tante cure Vestra preficeret Beatitudo animum inclinavimus. Igitur de nobis et Regni nostri re publica bene meritum Venerabilem in Christo Patrem Robertum Schawe in Cenobio de Pasleto Cluniacensis ordinis in diocesi Glasguensi multis jam annis Abbatem, ad Episcopalem huius Moraviensis Ecclesie dignitatem promoveri cupimus cum omnibus exemptionum privilegiis quibus vel novissime defunctus, vel alii Moravienses Episcopi gavisi sunt, et quod possit secundum illius Ecclesie usum et consuetudinem divina celebrare. Ceterum cum nobis aliquando familiarior est futurus, cuius etiam consilio in nostris negotiis usuri sumus, Vram Beatitudinem quam possimus maxime rogatum facimus illo cum eadem Vra Beatitudo dispenset, vestem possit episcopalem, rochetam lineam albam induere, atque quolibet illa incedere, modo sui ordinis signum scapulare subtus togam prope deploidem gestet. Et quid nobis in animo est Regni nostri proceribus, iis presertim qui nobis areta sanguinis necessitudine devincti sunt, et ob Regni nostri regimen vires expendunt morem gerere, nosque gratos reddere; Johannem Hamyltoun Monachum Ordinis divi Benedicti in Monasterio de Kylwynnyng, Glasguen etiam dicesis professum, charissimi consanguinei nostri Jacobi Aranie Comitis filium naturalem, in Abbaciam de Pasleto per ipsius Roberti promocionem ad Episcopatum Moraviensem suffici desideramus. Verum quid annum adhuc agit decimum quartum, impediuntque natales, quia genitus ex consanguineo nostro extra maritale vinculum, et sine Vestre Sanctitatis beneficio huiusmodi abbacia gaudere nequit, eidem Vra Beatitudo et etatis et natalium obstacula dimoveat. Et quia in prefatum consanguineum nostrum, et Robertum antedictum propensiori sumus animo, et multo amoris affectu, optamus vehementer utrumque uno consistorio hunc ad Episcopatum, Johannem illum ad abbaciam Sanctitas Vestra promoveat, cui longissimos dies, summamque felicitatem ab eterno precamur. Ex Castro nostro Edinburgensi tertio idus Januarias anno salutis nostre millesimo quingentesimo vicesimo quarto.

"E. V. S.

"Devotus filius Scotorum Rex,

"Jacobus R.

"L. ✠ S.

"Foris.

"Sanctissimo Domino Nostro Pape."

*Cottonian MSS., Caligula, B. III., fo. 232.—James V. to Henry VIII., dated 20th Jan., 1525.*

"Richt Excellent, Richt Hie, and michtie Prince, Our derrest bruder and vnc[le, In our] mast hartlie maner we can we commend ws vnto yow, And pleis ye samyn till vnderstand That [our ric]ht traist cousing and counsalour James erll of arane Is daylie and contynewallie In our seruice [and in our] Derrest modir's your sister, And to ws Richt tender be gret neirnes and proximite of blude. And R . . . ane venerabill fader in god, and our traist Counsalour Robot abbot of paslaye Is vnto ws and our said derrest moder Richt thankfull and obeysaunt seruitor, For ye quhilkis causse and vyeris moving ws we h[aue] grauntit and gevin to ye said venerabill fader The bischopryke of Murray, now vacand be decese of . . . . ane Reuerend fader in god James, last bischope yerof, And to our louit orato[ur] Dene Jhonne [Hammiltoune], naturale svn till our said Cousing, proffessit monke of ye samyn ordour of our said abbay of [paslaye q]uhen ye samyn abbay sall happin to waike be promocioun of ye said venerabil fader vnto ye s[aid bischo] prike of murray, or ony vyir manir of waye yat It sall happin to waike. And has givin to ye said venerabill fader and dene Jhonne our effectuus writings of nominacioun and supplicacoun to ye papis [haly]nes yerupoun. Herifor, Richt excellent, Richt Hie, etc., our Derrest bruder and vnclle, we pray you to [write] effectuislie to ye papis Halynes for expedicioun of ye bullis of baith ye said bischopryke and abbot . . . . . said venerable fader and Dene Jhonne Hammiltoune, baith to be sped attanis an[d] . . . . . ne Cousin . . . . otyir [m]aner, conforme till our wrytings aboue mencionat. Forthir, Derrest vnclo, pl[eis it] you t[o] . . . [req]uest and desyr and to cause ye samyn be sped with deligence apon . . . . . . . . . . . . . And his seruand, yis present bearer, to haue your saufconduct to cum, pass, and repass . . . . . . . within yat your realme of Ingland, To mak fynanc with your bancours or marchandes in london [and] oyer placis within yat your realme expedient to yat effect, lovsing and hamebringin of ye said b[ullis], because our said derrest Cousing, and ye said venerabill fader, dare nocht awentur yar fynanc and . . In vyer realmes be sey [by sea] because of werres. And yat yer is na seker peax* betuix ws and fraunce. A[nd[ for yat cause we desyr yis fynance to be maid within yat your realme, and saufconducts to be ma[de to] ye effect aboue writtin, with all claussis necessarie quhilkis ar Conuenient to be had in ye samyn. And . . . . ye space of ane yer efter ye day of ye date yerof till Indure, and ye samyn to be deliuerit to yis pres[ent bea]rar ; and als y[t] we may haue your speciall writings to your oratours in Rome To Conwoye and . . . . . . . said Cousing and ye said venerabill fader's seruands to ye papis Halynes for expedicioun of ye s[aid bu]llis. Allswa, Derrest Vncle, we desyre effectuuslie That we may have spede in your licence and . . . [p]asport w[t]in ye landes of flandars, Almanye, and vyeris landes pertenyng to ye empriour yat y . . . . . . . . tour and governour of. To our said Derrest Cousing and ye said venerable fader's seruands and . . . . . With yar horses, money, lettres, bullis, wrytings, and all vyeris necessary to pass and Repass thro[ugh] . . landis and cuntreis without ony truble or Impediment, be sey or land, within ye saide bounds . . . ye said licence and pasport Inlikwyse for ye space of ane yeir Till Indure. Richt excellen[t, Richt] Hie, and michty prince, Our Derrest bruder and Vncle, we pray eternall god haf you in His . . . keping. Gevin vndir our Signet At . . . . . xx[t] Day of Januar.

"Your lovyng [br]uder, Cusyng,
"[and Nephew],

"JAMES R.

* The Calendar quotes the words as "sicker peace."

[Addressed] "To Richt the Excellent, Richt [Hie], and michtie
Prince, oure [Derre br]uder and Vncle
The King of [Ingland]."

---

*State Papers, Scotland, Henry VIII., Vol. 3, No. 2.—30th January, 1525.—Dr. Magnus to Wolsey.*

"Please it your grace to be aduertissed it haith pleased the Kingg's grace here w^t the consent of his derriste moder, the Quene's grace, to promoote to the Busshopricke of Murray a right woorshipfull man, the Abbot of Paslay, as by the Quene's ltres directe booth to the Kingg's Highnes and to your grace moore at large, it doth appere. In my mooste humble and lawly maner I beseche your grace not oonly to be good and gracious lorde towardes the avauncement of the saide Abbott's causes, but that it may like youe also to vnderstande and shewe vnto the Kingg's saide Highnes this saide Abbot is the man of woorship amonggis many other that bereth his faste and faithfull seruice accoording to his naturall duety to the King, his soveraine lorde and maister, w^toute leanyng any waye, but for the weall and surety of his saide soveraine lorde, and of this his realme, soe that therfore booth he and all his be had in high displeasure w^t the ffrenshemen. At my reparing into these parties, my Lorde of Norffolke advised me to leene to the counsaill of the saide Abbot, and soe I haue doon ever sethenne my commyng hider, and have not oonly founden grete counforte of hym at all tymes, but also, he hath bene the mooste forwarde of any man to folowe the Kingg's high pleasure and youres in suche causes as have concerned the weall and surety of the yong King, and for the conioynnyng of booth these realms in profite, love, and amyte, and accoordingly I am sure he woll reste and contynue in suche maner, as woolde to God there were a good noumber of his oppynnyun. Wherfore I accompte my self bounden to declare, and shewe vnto your saide grace, the goodnes of the saide Abbot. The saide Abbot haith ordeynned his seruante, this berer, to sewe for th expedicon of his bulles, and to compounde w^t the Lombardes and bankers ther, for the same, and woll haue money in rediness for that purpoos. And for somyche as the saide Abbot and his seruaunte have noe maner of acquayntaunce in thoos parts, the saide Abbot therfor humble besecheth your grace for the poor seruice and prayer he bereth vnto youre saide grace, that it may like the same to accept and take his saide seruaunte into your gracious favour and proteccon, during the tyme of his busynes to be had for the cause aforesaide in thoos parts. And as it may lye in the saide Abbott's power, your grace is and may be well assured to haue hym at your pleasure and commaundement during his liff, for your grete goodnes to be shewed vnto hym at this the tyme of his grete nede of assistaunce and furtheraunce of his causes concernyng his promocon. And almighty god haue youre saide grace in his mooste blessed tuicon and gouernaunce. At Edinburgh, the xxxth day of January.

"Your mooste humble
Preiste and bideman,

"T. MAGNUS."

[Addressed] "Vnt[o my L]orde Legates
goo[d gr]ace."

---

*Cottonian MSS., Caligula B. II., fo. 132. Dated 2nd Feb. 1525.—Magnus to Wolsey.*

"Howe be it my commyng to the quene's presence for any my poor aduertisments to be geven to her grace, is moore by poore polecy vsed thenne by any commaundement or calling to the same. And after the same manner, ofte and many tymes, the Abbot of Holy Rood House, and the Abbot of Pasley be vsed, insomyche thay being the mooste sadde and auncient counsaillours here, shewe vnto me thay were never made prived to any parte of suche proclamacons as ar goon and paste furth at this season."

*British Museum, additional MSS., No. 15387 (? Transcripts of Documents in the Papal Archives at Rome) pencil, fo. 157.—Henry VIII. to Clement VI., dated 23d Feb. 1525, (i.e., 1524-5.)*

"Regis Anglie de promovendo Roberto Abbate de Paslay ad Episcopatum Moraviensem in Scotia.

"Ann, 1524.

"Ex litteris autographis Henrici VIII.

"Arm. XI., Cap. I., n°. 10.

"Foris Sanctissimo clementissimoque Domino nostro Pape.

"L. ✠ S.

"Intus. Beatissime Pater, post humillimam commendationem et denotissima pedum oscula beatorum. Optatissimum semper nobis est, quotiens ulla sese offert occasio rem gratam Serenissimo domino Regi Scotie fratri ac nepoti nostro charissimo, illustrissimeque Regine eius matri, nostre ibidem dilectissime Sorori prestandi, non solum quod utrique ex corde bene uolumus cumulateque satisfactum cupimus, sed etiam quod uehementer optamus haud obscuro indicio ab his perspici, intercessionem precesque nostras non exique gratie et authoritatis apud Vestram Beatitudinem extare, qui esti eam suis impresentia litteris rogent ut ad Episcopatum Morouien per obitum R^dl patris domini Jacobi eius ultimi Episcopi in dicto Scotie Regno uacantem; suoque presule orbatum, Venerandum dominum Robertum Abbatem de Pallay* promouere, atque suam abbatiam per huiusmodi translationem uel alio quocunque modo uacaturam religioso viro Don* Johanni Hamulton illius loci Monacho firmissimum in modum conferre dignetur, uoluimus tamen, et nos quoque fauorem partesque nostras pro uiribus interponere, Vestram Sanctitatem uehementissime rogantes, ut dicti nepotis nostreque Sororis desiderijs et uotis in precipuam nostram gratiam adnuere uelit, quod ut in dicti Regni quietem haud dubie redundabit, sic nos qui prefatum Nepotem nostrum unice amamus, Vestre Beatitudini eo nomine non mediocriter debebimus, suam erga nos facilitatem ac benignitatem memori semper animo seruaturi, hoc enim negocium quante cure nobis sit, ex nostro isthic Oratore ipsa uberius cognoscet, que diutissime, ac felicissime ualeat. Ex Regia nostra Londini Die xxiij febr. M.D.xxiiij. E. V. Stis. Devinus atque obsequentissimus filius Dei gratia Rex Anglie et Francie fidei defensor, ac Dns Hybernie.

"HENRICUS."

---

*Cottonian MSS., Vitellius B. VII., fo. 84. John Clerk to Wolsey, dated "At rome, the xix day off Marche" (A.D., 1525.)*

"I haue allso receyvyd the Kyng's letters in recommendation off the bushopricke off Murraye and the abbay off paslaye."

---

*Ibid, fo. 43. Dated 31st May, 1525. Magnus to Wolsey.*

"At the convenyng and meting of these Lordes and other the Lordes of the Prived Counseill, it was spoken that there were vj Scotts right good Englisshe men—that is to say, the abbots of Holyroode House and Pasley, the lorde of saint Johns, the Dean of Glasco, Patrik Synkler, and Mr. John Cheseholme."

April 2, 1547.

* Paslay.

*State Papers, Scotland—Edward VI., Vol. I., No. 13.*

"To Mye lord Whartton and Mastre bessop, these :—

"Yese serve to avertese yv y^t I rasavit your Writings, also Weyll [as well], of y^e dayt of y^e x of Marche, is* of y^e dayt y^e xvj of marche ; q^lk rasayt of Writings was y^e first of Apryll. & as to your long karye† for sendeyng to yv of newis, I intendet to hayf sent Putersone, bot schortlye I was informeit how y^e guvernowr beres steyf apone me, aye mye intellygense Wy^t yngland in avertesseyng of mye lord of lennox ; & I dibayt & answarris yerta acoordeyng to y^e sayinges, & so q^ll I maye na mair. I suspeck sorlye scottis men in carleyll for newis. at yese [At this] conversashone y^e porpose was [th]at y^e guvernour wald hayf y^e prenses [Princess] ; he knawane y^t ane gret part of y^e lordes be solesting of y^e quene's grace ; and heir [he] wald not consent yerto, ferret to propous y^e mater in plaine, bot wrocht secretlye to y^e consentes of yame at he myt susdus yerto ; quha hes gottyn argilles, huntlye, & y^e erll of angus, as I ame informet. & because y^e quenis grace mynd & diverrus oderres [others], heir assestores, is not contentet yerwy^t, it is divyset at y^e abbat of paslaye secretlye sall ga in francse for y^t cause, & for to get y^e Keyng of france's consent yerto, & to get y^e red hat to hymself to be Cardenall, & y^e bessoprye of merypoys yn godd. he parttes incontynent & passes at dumbartayne in ane Jamie Howmes schip, quha is laytle cum in wy^t two ynglese pryses. He hes gart prepare ane oder schep in sycrelye seklyk seklyk‡. bot because of y^e taking of ye lyoun§ be yngland, I am sorlye adverteyset he passes at dumbartayne. Yerfor he may be ysalye had wy^t delygense. at ye sayd conwersashone it is ordanit y^t all maner of man selbe radye wy^t iiij dayis warneyng & ane monetht wettall. yes [This] warneyng is mayd, & y^e Kyng of fransses mynd be gottyn to yes [this] porpose geyf [if]," &c. * *

* * * * * * * * *

he hed for I ded all at was possebell to wet yes proceedings, & as I could lernyng I writ to yv. & w^t elles peter tomsone sayd to y^e abbot of paslaye in counsell [th]at y^e gret men of ynglond was skac [scarce] content [th]at subern|| men had y^e rowlme in gyding, I praye yv harst [ask] me answer agayn of all things wy^t delygense. & yes," &c.

---

April 3, 1548.

*State Papers, Scotland—Edward VI., Vol. IV., No. 1.*

It may please your grace I haue at lenkethe spoken wt^h th'erle of Huntelie, who declareth vnto me the skottish quene, as he vnderstoude by his brother, addressed towarde hym a letter w^ch he thinks to be cumme to your grace's hands. And th effecte shuld be to requyer his helpe in frendship of the french Kinge to convey the yonge quene thether, w^ch lieth not in her to do bicawse, as he saith, w^th out dowpte Dunbarton is as yet in kepinge of the governor's men, and wolde th erle Huntelye travaile his best herein the quene promyseth Earledom of skotland and many other fayer gyftes. And now the Abbot of Paselie havinge advertised th erle that he woll cumme to barwicke wt^h a large comyssion to intreate of pease. And the governor, stondinge stiflie againste vs, cheflie in hope to marye his sunne w^th the yonge quene, shulde th erle Huntelie beleave be removed from that expectacon, and so the more easylie inclene to vs, if th erle had at that metinge w^t th abbot of Paselie the quene's letter to shew hym, syned w^th her awne hande, whereby it war to perceayve how se [she] abuseth the governor w^th daliance, not myndinge as she

* Should be "&."

† Charge.

‡ Word repeated.

§ The ship "Lion."

|| Stubborn.

wolde seme and as he beleveth. And yet Th erle Huntelie, beinge in dowpte whether that letter came to your grace's hands or no, hath towlde his brother to sutch words w[th] out wyttch in wrytinge he woll not aunswer the quene marie; had he from her an other letter delyvered to his awne hands he saith he wolde, and to me semeth of mynde to vse it as is before remembred. & so if it please your grace I cannot saie but the man speketh well, and as it war of ernest harte. märe [marry] of what disposition he is indede to be thought I know not, bycawse in mynde they haue differed ofte from their professions. Nevertheles if the abbot of Paselie shall so seke to debate that matter, your grace may please t' advertice how, by whome, and of what articles he shalbe receyved, felte, and debated w[th], for I beleave w[th]in viij daies assuredlie to know the tyme of his commynge. Also Th'erle of Huntelie sheweth me that th erle Boythell saide to hym at London he was by restrainte ther from his countreth [country], forced to condiscend and agre to your graces pleasure, and therfor th erle Huntelie thinketh it good whan he shall thrououtlie be confirmed vppon every pointe that your grace expreslie will hym well to remembre that it is of his awne mere and franke disposition to geue hym self to the King's Ma[ties] godlie purpose, and that the more apparauntlie he may confes the same, your grace may vnderstond the opinion of th erle is. It war good he shulde be remytted to his awne cowntreth [country], and in a seasonable tyme lymytted to reenter hym self to me, as it war only of hym self to confirme his former promyses wherby the open confession mowght bynde hym the rather to observe the same. And thus I take my leave of your grace, from Tynmouth the iij[de] of Aprell.

"Your grace's assured to commaunde,

William Grey."

[Addressed] "To my lord<br>Protectouris grace.<br>Hast Hast<br>Post Hast<br>w[t] all dilligence<br>possible.<br>Hast Hast Hast."

---

### Letter of Abbot Hamilton.

*State Papers, Scotland—Elizabeth, Vol. XX., No. 28.*

Quhair It alleigit violatioun of the Abstinence—the taking of the abbay of Paslay ? Answer, It will pleis the Quenis Ma[tie] of england to call to Hir Rememberence, Erst the cumyng of our soueraine the Quenis Ma[tie] of skotland In Hir grace realme of england to sute Hir help and mentenance, And that the earle of Murray that tyme proclamit ane pretendit parliament in his maner, And summondit ane greit part of the Nobilite to the said parliament to be forfaltit for assisting and obeying of our native quene and prince. And I ves summond amongis the rest to that parliament, Quhair vpone we wient and complenit to the Quenis Mat[ie] of engl.; oure soveraine beand in Hir handis, And als we preparit oure selffis againe that parliament to haue stayit it. And thair vos ane army on the feildis reddy to have fulfillit oure Interprise and stayit ye parliament onto the tyme the Quene of engl. wreit to us, and als causit our Quene Ma[tie] to cause ws to desist and ceise fra Armes. And the Quene of engl. tuik on Hir that na parliament suld be haldune, or ony thing done to ony man's hurt, bot that it suld have bene ony bot ane assemblie and na parliament. Nochtyeles vndir Hir promes thayy procedit in thair pretendit parliament to the forfaltour of sundry, And quhen we Immediatlie eifter that we complenit, and wreit to Hir that thay hed procedit nochw[t]standing Hir promes, and vsit on thair maner the protest of forfaltour. And than sche wreit to ws that the said protest suld tak na executioun agains ony man, or to thair hurt ony of thame na mair nor It hed nevir bene. And this Hir lettre your L. saw In Dunbartane or your departing in engl. And so all the skayth that ony of ws hes sustenit hes bene onder the Quene of engl. sic promess. And ay sensyne thay reft my place and Levyng sa far as they could get. And quhair my Lord Sempill vas maist maister and vndir his feite And vther partis quhair I mycht be maist, I tuik ay my Levying as I mycht cum to it, And swa [so] vas nevir out of possesioun of it, albeit I wes reft, and that for trew seruice done to my Prince and Realme and for na falt. And I knew that thay vsurpit allennerlie by all Reasoun oure soueraine's authorite, and hes na powar bot be tyranny and tressoun to thair Native borne Quene to ws Hir fai'full subiectis as thay do, And in reifing and spoilzeing of thaime of thair places and Levyngis, and me in speciall as ane. And quhair it is complenit of my serwands as wiolaris of abstinence for melling [meddling] w^t my awne place, It can be na breking nor violating thairof, In respect the place Is my awne, and hes had It thir xlv. yeires, And I nevir recognoscit ony aucthorite, bot nor man of oure surname, bot our Quenis Ma^tie only, Nor nevir obeyit the vther authorite or Lawes. And als my said place of Paslay vas standing waist, and na man in it but onlie ane boy that hed the key of ye yeit, And my serwandis dide no violence to ony man, bot Interit in my awne place without troble to ony man, And it can nocht be to enter In my awne place doand [doing] na violence. And als that the lord Sempill that had vsurpit that place of befoir wos content I had my awne place, for it dide him no proffeit bot cummer and expens; And heirfor [therefore] It can be no violations of the abstinence, And quhair It is said that I wos in Paslay and held courtis in our Souerain's name, that is manifest fals, for I wos not thair [these] thre yeiris and mair. As to courtis halding, all that evir I held, or thinkis to hald, salbe in the Quenis name So long as Hir Ma^tie beis on liff. And quhair Erle Lennox alleiges my seruaundis to have tane gair of his landis of Cruixtoun, It is manifest Inventit tales to cause scince that man do is Iniuries quhair man Is bot to check the rebellioun, oppressioun, and reiff that thay do vpon ws. And thay baycht dois the vrangis and complenyeis. Alvay yis assurance Is manifest brokine on me In sending be the erle of Lennox his souldeouris and Inclusit my place and seruaunds in It (thay doand no man vrang, but remanend in the place viij dayis), and slew certane in It and hurt otheris or evir that place vas desyrit to be deliuerit be the erle of Lennox proclamacioun. And eifter [after] the charge and proclamacioun (albeit Lennox had na authorite to gif [give] it bot vsurpit). That our souerain's materis suld not stay thay var content to render the place agane without ony manassing or schoittin at thair folkis (quhairof thay mycht have slane mony of thame). And als thay promesit to the men in the place that thay sould pass frelie w^tout troble in thair bodeis or geir. And quhen thay deliuerit the place and [ought] to have gane frelie away be that promeis, thay vor led captive as presouners to be hangit and yit be *ista* to be hangit. And yis is the assurance and abstinence kepit to vs, and not this onlie bot to all that obeyis our soueraine, and geve [if] the Quene of engl. Ma^tie vald cease fra thair help to owir ryne ws the Quenis fai^t full subiectis, it wald not be at this point, and thairfor sche maun put order to thame, for sum speikis they durst not brek this assurance or abstinennce without they belevit sche vald not crab at thaime thairfor. Albeit we beleiff the contrar of that nobill princess that hes our princes in Hir custody and mentenance. And to be schort your L. may declair, and sould declair, that all thir thingis amongis ws subiectis is bot particulareteis, and thay ar cassin in of set purpose be troust to stay oure souerain's libertie (gyfe thay can), for that is all that oure aduersareis vork for, and fyndis all thir fals invenciouns. And thairfor mak and labour our soveraine's Ma^tie to pass fordvart. And for all the subiectis, baycht we that ar oure Quenis fay^tfull subiectis, and als hir aduersiris and rebellis matteris, caussis and querrillis (quhilkis ar particularetes amongis our selffis), let thame com befoir ony men of reasoun deput thairto, other be ye Quene of engl. or vther ways, and we sall answer and redress for all attemptis and Iniuries done be ws or ony obedient to Hir Ma[tie] at all tyme and hour, swa that we may have the lyk. And quhair evir they can alleige (albeit it be fals) ane penny tane fra ony of that party we sall verife an hundret tane from vs, and that sen the tyme of the abstinence. And lat commissiouner be deput to this, and nocht to stay our Quenis cause, for thir trifflis are done allennerlie to stop thame. And thairfor ye may be the mair quyk that thair falset tak no place aganis yow and hir cause, and als ws againes, the treucht, and the thing that is trew ; and we wreit to yow that thing planle quhilk is trew, and thay vndir hand continewallie dois the iniurie and als complenis, bot thair falsset will not serve thame quhen it cumis befoir ony reisonabill answer. And this your L. may byd be to be of treuth for this article."

[*Endorsed*] "Ap[i]ll, 1571—The copie of the B. of Santtandy Lettre sent for defens of the medling with Paslay."

---

*State Papers, Foreign—Elizabeth, Vol. CXVI., No. 1016 (No. 1514 in the Calendar)—Sir William Drury to Cecil, dated 25th January, 1571 (*i.e.*, 1570-1).*

"The ambletons* hathe taken Passeley wytheowt stroke or contradyktyone, wyche the L. symple [Semple] had off late the vse off, whereby appeares the suspytyon conseyved off hym as by Kapten Yakeseley I dyd syngnyffe [signify] to be apone cawse, and some thyng more towchyng that praktyse wyll appeare."

---

*State Papers, Scotland—Elizabeth, Vol. 20, No. 10 (Numbered 1529 in the Calendar of State Papers, Foreign)—Memorandum by Abbot of Dunfermline, not dated, but the date January, 1571 (*i.e.*, 1570-1), supplied in Calendar.*

"Giff the quenis Ma[ties] intentioun be that the abstinence begvn be treulie keipit be ather of the parteis, than in my opinioun It war mete that Hir Hienes gaif Declaratioun that all attemptatis and Iniuries notoriouslie don, be way of deid, wy[t]out ony ordour of law specialie sen the renewing of the last abstinence, sik as the taking of the abbay Paslay, the slauchtir of the laird of garleis men, the thingis committit be the lard of grange and wtheris, as is at mair lenth contenit in the notes presentit be me to Hir Ma[tie] at Hamptoun coort and on settirday last wes, be redressit and amendit presentlie, but delay and every man put in *statu quo prius*, Or ellis that Hir Hienes will no[t] find falt that my Lord Regent wy[t] sik as professis the Kingis obedience tak remede thairoff as thai may best, wpoun thair awn perrell. And on the other parte, that all sik as hes evir professit the quene, the Kingis motheris, obedience, and hes at na tyme gevin thair aith and hand wrait to the King and his Regent, for the tyme be incontinent inlykwyse restorit to all thair possessionis and guidis extant, quhilkis war taking from thame onelie for the acknawlegeing of the quene, and noth acknawlegeing the Kingis authoritie.

"This being don, that Hir Hienes declair to bayth the parteis that Hir pleasure is, that nather of thame molest or mak ony prouocatioun of Iniurie during the tyme of the treaty to otheris.

"This far I speik onelie for my awn opinioun, Referring allwayis the conclusioun to theis to quhom it pertenis.

[Endorsed] "The Abbot of Dunfling." [Also, in pencil,† by the Record Office authorities—Eliz. probably 1569. The Abbot of Dumfermling was in Eng. 1569—Prob. Dec., 1570—query May, 1570.]

* Hamiltons.

† These remarks, I suppose, are overridden by the date fixed in the Calendar.

*State Papers, Foreign—Elizabeth, Vol. CXVII., No. 1081-1 (No. 1598 in Calendar)—Kirkcaldy of Grange to Drury, dated 6th March, 1571.*

"Vpon fryday last thair uas xv of the men $y^t$ uer tane in paislay condemnet and $y^r$ handes bound; quhat is becum of them sence I cannot presently assure you."

*Ibid, Vol. CXVI., No. 1059 (No. 1567 in Calendar)—Lord Scrope to the Earl of Sussex, dated 22nd Feb., 1571.*

"It may pleas your good Lordshippe to be aduertized: that synce the dispatche of my lres of yesternight, I haue this morning recyved intelligence, that the Lorde Regent on Mondaye last dyd wyn Pasley, and hath caryed them that were $w^{th}$n prisoners to Glascoo. What the Lordes $He^r$yes and Maxwell will doe now vpon this, I knowe not, but by my next your L. shall vnderstande, Althoughe I am aduertised that on Saterday next they mynde to set forwarde. And so I take my leave of your good L. At Carlisle the $xxij^{th}$ of februarie, 1570.

"Your good L. assured to commaunde,

"H. Scrope."

*Ibid, No. 1025 (No. 1525 in Calendar)—Sir William Drury to Cecil, dated 29th January, "1570" (that is 1571).*

"Passeley was taken by the L. symples [Sempill's] owne compotyane [composition], and the ambletons [Hamiltons] and he agreed as ys supposed."

*State Papers, Foreign—Elizabeth, Vol. CXVI., No. 1062 (No. 1570 in Calendar)—Sir William Drury to Cecil, dated 23rd February, 1571* (i.e., *1570-1*).

"The $xvij^{th}$ of this present Paisley* House was rendred vp to the Regent, and so many as were $w^{th}$in the same yelded them selues to his mercye, who graunted them their lyves condicionally that the Lord Simple might be restored to his libertie $w^{th}$in three daies next following, sauing and alwaiss reserued such as had bin before taken in Brykin, who at the rendring of the same then promised and sweare neuer after to beare armes against the King, whome as I heare, are, or els shortly shalbe, executed. And as I am farther aduertised the L. Simple hath no lyking of their Composicon; forsomoch as he holdeth not him self in case to lyue by reason he thinketh that he is poisoned.

The Regent also the same daye caused proclamacon to be made in Glasco wherein he charged all the Duke's ffrynds and Tenaunts, and so many as belonged to the chief of the Hambletons $w^{ch}$ had denied the gouernement of the King, to bring in their rents and Dueties $w^{th}$in three daies next after the proclamacon made, or els that they shold be rydden on $w^{th}$ fyer and sword, so that some of them haue already obeyed.

"From Barwike, the $xxiij^{th}$ of February, 1570."

*Ibid, No. 1055, I (No. 1563 in Calendar)—Lord Scrope to Lord Herries, dated 21st Feb., 1570 (i.e., 1571.)*

"My Lorde, I have this daie Receyved a ltre from your L. conteining that the $xvij^{th}$ of this monethe the abbot of Arbrothe came to that towne of Drumfreyse to desyre supplie of that Countrie to $w^{th}$stande the Erle of Levenox presentlie beseiging Pasley," &c.

* Query, if not written Pausley.

*State Papers, Foreign Elizabeth, Vol. CXVI., No. 1054 (No. 1561 in Calendar), Lord Scrope to Cecil, dated 20th February, 1570 (i.e., 1571).*

"It may pleas you, S^r^, to be aduertized, that a man of myne was yesterdaye at Drumfreise who is presentlie retourned vnto me w^th^ aduertisement that the Abbot of Arbrothe ys come in to those partes, w^th^ whom ehave assembled the Lorde Maxwell, the Lorde Herys, the Larde Lowqhenber, and dyvers other Lardes of that faccion, who have concluded, at his desier, on frydaye next to send some men furth to the relieff of Parsley, being presentlie beseged by the Regent, and if they shall holde theyr iournaye, yt is lykewise thought that Drumlangrick will goe w^th^ his powre to the ayde of the Regent. So, as of their proceedinges or staye, I shall not fayle by my next ltres to gyve you aduertisment. And so I commyt you to the proteccion of th almightie. At Carlisle, the xxth of Februarie, 1570.

"Your Honour's assured to commande,

"H. Scrope.

Post.—Yt is thought the Regent shall haue woone the Howse before that tyme. I pray you S^r^ pardon my boldnesse in that I haue in this pacquet sent a ltre to my seruaunte, James Phillippes, the w^ch^ I beseche your Honour, by one of your seruaunts, maye be delyvered vnto him at the Rose, at Holburn bridge."

---

*W. Kyrkaldy of Grange to the Commissioners of the Quen of Scots in England, March 20th, 1571.*

---

*State Papers, Scotland—Mary Queen of Scots, Vol. 6, No. 20.*

"Albeit y^t^ eftir that thay hade ondirstand the queinenis ma^tie^ of ingland guid intentione for performance of ye treatie, be your Ll. ltres, thai willinglie accordit thairto:, Notw^t^standing the erle of lennox hes vsit him self moir vttraigiouslie sensyn upon the Q. guid subiectis (ein quhen thai luikit for greattest quyetnes) nor at ony vthir tyme befoir ye takin of ony abstinence. As of lait thai haif not ceissit eftir ye randering of Paslay to put to deid nyne men vt come in his will.

---

**Sept. 10, 1583.**

*State Papers, Scotland—Elizabeth, Vol. 33, No. 32.*

"Th abbotts of Cambiskyneth and Paslay (nare kynsmen to Marre) ar chardged to Ward. But they will not enter, faringe the malyce of theire enemies in courte. And theron their beniffices & Lyvings are like to be disposed and geuen to others.

* * * * * * * * *

"Marre is presentlie w^th^ Argile by the King's direccon, and in nature of a Ward. He traueleth by his seruaunte now at courte, for relieffe of th abbotts his kinsmen aforesayd, offringe to putt him selfe in Ward in any such place as the King shall appointe, So that his kinsmen and seruaunts maye be free, and retains their Lyvings."

---

*State Papers, Scotland—Edward VI., Vol. 4, No. 53.*

"The Abbot of Paisley shal be made Cardnall and great lyueyngs geven him."

Sept. 20, 1583—R. Rowes to Walsburgh.

*State Papers, Scotland—Elizabeth, Vol. 33, No. 46.*

"It maye please your Honour, your laste of the xvijth hereof I receued yesterdaye in the fornoone, being sorie that the gentlemen did so plainelie discouer them selfes by the waie & in the towne, whereby their beinge at Barwa* is comonlie knowne here; I looke to be roondlie charged wth that matter: ffor I am presentlie aduised yt some in courte do buselie seeke a quarrell against me, gevinge me occasion to send oute of this house all such wrytings & papers as I would not haue seene. Your good consideracon & well handelinge of the cause shall (I trust) acquite me in this behalfe. In all others I shall stand to my lott, and allwaies imploye my selfe to aduance Her Maties seruice so farre as I can.

"The King hitherto contynueth at faukland wth a small nomber purposinge to remoue to sterlinge, about th' end of this monthe. And he pretendeth to be amynded to come to Edinburgh soone after to prepaire all bills and matters for the parliament. Aboute wch things the King & his counsellours haue had late consultacon. But I am informed that the parliament shalbe proroged for some tyme, excepte that these counsellours shall see Marre, Boyde, Glames, & others departed oute of the Realme, and that they shalbe able to carie their matters by pluralitie of votes. Besydes yt is thought that the cheife cause of the King's returne to Edenburgh, is both to put the Castell of Edenbr' in th'ands of Arren (who is said to seeke the same earnestlie), and also to make Sir William Stewarde (Arren's brother) Provost of Edenburgh, a matter so full of difficultie, as I think it shall either soone be leafte of, or ells not attempted.

"Th' erle Marshall is entred into the lands of the Lard of Bowgwhane (now passed vnto Carlyle) by assignment of the said Lard, and Huntley woulde gladlie haue possession thereof, for wch purpose, I heare that the King was moued to chardge Marshall to render those lands vpp to the King, but no such chardge is yett granted. On Tuesdaie last, Arkynlesse, comptroler of the King's house, was sent to Argile, to will Marre to prepare & prouide to departe out of the Realme before the first of Nouember next, duringe wch tyme of his aboade, he must not remaine in Argile, who is directed to see Marre accomplish the King's pleasure. And Argile is desiered to come to the courte at the King's cominge to Stryuelinge.

Marre, by his seruaunte, presented his supplicacon to the King on Mondaye last, prayinge his fauour to him selfe and his frends. Butt the supplicacon was not ouer redd. Argile and Marre ar at horne for default of payment of their taxes granted to the King. But the horninge is not yett registred, and therby the matter is of small effecte.

Boyde prepareth to departe into ffrance within xxtie daies, But his ould yeares & the wynter approchinge may happelie staye him.

223* remaineth in his owne house gretlie disquietted & complayninge that he knoweth not wch waie to addresse himselfe, in case as he nowe standeth. Hereon one of his frends aduised him to Δ ⊦ ⟡ ✕ 8 7Λ6 6 ◇ Z 8 6 8 ◇– 8 ‡ Ø ⟡.† whereby he might recouer couer trust and good opynion of his former ffrends.

John Maitlande hath obtayned the King's signature for the office of Secretarie. It is said Collonell Stewart is in good hope to haue the benefice of Dunfermlinge, or at lest the lands lyinge ner to Pettenweme.

Huntley hath gotten the King's graunte of th escheite of the Abbott of Pasley & the benefyce. And Crayford hopeth to haue Cambuskynnethe.

The foure Erles, viz., Arren, Huntley, Crayford, & Montrose were appointed to have lysted and kept at Courte at theire owne charges fyfty horsmen a peece. And one hundreth footemen

* E. of Rothes (in pencil), † h a n g e s i r r o b e r t m e l i n (in pencil).

should haue bene added to the garde vnder Collonell Stewart. But lacke of money hath defeite th establishment of these forces, w^ch^ shall neuertheless be provided in case monie can be gotten.

"Arren and Collonell Steward, contendinge for th' escheate of gilbert Dicke (to be forfeyted for the killinge of a man that still liueth), ar reconsiled by the mediation of William Steward, Capten of Dumbarton, who laied before them a huge masse of inconveniences growinge by discord betwixt them, wherevppon Arren went to Collonell Steward, franklie reconsiled him selfe to him w^th^ promise of all frendshippe.

"I haue harde that Loughleuen is alredie put to the horne. The rest I committ to the reporte & sufficiency of this bearer, my seruaunte, John Aleyn, to whom I praye you geue credite. Thus w^th^ myne humble duetie I pray god have you in His blessed kepinge.

"Edenbr', the xix^th^ of September, 1583.

"Your Honour's at comandment,

"ROBERT BOWES."

[Addressed] "To the Right Honorable S^r^ ffrancis Walsingham, knight, Principall Secretarie "to Her Ma^tie^, and one of Her Honorable Priuie Counsell."

---

*State Papers, Scotland. Elizabeth, Vol. 41, No. 26. Sept. 20, 1586.*

"My verie guid lord ester my maist hartlie commendatiounes. I am to craue your Lo. pardoun yat since my cuming out of france I have not wrettin to your Lo. gifing your honour thanks of the greate courtesseis and fauour schewed to me at my being in that countrey q^r^off I will never be forgetfull bot salbe ever willing to acquyte the same to my pouer. And now hering yat I am accompted be Mr. Welsinghame (in ane lre send be him to my Lo. my brother) ane double dealler, in sua far as I professed my selff outwartlie ane freind to Hir Ma^tie^ of Ingland, and that as he allegis ye contrairie y^r^off is maid manifest to the world be Intercepted lres of Charles Pagettis, whairin is mentioned the forsaiking of my relligioun and becuming ennemie to that estait. As to my relligioun, it is weill knawin in all pairtes quhaire I haue bene quhat relligioun I have professed since my tender yeires. As for Hir Ma^tie^ and estait, I have never meinnit Inuartlie bot yat quhilk I have professit outwartlie, q^lk^ is that I acknawlegit my selff moir oblist to Hir Hieness and countrey than to ony uther foran prince and natioun in the world, and yat in respect of the benefites I did ressaue of Hir Ma^tie^ and dyuers Hir subiectis during the tyme of my exile. As to these calumneis conteint (as is allegit) in the said Charles Pagettis lres to my dishonour as is meinnit, gif he or ony uther will accuis me thairoff, I will answer thairto as it becumeth me in honour. But seing vpon the occasioun of Intercepted lres but farther tryall or wretting y^r^off to my selff be the said Mr. Welsinghame befoir he haid dreaittet me sua dishonourablie in his lre foirsaid I can not bot think me evill entreatted be him quho being estemit ane wyse man juges sua raschelie befoir ony guide pruif or certaintie. Sua be this his dealling hes he maid manifest his evill will w^t^hout ony just occasioun ever offerit be me. Thairfore as your honour at all tymes hes schewin your selff my speciall freind now maist effecteouslie will I request your Lo. to do me that honour as to impart this my lre to Hir Hienes craveing Hir Ma^tie^ in my name to consave no sinistrous nor wrong opinioun of me vpoun sua slight occasiounes as ether ar Intercepting of fals letters or misreportis of evill willaris, for I hoipe Hir Ma^tl^ is myndfull how wprytlie I behauvit my selff in Hir countrey, and takis god to witnes yat nether than nor sensyne haue I practissed ony thing preiudiciall to Hir Ma^tie^ or estait, and wald be sorie that the meinnest w^t^in Hir Hienes countrey sould haue Just occasioun to accuis me of Ingratitude, lat be of double dealling, bot mekle moir Hir Ma^tie^. Sua luikeing for your Lo. answer w^t^ sic expeditioun as your Lo. lays[r] and occasioun will best permit. Committ your Lo. to the protectioun of god. Frome Paslay, the tuentie of September, 1586.

"Your Lo. assuirit at all pouer,

"CLAUD HAMILTON.

[Addressed] "To the richt Honorable
My Verie guid lord
my Lo. burlie Thesaurir
to Hir Ma[tie]."

---

## G.

## BULLS REFERRING TO THE ABBEY OF PAISLEY, FROM THE VATICAN MSS., BRITISH MUSEUM.

*British Museum, Additional MSS., No. 15,369, fo. 247. (Dated 24th Nov., Ao. 14—A.D. 1329.)*

"Anno XIV. Epist. 153.

"Ex Regesto litterarum Comunium Johannes XXII.

"Dilecto filio Roberto de Caral, Clerico Sancti Andree."

"Sedis Apostolice providentia circumspecta personarum qualitatem considerans illos non immerito munificentia sue liberalitatis attollit, quibus ed id propria virtutum merita fidedignorum adiuta testimoniis conspicit laudabiliter suffragari. Volentes itaque tibi meritorum tuorum intuitu, super quibus apud nos laudabiliter commendatis gratiam facere specialem beneficium ecclesiasticum consuetum abolim Clericis secularibus assignari, cuius fructus, redditus, et proventus si cum cura Viginti, si vero sine cura fuerit decem Marcharum Argenti iuxta taxationem decime valorem annuum non excedant ad dilectorum filiorum. . . . Abbatis et Conventus Monasterii de Passeret oordinis Eluniacen Glasguen Diocessis collationem, provisionem, presentationem, vel quamvis aliam dispositionem comuniter vel divisim pertinens, si quod vacat ad presens, vel quamprimum vacaverit, quod per te vel procuratorem tuum ad hoc legittime constitutum infra unius mensis spatium postquam tibi vel eidem procuratori de illius vacatione constiterit, duxeris acceptandum, conferendum tibi post acceptationem huiusmodi cum omnibus iuribus et pertinentiis suis donationi Apostolice reservamus. Districtuis inhibentes eisdem Abbati et Conventus ne de huiusmodi benefitio interim etiam ante acceptationem eandem, nisi postquam eis constiterit, quod tu vel procurator predictus Benefitium ipsum nolueritis acceptare disponere quoquomodo presumant, ac decernentes ex nunc irritum et inane si secus super hiis a quoquam quavis auctoritate scienter vel ignoranter attemptari. Non obstantibus si aliqui super provisionibus sibi faciendis de beneficiis ecclesiasticis in illis partibus speciales vel generales, dicte sedis, vel Legatorum eius litteras impetrarint etiam si per eos ad inhibitionem reservationem et decretum vel alias quomodolibet sit processum quibus omnibus preter quam auctoritate nostra huiusmodi beneficia expectantibus te in assecutione dicti beneficii volumus anteferri, set nullum per hoc eis quo ad assecutionem aliorum beneficiorum preiudicium generari. Seu si eisdem Abbati et conventui vel quibusvis aliis comuniter vel divisim ab eadem sit sede indultum quod ad receptionem vel provisionem alicuius minime teneantur, et ad id compelli non possint quodque de beneficiis ecclesiasticis ad eorum collationem, provisionem, seu presentationem, aut quamvis aliam dispositionem coniunctim vel separatim spectantibus nulli valeat provideri per litteras apostolicas non facientes plenam et expressam ac de verbo ad verbum de indulto huiusmodi mentionem, et qualibet alia dicti Sedis indulgentia generali vel speciali cuiuscumque tenoris existat per quam presentibus non expressam vel totaliter non insertam effectus huiusmodi nostre gratie impediri valeat quomodolibet vel differi, et de qua cuiusque toto tenore habenda sit in nostris litteris mentio specialis. Nulli ergo, &c., nostre reservationis, inhibitionis, et constitutionis infringi, &c. Datum Avinion viii. Kalendas Decembris Anno Quartodecimo.

In e. m. dilectis filiis Johanni Wischard Glasguen et Guillelmo Gomorii Laudonie Sancti Andree in Scotia Archidiaconis ac Galtero de Twynam Canonico eiusdem Glasguen ecclesiarum salutem.

Sedis Apostolice providentia circumspecta, &c., usque mentio specialis. Quocirca mandamus quatinus vos, vel duo, aut unus vestrum per vos vel alium, seu alios huiusmodi reservationis nostre tempore vacabat, vel extunc vacavit, aut quamprimum illud vacare contigerit prefato. Roberto vel procuratori suo eius nomine post acceptationem predictum cum omnibus iuribus et pertinentiis suis auctoritate nostra conferre et assignare curetis, inducentes ipsum vel dictum procuratorem pro eo in corporalem possessionem beneficii, ac iurium et pertinentiarum predictorum, et defendentes inductum, sibique facientes de ipsius beneficii fructibus, redditibus, proventibus, iuribus, et obventionibus universis integre responderi. Non obstantibus omnibus supradictis. Aut si eisdem Abbati et Conventui, vel quibusvis aliis comuniter vel divisim a Sede sit indultum predicta, quod interdici suspendi vel excomunicari non possint per litteras Apostolicas non facientes plenam et expressam ac de verbo ad verbum de indulto huiusmodi mentionem. Contradictores per censuram ecclesiasticam, &c. Datum ut supra."

---

*British Museum, Additional MSS., No. 15,383, fo. 570.* [*Dated 8th August, 1494, A.D. sic, but read 1459.*]

"Anno I., pag 40 to.

"Pius II.

"Dilecto filio Petro tituli Sancti Marci Presbitero Cardinali salutem, &c.

"Decens reputamus et congruum ut Sancte Romane Ecclesie Cardinales quos Altissimus et tamquam precipuas et sublimes ipsius Ecclesie columnas prerogativa sublimavit honoris, quique in Ecclesiarum omnium earumdemque personarum defensione nec non conservatione libertatum et iurium studia laboresque indesinenter impendant ab eisdem Ecclesiis et personis suscipiant in suis oportunitatibus relevamen. Cum itaque nos de persona nuper dilecti filii Henrici Grethon Monaci Monasterii Dumfermlie ordinis Sancti Benedicti Sancti Andree Diocesis Monasterio Sancti Mereni de Pasleto ordinis Eluniacen Glasguen Diocesis in Scotia a Monasterio principali eiusdem ordinis dependenti per obitum Thome illius ultimi Abbatis regimine destituto de consilio fratrum nostrorum Apostolica auctoritate providerimus preficiendo cum illi in Abbatem prout in nostris inde confectis litteris plenius continetur. Nos tibi ut expressarum onera que te vigisti de necessitate subnec oportet facilius supportare valeas de alterius subventionis auxilio providere specialemque gratiam facere volentes motu proprio non ad tuam vel alterius pro te nobis super hoc oblate petitionis instantiam sed de nostra mera liberalitate pensionem annuam trecentorum florenorum auri de Camera super fructibus, redditibus et proventibus dicti Monasterii Sancti Mereni qui duorum milium et quingentorum florenorum sterlingorum secundum comunem extimationem valorem annuum ut accepimus non excedunt quoad vixeris vel procuratori tuo legittimo per Henricum predictum et successores suos interim dicti Monasterii Sancti Mereni Abbates existentes pro una in Domini nostri Jesu Christi et reliqua medietatibus in Sancti Johannis Baptiste Nativitatum festivitatibus annis singulis in Romana Curia persolvendam auctoritate apostolica reservamus, constituimus et assignamus decernentes eosdem Henricum et successores Abbates prefatos ad solutionem faciendam pensionis huiusmodi iuxta concessionis, constitutionis, et assignationis predictarum tenorem fore efficaciter obligatos ac volentes et eadem auctoritate statuentes quod quilibet ex Henrico et successoribus abbatibus prefatis quotiens in aliqua festivitatum earumdem vel saltem infra triginta dies tunc immediate sequentes tibi pensionem tunc debitam huiusmodi non persolverit cum effectu lapsis diebus eisdem excomunicationis sententiam eo ipso incurrat a qua donte tibi de eadem pensione integre fuerit satisfactum, seu alias tecum vel cum dicto. Procuratore super hoc amicabiliter concordatur preter quam in mortis articulo absolutionis beneficium ab huiusmodi excomunicationis sententia nequeat obtinere. Si vero per sex menses dictos Triginta dies immediate sequentes huiusmodi excomunicationis sententiam animo quod absit sustinuerit indurato ex tunc lapsis mensibus eisdem regimine et administratione dicti Monasterii privatus existat ipsumque Monasterium vacare censeatur eo ipso non obstantibus Constitutionibus et ordinationibus Apostolicis, nec non Monasterii Sancti Mereni et alterius a quo dependet et ordinis predictorum iuramento confirmatione Apostolica vel quavis alia firmitate roboratis statutis et consuetudinibus contrariis quibuscumque sint si Henrico et Successoribus Abbatibus prefatis vel quibusvis aliis comuniter vel divisim a Sede Apostolica sit [in]dultum quod ad solutionem vel prestationem alicuius minime teneantur, et ad id compelli non possint per litteras Apostolicas non facientes plenam et expressam ac de verbo ad verbum de indulto huiusmodi mentionem et qualibet alia dicte Sedis indulgentia generali vel speciali cuiuscumque tenoris existat per quam presentibus non expressam vel totaliter non insertam effectus huiusmodi gratie impedire valeat quomodolibet vel differri, et de qua cuiusque toto tenore habenda sit in nostris litteris mentis specialis. Nulli ergo &c., nostre reservationis, constitutionis, assignationis, decreti, voluntatis, et statuti infringere, &c. Si quis autem, &c. Datum Mantue Anno, &c., MCCCCLVIII., Sexto Idus Augusti Pontificatus nostri Anno Primo.

"Venerabilibus fratribus Veronen. et Sancti Andree, ac Paretin. Episcopis salutem, &c.

"Hodie dilecto filio Petro tituli Sancti Mareti pensionem annuam Trecentorum florenorum auri de Camera super fructibus, redditibus, et proventibus Monasterii Sancti Mereni de Pasleto ordinis Eluniacen Glasguen Diocesis sibi quoad viveret vel Procuratori suo legittimo per dilectum filium Henricum Grethon et successores suos interim tenentes dicti Monasterii abbates in certis festivitatibus in Romana Curia sub excomunicationis et privationis penis annis singulis per solvendam reservavimus, constituimus, et assignavimus decernentes Henricum et Successores prefatos ad solutionem pensionis huiusmodi fore efficaciter obligatos, ac statuentes prout in nostris inde confectis litteris plenius continetur. Quocirca fraternitati vestre per Apostolica scripta mandamus quatinus vos vel duo, aut unus vestrum si et postquam dicte littere vobis presentate fuerint per vos vel alium seu alios faciatis auctoritate nostra pensionem predictam eidem Cardinali vel pro eo procuratori prefato iuxta reservationis constitutionis, et assignationis ac decreti huiusmodi continentiam atque formam integra persolvi et assignari. Et nichilominus quemlibet ex Henrico et Successoribus prefatis quem huiusmodi excomunicationis sententiam vobis incurrisse constiterit, et quotiens super hoc pro parte dicti Cardinalis fueritis requisiti tam diu in Ecclesiis Dominicis festivisque diebus dum maior inibi populi multitudo ad divina convenerit excomunicatum publice nunciatis, et faciatis ab aliis nunciari, ac ab omnibus artius evitari, donec et quousque ipsi Cardinali de huiusmodi pensione tunc debita fuerit integre satisfactum ipsique excomunicati ab eadem sententia meruerint absolutionis beneficium obtinere. Non obstantibus omnibus que in dictis litteris volumus non obstare. Seu si Henrici et Successoribus predictis vel quibusvis aliis comuniter vel divisim a Sede Apostolica sit indultum quod interdici, suspendi, vel excomunicari non possint per litteras Apostolicas non facientes plenam et expressam ac de verbo ad verbum de indulto huiusmodi mentionem. Contradictores per censuram ecclesiasticam appellatione post posita compescendo. Datum Mantue Anno, &c., MCCCCLXXXXIIII Sexto Idus Augusti Pontificatus nostri Anno Primo (1459)."

---

*British Museum, Additional MSS., No. 15,385, fo. 27.*

"Anno II., pag. 86.

"Paulus II.

"Venerabili fratri Patricio.

"Episcopo Sancti Andree, salutem, &c.

"Romani Pontificis providentia circumspecta Ecclesiis et Monasteriis universis que etiam de facti detenta vacationis incomoda deplorare noscuntur et detentorum eorumden cavillosis subterfugiis oportunis declarationibus, et decreto fueris, et gubernatorum utilium fulciantur pretidio prospicit diligenter et personarum ecclesiasticarum presertim pontificali dignitate preditarum in necessitatibus providere prout in Domino salubriter conspicit expedire. Dudum siquidem quondam Thoma Carwer Monacho tunc Abbate Monasterii Mireni de Pasleto Cluniacen ordinis Glasguen Diocesis regimini et administrationi dicti Monasterii Presidente fe : re : Pius Papa II. predecessor noster provisionem ipsius Monasterii cum vacaret dispositioni sue reservavit decernens irritum et inane si secus super hiis per quoscumque quavis auctoritate scienter ignorantur contigeret attemptari. Et deinde Monasterio per obitum ipsius Thome qui extra Romanam Curiam diem vite sue clausit extremum abbatis regimine destituto idem predecessor de persona dilecti filii Henrici tunc Monachi Monasterii de Dunfermlyn ordinis Sancti Benedicti Sancti Andree Diocesis ipsi Monasterio sic ut prefertur vacanti providit, ac pensionem annuam trecentorum florenorum auri de Camera super fructibus, redditibus et proventibus dicti Monasterii nobis qui tunc Cardinalatus tituli Sancti Marci fungebamur ad supportandum onera Cardinalatus quoad vitam duceremus in humanis vel procuratori nostro legittimo per dictum Henricum et successores suos ipsius Monasterii Abbatis pro tempore gerentes annis singulis in certis terminis, et loco tunc expressis apostolica auctoritate reservavit, constituit, et assignavit decernens Henricum et successores predictos ad solutionem pensionis huiusmodi iuxta reservationis, constitutionis, et assignationis predictarum tenorem et continentiam nobis faciendam fore efficaciter obbligatos, ac volentes, et eadem auctorite (*sic*) statuentes, quod illi ex Henrico et successoribus predictis qui in aliquo eorumdem terminorum, vel saltem infra triginta dies tunc immediate sequentes pensionem ipsam tunc debitam non persolveret cum effectu, lapsis diebus eisdem sententiam excomunicationis incurreret a qua donec nobis vel procuratori nostro prefatò de pensione huiusmodi tunc debita integre satisfactum, aut alias nobiscum, vel cum dicto procuratore desuper amicabiliter concordatum foret absolvi non posset preterquam in mortis articulo constitutus. Si vero per sex menses dictos triginta dies immediate sequentes sententiam ipsam animo sustineret indurato, ex tunc mensibus eisdem decursis regimine et administratione dicti Monasterii perpetuo privatus existeret ipsumque Monasterium ex tunc vacare censeretur certisque dedit indicibus in mandatis, quatinus Henricum et Successores predictos, ad integram solutionem pensionis huiusmodi, iuxta reservationis constitutionis, et assignationis, ac decreti predictorum continentiam nobis faciendam compellerent, et si eis Henricum et successores predictos excomunicationis sententiam incurris constitisset quotiens pro parte nostra forent requisiti tamdiu in ecclesiis Dominicis et festivis aliis diebus dum maior populi inibi multitudo conveniret ad divina excomunicatos publice nuntiarent, et ut tales ab hominibus evitari facerent donec nobis de pensione huiusmodi tunc debita integre satisfactum foret, ipseque excomunicatur ab huiusmodi sententia meretur absolutionis beneficium obtinere prout in quibusdam litteris euisdem predecessoris desuper confectis plenius continetur, et deinde orta inter nos et dictum Henricum super dicta pensione ad quam nobis solvendam iuxta earumdem litterarum continentiam nos dictum Henricum tunc teneri et illam recusasse ac litteras predictas et processus desuper de more decretos debite executioni demandare impedivisse, et impedire, et propterea dictam sententiam incurisse excomunicationis dicebamus, dictus vero Henricus e contra se ad dictam pensionem solvendam non teneri pretendebat materia questionis. Idem predecessor causam huiusmodi non obstantem quod ad Romanam Curiam legitime devoluta, et apud eam de iuris necessitate tractandam non esset dilecto filio nostro tunc Sancte Prisce Zamoreñ nuncupato imediate vero tituli Sancti Laurentii in Damaso presbitero cardinali cum potestate eundem Henricum in opido Brugis Tornaceñ Diocesis et alibi etiam per edictum cum communicatione quod si non compareret ad ulteriora etiam declarationem eundem Henricum incurrisse penam privationis predicte in dictis litteris contentam procederetur citandi audiendam, et sine debito terminandam. Et postquam idem Johannes Cardinalis dicto Henrico ut prefertur cum huiusmodi comminatione per edictum citato recte procedens eundem Henricum excomunicationis sententiam in eisdem litteris contentam propter non solutionem ipsius pensionis predicte incurrisse et illa irretitum fore per suam sententiam que nulla provocatione suspenta in rem transiverat indicatum declaraverat eundem Henricum in expressis legittimis in dicta causa pactis nobis nichilominus condemnando per nos et eidem predecessori exposito quod dictus Henricus non solum per citationem per Edictum sed et sibi per dilectum filium Johannem de Kalfur Procuratorem nostrum vigore presentium litterarum nobis ut premittitur concessarum, et processuum desuper habitorum in presentia plurimorum clericorum, et secularium factas requisitiones et instantias spernere non erubuit excomunicationis, et alias sententias, censuras, et penas etiam in litteris, et processibus huiusmodi contentas damnabiliter incurrendo quibus sic legatus per tres annos et ultra citra tamen quinquennium insordescens, et illa sustinens animo indurato divinis officiis palam et publice se immiscuit in contemptum non modicum Sedis apostolice, et Sacrosancte Romane Ecclesie ac pernisciosum exemplum plurimorum idem predecessor eidem Johanni Cardinali, ut causam quam nos super declaratione incursus pena privationis predicte monere intendebamus, audiret et sine debito terminaret successive commisit, nosque postquam idem Johannes Cardinalis in causa huiusmodi ad decretum citationis nondum executioni de mandato processerint, nosque dicto predecessore sicut Domino placuit rebus humanis exempto divina favente clementia eidem predecessori in Apostolatus officio successimus ad instantiam dilecti filii Magistri Antonii de Eugubio procuratoris fiscalis pro interesse Camere Apostolice propter nonnulla dicti Johannis impedimenta causam huiusmodi dilecto filio Nicolas tituli Sancte Cicilie, presbitero Cardinali reassumendam, et ulterius audiendam, et sine debito terminandam etiam commisimus, qui Cardinalis sicut accepimus in causa huiusmodi rite procedens sententiam per quam eundem Henricum regimine et administratione dicti Monasterii premissorum occasione fuisse, et esse privatum, et penam privationis huiusmodi incidisse, et dictum Monasterium vacasse, et vacare declaravit, ipsumque Henricum a dicti Monasterii, et bonorum eiusdem detentione, et occupatione amovendum fore, et amovit eundemque Henricum in expensis condemnando, que nulla provocatione suspensa similiter in rem transivit indicatam promulgavit. Cum autem secundum premissa dictum Monasterium per privationem, et declarationem huiusmodi vacare noscatur nosque dudum cum a nonnulis revocaretur indubium, an de Monasteriis et aliis beneficiis ecclesiasticis per eundem predecessorem dispositioni sue reservatis, et tempore sui obitus vacantibus aliquis preter Romanum Pontificem ea vice disponere potuisset sive posset ad huiusmodi ambiguitatis dubium submovendum cum similis interpositione decreti declaraverimus Monasteria, et alia Beneficia huiusmodi per eundem predecessorem dispositioni sue ut prefertur reservata, et tempore sui obitus vacantia per huiusmodi reservationem remansisse, et remanere affecta nullumque de illis preter Romanum Pontificem ea vice disponere potuisse, sive posse, ac propterea nullus de provisione ipsius Monasterii hac vice se intromittere potuerit, sive posset reservatione, declaratione, ac decretis obsistentibus supradictis. Nos eorundem Johannis et Nicolai Cardinalium processus, et sententias huiusmodi ac aliorum premissorum omnium tenores et compendia, ac si de verbo ad verbum insererentur presentibus pro expressis habentes, eaque, et prout illa concernunt omnia et singula in instrumentis et actis ac scripturis desuper confectis contenta quecumque ex certa nostra scientia de venerabilium fratrum nostrorum sancte Romane Ecclesie Cardinalium consilio, et assensu auctoritate apostolica approbates, et confirmantes pariterque et scientia ac potestate similibus omnes et singulos defectus tam iuris quam facti supplentes necnon Constitutionem quandam eiusdem predecessoris aut qua litteras suas super preservatione pensionum per eum reservatarum super fructibus beneficiorum ecclesiasticorum quibusvis personis absque consensu eius qui habet pensionem solutam expedire prohibuit in pensionibus Romane Ecclesie Cardinalibus motu proprio ipsius predecessoris reservata locum non habuisse, et observari non consuevisse nec debere et pretextu defectus consensus predicti Henri qui Monasterium predictum si gravem pensionem existimabat cum tali onere acceptare minime debebat in expeditione dictarum litterarum forsan non prestiti infringi aut annulari non potuisse nec posse, ac quascumque appellationes restitutiones nullitatum propositiones, et integrum restitutiones aliosque recursus et querellas interpositas, et interponendas, nec non commissiones si que desuper forsan emanassent vel in futurum emanarent nullas et invalidas fuisse, fore, et esse decernentes pariter et declarantes, ac causas si que si cet super predictis, et eorum occasione pendeant ad nos harum serie advocantes et lites penitusque extinguentes dictoque Henrico super regimine et administratione prefatis de consilio, et scientia predictis perpetuum silentium imponentes, ac tam dicto Monasterio ne longe vacationis exponatur incomodis de gubernatori utili, et ydones secundum cor nostrum per quem circumspecte regi et salubriter dirigi valeat que tibi ut statum tuum iuxta Pontificatis exigentiam dignitatis teneri valeas de alicuius subventionis auxilio providere volentes sperantesque quod dictum Monasterium per tue circumspectionis industriam regetur utiliter et prospere dirigetur, ac grate in spiritualibus, et temporalibus suscipiet incrementa Monasterium predictum sive per privationem et declarationem huiusmodi sive aliquovis modo, aut ex alterius cuiuscumque persona vacet et ex quavis causa illius dispositio ad Sedem Apostolicam specialiter vel generaliter pertineat cum omnibus irribus et pertinentiis suis tibi per te quoad vixeris, et una cum ecclesia tua Sancti Andree in Scotia cui preesse dinosceris et Prioratu de Petenwen tue Diocesis, ac quibuscumque aliis Beneficiis ecclesiasticis que auctoritate apostolica detines in titulum et commendam, et quorum omnes fructus, redditus, et proventus pro expressis habentes tenendum, regendum, et gubernandum de eorumdem fratrum consilii commendamus curam regimen, et administrationem ipsius Monasterii in eisdem spiritualibus, et temporalibus plenarie committendo, Volumus autem quod propter commendam huiusmodi solitus Monacorum et ministrorum numerus in dicto Monasterio non minuatur, quodque debitis et consuetis ipsius Monasterii ac dilectorum filiorum Conventus eiusdem supportatis oneribus de residuis illius fructibus, redditibus, et proventibus libere disponere, et ordinare valeas prout ipsius Monasterii Abbates qui pro tempore fuerunt disponere potuerunt seu etiam debuerunt alienatione tamen quorumcumque bonorum immobilium, et pretiosorum mobilium ipsius Monasterii tibi penitus interdicta Quocirca fraternitati tue per Apostolica scripta mandamus quatinus curam, regimen, et administrationem huiusmodi per te sic gerere studeas solicite fideliter et prudenter quod dictum Monasterium utili gubernatori, et fructuoso administratori gaudeat se commissum tuque preter eterne retributionis premium, nostram, et dicte Sedis Benedictionem et gratiam uberius prosequi merearis. Insuper dilectis filiis Electo Trasonem, et Priori Ecclesie

Sancti Andree, ac Abbati Monasterii de Londoris Sancti Andree Diocesis per Apostolica scripta mandamus," &c., &c.

"Datum Rome apud Sanctum Marcum Anno Incarnationis Dominice Millesimo quadringentesimo septuagesimo quinto,* quarto Idus Januarii [10th January] Pontificatus nostri Anno secundo [1466]."

---

*British Museum, Additional MSS., No. 15,385, fo. 194.*

"An. V., pag. 283.

"Ex lib. 7. Secretarum.

"Paulus II., &c., dilecto filio Henrico Crehtom Monacho Monasterii Sancti Merini de Pasleto Cluniacen ordinis, Glasguen diocesis, salutem, &c.

"Romani Pontificis copiosa benignitas de statu personarum quarumlibet Ecclesiasticarum, et Monasteriorum regiminibus preficiendarum attente considerans ad ea libenter intendit, per que persone predicte Ecclesiis, et Monasteriis sibi commissis salua conscientia, et cum animi quiete ualeant salubriter prouidere. Cum itaque nos Monasterio Sancti Merini de Pasleto Cluniacen ordinis Glasguen diocesis Abbatis regimine destituto de persona tua intervolamus hodie prouidere, teque illi preficere in Abbatem, nos capientes ut curam regimines, et administrationis dicti Monasterii ualeas salubriter exercere, te ab omnibus, et singulis, excommunicationis, suspensionis, et interdicti, aliisque Ecclesisticis sententiis, censuris, et penis a Jure, uel ab homine latis, si quibus forsan quomodolibet innodatus existis, quoad hoc dumtaxat, ut prouisio et prefectio de persona tua eidem Monasterio per nos, ut premittitur, faciende suum debitum sortiantur effectum, auctoritate Apostolica tenore presentium absoluimus, et absolutum fore censemus, omnemque inhabilitatis, et infamie maculam, siue notam per te quomodolibet forsan contractam penitus abolemus, tecumque super irregularitate, si quam sententiis, et censuris ligatus huiusmodi missas, et alia diuina officia, non tamen in contemptum clauium, celebrando, seu illis te immiscendo incurristi dispensamus. Nulli ergo, &c., nostre absolutionis, abolitionis, et dispensationis infringere, uel ei ausu temerario contraire. Si quis autem, &c. Datum Rome apud Sanctum Petrum anno Incarnationis Dominice millesimo, quadringentesimo sexagesimo septimo [octavo], tertio Kalendas Martii [27th February], Pontificatus nostri anno quinto [1468-9]."

---

*British Museum, Additional MSS., No. 15,385, fo. 196.*

"An. V., pag. 283.

"Ex. lib. 7. Secretarum.

"Paulus II., &c., dilecto filio Henrico Chrehtom Abbati Monasterii Sancti Merini de Pasleto Cluniacen ordinis Glasguen diocesis, salutem, &c.

Inter solicitudines uarias quibus assidue premimur, illa potissimum pulsat, ex excitat mentem nostram, ut status Ecclesiarum, et Monasteriorum omnium cure nostre diuina prouidentia commissorum spiritualiter, et temporaliter augeatur, quodque illis, que suis destitute Pastoribus, uacationis incommoda deplorare noscuntur, tales ministros preficere studiamus, per quorum regimen Ecclesie, et Monasteria ipsa utiliter et salubriter ualeant gubernari. Sane commenda Monasterii Sancti Merini de Pasleto Cluniacen ordinis Glasguen diocesis, ex eo quod Venerabilis frater noster Patricius Episcopus Sancti Andree, qui Monasterium ipsum in commendam huiusmodi una cum Ecclesia Sancti Andree, cui preesse dinoscitur, obtinebat *hod* in manibus nostris hodie sponte, et libere cessit, nosque cessionem ipsam duximus admittendam cessante

* This underlined, and 1465 written, in pencil, in the margin.

dicto Monasterio adhuc eo modo, quo tempore eidem Episcopo facte commende huiusmodi vacabat vacante. Nos dicto Monasterii vacatione alias etiam fide dignis relatibus intellecta, illiusque uerum, et ultimum uacationis modum, etiam si ex illo generalis resultet reseruatio, presentibus pro expressa habentes, et ad prouisionem dicti Monasterii celerem, et felicem, ne Monasterium ipsum longo uacationis exponatur incommodis, paternis, et solicitis studiis intendentes post deliberationem, quam de preficiendo eidem Monasterio personam utilem, et etiam fructuosam cum fratribus nostris habuimus diligentem, demum ad te Monachum dicti Monasterii, ordinem ipsum expresse professum, et in Sacerdotio constitutum, cui de Religionis zelo, litterarum scientia, uite ac morum honestate, spiritualium prouidentia, et temporalium circumspectione, ac aliis multiplicium uirtutum meritis apud nos fide digna testimonia perhibentur direximus oculos nostre mentis quibus omnibus debita meditatione pensatis, de persona tua nobis, et eisdem fratribus ob tuorum exigentiam meritorum accepta eidem Monasterio de dictorum fratrum consilio auctoritate Apostolica prouidemus, teque illi preficimus in Abbatem, curam, regimen, et administrationem ipsius Monasterii tibi in spiritualibus, et temporalibus plenarie committendo, in illo, qui dat gratias, et largitur premia confidentes, quod dextera Domini tibi assistente propitia, prefatum Monasterium per tue circumspectionis industriam prospere dirigetur, et grata in eisdem spiritualibus, et temporalibus suscipiet incrementa. Volumus autem, quod bona immobilia, et preciosa mobilia dicti Monasterii nullatenus alienare presumas, alioquin penas in quadam Constitutione per nos edita contentas eo ipso incurras. Quocirca discretioni tue per Apostolica scripta mandamus, quatinus impositum tibia Domino onus regiminis dicti Monasterii suscipiens reverenter, sic te in eius cura salubriter exercenda exhibeas solicitum, quod ipsum Monasterium gubernatori prouido, et fructuoso administratori gaudeat se commissum, tuque preter eterne retributionis premium, nostram et dicte sedis benedictionem et gratiam exinde uberius consequi merearis. Datum Rome apud Sanctum Petrum, anno Incarnationis Dominice millesimo, quadringentesimo sexagesimo octauo tertio Kalendas Martii, Pontificatus nostri, anno quinto.

Simila modo dilectis filiis Conuentui Monasterii Sancti Mereni de Pasleto Cluniacen ordinis Glasguen diocesis, salutem, &c.

Hodie Monasterio uestro, eius commenda, ex eo quod Venerabilis frater noster Patricius Episcopus Sancti Andree, qui Monasterium ipsum ex concessione et dispensatione Sedis Apostolice in huiusmodi commendam obtinebat, in manibus nostris sponte et libere cessit, nosque cessionem ipsam duximus admittendam cessante, dictoque Monasterio adhuc eo modo, quo tempore eidem Episcopo facte commende huiusmodi uacabat, uacante de persona dilecti filii Henrici de Crehtom ipsius Monasterii Abbatis de Venerabilium fratrum nostrorum consilio duximus auctoritate Apostolica prouidendum, preficiende ipsum dictu. Monasterio in Abbatem, curamque et administrationem illius sibi in spiritualibus, et temporalibus plenarie committendo, prout in nostris desuper confectis litterio plenius continetur. Quocirca discretioni uestre per Apostolica scripta mandamus, quatinus eidem Henrico Abbati, tamquam Patri, et Pastori animarum uestrarum humiliter intendentes, et exhibentes sibi obedientiam, et reuerentiam debitas, et devolas, eius salubria monita, et mandata suscipiatis humiliter, et efficaciter adimplere curetis. Alioquin sententiam, quam idem Henricus Abbas rite tulerit in rebelles, ratam habebimus, et faciemus, auctore Domino, usque ad satisfactionem condignam inuiolabiliter obseruari. Datum Rome apud Sanctum Petrum anno Incarnationis Dominice millesimo, quadringentesimo sexagesimo octauo, tertio Kalendas Martii, Pontificatus nostri anno quinto.

Simili modo dilectis filiis uniuersis Vassallis Monasterii Sancti Merini de Pasleto Cluniacen ordinis Glasguen diocesis, salutem, &c.

"Hodie Monasterio Sancti Merini de Pasleto Cluniacen ordinis Glasguen diocesis, eius commenda, ex eo quod Venerabilis frater noster Patricius Episcopus Sancti Andree, qui Monasterium ipsum ex concessione, et dispositione Sedis Apostolice in huiusmodi commendam obtinebat, in manibus nostris sponte et libere cessit. Nosque cessionem ipsam duximus admittendam cessante, dictoque Monasterio adhuc es modo, quo tempore eidem Episcopo facte commende huiusmodi uacabat, uacante, de persona dilecti filii Henrici Crehtom ipsius Monasterii Abbatis de Venerabilium fratrum nostrorum consilio duximus auctoritate Apostolica prouidendum, preficiendo ipsum dicto Monasterio in Abbatem, curamque et administrationem illius sibi in spiritualibus, et temporalibus plenarie committendo, prout in nostris desuper confectis litteris plenius continetur. Quocirca uniuersitati uestre per Apostolica scripta mandamus, quatinus cumdem Henricum Abbatem suscipientes denote, et debita honorificentia prosequentes, ei fidelitatem solitam, nec non consueta seruitia, et iura, sibi a nobis debita exhibere integre studeatis, alioquin sententiam, sine penam, quam idem Henricus Abbas rite tulerit, seu statuerit in rebellis, ratam habebimus, et faciemus auctore Domino, usque ad satisfactionem condignam inuiolabiliter obseruari. Datum Rome apud Sanctum Petrum, anno Incarnationis Dominice, &c., *ut supra*.

"Simili modo carissime in Christo filio Jacobo Regi Scotorum illustri salutem, &c.

"Hodie Monasterio Sancti Merini de Pasleto Cluniacen ordinis Glasguen diocesis, eius commenda, ex eo quod Venerabilis frater noster Patricius Episcopus Sancti Andree, qui Monasterium ipsum ex concessione, et dispensatione Sedis Apostolice in huiusmodi commendam obtinebat, in manibus nostris sponte, et libere cessit, nosque cessionem ipsam duximus admittendam, cessante, dictoque Monasterio, adhuc eo modo, quo tempore eidem Episcopo facte commende huiusmodi uacabat, uacante, de persona dilecti filii Henrici Crehtom ipsius Monasterii Abbatis de Venerabilium fratrum nostrorum consilis duximus auctoritate Apostolica prouidendum, preficiendo ipsum *in* dicto Monasterio in Abbatem, curamque et administrationem illius sibi in spiritualibus et temporalibus plenarie committendo, prout in nostris desuper confectis litteris plenius continetur. Quocirca Serenitatem tuam Regiam rogamus et hortamur attente, quatinus eumdem Henricum Abbatem una cum Monasterio suo commisso regimini habens pro diuina, et Apostolice Sedis reuerentia propensius commendatum, sic eidem te exhibeas fauore Regio beniuolum, et in opportunitatibus gratiosum, quod idem Henricus Abbas per auxilium tue gratie in commisso sibi Monasterii prefati regimine utilius proficere ualeat, tuque proinde consequaris premia felicitatis eterne, ac nos etiam Celsitudinem tuam Regiam condignis possimus in Domino laudibus commendare. Datum Rome apud Sanctum Petrum anno Incarnationis Dominice millesimo, quadringentesimo sexagesimo octavo, tertio Kalendas Martii [27th February], Pontificatus nostri anno quinto [1468-9]."

---

*British Museum, Additional MSS., No. 15,385, fo. 204.*

"An. V., pag. 284.

"Ex lib. 7, Secretarum.

"Paulus II., &c., dilecto filio Henrico Crehtom Abbati Monasterii Sancti Merini de Pasleto Cluniacen ordinis, Glasguen diocesis salutem, &c.

"Cum nuper Monasterio Sancti Merini de Pasleto Cluniacen ordinis, Glasguen diocesis tunc Abbatis regimine destituto de persona tua nobis, et fratribus nostris ob tuorum exigentiam meritorum accepta de fratrum eorumdem consilio auctoritate Apostolica duxerimus prouidendum, proficiendo te illi in Abbatem, prout in nostris inde confectis litteris plenius continetur, nos ad eaque ad tue commoditatis augmentum cedere ualeant, fauorabiliter intendentes, tuis supplicationibus inclinati, tibi, ut a quocumque malueris Catholico Antistite gratiam et communionem Apostolice Sedis habente munus benedictionis recipere ualeas, ac eidem Antistiti, ut munus predictum auctoritate nostra impendere libere tibi possit, plenam et liberam concedimus tenore presentium facultatem. Volumus autem, quod idem Antistes, qui tibi prefatum munus impendit, postquam tibi illud impenderit, a te nostro, et Ecclesie Romane nomine fidelitatis debite solitum recipiat iuramentum, iuxta formam iuramenti, quod te præstare contigerit, nobis de uerbo ad uerbum per tuas patentes litteras tuo sigillo signatas per proprium Nuncium quantocius destinare procures. Datum Rome apud Sanctum Petrum, anno Incarnationis Dominice millesimo CCCCLXVIII°. Kalendis Martii, Pontificatus nostri anno quinto."

---

## H.

### REPLEGIATION AS EXERCISED IN SCOTLAND, PARTICULARLY IN CONNECTION WITH THE COURT OF THE ABBOT OF PAISLEY. BY JOHN STUART, ESQ., LL.D., SEC. S.A. SCOT.*

In the early Celtic period of our history, when the population was divided into numerous tribes, each of these had its brehon or judge, who administered justice to the men of the clan, and the men of one tribe could not have been called to answer a suit in the court of another.

When the feudal system had for some time been established in Scotland, it became a custom for the Crown to grant to the great barons large tracts of land with the right of regality, in which was included the right of courts of exclusive jurisdiction. The same rights were also granted to the bishops and abbots, as owners of lands, at an early period. Thus in the reign of Alexander the First a royal charter invested the Abbey of Scone with the right of a court, and of giving judgment by combat, by iron, or by water, and with an exclusive jurisdiction over all the men of the abbey lands.

This power enabled the abbot, and all who enjoyed like rights, to vindicate their rights even in the King's courts, so as to exclude the interference of the royal judges.

The act by which the lord of regality enforced his rights in a foreign court to which his man had been summoned was called replegiation. It is recognised, and the proceedings under it are described, in one of our early codes of law known as Quoniam Attachiamenta, or the Laws of the Barons (§ ix. Acts, Vol. I. p. 284), where it appears that a claimant was bound to find surety that the law would be fully followed out in the court of his own lord to which he desired to be remanded. This surety or broch was known in our old law as a culrach.

The most remarkable instances in our history of replegiation are connected with the Law of Clan Macduff. Of this law, which seems to have combined the early Celtic idea of privilege of blood or kinship with that of girth annexed to a cross, we learn from Wyntoun that the black Priest of Wedale, the Thane of Fife, and the Lord of Abernethy, were the three judges.

We have two records exhibiting to some extent the working of the "Law." In the earliest we see Sir Alexander Moray, who was called before the King's justiciaries in the year 1391, accused of the slaughter of William of Spaldyne, protesting that he had already been indicted for the crime, and repledged to the Law of Clan Macduff by Robert, Earl of Fife; and in the next, when Hugh Arbuthnot and his accomplices were accused of the murder of John Melville, Laird of Glenbervy, we find by that by a writ dated 1st September 1421, the Stewart of Fife received them to the benefit of the Law of Clan Macduff, they finding three sicker burroise or

* The lamented author of this valuable paper kindly permitted me to use it. It was given at the Society of Antiquaries, March 8th, 1875, and is recorded in their transactions.

sureties, the first that they were law-worthy, the second that they were entitled to the privilege, and the third that they should "fulfil the lawes as the law will."

It thus happened that the barons or ecclesiastics who had received their lands with the right of regality, rescued, not only from the courts of other barons but from the royal courts, any of their men who happened to be cited into these foreign courts.

We have an early example of the exercise of this right in a case where in 1299 Sir John Comyn, Earl of Buchan, then Royal Justiciar of Scotland, was holding a court beside the Castle of Aberdeen in the place called the Castlesyd, and sitting in judgment on Adam de Fisto and four others, dwelling on the lands of Tulielt at Tarves, the property of the Abbot of Arbroath, accused of theft, when John of Pollok, the Abbot's steward, appeared and reclaimed the accused as men of the said Abbot, dwelling within his regality of Tarves, to the Abbot's court of said regality. (Chart. of Arbroath, p. 164.)

Other instances occur among the papers of the Earl of Airlie. Thus on 17th November, 1537, David, Abbot of Arbroath, granted authority to William Graham of Fintray and others to appear before the King, Council, or Great Justiciary at Edinburgh, and repledge James, Lord Ogilvy of Airly, the Abbot's tenant and indweller of the lands of Balischen and Brekko, and the said lord's tenants and subtenants, to the courts of the regality of Arbroath. And on 8th April, 1543, Cardinal Beaton, as Commendator of Arbroath and the convent thereof, empowered James, Lord Ogilvy of Airly, to repledge an indweller in the regality of Arbroath from the Governor of Scotland or Justiciaries of the same, he having been cited to Edinburgh by warrant of the Queen.

The following extract from the registers of the burgh of Dundee, dated 6th June 1521, affords an instance of the proceedings under a claim of replegiation :—

Curia balliuorum burgi de Dunde tenta in pretorio euisdem per Willelmum Gubit et Andream Barry balliuos, vj^{to} die Junii anno etc. quingentessimo xxj^{o}.

Quo die comperit Robert Meill and interit James Spalding to the instance of Margaret Moncur lady Telling as he that was souerte anent the clame of ane oix perseuit be hir on the said James and Hew Maxwell of Telling, his maister askit hym to be replegit to his court and it was fundyn be ward of court that he suld haf him replegit, and this efter the allegatione of Maister Daue Robertson forspekare for the said Margaret that he suld nocht be replegit, and the said lard offerit James Cunningham colreth and cautione for the said James that the said Margret suld haf ane day and court affixit to hir and iustice to be ministerit, the quhilk the said Maister David refusit.

In process of time many abuses arose from the exercise of these conflicting jurisdictions, and various enactments were made in Parliament for their regulation and restraint. In 1449, it was ordained that when regalities came into the hands of the king (as by ward) they should be holden as royalty, and that justice should be dispensed by the king's judges so long as they remained in the king's hands. In 1455 it was provided that all regalities then in the king's hands should be annexed to the royalty, and that in time to come no regalities should be granted without deliverance of Parliament (Acts, Vol. II. pp. 36, 43.) Two years later, another ordinance provided that all privileges of regalities should be kept according to their foundations, and "gif ony lorde haifande regalite abuse it in prejudice of the kingis lawis and brekin of the cuntre that they be punyst be the king and be the law as efferis." (Ib. p. 49.)

One of the documents exhibited by Mr. Martin, and which has suggested the foregoing remarks, is an Instrument of Replegiation by Robert, Lord Semple, bailie of the Abbot of Paisley, of a man of his regality accused before the king's judges, and then tried and acquitted in the court of the abbot. The process must have been a frequent one, but instances of the instruments themselves are comparatively rare :—

Robertus dominus Symple balliuus ac Justiciarius Regalitatis de Pasleto ac Abbatis et conuentos eiusdem Vniuersis et singulis ad quorum noticias presentes litere peruenerint salutem Noueritis quod comparens coram nobis Arthurus Maxwell filius Gavinii Maxwell in Badyland perprius summonitus coram Justiciario supreme Domine nostre regine suisve deputatis ad subeundum jura die decimo quarto mensis Nouembris anno Domini millesimo quingentesimo quinquagesimo sexto apud Edinburgh pro arte et parte crudelis necis et interfectionis quondam Joannis Sklater filii Roberti Sklater in Meikilriggis prout in literis supreme Domine nostre regine latius continetur Quo die dictus Arthurus coram magnifico viro Joanne Campbell de Lundye milite Justiciario deputato nobilis et potentis domini Archibaldi comitis Argadie domini Campbell et Lorne Justiciarii Generalis prescripti comparuit et ad curiam justiciarie dicte regalitatis ad subeundum jura pro dicto asserto crimine cautione inuenta pro justicia ministranda coram nobis replegiatus. Et dies decimus quintus mensis Januarii proxime sequens ad huiusmodi effectum prefixus fuit, Quo die ipso Arthuro in facie judicii coram nobis comparente nostram curiam in defectu acti adiornalis vsque ad diem duodecimum mensis Februarii proxime sequentem continuauimus Quo die adueniente comparens coram nobis dictus Arthurus in dicta nostra curia Justiciarii dicte regalitatis de Paslay perprius indictatus et summonitus vigore prefatarum literarum demum replegiatus ut premittitur et nunc accusatus et calumniatus pro arte et parte crudelis necis et interfectionis dicti quondam Joannis Sklater asserte commisse per eundem in mense vltimo elapso. Quamquidem necem et calumpniam Idem Arthurus in facie Judicii omnino denegauit et per condignam assisam quietus inde factus fuit penitus et immunis. Et hoc omnibus et singulis quibus interest notum facimus per presentes. In cuius rei testimonium sigillum meum proprium vnacum mea subscriptione manuali presentibus est affixum apud Paslay die duodecimo mensis Februarii anno Domini millesimo quingentesimo quinquagesimo sexto.

ROBERTUS LORD SYMPYLL, balze.*

---

## L.

## NOTES RELATIVE TO PAISLEY ABBEY FROM THE ACTS OF THE PARLIAMENTS OF SCOTLAND—(RECORD EDITION).

Vol. 1. p. 95—A.D. 1233.—Process by the Abbot and Convent before Papal delegates for recovery of the land of Monachkennaran, which they claimed as belonging to the Church of Kilpatrick.

A digest of the evidence offered is given, with the sentence of the delegates (Laurentius et Ricardus de Carric et de Cunigham decani et Allanus magister scolarum de Are), addressed to William, Bishop of Glasgow, finding the Abbot's case proven, and the defender, Gilbert, the son of Samuel of Renfrew, liable in costs. A letter to King Alexander follows (page 97), praying him to extend the

* See for various instances of replegiation, see "Pitcairn's Trials," I. 382.

secular arm to punish Gilbert for contumacy in not yielding. The Abbot's name is not given.

Vol. I. p. 425—A.D. 1250—1st June.—An Act of Alexander III., empowering the Abbot and convent to repair their fish-stake in the Leven, near Dunbarton. William, Bishop of Glasgow, is one of the witnesses.

" p. 441—A.D. 1289.—The Abbot one of these present at Queen Margaret's Parliament at Briggeham. His name not mentioned.

" p. 495—A.D. 1364—13th January.—The Abbot present at a General Council of David II. at Perth. His name not given.

Vol. II. p. 56—A.D. 1440—10th August.—Abbot Thomas present at a General Council at Stirling under James II.

Suppl. p. 22—A.D. 1450—7th May.—The Abbot (not named) appointed one of the auditors of a General Council under James II. at Perth.

Vol. II. p. 46—A.D. 1456—19th October.—At Edinburgh, the Abbot (not named) chosen to sit on Committee of Causes and Complaints. (James II.)

" p. 91—A.D. 1468.—At Edinburgh, the Abbot (not named) chosen "in the Articles." (James III.)

" p. 93—A.D. 1469—21st November.—At Edinburgh, the Abbot (not named) in Parliament. (Do.)

" p. 98—A.D. 1471—6th May.—At Edinburgh, Do. Do.

Suppl. p. 30—A.D. 1464-5.—The Abbot (not named) chosen among those to be with the King at Berwick during the meeting at Newcastle regarding the truce, with full power to advise as to the same. (Do.)

Vol. II. p. 102—A.D. 1471-2.—18th July, at Edinburgh, the Abbot (not named) in Parliament. (James III.)

" p. 114—A.D. 1476—10th July.—At Edinburgh, the Abbot (not named) chosen among others to negotiate as to the Royal Marriage. (Do.)

" p. 115—A.D. 1478—6th April.—At Edinburgh, the Abbot (not named) absent from meeting of Parliament. (Do.)

" p. 120—A.D. 1478-9—1st March.—At Edinburgh, the Abbot (not named) present in Parliament. (Do.)

" p. 124—A.D. 1479—4th October.—At Edinburgh, Do. Do.

" p. 133—A.D. 1481—11th April. Do. Do.

" p. 136—A.D. 1481-2—18th March.—Abbot absent.

" p. 142—A.D. 1482—2nd December.—Abbot present.

" p. 145—A.D. 1482-3—1st March.—At Edinburgh, the Abbot (not named) in Parliament, chosen to sit in Committee of Parliament. Do. Do.

" p. 146—A.D. 1483—27th June. Do. Do.

" p. 166—A.D. 1484—17th May. Do. Do.

" p. 167—A.D. 1484-5—21st March. Do. Do.

" p. 180—A.D. 1487-8—11th January. Do. Do.

" p. 199—A.D. 1488—7th October. Do. Do. (James IV.)

" p. 200—A.D. 1488—7th October.—Chosen to sit in Committee.

Vol. II. p. 212—A.D. [illegible]—17th October.—Abbot (not named) chosen in committee.

,, p. 229—A.D. 1491—6th February. Do. among those chosen "in the Articles."

,, p. 239—A.D. 1503-4—11th March. Do. present in Parliament.

,, p. 281—A.D. 1513—26th November.—Robert, Abbot of Paisley, in Parliament. (James V.)

,, p. 285—A.D. 1524—16th November.—The Abbot (not named) in Parliament.

Do. Do., and served in Committee of Causes.

,, p. 288—A.D. 1524-5—15th February. Do. Do.

,, p. 292—A.D. 1525—10th July. Do. Do.

,, p. 294—A.D. 1525—17th July. Do., among those chosen to remain with King from Hallowmas to Candlemas.

,, p. 339—A.D. 1535—10th June.—Abbot (not named) in Parliament.

,, p. 355—A.D. 1540—10th December. Do. Do.

,, p. 425—A.D. 1543—8th June.—At Edinburgh, the Abbot (not named) in Parliament. (Queen Mary.)

,, p. 427—A.D. 1543—4th December.—John, Abbot of Paisley, a Commissioner for holding Parliament, and chosen "in the Articles." (Do.)

,, p. 439—A.D. 1543—12th December.—John, the Abbot, one of the curators of Hamilton of Finnart. (Do.)

,, p. 443—A.D. 1543—15th December.—The Abbot in Parliament.

,, p. 445—A D. 1544—7th November.—John, the Abbot, treasurer, a Commissioner *ut supra.*

,, p. 446— Do. Do., chosen "in the Articles."

,, p. 448—A.D. 1544—24th November.—John, the Abbot, a Commissioner *ut supra.*

,, p. 595—A.D. 1545—26th June.—The Abbot signs a Bond with France against England. The signature is simply "Paslay."

,, p. 594—A.D. 1545—26th June.—The Abbot in convention at Stirling.

,, p. 595—A.D. 1545—28th June. Do. Do.

,, p. 595—A.D. 1545—29th June. Do. Do.

,, p. 454—A.D. 1545—28th September.—At Linlithgow, John, the Abbot, commissioner *ut supra.*

,, p. 455—A.D. 1545—1st October.—The Abbot in Parliament.

,, p. 465—A.D. 1546—6th April.—John, the Abbot, Commissioner *ut supra.*

,, p. 597—A.D. 1546—10th June.—At Stirling, the Abbot (not named) in the Lord Governor's Council.

,, p. 467—A.D. 1546—30th July.—The Abbot (not named) in Parliament.

,, p. 469—A.D. 1546—7th August.—John, Bishop-elect of Dunkeld [see next entry], one of the Commissioners for holding Parliament.

,, p. 480—A.D. 1546.—16th August.—John, the Abbot of Paisley, having been nominated by Queen Mary to the Bishopric of Dunkeld, according to the privilege belonging to the Queen and her predecessors to nominate to vacant sees, and having sent an intimation to the Pope, who in virtue thereof granted him the Bishopric, and having been opposed by Robert Crichton, provost of St. Giles, who produced an alleged decree from the Pope that the promotion of John was conditional upon himself being appointed Bishop of Ross, failing which he was himself to be Bishop of Dunkeld, whereas the Queen had promoted her secretary, David Painter, to the Bishopric of Ross—this alleged decree declared contrary to the royal privilege.

Vol. III. pp. 47, 54—A.D. 1658—18th August.—Claud Hamilton, Commendator of Paisley, son of the Duke of Chatelherault, with many others, forfeited for supporting Queen Mary and resisting the King at Langside. Their dignities, names, and memory to be perpetually extinct, their goods and lands to be confiscated, &c., &c. (James VI.)

,, pp. 125, 129—A.D. 1579—20th October. Do. Do., for the murder of the Regent Murray, withholding the Castles of Hamilton and Draffer, and for the murder of the Earl of Lennox.

,, p. 137—*Eo die.*—His posterity disinherited.—Cap. 5.

,, p. 159—A.D. 1579—11th November.—The Earl of Morton and others to search for and to administer justice to him.—Cap. 43.

,, p. 166—*Eo die.*—His feuars and tacksmen to enjoy their lands notwithstanding his forfeiture.—Cap. 49.

,, p. 195—A.D. 1581—30th October.—The Abbot of Paisley (not named) in Parliament. (James VI.)

,, p. 326—A.D. 1582—19th October.—The Abbot (Commendator) in Convention at Holyrood.

,, pp. 332, 336, 344—A.D. 1584—21st August.—William, Commendator of Paisley, forfeited, along with Earls of Angus and Mar.

,, p. 378.—A.D. 1585—10th December.—Claud, Commendator of Paisley, in the Privy Council. Cap. 10.

,, p. 383—A.D. 1585.—Claud restored from forfeiture, and receives the benefit of the pacification. Cap. 21.

,, p. 396—A.D. 1585.—A special Act passed in his favour and his domestics, restoring them. Cap. 26.

,, p. 413—A.D. 1585.—His forfeited lands excepted from a ratification to the Commendator of Pittenweem. Cap. 53.

,, p. 427—A.D. 1587—13th June.—The Abbot (not named) in Parliament.

,, p. 432—A.D. 1587.—The Temporalities of Paisley excepted from an Act annexing the temporalities of benefices to the Crown. Cap. 8.

,, p. 444—A.D. 1587.—The Commendator of Paisley (not named) in the Privy Council. Cap. 19.

,, p. 481—A.D. 1587.—An Act in favour of Claud, Commendator of Paisley, declares him titular of the parsonage and vicarage of Cambuslang. Cap. 79.

,, p. 482—A.D. 1587.—Act ratifying the Abbacy to his son Claud, with reservation of his own liferent. Cap. 80.

,, p. 523—A.D. 1588—4th April.—The Abbot of Paislay (not named) in Convention at Holyrood.

,, p. 587—A.D. 1592.—The infeftment of the temporality of Paisley exempted from the general Act of annexation. Cap. 90.

Vol. IV. p. 476—A.D. 1612.—"The Lord of Paisley" to convene his feuars at Paisley for apportioning a tax. (James VI.)

„ p. 583—A.D. 1617. Do. Do., (Do.)

„ p. 602—A.D. 1621. Do. Do., (Do.)

Vol. V. p. 171—A.D. 1625. Do. Do., (Charles I.)

„ p. 214—A.D. 1630.—"The Lord of Paisley" to convene his feuars at Paisley for apportioning a tax. (Charles I.)

„ p. 17—A.D. 1633. Do. Do., (Do.)

„ p. 106—A.D. 1633.—The teinds, parsonage, and vicarage of the parish church and "parochin of Inverwick," in the constabulary of Haddington, noted as having once been part of the patrimony of the Abbacy of Paisley, and as since to have pertained to James, Earl of Abercorn. (See Act in favour of James Maxwell.)

Vol. VI., Part II. p. 246—A.D. 1649—8th March.—Protest by the Earl of Abercorn that he be not affected by the Act anent the vassals of kirk lands, because the temporality of Paisley Abbey had never been annexed to the Crown, but expressly reserved in the Act of 1587; that the Act of 1633 proceeded on an agreement with him that he should have right to the superiority of the small vassals, and that he had disponed to the King the superiority of the great vassals, and he now prays that his rights of superiority, property, and regality be not prejudiced. (Charles II.)

Vol. VII. 533—A.D. 1665.—"The Lord of Paisley" to convene his feuars at Paisley for apportioning a tax. (Charles II.)

---

## J.

## IMMORALITY OF ABBOT HAMILTON.

This seems to have been too well proved. John Knox says—"While the inconstant governor was sometimes dejected and sometimes raised up, the Abbot of Paislay, who before was called 'chaster than ony madyn,' began to show himself. . . He took possession of his Ernes' (kinsman's) wife, the Lady Stanehouse. The woman is and has been famous, and is called Lady Gilston. Her Ladyship was holden always in property; but how many wives and virgins he has had since that time in common the world knows albeit not all; and his bastard birds bear some witness." This is the testimony of an enemy, but documents are extant which go to corroborate the Reformer's statement. There are letters of legitimation under the Great Seal granted to John and William Hamylton, bastard sons of Grizzel Sempill, daughter of Robert, Master of Sempill, dated 9th Oct., 1551. When William, third Lord Crichton, was slain by Robert, the father of this woman, he was acquitted by the governor 10th Sept., 1550, and it is said by Pitscottie that "he escaped punishment by means of John Hamilton, Bishop of St. Andrews, brother to the governor, who entertained the Lady Stenhouse, commonly called Lady Gilston, daughter of this Lord Robert Sempill, as his concubine." She died four years after the Archbishop. It has been said that the Archbishop was married to Lady Gilston before he was in holy orders, and had a son who legally succeeded him. The Abbot must have been in holy orders before she was born, for he was of an equal age with Lord Sempill. Any who care to investigate this unsavoury subject will find it discussed at length in Gordon's Scotichronicon, Vol. II., pp. 290, 291, 292.

---

## K.

### THE ASSEDATIOUN OF YE KIRKS OF PASLAY AND LOYTWINZOK TO MAST JOHNE STEWARD FOR XIX ZERIS.

"Be it kende till all men be yir pnt lers We Jhonne be ye permissioun of God Abbot of Paslay w[t] consent and assent of our convent chapter till haif set and in assedatioun lattyn and be ye tenor of yir or pnt lers settis and in assedatioun lattis tyll our familiar servand master Johne Steward in Paslay and his aires executoris and assignais factou[rs] and substitutis qlk sal be of na greter degre yan hym self is All and haill our vicarage and alterage of our Kirks of Paslay and Loy[t] Winzok w[t] all yair pertinants and causualiteis Togidder w[t] our corne myll of Paslay in y[e] Sedyll w[t] all sukconis profettis causualiteis and pertinants pertenand y[r]to or may perteine for all y[e] tyme space terms and zeirs and dayis of nynten zeirs togidder next & immediate following ye Entress of the said Master Johne his airis executoris and assignais factoris and substitutis of ye alterage and vicarage of ye saidis Kirkis of Paslay and Loy[t] Winzok w[t] yar pertinants The quhilkis entress of ye said Mast Johne or his airis executoris or assigniays in and to the saidis vicarages and alterages of Paslay and Loy[t] Winzok w[t] yar pertinants beand at the fest of ye Apostols Philip & Jacob callit belten in ye zeir of God ane thousand fyve hundrethe & fourty zeiris And ye Entress of our foresaid Corne Myll of Paslay to be at lamass in ye zeir of God ane thousand fyve hundretht & fourty zeiris. And yair efter to be peciable bruikit & possessit be ye said Mast Johne his airis executoris and assignias factoris and substituts for all ye tyme and terms togidder of nyntene zeiris as said is for ye quhilkis assedations and takis of our saidis alterages and vicarages of Paslay and Loy[t] Winzok w[t] yair pertnantis The said Master Johne Steward his airis executoris assignayis factouris and substitutis sall pay gyf and thankfully deliver till us o[r] officiares at o[r] command or yairntill our successoris zeirly all and haill ye soume of fyve scoir of poundis gude and usuall money of Scotland duyly at tua terms in ye zeir that is to say at ye fest of allhallowmass next following yair entress as for ye first terme and ye fest of ye Apostolis callit beltane imediat yairefter be equall portiones togidder w[t] y[e] ten pundis gude and usual monye of Scotland to be payit zeirly to ye curattis fee of Paslay and alsall conduce & fee y[e] curat of Loy[t] Winzok as he will be servit and pay him his fee zeirly induring ye saidis nyntene zeiris And also the said Master Johne his airis executoris and assignais factoris or substitutes sall pay zeirli for our Corne Myll of Paslay in ye Seedill ys soume of twenty-four pundis gude and usuall money of Scotland at twa usuall terms in ye zeir viz twelf pundis at ye next candilmas following ye entress of ye said Myll and otheris twelf pundis at lammas next yrefter and swa at candlemass and lamass q[lk] the saids nyntein zeirs be completly outrun and our cornes for us and o[r] successoris to be ground at o[r] said Myll rowm fre multure fre and causualtis fre as use and wont of before And failzeand at the said Mast[r] Johne his airis executoris or assignais factoris or substitutis mak thankfull payment till us and o[r] successoris at ye terms abonę writtin or w[t]in thretty dayis yairefter we will for us & o[r] successours yat yis prnt assedatioun and tak expyre in ytself and for ye mair securitie we bind and obliss us o[r] convent abbay successoris and assignais till observe and keip yis o[r] prnt assedation and tak in all pointis and to defend and warrand the said Maste Johne his airis executoris and assignays in peciable bruiking joysing and possedat yir forsaid takis in all points but ony contrary or obstacle of us our factoris or convent abbey or successoris quhatsomever but fraud or gyill or ony cawillatioun till be mowit in ye contrary quhatsoever In witness hereof till yis our prn[t] lers of assedation and tak subscribit w[t] our handis we haif appendit our commoun seil w[t] our supscriptiones at Paslay the twenty-fifth day of November the zeir of God ane thousand & fyve hundretht and thretty-nine zeirs before yir witnesses Mast James Fork vicar of Ruglan Sir Robert Sclater chaplain and Sir John Semisoun not[r].

Thir ar names of the Conv[t] yat hes subscribit yis Prn[t] Assedatione

Johne Abbat of Paslay
David Cant
Wilzam Sclat[r]
Richard Watsoun
Wilzam Leper
John Pade
James Taynne
Robert Morton
Robert Ker
David Brante
Johne Hamilton
Wilzam Lethem
David Mosman
Johne Alex[r]soun
Johne Fork
Johne Sandelandis

# RENTAL OF PAISLEY ABBEY.

---

ASSIDACIO TERRARUM INFRA DOMINIUM DE PASLETO FACTA APUD MONASTERIUM EIUSDEM VLTIMO DIE MENSIS APRILIS, ANNO DOMINI MILLESIMO QUADRINGENTESIMO SEXAGESIMO PER VENERABILEM, IN CRISTO PATREM ET DOMINUM, DOMINUM HENRICUM CRECHTOUN, ABBATEM MONASTERII DE PASLETO, PREDICTI ET WILIELMUM SIMPIL, EIUS BALLIUUM ASSISTENTE EIS VICECOMITE DE RANFREW AC CUM MULTIS ALIIS NOBILIBUS ET GENEROSIS.

*Auchingone, Balrogear cum lez burtreis.*

Assidantur per dominum abbatem, et eius balliuum predictum Johanni Stewart et Alano Stewart, filio suo naturali soluendo. Inde annuatim pro balrogear et bourtreis Lij solidos pecunie et xij denarios, et le bone siluer cum seruicio debito et consueto et dicta, assidacio fit eis coniunctim et diuisim plegius alter alterius.

*Merburn.*

Assidatur Johanni Stewart de bouchan, et dicto Alano Stewart, fratri suo coniunctim et diuisim soluendo Inde annuatim iiij libros, cum xij denariis, pro lez bone siluer ac cum seruicio debito et consueto plegius alter alterius.

*Mosside.*

Assidatur Johanni Stewart, fratri ——— prescripti Johannis Stewart, et filio Johannis Stewart senioris, Soluendo Inde annuatim xviij solidos pecunie, cum xij denariis de lez bonnesiluer necnon cum seruicio debito et consueto.

*Stokbrig.*

Assidatur pro dimedietate Johanni Knok, ex tollerancia matris sui et. Malcolmo Mareschal, suo marito, pro alia dimedietate et elezabeth de dunlop, vidue, quam diu fuerit vidua, soluendo annuatim xxxiiij solidos, iiij denarios, cum lez bonys siluer et seruicio debito et consueto plegius alter alterius. le bon siluer.

*Foulton.*

*Assidatur Johanni Simpile pro vna parte soluendo pro illa parte annuatim xx solidos.

Item, tantum de dicta villa assedatur roberto clidishede ut prius xx solidos.

Item, vna pars dicte ville assidatur maky thomson soluendo ut prius. xiij solidos iiij denarios.

Item, tantum eiusdem ville assidatur Wilielmo michalson, soluendo ut prius xiij solidos, iiij denarios.

* The lines underlined are erased in the original.

Item, vna pars eiusdem ville assidatur henrico brovne soluendo ut prius xxs xiij solidos iiij denarios.

Item, tantum assidatur Wilielmo brovne soluendo Inde annuatim ut prius xx s. xx s xiij s iiij d.

Item, vna pars eiusdem assidatur Johanni simpson soluendo Inde annuatim xl solidos.

Item, alia pars eiusdem ville assidatur Johanni paslay soluendo ut prius xx solidos.

Et statuendum quilibet tenens in dicta villa soluet annuatim quatuor bonys in autumno ij caragia vnum viz. in estate et aliud in hyeme vnam dietam cum harpicis vnam dietam in estate ad fenum anglice adawark of mawyn et quilibet soluit annuatim xij pultrias pro xij denariis cum aliis seruiciis debitis et consuetis plegius alter alterius. le bone siluer.

*Drumgrané.*

Assidatur pro vna parte thome bulle soluendo annuatim xxvij solidos viij denarios.

Item, tantum assidatur petro brovne soluendo inde annuatim ut prius xxvij solidos, viij denarios.

Item, tantum assidatur cristiane hering vidue soluendo Inde annuatim xxvij solidos viij denarios.

Item, tantum assidatur roberto glasfurde soluendo annuatim xxvij solidos viij denarios.

Item, tantum alia pars eiusdem ville assidatur Johanni stephani xxxviij solidos vj denarios.

Item, alia pars assidatur gilberto cochquharn soluendo annuatim xix solidos iij denarios.

Item, alia pars assidatur nicholao de bar soluendo annuatim ut prius xix solidos iij denarios.

Item, alia pars eiusdem assidatur Johanni jok et magistro Wilielmo arthorle soluendo annuatim ut prius xxv solidos viij denarios et statuendum quod tenentes in dicta villa soluunt annuatim viij duodecim pultrias pro quibus recipiunt viij solidos etiam soluent cariagios ut prius et quilibet duodena quatuor dietas in autumno cum seruicio debito et consueto.

Item, vna pars assidatur Roberto androwson soluendo annuatim xxvij solidos viij denarios.

pro vna introitu
pro tempore vite sue. *Summa.*

Robertus Glasfurde mutauit partem suam cum gylberto cochran ex tollerancia abbatis cum beneuolancia, etc.

*Lymbede Inde pecunie xl solidos.* viij s.

*Auchinch.*

Assidatur Jacobo tat inde annuatim liij solidos iiij denarios cum xiij pultriis quatuor dietis in autumno et 1 dieta cum harpicis et 1 dieta cum tonsura feni et cum seruicio et cariagio debitis et consuetis. xij denarios.

*Blaxton.*

In manibus abbatis pro grange inde pecunie xx solidos cum pultriis et seruicio debito et consueto.

*Fergusle Inde pecunie vj libras cum seruicio. Alia dimedietas non assidatur.*

Assidatur inde vna dimedietas vidue Matilde de crag Inde pecunie iij libras cum cariagiis et seruicio debito et consueto. ij s.

*Quhitcruk Inde pecunie xvj solidos cum seruicio.*

*Mekilriggis.*

Assedatur Johanni massoun Wilielmo roberti Wilielmo bully et thome Roberti soluendo inde annuatim equaliter et per equales portiones vi libras iij duodenas pultrias cum et quilibet duodena quatuor dietis metendum in autumno 1 dieta cum harpicis et 1 dieta aratio cum cariagio et seruicio debitis et consuetis.

Assidatur vna pars Andree tomsoun soluendo Inde annuatim xx solidos cum ix pultrie cum le bonis et seruicio debito et consueto.

Assidatur vna pars patricio tomsoun soluendo inde annuatim xx solidos cum seruicio ut supra. Plegiis alter alterius.

*Bridelande Inde pecunie xx solidos.*

Assidatur roberto hale soluendo Inde annuatim xx solidos cum seruicio debito plegio bricio kerwell. le bonis.

*Corsbar.*

Assidatur Alexandro logan soluendo inde annuatim xxvj solidos viij denarios iiij bollas auenarum xij pult cum quatuor dietis in autumno 1 dieta cum aratro 1 dieta cum harpica cum caragio et seruicio debitis et consuetis. le bonsiluer ij s.

*Corsbar.*

Assidatur make Johnsoun soluendo annuatim xxvj solidos viij denarios iiij bollas auenarum xij pultre cum quatuor dietis in autumno 1 dieta cum aratro 1 dieta cum harpicis cum cariagio et seruicio debitis et consuetis.

*Thomas bar.*

Assidatur bricio kerswell soluendo annuatim xl solidos iiij bollas auenarum xij pult cum le bonis et cariagio ac seruicio debitis et consuetis plegius alter alterius.

*Cariaghil.*

Assidatur Wilielmo henrisoun pro vna parte soluendo inde annuatim xxvj solidos viij denarios.

Item, alia parte Johanni murray inde pecunie xiij solidos iiij denarios.

Item, alia pars assidatur Johanni sclatar soluendo annuatim xiij solidos iiij denarios et dictus Wilielmus debet xij pultrias ac ipse et ceteri. Cum seruicio debito et consueto.

*Thodholm.*

Assidatur Thome luf soluendo inde annuatim ij solidos cum seruicio debito et consueto. le bonsil ij s.

*Todholm ij s.*

Assedatur Johanni Sclatar pro ij solidos et seruicio.

*Thornele.*

Assedatur domino de Haukat soluendo annuatim iij libras vj solidos viij denarios.

*Ruchbank.*

Assedatur patricio merchale soluendo annuatim xxvj solidos viij denarios cum seruicio.

Item, tantum assedatur Johanni merchale soluendo annuatim xxvj solidos viij denarios.

Item, alia pars eiusdem assedatur Andree bronside pro xiij solidos annuatim et ceruicio ut supra et dicti tenentes debent dietas ut prius. Cum cariagio et seruicio debito et consueto plegius alterius. le bonsiluer, iij s.

Assedatur vna pars Emme logan vxori quondam gilscristi lech que wlgaliter dicitur lyhill cum duobus ortis videlicet le craghall et le calsa syde soluendo annuatim xiij solidos.

*Villa de Pasleto.*

Assedatur vna pro vna parte Johanni murray soluendo annuatim xiiij solidos cum dietis ut prius ac eciam cum seruicio debito plegio Wilielmo quhit.

Item, alia pars assedatur alicie quhit soluendo annuatim viij solidos viii denarios cum quatuor dietis cum seruicio debito et consueto plegio Johanni murray. x s vjd. de le bonis.

Item, alia pars assedatur Johanni sclatar soluendo annuatim x solidos cum iiij bonis.

Item, alia pars assedatur gilcristo lech soluendo annuatim xj solidos.

Item, alia pars assedatur emote logane soluendo inde annuatim xj solidos.

*Castelhede.*

Assedatur roberto quhitfurde soluendo annuatim xiij solidos iiij denarios plegio. Johanne de morrauia. Arthuro Smale.

Assedatur arthuro smale pro soluendo annuatim xiij solidos iiij denarios cum cariagio et seruicio debito et consueto.

Assedatur thome mathe pro xiij solidis iiij denariis cum cariagio et seruicio debito et consueto pro terminis quinque annorum.

*Vj Acre de hile.*

Assedatur pro vna parte soluendo Inde annuatim xv solidos cum seruicio debito.

Item, alia pars assedatur.

*Litil Blakfalde.*

Assedatur thome Se—— soluendo inde annuatim vj solidos.

*Grerislande.*

Assedatur eidem thome schelis soluendo annuatim iij solidos.

*Mekil Blakfalde.*

Assedatur Wilielmo quhit soluendo annuatim viij solidos cum seruicio debito.

*Schankis tak.*

Assedatur Johanni halslokis soluendo annuatim xij denarios.

Assedatur Johanni alansoun et Johanni dule soluendo annuatim xviij solidos cum le bone et seruicio.

*Causaende.*

Assedatur de Jonete langshankis soluendo annuatim xviij solidos cum cariagio et debito et consueto seruicio debito et consueto plegio gilcristo lech.

*Terra Roberti Wilson.*

Assedatur Dauid tayt inde pecunie xvj solidos xij pultrie.

*Le Orchart.*

*Le Bernzarde.*

Assedatur thome sche solnendo annuatim iij pultrias.

*Causa.*

Ye causaende assedatur vna pars Johanni dule soluendo inde annuatim ix solidos cum seruicio debito et consueto cum le bonis twnis.

*Le Ochschawsian.*

*Oxschawside.*

Assedatur pro vna parte.

Item, alia pars eiusdem videlicet v acre cum dimedio assedatur Willielmo quhit soluendo annuatim x solidos quatuor le bonys cum seruicio debito et consueto.

Item, vna acra eiusdem assedatur thome schelis inde pecunie vj solidos et iiij bonis cum seruicio debito plegius alter alterius.

Assedatur vna acra arthuro smale soluendo annuatim ij solidos iiij denarios.

*Le Prior Croft.*

Assedatur iiij acre thome schelis soluendo annuatim xvj ix solidos iiij denarios cum le bonis et seruicio debito et consueto.

Item, iiij acre assedatur Wilielmo quhit soluendo annuatim ix solidos iiij denarios.

Item, alia pars assedatur Johanni denby.

*Cochranis tak.*

Item, cochranis tak assedatur domino Johanni wan inde pecunie vj solidos viij denarios.

*Oxschawhede.*

Assedatur Wilielmo quhit soluendo annuatim vj solidos cum seruicio.

*Bladozarde.*

Assedatur Johanni monypenny soluendo annuatim iiij solidos cum quatuor le bonis et seruicio.

*Le Sclatarisbank.*

Assedatur persual steil pro cariagio.

*Ox rane Wode.*

Assedatur dicto persual.

*Durschat side.*

Assedatur thome wilsoun soluendo inde annuatim xx solidos et dictus thomas custodiet siluam et sustentabit fossas circa dictam siluam cum seruicio debito et consueto.

Et post mortem dicti thome assedatur relicte eiusdem Jonete pro firme et seruicio et ut supra.

*Mernis cum lez Kirkhil.*

Assedatur Stephano walace soluendo annuatim xx solidos plegio Johanne bully cum seruicio debito et consueto.

*Kyrklande de Ouer Polloke.*

Assedatur Johanni harbartsoun soluendo annuatim viij solidos cum seruicio debito et consueto plegio Johanne curre.

*Ye Grenlaw.*

Assedatur dimedia pars thome ra luff inde auenarum ice auenarum.

*Le Snawdoun.*

Assedatur Negello lufy Johanni lufy soluendo annuatim xx s xiij solidos iiij denarios cum lez bonis et seruicio consueto plegio alano sunderlande.

Assedatur alia pars allano sunderlande soluendo annuatim xiii s iiij d xx solidos vedua non amota cum seruicio debito.

*Bridelande.*

Assedatur Johanni bulle inde pecunie xxvj solidos viij denarios xij pultrias cum cariagio et seruicio ut alii.

*Terra dominica de Pasleto.*

Assedatur dicto Johanni bulle Inde pecunia iij libros vj solidos viij denarios.

xij d le bonsiluer.

*Le Sedhill cuius una dimedietas.*

Assedatur cristiane de morrauia soluendo inde annuatim x solidos cum cariagio et seruicio consueto.

iij s de bonesiluer.

*Altera pars mior dimedietate.*

Assedatur roberto smytht que olim fuit elezabeth milner inde pecunie iiij solidos plegio se ipso.

*Jakis Zerde.*

Assedatur eidem roberto soluendo inde annuatim iij capones cum cariagio et seruicio debito et consueto plegio se ipso.

Memorandum quod locus qui dicitur nether crosflat. Assedatur thome hectore sculptore pro xx solidis et le quatuor bonys cum sectis curie et aliis omnibus consuetis et debitis quando locum in habitauit quondam Robertus sclatar ea condiciona interueniente quod dictus thomas promptum se prehebit et paratum dictis abbati et conuentui in omnibus concernentibus artem suam sculpture et opus nullius alterius in se recipiet quod ad artem suam spectat sine licentia abbatis et conuentus obtenta et dum ad opus sculpture monasterii per ipsum abbatem et conuentum requisitus fuerit opus sculpture quod in manibus suis habuit omnino dimittat et ad opus monasterii remeabit(?) infra mensem sub pena forisfactura hujusmodi sue assedacionis et sub pena centum solidorum.

ij s de le bonesiluer.

Terre assedate pro auenis.

*Hillintown.*

Assedatur Johanni norvel pro dimedietate soluendo annuatim quatuor celdras auenarum xij pultrias cum iiij bonis 1 dieta cum aratro et 1 dieta cum harpicis necnon et cum cariagio et seruicio debitis et consuetis.

Item, alia pars assedatur andree de morray soluendo annuatim ij celdras quatuor bollas auenarum xij pultrias cum dietis et seruicio ut supra.

Item, alia pars assedatur roberto de burn soluendo annuatim ij celdras quatuor bollas auenarum xij pultrias cum bonis et dictis ut supra plegius alter alterius. iij s de le bo.

*Ricardis bar.*

Assedatur Jacobo thomsoun soluendo iij celdras auenarum cum seruicio debito et consueto plegio Johanne robinsoun. xij d le b.

*Newtoun.*

Assedatur thome lech et R. ber per equales porciones soluendo annuatim iiij celdras auenarum et ij duodecim pultre cum le bonis et seruicio debito et consueto ut prius plegio.

*Erklistoun.*

Assedatur Stephano de brounside Johanni landell juniori et Johanni landell seniori soluendo annuatim ix celdras auenarum absque decimis ij duodecim pultre cum bonis et cariagio ac seruicio debito et consueto plegius alter alterius et plegio pro omnibus Johanne bully. iij s de b.

*Inch.*

Assedatur Johanni achinlose pro vna parte soluendo annuatim xxx bollas auenarum cum seruicio debito et consueto.

Item, tantum assedatur M^cke calban soluendo ut prius xxx bollas cum seruicio consueto plegius alter alterius.

Item, alia pars eiusdem assedatur thome kebil soluendo xx bollas auenarum.

Item, vna pars assedatur Johanni finlawsoun soluendo xxiiij bollas auenarum cum seruicio debito et consueto plegius alter alterius.

Item, vna pars Johanni johnsoun et Wilielmo johnsoun soluendo annuatim iij celdras auenarum plegius alter alterius.

Item, alia pars assedatur Simoni Johanni et Stephano johnsoun soluendo inde annuatim iiij celdras viij bollas auenarum plegius alter.

Item, vna pars assedatur thome johnsoun thome jonson Johanni wilsoun soluendo annuatim ut alii xxiiij bollae auenarum plegio Stephano johnsoun.

Item, vna pars assedatur finlao johnsoun et Johanni soluendo annuatim henrisoun soluendo ut prius ij celdras, ij bollas auenarum cum seruicio ut supra seruicio ut prius plegius alter alterius.

*Neuton.*

Assedatur roberto adamsoun et roberto Johnsoun per equales porciones iiij celdras auenarum ij duodenas pultrias cum bonis cariagio et seruicio ut prius plegius alter alterius.

Et illa pars quam habuit thomas kebil, nunc post mortem ipsius assedatur dauid kebil filio suo pro firma superscripta.

*Berschawan.*

Assedatur Roberto ada dimedia pars et inde ij celdras auenarum.

Item, alia pars vidue relicte Johannis robynsoun et inde ii celdras auenarum.

Assedatur vna pars finlao johnsoun juniori cum vna marcatu terre soluendo annuatim xviij bollas auenarum cum xiij solidis iiij denariis et seruicio debito et consueto, etc. ij s.

*Ofer-galohill.*

Assedatur Johanni bulle soluendo annuatim ij celdras auenarum xii pultrias cum cariagio et seruicio consueto.

*Nedir-galohill.*

Assedatur dicto Johanni bulle soluendo ut prius xx bollas xij pultrias cum seruicio ut supra. ij s de le bonis.

*Le grenlaw.*

Assedatur predicto Johanni bulle soluendo ut supra ij celdras auenarum xij pultrias cum cariagio et ceteris.

Vna pars assedatur thome morsoun soluendo 1 celdram auenarum vj pultrie cum cariagio et seruicio debito, et altera pars assedatur Johanni Morsoun filio eius soluendo ut supra 1 celdram auenarum cum seruicio debito et consueto.

*Lylislande.*

Assedatur thome luff soluendo annuatim xx bollas auenarum cum seruicio debito et consueto. xij d de le bonis ; xij de lilislande.

Terra assedata pro auenis.

*Lyncleyff.*

Assedatur Johanni cochran soluendo annuatim iiij celdras auenarum cum le bonis et seruicio debito et consueto. xij d de le bonis ; de canderene xij d.

Summa terrarum dominij de pasleto in termino pentecostes, videlicet, merborn, fultoun, drumgran, cum mollendino, mernis, estwod, thornle, cariagishill, todholm, corsbar, thomas bar, brydeland, mekylrygis, ferguale, quhytcrux, inche, snadoun, ye mains, brydelande, corsflat, sedhyl, banerakyr, willa de paslay, cum feodafermis cum annuis reditibus, videlicet, hustoun, porterflede, ruglen, renfrew, et glasgu. lv libri xiiij solidi v denarii obolo cum quadrante.

Item, in termino Sancti Martini de eisdem terris et annuis reditibus supradictis. l.vij libri ij solidi v denarii obolo cum quadrante.

Summa totalis cxij lib xvj s ; xi d cum obolo.

*Granis xv^xx petre casei.*

Assedatur vna pars inde Joanni crag soluendo inde annuatim iij^xx petras casei ad tres anni terminos et tres vitulos et x solidos pro aliis tribus vitulis plegio thome bulle.

Alia pars inde assedatur Johanni crag seniori soluendo inde iij^xx petras cassei ad tres anni terminos consuetos et tres vitulos et x solidos pro aliis tribus vitulis plegio thome bull.

Alia pars assedatur Johanni flege soluendo annuatim iij^xx petras casei et iij vitulos et x solidos ad tres anni terminos cum seruicio inde debito et consueto plegio Johnne cochran.

Assedatur vna pars eiusdem Johanni gemmyll soluendo inde annuatim iij^xx petras casei iij vitulos et x solidos cum seruicio inde debito et consueto plegio Roberto Gemmyll.

Assedatur vna pars Wilielmo gemmyll soluendo annuatim iij^xx petras casei et iij vitulos et x solidos cum seruicio inde debito et consueto plegio patre suo.

Anno 1^mo xxvij^o Octobris.

Assedatur vna pars Wilielmo Wilsoun illam terrarum de granis illam quam jam occupat robertus gemmyl post decessum eiusdem intrando soluendo annuatim iij^xx petras casei ad tres anni terminos et tres vitulos et x solidos pro aliis tribus vitulis Et si dictus Wilielmus decesserit ante decessum dicti roberti tunc Johannes Wilsoun frater eius succedit ad locum dicte Wilielmi absque aliquam alia solutione nobis aut successoribus nostris reddendo ante dictus robertus viz. xij vaccas pertinentes abbati et conuentui.

Anno I^mo xx^mo Januarii.

Assedatur vna pars de granis bartholomeo gilmur soluendo annuatim iij^xx petras casei ad tres anni terminos consuetos et tres vitulos et x solidos pro aliis tribus vitulis plegio Wilielmo Vilsoun.

Assidacio terrarum dominii de Glene facta apud monasterium de Pasleto primo die mensis Junii anno Domini et cetero sexagesimo.

*Le West Kers.*

Assedatur Johanni Kirklbode hugoni de Kirklbode pro dimedietate de qua sustentabunt ele esabel de hesilhede matrem suam pro toto tempore vite sue cum suis necessariis sub pena amissionis terrarum suarum et pro alia dimedietate assidatur andree kirkwode soluendo inde annuatim xliij solidos iiij denarios necnon duodecim denarios de le bonesiluer cum cariagio et seruicio debito et consueto plegius alter alterius et quilibet soluet 1 pultre.

*Balrany viz.* **Neder Kers.**

Assedatur Wilielmo Simpil inde pecunie xliij solidos iiij denarios cum le bonesiluer et seruicio plegio seipso.

*Joffrais tak.*

Assedatur Johanni Adamsoun Johanni hore Inde pecunie xxiij solidos iiij denarios cum duodecim denariis pro le bonesiluer 1 pultre pro vno denario cum cariagio et seruicio debito et consueto plegio roberto adamsoun Wilielmo hor seriando, etc.

*Barnklaw.*

Assedatur thome norvel inde pecunie annuatim x solidos cum duodecim denariis de le bonsiluer 1 pultre ut prius cum cariagio et seruicio debito et consueto plegio roberto Johnsoun.

*Mawisbank.*

Assedatur roberto adamsoun Johanni Robertsoun inde pecunie x solidos cum le bonesiluer 1 pultre cum cariagio et seruicio debito et consueto plegio Johanne adamsoun.

*Langstane le.*

Assedatur gilberto Johnsoun soluendo annuatim xv solidos cum le bonesiluer 1 pultre et cariagio ac seruicio debito et consueto plegio thoma alani.

*Le Camhile.*

Assedatur andree or et roberto Johnsoun Johanni Johnsoun Inde pecunie xx solidos cum le bonesiluer plegius alter alterius cum seruicio debito et consueto plegio roberto Johnsoun.

*Lourensbank vna particula de Auchinane.*

Assedatur Wilelmo gilberto Wylsoun Johanni Glen de lourensbank inde pecunie xiij solidos iij denarios 1 pultre cum le bonesiluer et cum cariagio et seruicio debito et consueto plegio roberto Johnsoun.

*Langzarde.*

Assedatur rogero Or thome hor pro vna dimedietate et pro alia dimedietate Wilielmo snap Ricardo Johnsoun in qua supportabit Jonetam logan viduam pro voluntate domini Inde pecuniam xxvj solidos viij denarios cum le bone siluer ij pultre et cariagio ac seruicio debito et consueto plegius alter alterius.

Item, dande dimedia pars loci quam inhabitant Johannes hor thome hor cum seruicio debito et aliis vt supra consuetis assedatur.

*Le aldzarde cum le farhyle.*

Assedatur Willelmo logan Jacobo glen Indo pecunie xxxvj s. xxviij s. cum le bonsiluer 1 pultre cariagio et seruicio ut presens prius plegio rogero Or.

Assedatur vna pars de aldzarde Johanni or pro viij solidos et le bonsiluer cum seruisio debito et consueto plegio Ronaldo Or.

*Le farhill cum le Gavilmos.*

Assedatur Jacobo glen Wilelmo logan inde pecunie xx xij solidos cum bonesiluer pultre cariagio et seruicio ut presens prius plegio Wilelmo logan Jacobo Glen.

*Gilliszarde.*

Assedatur Wilelmo glene Inde pecunie xxiij solidos, cum bonsilu pul cariagio et seruicio ut presens.

Assedatur roberto glene et Wilelmo glene fratribus soluendo annuatim xxiij solidos cum le bonisiluer et seruicio ut presens prius et dictus robertus et Wilelmus non possedebant dictam firman le girszarda donec obitum Villelmi patris eorum.

*Le gerzarde.*

In manibus domini abbatis.

Assedatur alano glene Inde xxx s. bonsiluer pul cariagio et seruicio ut.

Assedatur gilberto Cunyngam pro soluendo annuatim xxx solidos cum le bonesiluer pultre et cariagio.

*Le Vferton cum le brigende.*

Assedatur Wilelmo Glene Inde pecunie iiij libras cum bonesiluer pultre cariagio et seruicio ut presens prius prout continetur in litera assedacionis sibi data. Sub sigillo communi.

*Le bar.*

Assedatur dicto Wilelmo Glene ut prius Inde pecunie iiij libras xiij solidos iiij denarios cum seruicio ut prius plegio seipso.

*Le mylnbanke.*

Assedatur Wilelmo Or et Johanni Or Inde pecunie xxiiij solidos cum seruicio ut prius plegius alter alterius.

*Le litilclooch.*

Assedatur Johanni logan Inde pecunie x solidos cum seruicio pultre et cariagio ut prius ricardo Johnsoun plegio Johanne or Wilelmo Glene.

*Le langcroft.*

Assedatur thome thome Jacobo thome et Johanni thome Elizabeth Houstach Inde pecunie x solidos cum seruico ut presens debito et consueto per equales porciones.

Assedatur vna assedatur thome thomsoun alano alansoun et elesabeth houstach Inde pecunie x solidos cum seruicio debito et consueto etc. per equales portiones.

Assedatur vna assedatur alano alansoun pro vj solidos viij denarios cum seruicio debito et consueto.

Assedatur altera pars elisabeth henrici pro iij solidis iiij denariis cum seruicio debito et consueto.

*Le quensidmur.*

Assedatur dictis thome Jacobo et Johanni et alano soluendo annuatim xl solidos et pascent in estate xxiiij sowmez abbatis plegio alter alterius.

Assedatur vna pars alano alansoun pro xxvj solidos viij denarios cum xvj sowmez in estate domini abbatis plegio manu propria.

Assedatur altera pars elisabeth henrici pro xiij solidis iiij denariis cum viij sowmez in estate et alio seruicio debito et consueto.

*Le Came.*

Assedatur equaliter ro—— alansoun Gilberto Jacobo wilsoun Jamyson Johanni broune alexandro blakburn Inde pecunie iiij libras cum quatuor solidis de le bonesiluer quatuor pultre cariagio et seruicio debito et consueto.

*Bernaucht Wester.*

Assedatur dauid glene inde pecunie xxx solidos cum le boue siluer pultre cariagio et seruicio debito et consueto.

*Molendinum bladorum.*

Assedatur husbandis Inde pecunie xxvj solidos viij denarios cum seruicio ut prius plegio andro kirkwod et Johanne brovne.

*Esterbernacht.*

Assedatur Johanni alansoun et recipet annuatim ad non in primo assedacione.

Memorandum de le bone siluer.

*Tandilmure.*

Assedatur ranaldo or pro dimedietate et alano bride ac Margarete hugoni or vidue pro alia dimedietate soluendo annuatim 1ᵉ petras casei vj stirkis plegius alter alterius.

*Clouchok.*

Assedatur roberto marchande pro dimedietate loci ½ quarterie eiusdem et residuum patricio Kebil Johanni Kebil soluendo annuatim 1ᵉ petras casei vj stirkis plegiis alter alterius.

*Monyabro.*

Assedatur Johanni luf pro dimedietate et thome luf et alano or pro alia dimedietate soluendo Inde annuatim 1ᵉ petras casei vj stirkis plegius alter alterius.

*Auchinane.*

Assedatur simoni luf et wilelmo luf equaliter pro quinque annis soluendo annuatim 1ᵉ petras casei viij stirkis et recipient.

Assedacio terrarum dominii de kilpatrik facta apud monasterium de pasleto penultimo die mensis maii anno domini et cetero sexagesimo quinto pro terminis quinque annorum.

*Wester kilpatrik.*

Assedatur vna dimedietas wilelmo bulle quinta pars hugoni de bronsyde soluendo Inde annuatim iij libras vj s xxx solidos viij denarios cum duobus solidis de le bonesiluer et seruicio debito et consueto.

Item, alia pars assedatur relicte andree lang Inde pecunie xxxiij solidos iiij denarios cum le bonesiluer et seruicio debito et consueto.

Quarta pars assedatur symoni de bra soluendo inde annuatim xxxiij solidos iiij denarios, cum le bonesiluer et seruicio debito et consueto plegius alter alterius.

Item, assedatur quarta pars cum dimedia per vita quarte thome de galbratht inde pecunie.

vj lib. xiij s. iiij d.

*Morislande et huchon lande.*

Assedatur richardo smale soluendo Inde annuatim xxvj solidos viij denarios cum duodecim denariis pro le bonesiluer et seruicio debito et consueto plegio Wilgrewe plegio Johanne betoun.

*Estir kilpatrik.*

Assedatur pro quinta sexta parte Johanni betone Johanni Strabrok soluendo annuatim xxij solidos ij denarios.

Assedatur insuper Wilelmo Johnsoun tantum Inde pecunie xxij solidos ij denarios ut supra.

Assedatur Johanni thomsoun quarta pars ville Inde pecunie xxxiij solidos iiij denarios.

Assedatur mariote vidue alano donaldsoun vna sexta pars ville Inde pecunie xxij solidos ij denarios,

Assedatur Wilelmo greve quarta pars Inde pecunie xxxiij solidos iiij denarios cum le bonesiluer quilibet teneris duodecim denarios cum seruicio debito et consueto plegius alter alterius.

Assedatur vna pars Johanni moris inde pecunie xj solidis i denario cum tertia parte denarii. vj lib. xiij s. iiij d.

Assedatur alia pars Wilelm greff pro xxij solidis ij denariis cum obolo et ceruisio debito et consueto.

*Auchintochan.*

Assedatur Donaldo Wilsoun Inde pecunie xv solidos cum bonesiluer et seruicio consueto.

Assedatur Johanni Werkman alia pars ville soluendo annuatim x solidos cum le bonsiluer.

Assedatur Johanni roberti alia parte ville Inde pecunie x solidos cum le bonsiluer.

Assedatur Jacobo hog alia pars Inde pecunie annuatim xv solidos cum le bonsiluer.

Assedatur Wilelmo forsithe vna pars ville Inde pecunie x solidos cum le bonsiluer.

Assedatur alia pars Johanni Jamesoun Inde pecunie xx solidos cum le bonesiluer et cum seruicio debito et consueto plegius alter alterius.

Assedatur ester d tris Jacobo Kyncad inde pecunie xlv s cum le bonesiluer plegius ut supra alter alterius.

Assedatur vna pars Roberto quhyt Inde pecunie xxv solidos cum ceruisio debito et consueto. iiij lib.

*Duntrachman.*

Assedatur pro vna parte patricio Wilsoun soluendo Inde annuatim xv solidos viij denarios cum le bonsiluer.

Assedatur andre thomsoun vna alia pars soluendo annuatim vij solidos viij denarios cum le bonsiluer.

Assedatur alia pars dicte ville Johanni mur Ricardo Fordon Inde pecunie xv solidos vj denarios cum le bonesiluer.

Assedatur alia sexta pars Johanni thomsoun Inde pecunie xv solidos vj denarios cum le bonsiluer.

Assedatur illa pars quam habuit Wilelmus thomsoun Johanni Wilsoun filio dicti Wilelmi soluendo Inde annuatim xv solidos viij denarios et sustentabit patrem suum pro toto tempore sue sub pena amissionis dicte terre.

Assedatur vna quarta pars Johanni Strabroke soluendo annuatim xxiij solidos iiij denarios cum le bwn et seruicio debito. iiij lib. xiij s. iiij d.

*Wester Cochnoch.*

Assedatur inde Jacobo kincade vna pars soluendo inde annuatim l solidos cum le bonesiluer.

Assedatur alia pars finlao Jamyson Richardo gibsoun Inde pecunie xvj solidos viij denarios cum le bonesiluer.

Assedatur alia richardo Glenra Inde pecunie xxxiij solidos iiij denarios cum le bonsiluer.

Alia pars assedatur roberto alansoun Inde pecunie xvj solidos viij denarios cum le bonesiluer.

Assedatur quinta pars Wilelmo alansoun Inde pecunie xvj solidos viij denarios cum bonesiluer plegius alter alterius. vj lib. xiij s. iiij d.

*Ester Cochno.*

Assedatur vna pars inde Roberto forsytht soluendo annuatim xvj solidos viij denarios cum le bone siluer et seruicio consueto plegio Ricardo fordoun.

Assedatur Inde Johanni thomson pleuchwricht.

Assedatur alia pars Johanni lee Inde pecunie xvj solidos viij denarios cum le bonesiluer.

Assedatur alia pars andree wilsoun Inde pecunie xvj solidos viij denarios cum le bonesiluer.

Assedatur alia pars roberto lee Inde pecunie xxxiij solidos viij denarios cum bonesiluer cuius dimedietas assedatur Wilelmo lee.

Assedatur alia pars Johanni Gibsoun Katrine vidue Inde pecunie xvj solidos viij denarios cum bonesiluer.

Assedatur alia pars quam habuit Marioria vidua de consensu ipsius Johanni donaldsoun filio dicte vidue Inde pecunie xvj solidos viij denarios et sustentabit matrem suam pro toto tempore vite sue plegius alter alterius.

Item, assedatur filio thome zong inde pecunie xvj solidos viij denarios. Item, tantum Willelmo Lee.

Assedatur vna pars andree glwwar soluendo inde annuatim viij solidos iiij denarios cum le bonsiluer et seruicio debito et consueto plegio Ricardo fordoun.

vj lib. xiii s. iiij d.

*Edinbernan.*

Assedatur Inde quarta pars mauricio flemyn Inde pecunie xx solidos xx denarios cum bonesiluer.

Assedatur inde vna bouata Lowre Johnsoun Inde pecunie x solidos x denarios cum bonsiluer.

Assedatur Johanni gilmorson vna quarta Inde pecunie xxj solidos viij denarios cum bonsiluer.

Assedatur inde Stephano talzour octaua pars Inde pecunie x solidos x denarios cum bonsiluer.

Assedatur inde hugoni le tantum Inde pecunie x solidos x denarios cum le bonsiluer.

Assedatur vltima pars Jacobo rede Inde pecunie x solidos x denarios cum le bonsiluer plegius alter alterius. iiij lib. vj s. viij d.

*Aschlek.*

Assedatur Johanni le vna quarta Inde pecunie xxv solidos cum le bonsiluer.

Assedatur Wilelmo patonsoun octaua quarta pars Inde pecunie xij solidos cum bonesiluer.

Assedatur donaldo androsoun tercia quarta alia octaua pars Inde pecunie xij solidos cum bonesiluer.

Assedatur synnysoun ye colzar Johanni brisane vltima quarta Inde pecunie xxv solidos cum le bonsiluer et seruicio consueto plegius alter alterius.

Assedatur Johanni Mwr vna octaua pars Inde pecunie xij solidos vj denarios cum le bonsiluer.

Assedatur Johanni thomsoun vna octaua pars Inde pecunie xij solidos vj denarios cum le bonsiluer.

Assedatur Patricio vilson vna octaua pars Inde pecunie xij solidos vj denarios cum le bone.

Assedatur vna octaua pars Christoforo Donaldsoun Inde pecunie xij solidos vj denarios cum le bone. v lib.

*Miltoun.*

Assedatur inde thome Strabrok Inde pecunie xliij solidos iiij denarios cum le bonsiluer.

Assedatur Johanni lang alia pars Inde pecunie xxj solidos viij denarios cum le bonkil.

Assedatur Wilelmo Stephani Inde pecunie xiiij solidos vj denarios cum bonesiluer.

Assedatur alia pars Johanni wilson Wilelmo Stewynson Inde pecunie vij solidos ij denarios cum bonsiluer plegius alter alterius cum seruicio consueto.

iiij lib. vj s. viij d.

*Molendinum bladorum.*

Assedatur dicto thome de Strabok soluendo Inde annuatim xx lib.

*Le Bradfeld.*

Assedatur domino alano capellano Johanni de malyny andree murhed Johanni Wodrufe et angusio denby per equales portiones soluendo annuatim iiij libras cum quatuor solidis de le bonesiluer et seruicio consueto plegius alter alterius.

Assedatur vna pars Johanni brysoun soluendo in annuatim xxv solidos cum le bonsiluer et ceruisio debito et consueto plegio Ricardo fordoun et domino alano. patet.

*Litilculboye.*

Assedatur relicte Wilelmi flemyng thome de wardlaw vna quarta Inde pecunie xxv solidos.

Assedatur vna alia quarta roberto M'Cunyn Inde pecunie xxv solidos.

Assedatur alia dimedietas michaeli donaldi Inde pecunie annuatim l solidos et dicta villa soluet tres solidos de le bonesilu plegius alter alterius. v lib.

*Mekilculboy.*

Assedatur alano huchonson Inde pecunie xliij solidos iiij denarios cum le bonesiluer.

Assedatur alia pars Wilelmo brisson Inde pecunie xxxij solidos vj denarios cum bonsiluer.

Assedatur alia pars alano richartsoun Inde pecunie xxj solidos viij denarios cum bonesiluer.

Assedatur roberto wilsoun tantum Inde pecunie xxj solidos viij denarios cum bonsiluer.

Assedatur Inde cristiane vidue Roberto Wilsoun Inde pecunie x solidos x denarios cum le bonesiluer cum seruicio debito et consueto plegius alter alterius. vj lib. x s.

*Mauchandran.*

Assedatur Wilelmo Johnsoun vna dimedietas Inde pecunie iij libros vj solidos viij denarios.

Assedatur alia pars margarete heriot vidue Inde pecunie xxij solidos iij denarios.

Assedatur alia pars relicte Walteri gilchrist roberto quhit Inde pecunie xxij solidos l denarium.

Assedatur alia pars richardo alaneson Inde pecunie xxij solidos l denarium cum le bonesiluer et seruicio consueto plegius alter alterius. v lib. xiij s. iiij d.

Assedatur tota terra de machandran fynlayo hustoun pro terminis decim annorum Inde pecunie vj lib. xiij solidos iiij denarios cum le bonsiluer et seruicio debito et consueto introito ejus in ipso intrante ad festum pentecostis.

*Ferchlay.*

Assedatur thome Strabrok Jhon off Strabrok Inde pecunie xx solidos cum le bonesiluer plegio brasio flemyn.

Assedatur Roberto Stensoun soluendo annuatim xx solidos cum le bonsiluer et seruicio debito.

*Le bernis.*

Assedatur thome hasty et thome knok soluendo annuatim iij celdras farine cum octo bollis frumenti et octo bollis ordei seruando partem pratum in manibus abbatis plegius alter alterius. iiij lib.

*Auchingre.*

In manibus abbatis pro suis equis siluestribus Inde pecunie xxvj solidos viij denarios.

*Cragbanzo.*

In manibus abbatis ut prius Inde pecunie vj solidos viij denarios. Item, vj solidos viij denarios. xl s.

*Domus Margarete Sclatar.*

Assedatur Margarete Sclatar vidue soluendo annuatim xij capones.

Assedacio terrarum infra dominium de Kill facta apud Monktoun octauo die mensis maii anno domini et cetero sexagesimo.

*Monktonhil cuius vna pars.*

Assedatur Thome Cuthtbert soluendo inde annuatim xv solidos iiij denarios.

Assedatur alia pars eiusdem vilelmo Istoll inde pecunie xv solidos iiij denarios.

Assedatur alia pars thome broun inde pecunie xv solidos et iiij denarios.

Assedatur alia pars nicholaio boghous inde pecunie xxiiij solidos.

Assedatur alia pars Rankino Rig inde pecunie xxiiij solidos.

Assedatur alia pars patricio pecunie xxiiij solidos.

Summa huius ville v lib. xviij s.

Assedatur vna pars Inde dauid Scot soluendo annuatim viij solidos cum seruicio inde debito et consueto.

Assedatur vna pars inde Johanni fyndlo soluendo annuatim xxx solidos cum seruicio inde debito et consueto.

Assedatur vna pars inde matheo Nele Inde pecunie liij solidos iiij denarios.

*Monkton cuius vna pars.*

Assedatur Johanni nele inde pecunie liij solidos et iiij denarios.

Alia pars assedatur Johanni nicoll soluendo annuatim xxv solidos plegio matheo nell cum seruicio debito et consueto.

Alia pars assedatur Johanni nele soluendo annuatim xxix solidos cum seruicio debito et consueto plegio matheo nele.

Assedatur matheo hulsoun inde pecunie xliiij solidos.

Assedatur Roberto chapell inde pecunie xxij solidos.

Assedatur Roberto Jurden inde pecunie xiiij solidos.

Assedatur Johanni Oglacht inde pecunie xviij solidos.

Assedatur Johanni Dawe inde pecunie xj solidos viij denarios.

x pars Johannis Dawe assedatur nicolaio morisoun soluendo annuatim xj solidos viij denarios plegio Johanne Wilsoun.

Assedatur Jonete Oglacht inde pecunie xxxvj solidos.

Assedatur Cristoforo thomsoun inde pecunie xvj solidos.

Assedatur Agnete Scot inde pecunie xvj solidos.

Assedatur finlaio talzour inde pecunie xxx solidos.

Item, terra alani gardiner in manibus abbatis liij solidos iiij denarios.

Summa huius ville xv lib. xiiij s. iiij d.

Assedatur vna pars allexandro stewinsoun inde pecunie xx solidos.

*Brockat cuius vna pars.*

Assedatur vidue eiusdem inde pecunie xx solidos.

Assedatur Wilelmo nicholl inde pecunie xx solidos. Summa huius xl s.

*Brerisyarde cuius tota pars.*

Assedatur Johanni stewinson inde pecunie vj solidos viij denarios jactando et laborando sequelem molendini.

*Cuchat mur cuius tota pars.*

Assedatur Vilelmo Wite inde pecunie xxxvj solidos viij denarios.

Summa huius xxxvj s. viij d.

*Le Wardhous.*

In manibus abbatis et solet assedari pro iij solidis iiij denariis.

*Molendinum.*

Assedatur Inde pecunie vj libras xiij solidos iiij denarios.

Summa terrarum de Mownktoun patet xij s. iiii d.

*Terre dominice.*

Assedatur inde vna pars Johanni hunter seniori inde pecunie xxv solidos.

Assedatur etiam alia pars Johanni hunter juniori inde pecunie xxxvij solidos vj denarios.

Assedatur tantum archibaldo cunyngam inde pecunie xxxvij solidos vj denarios.

Assedatur insuper alia pars stephano colrath Inde pecunie iij libras vj solidos viij denarios.

Assedatur etiam alia cristofero balze Inde pecunie xxxiij solidos iij denarios.

Assedatur alia pars earundem Johanni grefe Inde pecunie l solidos.

Assedatur alia pars Wilelmo hunter Inde pecunie l solidos.

Assedatur etiam relicte quondam Wilelmi greve Inde pecunie v libras cum seruicio et cariagio debito et consueto plegius alter alterius quatuor duodecim capones.

Summa huius xx lib.

Et statuendum quod quilibet tenens in dicto dominio debet annuatim pro suo seruicio vnum cariagium ad pasletum semel in anno quinque dietas cum messoribus in autumno anglice fyve days scheryn et quodlibet aratrum arabit abbati vnam acram et harpicabit vnam acram et quilibet habens dimedietatem aratri arabit dimedietatem acre et tantum harpicabit et quibus tenens dabit et importabit ad aulam de munktown in anno duo onera carbonis et qui non habet aratrum harpicabit vnam acram et tenentes de terra dominica dabunt in anno quatuor duodecim capones.

Memorandum, de sex marcatis terrarum dominicalium in manibus abbatis iiij lib.

*Dalmulyne.*

*Kirklandholm cuius vna dimedietas.*

Assedatur alexandro galway Inde pecunie annuatim xxvj solidos viij denarios cum seruicio ut supra.

Assedatur altra dimedietas Johanni clerk Inde pecunie xxvj solidos viij denarios cum seruicio ut prius. Summa huius iij lib. xiij s. iiij d. liii s. iiij d.

*Kirk hile.*

Assedatur inde vna pars Wilelmo haufe Inde pecunie xlix solidos cum seruicio ut supra.

Assedatur inde altra pars malcolmo huntar Inde pecunie xxiiij solidos iiij denarios cum seruicio et cariagio ut prius plegius alter alterius.

Summa iij lib. xiij sol : v d. iiijd.

. . . *le Sauquhar vi s. viij d.*

*Dalmulyn.*

*Dalmulyn.*

Assedatur inde vna pars inde pecunie alexandro osborne inde pecunie xx solidos assedatur inde altra pars Johanni hauffe juniori Inde pecunie xxxiij solidos iiij denarios.

Assedatur inde alia pars pery foulartoun Inde pecunie xv solidos viij denarios.

Assedatur et alia relicte quondam Johannis gray Inde pecunie xv solidos viij denarios.

Assedatur etiam et alia Johanni M'Cowlo Inde pecunie xv solidos viij denarios.

Assedatur et alia Johanni thomsoun seniori Inde pecunie xlvij solidos.

Assedatur etiam hog balza Inde pecunie xxxv solidos.

Assedatur alia pars Johanni thomsoun juniori Inde pecunie xj solidos viij denarios.

Assedatur et vltima pars Johannie hauffe seniori inde pecunie xlvj solidos viij denarios plegius alter alterius cum seruicio et cariagio ut supra.

Ut torra ade alexandri se extendit ad xl solidos non assedatur.

Summa huius xiiij lib. viij d.

*Miltoun.*

Assedatur Inde pars prima patricio quhit soluendo annuatim xxvj solidos viij denarios.

Assedatur et alia pars relicte Johannis Wilsoun Inde pecunie xiij solidos iiij denarios.

Assedatur etiam alia pars ade de gaulstoun Inde pecunie xiij solidos iiij denarios.

Assedatur et alia pars roberto Myln Inde pecunie xxvj solidos viij denarios.

Assedatur etiam alia pars Johanni Makkysoun Inde pecunie cum thoma androu xiij solidos iiij denarios plegius alter alterius cum seruicio et cariagio ut supra.

Summa iiij lib. xiij sol. iiij d.

*Molendinum bladorum.*

Assedatur patricio quhit Agneti vidue Inde pecunie x libras.

Cuius vna pars assedatur henrico karnys soluendo inde annuatim v libras ad duos anni terminos ut solitum est.

*Anuale de Adamton.*

Debentur annuatim per dominum de Adamtoun xl solidos.

*Annuale de russallande.*

Debentur inde annuatim per dominum de Auchinlek annuatim xx solidos.

*Annuale de Auchinlek.*

Debentur per dominum de auchinlek annuatim xx solidos.

*Pensio de Corsraguel.*

Debentur annuatim de abbate de Corsraguele vj hbras xiij solidos iiij denarios.

*Piscaria.*

Assedatur pro tercio pisce. Terrarum de Dalmulyn xliij lib. xiij s.

Totalis firmarum terrarum iij^xx xiiij^lb

Assedacio terrarum abbatis et conuentus monasterii de pasleto infra kyll facta apud munkootown per venerabilem in Christo patrem et dominum dominum henricum crechtoun abbatem monasterii de pasleto xxiiij° die mensis Julii anno domini M° CCCC° sexagesimo quarto pro terminis quinque annorum proximo et immediate sequentibus a termino pentecostes proximo futuro cum seruicio et cariagio ut supra videlicet in vltima assedacione.

*Monktounhill cuius vna pars.*

Assedatur thome cuthbert soluendo annuatim xv solidos iiij denarios.

Assedatur alia pars eiusdem Wilelmo Cristoll inde pecunie xv solidos iiij denarios.

Assedatur alia pars thome broune inde pecunie xv solidos iiij denarios.

Assedatur alia pars nicholayo boghous inde pecunie xxiiij solidos.

Assedatur alia pars Rankino Rig inde pecunie xxiiij solidos.

Assedatur alia pars relicte quondam patricii M'spaden inde pecunie xxiiij solidos plegius alter alterius cum seruicio ut supra. Summa v lib. xxiij s.

*Monktoun cuius vna pars.*

Assedatur Johanni nell inde pecunie liij solidos iiij denarios.

Assedatur alia pars phillippo broun inde pecunie liij solidos iiij denarios.

Assedatur alia pars matheo houstoun inde pecunie xliiij solidos.

Assedatur alia pars Roberto chapel inde pecunie xxij solidos.

Assedatur alia pars quondam roberti Jurden proportionaliter relicte dicti roberti et roberto chapell pro xiiij solidis.

Assedatur alia pars quondam Johannis Oglacht patricio Stenson inde pecunie xviij solidos.

Assedatur alia pars quondam Jonete Oglacht Johanni Oglacht inde pecunie xxxvj solidos.

Assedatur alia pars cristofero seriand inde pecunie xvj solidos.

Assedatur alia pars Agnete Scot inde pecunie xvj solidos.

Assedatur alia pars Johanni Daw inde pecunie xj solidos viij denarios.

Assedatur alia pars ffinlayo talzour inde pecunie xxx solidos plegius alter alterius cum seruicio ut supra Summa xv lib. xiiij s. iiij d.

*Brockat cuius vna pars.*

Assedatur Johanni Rig inde pecunie xx solidos.

Summa xl s.

*Cuthatmur cuius tota pars.*

Assedatur Wilelmo Wily inde pecunie xxxvj solidos et viij denarios.

Summa patet.

*Le Wardhous.*

*Molendinum de Munktown cuius vna pars.*

Assedatur Johanni oglatht inde pecunie xxxiij solidos iiij denarios.

Assedatur alia pars Relicte quondam Wilelmi gref inde pecunie xxxiij solidos iiij denarios.

Assedatur alia pars Johanni greff inde pecunie xxxiij solidos iiij denarios.

Assedatur alia pars matheo housoun inde pecunie xxxiij solidos iiij denarios plegius alter alterius cum debito seruicio. Summa vj lib. xiij s. iiij d.

*Le Manys de Munktaun cuius vna pars.*

Assedatur Johanni huntar juniori inde pecunie xxxvij solidos et vj denarios.

Assedatur alia pars archibaldo cunyngam inde pecunie xxxvij solidos vj denarios.

Assedatur alia pars Johanni greff inde pecunie l solidos.

Assedatur alia pars Wilelmo huntar inde pecunie l solidos.

Assedatur alia pars Relicte quondam Wilelmi greff inde pecunie v libros.

Assedatur alia pars Johanni huntar mercatori inde pecunie xxx xvj solidos et viij denarios.

Assedatur pars stephano colratht inde pecunie l solidos.

Assedatur alia pars Jacobo andree inde pecunie xxxiij solidos iiij denarios cum seruicio et cariagio debito et consueto et iiij duodecim capones plegius alter alterius. Summa xx lib.

*Dalmolyng.*

*Dalmolyn Kyrkhill cuius vna pars.*

Assedatur malcolmo huntar inde pecunie xxiiij solidos iiij denarios.

Assedatur alia pars Wilelmo hanffy inde pecunie xxiiij solidos vj denarios.

Assedatur alia pars Johanni hanffy seniori inde pecunie xxiiij solidos vj denarios plegius alter alterius cum seruicio debito. Summa xiiij lib. viij d.

*Kyr land holm cuius vna pars.*

Assedatur vna pars alexandro galoway inde pecunie xxxiij solidos iiij denarios.

Assedatur alia pars Relicte quondam Johannis clince inde pecunie xx solidos plegius alter alterius cum seruicio debito. Summa liij s. iiij d.

*Maneholm cuius tota pars.*

Assedatur Johanni locart inde pecunie iiij libras xiij solidos iiij denarios cum seruicio debito.

Assedatur tota Alexandro schawe soluendo annuatim iiij libras xiij solidos iiij denarios cum seruicio inde debito et consueto.

Assedatur vna inde Johanni Willes soluendo annuatim xx solidos cum seruicio debito et consueto.

Assedatur alia pars roberto galloway soluendo annuatim xx solidos cum seruicio debito et consueto.

*Mylquarter cuius vna pars.*

Assedatur Roberto myllar inde pecunie xxvj solidos viij denarios.

Assedatur alia pars henrico karnis post obitum patricii quhite soluendo inde annuatim xl solidos xxvj s. viij d. cum seruicio inde debito et consueto.

Assedacio terrarum infra dominium de kilpatrik facta apud le bernys penultimo may anno domini M°CCCLXV° pro terminis quinque annorum.

*Westir Kilpatrik.*

Assedatur vna quinta pars hugoni brounsyd soluendo inde annuatim xxv solidos cum le bone et seruicio debito.

Assedatur vna octaua pars Johanni morysoun inde pecunie xvj solidos viij denarios cum le bon siluer.

Assedatur octaua pars Wilelmo lang inde pecunie xvj solidos viij denarios cum le bone.

Assedatur vna domus cum pertinenciis soluendo annuatim xij capones.

*Patricio Donaldsoun.*

Assedatur vna pars donaldo vilsoun inde pecunie xxxv solidos iiij d.

Assedatur finlaio Jameson vna quarta pars octaua pars soluendo annuatim l solidos cum le bone.

*Morysland et Huchonland.*

Assedatur.

*Ester kilpatrik.*

Assedatur vna sexta pars Johanni Strabrok soluendo annuatim xxij solidos ij denarios.

Assedatur vna sexta vilelmo greyff inde pecunie xxxij solidos viij d. xxij solidos ij denarios cum obulo.

Assedatur Johanni lang dimedia vna quarta inde pecunie xvj s. viij d. xxxiij solidos iiij denarios cum le bonsiluer.

Assedatur vna sexta pars vilelmo Johnsoun inde pecunie xxij solidos.

Assedatur octaua pars Johanni tomsoun inde pecunie xvj solidos viij denarios.

Assedatur vna sexta pars inde pecunie xxij solidos ij denarios.

Assedatur vna pars Johanni moris inde pecunie xj solidos 1 denarium cum seruicio debito et consueto.

*Auchinthoythan.*

Assedatur.

Assedatur.

Assedatur.

Assedatur.

*Auchinlek.*

Assedatur cristofero donaldsoun vna octaua pars Inde pecunie xxij solidos cum le bone.

Assedatur mauricio malcumsoun vna octaua pars Inde pecunie xij solidos vj denarios cum le bon siluer et cer[uicio debito.]

Assedatur cristofero donaldson vna pars Inde pecunie xij solidos vj denarios cum le bon siluer et ceruisio de[bito.]

Assedatur.

*Drumtochunan.*

Assedatur vna tertia pars Ricardo fordun Inde pecunie xxxi solidos cum le bwne et seruicio debito.

Assedatur thome Strabroke.

Alia pars assedatur Ricardo fordoun pro xv solidis vj denariis cum le bonsiluer et serucio debito et consueto.

*Lytyl Colboy.*

Vna pars inde assedatur georgio morisoun Reddendo inde annuatim xviij solidos ix denarios cum le bonsiluer et alio ceruisio debito et consueto plegio Roberto fynne.

*Vestir couchnow.*

Assedatur vna quarta pars alexandro Stuart soluendo annuatim xxxiij solidos iiij denarios cum le bwne.

Assedatur vna duodecima pars assedatur uxori Jacobi hor mareote hog pro xj solidos 1 denario cum ceruisio ut supra.

Assedatur duodecima pars Wilelmo hog pro xj solidis 1 denario cum le bonsiluer et seruicio debito et consueto plegio Ricardon.

*Estir Cochnow.*

Assedatur vna octaua pars Jacobo lenax soluendo annuatim xvj solidos viij denarios cum le bone et seruicio.

Assedatur.
Assedatur.
Assedatur.
Assedatur.
Assedatur.

*Edinbernane.*

Assedatur quarta pars mauricio flemyn Inde pecunie xx solidos xx denarios cum le bwne.

Assedatur quarta pars Johanni gilmorson Inde pecunie xx solidos xx denarios cum le bone.

Assedatur Johanni Allansoun quarta pars Inde pecunie xx solidos xx denarios cum le bone.

Assedatur Wilelmo le vna octaua pars Inde pecunie x solidos x denarios.

Assedatur Johanni tomsoun quarta pro xx solidis xx denariis cum ceruisio debito et consueto.

*Vestir Colboy.*

Assedatur quarta pars eiusdem patricio Roberto fynneson pro xxxij solidis vj denariis cum le bonsyluer et seruicio debito et consueto plegio alano huchinsoun.

Assedatur vna pars nycholayo huchinsoun pro xxi solidis viij denariis cum le bonsyluer ac seruicio debito et consueto plegio allano huchinson.

*Moreisland.*

Assedatur Johanni flemyn pro xxvj solidis vj denariis cum seruicio debito et consueto ut prius solebat esse plegio Ricardo fordoun. kylpatrik.

*Auchynlek.*

Assedatur vna pars mariote leys et roberto leis pro xxv solidis cum seruicio debito et consueto videlicet quarta pars plegio Wilelmo le of edynbernan. kylpatrik.

*Le langcroft.*

Langcroft vna pars assedatur malcolmo broun pro iij solidis iiij denariis cum seruicio debito et consueto cum tertia parte de quensate pro xiij solidis iiij denariis. glen.

*Ye Came.*

Assedatur vna paos waltero broun ex tollerancia patris sui pro xv solidis et cum seruicio debito et consueto et le bonsyluer plegio allano brydyn et Johanne merchande. glen.

No. { Altera pars assedatur Wilelmo Robis pro x s
Altera pars assedatur Mariote Snape pro x s } cum seruicio debito et consueto.

*Clochon.*

Vna pars assedatur Johanni Marchande pro xxx iij xx x petris casei et seruicio debito et consueto plegio Waltero brown et allano brydyne. glen.

*Gawilmos.*

Vna pars assedatur Wilelmo logan pro viij solidos cum seruicio debito et consueto.

Alia pars assedatur thome logane pro iiij solidis cum seruicio debito et plegio Johanni or

*Hillyntown.*

Vna pars assedatur Johanni norwel pro vj celdris xij boll auenarum vedue remanente in octaua parte ad voluntatem abbatis plegio thoma leche.

Auchinche assedatur Jacobo tate ut supra.

*Dunterclunan.*

Vna pars assedatur georgio morisoun pro xv solidos vj d. cum seruicio debito et consueto plegio Ricardo fordoun et Wilelmo Stewart.

Alia pars assedatur alexandro Stewart pro xv solidis vj denariis cum seruicio debito et consueto plegio Ricardo fordoun teste.

Alia pars.

*Ester cochnay.*

Vna pars assedatur andree Jonsoun pro xvj solidis viij denariis plegio Ricardo fordoun cum seruicio debito et consueto etceteris.

*Cam logan.*

Cera que est in manibus emote logan assedatur Johanni langmur pro xj solidis a duos anni terminos cum seruicio debito et consueto plegio.

*Lytilhillis lynt Auchynh.*

Assedatur gilberto cwnyngam pro iij libris vj solidis viij denariis per soluendo annuatim cum ceruisio debito et consueto et per se plegium et debitorem Ranaldo or et Wilelmo logane.

*Foultoun.*

Vna pars de foultoun assedatur Roberton Synsoun pro x solidis annuatim soluendo cum vj pultreis et le bonsiluer cum seruicio debito et consweto plegio et debitore Johanne paslay.

Assedatur alia pars Jonete cwper uxori malcome sancer pro x solidis annuatim soluendo cum ceruisio debito et consweto et le bonesiluer.

*Aldzarde.*

Vna pars assedatur Johanni or pro viij solidis ut supra in, . . . . . . . . .

Assedacio terrarum dominii de pasleto facta apud monasterium eiusdem . . . . die mensis . . . anno domini millesimo quadragentesimo sexagesimo ix° per venerabilem in Cristo patrem et dominum henricum Crechone pro terminis quinque annorum.

Assedacio terrarum infra dominium de Pasleto facta apud monasterium eiusdem post festum qui dicitur ad uincula sancti petri anno domini M° CCCC° septuagesimo secundo per venerabilem in Cristo patrem et dominum dominum georgium schaw abbatem monasterii de pasleto predicti pro terminis videlicet de anno in annum.

*Auchingone xl s.*

Assedatur tota pars Inde Alano Stewart soluendo annuatim xl solidos cum seruicio inde debito et consueto plegio Malcomo merschel.

*Balrogear cum le xijs Burthreis.*

Assedatur tota pars inde Alano Stewart soluendo annuatim xij solidos cum seruicio inde debito et consueto.

Assedatur altra pars Johanni Schaw soluendo inde annuatim xviij s. et xij d de le bonsiluer et cariagia et alia seruicio inde debita et consueto.

Assedatur altera pars inde gilberto Steuuart soluendo inde annuatim xviij solidos et xij denarios de le bonsiluer et cariagia ac alia onera debita pro huiusmodi parte terre et consueta.

*iiij lib. Merburn.*

Assedatur dimedia pars inde allano Stewart soluendo inde annuatim xl solidos cum seruicio debito et consueto.

Assedatur alia pars inde Johanni Stewart soluendo annuatim xl solidos cum seruicio debito et consueto plegio allano Stewart.

*xviij Mossyde.*

Assedatur tota pars inde Johanni Stewart soluendo inde annuatim xviij solidos cum seruicio inde debito et consueto plegio Alano Stewart.

*Stokbrig xxxiij s. iiij d.*

Assedatur vna pars inde malcomi merschel soluendo annuatim xvj solidos viij denarios cum seruicio et consueto.

Assedatur vna pars inde vidue elisabethe galbrathe soluendo annuatim xvj solidos viij denarios cum seruicio inde debito et consueto plegio malcomo merschel.

Altra pars inde assedatur Johanni allano Knox soluendo inde annuatim xvj solidos viij denarios cum seruicio debito et consueto plegio Johanne m'gregor.

Summa ix lib. s. iiij d.

*Foultovn.*

Cuius vna pars assedatur wilelmo Symson soluendo inde annuatim xl solidos ad duos anni terminos cum seruicio debito et consueto plegio pro se Roberto symson.

Assedatur vna pars eiusdem Roberto malcomi soluendo inde annuatim x solidos cum le bonesiluer et *le cane* et seruicio inde debito et consueto plegio Roberto bar.

Assedatur vna pars wilelmo methel soluendo annuatim xiij solidos iiij denarios cum seruicio inde debito et consueto plegio Johanne paslay.

Assedatur altra pars Johanni paslay soluendo annuatim xx solidos cum seruicio inde debito et consueto.

Due partes istius ville quas habebant Johannes Sempil et Robertus clydishede assedantur petro brown soluendo inde annuatim xl s. cum seruicio debito et consueto et prout dicti Johannes et Robertus temporibus retroactis fecerunt pro termino quinque annorum intrando idem petrus in assedacione dictarum terrarum in festo pentecostes anni lxxv etc.

*Ye lenwode xl s.*

Assedatur Johanni Simpill soluendo inde idem Johannes —— xl^ta s. cum seruicio debito et consueto.

*Claxton xx s.*

*Auchinch liij s. iiij d.*

Summa xj lib. xvj s. vii d.

Summa huius domus xiiij lib.

Assedatur vna pars inde Johanni Anderson post decessum cristiane herryng soluendo inde annuatim xiij s. x d. cum seruicio debito et consueto.

*Drumgrane.*

Vna pars assedatur wilelmo glasfurde soluendo inde annuatim xix s. iij d. cum *le cane* fowlis cariagio et ceruisio debito et consueto.

Assedatur vna pars inde wilelmo gemyl pro tempore cristiane heryn soluendo inde annuatim xiij s. iiij d. cum seruicio inde debito et consueto.

*Auchinch.*

Assedatur Jacobo tate soluendo inde annuatim liij s. iiij d. cum seruicio debito et consueto plegio et debitore henrico frog.

*Drumgrane.*

Assedatur vna pars inde thome dunbar soluendo annuatim xix s. iij d. cum obulo cum cariagio le bonsiluer et alio seruicio inde debito et consueto et predictus thomas sustentabit matrem suam quamdiu ipsa vixit in humanis et tenetur soluendo annuatim liij s. iiij d. pro fermis molendini dicte ville de drumgrane et pro eo plegio thoma bulle.

Assedatur Johanni Stenson vna pars soluendo inde annuatim xxxviij s. vj d. cum seruicio inde debito et consueto Johanni Jope.

Assedatur vna pars inde Johanni Jope soluendo annuatim xvij s. iiij d. xxv s. iiij d. cum seruicio inde debito et consueto plegio Johanne Stenson.

Assedatur vna pars eiusdem thome bulle soluendo annuatim xxvij s. viij d. cum alio seruicio debito et consueto.

Assedatur vna pars gilberto cochran soluendo annuatim xxvij s. viij d. cum seruicio inde debito et consueto plegio Johanne Andersoun.

Summa ix lib. iiij s. viij d. obulo.

*Molendinum de Drumgrane liij s. iiij d.*

*liij s. iiij d. Auchinch.*

*xx s. Blaxtown.*

*vj lib. Ferguslе.*

*xvj s. Quhytcruk.*

*viij lib. Mekilriggis.*

Assedatur vna pars eiusdem thome Robys soluendo annuatim xl s. cum seruicio inde debito et consueto plegio wilelmo bulle.

Assedatur alia pars eiusdem Andree thome soluendo annuatim xx s. cum seruicio ut supra plegio thome Robys.

Assedatur altra pars patricio thome soluendo annuatim xx s. cum seruicio ut supra plegio thome Robis.

Assedatur vna pars vilelmo bulle soluendo annuatim iiij lib. cum seruicio ut supra.

Assedatur quarteria ville thome Robisoun seniori et thome Robisoun juniori filiis thome Robisoun soluendo annuatim xl s. ad duos anni terminos consuetos cum ix pultriis cum iij bwnys et seruicio inde debito et consueto plegius alter alterius.

*xx s. Brydelande.*

*Corsber.*

Assedatur vna pars inde magistro Dauid logane soluendo annuatim xxvj s. viij d. et quatuor bollas auenarum cum seruicio debito et consueto plegio Johanne Alexandri.

*xl s. Corsber xxvj s. viij d. viij b. auenarum.*

Assedatur vna pars inde elsobethe logane soluendo annuatim xxvj s. viij d. et liij bollas auenarum cum seruicio debito et consueto plegio wilelmo bulle.

Assedatur altra pars inde brisio kerswele soluendo inde annuatim xl s. et quatuor bollas auenarum cum seruicio debito et consueto plegio Johanne Ricardo bar.

*Ye Inch xiij s. iiij d.*

Cuius tota pars assedatur fynlayo henrisoun pro xiij s. iiij d. cum seruicio debito et consueto plegio Johanne bulle.

*Thomebar xxvj s. viiij d.*

*Cariagehyl liij s. iiij d.*

Assedatur vna pars inde Johanni Sklater soluendo annuatim xiij s. iiij d. cum seruicio debito et consueto plegio Johanne cochran.

Assedatur vna pars inde Johanni wilsoun post decessum matris sue soluendo annuatim xiij s. iiij d. cum seruicio debito et consueto plegio allano suddyrland.

Assedatur vna dimedia pars inde malcomo Sklater soluendo inde annuatim xxvj s. viij d. cum xij pullis et quatuor bunis et seruicio debito et consueto.

*Todholme ij s.*

*Ruthbank.*

Assedatur Alexandro Schaw soluendo inde annuatim iij lib. vj s. viij d. cum seruicio debito et consueto sicut alii tenentes faciunt.

*Thornle vj lib. xiij s. iiij d.*

*Ruthbank.*

Vna pars inde assedatur patricio merschel soluendo annuatim xxvj s. viij d. cum ceruisio inde debito et consueto plegio Johanne merschel.

Assedatur vna pars inde Johanni merschel soluendo annuatim xxvj s. viij d. cum seruicio debito et consueto plegio patricio merschel.

Assedatur altra pars inde Alexandro bronside soluendo annuatim xiij s. iiij d. cum seruicio ut supra plegio Johanne merschel.

*xiiij s. Willa de Jhone of Morray.*
*Pasleto.*

*viij s. viij d.——Alis Quhyt.*

Assedatur Johanni Sklater soluendo annuatim viij s. viij d. cum seruicio inde debito et consueto plegio ut supra.

*x s.——Jhone Sclater.*

Assedatur Johanni Sklater soluendo annuatim x s. cum seruicio debito et consueto.

*xj s.*——Relicte quondam gilgriste leth viz. ye syde.

*xviij s. ye Causaside.*

*xv s. ye Ward vna pars.*
*xv s. altra pars.*

Cuius vna pars assedatur Johanni quhytfurde soluendo annuatim v s. cum seruicio inde debito et consueto plegio Johanne çochran.

Assedatur altera pars Johanni quhytfurde soluendo annuatim xxi s. et memorandum quod ista assedacio est facta dicto Johanni cum contingat ipsum optinuere consensu relicte alani quhit plegio Johanne cochran.

*Castalhed xiij s. iiij d.*

Assedatur thome mathe soluendo annuatim xiij s. iiij d. cum seruicio inde debito et consueto.

*vjs vj Acre in ye hil.*

Terra quam habebat thomas Stewart assedatur Johanni quhitfurde soluendo annuatim xij s. iiij d. cum vna acra de prior corffit.

*Lytyl blakfalde v s.*

Assedatur vna pars Johanni quhitfurde soluendo annuatim ij s. vj d. cum seruicio inde debito et consueto plegio Johanni Sympil.

Altera pars assedatur dicto Johanni quhitfurde soluendo xxx d. ut supra.

*viii s. Grevysland.*

Assedatur Johanni quhytfurde soluendo annuatim iij s. cum seruicio inde debito et consueto.

*Mekyl blakfalde viij s.*

*Schankis tak.*

Assedatur vna pars Johanni hecture soluendo inde annuatim ix s. cum seruicio debito et consueto plegio Johanni Sclatter cum propria manu.

*Casaende.*

Cuius vna pars assidatur Johanni Dule soluendo inde annuatim ix s. cum seruicio debito et consueto plegio.

Assedatur Johanni Alansown soluendo inde annuatim . . . cum . . . le bonis et seruicio debito et consueto.

*Ye Orchat.*

Assedatur relicte domini quhitfurde soluendo annuatim xvj s. cum xij pultre et le bonsiluer et seruicio debito et consueto plegio Johanne cochran.

*Ye bernzard.*

Assedatur alano sunderland pro vj caponibus.

*v s. le ocschauside v acre.*

*iiij s. ochauside iiij acre.*

*vij s. Item 1 akir in eodem loco.*

*vj s. ye ocschawhede.*

Assedatur vna acra eiusdem Johanni quhytfurde soluendo annuatim vj s. cum xij d. de le bonsiluer et alio serucio ut supra.

*Molendinum bladorum de Paslay.*

xiiij lib.
xiij s.
viij d.

*ix s. le priorcrofft quatuor acre iiij d.*

Assedatur vna pars inde viz. iij acre terre Johanni quhytfurde soluendo annuatim vij s. cum seruicio ut supra.

Item quatuor acre ix s. iiij d.
Item ij acre iiij s. viij d.
Item 1 akir ij s. iiij d.
Item 1 akyr ij s. iiij d.

Domus Johannis ross vid post in feodo vj s.

xiij s. iiij d. Domus Johannis valace.

xiij s. iiij d. Domus Roberti Morray.

xiij s. iiij d. Domus thome Stewart.

ij s. Ortus Dauid narne.

ij s. ye Bernzarde.

v s. Item, alia domus domini Johannis ross vna botha.

v s. Item, alia botha.

v s. Item, alia botha.

*iij s. Bladouchzarde.*

x s. Terra olym Domini de kelsolande. Assedatur David tate pro soluendo inde annuatim x s. ad duos anni terminos.

ij s. vj d. Domus Andree Smitht.

viij s. Ye walk mil cum le dame.

xvj s. Magnus ortus.

iiij s. Domus domini Johannis Ross.

vj s. Item, alia domus domini Johannis Ross.

*Ye Slaterisbank xiij s. iiij d.*

Assedatur Roberto Caueris et Maldavene spens soluendo Inde annuatim xiij s. iiij d. cum seruicio et le bonsiluer Inde debito et consueto.

*Ye Oeschauwode vj s.*

Assedatur Johanni brangy cum custodia silue soluendo inde annuatim xx s. et pro seruicio seruabit siluam pro qua.

*xx s. Durshachsyde.*

*xiij s. iiij d. Roben flemenis tak in estwod.*

*xx s. Ye Mernes.*

*Ye kirkhill in Polloc viij s.*

Assedatur Johanni harbardson soluendo inde annuatim viij s. cum seruicio debito et consueto plegio alano sunderlande.

*xl s. Snaldovn.*

*xxvj s. viij d. Brydelands.*

*xxxiij s. iiij d. Ye Manys of Paslay vna pars.*

*xxxiij s. iiij d. altra pars.*

Assedatur vna pars inde Jacobo bulle soluendo annuatim xxviij s. iiij d. cum seruicio debito et consueto plegio Johanne Cochran.

*x s. ye Sedhil vna pars.*

*x s. Item altera pars pertinens ad molendinum.*

iij lib. ye estwode<br>vj s. viij d. — Ye Aldhous assedatur allano flemyng post decessum sue matris soluendo annuatim xiij s. iiij d. cum seruicio inde debito et consueto illa pars viz. quam habebat Robertus flemyng pater dicti allani.

iij Capones.

*Falkis zarde.*

*iiij s. Ye banar akyr.*

Assedatur Alexandro wache soluendo inde annuatim iiij s. cum seruicio inde debito et consueto cum quatuor le bonis plegio waltero Scot assedacione durante pro voluntate domini abbatis.

*xl s. ye Corsflate.*

*Ffeode ferme.*

viij s. In primis domus vilelmi quhit cum acra.
viij s. Domus domini Johannis Vane.
vj s. Domus dauid Narne.
Domus domini vilelmo vilsoun iij s.
xj s. Domus domini haukhede.
iiij s. Domus vilelmi masson.
iiij s. Domus Johannis Lang.
iiij s. Domus Johannis logane.
ij s. Domus Johannis Alexander.
ij s. Domus Alano Sunderlande.
v s. Domus domini wilelmi Vilsoun in le mos raw.
v s. Domus michaelis paslay.
v s. Domus dauid rede.
v s. Domus Roberti bryntschelis.
vj s. Domus Roberti bryntschelis.
xij d. Domus Johannis forest.
x s. Domus Johannis mur.
x s. Domus Alexandry belhous.
viij s. Domus Roberti Sympil.
iiij s. Item alia domus Roberti Sympil.
Domus Roberti quhit xiij s. iiij d.
Domus andree cwke xiij s. iiij d.
viij s. Domus fynlay thomson.
viij s. Domus thome kyngorne.
ij s. Domus Johannis paslay.
xij d. Item alia domus Johannis paslay.
ix s. Domus thome schelis.
vj s. Domus Johannis logane.
vj s. Item alia domus Johannis logane.
vj s. Domus gilcriste lech.
xviij d. ye crag hale, viz. eme logane.
xviij d. ye langzard viz. eme logane.
xviij s. Domus thome steuart.
iij s. Domus Johannis pynkarton.
ij s. Domus Johannis quhit.
iiij s. iiij d. Domus emme logane prope causasid.

*Terre assedate pro auenis.*

*Hillentovn.*

ix celdre auenarum.

Assedatur vna pars Andree Morray soluendo Inde annuatim ij celdras quatuor bollas auenarum xij pullis et quatuor le bonis cum ceruisio debito et consueto plegio.

Assedatur vna pars Roberto bar soluendo inde annuatim 1 celdram auenarum cum seruicio debito et consueto.

*Rycardysbar.*
iij celdre auenarum cum xij pultre et iiij le bonis.

Assedatur vna pars Johanni Ricardis bar soluendo annuatim xvj bollas auenarum cum seruicio inde debito et consueto plegio brisio korswel.

Assedatur altra pars Inde Jonete norwell soluendo Inde annuatim xvj bollas auenarum cum seruicio debito et consueto plegio Johanne norwell.

Altera pars assedatur Johanni Wilson post decessum Jonete norwell soluendo Inde annuatim xvj bollas auenarum cum seruicio debito et consueto, viz. iiij pultre iiij bonis iiij cariagiis.

*Newtovn.*
iiij celdre auenarum cum xxiiij le pultre et viij le bonis.

Assedatur vna pars assedatur Johanni Wilson soluendo inde annuatim ij celdras auenarum cum seruicio inde debito et consueto.

*Erklyston.*

Vna pars assedatur Johanni morgan soluendo inde annuatim ij celdras iiij bollas auenarum cum quatuor le bonis et cariagio et ceruisio debito et consueto plegio Johanne bulle ut supra decimo augusto anno etc. septuagesimo secundo.

Assedatur altra pars inde Johanne landalis juniori soluendo annuatim iiij celdras viij bollas auenarum cum xij pultre cum le bwnis et cum alia serucia inde debita et consueta.

Assedatur altra pars duncano bulle loure soluendo inde annuatim ij celdras iiij bollas auenarum cum alio seruicio inde debito et consueto plegio Johanne morgan.

Assedatur vna pars stephano urre soluendo inde annuatim ij celdras iiij bollas auenarum cum quatuor le bonis et cariagio et seruicio debito et consueto Alexandro brone Remanente cum dimedietate quam dominus ipse gaudeat soluendo dimedietatem dicte ferme et dimedietate plegio Duncano de Arkliston.

*Ye Inch.*
xviij celdre auenarum.

Vna pars assedatur fynlayo henrison pro xviij bollis auenarum et cum seruicio debito et consueto et pro se debitori et plegio Johanne bulle.

Assedatur vna pars inde Stephano Jonson soluendo annuatim ij celdras iiij bollas auenarum cum seruicio debito et consueto.

Assedatur vna pars inde Symoni Johnson soluendo annuatim ij cd. iiij b. auenarum cum seruicio ut supra.

Assedatur altra pars malcomo Jonson soluendo annuatim xxx b. auenarum cum seruicio ut supra.

Assedatur altra pars Johanni Johnson soluendo annuatim xxiiij bollas auenarum cum seruicio ut supra.

Assedatur vna inde wilelmo Johnson soluendo annuatim xxiiij bollas auenarum cum seruicio ut supra.

Assedatur vna pars inde thome Johne soluendo annuatim xxiiij bollas auenarum cum alio seruicio ut supra.

Assedatur vna pars Johanni auchinlos nunc relicte eiusdem Johannis soluendo annuatim xxx bollas auenarum cum seruicio ut supra.

Assedatur vna pars inde Johanni fynlay soluendo annuatim xxiiij bollas auenarum cum seruicio ut supra. Et post decessum eiusdem Johannis assedatur ista pars Johanni finlayo filio dicti Johannis.

Assedatur vna pars inde fynlay talzeour soluendo annuatim xviij bollas auenarum cum seruicio ut supra plegiis alter alterius per totum.

Assedatur vna pars inde mariote byrsbane soluendo annuatim xxiiij bollas auenarum cum seruicio et consueto.

Assedatur altra pars relicte quondam malcomi gawane soluendo annuatim xxx bollas auenarum cum seruicio debito.

Assedatur ista pars Roberto cowan post decessum Katrine cowan eius matris soluendo inde annuatim xxx bollas auenarum cum seruicio debito et consueto plegio Johanni sympill.

Assedatur vna pars Roberto symson et Johanni symson fratribus soluendo inde annuatim ij celdras iiij bollas auenarum cum seruicio inde debito et consueto.

Assedatur vna pars Johanni Auchinlos juniori soluendo annuatim xxx bollas auenarum cum seruicio debito et consueto.

Idem pars assedatur thome norwele ut supra plegio Johanne nowell teste Roberto quhyt.

*Corsbar.*

Assedatur vna pars inde malcomo tomson soluendo inde annuatim xxx bollas auenarum cum seruicio debito et consueto plegio wilelmo Jonson.

Memorandum de vna parte de berskawe assedat malcomo Vilson soluendo inde annuatim x bollas ij firlot ij peccas cum tercia parte j pece auenarum plegio Johanne cochran cum seruicio debito et consueto.

Memorandum quod pars de berskawe assedatur mariote mathe soluendo annuatim xxi bollas 1 firlot 1 pecce auenarum cum seruicio debito et consueto viij pultrie le bone seruicium plegio thome mathe.

*Berschawan.*
iiij c. auenarum
duobus duodenis
le pultrie et vjjj
le bonis.

Assedatur vna pars Inde Roberto Adamson soluendo annuatim xxi bollas 1 firlot cum tertia parte firlotæ auenarum cum alio seruicio inde debito et consueto plegio.

Vna pars assedatur Alexandro wilson Inde soluendo annuatim xxj bollas 1 firlot cum tercia parte firlote auenarum cum alio seruicio Inde debito et consueto plegio Johanne Cochran.

Assedatur vna pars relicte quondam Roberti Adamson soluendo inde annuatim 1 celdram auenarum cum seruicio debito consueto plegio Alexandro vilson.

Assedatur altera pars alexandro superiori soluendo annuatim ij celdras auenarum cum seruicio consueto et debito plegio manu propria.

*Ouer gallohil.*
1 c. viij b. auenarum.

Assedatur altera pars Johanni barstawyne post decessum sue matris soluendo inde annuatim tertiam partem quatuor celdrarum avenarum cum seruicio debito et consueto.

Assedatur vna pars Ade Robeson soluendo annuatim terciam partem duarum celdrarum auenarum cum seruicio inde debito et consueto.

Assedatur vna pars Johanni Wilson soluendo inde annuatim ij celdras auenarum cum seruicio inde debito et consueto plegio manu propria.

*Neder gallohil.*
ij c. auenarum.
*Ye grenlaw.*
ij c.

Eiusdem media pars assedatur Stephano vrre pro vna celdra auenarum et faciendo idem seruicium solidum et consuetum.

*Lylyslande.*
xx b. auenarum
que thruscrag
dicitur.

Assedatur thome hiff soluendo annuatim xx bollas auenarum cum seruicio inde debito et consueto plegio thome mathe Johanne Ricardisbar.

Assedatur Rotulando mur soluendo inde annuatim xx bollas auenarum cum seruicio debito et consueto plegio Johanne murray.

*Lyncleff.*
iiij c. auenarum.

Assedatur Johanni cochran soluendo annuatim iiij celdras auenarum cum seruicio Inde debito et consueto plegio Johanne Sympill.

*Candrane.*
v c. auenarum.
*Ye blaklyn.*
viij b. auenarum.

Molendinum de pasleto assedatur Johanni millar pro terminis quinque annorum soluendo Inde annuatim durantibus illis quinque annis iiij celdras xj bollas farine cum 1 celdra ordei brasei et dictus Johannes subibit omnia onera eiusdem molendini et dimedia parte terre pertinente.

Pertinente ad dictum molendinum remanebit cum vilelmo coco soluendo annuatim ipse vilelmus iij bollas farine pelegiis et debitoribus Johanni sclatter persuelo steill Johanne murray alano quhit et Thoma morsoun quos plegios ipse Johnnes remanebit ad placitum abbatis.

Assedacio terrarum dominii de glen.

*Wester kers* xliij s. iiij d.

Assedatur vna pars Andree kyrkwode soluendo annuatim xxj s. viij d. x s. x d. cum seruicio Inde debito et consueto plegio wilelmi or.

Assedatur altra pars Johanni kirkwode soluendo annuatim x s. x d. cum seruicio debito et consueto plegio Johanne Or.

Assedatur hugoni kyrkwode soluendo annuatim x s. x d. cum seruicio debito et consueto plegio Johanne Or.

Assedatur vna pars Wilelmo kyrkwode soluendo inde annuatim xx s. x d. cum seruicio debito et consueto plegio hugone kyrkwode.

*Balray*, viz.
ye neder kers
xliij s. iiij d.

Assedatur vna pars quam Wilelmus kyrkwode habuit et altra quam habuit andreas kyrkwode Alano et Johanni kirkwode filiis superscripti Andree kyrkwode coniunctim et diuisim soluendo inde annuatim xx s. xx d. cum seruicio debito et consueto alter alterius plegius.

*Joffrays tak.*
xxiij s. iiij d. xviij pultre.

Assedatur Johanni or soluendo annuatim xxiij s. iiij d. cum seruicio debito et consueto plegio Johanne Robisoun.

Assedatur Johanni Or filio Johannis Or soluendo annuatim xxiij s. iiij d. cum seruicio pullis et cariagio et alio seruicio debito et consueto plegio Jacobo Or.

*Barnklaw*, x s.

Assedatur Alexandro norwel soluendo annuatim x s. cum seruicio debito et consueto plegio Johanne Or.

*Mawysbank*, x s.

Assedatur Johanni Robisoun soluendo annuatim x s. cum seruicio inde debito et consueto plegio Alexandro norwell.

*Langstanle*, xv s.

Assedatur Johanni lufe soluendo annuatim xv s. cum seruicio debito et consueto plegio Johanne canshil.

*Ye Caymhil*, xx s.

Assedatur vna pars Johanni Jonsoun soluendo annuatim x s. cum seruicio debito et consueto plegio Andrea Or.

Assedatur altra pars Andree or soluendo annuatim x s. cum seruicio debito et consueto plegio Johanne Jonsoun.

Assedatur vna pars Wilelmo Or filio andree Or soluendo inde annuatim x s. cum seruicio.

*Lourensbank.*
xiij s. iiij d.

Assedatur gilberto lourencebank Johanni glen soluendo annuatim xiij s. iiij d. cum seruicio debito et consueto plegio Ricardo langmuir Alano glen.

*Auchinhane.*
iij lib. viij s. viij d.

Cuius vna pars assedatur Johanni langmur soluendo inde annuatim iii$^{xx}$x petras casei et iij vitulos cum dimedio cum seruicio debito et consueto plegio malcomo broun plegio dompno Johanne menson.

Assedatur altra pars thome Jamesone pro terminis quinque annorum soluendo inde annuatim iij$^{xx}$x petras casei et iij vitulos cum dimedia cum seruicio Inde debito et consueto plegio alano glen.

Quarta pars inde assedatur patricio Allansone soluendo inde annuatim xxxij petras viij lib. casei 1½ vituli cum alio seruicio debito et consueto plegio Alexandro atkyn.

*Langzarde.*
xxvj s. viij d.

Assedatur vna pars Inde Ricardo langzarde soluendo xiij s. iiij d. cum seruicio debito et consueto ut supra plegio thoma Or.

Assedatur altra pars Inde thome Or soluendo annuatim xiij s. iiij d. cum seruicio debito et consueto plegio Ricardo langzarde.

Assedatur vna pars assedatur Jacobo glen Johanni lufe soluendo annuatim viij s. cum seruicio debito et consueto plegio Johanne Or.

Assedatur altra pars inde Johanni Or soluendo viij s. cum seruicio debito et consueto plegio Jacobo glen.

*ye aldzarde cum le farhil* Assedatur tota vna pars inde Roberto glen soluendo Inde annuatim x s. cum seruicio Inde debito et consueto.

xvj s.
xxviij s.
xx s.
Assedatur vna pars inde Roberto brydyn pro soluendo Inde annuatim x s. cum seruicio debito et consueto plegio Jacobo glen wilelmo snape.

*Ye gavilmos.* xij s. Assedatur vna pars wilelmo logane soluendo annuatim viij s. cum seruicio debito et consueto plegio Roberto glen.

Assedatur altra pars thome logan soluendo annuatim iiij s. cum seruicio debito et consueto plegio Roberto glen.

*Gilgiszarde.* xxiij s. Assedatur vna pars Roberto glen soluendo annuatim xiij s. iiij d. cum seruicio debito et consueto plegio Wilelmo glen.

Assedatur altra pars wilelmo glen Dauid blakburn soluendo annuatim xiij s. iiij d. cum seruicio debito et consueto plegio Roberto glen.

*le gerszarde* xxx s.

In manibus domini abbatis xxx s.

*Le ouertoun.*

Assedatur vna pars Johanni Schawe soluendo annuatim x s. cum seruicio debito et consueto.

Altra pars in manibus domini abbatis xxx s. in pascuis annuatim per pastores, viz.: nigellum or et patricium luff.

xl s. *Ye brigend.*

*Ye bar.*
iiij lib. xiij s. iiij d.

Assedatur vna pars Wilelmo lor soluendo inde annuatim xij s. cum seruicio debito et consueto.

*Ye Mylnbank* xxiiij s.

Assedatur vna pars wilelmo or soluendo annuatim xij s. cum seruicio debito et consueto plegio Johanne or.

Assedatur altra Johanni or soluendo annuatim xij s. cum seruicio debito et consueto plegio Wilelmo or.

Vna pars inde assedatur Jacobo or soluendo inde annuatim xij s. et xij d. pro le bone syluer plegio Johanne or.

*lytyl clochok* x s.

Assedatur alano Wilelmo bryde cum consensu patris sui soluendo annuatim x s. cum seruicio debito et consueto plegio Alexandro atkyn.

x s. *ye langcroft.*

Assedatur vna pars vidue Elisobethe henrici alano alansoun soluendo annuatim soluendo iiij s. iiij d. iij s. iiij. cum seruicio ut supra x s. cum seruicio.

*Quensidmuir* xl s.

Assedatur vna pars Elisobethe henrici alano alanson soluendo annuatim xl s. xiij s. iiij d. cum seruicio debito et consueto et sustentabit viginti quatuor le swmys in estate in eadem pascua cetera summa.

Assedatur pars illa quam habuit Walterus broun agneti relicte ipsius soluendo annuatim x s.

*Ye Caym* iiij lib.

Assedatur vna pars assedatur malcomo broun soluendo inde annuatim x s. cum le bon siluer et ceruisio inde debito et consueto.

Assedatur Jacobo Jameson alias cochran soluendo annuatim xl petras casei cum seruicio debito et consueto plegio Dauid Sandeson.

Assedatur vna pars gilberto Jameson soluendo annuatim xx s. cum seruicio debito et consueto plegio Wilelmo Alansone.

Assedatur altra pars Wilelmo Alanson soluendo annuatim x s. cum seruicio ut supra plegio gilberto Jameson.

Assedatur vna pars Johanni Jonsoun filio Johannis Robertson soluendo pro xv s. land .......... xxx[ti] petras casei cum seruicio debito et consueto plegio Johanni Robertson.

Assedatur alia pars waltero broun soluendo annuatim x s. cum seruicio debito et consueto plegio Malcomo Broun.

Assedatur alia pars meriote snape soluendo annuatim x s. cum seruicio debito et consueto plegio Wilelmo Alansoun. Et isto pars assedatur Johanni Robertsoun filio dicte mariote snape post decessum ipsius mariote soluendo.

Assedatur dauide blakborn wilelmo glen soluendo annuatim xx cum seruicio debito et consueto plegio Alano bryde.

Assedatur vna pars Johanni Alansoun soluendo annuatim x s. cum seruicio debito et consueto.

*bernauch wester* xxx s.

Cuius vna tota pars assedatur henrico frog soluendo inde annuatim xxx s. cum le bonsiluer pultrias et seruicio debito et consueto.

xxx s. *bernauch wester.*

Assedatur Jacobo crafurd soluendo annuatim xxx s. cum seruicio debito et consueto.

xl s. *ye lyntell.* **Occupat cum propriis monasterii.**

*Ester bernautht.*

x s. *barnuiklaw.*

**Assedatur Jacobo Schaw post decessum Johannis Schaw sui patris et soluendo inde annuatim x s.** cum seruicio inde debito et consueto.

*Molendinum bladorum.*

*Candilmur.*

Assedatur vna pars Ranaldo or soluendo annuatim iii$^{xx}$ petras casei cum tribus vitulis cum seruicio debito et consueto plegio Wo. Snape.

Assedatur alia pars waltero Snape soluendo annuatim xxx petras casei et 1 vitulum cum dimedio cum seruicio ut supra.

*Summa casei.*
vj$^{xx}$ vj vituli.

Assedatur **altera pars hugoni or soluendo annuatim xxx petras casei** cum vno vitulo et dimedio.

*Clochog.*

Cuius **vna pars assedatur Alexandro Atkyn soluendo inde** annuatim x petras casei et duos vitulos cum dimedio et cum seruicio debito et consueto Et predictus Alexander obligatur non displicere patricium kebil in ocupatione predicte assedacionis.

*Casei* vj$^{xx}$.
et vj vituli.

Assedatur altra pars Johanni merschande soluendo annuatim iij$^{xx}$ petras casei cum tribus vitulis et dimedio plegio Alexandro Atkyn.

Et predicta villa dividitur in duas partes equales inter dictos Alexandrum et Johannem cum consensu abbatis.

Assedatur vna pars de Mekil clochog Johanni Atkyn juniori filio Johannis viz. ye xx s. land de bawgren soluendo annuatim xij$^{xx}$ petras cum tribus vitulis plegio niniano or de westir bracht.

*Monyzabrok* xl s.

In manibus domini de hawkhede xl s.

Vna pars de clochog assedatur wilelmo mungumbry cum vidua margareta viz. xx s. land soluendo annuatim iij$^{xx}$ petras casei cum tribus vitulis cum alio seruicio debito et consueto.

*Molendinum.* In manibus tenandorum xxvj s. viij d.
*bladorum de Glen*
xxvj s. viij d.

*Ye Grange* **Assedatur vna pars Inde relicte Stephani crag** soluendo annuatim iij$^{xx}$ petras casei
xv$^{xx}$ *petre casei.* ad terminos consuetos vna cum tribus vitulis et x s. plegio et debitore hugone bronside.

Assedatur vna pars Inde Johanni crag soluendo inde annuatim iij$^{xx}$ petras casei xx s. pro vitulis ipso Johanne intrante post recessum Jonete ker vel cum sit coniugata plegio.

*Caym.* Assedatur pars quam habuit gilbertus Jameson Johanni gybson et Wilelmo gybson filiis predicti gylberti post dissessum patris ipsius placente matre cum consilio et voluntate domini abbatis soluendo Inde annuatim xx s. et v marcas in Introitu ipsorum Johannis et wilelmi cum omni alio seruicio debito et consueto.

*Assedacio terrarum dominii de kylpatrik.*

Cuius vna pars assedatur alano bryson soluendo Inde annuatim xxxiij s. iiij d. cum le bonsiluer et seruicio debito et consueto plegio Roberto quhyte.

Assedatur inde alia pars Roberto bronsyde soluendo xvj s. viij d. cum le bonsiluer et seruicio debito et consueto plegio Ricardo fordoun.

*Vester kylpatrik.*

vj lib. xiij s. iiij d. Cuius vna pars assedatur fynlayo Jamyson soluendo inde annuatym l s. cum le bonsiluer et seruicio debito et consueto plegio Johanne morisoun.

Assedatur alia pars inde Johanni morisoun relicte Johannis morisoun malcomo morisoun soluendo Inde annuatim xvj s. viij d. cum le bon siluer et seruicio debito et consueto plegio hugone bronside.

Altera pars assedatur hugoni bronsid soluendo annuatim xxv s. cum le bonsiluer et seruicio debito et consueto plegio Johanne morisoun.

Altera pars assedatur Wilelmo lang soluendo annuatim xvj s. viij d. cum seruicio debito et consueto plegio fynlayo Jameson.

Altera pars assedatur donaldo Vilson soluendo inde annuatim xxv s. cum le bonsiluer et ceruisio debito et consueto plegio finlayo Jamesoun.

Illa domus quam habuit patricius donaldson cum orto eiusdem assedatur Johanni logane soluendo inde annuatim duodecim capones cum seruicio debito et consueto.

*Moreslande & huchonisland.*

xxvj s. viij d. Inde Assedatur Johanni flemyn soluendo annuatim xxvj s. iiij d. cum seruicio debito et consueto sicut alii tenentes faciunt plegio Ricardo fordoun.

*Ester Kilpatrik.*

Cuius vna pars assedatur Johanni beton soluendo inde annuatim xxij s. ij d. cum seruicio debito et consueto plegio Wilelmo Patonson.

Altera pars assedatur Alano donaldson soluendo inde annuatim xxij s. ij d. cum seruicio debito et consueto plegio W° Jonson.

Altera pars Inde assedatur Wilelmo Jonson soluendo inde annuatim xxij s. ij d. cum seruicio debito et consueto plegio Alano Donaldson.

Altera pars assedatur Johanni Jameson soluendo annuatim xxij s. ij d. cum seruicio debito et consueto plegio Johanne beton.

Altera pars Inde assedatur relicte Johannis morisoun Johanni morisoun malcolmo morisoun wilelmo morisoun soluendo annuatim xj s. j d cum seruicio debito et consueto plegio hugone bronside.

Item, pars illa que assedebatur alano donaldson nunc diuiditur in duas partes.

Quarum vna assedatur Simoni donaldson soluendo inde annuatim xj s. j d.

Et altera assedatur thome makscuben soluendo inde annuatim xj s. j d. cum seruicio consueto.

Assedatur alia pars Johanni lang soluendo inde annuatim xxxiij s. iiij d. xxij s. ij d. cum ceruisio et le bonis plegio vilelmo Jonsoun.

Alia pars assedatur Jacobo Johnsone soluendo inde xj s. ij d. cum seruicio debito et le bonis.

Dimedia pars terre que possidebat alanus donaldson assedatur cristoforo donaldson soluendo inde annuatim xj s. j d. cum seruicio debito et consueto et le bonis.

Vna pars assedatur thome donaldson soluendo Inde annuatim xviij s. iiij d. cum le bonsiluer et seruicio debito et consueto plegio Roberto quhit.

*Auchinchoschan* iiij lib.

Cuius vna pars assedatur donald Wilson soluendo Inde annuatim xiij s. iiij d. cum bonsiluer et seruicio debito et consueto plegio roberto quhit.

Altera pars assedatur mergrete heriot Jacobo brisone soluendo Inde annuatim xx s. cum seruicio debito et consueto plegio donaldo Wilson.

Altera pars roberto quhit soluendo Inde annuatim xxvj s. viij d. xxv s. cum seruitio Inde debito et consueto plegio andree murhede.

Assedatur altera pars Johanni Robysoun soluendo Inde annuatim x s. cum ceruisio Inde debito et consueto et bonsiluer plegio donaldo Wilson.

Assedatur vna pars Roberto quhyt pro v. s. annuatim.

alia pars thome donaldson soluendo annuatim xx d. cum seruicio debito et consueto.

Assedatur alia pars Johanni Wilson soluendo Inde annuatim vj s. viij d. cum ceruisio inde debito et consueto plegio donaldo Wilson.

Pars quam habuit Johannes Robyson assedatur vilelmo hog soluendo inde annuatim x s. cum seruicio et bonsiluer et alias seruicio consueto.

*Dunterclunan.*

iiij lib. xiij s. iiij d.

Cuius vna pars assedatur Ricardo fordoun Johanni alanson soluendo inde annuatim xxiij s. iiij d. cum le bonsiluer et seruicio debito et consueto plegio Ricardo fordoun.

Assedatur alia pars inde assedatur alano lang soluendo inde annuatim xxiij s. iiij d. cum seruicio debito et consueto plegio Ricardo fordoun.

Assedatur ista villa in toto Ricardo fordoun preter illam partem quam habuit andreas thomson soluendo inde vt hic Scribitur cum seruicio debito et consueto.

Assedatur alexandro Stewart soluendo annuatim xv s. ix d. cum ceruisio Inde debito et consueto plegio Rycardo fordoun.

Assedatur altera pars andree tomsoun soluendo annuatim vij s. x d. cum obolo plegio Alexandro stewart.

Assedatur illa pars quam habebat alexander Steuuart Ricardo fordoun soluendo inde annuatim xv s. ix d. cum seruicio debito et consueto plegio Johanne Alanson.

Assedatur tota ista villa predicto Ricardo fordoun preter illam partem.

*Ferchlay* xx s.

Assedatur Roberto Stenson Johanni brisone soluendo annuatim xx s. cum alio ceruisio Inde debito et consueto plegio Andrea murhede.

Assedatur eciam filio suo Wilelmo Stevinson post decessum patris sui antedicti soluendo xx s. cum seruicio debito et consueto plegio Ricardo fordoun.

Assedatur vna pars Roberto ffordon post discessum Wilelmi Alanson soluendo inde xvj s. viij d.

*Wester Cochnoch.*
vj lib. xiij s. iiij d.

Assedatur vna inde Wilelmo Alanson soluendo Inde xvj s. viij d. cum seruicio debito et consueto plegio roberto fynneson.

Assedatur alia pars Wilelmo hog soluendo Nicholais strabrok Inde annuatim xj s. ij d. cum seruicio debito et consueto plegio Johanne Jamson.

Assedatur vna pars Jacobo Jonson pro xvj s. viij d. cum seruicio debito et consueto pro plegio Ricardo fordoun.

Assedatur Johanni Jameson Johanni Alanson soluendo Inde annuatim xxij s. ij d. cum seruicio Inde debito et consueto plegio Ricardo gibson.

Assedatur alia pars Roberto alanson soluendo annuatim xvi s. iiij d. cum seruicio Inde debito et consueto plegio Johanne Jameson.

Assedatur Ricardo gibson alia pars soluendo annuatim xxij s. ij d. xvj s. viij d. cum seruicio Inde debito et consueto.

Assedatur altera pars Johanni hog soluendo annuatim xj s. i d. cum seruicio Inde debito et consueto plegio Ricardo fordoun.

Assedatur alia pars Jacobo Sclatter soluendo inde annuatim post decessum Ricardi gybson cum seruicio debito consueto v s. vj d.

Assedatur vna pars thome lecht Waltero Scot soluendo inde annuatim xvj s. viij d. et alia seruicia debita et consueta sicut ceteri tenentes.

Assedatur vna pars Jacobo lenax soluendo inde annuatim xvj s. viij d. cum seruicio Inde debito et consueto plegio andrea Wilzongson.

*Nota*

*Ester Cochnoch.*
vj lib. xiij s. iiij d.

Assedatur vna Johanni donaldson soluendo inde annuatim xvj s. viij d. cum seruisio debito et consueto plegio roberto fynne.

Assedatur vna pars roberto forsytht soluendo annuatim xvj s. viij d. plegio thoma Tomsoun.

Ista pars assedatur Jacobo Jonson post decessum eius patris Johannis Tomson soluendo annuatim xvj s. viij d. cum seruicio debito et consueto.

Assedatur thome Johanni tomson soluendo inde annuatim xvj s. viij d. cum seruicio debito et consueto plegio Andrea Wilzongson.

Altera pars inde assedatur Wilelmo le soluendo Inde annuatim xvj s. viij d. cum seruicio Inde debito et consueto plegio Andrea Jonson. Et dimedietas eiusdem assedatur Johanni filio ipsius Willelmi post eius decessum.

Altera pars inde assedatur Roberto forsytht soluendo annuatim xvj s. viij d. cum seruicio debito et consueto plegio Wilelmo le.

Alia pars inde assedatur Andree glwwar soluendo annuatim viij s. iiij d. cum seruicio debito et consueto plegio Wilelmo le.

Assedatur alia pars Inde donaldo sklater soluendo inde annuatim viij s. iiij d. plegio Johanne lang teste Johanne sympyl et notandum quod ista assedacio est facta ipso donaldo post mortem roberti le et non alias.

Assedatur altera pars Johanni tomson soluendo annuatim xvj s. viij d. plegio Andree Wilzongson.

*Edynbernan.*
iiij lib. vj s. viij d.

Cuius vna pars assedatur mauricio flemyn soluendo annuatim xxj s. viij d. cum seruicio Inde debito et consueto plegio.

Altera inde assedatur Johanni Allanson Johanni Jameson soluendo annuatim xxj s. viij d. cum seruicio Inde debito et consueto plegio Ricardo fordoun.

Assedatur alia pars Johanni bochlay soluendo annuatim x s. x d. cum seruicio Inde debito et consueto plegio Wilelmo le.

Assedatur alia pars bartholmo flemyn Johanni Alanson soluendo annuatim x s. x d. cum seruicio Inde debito et consueto plegio fynlayo Jameson.

Ista pars quam habebat mauricius fleming assedatur Jacobo fleming et bartholomeo fleming soluendo inde eorum quilibet per se x s. x d. cum seruicio etc.

Assedatur alia pars elisobethe dare Johanni Alanson soluendo annuatim x s. x d. et seruicio Inde debito et consueto plegio Johanne bochlay.

Assedatur altera pars Wilelmo le soluendo annuatim x s. x d. cum seruicio Inde debito et consueto plegio Johanne Alanson.

Assedatur illa pars quam habuerunt bartholomeus fleming et ebota darro Johanni Alansone soluendo inde annuatim xx s. xx d. cum seruicio debito et consueto plegio Ricardo fordoun.

*Auchenlec.*
v lib.

Cuius vna pars assedatur Johanni bryson soluendo inde annuatim xxv s. cum seruicio debito et consueto plegio Johanne Mwr.

Altera pars assedatur Johanni Mwr soluendo inde xij s. vj d. cum seruicio debito et consueto plegio Johanne bryson.

Assedatur alia pars Johanni m'gregor soluendo annuatim xxv s. cum seruicio debito et consueto plegio Johanne bryson.

Item, eodem assedatur pars Johannis Mwr soluendo annuatim xij s. cum seruicio etc.

Assedatur mauricio makkeson soluendo annuatim xij s. xj d. cum seruicio inde debito et consueto plegio Johanne brysoun.

Assedatur alia pars Roberto le soluendo annuatim xij s. vj d. cum seruicio inde debito et consueto plegio Johanne bryson.

Altera pars assedatur patricio Wilsoun soluendo inde annuatim xij s. vj d. cum seruicio inde debito et consueto plegio Johanne.

*Mylntown.*
iiij lib. vj s. viij d.

Cuius vna pars assedatur Andree murhede soluendo inde annuatim xliij s. iiij d. cum seruicio inde debito et consueto plegio Johanne lang.

Altera pars assedatur Johanni lang soluendo inde annuatim xxj s. viij d. cum seruicio debito et consueto plegio Andrea murhede.

Assedatur alia pars Wilelmo Stenson soluendo annuatim xxj s. viij d. cum seruicio inde debito et consueto plegio Andree murhede.

Assedatur vna pars inde Johanni lang juniori soluendo xxj s. viij d. cum seruicio debito et consueto plegio Ricardo fordoun.

*ye bradfeld.*
iiij lib. Assedatur vna pars inde Johanni Wodruff soluendo inde annuatim xx s. cum seruicio debito et consueto plegio georgio morisoun.

Assedatur altera pars inde Johanni bryson soluendo inde annuatim xx s. cum seruicio inde debito et consueto plegio Alano ricardi.

Assedatur altera pars Angucio denby soluendo annuatim xx s. cum seruicio inde debito et consueto plegio ricardo fordo.

Altera pars assedatur Ricardo Knox soluendo inde annuatim xx s. cum seruicio inde debito et consueto.

Assedatur vna pars relicte Wilelmi Wodruff Mariote patrikson pro tempore viduetatis sui sicut alii tenentes habent assidaciones plegio andree murhede.

*lytil culboy.*
v lib. Assedatur vna pars georgio morisoun soluendo inde annuatim xviij s. ix d. cum ceruicio debito et consueto plegio Johanne Wodruff.

Altera pars inde assedatur thome sym soluendo inde annuatim xxv s. cum seruicio inde debito et consueto plegio nicholayo huchinson.

Assedatur alia pars Wilelmo Stenson soluendo annuatim vj s. ij d. cum seruicio Inde debito et consueto plegio morisoun.

*Mekil culboy.*
vj lib. x s. Cuius vna pars assedatur Vilelmo bryson soluendo inde annuatim xxxij s. vj d. cum seruicio Inde debito et consueto plegio Andrea murhede.

Altera pars assedatur roberto fynne soluendo Inde annuatym xxxij s. vj d. cum seruicio debito et consueto plegio Alano richeson.

Altera pars alano richeson soluendo annuatim xxj s. viij d. plegio roberto fynne cum ceruisio debito et consueto.

Assedatur alia pars nicholayo huchsoun soluendo annuatim xxj s. viij d. cum seruicio debito et consueto plegio roberto quhit.

Assedatur alia pars Johanni denby soluendo annuatim x s. x d. cum seruicio Inde debito et consueto.

*Mauchquhaurane.*
vj lib. viij s. iiij d.

*ye bernys.*
iiij lib.

*Auchingrey.*
xxvj s. viij d.

*Cragbanzok.*
xiij s. iiij d.

xij *capones.* Domus mergrete solater assedatur patrik donaldson soluendo annuatim xij capones.

*Molendinum de Drumtochyr.*
xx lib. Assedatur tenentibus pro j[a] markis.

Terra capelle de vester cochnay assedatur Johanni Alani per venerabilem patrem Dominum georgium abbatem cum omnibus libertatibus ad eandem capellam pertinentibus.

Assedacio terrarum dominii de Kile vt supra facta apud munkton vij$^{mo}$ die Octobris anno domini M° iiij$^{c}$ lxxij$^{do}$ de anno in annum per venerabilem in cristo patrem et dominum dominum Georgeum Schaw abbatem monasterii de Pasleto.

*Monktvon hil.*
v lib. xviij s.

Cuius vna pars assedatur thome Cuthtbert pro xv s. iiij d. annuatim cum seruicio Inde debito et consueto plegio thoma broun.

Alia pars assedatur thome brone pro xv s. iiij d. annuatim cum seruicio inde debito et consueto plegio thoma Cuthtbert.

Alia pars assedatur thome grefe pro xxiiij s. annuatim cum seruicio Inde debito et consueto plegio nicholayo Boghouse.

Alia pars assedatur Wilelmo patone pro xij s. annuatim cum seruicio inde debito et consueto plegio nicholaio Boghous.

Alia pars assedatur nicholaio Boghous pro xxiiij s. annuatim cum seruicio inde debito et consueto plegio thome grefe.

Alia pars assedatur mage oglatht pro xij s. annuatim cum seruicio inde debito et consueto plegio Wilelmo Patone.

Alia pars assedatur henrico hosbar pro xv s. iiij d.

Alia pars assedatur Johanni Osberne juniori pro xxxvj s. annuatim plegio Wilelmo Coningham.

Summa huius ville annuatim, v lib. xviij s.

*Monktovn.*
xv lib. xiiij s. iiij d.

Cuius vna pars assedatur Johanni nell pro liij s. iiij d. annuatim cum seruicio Inde debito et consueto plegio et debitore Johanni Philipo Broune.

Alia pars assedatur Philipo brone pro liij s. iiij d. annuatim cum seruicio inde debito et consueto plegio Johanne nelle.

Assedatur Roberto Schaw soluendo annuatim pro firma decima et omnibus aliis seruicio consuetis viij lib.

Alia pars assedatur Roberto chapele pro xxix s. annuatim cum seruicio inde debito et consueto plegio et debitore cristofero sergeando.

Alia pars assedatur Johanni Daw pro xj s. viij d. annuatim cum seruicio inde debito et consueto plegio Johanne Oglatht.

Alia pars assedatur Johanni Oglatht pro xxxvj s. annuatim cum seruicio inde debito et consueto plegio Johanne Daw.

Alia pars assedatur Johanni clerico pro viij s. annuatim cum seruicio inde debito et consueto plegio et debitore Johanne Wilsone.

Alia pars assedatur Johanni Wilsone pro viij s. annuatim cum seruicio inde debito et consueto plegio et debitore Johanne clerk.

Alia pars assedatur ffinlaio talzeour pro xxx s. annuatim cum seruicio inde debito et consueto plegio cristofero sergeando.

Alia pars assedatur cristofero sergeando pro xvj s. annuatim cum seruicio inde debito et consueto ffinlaio talzoure.

Alia pars assedatur vilelmo Adamson pro xliiij s. annuatim cum seruicio.

Alia pars assedatur patricio nichole pro xxv s. cum vno seruicio et dimedio.

Alia pars quam prius possidebat Johannes ogloch assedatur Wilelmo hunter pro xxxvj s. annuatim cum seruicio inde debito.

Summa huius xv lib. xiiij s. iiij d.
Roberto Schaw excepto.

xl s. *Brokat.*

Cuius vna pars assedatur Alexandro nicholl pro xx s. annuatim cum seruicio inde debito et consueto plegio et debitore Johanne Rig eiusdem.

Alia pars assedatur Johanne Rig pro xx s. annuatim cum seruicio inde debito et consueto plegio Alexandro nicholl supra.

*Bronsyde cuius tota pars.* Assedatur Johanni Thome Rig inde pecunie vj s. viij d. et jactando et laborando sequelam molendini.

*Cuchatmur, viz.* xxxvj s. Cuius tota pars assedatur Elene wile pro xxxvj s. viij d. annuatim cum seruicio indedebito et consueto plegio et debitore Roberto Schaw de monktone.

*Vileis tak* viij d.

*le Wardhous.* iij s. iiij d. Cuius tota pars assedatur domino roberto greve prius pro iij s. iiij d. annuatim pro toto tempore vite sue sub communi sigillo capituli ut patet plegio Johanne greve.

*Terre domini. de le manys.* xx lib. iij s. iiij d.

Cuius vna pars assedatur Johanni huntar seniori pro xxxvij s. vj d. cum seruicio inde debito plegio Roberto Schaw de Munkton.

Alia pars assedatur Johanni grefe pro l s. annuatim cum seruicio inde debito plegio Roberto chapele.

Ye byrquarter assedatur domino roberto greve prius pro toto tempore vite sue sub sigillo communi capituli nostri pro v lib. annuatim et duodecim caponibus et seruicio inde debito et consueto ut patet in litera sua plegio Johanne greve.

Alia pars assedatur vilelmo symson pro l s. annuatim cum seruicio debito plegio roberto chapel.

Alia pars assedatur Dauid masson pro xxv s. annuatim cum seruicio debito plegio roberto schaw.

Alia pars assedatur vilelmo hunter pro l s. annuatim cum seruicio debito plegio Malcomo hunter de kirkhille.

Alia pars assedatur Archibaldo Coninghame xxxvij s. vj d. cum seruicio inde debito et consueto plegio Roberto chapele.

Item, predictus dominus Robertus greyfe pro le warhouse soluit annuatim xl d.

Summa vtriusque lateris Roberto Schaw excepto xlv lib. xiij.

VS, Robert, be ye permission of God, Abbot of Paslay, grantis ws til haf rentallit our seruand Sir William hwyme, curet of our kirk of Auchinlek, in the hail kirkland of ye samyn, payand yerfor zeirlie as it was wont to do, and alse we ordain and makis ye said William our curet of our said kirk for al ye tyme of his life, and quhen ye said Sir William may nocht mak seruis in ye parochin, he sal cause ane other to mak seruis for him that sal be sufficient.———

In witnes quherof we haif subscrivit this writ with our hand at Paslay, ye xvij day of Aprile, ye zeir of God a thousand fife hundreth and xxiij zeris, befor Dene Richart Watson, Johne Abernethy.

*Molendinum.*

x lib. *bladorum de Monkton.*

*Dalmulyng.*

liij s. iiij d. *kyrlandholme.*

Cuius vna pars assedatur Alexandro galouai pro xl s. annuatim cum seruicio inde debito et consueto plegio et debitore Roberto Schaw de munkton.

Altera pars de kirklandholme assedatur Johanni Ingeram pro xiij s. iiij d. cum seruicio debito et consueto.

*Kyrkhil.*

iij lib. xiij s. iiij d.

Cuius vna pars assedatur Johanni haufe juniori inde pecunie annuatim xxiiij s. vj d. cum seruicio debito et consueto plegio cristofero sergeando.

Secunda pars assedatur pro xxiiij s. v d.

Tercia pars assedatur macolmo hunter pro xxiiij s. v d. annuatim plegio vilelmo hunter cum seruicio debito.

Ye Wodquarter Is set to ye men vnder-writin kepand ye wode clene of gulde that thai eire in it vnder ye pane and tinsal of ilka manis awne tak.

*ye Wodquarter.*

iiij lib. xiij s. iiij d.

Cuius vna pars assedatur Johanni thomson seniori pro xxiij s. iiij d. annuatim cum seruicio inde debito et consueto plegio Nigello thomson.

Alia pars assedatur Nigello thomson pro xxiij s. iiij d. cum seruicio inde debito et consueto plegio Johanne thomson supra.

Alia pars assedatur Elene forsithe pro xv s. x d. annuatim cum seruicio inde debito et consueto plegio ade Alexanderson de taitis quarter.

Alia pars assedatur Alexandro Grey pro vij s. x d. cum seruicio debito plegio Alexandro osborne.

*Octauo Maii.*

*ye maynholme quarter.*

iiij lib. xiij s. iiij d.

Assedatur maynholme quarter henrico carnis anno quingentesimo quinto soluendo annuatim iiij lib. xiij s. iiij d. cum seruicio inde debito et consueto plegio Alexandro Obsberne.

Milquartar assedatur Matheo Rodman anno v^ma^

Assedatur vna pars inde viz. xl^ti^ solidi terrarum matheo Rodman cum consensu nostro de dimedietate molendini de dalmullyng soluendo annuatim xl^ti^ solidos cum seruicio debito et consueto pro terra tantum plegio.

*Taytis quartar.*

iiij lib. xiij s. iiij d.

Cuius vna pars assedatur Alexandro osberne pro xx s. annuatim cum seruicio inde debito et consueto plegio et debitore patricio quhit.

Alia pars assedatur Johanni haufe seniori pro xvj s. viij d. annuatim cum seruicio Inde debito et consueto plegio Nigello thomson de Wodquartar.

Alia pars assedatur Ade Alexanderson pro xl s. annuatim cum seruicio Inde debito et consueto plegio Johanne haufe seniori.

Alia pars assedatur valtero haufe pro xvj s. viij d. annuatim cum seruicio Inde debito et consueto plegio Johanne haufe seniori.

*Ye Myln quartar.*

Cuius vna pars assedatur Roberto Millar pro xxvj s. viij d. annuatim cum seruicio Inde debito et consueto plegio malcolmo huntar de kirkhile.

Altera pars assedatur Agnete vedue pro xiij s. iiij d. annuatim cum seruicio inde debito et consueto plegio Roberto millar supra.

x lib. *Molendinum bladorum de Dalmulyng.*

Summa totalis ferme de Dalmolyn cum molendino xxxv lib. vij s. ix d. cum vij s. ix d. datis per dominum de kethkert pro vno lumine ardente in ecclesia Sancte Kenote.

*Ye Movnthous.*

xx s. Assedatur Dauid tate soluendo Inde annuatim xx s. ad duos anni terminos debitos et consuetos plegio et debito henrico frog. Et memorandum quod dicta assedacio facta fuit dicto dauid sub condicione si ipsius erat tenens in dicta terra.

*terra in teuedale.*

*Anni reditus.*

In primis vj s. viij d. per dominum houstone.
Item, vj s. viij d. in portarfield.
Item, xiij s. iiij d. per molendinum in refru.
Item, vij s. per teram prope le kyngis orchat.
Item, v s. pro le monkdyk.
Item, xij d. per terram Jonete Sperlyne.
Item, pro le thortur landis viij d.
Item, ij s. vj d. per domum patricii glouer in glasgow.
Item, iij s. iiij d. per domum Johannis chalmer in ruglen.
Item, iiij s. per le tend zettis in Ruglen.
Item, xv d. per domum Johannis byrkinschaw in ruglen.
Item, vij d. cum obolo per domum Roberti Symson in Ruglen.
Item, vij d. cum obolo per domum mergarete mersanton in Ruglen.
Item, vij d. cum obolo per domum locarde in Ruglen.
Item, xl s. per dominum de Adamtovn in kile.
Item, viij s. per dominum de Corsbe in kile.
Item, xx s. per dominum de Auchinlek in kile.
Item, vj lib. xiij s. iiij d. pro pensione in korraguel.

*Piscarie in primis.*

Ye annuel of kelsoland in ye largis zerly 1 stane of wax.
Ye annuel of Ryswin half a stane of wax zerly.
Ye annuel of kilmacolme 1 libra of sema. (?)
Ye annuel of ye chapel of Renfru 1 libra of wax.

*Firme domus monachorum in glasgo.*

In primis 1 loff 1 cellar 1 zarde assedatur Johanni kyrkland pro xxviij s.
Item, 1 bothe wast.
Item, v cellaris 1 thruggang wast in glasgo.
Item, quatuor lofftis wast in glasgo.

*Kyrlandis.*

In primis Ecclesia de Auchinle xl s.
Ecclesia Sancte kenote.
Ecclesia de largis.
Ecclesia de lochwynok.
Ecclesia de neilstone.
Ecclesia de Rosneth.
Ecclesia de lydzardvode.

Assedacio terrarum dominii de kill facta per venerabilem in cristo patrem Robertum abbatem monasterii de pasleto et dominum de adamtoun eius balliuum apud munktoun octauo die mensis maii anno domini millesimo quingentesimo quinto pro tribus annis duratura sub stilis et condicionibus viz.:

Munktoun hill v lib. xviij s.

Paton riche xv s. iiij d. 1 capon 2 pultre ij chekins ij sartis sarcinae carbonum.

Alexander Conighame xv s. iiij d. 1 capon ij pultre ij chekins ij sartis sarcine carbonum.

Ninianus legat xv s. iiij d. 1 capon ij pultre ij chekins ij sartis sarcine carbonum.

Johannes Osbern junior xxxvj s. iij capones iiij pultre vj pulli iij sartis sarcine carbonum.

*plegius alter alterius.* { Allan greif xxiiij s. ij capones ij pultre iiij pulli iij sarcine carbonum plegius alter alterius.
locus Wilelmi patoun xij s. 1 capo 1 pultre ij pulli 1 sarcina carbonum. }

Summa pecunie v lib. xviij s. ix capones xiij pultre xviij pulli xij sarcine carbonum.

*Munktoun* xv lib. xiiij s. iiij d.

*plegius alter alterius.* {
Wilelmus hunter xxxvj s. iij capones iij pultre vj pulli ij sarcine carbonum.
Johannes Wilson xvj s. 1 capones 1 pultre iij pulli ij sarcine carbonum.
Johannes fyndlaw xxx[d] s. ij capones iij pultre v pulli ij sarcine carbonum.
Johannes neyl senior xxix s. ij capones iij pultre iiij pulli ij sarcine carbonum.
Johannes adamson liij s. iiij d. iiij capones iiij pultre viij pulli ij sarcine carbonum.
Dauid Gottray xxv s. ij capones ij pultre iiij pulli ij sarcine carbonum.
Nicholaus morys xj s. viij d. 1 pultre ij pulli ij sarcine carbonum.
Matheus neill liij s. iiij d. iiij capones iiij pultre ij sarcine carbonum.
Wil adamson xliiij s. iiij capones iij pultre ij sarcine carbonum—plegius alter alterius.
Robertus clerk / Johannes neyl junior } xvj s. 1 capo 1 pultre iij pull ij sarcine carbonum. }

Summa pecunie xv lib. xiiij s. iiij d. xxiij capones xxv pultre xlix pulli xx[ti] sarcine carbonum.

*Brokat et Cuchatmur* iij lib. xvj s. viij d.

Robertus Wilson xx[ti] s. }
In manibus domini xx[ti] s. } iij capones iij pultre vj pulli ij sarcine carbonum.

Dominus de Adamtoun xxxvj s. viij d. iij capones iij pultre vj pulli ij sarcine carbonum.

Dauid blair xxij°. Summa pecunie iij lib. xvj s. viij d. vj capones vj pultre xij pulli vj sarcine carbonum.

Munktoun manys xx[ti] lib. iiij duodecim caponum.

Robertus hunter........................l[ti] s.
locus roberti greif......................l[ti] s.
Willelmus huntar.................. ...l[ti] s.
Charle Wilson Wilelmus conigham...................liiij s. ij d. enter to Wilzem Conigham steid.
Wilelmus Wily.........................iij lib. ij s. vj d.
Adam Schaw.............................xxxiij s. iiij d.
Johannes huntar....... ..............l[ti] s.
Johannes osberne.......................l[ti] s.
Locus ade Schaw prope munktoun iiij lib.
Adam Schaw iiij lib. vj capones vj pultre xij pulli.
le Wardhous x s. prope domum vicarii.
Magister Alexander Schaw x s.

The ouer manis of munktoun, alias Adam of Schawis steid set to mergret mwr for seruis done till ws be hyr and od gratuiteis, payand therfor zheirly, iiij lib. of mail, wyth vj capons, vj pultre, xjj pulli, allanerly mayd at Paslay xix[no] Januarii, in anno xix[no], befor thir Witness m person of cardross, master Wilzem Stewart, george houstoun.

Item, set till mergret mur ye tendis of ye ouer manis for vj merkis, and ye tendis of ye nether manis, for x lib., sic lik as thai pait of befor be Robyn of Schaw, Adam of Schaw, and Adam Wallace. Item, set to the said mergret the myllis of munktoun and Dalmilling, for ilk myl for ten lib., sic lik as thai pait be forsaid robyn Schaw, Adam Schaw, and Adam Wallace, maid this rentilling, maid at paslay xix of Januar, in anno Domini, etc., xix[mo] iij°, befor thir witness, person of Cardross, master patrik Schaw, master Wilzem Steuart, and george houstoun. Wyth our hand, Robert, Abbot of Paslay, etc.

Item, set to mergret mwr, and to thomas schaw, hyr sone, ye tendis of the ouer manis, the quhilkis scho dwellis in, extendand to xij bollis of meill and beir, for vj merkis of vsuale money zerly, and the tendis of the nether manis for x lib., sic lik as thai pait of befor be auld robyn of Schaw, Adam of Schaw, and Adam Wallace. Item, set to the said mergret mwr, and thomas, hyr sone, the myllis of munktoun and Dalmillyn, for ilk myl ten lib., sic lik as was pait be the forsaidis robert Schaw, Adam of Schaw, and Adam Wallace; and als the vj merkis land of the ouer manis for vj merkis of mail, as the forsaid tenandis pait, and for cariage, foullis, and all oder dewy seruis, j lib. allanerly. this rentilling maid at Paslay the xx day of Julij, in anno

Domini, etc., xxiiij°, befor thir witness, george schaw of knokhill, master Wilzem Steuart, vicar of croy, robyn Schaw of the maynhom, John of Abernethy, and oder diuers.

*Assedacio terrarum Infra dominium de Pasleto facta per venerabilem in Cristo patrem georgium permissione diuina.*

*Dominum de Kyl.*

locus Wilelmi huntar de munktoun assedatur filio suo Ade huntar pro xxxvj s. cum pullis et cariagio et alio seruicio debito et consueto anno Domini, etc., quingentesimo xij° xx° augusti.

Item, vna pars de neder manis quam occupat Adam Schaw ortulous assedatur ade gylcrist de consensu dicti Ade soluendo annuatim xxxvij s. vj d. sicut dictus Adam solebat soluere cum auenis et caponibus sicut ceteri tenentes soluunt plegio pro eo Johanne osberne.

*Assedacio terrarum dominii de pasleto facta per venerabilem in cristo patrem georgium abbatem dicti monasterii ad terminum pentecosten in anno Domini etc. lxxxiiij^to pro voluntate dicti domini Abbatis duratura.*

*Auchingone*

*Balroger* xl s. Assedatur vna pars de balroger et burtreis Andree Stewart soluendo inde annuatim
*Burtreis* xij s. xvij s. iiij d. cum le bonis et seruicio Inde debito et consueto post mortem patris
xij d. *de bonis.* ipso intrante vel ad voluntatem patris.

Alia pars Inde assedatur dauid Stewart soluendo annuatim xvij s. iiij d. cum le bonis et seruicio Inde debito et consueto.

Alia pars Inde assedatur matheo Stewart soluendo Inde annuatim xvij s. iiij d. cum seruicio Inde debito et consueto.

Altera pars Inde assedatur domino Alexandro Stewart soluendo inde annuatim xvij s. iiij d. cum le bonnis et alia seruicio inde debito et consueto.

*Merborne* iiij lib.
xij d. *de le bonis.*

Assedatur vna pars Inde Jacobo Stewart soluendo Inde annuatim xx s. cum le bonis et seruicio Inde debito et consueto.

Alia pars Inde assedatur thome Stewart soluendo Inde annuatim xx s. cum le bonys et seruicio Inde debito et consueto.

Assedatur vna pars Johanni Stewart filio Dauid Stewart soluendo Inde annuatim xl^ti s. et xij d. pro le bon siluer cum le cane foullis et alio seruicio inde debito et consueto plegio domino Alexandro Stewart.

Assedatur vna pars inde Johanni Stewart et Dauid Stewart filio suo et eorum diutius viuenti pro terminis ut supra soluendo annuatim xl s. et xij d. pro le bone syluer cum seruicio inde debito et consueto plegius alter alterius.

*Mos side.*

Assedatur alia pars inde Malcomo merschel juniori soluendo inde xvj s. viij d. cum seruicio inde debito et consueto.

*Nota.* Alia pars assedatur gilberto Stewart soluendo xviij s. annuatim cum le bone siluer et ceruisio inde debito et consueto plegio Johanni glen.

*Stokbrig.*

Assedatur vna pars inde Alano Knok soluendo annuatim xvj s. viij d. cum bonsiluer et seruicio inde debito et consueto plegio dauid Stewart.

*Nota.* Pars gilberti Stewart assedatur thome Stewart filio dicti gilberti post mortem patris soluendo annuatim xviij s. cum le bone siluer et seruicio inde debito et consueto plegio Andrea Stewart.

*Auchingone per totum.*
in anno ix lib.
iij s. iiij d.
xiij½ dd. pultrie.

Assedatur vna pars inde roberto clerk soluendo annuatim xvj s. xviij d. le bon siluer et cane foullis cum alio seruicio debito et consueto plegio Jacobo or.

Assedatur Johanni Mwr de Estir Caldwell et filio suo naturali Wil. Mwr soluendo annuatim xl[ti] s. et xij d. pro le bonesiluer viz. de neder . . . . . xl[ti] s. land besyd Sanct Ninianis chapell cum alio seruicio debito et consueto facta in Augusto in anno Domini xxxiiij • coram hiis testibus Jacobo Schaw vicario de Kilibarquhan Matheo Walker vicario de Troon et Johanne Abernethy cum aliis diuersis.

*ffultone.*
viij lib. vj s. viij d.
*et* xij dd. vj *pultrie.*

Assedatur vna pars inde Jacobo bute post dimissionem relicte Johanni paslay soluendo annuatim xx s. cum seruicio debito et consueto.

Assedatur vna pars inde petro brone soluendo liij s. iiij d. cum seruicio inde debito et consueto.

Alia pars inde assedatur Johanni mechelson soluendo inde annuatim xiij s. iiij d. cum seruicio inde debito et consueto sicut alii tenentes faciunt.

Assedatur vna pars Johanni broun soluendo annuatim liij s. iiij d. cum seruicio inde debito et consueto plegio Roberto Symson.

Assedatur vna pars Alexandro bute soluendo annuatim xx s. cum seruicio inde debito et consueto plegio Wilelmo Symson.

Assedatur vna pars Roberto Symson soluendo annuatim xx s. cum le bonys et seruicio inde debito et consueto plegio Wilelmo Symson.

Assedatur vna eiusdem Johanni brone soluendo annuatim xiij s. iiij d. cum seruicio inde debito et consueto plegio Johanne brone.

Assedatur alia pars Johanni Symson soluendo annuatim xx s. xij pultrie cum le bonys et cariggio et seruicio debito et consueto.

Assedatur vna pars de lynwode Roberto sympil de caldorhawe soluendo inde annuatim xx s. vj pultrie cariagia et cum seruicio inde debito et consueto.

*lynwode* xl s.
iii dd. *pultrie.*

Assedatur vna pars Inde patricio Sympill soluendo Inde annuatim xx s. vj pultrie cum seruicio Inde debito et consueto.

Alia pars Inde assedatur Roberto sympill soluendo annuatim xx s. cum vj le pultrie cum alio seruicio inde debito et consueto et memorandum quod dicti patricius et Robertus non habebunt introitum ad dictam assedacionem quam diu parentes lorum vixerint in humanis.

*Auchynche.* Auchynche assedatur matheo walace soluendo annuatim liij s. iiij d. cum xij pultre
liij s. iiij d. quatuor dietis in autumno vna dieta cum harpicis 1 dieta falcando fenum cum
ij dd. *pultrie.* cariagio et alio seruicio debito et consueto.

Tota terra de Auchinche assedatur Waltero Scot soluendo annuatim liij s. iiij d. xij pultre quatuor dietas in autumno vnam dietam cum harpicis vnam dietam falcando cum alio seruicio inde debito et consueto.

Auchynche assedatur Johanni Atkyn et Johanni knokis coniunctim et diuisim soluendo annuatim viij lib. cum iiij le wederis 1 dusan ancaris vel ij merkis in festum Sancti Thome minoris viz. fair of Gasgu et alio seruicio plegius alter alterius in anno xix° viij° februarii.

Llynwode assedatur Johanni sympyll soluendo annuatim xl s. xij pultrie quatuor dietas in autumno cum cariagio et seruicio Inde debito et consueto.

Vna pars assedatur patricio sympyl soluendo annuatym xx s. cum seruicio inde debito et consueto et ix capo xviij pullis.

*Blaxtoun* xx s.

In manibus domini.

Item, vna pars inde assedatur fra the wod wast Johanni Syme et Jacobo erskyn soluendo annuatym x lib. libere ab omni alio seruicio.

*Cariagishill.*
*Inde pecunie*
liij s. iiij d. Assedatur vna pars Roberto morray soluendo annuatim xiij s. iiij d. cum le bone-
*quatuor* dd. syluer cariagio et vj pultrie et seruicio inde debito et consueto.
*pultrie.*

Alia pars assedatur Dauid Sklater soluendo annuatim xiij s. iiij d. vj pultre le bonsiluer et cariagio et seruicio inde debito et consueto plegio Johanne Sklater.

Alia pars assedatur Johanni Sklater juniori soluendo annuatim xiij s. iiij d. xx s. cum vj s. viij d. ix pullis cum seruicio Inde debito et consueto.

Alia pars assedatur Johanni hector seniori soluendo annuatim vj s. viij d. iij pultre et seruicio inde debito et consueto.

*Todholme.*
*Inde pecunie* ij s.

*Rochbank.*
*In pecunie* iij lib. vj s.
viij d. Assedatur vna pars Inde thome Stewart soluendo annuatim xxvj s. viij d.
v dd. *pultre.*

Assedatur nicholaio Stewart pro xxvj s. viij d. cum soluendo annuatim cum seruicio inde debito et consueto.

*thornle nethyr.*
*Inde pecunie* iij lib.
vj s. viij d. v dd. *pultrie.*

*Rochbank.*

*Inde pecunie* iij lib. vj s. viij d. Assedatur vna pars inde Johanni merschel soluendo inde annuatim xxvj s. viij d. cum seruicio debito et consueto plegio Johanne cochran.

Assedatur alia pars inde Dauid merschel post decessum andree bronside soluendo annuatim xiij s. iiij d. cum cariagio et seruicio inde debito et consueto et plegio Roberto.

*nota.* Assedatur vna pars dauid merschell cum consensu andree brounside soluendo annuatim xiij s. iiij d. cum cariagio et seruicio inde debito et consueto plegio Johanni Sklater juniori.

*nota.* Assedatur alia pars Johanni merschell juniori soluendo annuatim xxvj s. viij d. cum seruicio debito et consueto plegio Johanne Sclatar juniori.

*Villa de Paslay.*

Assedatur vna pars Roberto murray soluendo annuatim xiiij s. cum seruicio Inde debito et consueto.

Assedatur quatuor acre Johannis Sklater et quatuor acre quas habuit Alicia quhit Johanni Sklater juniori soluendo Inde annuatim x s. cum quatuor le bonis et seruicio inde debito et consueto plegio patre dicti Johannis.

*Castelhede.*
xiij s. iiij d.
vj *acre de hyl.*
xv s.

*lytyl blakfalde.*
vj s. Assedatur Johanni quhitfurde soluendo annuatim vj s. cum seruicio debito et consueto.

*Ye bromlandis.*
*cum le Ward bodom.*

Assedatur Johanni quhitfurde soluendo annuatim.

*Mekyl blakfalde.*
viij s. Assedatur Roberto quhyt Johanni ersman et dauid quhyt soluendo Inde annuatim viij s. cum seruicio Inde debito et consueto.

*grevislande.*
iij s. Assedatur Johanni quhitfurde soluendo annuatim iij s.

*Causa ende.*
xviij s.

*Mekyl Zarde.*
xvj s. xij *pultrie.*

Assedatur domino henrico morisoun soluendo annuatim xvj s. xij pultre cum seruicio debito et consueto.

*Bernzarde.* Assedatur Alano Sunderlande soluendo Inde.

*Oxschawhede.*
vj s. Assedatur Roberto quhyt Johanni ersman soluendo annuatim vj s. cum seruicio debito et consueto.

*Oxschawsyde.*

Assedatur quatuor acre Roberto quhyt Johanni ersman et dauid quhyt pro iiij s. soluendo annuatim cum quatuor le bonys.

Assedatur vna acra Johanni quhytfurde soluendo annuatim vij s. cum quatuor le bonis.

Assedatur vna pars assedatur Johanni quhitfurde soluendo annuatim vj s. cumo quatuor le bonis in autumno.

*Prior crofte.*

Assedatur vna pars Inde viz. quatuor acre Roberto quhyt Johanni ersman soluend annuatim ix s. iiij d.

Assedatur vna acra andree Kuke soluendo annuatim ij s. iiij d.

Assedatur vna acra relicte Ade Smythe soluendo annuatim ij s. iiij d.

Assedatur quatuor acre Inde Johanni quhitfurde soluendo annuatim ix s. iiij d.

*Terre assedate pro auenis.*

*hyllyngtoun.*
ix c. *auenarum*
iiij dd. *pultre.*

Assedatur vna pars Andree murra soluendo annuatim ij celdras quatuor bollas auenarum xij pulli et quatuor le bwnys cum cariagio et seruicio inde debito et consueto.

Assedatur alia pars thome mathe soluendo annuatim ij c. iiij b. auenarum xij pul. quatuor bonys et seruicio inde debito et consueto plegio Johanne cochran.

Assedatur vna pars Roberto Stene soluendo inde annuatim ij c. iiij b. auenarum cum seruicio inde debito et consueto plegio thoma Mathe.

Alia pars inde assedatur Johanni kebil soluendo annuatim ij c. iiij b. auenarum xij pultre quatuor le bonys cum cariagio et seruicio inde debito et consueto plegio thoma Kebill.

Alia pars patricio bulle soluendo annuatim ij c. iiij b. auenarum xij pullos quatuor le bonys cum cariagio et seruicio inde debito et consueto plegio Johanne bulle de grene law.

Assedatur vna pars inde roberto Wry soluendo annuatim ij c. iiij$^{or}$ b. auenarum cum caponibus et cariagio ut prius.

*Erkliston.*
ix c. *auenarum*
iiij dd. *pultre.*

Assedatur vna pars Inde Stephano Urre soluendo annuatim ij c. iiij b. auenarum xij pulli cum cariagio & seruicio Inde debito et consueto plegio duncano erklistoun.

Assedatur vna pars inde duncano de Erklistoun soluendo annuatim ij c. iiij b. auenarum xij pultre cum cariagio et seruicio inde debito et consueto plegio Stephano urre.

Assedatur alia pars Johanni landalis soluendo inde annuatim viij c. vj b. auenarum et ix pultre cum bonsiluer et cariagio Inde debito et consueto plegio thoma landalis filio suo.

Assedatur vna pars inde Dauid crag soluendo annuatim ij c. iiij b. auenarum xij pultre cum cariagio et seruicio inde debito et consueto facta in anno Domini quingentesimo xvj$^{o}$ xxiiij$^{o}$ Julii.

Assedatur vna pars Roberto landalis juniori soluendo annuatim ij c. iiij b. auenarum vj pultre.

Assedatur vna pars domino Andree Anderson soluendo inde annuatim ij c. iiij b. xij pult cum seruicio inde debito et consueto plegio patricio bulle.

Assedatur vna pars Wilelmo purlie soluendo inde annuatim vj c. vj b. iii c. iiij b. auenarum cum pullis boniesiluer et cariagio debito et consueto.

Assedatur vna pars inde Johanni tomson juniori soluendo annuatim ij c. iiij b. auenarum cum pullis bonsiluer et cariagio debitis et consuetis plegio malcomo tomsoun de Inche.

*Canderane* v c. *auenarum* xxiiij *pultre.*

Assedatur vna pars petro tomsoun soluendo annuatim xxiiij b. auenarum cum seruicio et pultre debito et consueto.

*ye Inche.* viij dd. *pultrie.* Assedatur vna pars malcomo thomson soluendo annuatim xxiiij b. auenarum cum seruicio debito et consueto plegio W° Jonsoun.

Assedatur malcolmo tomson et Johanni tomson eius filio pro secundo soluendo annuatim xviij b. auenarum cum seruicio etc. plegio Wilelmo tomson in anno xi°.

Assedatur vna pars Johanni Jonson soluendo annuatim xviij b. auenarum cum seruicio inde debito et consueto plegio Wilelmo Jonson.

Assedatur vna pars inde Johanni Wile pro xxiiij b. auenarum cum seruicio inde debito et consueto plegio Johanne cochran.

Assedatur vna pars malcolmo Jonson soluendo annuatim xxiiij b. auenarum cum seruicio inde debito et consueto plegio Wilelmo Jonson.

Assedatur vna pars Johanni fynloson juniori soluendo xxiiij b. auenarum cum seruicio inde debito et consueto plegio Wilelmo Jonson.

Assedatur vna pars inde duncano hector soluendo annuatim xviij b. auenarum cum seruicio debito et consueto plegio in anno xj° x° Junii.

Assedatur vna pars Inde assedatur thome kebil soluendo inde annuatim xxiiij b. auenarum cum seruicio inde debito et consueto plegio Wilelmo Jonson.

Assedatur vna pars Roberto symson soluendo annuatim xviij b. auenarum cum seruicio inde debito et consueto plegio Johanne Symson.

Assedatur vna pars malcolm Symson soluendo annuatim xviij b. auenarum cum seruicio debito et consueto in anno domini etc. xv$^{to}$ xxvj$^{to}$ Junii.

Assedatur vna pars Johanni symson soluendo annuatim xviij b. auenarum cum seruicio Inde debito et consueto plegio roberto Symson.

Assedatur fynlay henryson soluendo annuatim xviij b. auenarum cum seruicio Inde debito et consueto plegio Johanne Stenson.

Assedatur malcolmo smyth alia pars soluendo annuatim xxx b. auenarum cum seruicio Inde debito et consueto plegio Johanne quhitfurde.

Assedatur vna pars Johanni hectori juniori soluendo annuatim xxiiij b. auen-

Assedatur vna pars Johanni fynloson juniori soluendo inde annuatim xxiiij b. auenarum cum seruicio inde debito et consueto plegio Wilelmo Jonson.

Assedatur vna pars Ade Erskyne soluendo inde annuatim 1 c. xxiij b.

arum cum seruicio debito et consueto facta in anno domini quingentesimo xvj° xxvj° Julij etc.

auenarum cum seruicio inde debito et consueto plegio Macolmo thomsone n anno xx° x° nouembris.

Assedatur vna pars Johanni Jonson juniori soluendo annuatim xxiij b. auenarum cum seruicio inde debito et consueto plegio Johanni fynloson.

Assedatur vna pars inde Elisobethe relicte fynlay henryson soluendo inde annuatim xviij b. auenarum cum seruicio inde debito et consueto plegio Johanne fyndloson.

Assedatur vna pars Johanni flyndlawson juniori soluendo annuatim xxiiij b. auenarum cum seruicio debito et consueto facta xxv Julii anno xvij[c].

Anno xij° xx[mo] Decembris pro tribus annis.

Assedatur vna pars inde roberto fyndlawson filio Johanni fyndlawson soluendo annuatim xviij b. auenarum cum seruicio inde debito et consueto plegio Adam Erskyne.

Assedatur roberto smyth vna pars soluendo annuatim xxx b. auenarum cum pult et bown siluer facta eiusdem occupando dimedietate eiusdem assedacionis pro tribus annis.

Assedatur vna pars inde Johanni kebill soluendo Inde annuatim . . . auenarum cum seruicio inde debito et consueto plegio thoma kebill.

*ye merkis worthe of ye Inche.* xij pultrie.

Assedatur Wilelmo quhit soluendo annuatim xiij s. iiij d. cum seruicio debito et consueto.

Assedatur Wilelmo tomsoun soluendo annuatim xiij s. iiij d. cum seruicio debito et consueto et xij pultre.

Assedatur Johanni Smyth et mergret Schaw eius sponse — quinque acre de west medo de Inche x acre quinque firlotas eidem annuatim facta xviij° martii coram his testibus in anno xxiiij° domino Jacobo Schaw vicaro de Kilbarquhan Johanne Schaw et Johanne abernethy.

*Assidatio terrarum dominii de Kilpatrik:*

*Auchinlek.*

Auchenlek vna pars assedatur roberto forsythe soluendo annuatim xij s. vj d. cum le bonis et cariagio et seruicio Inde debito et consueto.

*Farchlay.*

ffarchla assedatur roberto forsythe soluendo inde annuatim xx s. cum le bonys cariagio et seruicio inde debito et consueto.

Patrik comyng sal draw the browne of caudrane by the loch on the west syd down to the bryg of caudran wyth the clowse maid on the best fasson and the laid sufficand that all the browne sal ryn by the loche and he sal do this or Witsonday and sal haue therfor xij bollis of meil and his buntat.

*Bradfelde.*

Vna eiusdem assedatur waltero denby soluendo annuatim xx s. cum le bonys cariagio ac alio seruicio inde debito et consueto.

*Kylpatrik ester.*

Vna pars eiusdem assedatur wilelmo Jonson soluendo inde annuatim xj s. ij d. cum vj d. de bonsiluer et cariagio inde debito et consueto plegio ricardo fordoun.

Assedatur altera pars inde patricio fynlo soluendo inde annuatim xj s. ij d. cum vj le bonsiluer cariagio inde debito et consueto plegio Johanne m'gregor.

---

*Assidacio terrarum dominii de glen facta per venerabilem in Cristo patrem georgium abbatem dicti monasterii de P. ad terminum pentecosten anno domini etc. lxxxiiij° pro voluntate dicti domini abbatis duratura :—*

*wester kers.*

xliij s. iiij d. iij dd. pultrie. Assedatur vna pars allano kyrkwode soluendo inde annuatim x s. cum cariagio et bonsiluer et alio seruicio inde debito et consueto plegio Jacobo Or.

Assedatur alia pars hugoni kirkwode soluendo annuatim x s. x d. cum le bonsiluer et seruicio inde debito et consueto plegio Johanne Or seniori.

Assedatur vna pars Johanni kyrkwode seniori soluendo annuatim x s. x d. cum cariagio et seruicio inde debito et consueto plegio Johanne kirkwode juniore.

Assedatur alia pars Johanni kyrkwode juniori soluendo annuatim x s. x d. cum cariagio et bonesiluer et alio seruicio debito et consueto.

Assedatur Alexandro conwal pro tempore sue uxoris soluendo annuatim vj s. viij d. cum seruicio debito et consueto.

Alia pars assedatur thome kirkwode soluendo annuatim x s. x d. cum le bonissiluer et seruicio inde debito et consueto plegio gilberto Stewart.

*Ester kerse.*

iij dd. pultrie. Alia pars assedatur andree belze for tempore vxoris ad vtilitatem filiorum x s. x d. land soluendo annuatim cum seruicio debito et consueto plegio Jacobo Or.

*Joffratak* iij s. iiij d.

xviij pultrie. Assedatur Johanni Or juniori soluendo annuatim xxiij s. iiij d. cum bonsiluer et seruicio inde debito et consueto plegio hugone kirkwode.

*Bermoklaw* x s.

ix pultrie. Assedatur Alexandro norwal soluendo annuatim x s. cum le bonesiluer et seruicio inde debito et consueto plegio Johanne Or seniori.

*Mawsebank,* x s.

ix pultre. Assedatur Johanni Jonson soluendo inde annuatim x s. cum cariagio le bon siluer et alio seruicio inde debito et consueto plegio Johanni Cochran.

Anno viij° xij° decembris.

Assedatur ricardo or filio Jacobi or de milbank soluendo annuatim x s. et xij d. pro le bonsiluer et alio seruicio debito et consueto et ix pultrie.

*lynstanele* xv s.

xij pultrie. Vna pars assedatur Jacobo or soluendo annuatim xv s. cum seruicio inde debito et consueto plegio Johanne or.

*Caymhyll* xx s.

xviij pultrie. Assedatur vna pars Wilelmo or soluendo annuatim xiij s. iiij d. cum bonsiluer et seruicio inde debito et consueto plegio Wilelmo Snape.

Assedatur Wilelmo kyrkwode soluendo annuatym x s. cum le boniss et seruicio inde debito et consueto plegio Jacobo or.

Assedatur Johanni kyrkwode soluendo annuatim vj s. viij d. cum boniss et seruicio debito et consueto.

*lorensbank* xiij s. iiij d.

xij pultrie. Assedatur Johanne glene soluendo annuatim xiij s. iiij d. cum bonsiluer et seruicio inde debito et consueto plegio gilberto Stewart.

Assedatur Alano glen soluendo annuatim xiij s. iiij d. cum bonsiluer et seruicio inde debito et consueto plegio Johanne glen patre suo.

*langzarde* xxvj s.

viij d. xxiijj pultrie. Assedatur vna pars inde Roberto or soluendo inde xiij s. iiij d. annuatim cum le bonsiluer et cariagio et seruicio inde debito et consueto plegio Jacobo or.

Assedatur vna pars inde Wilelmo Ricardi soluendo xiij s. iiij d. cum seruicio inde debito et consueto plegio Ricardo.

*Aldzarde* xvj s.

xiiij pultrie. Assedatur vna pars inde roberto glene soluendo annuatim viij s. cum bonsiluer et seruicio inde debito et consueto plegio Johanne or de farhillis.

Assedatur alia pars Andree gybson soluendo inde annuatim viij s. cum bonnys et seruicio inde debito et consueto plegio Alano glen.

*Ffayr hill* xx s.

xviij pultre. Assedatur vna pars Roberto bridyn soluendo annuatim x s. cum le bonsiluer et seruicio inde debito et consueto plegio thome Jameson.

Assedatur alia pars inde Johanni Or filio Rolandi Or soluendo annuatim x s. cum bonsiluer et alio seruicio inde debito et consueto plegio Roberto glen.

Assedatur predicta pars Wilelmo Or soluendo annuatim x s. cum seruicio ut supra plegio Roberto bryden.

*Gawjlmoss* xij s.

x pultre. Assedatur Wilelmo logane soluendo annuatim viij s. cum le bonsiluer et seruicio inde debito et consueto plegio Roberto glen.

Tercia pars eiusdem assedatur dicto Wilelmo soluendô inde iiij s. cum seruicio ut supra.

Assedatur Jacobo logan filio Wilelmi logan viij s. land soluendo annuatim viij s. cum le bonsiluer et caragio et seruicio debitis et consuetis anno xxij° xiij° octobris.

*Gylliszarde* xxiij s.

xx pultre. Assedatur vna pars Roberto glen soluendo annuatim xj s. vj d. cum bonsiluer et seruicio inde debito et consueto plegio Wilelmo glene.

Assedatur alia pars Wilelmo glen soluendo annuatim xj s. vj d. cum bonsiluer et seruicio inde debito et consueto plegio Roberto glene.

Assedatur vna pars assedatur Jacobo glen soluendo annuatim xj s. vj d. cum bonsiluer et seruicio inde debito et consueto plegio Wilelmo glene.

Assedatur vna pars allano Jonson soluendo annuatim xj s. vj d. wyth bwnsiluer malis pullis et cariagio wyth oder seruis acht and wont plegio Jacobo Or.

*Gyrsszarde* xxx s.

xviij pultre. Assedantur ij acre terre arabilis et cum pastura duorum animalium in le Innerwarde et vj animalium ad extra soluendo inde annuatim.

Assedatur seruicium nigelli Or post mortem dicti nigelli Johanni Or cum seruicio pastoris.

*Lynthillis* xl s.

xxxvj pultrie. Assedatur vna pars inde Jacobo Schawe soluendo annuatim x s. cum le bonsiluer cum seruicio inde debito et consueto plegio Roberto glen.

Vna pars inde assedatur Jacobo Schawe cum tribus acris de gyrszarde soluendo inde annuatim x s. inde debito et consueto plegio Roberto glen de gilliszarde et cum pastura duorum animalium.

Assedatur dimedia pars Inde pro custodia boum Jacobo barde pro seruicio sicut nigellus ore solebat habere tempore sui introitus.

Assedatur Jacobo barde ij acre terre arabilis cum pastura duorum animalium in le ener warde et vj animalium in le vter warde soluendo inde annuatim.

*Brygende* xl s.

xxxvj pultrie.

ij lib. land of ye bar set to thir tenaandis wnder wryttin:

Vna pars inde assedatur Jacobo Schaw soluendo xliiij petras ij le stirkis annuatim cum seruicio debito et consueto plegio Johanne fyschar.

*Ye bar* iiij lib. xiij s.

iiij d. vij dd. pultre.

Alia pars inde assedatur Johanni fyschar soluendo annuatim xxij petras casei 1 le stirk cum seruicio debito et consueto.

Alia pars inde assedatur Johanni or soluendo annuatim xliiij petras casei et ij le stirkis cum seruicio debito et consueto.

Assedatur vna pars inde roberto Or filio Jacobi Or clentis soluendo annuatim xij s. et xij d. pro le bonsiluer cum alio seruicio debito et consueto in anno Domini etc. viij° xij° decembris.

*Mylbank* xxiiij s.

xx pultrie. Assedatur vna pars inde Jacobo Or soluendo annuatim xij s. cum le bonsiluer cariagio et alio seruicio inde debito et consueto plegio Wilelmo Or.

Assedatur alia pars Wilelmo soluendo inde xij s. annuatim cum le bonsiluer cariagio et alio seruicio inde debito et consueto plegio Wilelmo Or.

Assedatur alia pars Wilelmo Or soluendo inde xij s. annuatim cum le bonsiluer cariagio et alio seruicio inde debito et consueto plegio Jacobo Or mortuo Wilelmo assedatur vna pars Inde Roberto or soluendo Inde annuatim vj s. cum seruicio inde debito et consueto plegio Jacobo crawfurd de sedhill.

Alia pars assedatur Johanni or soluendo annuatim vj s. cum seruicio inde debito et consueto.

Altera pars inde assedatur Jacobo Or juniori soluendo annuatim vj s. cum seruicio inde debito et consueto plegio Jacobo or seniori seniorie.

*lytl clohog* x s.

ix pultre. Assedatur vna pars alexandro Atkyn soluen Wilelmo brydene soluendo annuatim x s. cum le bonsiluer et seruicio inde debito et consueto plegio Roberto bryden.

*Moniabrocht* xl s.

Moniabrocht xj s.

*langcrofft* x s.

ix pultre. Assedatur alano alanson pro x s. annuatim cum bonsiluer et seruicio inde debito et consueto plegio Johanne luff de Came.

Assedatur vna pars alano alanson soluendo annuatim v s. cum seruicio inde debito et consueto plegio.

Alia pars assedatur thome alanson soluendo annuatim v s. cum seruicio inde debito et consueto plegio.

*Quensidmur* xlviij s.

Assedatur alan alanson soluendo annuatim xl s. cum seruicio inde debito et consueto plegio Johanne luff.

Assedatur vna pars inde alano alanson soluendo annuatim xx s. cum seruicio inde debito et consueto plegio.

Alia pars assedatur thome alanson soluendo xxx s. cum seruicio inde debito et consueto xxiiij^or^ summis animalium nobis reseruatis.

Assedatur xxiiij^or^ summe animalium nobis reseruatis Jacobo Jonson et Roberto Jonson soluendo inde annuatim viij s. ad festum sancti mertine plegius alter alterius.

*Came* iiij lib.

vj dd. pultre. Vna pars assedatur cutbert Jameson soluendo annuatim x s. cum seruicio inde debito et consueto plegio gilberto Jameson.

Assedatur alia pars Johanni alanson soluendo annuatim x s. cum bonesiluer et seruicio inde debito et consueto plegio Alexandro atkyn.

Assedatur vna pars inde Jacobo gybson soluendo annuatim x s. cum seruicio inde debito et consueto plegio gilberto patre dicti Jacobo.

Vna pars assedatur waltero Robison soluendo annuatim x s. cum seruicio inde debito et consueto plegio alano glene etc.

Assedatur x s. eiusdem soluendo annuatim x s. cum seruicio debito et consueto Jacobo blakburn.

Assedatur vna pars dauid blakburne soluendo annuatim x s. cum seruicio inde debito et consueto plegio Johanne Robyson.

Alia pars inde assedatur Johanni Robynson soluendo annuatim xx s. xv s. cum seruicio inde debito et consueto plegio dauid blakburne.

Alia pars inde assedatur Jacobo brone soluendo inde x s. annuatim cum seruicio inde debito et consueto plegio Alano glene Johanne luff habente assedacionem pro vita sue vxoris.

Assedatur vna pars Jacobo Jonson soluendo annuatim v s. cum seruicio inde debito et consueto plegio Johanne alanson.

Assedatur vna pars Johanni alanson juniori soluendo annuatim x s. cum le bonys cariagio et alio seruicio inde debito et consueto plegio Jacobo Jonson.

Wester bernacht assedatur xv s. nacht inde Johanni Jameson soluendo annuatim xl [ti] petras casei cum.

*Bernache vester* xxx s.

xxvj pultre. Assedatur Jacobo craufurde soluendo annuatim xxx s. cum le bonesiluer et seruicio inde debito et consueto et dicto assedacio assedatur nicholao Stewart post decessum dicti Jacobo soluendo ut supra.

Alia pars inde niniano or soluendo annuatim xv s. ac xl[ti] petras casei.

Assedatur bernache wester roberto schaw soluendo annuatim xxx[ti] s. cum alio seruicio debito et consueto.

*Bernache ester.*

Assedatur Johanni Lowe soluendo annuatim vj[xx] petras casei et vj vitulis cum seruicio inde debito et consueto.

Assedatur vna pars thome or soluendo annuatim iij[xx] petras casei iij vituli cum seruicio inde debito et consueto plegio Jacobo Or de milbank.

Alia pars inde assedatur Johanni atkyn soluendo annuatim iij[xx] petras casei iij vitulis cum alio seruicio debito et consueto anno domini x[to].

*Molendinum cum terris pertinentibus.* Assedatur Jacobo glene soluendo inde consuetam firmam et seruicium sicut prius

xxvj s. viij d. soluere solebat cum terris dicto molendino pertinentibus plegio Alano glen.

Molendinum de glene assedatur alano glen Jacobo or thome kyrkwode et Roberto glen soluendo inde annuatim xxiiij[or] bollas farine. Memorandum quod dicta assedacio est ad usum omnium tenentium de glene.

Molendinum de glen assedatur henrico Cummyng soluendo annuatim xxiiij b. farine xxvj s. viij d. pro firma molendini et aprum ad vsum abbatis et monasterii promittendo eidem henrico quod gaudebit terras molendini cum multura omnium tenandorum bladorum ad xxiiij le fail of ye parrochin plegio.

Molendinum de glen assedatur thome kyng soluendo annuatim xxiiij bollas farine communis mensure plegio Johanne kyng et Jacobo Johnson sustentabit et edificabit dictum proprius expensis ad vsum et abbatis et conventus et gaudebit multuras omnium tenentium glen pertinentium abbati et conventui ad xxiiij le fait parrochin xix[no] xxvi[to] Januarij.

Auchynhaue vna pars assedatur Wilelmo Jonson soluendo Inde annuatim xxx petras casei cum 1½ stryk cum seruicio Inde debito et consueto plegio thoma strache.

Auchinhaue vna pars inde assedatur thome strache soluendo inde annuatim xxx petras casei cum seruicio Inde debito et consueto cum 1 le styrk.

Assedatur vna pars inde thome Jameson soluendo annuatim iii[xx] petras casei et tres vitulos cum seruicio inde debito et consueto plegio Roberto brydyn.

Alia pars assedatur patricio alanson soluendo annuatim xxx petras casei cum 1 le stirk et seruicio inde debito et consueto.

Assedatur vna pars Ranaldo Jameson soluendo annuatim iij$^{xx}$ petras casei et vitulos cum seruicio inde debito et consueto plegio patricio alanson.

Vna pars assedatur Johanni Atkyn soluendo inde iii$^{xx}$ petras casei et iij vitulos cum seruicio inde debito et consueto plegio patre suo Alexandro atkyn.

*Mekyl clochog.*

Assedatur vna pars alexandro atkyn soluendo annuatim iij$^{xx}$ petras casei et tres vitulos cum bonsiluer et seruicio inde debito et consueto plegio Johanne or de Joffra tak.

Assedatur vna pars roberto atkyn soluendo annuatim iij$^{xx}$ petras casei et vitulos cum seruicio inde debito et consueto plegio Jacobo or de milbank.

*Candilmure.*

Assedatur vna pars Dauid or soluendo annuatim xl petras casei et duos vitulos cum seruicio inde debito et consueto plegio Johanne or.

Assedatur vna pars inde niniano or soluendo annuatim xxxv petras casei cum le strykis et alio seruicio debito et consueto et pro tribus annis factum iij • februarii anno xl• plegio Johanne fyschar.

Assedatur vna pars thome snape soluendo annuatim xv petras casei et 13 (1½) vituli cum seruicio inde debito et consueto plegio thome kebil.

Assedatur Johanni kebill filio dicti thome soluendo annuatim xxx petras casei et jȝ vituli cum seruicio debito et consueto pro x s. land.

Alia pars assedatur thome kebil soluendo annuatim xxx casei petras et jȝ vituli cum seruicio inde debito et consueto plegio alano or de monabrok.

Assedatur vna pars thome or soluendo annuatym xx xxxv petras casei j le stirke cum seruicio inde debito et consueto plegio manu propria.

*Lynthillis ye graszarde.*

Assedatur quarta pars eiusdem Johanni or seniori soluendo annuatim xlij petre viij lib. casei et ij le stirkis cum seruicio inde debito et consueto plegio Jacobo or.

Assedatur alia pars viz. quarta pars Johanni or juniori soluendo annuatim xlij petre viij lib. casei et duos vitulos cum seruicio inde debito et consueto plegio Jacobo or.

Assedatur alia pars viz. octaua pars assedatur Jacobo barde soluendo xxj petras iiij lib. casei et vnum vitulum cum seruicio debito et consueto plegio Johanni fyschar.

Assedatur alia pars viz. octaua pars Johanni fyschar soluendo xxj petras iiij lib. casei et vnum vitulum cum seruicio inde debito et consueto plegio Jacobo barde.

*ye gerszarde.*

Vna pars inde assedatur Johanni or seniori soluendo annuatim xl$^{ti}$ petras casei ij le strikis cum seruicio debito et consueto plegio Jacobo or.

Alia pars assedatur Jacobo barde soluendo annuatim xx[ti] petras casei et 1 le stirk cum seruicio debito et consueto plegio Johanne or seniori.

---

*Assedatio terrarum et possessionum monasterii de pasleto facta per venerabilem in Christo patrem Robertum Schaw Die gracia dicti monasterii abbatem facta apud monasterium antedictum.*

In primis, that na man takar of land or tenent within the abbotis land mak tenent na set na mak interchangin off land onder him, bdt leiff of the abbot askit and vpteinit onder ye pane of ane hundred s. and forfaltour off his malyng and removing of it but mercy.

Item, at he purchess na lordschip to spek na to pled agane his lord ye abbot, na agane his nychburis, onder ye pane forsaid.

Item, quhat sa euer he be at harbreis nocht ye abbotis seruandis in to his seruis sal be in xl s. on forgiffin for his defalt.

Item, at he be na manis man bot anerly ye abbotis, na at he ryd nocht with na man but special leiff off ye abbot, or quhom ye abbot deputis or leiffis him to ryd with, onder ye pane forsaid.

Item, at he sal set na quhyt land to na man without special lieff of the abbot, under the pane of forfalt of his maling.

Item, at na man purchess lordschip agane the abbot be ony way be hurtyn off him, or commond profyt of the hous, or sclanderis him or his monkis in word or in ded, onder the pane of a hundreth s. and forfaltour of his maling and removing of it, but mercy as it is befor writin.

Item, he that fylis his maling with guld, and clenge it nocht be lammess, sal pay a merk without mercy, and efteruart the land beand fund foule al his guidis sal be eschetit.

Item, quha sa euer he be at makis wrangus landmers, or zet consalis thame, or sufferis men to occupy thame, sal certify the abbot and the conuent within sufficient tym, that is to say, within the space of six monthis folowing fra the tym he haff knavledge thairof, onder the pane for writin.

Item, quha sa euer has gudis to be sauld, other martis or wederis or fedis swyne, sal proffir thai gudis of vsuel and compatabil price to the abbotis officiaris or thai pas til ony merkat, onder the pane forsaid.

Item, at na man be fundin be an Inquest a commone tulzeour, na ane onlauchful nychbur, bot ilk malar do til other nychburschip, onder the pane of law.

Item, that ilk malar be redy, without obstakil or debat, to comper to court or to witsonday quhen thai ar warnyt be the sereand on the day befor to cum on the morn, as lauchful day and lauchful warnyng, onder the pane off ane vnlaw off the court.

Item, that na man pas with thar corne and thar multour fra the abbotis myl, onder the pane off forfaltour off thar malyng and ane vnlaw off ane hundreth s.

Item, quha sa euer malar of the sukkin of the myl of Dalmvlyne, or of the sukkin of ony other myl of the abbot and conuent forsaid, quhar euer it be within the abbotis land that vphaldis nocht his part off the damme sufficientlie, or zet cumis nocht quhen he is warnyt be the fermour to mend and mak wp gif oucht be failzet, for the first falt he sal pay v s., and for the secund x s., and the thrid tym forfaltour of his maling but ony mercy.

Item, at na man be fundin be ane inquest a common distroyar of the abbotis wod onder the pane of forfaltin of his malyng and the vnlaw, viz.——

Item, at na tenand man or woman be fundin adulterar be an inquest of thar nychburis onder the pane of forfaltyn of thar maling but mercy.

Item, quhatsumeuer malar or femour at pays nocht his mail and ferm with seruis in detfull tym, he forfaltis his malyng, and at he presume nocht to tak his maling in tym to cum.

Item, that quhat tym thai be chargit with thar bwyns in hervist and other tymis of the zher in thar aucht seruis, gif thai cum nocht the day that it hapiunis thame to be warnyt, the sereand sal rais of ilk faltour a wedder, and the secund tym ij wedderis, and the third tym ane ox or ane cow, but Remission to the abbotis behuffe.

Item, at nane be fundin onlauchful nychbure, na tulzeour with the abbotis seruitoris of his house or of his Retinev, na strik of tham na of na otheris, his tenentis, onder the pano of v lib. and forfaltour his maling.

Item, that ony tenent within the abbot land in to the landis of kilpatrik, in to the lennax, haldin nychburis and pluwyne til his nychbur eftir the auld stent, and as awcht and custumn requiris within the forsaidis landis, vnder the pane of forfaltour his maling, bot gif he haff special leiff askit and vptenit of the abbot.

Item, at the payment of thir poyntis forsaid, to thame at defaltis therin, is ane hundretht s. to the abbot, vnrecouerabil, to be Rasit and the malingis of the defaltouris to be in the abbotis.

Item, with other statutis and stilis, awcht and wontsum, bath anent grene wod, guld, and swyne, and otheris of nychburschip, sic as ar requirit of law.

Item, it is statut at ilk tenent duelland within the abbotis landis of the lennax, or ony otheris landis of the abbotis, that ilk ane of them supple and assist to other to pwnd outcovnys catal and gudis at vsurpis til distroy or occupy the abbot land, and he at cumis nocht to supple his nychbur quhen he is warnyt to suple, and helpis nocht his nychburis to pwnd outcovnys catal and suppleis nocht his malyng his malyng sal be in the abbotis hand.

---

The xl[ti] s. land of the kyrkland of the largis Set to James Crafurd of the choche and mergrat Kelso his spouse payand therfor zheirly xl[ti] s. of maile, with oder sic lik seruis as the said land payit of befor in the said James faderis tyme, the gersum of the said land xx[ti] merkis pait in hand the viij day of september in the zheir of god a thowsand v[c] & xvj zheiris.

Auchynche assedatur Willelmo Conigham de craganis soluendo annuatim liij s. iiij d. cum ij dusan pultre cum aliis seruiciis debitis et consuetis facta primo maii in anno quingentesimo v[to] coram testibus domino henrico Beuerage domino Waltero morton et archibaldo Warnokis cum diuersis aliis.

---

*Assedacio terrarum domini de pasleto facta per venerabilem in Cristo patrem Robertum abbatem dicti monasterii ad terminum pentecosten in anno domini millesimo vc 2o pro tribus annis duratura sub stilis et condicionibus vt supra.*

*ffulton*, viij lib. vj s. viij d. xijdd vj pultrie.

Assedatur vna pars Johanni brown janitori roberto brown filio dicti Johannis soluendo inde annuatim liij s. iiij d. iiij dd. pultre cum seruicio inde debito et consueto plegio andrea cochran.

Alia pars inde assedatur Johanni brown juniori soluendo annuatim xiij s. iiij d. xij pultre cum seruicio debito et consueto plegio Johanne brown seniori in anno xxiiije.

Alia pars inde assedatur alexandro but soluendo inde annuatim xxti s. xviij pultre cum alio seruicio inde debito et consueto plegio valtero scot.

Alia pars inde assedatur vxori olim roberti symson soluendo annuatim xxti s. xviij pultre cum alio seruicio inde debito et consueto plegio Johanne brown seniori.

Alia pars inde assedatur Wilelmo symson soluendo annuatim xlti s. iij dd. pultrie cum alio seruicio inde debito et consueto plegio.

Alia pars inde assedatur Jacobo but soluendo annuatim x s. et Cristiane crafurd x s. annuatim xviij pultrie cum seruicio debito et consueto plegio.

*Lynwood* xlti s. iij pultrie.

Assedatur vna pars patricio Sympill soluendo annuatim xxti s. xviij pultre cum seruicio inde debito et consueto plegio Andrea cochran.

Assedatur vna pars Johanni Sympill filio patricio Sympill soluendo annuatim xxti s. xviij pultrie et bonsiluer et alio seruicio debito et consueto.

Alia pars inde assedatur roberto cochran soluendo annuatim xxti s. xviij pultrie cum seruicio inde debito et consueto plegio patricio Sympill facta xxiijo nouembris in anno xixno

*Auchynche* liij s. iiij d. ijd. dd. pultrie.

*Auchynche.*

Assedatur auchynche Waltero Scot soluendo inde annuatim liij s. iiij d. cum ij dd. pultre iiij dietis in autumno vna dieta cum harpicis 1 dieta falcando fenum cum cariagio et alio seruicio debito et consueto.

Assedatur auchynche Johanni knok et Elisbetht knokis his spous soluendo inde annuatim liij s. iiij d. cum ij dd. pultre vel 1 dd. caponum iiij dietis in autumno vna dieta cum harpicis 1 dieta falcando fenum cum cariagio et alio seruicio debito et consueto testibus Johanne knok wilelmo et Johanne mortown sub stilis et condicionibus vt supra.

*Blaxton* xxti s. in manibus domini.

*Lyncleiff* in manibus domini assedatur.

*Durschawsyd.*

Assedatur Johanni Steuart alias roger soluendo annuatim xxti s. et dictus Johannes custodiet siluam et sustentabit fossas circa dictam siluam cum alio seruicio debito et consueto plegio Johanne schaw.

Lyncleff assedatur Johanni cochran et mergaret mortoun sponse dicti Johannis soluendo annuatim iiij cheldras auenarum cum alia seruicio debito et consueto facta die vicesimo nouembris in anno domini, &c., quingentesimo decimo plegio Ade mortoun de Walkynschaw et alano steuart de orchat.

*Auchyngown* ix lib. iij s. iiij d. xiij dd. pultre et filio suo Wilelmo mur.

Assedatur Johanni Mur de estir Caldwell xl[ti] s. land de neder murbvrn soluendo annuatim pro dictis terris xl[ti] s. et xij d. pro le bon siluer cum alio seruicio debito et consueto coram hiis testibus domino Jacobo Schaw vicario de Kilbarquhan magistro W° Steuart vicario de cragy et Johanne Abyrnethy cum aliis diuersis facta in anno xxiiij° xviij° martii apud Paslay.

Assedatur vna pars Johanni mur de Ester Caldwell et Roberto mwr eius filio soluendo annuatim xx[ti] s. cum seruicio debito et consueto illam partem videlicet quam occupabat thomas Steuart de murbvrn.

David Stewarti assedatur vna pars pro terminis vite sue soluendo annuatim xl[ti] s. et xij d. pro le bownsiluer cum le cane foullis et alio seruicio inde debito et consueto plegius alter alterius.

Assedatur vna pars de balroger Andree Stewart soluendo inde annuatim xvij s. iiij d. cum le bownsiluer et le cane foullis et alio seruicio debito et consueto.

Assedatur vna pars Jacobo Stewart soluendo annuatim xx[ti] s. cum bown siluer et le cane foullis et alio seruicio debito et consueto.

Assedatur vna pars thome Steuart soluendo annuatim xx[ti] s. cum bown siluer et le cane foullis et alio seruicio debito et consueto.

Assedatur vna pars matheo Steuart pro terminis vite sue soluendo annuatim xvij s. iiij d. pro terminis vite sue soluendo annuatim cum bown siluer et le cane foullis et seruicio debito et consueto.

Assedatur vna pars domino Alexandro Steuart soluendo annuatim xvij s. iiij d. cum le bown siluer et le cane foullis et seruicio debito et consueto.

Assedatur vna pars gilberto Steuart soluendo annuatim xviij s. cum le bown siluer et le cane foullis et alio seruicio debito et consueto.

### *Murbvrn.*

Assedatur vna pars malcolmo merschell soluendo annuatim xvij s. iiij d. cum le bown siluer et le cane foullis et alio seruicio debito et consueto.

Assedatur alia pars Allano knok soluendo annuatim xvij s. iiij d. cum le bown siluer et le cane foullis et alio seruicio debito et consueto.

### *Auchynche.*

Assedatur Waltero Scot tota terra de auchynche soluendo annuatim liij s. iiij d. cum ij dd. pultrie quatuor dietis in autumno vna cum harpicis vna falcando fenum cum alio seruicio debito et consueto.

*the newtown,* iiij c. auenarum.

Assedatur vna pars alexandro newtown soluendo annuatim ij c. auenarum cum le cane foullis et alio seruicio debito et consueto plegio thoma mathe.

Alia pars.——

*barskawan,* iiij c. auenarum xxiiij pultre.

Assedatur vna pars Jacobo vrre soluendo annuatim ij c. auenarum xij pultre cum alio seruicio debito et consueto ad barskawan.

Alia pars inde assedatur ade barskauan soluendo annuatim ij c. auenarum xij pultre cum alio seruicio debito et consueto plegio Jacobo vrre.

*Mekilrigis,* viij lib. xij dd. pultre.

Robert of caueris xl^ti^ s. iij dd. pultre cum alio seruicio plegio dauid sclater.

thomas robyson xl^ti^ s. iij dd. pultre cum alio seruicio plegio Ad hall.

Andro mekilrigis xx^ti^ s. xviij pultre cum alio seruicio plegio thoma robison.

Dauid sclater xx^ti^ s. xviij pultre cum alio seruicio plegio thoma robison.

Malcolm mosman xx^ti^ s. xviij pultre cum alio seruicio debito plegio dauid sclater.

Richardo Brigton assedatur iiij lib. de mekilrigis cum pultre et alio seruicio debito et consueto anno xx° octobris.

Johanni mortoun assedatur iiij lib. de mekilrigis cum pultre et bonsiluer et alio seruicio debito et consueto xxij° Januarii in anno domini et octauo.

*brideland.*

Assedatur bridelend gavino Maxwell soluendo annuatim xx^ti^ s. cum xviij pultre cum alio seruicio debito et consueto.

*brideland* x^ti^ s. xviij pult in manibus domini.

*Corsbar.*

thomas bar. Assedatur Johanni Maxwell et roberto Maxwell eius filio soluendo annuatim quinque merkis monete cum duobus cariagiis cum a dusan caponum termino pro omni alia firma cum seruicio debito et consueto coram hiis testibus magistro Wilelmo Steuart george de knokhill Johanne Abyrnethy cum domino roberto sclater.

*Corsbar* xxvj s. viij d. xxiiij pult.

Assedatur Wilelmo Crafurd corsbar soluendo annuatim xxvj s. viij d. xxiiij pultre cum alio seruicio debito et consueto plegio bris kerswell.

*Thomasbar* xl^ti^ s. iij dd. pultre.

Assedatur vna pars inde bris kerswell soluendo annuatim xxviij s. viij d. xxiiij pultre cum alio seruicio inde debito et consueto plegio wilelmo crafurd.

Alia pars inde assedatur georgio crafurd soluendo annuatim xxiij s. iiij d. 1 dd. pultre cum alio seruicio debito et consueto plegio wilelmo crafurd.

*Cariaghill* liij s. iiij d. iiij dd. pultre.

Malcum sclater xxvj s. viij d. xxiiij pultrie cum seruicio plegio roberto caueris.

Johanni Sclater elder xiij s. iiij d. xij pultre cum seruicio plegio roberto caueris.

Johanni Sclater songer vj s. viij d. vj pultre }
Johanni hector elder vj s. viij d. vj pultre } plegius alter alterius.

*the thurscrag* xx b. auenarum in manibus domini.

Corsflat, that ald hector brukyt the xx^ti^ s. land of the sammyn on the ester sid of the commyn bezound the dik set to george houston for xx s. of mail, wyth oder deutis.

*The Rockbank* iij lib. vj s. viij d. v dd. pultre.

Assedatur thome bard ij merkland de rouchbank pro viij merkis annuatim sine alio seruicio vij° Junii in anno xxiij°.

Assedatur Johanne quhytfurd soluendo annuatim v lib. vj s. viij d.
Nicolao Steuart xxvj s. viij d. xxiiij pultre
Johanni merschell xxvj s. viij d. xxiiij pultre } plegius alter alterius.
Andree brownsed xiiij s. iiij d. xij pultre.

Vna pars inde assedatur thome hunter soluendo annuatim viij s. iiij d. equaliter plegio dauid Sclater.

*Methyr thornle* iij lib. vj s. viij d. in manibus domini.

*Dungrane*, xj lib. xvj dd. pultre.

Assedatur Andre sprewaill xxvij s. viij d. cum pultre et alio seruicio solito et consueto.

Riche brigton xxvij s. viiij d. xxiiij pultre
Ville glen xxvij s. viij d. xxiij pultre } plegius alter alterius.
Johanni Androson elder xx^ti s. vj d.
Johanni Androson zonger xiij s. x d. xij pultre
thom of cochran xxvij s. viij d. wyth cane foullis. } plegius alter alterius.

Johanni Stensonis maling wes xxxviij s. vj d. in my lordis hand.

xix s. iij d. Wilelmo glasfurd xvj s. viij d. wyth cane foullis
xix s. iij d. Nichol of bar xvj s. viij d. wyth cane foullis } plegius alter alterius.

Johanni Jobson xxvj s. viij d. xxiiij pultrie plegio thoma Jopson.

*Molendinum* liij s. iiij d. xij capones.

Assedatur constancio quhyt.

Assedatur vna pars de Dumgrane thome cochran zonger soluendo annuatim xix s. iij d. cum bonsiluer et pullis et alio seruicio debito et consueto plegio thoma cochran.

In anno viij° xij° februarii.

Assedatur vna pars de Drumgrane Alexandro raffe soluendo annuatim xix s. iij d. cum le bwyne syluer et pultre et omni alio seruicio Inde debito et consueto plegio magistro Johanne reid. In anno domini M° v° xiiij^to xj° Septembris.

Item, [the mis xv petras casei set] inde Wilelmo gilmor Alexandro Striuiling soluendo annuatim iij^xx petras casei x s. cum alio seruicio debito et consueto facta in anno xvj^to xxvj^to Augusti et x s. pro.

Assedatur vna pars inde Alexandro Striuiling soluendo annuatim iij^xx petras casei cum alio seruicio debito et consueto pro tribus annis plegio bartholomeo gilmor et x s. pro stirk siluer.

Assedatur vna pars inde Johanni Wilson juniori soluendo annuatim iij^xx petras casei et x s. pro le stirk siluer cum alio seruicio debito et consueto.

Assedatur vna pars inde Johanni                soluendo annuatim iij^xx petras casei et x s. pro le stirk siluer cnm alio seruicio debito et consueto.

Assedatur vna pars inde (bartholomo) Johanni Gilmuyr soluendo annuatim iij^xx petras casei et x s. pro stirk siluer cum alio seruicio debito et consueto.

Assedatur vna pars inde bartholomo gilmor soluendo annuatim iij$^{xx}$ petras casei et x s cum alio seruicio debito et consueto.

*Auchynche.*

Assedatur Johanni Atkyn et Johanni knok coniunctim et diuisim in anno xix$^{no}$ soluendo annuatim viij lib. cum iiij le wedderis at the fair of glasgw 1 dusan ansarum at Sant mirrens-day vel duas mercas—plegius alter alterius.

*Auchyngown* ix lib. iij s. iiij d.

Assedatur vna pars inde viz. so de merborn archbaldo boid soluendo annuatim xvj s. viij d. a dusan pultrie cum cariagio et bon siluer et alio seruicio debito et consueto plegio Johanne brown viij$^{o}$ martij anno 6$^{to}$.

Vna pars inde Johanni Steuart filio quondam Jacobi soluendo annuatim xvj s. viij d. 1 dusan pultre et xij d. de bown siluer cum alio seruicio debito et consueto plegio magistro Wilelmo Steuart xxvj Junii in anno xviij$^{o}$.

Anno 6$^{to}$ xxv$^{to}$ Januarii.

*Cariaghill* liij s. iiij d. iiij dd. pultre.

Assedatur vna pars inde Johanni sclater xiij s. iiij d. soluendo annuatim cum alio seruicio debito et consueto plegio ricardo brigton.

Assedatur Inde vna pars patricio schelis soluendo annuatim vj s. viij d. cum alio seruicio debito et consueto plegio Johanni Sclater.

Assedatur alia pars Alexandro Dawson Johanni Wilson xxvj s. viij d. soluendo in anno cum alio seruicio et cariagio debito et consueto facta anno xvij$^{o}$ x$^{o}$ maii.

Assedatur pars quondam Johannis sclater Johanni hector juniori soluendo annuatim xiij s. iiij d. cum alio seruicio debito et consueto plegio Dauid Sclater de mandato abbatis vj$^{o}$ februarii anno Domini M$^{o}$ quingentesimo xx$^{o}$ etc.

*Mekilrigis* viij lib.

Item, vna pars Inde assedatur Jacobo Wilson soluendo annuatim xx$^{ti}$ s. cum vij pult cum bownis et alio seruicio debito et consueto plegio.

Item, vna pars Inde assedatur Jacobo Vylsone soluendo annuatim xx s. et xij pultre et bownis alio seruicio debito et consueto primo octobris anno xviij$^{o}$.

Item, assedatur roberto Sclater iiij lib. land quam nunc occupat Vidua Joneta brownheid soluendo annuatim iiij lib. cum pultre et seruicio et cariagio debitis et consuetis plegio dauid Sclater.

ROBERTUS, abb. de pasleto.

*Dumgrane.*

Item, componit wyth John cochran, son to thomas cochran of Dumgrane, for his faderis maling, payand zheirly therfor xxvij s. viij d., wyth foullis and cariage and oder dew seruis as nychbour and oder does facta in anno xvj$^{to}$ xv$^{to}$ martii.

Assedatur elisabeth edmonston xxxviij s. vj d. quam nunc occupat in Drumgrane pro dicta firma annuatim cum bon siluer et pultre et alia seruicia debita et consueta insuper concedimus dicte elisabetht nostram licenciam ad contrahendum matrimonium cum Jacobo hammiltoun non obstante actis et stilis curie nostre in contrarium habitis et factis Et fatemur nos recipisse xl$^{to}$ libras vsualis monete pro gersuma dicti loci actum apud paslay x$^{o}$ Junii anno Domini M$^{mo}$ V$^{cmo}$ xx quarto teste nostra subscriptione manuali.

*Estwod.* Oswald maxwell rentillyt in the chantor land at the kyrk stil of the est wod the xxviij day of october, payand therfor zheirly to the saidis chantoris $xl^{ti}$ s. at twa termis vsuale in zheir, et thom of maxwell, his fader and his wyf, brukand it for thar tym at paslay day forsaid in $xx^{ti}$ zheir of god.

*Glen.*

*Barmoklow.* Assedatur Johanni Norwoll soluendo annuatim x s. cum xii d. pro bwnys siluer 1 x pultre cum seruicio debito et consueto plegio Jacobo Or de mylbank facta xxvij° aprilis in anno Domini etc. $xix^{no}$.

*Wester Kerss.*

Assedatur vna pars inde Johanni kyrkwode filio Johannis kyrkwod soluendo annuatim x s. x d. cum cariagio et pultre et alio seruicio debito et consueto plegio patre suo.

*Galwysmos.* Assedatur vna pars inde Jacobo logan soluendo annuatim viij s. cum cariagio et pultre et aliis seruiciis debitis et consuetis plegio W° logan patre eiusdem.

*The gerssarde Lintellis* xx° Februarii anno $6^{to}$ $viij^{xx}x$ petras et viij le stirkis.

Assedatur vna pars inde Johanni fischar xiiij s. terrarum soluendo annuatim firmam casei et le stirkis cum alio seruicio debito et consueto secundum portionem terrarum plegio Jacobo bard.

Alia pars inde assedatur Jacobo bard xiiij s. terrarum scilicet soluendo firmam casei et le stirkis cum alio seruicio debito secundum portionem terrarum plegio thome fischar.

Anno viij° xxvij° Junii.

Assedatur vna inde Jacobo roberto glen viz. xiiij s. terrarum soluendo annuatim firmam casei et le stirk siluer et bonis cum alio seruicio debito et consueto secundum portionem terrarum plegio thoma Steuart.

*Came hill*
$xx^{ti}$ s. xviij pult.
ij s. of bonsiluer.

Inde vna pars assedatur Wilelelmo Or de Caymhill soluendo annuatim xiij s. iiij d. a dusan pultre xviij d. of bwnsiluer wyth cariag and seruis aucht and wont plegio manu propria secundum firmam rentallis pro tribus annis.

*gillizarde* xxiij s.
xx pultre ij s. bwnsiluer.

Inde vna pars assedatur roberto glen filio Jacobi glen post decessum patris soluendo annuatim xj s. vj d. cum bonsiluer et cariagio debito et consueto plegio Jacobo facta anno Domini quingentesimo $xv^{to}$ et secundum formam rentallis pro tribus annis.

*Milbank* xxiiij s.
ij s. bonsiluer. xx pultre.

Inde vna pars assedatur roberto or filio Jacobo or soluendo annuatim xij s. et xij d. pro bwnsiluer et x pultre cum alio seruicio debito et consueto anno Domini etc. quingentesimo viij° xij decembris.

Alia pars inde assedatur thome or filio Jacobi or soluendo annuatim vj s. cum bwnsiluer et pultre et alio seruicio debito et consueto anno Domini quingentesimo $xv^{to}$ 1° octobris.

Vna pars inde assedatur Johanni Jameson soluendo annuatim vj s. cum bown siluer cariagio et pultre et alio seruicio debito et consueto.

Primo Martii anno 6to Camen viij$^{xx}$ casei.

In primis assedatur vna inde viz. xx s. land Jacobo broun soluendo annuatim xx$^{ti}$ s. xl$^{ti}$ petras casei cum alio seruicio debito et consueto plegio.

Vna pars inde assedatur Jacobo Allanson soluendo annuatim xx$^{ti}$ s. cum xxx$^{ti}$ petras casei et alio seruicio debito et consueto wythin the lordschip x° Junii in anno xxj°.

Assedatur vna pars inde Johanni Jonson soluendo annuatim pro xx$^{ti}$ s. land xxx$^{ti}$ petras casei cum alio seruicio debito et consueto plegio.

Item, vna pars inde assedatur Johanni Allanson soluendo annuatim xxx petras casei 1½ stirkis cum alio seruicio debito et consueto facta in anno Domini quingentesimo xv$^{to}$ pro tribus annis.

*Auchynhan* petre casei vj stirkis.

Item, vna pars inde assedatur Johanni Jameson filio rannoldi Jameson soluendo annuatim iij$^{xx}$ petras casei cum tribus vitulis cum alio seruicio debito et consueto facta xxvj° Junii in anno xviij°.

Item, dimedia pars assedatur thome or soluendo annuatim iij$^{xx}$ petras casei cum tribus vitulis cum alio seruicio debito et consueto plegio.

*Mekil clook.*

Assedatur vna pars inde Johanni Atkyn juniori soluendo annuatim pro xx s. land iij$^{xx}$ petras casei et iij stirkis cum alio seruicio debito et consueto dicta assedacio facta fuit xv$^{to}$ Januarii in anno xvj$^{to}$.

Assedatur vna pars inde Jacobo Or de clook ye half of sammyn soluendo annuatim pro xx$^{ti}$ s. land iij$^{xx}$ petras casei et iij stirkis cum alio seruicio debito et consueto plegio for ye sammyn rannald Or et rob or of mylbank.

*Litil clooche* x s. land quam nunc occupat Valterus bridyn assedatur roberto bridyn filio suo de consensu patris soluendo annuatim x s. cum cariagio et alio seruicio debito et consueto.

*Wester kerss.*

Assedatur vna pars eiusdem Johanni kyrkwod filio thome kyrkwod soluendo annuatim x s. x d. cum bownis et alio seruicio debito et consueto quiquidem Johannes debet de sua girsuma x merkis soluendo immediate postquam fuerit legittime nuptus facta iij Junii in anno xviij°.

*Dominium de Kilpatrik.*

*Ester Kylpatrik.*

In primis assedatur vna pars inde de ester kilpatrik Johanne purvhe soluendo annuatim xj s. 1½ d. cum cariagio et bonsiluer et alio seruicio debito et consueto plegio Johanne bulle de grynlaw anno 6ot viij$^{to}$ marcii.

*Allan lang.*

Assedatur vna pars inde allano lang soluendo annuatim xj s. cum cariagio et bon siluer et alio seruicio debito et consueto plegio Johanne Strabrok facta vj° Januarii in anno xiij°.

*Rob. Strabrok.*

Assedatur vna pars inde de ester kilpatrik roberto Strabrok soluendo annuatim xxij s. iij d. cum seruicio inde debito et consueto plegio Johanne Strabrok viij° marti anno.

Assedatur vna pars inde roberto Jacobo Strabrok soluendo annuatim xxix s. iij d. cariagio bown siluer et alio seruicio debito et consueto facta xxvj° Octobris Decembris in anno xviij°.

Assedatur vna pars inde Jacobo fyndlaw soluendo annuatim xj s. 1½ d. cum cariagio et bown siluer et alio seruicio debito et consueto in anno domini M^mo etc. xviij° x° martii.

*Morysland.* Assedatur vna pars inde fyndlao merchant illam quam nunc occupat Joneta Sclater cum domo et orto ad occidentalem partem ecclesie etc. cum consensu Jonete Sclater soluendo annuatim xiij s. iiij d. et xij capones pro domo et orto cum alio seruicio debito et consueto.

*Wester Kilpatrik.*

In primis assedatur Wilelmo symson vna pars soluendo annuatim xvj s. viij d. cum seruicio debito et consueto viz. bonsiluer et cariagio etc. pro tribus annis factum apud paslay anno Domini quingentesimo xiij° xxviij° octobris.

Assedatur vna pars inde Conuallo brownsid soluendo annuatim xxvj s. cum seruicio bonsiluer et cariagio debito consueto apud paslay x° augusti in anno xviij°.

Assedatur vna pars roberto brok soluendo annuatim viij s. iiij d. cum cariagio et bonsiluer et alio seruicio debito et consueto in anno xviij° xx^me octobris.

Assedatur vna pars inde georgio brownsid filio roberti brownsid soluendo annuatim xxxiij s. iiij d. cum cariagio brownsiluer aucht and wont plegio James Dowglas.

Assedatur vna pars inde Wilelmo lang soluendo annuatim xvj s. viij d. cum cariagio et bown siluer aucht wont as nychbour and oder pais.

Assedatur vna pars inde vnfredo brousid soluendo annuatim xvj s. viij d. cum cariagio at bwn siluer debito et consueto facta in anno xxxiiij^to primo octobris.

*Dunterclunan* iiij lib. xiij s. iiij d.

Assedatur vna pars inde Andree Allanson j d. filio domini roberti Allanson soluendo annuatim xxxiij s. iiij d. cum seruicio inde debito et consueto cum xij d. de bon siluer plegio Johanne lang in anno xj° in vigelia Sancti Andree.

Assedatur Johanni forsyth terciam partem de Duterclunan extendentem xxxj s. ij d. cum seruicio debito et consueto cum cariagio et xvj d. bonsiluer facta in anno xxj° xxvij° Aprilis.

Assedatur vna pars inde georgio forsyth xxiij s. iiij d. land soluendo annuatim xxiij s. iiij d. cum seruicio cariagio et bwn siluer debito et consueto.

Assedatur Jacobo Dowglais xj s. viij d. land in Dunterclunan post decessum mariote logan et Johannis forsyth quam occupant predictum qua assedacio fuit Jacobis Sclater defuncti soluendo dicti Jacobi quinque mercas.

*Dominium de kylpatrik.*

*Auchyntosschen* iiij lib. Auchyntosschen vna pars inde assedatur wlo Patrikson Reddendo inde annuatim xx s. cum cariagio et le bwnesiluer et cum omni alio seruicio inde debito et consueto plegio thoma Donald et Jacobo flemyn.

Vna pars assedatur roberto lang alias cleme xiij s. iiij d. cum seruicio debito et consueto et bwnsiluer plegio Wil. hog.

Vna pars inde assedatur viz. x s. Johanni Jonson reddendo inde annuatim x s. cum cariagio et alio seruicio debito et consueto plegio Wilelmo Jonson de afflec facta xj° maij in anno xvj^to etc.

Assedatur Martino cuthbert de Auchynche ij akyris terre cum iiij sowmys and a hors girs wyth hous and zard as he brukis now payand therfor sheirly alanerly xiij s. iiij d.

Alia pars assedatur Wilelmo donald soluendo inde annuatim xxvj s. viij d. cum cariagio et le bown siluer et alio seruicio debito et consueto plegio in anno xvj° xxij° mensis nouembris pro tribus annis.

Alia pars inde assedatur Johanni Jacobo M'reryk soluendo annuatim xl s. cum bonsiluer et alio seruicio debito et consueto wyth ij gud chaip wedderis.

Ferclay assedatur Johanni brownsid xx[ti] s. land of the ferclay wyth cariage and bwn siluer plegio bartholomeo flemyn.

*Auchynlek* v lib. ij c. ordei et xl[ti] wedderis custodia et pastura.

Auchynlek vna pars Inde assedatur Johanni edmunston soluendo Inde annuatim xxv s. cum le bwnesyluer et omni alio seruicio Inde debito et consueto Et post decessum Johannis bris assedatur dicto Johanni Edmunston xxv s. quam nunc occupat dictus Johannes bris simili modo ut supra non remouendo viduam nisi cum suo beneplacito super expensis Domini abbatis.

Assedatur Johanni Edmonston vna pars inde soluendo annuatim xij s. vj d. cum bwnsiluer et alio seruicio inde debito et consueto etc.

Assedatur vna pars inde Willelmo Jonsoun soluendo inde annuatim xij s. vj d. cum le bwnsiluer et alio seruicio debito et consueto plegio etc de consensu vidue uxoris patris alias nostri facta iij° Junii in anno xiij°.

Assedatur vna pars inde bartholomeo flemyn soluendo annuatim xxv s. cum bwnsiluer et alio seruicio debito et consueto.

Assedatur vna pars Inde Johanni flemyn soluendo annuatim xxv s. cum bwnsiluer et cariagio et alio seruicio debito et consueto cum vj b. ordei et custodia et pastura de x wedderis.

Assedatur vna pars inde Elizabetht holmylton soluendo annuatim xxv s. cum le bown et alio seruicio Inde debito et consueto illam assedacionem quam nunc occupat Johannes brison post mortem vxoris.

Assedatur vna pars inde fynlao M'gregor soluendo annuatim xxv s. cum le bown siluer cariagio et alio seruicio debito et consueto facta pro tribus annis in anno Domini etc. xv[to] xv[to] martii.

Assedatur vna pars inde Jacobo M'reryk soluendo annuatim xii s. vj d. iij b. ordei communis mensure cum pastura quinque ouium et seruicio iij decimo in dominio.

*Terre capelle de West Cochnay vel Warthill.*

Assedatur le belwarthill Jacobo Dowglas soluendo annuatim xiij s. iiij d. Et dictus Jacobus sustentabit lectum omni tempore pro pauperibus et sustinebit capellam in tecto et honestate.

Assedatur le belwarthill Wilelmo Alanson soluendo annuatim xiij s. iiij d. Et dictus Wilelmus sustentabit lectum omni tempore pro pauperibus et sustinebit capellam in tecto et honestate.

*Dominium de kilpatrik.*

*Wester Cochnay.*

vj lib. xiij s. iiij d. Wester Cochnay vna pars inde assedatur Alexandro prowand Reddendo Inde annuatim xxvj s. viij d. cum cariagio et bwnsiluer et alio seruicio inde debito et consueto plegio Roberto fyne xiiij$^{to}$ die mensis nouembris anno Domini m$^{o}$ v$^{c}$ viij$^{o}$.

Alia pars Inde assedatur Jacobo brison Reddendo inde annuatim xvj s. viij d. cum cariagio et bwnsiluer et alio seruicio debito et consueto plegio georgio morison xiij$^{o}$ die mensis februarii anno domini v$^{o}$ x$^{o}$.

Alia pars inde assedatur gilberto boill reddendo Inde annuatim xvj s. viij d. cum cariagio et bwnsiluer et alio seruicio debito et consueto plegio Wilelmo hog xviij$^{o}$ mensis Julii in anno xiiij$^{a}$.

Alia pars inde assedatur Jacobo tomson soluendo annuatim xv s. cum cariagio et bwnsiluer et alio seruicio debito et consueto post decessum roberti fordoun soluendo iiij merkis pro introitu xxvj$^{o}$ aprilis in anno Domini quingentesimo.

Alia pars inde assedatur roberto Sclater filio quondam Donaldi Sclater soluendo annuatim viij s. cum cariagio et bwnsiluer qui robertus sustentabit matrem facta xxiiij$^{o}$ octobris anno xvij$^{o}$.

Assedatur vna pars inde Johanni lee soluendo annuatim xvj s. viij d. cum cariagio et bwnsiluer et alio seruicio debito.

*Drumtochyr alias myltown.*

Assedatur vna pars inde Jacobo symson soluendo annuatim xx$^{ti}$ s. xx$^{ti}$ d. pro ferma terre cum wyth wache mell et myll mail plegio Wilelmo Donald facta xxix$^{mo}$ octobris in anno xx$^{mo}$.

Assedatur vna pars inde georgio houston soluendo annuatim xx$^{ti}$ s. xx$^{ti}$ d. cum wache mail et myl malis et aliis seruiciis debitis et consuetis.

Assedatur vna pars Jacobo Dowglas assedatur soluendo annuatim xx$^{ti}$ s. xx$^{ti}$ d. cum wache mail et myl malis et aliis seruiciis debitis et consuetis.

*Kylpatrik.*

*The bradfeld.*

Vna pars de Bradfeld assedatur W$^{to}$ brison Reddendo Inde annuatim xx s. cum cariagio et le bwnesyluer et cum omni alio seruicio Inde debito et consueto plegio Johanne brison suo patre xix$^{o}$ die mensis Decembris anno Domini M$^{o}$ v$^{c}$ viij$^{o}$.

Alia pars inde assedatur Jacobo Dowglas. — Altera pars Inde assedatur Jacobo roberto brison Reddendo Inde annuatim xvj s. xx$^{ti}$ s. cum cariagio et le bwnsiluer et cum omni alio seruicio Inde debito et consueto plegio georgio morison xiij$^{o}$ die mensis februarii anno Domini v$^{c}$ x$^{o}$.

Alia pars indo martino cuthbert soluendo annuatim x s. cum cariagio et bwnsiluer et omni alio seruicio debito et consueto xvj$^{o}$ Junii in anno xvj.

Assedatur xx$^{ti}$ land de braidfeld fyndlas M'gregor pro Tenple vidue roberti brison qua dedimus consensum nostrum eidem vidue matrimonium contrahere cum dicto fyndlaw hoc factum fuerit primo octobris in anno xxiiij$^{o}$.

*Miltoun alias Drumtocher* v lib. cum terris molendini ij c. iiij b. ordei.

Cuius vna pars assedatur Johanni Sprewil pro tribus annis soluendo annuatim lvj s. viij d. cum le bonsiluer et alio seruicio debito et consueto plegio roberto Sprewil octobris anno Domini M° v° ix°.

Vna pars inde videlicit xx s. xx d. land vna pars inde assedatur Jacobo M'raryk soluendo annuatim x s. x d. et iiij b. ordei communis mensure cum firma molendini et decimis debitis et consuetis et seruicio communi seruicio in dominio.

Alia pars assedatur Johanni Lang soluendo annuatim x s. x d. et iiij b. ordei cum ferma molendini et decimis debitis et consuetis pro fermis ix Septembris in anno xvj°.

Vna pars inde assedatur Domony lang soluendo annuatim xx[ti] s. xx d. et viij b. ordei communis mensure cum ferma molendini wathe meil et decimis debitis et cousuetis et seruicio communi in dominio de lenax plegio Jacobo Dowglas anno xviij° xv° Junii.

*kylpatrik.*

*wester culboy.*
vj lib. xiij s. iiij d.
et iij c. ordei.

Vna pars inde assedatur patricio morison pro tribus annis Reddendo inde annuatim xxxiij s. iiij d. pro firma cum xij b. ordei cum omnibus aliis oneribus inde debitis et consuetis longo cariagio excepto plegio Georgio morison suo patre xxiiij[to] die mensis nouembris anno Domini M° v° ix°.

Vna pars inde assedatur roberto angus soluendo xxj s. viij d. v b. ordei pro ferma x firlotas farine j b. ordei pro decima reseruando in manibus abbatis iij½ acris prati proximo le barnis.

Altera pars assedatur Jacobo anghus pro tribus annis Reddendo Inde annuatim xxxiij s. iiij d. cum xij b. ordei pro ferma eiusdem cum omnibus aliis oneribus Inde debitis et consuetis longo cariagio excepto plegio Waltero anghus et Jacobo Donaldo xxiiij[to] nouembris anno Domini M° v° ix° etc.

Alia pars Jacobo Angus soluendo annuatim xxj s. viij d. v b. ordei pro ferma x fir. farine j b. ordei pro decima cum aliis oneribus debitis et consuetis reseruando in manibus abbatis iij½ acris prati proximo le barnis.

Alia pars assedatur Allano Johanni Riche et Roberto anghus pro tribus annis Reddendo Inde annuatim xxxiij s. iiij d. cum xij b. ordei cum omnibus aliis oneribus Inde debitis et consuetis longo cariagio excepto plegio pro roberto anghus Jacobo Anghus plegio pro Johahanni ryche.

Quarta pars de Vester culboy assedatur Johanni fynnes pro tribus annis Reddendo Inde annuatim pro ferma xxxiij s. iiij d. et xij b. ordei cum omnibus aliis oneribus Inde debitis et consuetis longo cariego excepto plegio.

Alia pars fyndlaw Riche soluendo annuatim xxj s. viij d. viij b. ordei facta in anno xxj° xxvj° aprilis ordeum iiij b. vij pec. j clyt.

*Ester Cwlboy.*
v lib. xxx b. ordei.

Ester Cwlboy vna pars Inde assedatur Johanni fyneson pro tribus annis Reddendo Inde annuatim pro ferma xxxiij s. iiij d. cum x b. ordei cum omnibus aliis oneribus Inde debitis et consuetis lango cariegio excepto plegio Roberto Sprewill in festo sancti mertini in anno Domini m° v° xij° etc.

Alia pars Inde assedatur Johanne Denbe pro tribus annis Reddendo inde annuatim pro ferma xxxiij s. iiij d. cum decim b. ordei cum omnibus aliis oneribus inde debitis et consuetis lango cariagio excepto plegio Roberto Sprewill.

Alia pars Inde assedatur Ade morison cum matre pro tribus annis Reddendo Inde annuatim pro ferma terre xxxiij s. iiij d. cum x b. ordei cum omnibus aliis oneribus inde prius debitis et consuetis lango cariagio excepto plegio patricio morison facta in anno Domini M^mo v° xviij° in termino Sancti Martini.

*Kilpatrik.*

Anno x°.

*Edinbernan*
iiij lib. vj s. viiij d.

Edinbernan set to master Patrik Schaw for thre zheiris payand therfor zheirly xxiiij merkis at thwa termys at vitsonday his entress in anno Domini etc. quingentesimo decimo souerte for this mail his and his hand wryt.

Magister patricius schaw manu propria.

Item, Cragbanzok xiij s. iiij d. set to the said master patrik for thre zheiris for the said merkis of mail alanerly.

*Edynbernane*
iiij lib. vj s. viij d.

Edynbernane in anno Domini M° v° xij° in festo Sancti Mertini dimi pars assedatur Roberto Sprewill Reddendo Inde annuatim xliij s. iiij d. cum cariagio et le bwne syluer et cum omni alio seruicio Inde debito et consueto plegio bartholomus flemyn.

Assedatur Johanni Edmonston de Edinbernan xx s. xx d. quam habuit Bartholomeus flemyn soluendo tantum pro firma in anno cum alio seruicio debito et consueto.

Alia pars assedatur bartolomomeo flemyn anno et die ut supra Reddendo Inde annuatim xx s. xx d. cum cariagio et le bwne syluer et cum omni alio seruicio Inde debito et consueto plegio Roberto Sprewill.

Alia pars assedatur alexandro hustone anno et die quo supra Reddendo Inde annuatim xx s. xx d. cum cariagio et le bwne siluer et cum omni alio seruicio Inde debito et consueto plegio Roberto Sprewill.

Alia pars Inde assedatur thome Sprewil reddendo inde annuatim xx s. xx d. cum cariagio et bwnsiluer et alio seruicio debito et consueto xvj° Julii in anno xiiij°.

The chapelland of Boquhanran set to Will Atkyn payand therfor zheirly xiij s. iiij d. wyth ane bed to trawellouris for goddis sak and our fundouris wyth all fredomys wsyt of befor xxvj° decembris in anno xviij°.

*Terre pro auenis.*

*hillyntoun.* Item, vna pars inde assedatur henrico lochheid soluendo annuatim ij c. iiij b. auenarum vj capones iiij bwnis cum alio seruicio debito et consueto.

*Molendinum fulonis de Sadill.*

Assedatur allano mosman soluendo annuatim quinque merkas et duas petras de le nopis ad duos anni terminos viz. ad festum petri ad vincula et purificacionis beate martine et le ij petre nopis in festo sancti thome applicandis.

---

*Rentale tenandorum dominii de pasleto scriptum per manum roberti abbatis eiusdem xviij^o^ maij in anno xxij^o^ qui tenandi suas assedaciones ad vitam gaudere debent seruando stilos curie abbatis in libro curie sue contentis vt ibidem patet qui etiam tenandi sunt series in rentale set hic tamen clarius inveniuntur.*

*The Inche* xviij merkis land assedatur pro xviij c. auenarum antique mensure xij dd. pultre subscriptis tenentibus.

Assedatur vna pars Johanni langmur soluendo annuatim xxxvj b. auenarum xviij pultre vel ix capones.
Johanni fyndlawson zonger xxiiij b. auenarum xij pultre vel vj capones.
Roberto Smyth xxx^ti^ b. auenarum xij pultre.
Adam erskyn zonger xxx b. auenarum xv pultre.
Petyr tomson xxiiij b. auenarum xij pultre.
~~Hobe fyn~~dlaw xviij b. auenarum ix pultre.
Johannes Johson the lard xxiiij b. auenarum xij pultre.
Duncan hector xviij b. auenarum ix pultre.
John Kepbill xxiiij b. auenarum xij pultre.
John tomson xviij b. auenarum ix pultre.
John Symson xviij b. auenarum ix pultre.
John Smyth and mage Schaw v akyris of the wester medo assedatur pro vj b. 1 f. ordei.
The ester peys of medo assedatur tenentibus Wille pro v b. ordei.
Make Jonson xxiiij b. auenarum in manibus abbatis qua non soluit pro rentali.

*Arkylston* ix merkis land assedatur pro ix c. auenarum ij dd. caponum.

Rob Wry xxxvj b. auenarum vj capones.
John tomson xxxvj b. auenarum vj capones.
Rob landalis xxxvj b. auenarum vj capones.
Dauid crag xxxvj b. auenarum vj capones.

*helyntown* ix merkis land assedatur pro ix c. auenarum ij dd. caponum.

henry lochheid xxxvj b. auenarum vj capones.
Rob Sten xxxvj b. auenarum vj capones.
John Kebill xxxvj b. auenarum vj capones.
Wille bully xxxvj b. auenarum vj capones.

*Grenglaw* xxvj s. viij d. land.

Assedatur vna pars Waltero bully viz. ester part pro viij b. ordei.
Altera pars assedatur diuersis tenentibus wille pro xvij b. 1 f. ordei.

*Corsflat* xl[ti] s. land.

Vna pars assedatur georgio houston soluendo annuatim xx[ti] s.
Altera pars assedatur diuersis tenentibus ville pro xvij b. ordei.

*Brablo* xxviij s. iiij d. land assedatur diuersis tenentibus ville paslete pro ij c. j b. ij f. ordei.

*Gallowhillis ouer* xliiij s. land cum bonis monasterii per Robertum abbatem in manibus tenandorum qui habunt bonos semen et pabulum.

Vna pars assedatur Jacobo Wilson soluendo xl s. xij b. auenarum communis mensure et iiij b. ordei vj capones cum alio seruicio debito et consueto.
Alia pars assedatur roberto bully soluendo annuatim xl[ti] s. xij b. auenarum communis mensure iiij b. ordei et vj capones cum alio seruicio debito et consueto.

*Gallowhillis nethir* xxvj s. viij d. land ij dd. pultre.

Assedatur vna pars Wilelmo quhyt pro xiij s. iiij d. 1 cariagio xij d. pro le bonsiluer et xij pultre.
Altera pars assedatur Johanni Abernethy Andree bully pro xiij s. iiij d. 1 cariagio xij d. pro le bonsiluer et xij pultre.

*Lilysland* assedatur egidie Dunlop pro xl[ti] s. annuatim.

Item, *toddisholme* ij s. land assedatur predicte Egidie scilicet.

*Cariagehill* iiij merkis land iiij dd. pultre ij lang cariages.

Assedatur vna pars Johanni Wilson xxvj s. viij d. xij d. pro le bonsiluer ij dd. pultre 1 lang cariage vel x s. for le cariage.
Altera pars assedatur Johanni hector zonger soluendo xiij s. iiij d. 1 dd. pultre.
Altera pars assedatur Johanni hector elder soluendo vj s. viij d.
Altera pars assedatur vxori patricii chelis soluendo annuatim vj s. viij d. 1 cariage 1 dd. pultre.

*Ricarbar* xl[ti] s. land assedatur pro iij celdris auenarum.

Assedatur vna pars Johanni ralston pro dimedia parte vj pultre.
Altera pars assedatur Jacobo mekilrigis pro altera dimedia parte.

*Mekilrigis* assedatur pro viij lib. iiij lang cariages viij dusan pultre.

Assedatur vna pars roberto sclater soluendo annuatim iiij lib. ij s. pro le bonsiluer iiij dusan pultre ij lang cariages vel xx[ti] s. cum alio seruicio.
Altera pars assedatur dauid Sclater soluendo annuatim ij lib. ij s. pro le bonsiluer ij dusan pultre 1 lang cariage vel x s.
Altera pars assedatur Johanni robison soluendo annuatim xx[ti] s. xij pro le bonsiluer xij pultre 1 single cariage vel fyf s.
Altera pars assedatur roberto mekilrigis soluendo xij s. annuatim xij d. pro le bonsiluer xij pult. a singil cariage vel v s.

*fferguslay* assedatur pro vj lib. niniano Wallace pro toto tempore vite sue secundum formam rentalis.

Assedatur niniano Wallace soluendo annuatim vj lib. ij cariages ij pultre iiij s. pro le bonsiluer pro toto tempore vite sue secundum formam rentalis facta primo Maii in anno Domini etc. quingentesimo xxiij°.

*barskawan* assedatur pro iiij c. auenarum xxxij pultre.

Item Andro Vre Jno. Hoggzard xxxij b. auenarum xvj pultre.

Jok barskawan xxxij b. auenarum xvj pultre.

*Newton* assedatur pro iiij c. auenarum xxxij pultre.

Allan newton xxxij b. auenarum xvj pultre.

Altera pars vacat xxxij b. auenarum xvj pultre.

*Dulskaitht* assedatur pro xx s. 1 dusan pultre.

Assedatur Johanni Steuart coqino pro xx$^{ti}$ s. 1 dd. pultre cum sustentacione fossarum silue de Dulskaitht et custodia eiusdem.

*Candrane* v merkis land et x s. pro quhyt cruk assedatur pro viij c. auenarum preter xxxij merkis x b. ordei 1 c. petre casei xij stirkis preter iij lib. sine dictis.

John Arche gibson dimedia pars dicte wille.

Altera pars assedatur filio Johanni Alexr. beyond ye mos thyr tennandis hes of gudis of the abbay xlviij b. auenarum vj b. ij f. of secundbere x akyris of medo wyn and stakyt, 1 c. of hors corn, iiij oxin, xxiiij tidy ky, ilk tenand elik to deliuer at thair first in gangin.

*lynclef* assedatur pro iiij c. auenarum ij dusan pultre.

Johanni cochran et mergarete morton vxori dicti Johannis et vna celdra vltra allocata pro supportacione le crill.

*The brideland* assedatur pro xx$^{ti}$ s. xviij pultre xij in bwn siluer.

Assedatur gavimo maxwell pro xx$^{ti}$ s. xviij pultre xij d. in bwnsiluer j lang cariage in summer and wynter, cum alio seruicio debito et consueto.

*Corsbar* et thomas bar iij lib. vj s. viij d.

Assedatur Johanni Maxwell de Stanle et roberto maxwell eiusdem filio soluendo annuatim fyf merkis cum ij le cariages 1 dusan caponum cum alio seruicio debito et consueto.

*The rochbank* iij lib. vj s. viij d.

Assedatur vna pars thome bard ij merkland pro viij merkis sine alio seruicio viz. cariagio.

Altera pars vij 1 merkland assedatur thome hunter pro iiij merkis sine seruicio annuatim.

Altera pars ij merkland assedatur Johanni merschell soluendo ij merkis annuatim ij lang cariage 1 in symmer and a in wyntyr ij s. in bwn siluer ij dusan pultre.

*The neder thornle* iij lib. vj s viij d. land.

Solet soluere v chalder auenarum v dusan pultre iij s. in bwn siluer occupat per dominum ross sine assedacione abbatis.

*The neder thornle* set to the John lord roos payand therfor zherly iij lib. vj s. viij d. wyth oder do serius.

Knasland v s. in manibus relicte Johannis bully prope le Ward pro custodia auenarum.

*Monthouse* prope pleblis xx^ti s. land assedatur magistro Wilelmo Stewart.

Assedatur Wilelmo Stewart rectori de lochmaben pro xx^ti s. annuatim.

*Auldhous fyf merkisland.*

Assedatur Dauid Schaw filio fratris abbatis pro fyf merkis annuatim 1 dd. caponum.

*the kyrkland of the mernys* xx^ti s. land.

Assedatur Johanni Wallace pro xx^ti s. xij caponum xij d. in bwn siluer.

*the kyrk in pollok in mernys.*

Assedatur Johanni harberson pro viij s. vj pultre vj d. in bwn siluer.

*The kyrkland of estwod* j merk land.

Assedatur thome maxwell pro ij lib. soluendo cantoribus chori de pasleto annuatim.

*Tofta de Stewart* vj s. viij d.

Assedatur Johanni fergusson pro vj s. viij d. cum hospitalitate seruorum abbatis et cariagis inter munktown et paslay.

*the kyrkland of kilmacolme* xij s.

Assedatur george flemyn de Kilmacolm pro xij s. annuatim cum recepcione decimarum congregatarum cum contingerit et conservacione eiusdem in terra nostra.

*The Kyrkhouse of lochwynzoll* at John luff duellis in vj s.

*The Kyrkhouse* on the south syd at the largis xiij s. iiij d.

*The xl^ti s. land* besid the kyrk of the largis.

Assedatur Jacobo Crafurd et mergret Kelsoland sponse dicti Jacobi pro ij lib. annuatim vna cum equis et le Kartis pro congregacione decimarum in dicta terra et conseruacione eiusdem.

*Dominium de The glen.*

In the bar and brygend assedatur thome Schaw sub sigillo commune pro vj lib. xiij s. iiij d. annuatim cum alio seruicio debito et consueto.

*Milbank.* Assedatur vna pars roberto or clienti pro xij s. ferme annuatim x pultre xij d. in bown siluer. Altera pars assedatur Jacobo or et Johanni Jameson pro xij s. annuatim x pultre xij d. pro bownsiluer 1 lang cariage.

*Wester Kerss.*

Assedatur vna pars Johanni kyrkwode soluendo annuatim x s. x d. vj d. pro le bownsiluer 1 lang cariage cum alio seruicio debito et consueto.

Altera pars assedatur Allano kyrkwod pro x s. x d. annuatim.

Altera pars assedatur Johanni kyrkwod juniori x s. x d. annuatim.

Quarta pars assedatur roberto kyrkwod pro x s. x d. annuatim.

*Ester kers.*

Ester kerse xliij s. iiij d. in manibus abbatis occupat pro dominum sympill sine assedacione viij^xx petre casei tenentes soluent etiam vj vitulos et xliij s. iiij d. annuatim soluent tenandi occupatores.

*Joffraistak.*

Assedatur Johanni or pro xxiij s. iiij d. ij lang cariages ane symmer et ane wynter xij d. pro le bown siluer et xviij pultre.

*barmochlo.*

Assedatur Johanni Norwell pro x s. annuatim xij d. bown siluer ix pultre 1 singil cariage.

*Mawysbank.*

Assedatur ricardo or soluendo annuatim x s. xij d. bownsyluer ix pultre 1 singil cariage.

*lanstale.*

Assedatur Jacobo Or soluendo annuatim xv s. xij pultre xij d. bownsiluer 1 lange cariage.

*Camhill.*

Assedatur vna pars wilelmo Or soluendo annuatim xiij s. iiij d. 1 lange cariage xij d. bwnsiluer xviij pultre.

Altera pars Johanni kyrkwod soluendo annuatim vj s. viij d. xij d. bwnsiluer ix pultre.

*Gawilmos.*

Assedatur Jacobo logane et Johanni anderson soluendo annuatim xij s. xij d. bowne siluer x pultre 1 singil cariage.

*Lourensbank.*

Assedatur Allano glen soluendo annuatim xiij s. iiij d. 1 lange cariage xij d. bwnsiluer xij pultre.

*Auldzard.* Assedatur vna pars roberto glen soluendo annuatim viij s. vj d. bownsiluer vij pultre.

Altera pars assedatur Andree Gipson soluendo annuatim viij s. vj d. bownsiluer vij pultre 1 lange cariage.

*langzard.* Assedatur vna pars roberto Or soluendo annuatim xiij s. iiij d. xij d. bownsiluer xij pultre 1 lange cariage.

Altera pars assedatur Wilelmo riche soluendo annuatim xiij s. iiij d. xij d. bownsiluer xij pultre 1 lang cariage.

*Fairhillis.* Assedatur vna pars Wilelmo Or soluendo annuatim xj s. xij d. bownsiluer ix pultre 1 single cariage.

Altera pars assedatur roberto bridyn soluendo annuatim x s. xij d. bownsiluer ix pultre 1 single cariage.

*gilliszard.* Assedatur vna pars allano Jonson soluendo annuatim xj s. vj d. x pultre vij d. bown siluer 1 lang cariage.

Altera pars assedatur roberto glen soluendo annuatim xj s. vj d. x pultre xij d. bownsiluer 1 lang cariage.

*litillclook.*

Assedatur roberto bridyn soluendo annuatim x s. cum le bonsiluer et alio seruicio debito et consueto.

*Moniabrocht* xl[ti] s. land in manibus abbatis.

*langcrofft.*

x s land. Assedatur vna pars Jacobo Cochran
Altera pars roberto cochran } soluendo annuatim x s. 1 singil cariage.
Altera pars allano allanson

*The Quensidmur.*

Assedatur Jacobo et roberto soluendo annuatim xlviij s. in festo sancti mertini.

The ferm placis of the glen for cheys and stirkis.

*Moniabrocht* xl[ti] s. land set to Jhone lord roos.

Moniabrocht in manibus abbatis propter non solucionem firmarum occupat per dominum roos xl[ti] s. land of auld extent et soluit annuatim viij[xx] petras casei vj stirkis preter pecii vj s. viij d. et xl[ti] s. pro firma annuatim.

1 c. stane Auchynhayn xl[ti] s. land assedatur Rannaldo Johanni Allanson soluendo annuatim xxx petras casei 1 stirk cum allo seruicio.

Altera pars Wilelmo Maldished pro xxx petris casei 1 stirk.

Altera pars thome or soluendo annuatim iij[xx] petras casei iij stirk.

viij[xx] stane. *The lyntellis* viij[xx] stane viij stirkis.

Assedatur vna pars Johanni fyschar pro iij[xx] viij petris casei iij stirkis.

Altera pars Johanni Or juniori pro xxxiiij petris casei.

Altera pars Jacobo bard pro xxxiiij petris casei.

Altera pars thome Schaw pro xxxiiij petris casei.

*The candilmur* xl[ti] s. land 1[e] stane vj stirkis.

Assedatur vna pars dauid or pro xl[ti] petris casei vj stirkis.

Niniano or pro xl[ti] petris casei.

Johanni kebill pro xl[ti] petris.

*Nethyr barnatht* xl[ti] s. land.

Assedatur thome Or et Johanni Atkyn pro 1[e] petris casei per equales portiones et vj stirkis.

*Ouer barnatht* xxx[ti] land.

Assedatur roberto schaw soluendo annuatim xxx[ti] s. et xij d. pro le bonsiluer.

*Clookis* xl[ti] land.

Assedatur vna pars Wilelmo mungumbry soluendo annuatim iij[xx] petras casei et iij stirkis.

Altera assedatur Johanni Atkyn soluendo annuatim iij[xx] petras casei et iij stirkis.

*litill clook* x s. land.

Assedatur roberto bridyn soluendo annuatim x s. xij d. pro le bonsiluer x pultre 1 singil cariage non soluit introitu post decessum patris tamen prius fuit in rentale.

*The came* iiij lib. land.

Assedatur vna pars Jacobo brown viz. xx[ti] s. land pro xxx petris casei.

Altera pars xx[ti] s. land assedatur Johanni robisoun pro xxx petris casei.

Altera pars xx[ti] s. land assedatur Jacobo Sandeson pro xxx petris casei.

Altera pars xx[ti] s. land assedatur Jacobo cochran pro xxx[ti] petris casei.

---

*Rentale assedacionis dominii de lennax facta in anno Domini v^c etc. videlicet in anno Domini quingentesimo xxj^o.*

*Wester Kilpatrik* vj lib. xiij s. iiij d. v cariagis v s. pro le bonsiluer assedatur subscriptis tenentibus.

Johanni assedatur vna pars soluendo annuatim xxv s.
george brown assedatur altera soluendo annuatim xxxiij s. iiij d.
Winfra brownsid soluendo annuatim xvj s. viij d.
Roberto brok viij s. iiij d. annuatim.
Wall bronsid soluendo annuatim xxv s.
Wille brison viij s. iiij d. annuatim.
Wille lang xvj s. viij d. annuatim.

*Ester Kilpatrlk* vj lib. xiij s. iiij d. land v cariagis v s. pro le bonsiluer.

Johanni fyndlawson et Johanni Allanson xxij s. ij d. annuatim.
James brok xxij s. ij d. annuatim.
Janete brownsid xvj s. viij d. annuatim.
Johanni bryson xvj s. viij d. annuatim.
Jame angus xvj s. viij d. annuatim.
Jame fyndlaw xj s. i d. annuatim.
Dauid henrison xi s. ij d. annuatim.
Allan laing xvj s. viij d.

*Morysland* xxvj s. viij d. land. xij d. in bonsiluer a lang cariage.

Patrik laing xiij s. iiij d.
fynlaw merchand Sclater xiij s. iiij d.
The ostlar hous wyth the zard at the west end of kyrk in fynlaw merchandis hand a dusan of capon vel xiij s. iiij d. annuatim.
Schyr Wilzem Schawis hous and zard at the est end of the kyrk xiij s. iiij d. annuatim.
The ~~smyths~~ hous assedatur Jacobo angus pro xiij s. iiij d. annuatim.

*Auchynlochan* iiij lib. land iiij s. bonsiluer iij cariage.

Assedatur vna pars Wilelmo donald soluendo annuatim xxvj s. viij d.
Will paterson xx^{ti} s. et pro hostellaria viij ^{d.} xij capones annuatim.
Will Jonson x s. annuatim.
Johanni M^crerikis steid xiij^{s.} iiij^{d.}
Jame M^creryk xl^{ti} s.

*Dunterclunan* iiij lib. xiij s. iiij d. land iiij s. in bonsiluer iij cariage.

Assedatur vna pars Johanni lang soluendo annuatim xxiij s. iiij d.
Altera pars georgio forsyth pro xxiij s. iiij d. annuatim.
Altera pars Andree Allanson pro xxiij s. iiij d. annuatim.
Altera pars bartholomeo flemyn pro xxiij s. iiij d. annuatim.

*Vester cochnay* vj lib. xiij s. iiij d. land v cariagis v s. in bonsiluer assedatur subscriptis tenentibus.

Assedatur vna pars gilberto boil soluendo annuatim xvj s. viij d.
Rob Sclater viij s. iiij d. annuatim.
Anne Boquhannan viij s. iiij d. annuatim.
Jhon of lee zonger xvj s. viij d.
Wil Nelwyn xiij s. x d.
John Paterson xiij s. iiij d.

Jame brison xvj s. viij d.
Wille hog xxv s.
Jame Tomson xv. s.

*Chapelland of West cochnay* xiij s. iiij d. assedatur Wilelmo Allanson.

*Ester cochnay* vj lib. xiij s. iiij d. assedatur georgio schaw per sigillum communem.

*Druntochyr* iiij lib. vj s. viij d. ij cariage iiij s. in bonsiluer.
James Dowglas xx^ti^ s. xx^ti^ d. zheirly.
James fynneson xx^ti^ s. xx^ti^ d.
Item, georgio houston viij b. ordei soluendo per Jacobum fynneson.
Johanni Sprewil xliij s. iiij d.

*Tho Mylland* xiij s. iiij d. 1 dd. caponum iiij b. ordei.
The myll of the lennax callyt Drumtochyr myll assedatur tenentibus dominii de lennax pro 1^e^ merkis soluendis in festo sancti mertini et pentecostes per equales portiones.

*Inbernan* iiij lib. vj s. viij d. iij cariages iiij s. of bonsiluer assedatur subscriptis tenentibus.
Rob. Sprewil et Stein Sprewil his son xliij s. iiij d.
Dauide houston xx^ti^ s. xx^ti^ d.
Jhon Edmonston xx^ti^ s. xx^ti^ d.

*Cragbanzoch* xiij s. iiij d. set to the tenandis of Inbernan.

*Afflec* v lib. iij cariages iiij s. bonsiluer assedatur subscriptis tenentibus.
ffyndlaw m'gregor xxv s.
Wille Jonson xij s. vj d.
Jhon brison xxv s.
Jhon edmonston xij s. vj d.
Jhon flemyn xxv s. vj b. ordei.

*ffarklay* xx^ti^ s. land assedatur.
Jhon brownsid xx^ti^ s. xij d. bonsiluer.

*Braidfield* iiij lib. land iij cariage iiij s. bonsiluer assedatur subscriptis tenentibus.
Jame Dowglas xxx^ti^ s.
Wille brison xx^ti^ s.
fyndlaw M'gregor xx^ti^ s.
Martin Caitberoht x s.

*Wester culboy* vj lib. x s. land assedatur tenentibus subscriptis.
Adam morison xxj s. viij d. and Janet Schaw x s. x d. zheirly v b. ordei. (Nota, set to thome m'reryk.)
Jame Angus xxj s. viij d. and John Angus x s. x d. zheirly et v b. ordei.
Allan richarson xxj s. viij d. and elyn allanson x s. x d. et v b. ordei.
Elyn Wodruff xxj s. viij d. et Jhon fynnyson x s. x d. et v b. ordei.

Item, the said tenandis has giffin our to the abbot xxiiij akyris of medo of the samyn town at lyis apone the medo of the barnis the abbot payand for mawyn and wynyn ther of.

*Ester culboy* v lib. land assedatur tenentibus subscriptis.

Pate morison xxxiij s. iiij d. and vij b. ordei.
Wille henrison xxxiij s. iiij d. and vij b. ordei.
Jhon henrison xxxiij s. iiij d. and vij b. ordei.

*Boquhanran* vj lib. xiij s. iiij d. land assedatur Wilelmo edmonston secundum formam rentalis soluendo annuatim vj lib. xiij s. iiij d. cum aliis servitiis debitis et consuetis sic pater et auus habuerunt per prius.

*Achynge* xvj s. viij d. land assedatur tenandis de boquhanran. It is ane mur sted t. payis at mertmess ye hail maill.

The chapelland of boquhanran set to Andro Atkyn for xiij s. iiij d.
The barnis iiij lib. land set for ij c. viij b. farine j c. ordei to rob of knock ye tane half t. thom of knock ye toder half the medow of ye barnis won mawing and and stakhyt be ye tenandis of ye samyn fre. It was in auld tymis manis t. payit.

Memorandum, at ye tenandis of ye barnis pais j merk zheirly for quhyt silver.
Memorandum, at ye land of ye lordschip of kilpatrik pertenand to ye abbay of Paslay pais na cane foullis becaus yai ar thryllyt to fyff chalder of wache meil to ye castell of Dumbertane t. quhilk towne pais elik.

*The lordship of Munktown in Kilsteuart.*

Memorandum of ye statut of ye doseruice of y[t] lordschip y[t] ilk merk land iij capones ye price of ilk capon unspendit viij d. ilk pultre iiij d. ilk chekyn ij d. ye laid of mail colis iiij d. ilk laid thre hutchis or thre crelis t. to be pait in ye abbotis place of Munktown betwex Witsonday t. mychaelmas or ye price fre t. gif ye abbot misteris may colis yan his mail colis ye tenandis sal leid als many as he mysteris ye abbot payand for yame the entresse of ye foullis begynnis at pasche caponis t. chekynnis to mychaelmes t. fra mychaelmes pultre to fastrenis ewyn.
Item, for oder doseruice it is statut at ilk tenand at makis ane hail pleucht suld teyl ane akyr of land t. harrow ye sammyn or yan pay for ye pleuche telling ij s. and ye akyr hairowyn vj d. t. for ilk dais schering iij d. ye penny mail to be pait at Witsonday t. mertimes as wse is oder doseruice to be pait at mertimes.

The rentale of ye malis foullis colis and oder doseruice of ye lordschip of Munktown t. Dalmilling to be zheirly pait at wsuale termes as ye memorial befor proportis.

*Munktown hill* v lib. xviij s. land set to yir tennentis wnder wryttin.

Patoun riche tak xv s. iiij d. ij capones ij pultre ij chekyns ij laid of colis ½ pleuche ½ bed a cariage v dais schering.

*Munktown hill* set to thyr tennantis.

Alexander Conigham tak xv s. iiij d. ij capones ij pultre ij chekyns ij laid of colis ½ pleuche ½ bed a cariage v dais schering.
John Dermont tak xxvjj s. iij d. iij capones iij pultre ½ laid of colis a pleuche a cariage a bed a ridand man viij dais schering.
Jhon Osborn tak xxxvj s. iiij capones iiij pultre viij chekynis iiij laid of colis a ridand man a cariage a bed a pleuche viij dais schering.

Allan greyffis tak xxiiij s. ij capones ij pultre vj chekynis ij laid of colis a bed a pleuche a cariage v dais schering.

Summa huius ville v lib. xviij s. xiij capons xv pultre xxiiij chekynis xiij laid of colis iiij plowis iiij beddis ij ridand men v cariagis xxx dais schering.

*Munktown* set to yir tennandis at foullis.

Jhone adamsoun tak liij s. iiij d. iiij capones iiij pultre viij chekynnis ij laid of colis a ridand man a cariage a pleucht a bed v dais schering.

kateryn neillis tak liij s. iiij d. iiij capons iiij pultre viij chekynnis ij laid of colis a ridand man a cariage a pleucht a bed v. dais schering.

Jhekyn osbern tak xxviij s. iij capones iij pultre vj chekynnis iij laid of colis a ridand man a cariage a pleucht a bed v dais schering.

Jok Willo tak xxviij s. iij capon iij pult vj chekynnis iij laid of colis a ridand man a cariage a pleucht a bed v dais schering.

Jok Cristollis tak ye ostellar land xiij s. iiij d. alanerly.

Jok nelyn tak xxix s. iij capons iiij pultre vj chekynnis iij laid of colis a redand man a cariage a pleucht a bed v dairs schering.

Dauid gottra tak xxxvj s. viij d. wyth nychol moris tak iiij capones iiij pultre viij chekynnis iiij laid of colis a ridand man a cariage a pleucht a bed x dais schering.

Adam hunter tak xxxvj s. iiij capones iiij pultre viij chekynnis ij laid of colis a ridand man a cariage a pleucht a bed v dais schering.

James clerk t. thome loury tak xvj s. ij capones ij pultre iiij chekynnis ij laid of colis a cariage 1 half pleucht z half bed v dais schering.

Jhon fyndlawis tak xxx[ti] s. iij capones iiij pult vj chekynnis ij laid of colis a ridand man a pleucht a bed v dais schering.

The ouer place callyt robynschawis tak set to Mergret Mwr t. hyr son Jhon of Schaw for iiij lib. xij capones xij pultre iiij laid of colis a ridand man a cariage a pleucht a bed x dais schering wnder ye conuentis seill.

The Wardhouse wyth Allan Smythis house besid ye kyrk xiij s. iiij d. alanerly.

The bronsyde John rig tak vj s. viij d. iiij capones casting ye mill laid.

The brokat rob Wilson tak xx[ti] s. ij capones iij pultre iiij chekynnis ij laid of colis a cariage a half pleucht a half bed v dais schering.

Jhon conighamis tak y[r] in brokat xx[ti] s. ij capones iij pultre iiij chekynnis ij laid of colis a cariage a half pleucht a half bed v dais schering.

blairis tak of Adamtoun in Cwquhatmur xxxvj s. viij d. land iiij capones iiij pultre iiij chekynnis ij laid of colis a ridand man a cariage a pleuche a bed v dais schering.

Summa huius ville xxiiij lib. xiij s. iiij d. l capones liiij pultre iij[xx] xij chekynnis xxxvij laid of colis xvj½ plowis xj½ beddis x ridand men xj cariag iij[xx] xv dais schering.

Dalmilling land in Sanct Kenotis parochin ye foullis of yat land is all capons set to ye tenandis wnderwryttin :—

*Kyrkland holme.* Jhok conighamis tak xxxiij s. iiij d. xxvj s. viij d. v capones ij laid of colis a ridand man a cariage a half pleucht a bed v dais schering.

Jame Galloways tak xxvj s. viij d. vj capones ij laid of colis a cariage a half pleuche v dais schering.

*Kyrkhill.* Rob fergushill tak ij lib. ix s. x capones iiij laid of colis a ridand man a cariage a pleucht a bed v dais schering.

henry hunteris tak in kyrkhill xxiiij s. iiij d. v capon ij laid of colis a cariage v dais schering.

*Dalmilling town.*

The myl quarter (the chapelland at ya bryg-end of air) xiij s. iiij d. iij capones ij laid of colis a half pleuche v dais schering in Adam Wallace hand of ye newtown.

The blakhouse in ye sammyn quarter Wilzem Wallace tak xxvj s. viij d. vj capones ij laid of colis a pleucht a bed a cariage a ridand v dais schering.

Wilke blairis tak in yat quarter xiij s. iiij d. iij capon ij laid of colis a half pleucht a cariage v dais schering.

katrin holmyltown tak in yat quarter ij lib. ix capon iiij laid of colis a ridand man a cariage a pleucht a bed v dais schering.

The myll land vj capones.

The maynholme quarter robyn of Schawis tak iiij lib. xiij s. iiij d. xxi capones vj laid of colis a ridand man a pleuch a bed v dais schering set under ye conuentis seill.

*Cantis quarter.*

huchsoun osbern tak set to thom of galloway payand 1 lib. ix capones iiij laid of colis a ridand man a cariage a pleuch a bed v dais schering.

Jasper Stenis tak xvj s. viij d. iij capon ij laid of colis a cariage a half pleucht v dais schering.

lawrence Striuiling tak xx[ti] s. iiij capones iij laid of colis a cariage a half pleucht v dais schering.

Jhon Stenisounis tak xvj s. viij d. iij capones ij laid of colis a cariage a half pleucht v dais schering.

*Wod quarter.*

Wille richmont xviij s. xj d. iiij capones ij laid of colis a cariage a half pleuche v dais schering.

Rob Galloway tak xviij s. xjd. iiij capones ij laid of colis a cariage a half pleucht v dais schering.

Edward Trumbellis tak xlij s. ix capones iiij laid of colis a cariage a ridand man a pleucht a bed x dais schering.

Pate tomsonis tak xxvj s. viij d. vj capons iij laid of colis a cariage a ridand man v dais schering.

Adam tomsonis tak vij s. ij capon a laid of colis v dais schering.

Sandy grais tak vj s. viij d. ij capones 1 laid of colis v dais schering.

*The Manis of Munktown* x lib. land set for dwble mail and 1 c. of horse corn set yir tennandis followand iiij ddis. caponum.

george nychollis tak at ye hall l[ti] s. zheirly vj capon ij b. of corn.

Jhon hunter tak set for xij b. farine price bolle vj s. viij d. et iiij b. ordei price bolle viij s. iiij d. Inde pecunia v lib. xiij s. iiij d.

Charlgis Wilsoun lvj s. vj d. zheirly wyth capones t. horse corn a ridand man to his part.

Alexander bellis tak lvj s. vj d. wyth oder dwytis sic lik.

Mathew mwry lv s. vj d.

Rob hunter of ye quhyt sid $l^{ti}$ s.
Jhon hunter of ye quhyt side $l^{ti}$ s. land at was Robyn nycholl steid.
Adam gilcrist t. Adam Schaw xxxij s. iiij d.

---

*Rentale Reuerendi patris domini Johannis hammilton commendatarii monasterii de pasleto et abbatis futuri eiusdem ac assedaciones omnium terrarum dicto monasterio spectantium et pertinentium factum in mensibus Octobris et nouembris Anno Domini millesimo quingentesimo vigesimo quinto scriptum manu religiosi viri domini Alexandri Walcar prioris tunc claustralis prefati monasterii necnon dicti domini commendatarii administratorii deputati.*

*The ynch* xviij merk land assedatur pro xviij c. auenarum antique mensure xij dd. pultre.

Pars vilhelmi Sympill cum consensu eiusdem assedatur Jacobo Snodgers soluendo vt supra factum apud paslay anno 1554.

Vna pars assedatur Jhoani langmur pro xxx b. auenarum xviij pultre vt nunc assedatur Roberto hammilton burgensi pasleti soluendo vt supra xxix° Aprilis anno &c. xxxi° Qui mortuus est nunc autem assedatur Joanni hamylton filio dicti roberti cum consensu sui patris soluendo ut supra Et nunc cum consensu dicti Joannis assedatur Joanni hammylton de fergusly granatarii soluendo vt supra factum apud paslay xxv octobris anno 1548 Et nunc cum consensu dicti Joannis assedatur Willelmo Sympill de Thridpairt soluendo vt supra factum apud $Ed^{r}$ xxv augusti anno 1550.

Alia pars assedatur Jhoanni findlason juniori pro xxiiij b. auenarum xii° pultre.

Alia pars assedatur roberto smyth pro xxx b. auenarum xv pultre.

---

Dimedietas assedatur Joanni Smyth eius fratri soluendo xv boll auenarum et vij½ pultre.

anno domini etc. xxxvj mense octobris.

Et altera pars huius assedatur Joanni quhit soluendo xv b. auenarum et vij½ pultre qui mortuus est Et nunc assedatur Joanni quhit eius filio soluendo vt supra factum apud paslay xvij decembris anno 1551.

Alia pars assedatur Ade erskyn pro xxx b. auenarum xv pultre quhilk adam erskyn has gevyn his kyndness to Dauid crag & admittit be my lord t. ye convent and so ye said Da. is tenend paiand all dewteis to ye place vait t. wont Megge schaw ye wedo browkand ye tane halff for hyr lyff tyme. Et nunc assedatur Johanni crag filio primogenito dicti dauid soluendo ut supra factum apud hammylton xxij° maii anno Domini $j^{m}$ $v^{c}$ xliij°.

Pars olim Joannis thomson qui mortuus est assedatur Jonete thomson eius sorori seniori soluendo in omnibus vt supra factum apud lythgw vj februarii 1552.

Alia pars assedatur petro tomson pro xxiiij b. auenarum xij pultre.

Et nunc assedatur Johanni tomsone juniori soluendo vt supra anno domini m $v^{c}$ xxxiiij° primo Septembris Et mortuus est t. nunc hec pars t. alia media pars quam possedebat olim malcolmus Johneson assedatur thome thomson soluendo annuatim xxxvj b. auenarum xviij pultre qui mortuus est Et nunc assedatur Joanni thomson eius filio primogenito soluendo vt supra factum apud paslay xvij decembris anno 1551.

Eodem die dicta pars terre cum consensu dicte Jonete assedatur Jacobo Adam alias vilson soluendo in omnibus vt supra die et loco predictis.

Alia pars assedatur Roberto fyndloson pro xviij b. auenarum ix pultre et nunc eadem pars Alexandro robisone soluendo vt supra plegio Dauid craig.

Alia pars assedatur Jhoani Jhonson elder pro xxxiiij b. auenarum xij pultre et mortuus est et nunc assedatur Willelmo Johneson filio seniori Joanis Johneson soluendo vt supra factum vltimo Januarii anno domini m° v° xxxviij qui mortuus est Et nunc assedatur Joanni Jhonston eius filio primogenito soluendo vt supra factum apud paslay xvij decembris anno 1551.

Pars olim thome bard nunc assedatur Joanni bard eius filio primogenito soluendo vt supra factum apud hammylton xxvij Aprilis anno 1551.

Alia pars assedatur Duncano hector pro xviij b. auenarum ix pultre Et nunc assedatur patricio bard soluendo vt supra anno Domini etc. xxxvj° mense octobris Et nunc heć pars t. illa alia pars quam occupabat Johannes thomson t. post eum patricius bard assedatur thome bard soluendo xxxvj b. auenarum xviij pultre factum xxviij aprilis anno Domini m° v° xl°.

Alia pars assedatur Jhoani kebill pro xxiiij b. auenarum xij pultre nunc cum consensu dicti Joannis Eius due partes viz. xviij boll auenarum assedatur alexandro Robison Et altera tertia pars eius assedatur thome kebill filio dicti Joannis soluendo eorum quilibet pro sua parte vt supra factum apud lynlythgw xxix mercii 1554.

Alia pars assedatur Jhoani tomson pro xviij b. auenarum ix pultre.

Et nunc eadem pars assedatur patricio bard pro xviij b. auenarum ix pultre.

Alia pars assedatur Jhoanni Symson pro xviij b. auenarum ix pultre.

Alia pars assedatur Malcolmo Jhonson pro xxiiij b. auenarum xij pultre et mortuus est et nunc eius medietas assedatur Joanni kebill juniori soluendo pro illa parte xij b. auenarum vj pultre factum viij februarii anno domini m° v° xxxij.

Et nunc illa pars quam occupabat Johannes kebill assedatur thome kebill ejus fratri soluendo ut supra factum apud lynlythgw x Augusti 1547.

Et altera pars assedatur Joanni thomson juniori soluendo pro illa parte xij b. vj pultre factum anno domini m° v° xxxiiij primo Septembris.

The merkis worth assedatur tenenti de ynche pro xiij s. iiij d. xij pultre t. seruicio.

The medow of ye ynche ye est part v acres land set to tenendis of ye ynche for vij b. ij f. ordei.

The west part of ye medow of ye ynche v acres set to Jhon Smyth for vj b. i f. ordei.

*Arkliston* assedatur ix merkland assedatur pro ix c. auenarum ij dd. caponum.

Vna pars assedatur roberto wrry pro xxxvj b. auenarum vj capones vel xij pultre iiij bwnys.

Et nunc assedatur Joanni wrry filio roberti supra scripti soluendo vt supra factum anno etc. xxxvj mense octobris t. mortuus est t. nunc assedatur Joanni wry fratri supra scripti Joannis wry soluendo vt supra.

xxv Aprilis etc. xxxviij[d].

Alia pars assedatur Jhoanni thomson pro xxxvj b. farine auenarum xij pultre vel vj capones ii bwnys.

Et nunc assedatur Johanni thomsoun primogenito dicti Johannis soluendo ut supra factum apud hammyltown xv augusti 1544 Et mortuus est Et nunc assedatur hugoni hammyltown soluendo vt supra factum apud Edynburcht x Januarii anno etc. xlvj[e] Qui mortuus est nunc assedatur Joanni hammilton eius fratri soluendo vt supra factum apud Stirlyng v Januarii anno Domini 1547.

Et nunc cum consensu dicti Joannis hammylton assedatur patricio hammylton eius fratri soluendo vt supra factum apud Edinburcht xx Junii anno 1554.

Alia pars assedatur Roberto landelis pro xxxvj b. auenarum vj capon iiij bwnys Et nunc assedatur Johanni landelis soluendo ut supra factum xxiiij Julii 1545.

Alia pars assedatur Dauid Crag pro xxxvj b. auenarum vj capones iiij bwnys Et nunc cum consensu dicti Dauidis assedatur Willielmo crage eius filio reseruando tamen vsum fructu patri quo ad vixerit soluendo vt supra factum apud paslay augusti anno etc. 1547.

*Hyllynton* ix merkland assedatur pro ix c. auenarum ij dd. caponum.

Vna pars assedatur roberto Steyn pro xxxvj b. auenarum vj capones iiij bwnys Et nunc assedatur Joanni Steyne filio roberti steyn soluendo vt supra xxij decembris xxxviij[o].

Et cum consensu dicti Joannis Eius pars media assedatur Joanni (?) hammylton de fergusly et Roberto hammylton eius filio soluendo pro vt supra factum apud lynlythgw x Januarii anno 1553.

Alia pars assedatur henrico lochheid pro xxxvj b. auenarum vj capones iiij bwnys Qui mortuus est assedatur vero nunc lochheid eius filio primogenito soluendo in omnibus vt supra factum apud lythgw ix Januarii anno 1553.

Alia pars assedatur Jhoanni kebyll pro xxxvj b. auenarum vj capones iiij bwnys Et nunc assedatur Dauid kebil filio primogenito Joannis kebil soluendo vt supra factum anno Domini etc. xxxviij Et nunc cum consensu dicti dauidis eius media pars assedatur Jacobo vilson soluendo vt supra proportione cum aliis seruitiis debitis et consuetis factum [apud] paslay xxiiij Januarii anno 1555.

Mortuus est. Alia pars assedatur Wilelmo bully pro xxxvj b. auenarum vj capones iiij bwnys.

Assedatur thome darroch pro xxxvj b. auenarum vj capones iiij bwnis.

*Grenlaw* ij merkland.

Vna pars assedatur Waltero bully pro viij b. ordei.

Et nunc assedatur alexandro crage cum consensu walteri bully supra scripti soluendo vt supra factum xviij die mensis februarii anno Domini m[o] v[e] xxxiiij.

Alia pars assedatur diuersis tenentibus ville pro xvij b. j. f. ordei.

*Corsflat* xl s. land.

Vna pars assedatur diuersis tenentibus ville pro xvij b ordei.

Alia pars assedatur georgio houston pro xx s. xij pultre xij d. in bonsiluer 1 cariage.

*Brablo* xxviij s. iiij d. assedatur diuersis tenentibus pro ij c. 1 b. ij f. ordei.

*Gallohyllis ouer* xliiij s. iiij lib. cum bonis monasterii.

Vna pars assedatur Jacobo Wilson pro xl s. xij b. auenarum communis mensure iiij b. ordei vj capon & seruicio debito et consueto Et nunc assedatur Joanni vilson primogenito dicti Jacobi soluendo vt supra apud Hamiltoun xvij augusti 1544.

Alia pars assedatur roberto bully pro xl s. xij b. auenarum communis mensure iiij b. ordei vj cappn cum seruicio debito et consueto Et mortuus est nunc autem assedatur elizabethe M'Ge & Willielmo Stewart eius filio soluendo vt supra factum apud Edinburcht xij februarii anno etc. xlvj°.

knolandis assedatur Jacobo quhyt pro v s. cum seruicio alio debito et consueto Et nunc cum consensu dicti Jacobi assedatur Joanni quhit primogenito dicti Jacobi soluendo vt supra factum apud edinburcht xj augusti anno 1550.

*Gallohyllis nethyr* ij merkland ij dd. pullorum.

Vna pars assedatur Wilelmo quhit pro xiij s. iiij d. xij d. in bwn siluer xij pultre 1 cariage.

Et nunc assedatur Jacobo quhyit filio seniori dicti Willelmi quhit soluendo vt supra anno Domini m° v° xxxiiij° die augusti Nunc autem cum consensu dicti Jacobis assedatur Joanni quhit filio primogenito dicti Jacobi soluendo vt supra factum apud Edinburgh xj augusti anno 1550 reseruando vsufructum patri.

Alia pars assedatur Andree bully pro vj s. viij d. xij d. in bwn silver xij pultre 3 cariages.

Media pars assedatur karolo hammilton soluen. annuatim vj s. viij d. vj d. in bon siluer vj pultre 3 cariages.

[Margin: Media Roberti gylmour cum consensu eiusdem assedatur Joanni hammiltonde fergusly soluendo vt supra factum apud paslay xvj. . . . embro' anno 1551 nunc cum consensu dicti Joannis assedatur elene Maxwell et Roberto hamiltoun[eius] sponso et filio dicti Joannis reseruato tamen vsufructum patri soluendo vt supra factum apud paslay xx viij martii anno 1555.]

Alia pars assedatur gilchristo gilmwr pro xiij s. iiij d. xij d. in bwn siluer xij pultre 1 cariage anno domini m° v° xxxiiij xxij° Septembris Et nunc assedatur roberto gilmwr filio dicti gilchrist soluendo ut supra factum apud paslay xxj Januarii 1544.

*Lylisland* xx b. auenarum.

Assedatur egidie dwnlop pro xx$^{ti}$ b. auenarum.

*Toddisholm* ij s. land.

Assedatur egedie dunlop pro ij s.

*Cariage hyll* iiij merkland iiij dd. pullorum ij lang cariagis.

Vna pars assedatur Jhoanni Wilson pro ij merkis xij d. in bwn siluer ij dd. pultre 1 lang cariage vel x s. pro cariago et nunc assedatur Joanni wilsone filio supra scripti Joannis cum consensu eiusdem soluendo vt supra in omnibus.

anno etc. xxx vij°

Alia pars assedatur Jonete Sclater pro vj s. viij d. vj pultre cum quarta parte cariagii vj d. in bonsyluer et mortua est Et nunc assedatur domino Roberto Sclater capellano soluendo vt supra factum apud paslay quinto decembris anno Domini m° v° xxix°.

Alia pars assedatur Jhoanni hector seniori pro vj s. viij d. vj pultre cum quarta parte cariagii vj d. in bonsiluer mortuus est et assedatur domino Robert Sclater capellano vt supra xiijj° Januarii anno Domini etc. xxviij°.

Alia pars assedatur Jhoanni hector juniori pro xiij s. iiij d. xij pultre media pars cariagii xij d. in bonsiluer Et nunc assedatur petro algeo soluendo ut supra factum xj Januarii anno Domini m° v° xxxvij°.

*Ricardisbar* xl s. land assedatur pro iij c. auenarum xij pultre ij s. in bonsiluer.

Vna pars assedatur Jhoanni ralstone pro xxiiij b. auenarum vj pultre xij d. in bonsiluer Et nunc cum consensu suprascripti Joannis ralstone assedatur eadem pars dauidi ralstone filio dicti Joannis sicut tamen idem Joannes eandem possedebit terram quoad vixerit et dauid ralston soluet pro illa terra vt prius pater eius Joannes soluit factum xxvij[a] Januarii anno Domini m° v° xxxij°.

Alia pars assedatur Jacobo ricardisbar pro xxiiij b. auenarum vj pultre xij d. in bonsiluer Et nunc cum consensu dicti Jacobi assedatur matheo wilsone eius filio primogenito soluendo vt supra factum apud glasgw vltimo octobris anno Domini etc. xlviij Qui mortuus est Et nunc Assedatur thome vilson eius fratri soluendo in omnibus vt supra factum apud Edinburcht xviij Septembris anno 1550.

*Mekilriggis* assedatur pro viij lib. iiij lang cariages viij dd. pullorum.

Vna pars assedatur roberto Sclater pro iiij lib. ij s. in bwnsiluer iiij dd. pullorum ij lang cariagis vel xx s. cum alio seruicio Et nunc cum consensu dicti Roberti assedatur Arthuro Sclater eius filio primogenito soluendo vt supra factum apud glasgw vltimo octobris anno Domini etc. xlviij° reseruato tamen vsufructu dicto roberto quoad vixerit.

Alia pars assedatur Dauid Sclater pro xl s. xij d. in bwnsiluer ij dd. pultre 1 lang cariage vel x s. cum alio seruicio Qui mortuus est Et Joanni sclater nepoti dicti dauidis soluendo in omnibus vt supra factum apud . . . . xvij martii anno etc. 1548.

Alia pars assedatur Roberto Anderson pro xx s. xij pultre vj d. in bwnsiluer 1 . . . . vel v s. Et nunc cum consensu dicti Roberti assedatur Roberto Anderson primogenito dicti roberti Roberti sui patris ac alia accedente consensu Jo . . . alias Anderson filii primogeniti dicti roberti patris soluendo vt supra factum apud . . augusti anno 1550.

Alia pars assedatur Jhoanni robison pro xx s. xij pultre vj d. in bwnsiluer.

*ffergusly* vj lib. land assedatur pro vj lib. 1 c. xiiij b. farine 1 c. ordei ij dd. caponum ij lang cariagis.

*ffergusly.*

Assedatur niniano Wallace soluendo annuatim vj lib. ij lang cariages ij dd. capones iiij s. in bonsiluer pro toto tempore vite sue secundum formam rentalis prout continetur in rentali roberti olim abbatis facto xv Junii anno Domini M. v^c^ xxxj° coram his testibus M. Arthuro hamiltoun prepositi eiusdem Joanne hamiltoun de newton M. Jacobo foster clerico domino henrico Bereche capellano cum diuersis aliis Et mortuus est Et nunc eadem terra viz. ffergusly assedatur Joanni hammylton granatario pasleti soluendo annuatim vt supra factum iij marcii anno Domini m. v° xxxviij° Et nunc assedatur post mortem eius cum consensu eiusdem Joanni hammilton filio suo primogenito soluendo vt supra xx marcii anno Domini m° v° xlj zeir.

*The brydeland* assedatur gawino maxwell pro xx s. xviij pultre xij d. in bwnsiluer 1 lang cariage in symmer t. wynter cum alio seruicio debito et consueto.

Et nunc post obitum dicti gawini assedatur arthuro maxwell secundo genito gawini cum consensu sui patris t. Roberti maxwell sui fratris primogeniti soluendo in omnibus annuatim vt supra factum apud glasgw xvij mertii anno Dominii 1 m° v^c^ xlviij°.

*Corsbar and Thomasbar* v merkland ij c. iiij b. farine xij b. ordei xij capones.

Corsbar t. thomasbar assedantur magistro Waltero Maxwell pro vita eius Et post eum gabrieli maxwel filio et heredi quondam Joannis maxwel de Stanle Ita quod gabriel persoluat aut satisfaciat magistro Waltero de summa ducentarum quinquaginta mercarum vsualis monete Scotie quam quidem summam dictus magister Walterus persoluit et deliberauit wenerabili patri Joanni abbati de . . . . pro rentalatione eorundem in dictis terris soluendo annuatim dictus magister Walterus aut gabriel nobis et successoribus nostris nostro ve monasterio quinque mercas vsualis monete cum duabus cariagiis — caponibus pro omni alia firma cum alio seruicio debito et consueto factum pasleti xxviij februarii marcii anno Domini m° v^c^ xxxvij.

*Berskawen* iiij merkland assedatur pro iiij c. auenarum xxxij pultre ij s. in bwn silver.

Vna pars assedatur Jhoanni Adam pro xxxij b. auenarum xvj pultre xij d. in bwn siluer Et nunc cum consensu eiusdem Joannis assedatur eadem pars matheo Adam filio primogenito soluendo vt supra factum xv aprilis anno Domini M. v° xl° Nunc cum consensu dicti mathei assedatur gilberto Adam eius filio primogenito Reseruando usufructum patri Soluendo vt supra vna cum seruitiis et deuoriis debitis et consuetis et seruando acta et stilis nostre curie factum primo februarii anno.

Alia pars assedatur Wilelmo hoggiszard pro xxxij b. auenarum xvj pultre xij d. . . Et mortuus est et nunc eadem pars assedatur Jacobo hoggiszard soluendo ut supra factum xv Aprilis anno Domini M. v° xl°.

iiij merkland. *The Newton* assedatur pro iiij c. auenarum xxxij pultre.

Una pars assedatur allano newton pro ij c. auenarum xvj pultre xij d. in bwnsilver ½ akyr telyn 1 akyr harrowyn cum debito seruicio et consueto Et nunc assedatur Alexandro Wilsone filio Allani Wilsone alias newton cum consensu eiusdem

Alani soluendo vt supra factum viij augusti anno Domini M. v$^{c}$ xxxviij Et nunc assedatur Johanni Wilsoun filio primogenito dicti Alani soluendo ut supra factum apud hamtoun vltimo Junii 1544.

Alia pars assedatur roberto lech pro ij celdris auenarum xvj pultre xij d. in bwn siluer ½ akyr telyng 1 akyr harroing cum alio seruicio.

*Durskath* assedatur Jhoanni Steuard pro xx s. 1 dd. pullorum cum custodia silue et sustentatione fossarum eiusdem Et postquam decesserit Joannes Stuart senior suprascripti Joannis Steuarti coci soluendo in omnibus vt pater eius prius soluerat et nunc soluit factum primo Aprilis anno Domini M$^{o}$ v$^{c}$ xxxvj$^{d}$.

*Candren* v merkland et x s. of ye quhit cruyk assedatur pro viij c. auenarum xxxij merkis x b. ordei 1$^{a}$ petre casei xij styrkis preter iij lib. sine decima The tenandis of gudis of ye abbay xlviij b. auenarum vj b. ij f. of seid bee. . . . . x acris of medow won and skalit 1 c. of hors corn iiij oxen xxiiij tydy ky Ilk tenand in lyk mekill delyuerand at the furth gangyng and xij$^{xx}$ threffis of fodder.

*Candren* wythout ye gudis of ye place set ye ester halff part to Jhone Alexander payand yerfor zeirly xvj merkis v bollis beir iij$^{xx}$ stane cheys wyth other service wsit t. wont sine decima xvij Augusti 1544.

Nunc autem assedatur vna medietas Joanni Alexander juniori cum consensu sui patris soluendo vt supra pro parte dimedia factum apud edinburch xxiiij Septembris anno Domini 1548.

pars dicti Joannis Alex$^{r}$ assedatur cum consensu dicti Joannis Roberto Alex$^{r}$ filio secundo genito reseruando tamen vsufructum patri . . . . vixerit soluendo vt supra factum apud Hamiltoun xj Junii 1552.

The west half of ye samyn set to Jhone hoggiszard payand yairfor zeirly xvj merkis v bollis beir iij$^{xx}$ stane cheys wyth other seruice vsit t. wont sine decima xvij augusti 1544.

Vna medietas huius medietatis cum consensu dicti Johannis assedatur villelmo wallace filio Johannis wallace in Cartissyd qui ductus est in vxorem filiam dicti Johannis hoggiszard soluendo annuatim proportionaliter ut supra factum apud paslay ij Aprilis 1547.

Pars Joannis hogiszard cum consensu eiusdem assedatur Joanni hogiszard eius filio primogenito soluendo in omnibus vt supra reseruando tamen vsufructum patri Et seruando acta et stilos curie . . . . .

*Lyncleiff* iiij c. auenarum xij capones assedatur Joanni cochran de eodem soluendo annuatim iiij c. auenarum communis mensure xij capones cum alio seruicio debito et consueto factum xxix$^{o}$ Aprilis anno Domini M$^{o}$ v$^{c}$ xlj$^{o}$.

*Ruthbank* v merkland de nouo ix lib. vj s. viij d.

Vna pars assedatur Jhoanni merschell pro liij s. iiij d. xxvj s. viij d. ij lang cariages 1 in summer & 1 in wynter ij s. in bwnsiluer ij dd. pultre.

Set to Edward Steward for xxvj s. viij d. ij lang cariagis 1 in somer 1 in wynter ij s. in bwnsiluer ij dd. pultre vt supra siclyk as Jhone merschell pait of befor for ye samyn.

*nota.* Thom bard viij merkis sine alio seruicio non enterit.

In feu to James Hamilton. Pars eduardi Stuart qui mortuus est assedatur Joanni hammilton de cunnok soluendo vt supra in omnibus Reseruato tamen vsufructu Joanni merchell quamdiu viuit factum apud Stirlyng 5$^{o}$ Januarii anno domini 1547.

*nota.* Thom hunter iiij merk sine alio seruicio no enterit.

Partes olim thome bard t. thome huntar qui mortui sunt assedantur Joanni hammilton de Cunnok soluendo iij merkis iij dd. pultre ij cariage cum alio seruicio debito et consueto factum apud Sterlyng 5° Januarii anno domini 1547.

*Thornle nethyr* v merkland. Et nunc assedatur Niniano domino de ross soluendo annuatim iij lib. vj s. viij d. ad duos anni terminos vsitatos vnacum seruicio debito et consueto factum apud sanctum Andream x mensis decembris 1546.

*Knaflandis* v s. catrine watson pro vita quia pauperam.

*The monthouse* xx s. land in manibus Willi Steward.

Assedatur Roberto hammylton de bryggis soluendo xx s. Et nunc cum consensu dicti Roberti assedatur Joanni hammylton de stirkfeld soluendo vt supra factum apud lynlythgw xx februarii anno 1555.

*The aldhouse* v. merkland assedatur Joanni maxwell pro xxx b. farine xv b. ordei iij° nouembris anno 1526 xii capones Et mortuus est nunc assedatur Joanni maxwell filio dicti Joannis soluendo vt supra factum apud Edinburcht xx Junii anno etc. xlvj°.

*Kyrkland of Neilstoun* Infra assedatur.

*Kyrkland of ye mernys* xx s. land xij pultre assedatur Jhoanni Wallase pro xx s. ferme annuatim xij pultre xij d. in bonsiluer.

Et nunc assedatur Joanni Wallase juniori nepoti Joannis senioris cum consensu

anno xxix° xv augusti. Joannis eandem possedebit terram quoad vixerit soluendo vt supra etc.

In feu. *Kyrkland of pollok* viij s. land.

Assedatur Jhoanni herwy pro viij s. annuatim soluendo sacrista vj d. in bonsiluer et mortuus est Et nunc assedatur ex consensu subsequente Johanni harvy seniori et Johanni harvy juniori per dimedias partes soluendis annuatim equaliter vt supra cum aliis seruiciis debitis et consuetis factum apud hammiltown xxvij° aprilis anno Domini etc. 1551.

*Kyrkland of ye estwod* 1 merkland to ye chantoris.

Assedatur oswaldo maxwell pro xl s. soluendo annuatim cantoribus chori secundum formam rentalis roberti abbatis viz. xl s. pait in entra siluer Et mortuus est Et nunc assedatur hugoni hammilton soluendo xl s. vt supra apud paslay vj° decembris anno etc. xlv Qui mortuus est nunc autem assedatur Joanni hamilton eius fratri soluendo in omnibus vt supra factum apud Edinburcht xv novembris anno 1548.

In feu to Jhon Maxwell. Nunc Assedatur in feodofirma Joanni maxwell in Aldhous.

*Tofta in Stewarton* vj s. viij d. to ye sacristan.

Assedatur Jonete arnot pro vj s. viij d. soluendo sacriste annuatim cum hospitalitate seruorum abbatis et cariagis inter paslày et monkton.

*Kyrkland of kylmacon* xij s. xxiiij s. xij s. to ye sacristan.

Assedatur georgio flemyn pro xij s. annuatim cum recepione decimarum congregatarum cum contigerit et conseruacione eiusdem ac equitando nobiscum quum requisitus fuerit.

*The kyrkhouse in lochquhynzok* vj s. to ye sacristan.

The xl s. penny worth land of ye kyrk of largis wyth ye pertenans set to Dauid Sympil payand yarfor zeirly vj s. viij d. exceptand ye kyrkhouse of largis and payis xx s. at paslay ye ij day of Aprill anno xlvij°.

*The kyrkhous in ye largis* xx s. to ye sacristan.

ye pay maid in ye lord sympill hand Indurand his xix zeris. In few to lord sympill.

The kyrkland in ye largis xl s. of auld extent set to James Crafwrd payand yeirly xl s. wyth vther seruic vsit t. wont as nychbour t. vther doyis factum xxv Aprilis anno etc. xlj°.

*The huntlaw.*

In feu.

Assedatur Joanni hammylton de Stirkfeld soluendo xiij s. iiij d. et locum vocatum ane dog leche.

*Drumgrane* cum molendino xiij lib. xiij s. iiij d. ix cariage xviij dd. xvj dusan pultre ix s. in bonsiluer.

James hammylton.

Vna pars assedatur Jhoanni Anderson juniori pro xx s. vj d. xij pultre 1 cariage.

Alia pars assedatur Jhoanni cochran pro xxvij s. viij d. ij dd. pullorum 1 cariage ut nunc assedatur Andree Spreull cum consensu dicti Joannis soluendo vt supra Et nunc assedatur Andree Spreull et Cristine hammylton eius sponse et patricio spreull filio primogenito dicti Andree et Christine soluendis vt supra factum apud edinburcht xx Junii anno etc. 1549 Et nunc cum consensu dicti Andree assedatur Andree Cristine et patricio factum apud air xxviij mercii anno 1552.

Alia pars assedatur Jhoanni Anderson seniori pro xiij s. x d. xij pultre 1 cariage mortuus est.

Assedatur Johanni Anderson juniori filio istius Johannis senioris vt supra.

Et nunc assedatur Joanni hammyltone soluendo vt supra factum xxj octobris anno xxxv.

Alia pars assedatur thome jop pro xxv s. viij d. xxiiij pultre 1 cariage Et mortuus est Et nunc assedatur Joanni Jop filio seniori pro xxv s. viij d. xxiiij pultre 1 cariage xj Septembris etc.

anno xxxj

Alia pars assedatur Alexandro rawf pro xix s. iij d. xviij pulle 1 cariage t. mortuus est assedatur domino Alexandro Rawff eius filio pro xix s. iij d. xviij pulle 1 cariage et nunc assr Joni hammylton de newbrgynis cum consensu supra scripti Alexandre soluendo et supra factum anno domini m. v° xxxv xxviij mensis augusti.

Alia pars assedatur magistro roberto Steward pro xxvij s. viij d. ij dd. pultre xij d. in bonsiluer j lang cariage.

Alia pars assedatur Andree Sprewll pro xxvij s. viij d. ij dd. pullorum 1 cariage Et nunc cum consensu dicti Andree assedatur Cristine hammilton eius sponse et patricio spreull filio primogenito dicti Andree et Cristine ex eorum consensu soluendo vt supra factum apud Edinburcht xx Junii anno 1549 Et nunc assedatur dictis Andree cristine et patricio vt supra factum apud air xxviij martii anno 1552.

Alia pars assedatur Nicolao bar pro xix s. iij d. xviij pultre 1 cariage Et nunc cum consensu eiusdem assedatur margarete dicson et post eius mortem assedatur margarete M'ge et Willielmo Stewart eius filio soluendo vt supra factum xx nouembris anno Domini 1543.

*The myll of Drumgrane* assedatur constantino quhit pro liij s. iiij d. xij capones Et nunc assedatur thome quhit filio constantini quhit soluendo vt supra factum anno Domini M. v$^{c}$ xxxv. xxij augusti Et nunc assedatur mergrete dicson t. post mortem eius assedatur mergrete M'ge t. Willielmo Steuart eius filio soluendo vt supra factum xxvj Aprilis anno Domini M$^{o}$ v$^{c}$ xlj$^{o}$.

*The kyrkland of Neilstoun* assedatur Jacobo Zong pro xl s. soluendo cantoribus chori pro Domino glorioso cantandi in capelle beate marie infra capitulum monasterii de pasleto xviij$^{o}$ Septembris anno Domini etc. xxix$^{o}$ etc.

Et nunc assedatur Johanni Zoung filio dicti Jacobi soluendo vt supra factum apud Edinburcht xxij maii anno Domini 1 M. v$^{c}$ xlv$^{o}$ Et nunc cum consensu dicti Joannis assedatur Dauidi Zong soluendo vt supra Nunc vero cum consensu dicti dauidis Assedatur Jacobo pyncarton soluendo vt supra factum apud paslay vltimo februarii anno 1554.

*Drumgrane.*

Vna pars eius quam occupabat Joannes hammylton nunc assedatur mergrete dickson t. post mortem eius assedatur mergrete m'ge t. Willelmo Stuart eius filio soluendo pro illa parte xiij s. x d. vij pultre 1 carage factum xxvj$^{o}$ Aprilis anno etc. xlj$^{i}$ Et nunc assedatur Nicholao bar soluendo vt supra factum xx nouembris anno 1543 Et nunc assedatur Alexandro bar filio dicti nicholao soluendo ut supra factum apud paslay ij aprilis 1547.

Alia pars xix. s. iij d. quam prius occupabat Joannes hamtoun nunc assedatur Joanni Stuart t. mergrete makge eius sponse annuatim xix s. iij d. xviij pultre ane cariage factum xxvj aprilis anno etc. xlj$^{o}$

*The myll of Drumgrane* assedatur Alexandro bar filio nicholai bar soluendo liij s. iiij d. xij capon factum xxvj Aprilis anno Domini 1543.

*The Granys* xv$^{xx}$ petre casei v dd. auenarum vna pars assedatur bertylomeo gylmor pro iij$^{xx}$ petris casei xij aucis t. mortuus est Et nunc assedatur Joanni gilmor filio seniori suprascripti bertylomei soluendo vt supra.

xxviij Julii anno xlj.

Alia pars assedatur Alexandro Stirlyng pro iij$^{xx}$ petris casei xij aucis Et nunc assedatur cum consensu prefati Alexandri Johanni Stirlyng suo filio primogenito soluendo annuatim vt supra cum aliis seruitiis debitis et consuetis factum apud hammilton xxvij$^{o}$ aprilis anno Domini etc. 1551.

Alia pars assedatur Jhoanni Wilson pro iij$^{xx}$ petris casei xij aucis t. mortuus est.

Alia pars assedatur Johanni gemmyll pro iii$^{xx}$ petris casei xii aucis vt supra 3$^{o}$ marcii anno Domini etc. xxviij$^{o}$ Et nunc assedatur Andree hammylton soluendo vt supra factum v octobris anno Domini M. v$^{c}$ xl$^{o}$ Et nunc cum consensu eiusdem andree assedatur alexandro gammyll soluendo vt supra xxvij mertii 1544.

Alia pars assedatur Jhoanni crage pro iij$^{xx}$ petris casei xij aucis.

Et nunc eadem pars assedatur Willelmo crage filio supra dicti Joannis crage soluendo in omnibus vt supra anno Domini m$^{o}$ v$^{c}$ xxxj ix maij.

*Auchyngown* ix lib. iiij s. ix d. iiij s. in bwnsiluer xiiiȝ dd. powtre.

Vna pars assedatur thome stewart filio gilberti pro xviij s. xij d. in bwnsiluer xviij pultre et mortuus est Et nunc assedatur thome Stuard filio suprascripti thome soluendo vt supra xxv aprilis anno etc. xljo.

Alia pars assedatur Matheo Steward pro xxiij s. viij d. xxiiij pultre cum le bon siluer t. aliis seruiciis debitis et consuetis.

Et nunc assedatur Joanni Stewart filio seniori mathei Stuart cum consensu mathei patris eiusdem Joannis sed tantum matheus pater eius eandem possedebit terram
xxijo octobris quoad vixerit soluendo vt supra et Joannes post decessum patris libere eadem
anno xxixo etc. gaudebit terra.

Alia pars assedatur Johanni Steward filio Jacobi pro xlij s. viij d. iij dd. pullorum.

Alia pars assedatur Archibaldo boyd pro xvj s. viij d. xij pultre t. cum consensu suprascripti Archibaldi assedatur Jacobo boid filio dicti archibaldi Ita quod archibaldus eadem gaudebit terra quoad vixerit soluendo vt supra factum anno Domini mo ve xxxvijo xiij May.

Alia pars assedatur Jhoanni Steuard filio Andree pro xvij s. ix d. xvj pultre Et nunc assedatur Alano Stuart filio Joannis Stuart suprascripti soluendo vt supra Et nunc tertia pars eius assedatur Joanni Stuart filio Jacobo Stuart t. altera
anno xxxix tertia pars eius assedatur Jacobo Stuart filio thome Stuart t. altera tertia pars
xxijo nouembris assedatur Joanni Stuart filio Mathew Stuart soluendo vnusquisque v s. xj d. t. xvj pultre to be payit amang thaim thre . . .

Alia pars assedatur Jhoanni Steward filio seniori mathei Stuart pro xxvj s. viij d.
xiijo decembris ij dd. pulli cum le bonsiluer t. aliis seruiciis debitis t. consuetis.
anno xxvto

xiijo decembris Alia pars assedatur Jacobo Steward de Louchhed filio thome pro xl s. iij dd.
anno xxvto pultre.

*ffowlton* cum molendino auchynche blaxton t. mydilton xxxvij lib. xvj s. viij d. iiij lang cariagis xv dd. vj pultre.

Jhone brownys Sted iiij merkland assedatur Roberto brown pro liij s. iiij d. iiij dd. pultre cum seruicio inde debito et consueto viz. xij d. in bwn silver et 1 lang cariage pait no entra siluer Et nunc assedatur Johanni brown filio primogenito dicti roberti soluendo ut supra factum apud hammylton xxij may anno Domini 1 M vc xliijo

Alia pars assedatur Jhoanni buyt pro xxs. 1 cariage xij d. in bwnsiluer et viij pultre Et nunc assedatur Johanni hammyltown granatorio de paslay et archibaldo hamilton filio dicti Johannis soluendo ut supra factum apud paslay.

Apud paslay
xxliij xxiiij Julii.
Julii 1545. Alia pars quam prius possedebat archbaldus hamtoun cum consensu eiusdem assedatur Joanni Adam juniori soluendo annuatim xx s. pultre xij d. in bwnsiluer 1 cariage factum xv augusti anno domini mo vc xxxix.

Alia pars assedatur Jhoanni symson filio roberti pro xx s. xviij pultre xij d. in bwnsiluer 1 cariage et mortuus est Et nunc assedatur Joannis Symson filii primo geneti superiori Joannis symson soluendo vt supra Nunc Que quidem terra quam
x aprilis anno possedebat Johannes hamilton nunc cum consensu eiusdem assedatur arcbaldo
Domini mo vc hammilton fratri eius soluendo vt supra.
xxxix.

Alia pars assedatur Johanni Symson filio Wilelmi pro xl s. iij dd. pullorum xij d. in bwnsiluer 1 cariage Et mortuus est nunc assedatur Joanni symsone filio suprascripti Joannis soluendo vt supra factum viij februarii anno xxxij° Et nunc assedatur roberto Symson filio dicti Joannis cum consensu eiusdem soluendo vt supra factum apud Edinburcht xviij augusti 1550 reseruando dicto Joanni patri vsufructum quoad vixerit.

Alia pars assedatur Jhoanni knok de wrayes pro xx s. xviij pultre xij in bwnsiluer 1 cariage Et post mortem eius assedatur Joanni browne soluendo vt supra anno xxxv xxi februarii Et nunc cum consensu filii primogeniti dicti Joannis assedatur villielmo Sympill de Thirdpairt soluendo vt supra nunc postremo cum consensu dicti villielmo Assedatur Joanni hammylton de ferguslу et archibaldo hammylton eius filio soluendo vt supra factum apud Edinburcht xxv augusti anno 1550.

Alia pars assedatur Jhoanni brown pro xiij s. iiij d. xij pultre xij d. in bwn siluer 1 cariage Et post mortem Joannis knok in wrayis hec pars assedatur Joanni hall soluendo vt supra anno xxv^to^ xxj februarii.

*lynwod* vna pars assedatur Jhoanni houston pro xx s. roberto cochran pro xx s. xij d. in bwnsiluer xviij pultre 1 cariage qui mortuus est et nunc assedatur Andree cochran eius primogenito soluendo vt supra factum apud glasgow xxvij decembris anno 1547.

Alia pars assedatur Jhoanni Sympyll pro xx s. xij d. in bwnsiluer xviij pultre 1 cariage et nunc assedatur patricio Sympill soluendo xx s. xij d. in bwnsiluer xvjij pultre ane cariage factum xxviij° aprilis anno domini m° v^e^ xlj°.

*Auchynche* assedatur gabrieli cwnyghame de craganys soluendo annuatim nobis aut successoribus nostris liij iiij d. cum duabus duodecis le pultre et aliis seruiciis debitis et consuetis factum apud pasletum quinto mercii anno domini m. v^e^ xxxix coram his testibus magistro David hammylton rectore de thankertoun magistro Jacobo froster t. magistro gavino hamtoun.

*The Myll of ye foulton* assedatur gibberto cummyn pro vj lib. xiij d. assedatur Joanni cwmyng filio quondam gibberto cwmyng soluendo teme merkis nostro monasterio de pasleto anno domini m° v^e^ xj junii.

*Blakston* vna pars viz. myddilton x s. land assedatur Jacobo erskyn et Jhoanni Symmyr pro x lib. Pars Jacobi erskyn assedatur Joanni aitkyn cum consensu brown sponse dicti Jacobo et matris dicti Joannis Reseruando vitalem reditum dicto Jacobo et sui sponse quamdiu vixerint soluendo vt supra factum apud lythgw xiiij Januarii anno 1553.

Vna pars eius assedatur thome sympil pro—

Alia pars cum mansura et prato x s. land in manibus abbatis.

*The ward aboue the place* x s.

*The zard of Blaxstone* xx s. to pay at mertymess.

Vna mercata terrarum vocate ye le merkis wortht cum pertinentiis assedatur petro algeo secundum ritum et consuetudinem nostri rentalis inde soluendo annuatim xiij s. iiij d. ad duos anni terminos consuetos per equales portiones vnacum duodecim le pultre cum aliis debitis et seruiciis solitis et consuetis sicut willelmus quhit et ceteri tenandi in dicta mercata persoluerint factum apud nostrum monasterium de pasleto vltimo die mensis mertii anno domini m° v^e^ xxxix coram his testibus magistro Jacobo frostar vicario de ruglen Joanne sandelandis et andrea hamtoun cum diuersis aliis etc.

*Annui redditus ville de Paslay.*

*Snawdon* vj lib.

Peter neil iij lib.
James crag iij lib.

*Sclaterbank* xl s.

Wilzam pyrey xl s.

*Oxschawsyd* vj lib. xiij s. viij d.

Jhon quhitfurd xvij s.
Jhon symson xiij s. iiij d.
Andro quaryor xiij s. iiij d;
Jhon wes xiij s. iiij d.
Jhone sunderland xiij s. iiij d.
Stene henderson t. allan nowton xiij s. iiij d.
Conne Steyn xiij s. iiij d.
John bully xiij s. iiij d.
Robert brown xiij s. iiij d.
Robert wrry x s.

*The pryor croft* viij lib. iiij s.

Jhone quhitfurd xiiij s.
Patrik mosman xiij s. iiij d.
James paynter xiij s. iiij d.
Thom morton xiij s. iiij d.
Robert bissat xijj s. iiij d.
Elyn quhit xiij s. iiij d.
Wilzam brown xiij s. iiij d.
Jonet tech xiij s. iiij d.
Master Wilzam Steuard t. Wilzam pyrry xiij s. iiij d.
Jhone Alexander t. gilbert Alexander xiij s. iiij d.
Master Wilzam Steuard t. mathe Wilson xiij s. iiij d.
Thom quhit iij s. iiij d.
Arche gybson viij s. x d.
Rob Smyth iiij s. vj d.

*The Sedyll & ye welmedow* vj lib. x s. per capellanum.

*The town of Paslay* v. lib. ix s. viij d.

Dene Jhone Scot xv. s.
Patrik mosman vj s. 1 lib. cere.
Thom quhit ij s.
John bully xiij s.
Robert brown xiij s.
Jhone brown xiiij s.
Patryk thom viij s.
David crag x s.
Patrik mosman pro domo ij merkis 1 lib. cere.

*The know* ij s.

*The Cawsasyd* xv lib. ij s. ij d.

huchon mershell iiij s. vij d.

huchon forest vj s. viij d.
Schir robert sclater xiiij s. iiij d.
Jhone Allanson t. thom mekilriggis xxxiij s. iiij d.
Jhone hector elder xxvj s. viij d.
Jhone hector zonger xviij s. iiij d.
Andro Steuard xxx s.
Bertylmo Steuard v s.
Johne Luyf xvj s. ix d.
Dauid Sclater xvj s. viij d.
Jhone Sclater zonger xxvij s. viij d.
Patrik Schelis xxiij s. vij d.
Jhone symson xxviij s. 1 d.
Rob Luyf vij s. xj d.
Malcom Gardner xvij s. vij d.

*The Castelheid* iij lib. vj s. viij d.

Jhone Jop xxxiij s. iiij d.
Jhone Allanson xxxiij s. iiij d.

*The qwarell* xxvj s. x d. ½

Jhone quhitfurd xiij s. iiij d.
Andro quaryor vj s. viij d.
Wilzam ker vj s. x½ d.

*The brunelandis* wyth ye bodwin of ye ward t. sergiand akyr iij lib. xv s. iiij d.

Master Wilzam Steuard vj s. x d.
James payntor vj s. x d.
Wilzam pyrry vj s. viij d.
Matho Wilson t. Wilzam pyrry vj s. viij d.
Rob Smyth vj s. viij d.
Schir henry bard vj s. viij d.
nota. The bodwin of ye ward xxiiij s.
Robert bissat vj s. viij d.
Ye sergiandis akyr iiij s. iiij d.

*The Oxschawheid* xxxvj s.

Jhone quhitfurd xiij s. iiij d.
Megge quhit t. Elyn quhit xxij s. viij d.

*The ward medow* xxvj s. viij d. 1 lib. cere per Stephanum henderson et gilbertum Alexanderson.

Summa feodorum pasleti iij$^{xx}$j lib. xviij s. vii½ d.

*The walk myll* v merk t. ij stane noppis.

Alexander mosman iij lib. vj s. viij d. at witsonday and mertymes equaliter t. ij stane noppis to be pait zerly at sanct thomas day before zwill Nunc autem cum consensu dicti Alexandri assedatur Willielmo Stuert filio villielmi Stuart soluendo vt supra factum apud Edinburcht v mercii anno 1553.

Summa lateris x lib. iiij s. viij d.

*Annui redditus in diuersis partibus.*

Houston vj s. viij d.
Porterfield vj s. viij d.

Renfrew. { The monk dyk in renfrew, v s.
Bertylmo mungumry vij s.
Jhone cunnock xij d.
Wilzam Snaip viij d.
The myll of renfrew xiij s. iiij d.

ruglen. Annuel of ruglen x s. ij d.

Glasgw. { Master thomas leis of ye Stokwell v s.
Maryon Scot v s.
Thom walcar t. Wilzam baxter ij s. vj d.
The hous at ye wynd heid.
The ynnis before ye blak freris ij anwell xiij s. iiij d.

---

kyll. Adamtoun xl s.
Corsbe viij s. iiij d.
Auchynlek xx s.
Corsraguell vj lib. xiij s. iiij d.

ergyll. Gleba de kyllenon in ergyll xl s.
Stralachlan in ergyll xl s.

---

*Rentale de glene.*

*The bar and ye brygend* x merkland in bonsiluer ij s. ij lang cariage xx s. vij dusone pultre and ye auld mansione & ye zard & ye medo descendand downe betwex ye dykis to ye Lowch reseruit in ye abbottis handes set to James of glen for ten merk of mayll wyth dewteis t. dew seruice vsit t. wont siclyk as his fader wylzem glen browkyt ye said ten merk land of befor ye xiij day of august ye zer of god 1 m. v$^{c}$ xxviij zeris.

*The Mylbank* xxiiij s. land xx pultre ij s. in bwnsiluer ii cariagis.

In few. Vna pars assedatur roberto or pro xij s. x pultre xij d. in bwnsiluer 1 cariage Et nunc cum consensu eiusdem roberti assedatur Jacobo or filio dicti roberti soluendo ut supra factum apud paslay xx octobris 1545.

Alia pars assedatur Jacobo or et Jhoanni rannaldson pro xij s. xij d. in bwnsiluer x pultre 1 cariage Et nunc illa pars Jacobi or viz. vj s. land assedatur thome Schaw soluendo pro illa parte vt prius soluebat Jacobus or in omnibus factum vltimo maii anno Domini m$^{o}$ v$^{c}$ xxxix.

Et nunc pars Joannis rannaldson qui mortuus est viz. vj s. land Assedatur Joanni rannaldson eius filio primogenito soluendo vt supra factum apud glasgw xiiij mertii 1547 pars olim Thome Schaw nunc assedatur Jacobo glen de bar soluendo In omnibus vt dictis Thomas Schaw prius persoluebat ac etiam dotabit filiam seniorem dicti Thome Schaw pro qualitate t. facultate dicte terre de milband ac se eius pater viueret alioque presens locatio nullus erit momenti factum apud Edinburcht xxv augusti anno 1550.

*Wester Kerse* xliij s. iiij d. ferme ij s. in bwnsiluer iij dd. pultre ij cariagis.

Vna pars assedatur Allano Kyrkwod pro x. s. x d. ix pultre vj d. in bwnsiluer 3 cariagis Et nunc eadem pars post mortem huius Alani assedatur Jacobo Allasone qui ducturus est in vxorem filiam dicti Alani soluendo vt supra factum xiiij° Januarii anno domini m° v° xxxij°.

Alia pars assedatur Jhoanni kyrkwod juniori pro x s. x d. vj d. in bwnsiluer ix pultre ½ cariage.

Alia pars assedatur roberto kyrkwod pro x s. x d. vj d. in bwnsiluer ix pultre ½ cariage Et nunc cum consensu dicti Roberti assedatur Roberto kyrkwod filio eius soluendo vt supra factum apud air quarto aprilis anno 1552.

Alia pars assedatur Jhoanni Kyrkwod seniori pro x s. x d. vj d. in bwnsiluer ix pultre ½ cariage qui mortuus est Et nunc assedatur Jacobo Kyrkwod filio seniori dicti Joannis soluendo In omnibus vt supra factum apud paslay xxvj May anno 1553.

*The ester kerse* xliij s. iiij d. land iij dd. powtre ij s. in bonsyluer ij lang cariage.

*Joffray tak* xxiij s. iiij d. ferme xij d. in bownsiluer xviij pultre 1 lang cariag 1 schort cariag.

Assedatur Jhoanni Or pro xxiij s. iiij d. xij d. in bwnsiluer xviij pultre ij cariag.

Et mortuus est nunc autem assedatur Joanni or eius filio primogenito soluendo vt supra factum apud lynlythgw iij may anno 1552.

*Bermeklo* x s. land xij d. in bwnsiluer ix pultre 1 cariage assedatur Jhoanni norwell pro x s. xij d. in bwnsiluer ix pultre 1 cariage.

Et mortuus est Nunc assedatur Roberto norwell filio primogenito dicti Joannis norwell soluendo vt supra factum apud paslay xxviij May anno 1553.

*Mawysbank* x s. land assedatur Ricardo or pro x s. ferme xij d. in bwne syluer ix pultre 1 cariage et mortuus est Et nunc assedatur Joanni glene soluendo vt supra Et mortuus est Nunc autem assedatur Jacobo or filio primogenito soluendo vt supra factum apud glasgw xiiij martii 1547.

*Langscale* xv s. land assedatur Jacobo or pro xv s. ferme xij d. in bwnsiluer xij pultre 1 cariage Et post mortem Jacobi Or assedatur wilelmo Or filio huius Jacobi Or soluendo in omnibus vt supra xvij° Junii anno xxxj° Et nunc cum consensu dicti villielmi or assedatur Jacobo or eius filio primogenito et eo deficiente Joanni or eius secundo genito Reseruato tamen patri vitalem reditum In omnibus quamdiu vixerit soluendo vt supra factum apud paslay penultimo augusti anno 1554.

July anno xxxj. *Camehill* xx s. land vna pars assedatur wilelmo or pro xiij s. iiij d. in xij d. bwnsiluer xviij pultre 1 cariag Et post mortem huius villelmi assedatur ranaldo or eius filio soluendo in omnibus vt pater prius soluerat Et nunc cum consensu dicti ranaldi assedatur Roberto or filio primogenito eius Reseruato tamen vsufructu patri soluendo vt supra factum vltimo augusti anno 1554.

Alia pars assedatur Jhoanni kyrkwod pro vj s. viij d. vj d. in bwnsiluer ix pultre 3 cariagis qui mortuus est Nunc autem assedatur thome kyrkwod filio primogenito dicti Joannis soluendo vt supra factum apud paslay xxviij may anno 1553.

*Lowrensbank* xiij s. iiij d. assedatur Allano glen pro xiij s. iiij d. xij d. in bwnsiluer xij pultre 1 cariage xxix aprilis anno etc xlj° Et nunc cum consensu dicti Alani assedatur Jacobo glen de bar soluendo vt supra factum apud hamilton xxviij aprilis 1551.

*Aldzard* xvij s. land vna pars assedatur roberto glen pro viij s. vj d. vj d. in bwnsiluer vij pultre 1 schort cariage et mortuus est Et nunc assedatur filio eiusdem villelmo glene soluendo vt supra Et nunc autem cum consensu dicti willielmi glen assedatur Joanni glen soluendo vt supra reseruato tamen vsufructu dicto villielmo factum apud glasgw xiiij mertii 1547.

Alia pars assedatur andree gibson pro viij s. vj d. vj d. in bwnsiluer vij pultre 1 schort cariage Et nunc eadem pars assedatur thome kyng pro viij s. vj d. vj d. in bowne siluer vij pultre 1 schort cariag cum consensu andree gibsone t. filii sui
anno xxxij° factum anno m. v° xxxij xij Junii et mortuus est t. nunc assedatur willelmo
anno xxxv kyng filio suprascripti thome soluendo vt supra Et nunc assedatur villelmo
xxv die mensis Julii. cwmyng cum consensu Jacobo king eius fratris soluendo ut supra.

*Langzard* ij merk land vna pars assedatur roberto or pro xiij s. iiij d. xij d. in bwnsiluer xij pultre 1 cariage Ista pars assedatur Jacobo or pro xiij s. iiij d. xij d. in bonsiluer xij pultre 1 cariage xiij° decembris anno xxvj° Et cum consensu dicti assedatur Roberto or eius filio primogenito soluendo vt supra factum xvij filii anno 1554.

Alia pars assedatur Wilelmo riche pro xiij s. iiij d. xij d. in bwnsiluer xij pultre 1 cariage et nunc assedatur Jacobo ryche filio Willelmi riche pro xiij s. iiij d. xij d. xij d. in bown siluer xij pultre 1 cariage sed eius pater Willelmus eadem gaudebit terra quoad vixerit qui furti conuictus mortuus est nunc autem assedatur Joanni hammylton soluendo vt supra factum apud Paslay xiij augusti anno etc. 154—.

Et nunc cum consensu dicti Joannis assedatur Roberto domino Sympill soluendo vt supra factum apud lythgw vltimo mertii anno 1553 cum aliis seruiciis et consuetis.

*ffayrhyllis* xx s. land vna pars assedatur Wilelmo or pro x s. xij d. in bwnsiluer ix pultre 1 syngel cariage.

Alia pars assedatur roberto bryden pro x s. xij d. in bwnsiluer ix pultre 1 syngil cariage.

Et nunc assedatur Jacobo brydyn soluendo vt supra factum maii anno Domini 1$^{m}$ v° xliij.

Qui mortuus est nunc autem assedatur matheo brady eius filio primogenito soluendo vt supra factum apud hammylton v. Junii anno 1552.

*In few.* *Gawylmos* xij s. land vna pars assedatur Jacobo logan pro viij s. viij d. in bwn siluer vj pultre ½ cariage et nunc cum consensu dicti Jacobi assedatur Jacobo logan eius filio primogenito soluendo vt supra factum apud paslay xviij Julii anno 1554 Reseruato tamen vsufructu patri.

Alia pars Jhoanni Anderson pro iiij s. iiij d. in bwn siluer vj pultre ½ cariage et nunc cum consensu huius Joannis Anderson assedatur Joanni lauta soluendo vt supra factum xxj Januarii anno Domini m° v° xxxix$^{s}$.

*Gylliszard* xxiij s. land vna pars assedatur Allano Jhonson pro xj s. vj d. xij d. in bwn siluer x pultre 1 cariage et nunc assedatur Wilelmo Johnson filio supra scripti Alani soluendo vt supra factum anno Domini m° v° xxxiiij xxvij day of April et nunc cum consensu dicti Willelmi assedatur roberto allanson eius filio seniori soluendo vt supra factum xvij Julii anno 1554.

Alia pars assedatur roberto glen pro xj s. vj d. xij d. in bwnsiluer x pultre 1 cariage Et nunc assedatur willielmo glene filio primogenito dicti Roberti cum consensu eiusdem soluendo vt supra factum xxv Octobris anno 1549.

*Litil clook* x s. land assedatur roberto brydyn pro x s. xij d. in bwnsiluer ix pultre 1 cariage Et mortuus est nunc assedatur Vmfridi bridin cum consensu . . . . bridin sui fratris senioris soluendo supra factum apud glasgw xiiij mertii 1547.

*Langcroft* x s. land vna pars assedatur Allano Allanson pro iij s. iiij d. iiij d. in bwnsiluer iij pultre thrie pert cariagis et nunc assedatur Joanni Allanson filio seniori suprascripti alani cum consensu eiusdem soluendo vt supra factum anno etc. Domini M. V$^{c}$ xxxv v die februarii.

Alia pars assedatur Jacobo cochran pro iij s. iiij d. iiij d. in bwnsiluer iij pultre thre part cariage Et nunc assedatur roberto cochran soluendo ut supra factum apud blaxton xj decembris anno 1$^{m}$ v$^{c}$ xlv$^{o}$.

Alia pars assedatur Jhoanni Jhonson pro iij s. iiij d. iiij d. in bwnsiluer iij pultre thrid part cariage.

*Qwenesyd mur* xlviij s. assedatur tenenti pro xlviij s.

Ane thrid part of ye said quenesyd mwyr set to robert cochran sone to James cochran payand yairfor zeirlie xvj s. reseruand to ws of yis thrid part viij sowmys girs factum apud blaxtoun xj decembris anno 1$^{m}$ v$^{c}$ xlv$^{o}$.

*Monyabroch* xl s. Et nunc assedatur niniano domino de ross soluendo annuatim xl s. ad duos anni terminos vsitatos vnacum seruicio debito et consueto factum apud sanctum andream x mensis nouembris 1546.

*Wester bernach* xxx s. land assedatur niniano or et Jhoanni Jameson pro iiij$^{xx}$ petre casei.

Assedatur roberto schaw soluendo annuatim xxx$^{ti}$ s. et xij d. pro le bonsiluer.

Vna pars eius assedatur Richardo Or soluendo annuatim xl petre casei Et mortuus est Post cuius mortem assedatur Dauidi Ramsay soluendo vt supra Et nunc cum consensu eiusdem Dauid assedatur roberto or filio roberti or in mylbank soluendo ut supra factum apud edinburcht viij decembris anno 1544.

Altera pars eius assedatur vmfrido Jameson soluendo annuatim xl petras casei factum xviij Januarii anno Domini m. v$^{c}$ xxxviij.

The myll of ye glen xxiiij b. farine assedatur thome kyng pro xxiiij b. farine plegio roberto or Jhoanne atkyn et Jhoanne merschell.

Molendinum de glen assedatur Jacobo kyng soluendo annuatim xxiiij b. farine communis mensure qui sustentabit et edificabit dictum molendinum propriis impensis ad vsum tenendorum et abbatis et conuentus factum anno Domini etc. xxxv etc. xx Julii Qui mortuus est nunc autem assedatur Jacobo kyng eius filio primogenito soluendo vt supra factum apud paslay xxvij februarii anno 1554.

*Auchynhame* xl s. land pays 1$^{c}$ petre casei vj stirkis.

Vna pars assedatur thome or pro iij$^{xx}$ petre casei iij stirkis Et cum consensu dicti thome assedatur Jacobo or filio seniori dicti thome soluendo In omnibus vt supra reseruato tamen vsufructu patri quoad vixerit factum apud paslay xxvj may anno 1553.

Alia pars Johanni Allanson pro xxx petre casei 13 stirk Et nunc assedatur roberto paterson primogenito dicti Jhonnis soluendo ut supra cum seruicio consueto factum apud paslay xiij octobris 1545 Qui mortuus est absque liberis nunc autem cum consensu Joannis paterson senioris assedatur . . . . . . paterson filio dicti Joannis senioris reseruato tamen vsufructu patri factum apud paslay xij novembris anno 1554.

mortuus est. Alia pars assedatur Wilelmo maldisheid pro xxx petre casei 13 stirk.

Assedatur Eduardo ramsay de consensu vidue pro xxx petrie casei 1½ stirkis x° Julii 1526.

*Lynthyllis* in ye Corsezarde iij lib. x s. land pays viij$^{xx}$ x petre casei viij styrkis to be diuidit amang ye tenandis.

Vna pars assedatur Jhoanni fyschar iij$^{xx}$ viij petre casei Et nunc cum consensu dicti Joannis assedatur Roberto fyschir eius filio soluendo vt supra factum apud paslay xvij decembris anno 1551 Et nunc eius consensu dicti roberti assedatur glene de bar soluendo vt supra reseruando tamen Joanni fischar seniori vsufructum ad vitam factum apud air 4 aprilis anno 1552.

Memorandum dicti pars assedatur Jacobo Glene.

Alia pars assedatur Jhoanni Or pro xxxiiij petre casei et nunc assedatur Joanni or filio suprascripti Joannis soluendo vt supra factum xvij° may anno Domini M. v° xxxviij°.

viii stirkis.

Alia pars assedatur Jacobo bard pro xxxiiij patre casei et mortuus est Et nunc assedatur Joanni bard filio Jacobi bard soluendo vt Qui mortuus est Et nunc assedatur Joanni bard eius filio soluendo vt supra factum apud paslay xvij decembris anno 1551.

Alia pars assedatur thome schaw pro xxxiiij petris casei Et nunc illa pars assedatur Jacobo or soluendo vt supra factum vltimo aprilis anno Domini m° v° xxxix Et nunc cum consensu dicti Jacobi assedatur Jacobo glen filio Jacobi de bar t. brigend soluendo ut supra factum apud paslay vltimo aprilis 1546.

*Candylmur* xl s. land payis 1° petre casei vj stirkis.

Vna pars assedatur Jhoanni Kebyll pro xl petre casei ij stirkis Et nunc assedatur Joanni Cwmyng filio quondam henrici Cwmyng cum consensu dicti Joannis kebil soluendo vt supra factum anno Domini M. v° xxxvj xxvij Aprilis.

Alia pars Niniano or pro xl petre casei ij stirkis et mortuus est et nunc assedatur Johanni Schaw pro xl petre casei et ij styrkis Et mortuus est Nunc assedatur Joanni Schaw filio dicti Joannis senioris soluendo vt supra 1° martii anno xl v.

Alia pars assedatur Dauid or pro xl petre casei ij stirkis Et eadem pars cum consensu huius Dauid or assedatur thome or filio suprascripti Dauid soluendo vt supra factum xxviij Januarii anno Domini M. v° xxxix°.

Et nunc assedatur ranaldo or fratri dicti Dauid qui obiit sine liberis soluendo ut supra factum apud paslay xx octobris 1545.

Alia pars quam prius possedebat Joannes cumyng cum eius consensu assedatur Willelmo cwmyng fratri germano eiusdem soluendo xl st. casei ij stirkis xxviij Januarii anno Domini M° v° xxxix.

*Bernach nethyr* xl s. land 1° petre casei vj stirkis. Vna pars assedatur Jhoanni atkyn pro iij$^{xx}$ petre casei et iij stirkis.

Et nunc assedatur niniano atkyne filio dicti Joannis soluendo vt supra factum xiiij° may anno Domini M° v° xxxj° coram his testibus Joanne hamtoun de newbyggyn andrea hamtoun et Joanne browne et domino henrico Berect capellano.

Alia pars assedatur thome or pro iij$^{xx}$ petre casei et iij stirkis Et nunc assedatur Joanni or filio thome or suprascripti cum consensu eiusdem soluendo vt supra factum anno Domini M. v$^{c}$ xxxv vij die mensis maii.

*Clook* xl s. land pais 1$^{c}$ petre casei vj stirkis.

Vna pars assedatur Jhoanni atkyn pro iij$^{xx}$ petre casei iij stirkis Et nunc cum consensu dicti Joannis assedatur Jacobo aitkyne soluendo vt supra factum apud paslay 3$^{o}$ martii anno 1545.

Alia pars assedatur Wilelmo mungumry pro iij$^{xx}$ petre casei iij stirkis Et nunc cum consensu dicti Wilelmi assedatur Johanni mongumry filio primogenito dicti Wilelmi soluendo ut supra Sed dictus Wilelmus gaudebit eadem parte pro toto tempore vite sue factum apud Edinburcht ye xxiij day of august 1547.

*Cayme* iiij lib. land pais 1$^{o}$ petre casei.

Vna pars assedatur Jacobo browne pro xxx petre casei et mortuus est Et nunc eadem pars assedatur Joanni browne filio suprascripti Jacobi soluendo vt supra anno Domini M$^{o}$ v$^{e}$ xxxj die xviij may Et eius media pars assedatur Willielmo bradyne cum consensu dicti Joannis soluendo xv petre casei cum alio seruicio consueto et debito factum xxiiij aprilis anno xlvj Et nunc altera eius media pars cum consensu dicti Joannis broun assedatur dauidi hammylton de bothwell hawcht soluendo vt supra.

Pars dauidis hammylton viz. x s. land cum consensu dicti dauidis assedatur Joanni aitkyn et vmfrido eius filio post obitum dicti Joannis soluendo vt supra factum apud paslay xiij Julii anno 1554.

Alia pars assedatur Jacobo Allanson pro xxx petre casei Et mortuus est nunc assedatur thome alanson filio dicti Jacobi soluendo ut supra factum apud paslay 3$^{o}$ martii anno 1545.

Alia pars assedatur Jhoanni robison pro xxx petre casei et mortuus est Et nunc assedatur patricio cochrane soluendo vt supra cum alio seruitio debito et consueto factum xxviij Junii anno Domini M. v$^{c}$ xxxvij.

Alia pars assedatur Jacobo blakburn pro xxx petre casei.

Cuius tertia pars viz. vj s. viij land assedatur Joanni Jamesone cum consensu dicti Jacobi blakburn soluendo pro hac sua tertia parte proportionabiliter ad supra dicta anno Domini m$^{o}$ v$^{c}$ xxxij$^{o}$ et mortuus est et nunc eadem pars assedatur vmfrido Jameson filio primogenito Joannes Jameson soluendo vt supater eius prius pro eadem terra soluit factum xviij Januarii anno xxxviij$^{o}$ Item, alia pars quam possedebat Jacobus (*original torn*).

---

*Rentale de Kilpatrik.*

*Kylpatryk wester* vj lib. xiij s. iiij d. v s. in bonsiluer v lang cariage.

Vna pars assedatur georgio brownsyd pro xxxiij s. iiij d. Et nunc cum consensu dicti georgii assedatur Joanni bronsid eius ffilio primogenito et Issabelle has . . . eius sponse soluendo vt supra factum apud paslay xvj decembris anno 1551.

Alia pars assedatur wmfrido bronsyd pro xvj s. viij d. Et nunc eius media pars viz. viij s. iiij d. land assedatur roberto brownsyd soluendo pro illa parte viij s. iiij d.

anno xxxiiij$^{o}$

Alia medietas viz. viij s. iiij d. assedatur Joanni bronsyd filio primogenito dicti wmfridi soluendo ut supra factum 2° martii 1545.

2° decembris.

Alia pars assedatur Jhoanni Jhonson pro xxv s. et nunc assedatur Wilelmo Jhonson filio Johannis Jhonson et quod idem Joannes eaddem possedebit terram quoad vixerit et nunc tertia pars huius viz. viij s. iiij d. land assedatur georgio brownsyd juniori soluendo vt moris est.

x Septembris anno etc. xxxvj^to. Pars olim georgii bronsid assedatur villielmo bronsid viz. viij s. iiij d. land soluendo vt supra factum xxvj decembris anno 1552.

Alia pars assedatur roberto Strabrok pro viij s. iiij d. Et nunc cum consensu dicti roberti assedatur fynlay brok eius filio primogenito soluendo vt supra factum apud glasgw primo Januarii anno Domini 1547.

Alia pars assedatur Conando brownsyd pro xxv s. et mortuus est et nunc assedatur patricio brounsid primogenito dicti Conandi soluendo xxv s. cum cariagio et alio seruitio debitis et consuetis apud paslay xx Octobris 1545.

assedatur Joanni brounsyd eiusdem fratri.

Alia pars assedatur wilelmo brison pro viij s. iiij d. et mortuus est Et nunc assedatur roberto brownsyd soluendo vt supra factum anno Domini m° v° xxxiiij° xxv aprilis.

Alia pars assedatur willelmo lang pro xvj s. viij d. Et nunc assedatur Joanni howstowne pro xvj s. viij d. et mortuus est Et nunc assedatur Johanni houstown filio dicti Johannis soluendo ut . . . apud paslay xxj octobris 1545.

*Kylpatryk* ester x merk land v s. in bonsiluer v lang cariage.

Infra. Vna pars assedatur Jacobo fyndlason pro xj s. ij d. xvj s. viij d.

Alia pars assedatur allano layng pro xvj s. viij d. xj s. 1½d. Et nunc assedatur willelmo brownsyd cum consensu supradicti alani soluendo vt supra anno Domini m° v° xxxiiij zeris.

Alia pars assedatur Jonete brownsyd pro xxij s. ij d. Now set to vmfra layng for ye mayll abone writtyn wyth detweis t. dew seruice pertenand to ye said land.

Alia pars assedatur dauid henderson pro xj s. ij d. ½.

Alia pars assedatur Jacobo Strabrok pro xxij s. ij d. Et nunc cum consensu dicti Jacobi assedatur Joanni Strabrok eius filio primogenito Reseruandi vsufructum patri soluendo vt supra vnacum seruitiis debitis et consuetis de dictis terris factum apud paslay xiij novembris anno 1554.

Alia pars assedatur relicte quondam Joannis bryson pro xvj s. viij d. Of ye quhilk vj s. vj d. worth of land set to Dauid henderson vt supra wyth consent of ye said wedo callit cristiane forrest.

anno xxxiij x nouembris Illa pars relicte Joannis brison viz. xj s. j½ d. land assedatur Jacobo fynlay pro xj s. 1½ d. cum alio seruicio debito et consueto factum anno Domini m° v° xxxiij x nouembris.

Alia pars assedatur Willelmo fynlaws pro xj s. i d. et mortuus Et nunc assedatur Joanni patersone pro xj s. j d. cum alio seruitio debito et consueto.

Alia pars assedatur Johanni alanson pro xxij s. iij d. wyth dewteis t. dew seruice.

x nouembris anno xxxiijo.

Alia pars que prius assedebatur Jacobo fynlay nunc assedatur Joanni Jhonson cum consensu Jacobi fynlay pro xj s. j½ d. cum alio seruitio debito et consueto factum xx octobris anno Domini m° v° xxxiij° Et nunc cum consensu dicti Joannis assedatur Joanni Jhonson eius filio primogenito Reseruando vsufructum patri soluendo vt supra vnacum cariagio pro sua portione et aliis debitis et consuetis Et seruando stilos et acta nostre curie factum apud paslay xxiiij Januarii anno 1555.

*Morisland* xxvj s. viij d. xij d. in bonsiluer a cariage.

Vna pars assedatur patricio lang pro xiij s. iiij d. vj d. in bonsiluer ½ cariag et mortuus est Et nunc assedatur Jacobo lang filio patricij soluendo vt supra x mertii anno Domini m° v° xxxviij Et nunc cum consensu dicti Jacobi assedatur Jacobo eius filio primogenito Reseruato vsufructu patri soluendo vt supra factum apud paslay vltimo februarii 1554.

Alia pars assedatur fynlayo merchand pro xiij s. iiij d. vj d. in bonsiluer ½ cariage Qui obiit absque liberis Et assedatur Willielmo conyghame soluendo vt supra factum apud Edinburcht xv novembris anno 1548.

The hostilar house at ye west end of ye kyrk wyth ye zard xiij s. . . . or ellis xij capones.

Assedatur fynlayo merchand pro xiij s. iiij d. vell xij caponibus.

Schyr Wilzam schawis house at ye est end of ye kyrk xiij s. et mortuus est et nunc assedatur Jacobo lennox soluendo xiij s. iiij d. factum xxviij aprilis anno etc. xlj°.

The smythis house xiij s. iiij d. set to george schaw . . . of Schir James Denbe for xiij s. iiij d. allanerly Et mortuus est nunc autem assedatur Roberto hammylton sergiando . . . vt supra factum apud Edinburgh xxiij aprilis anno 1548.

Et nunc cum consensu dicti Roberti assedatur Jacobo colquhen soluendo vt supra factum anno 1544.

*Auchyntochan* v. lib. land iiij s. in bonsiluer t. iij.

Pars roberti donald viz. x s. land cum consensu eiusdem assedatur Roberto hammylton in Dunterclunan Et Roberto hammylton eius filio soluendo vt supra factum apud paslay xvij decembris 1551.

Vna pars assedatur Willelmo donald pro xxvj s. viij d. and also set to ye said wilzem donald iij s. iiij d. worth land quhilk was to be Jhon m'roryk cuius vna pars cum consensu eiusdem Willelmi assedatur Johanni Johneston filio vltimi Johne in auchinlek soluendo v s. cum sua parte de cariage t. bwnesiluer apud blaxton xj.

Vna pars viz. x s. land eius partis quam nunc occupat Wilelmus donald assedatur roberto donald filio primogenito dicti Wilelmi soluendo proportionabiliter ut supra.

Alia pars viz. x s. land eius partis quam nunc occupat villelmus donald cum consensu dicti wilelmi et consensu

Alia pars assedatur Wilelmo paterson pro xx s. t. pro ostralia xij capones.

Joannis Jhonson assedatur Jacobo Johnston filio dicti Joannis soluendo pro sua portione vt supra factum apud Edinburcht xxiij aprilis 1548.

Et nunc assedatur Joanni patersone eius filio cum consensu patris sed pater possedebit eandem terram ad vitam soluendo vt supra xvij Junii anno Domini m° v° xxxj° Et nunc cum consensu Joannis paterson assedatur Jacobo paterson eius filio primogenito soluendo vt supra Reseruato vsufructu patri factum apud Edinburcht xx° Januarii anno (*original torn*).

gevyn ower to Robe M'reryk. Alia pars ass' Jhoi Makreryk pro x s. has gevyn ower to Wille donald iij s. iiij d. worth.

Alia pars assedatur Isabelle Dauson pro xxx s. quhilk has gevyn owr t. now set to Wilze Atkyn ut s. . . . a . . . pro xxx s.

*(Original torn and defaced.)*

*Dunterclunan* iiij lib. xiij s. iiij d. land iiij s. in bonsyluer iij cariage.

Vna pars assedatur Johanni lang pro xxiij s. iiij d.

Et nunc assedatur Joanni Lang filio primogenito dicti Joannis cum consensu eiusdem Reseruando patri vsufructum quamdiu vixerit factum 2° martii 1545.

Nunc autem cum consensu dicti Joannis lang assedatur Roberto hammilton soluendo ut supra factum apud edinburcht xv Julii anno 1549.

Alia pars assedatur Johanni le pro xxiij s. iiij d.

Alia pars assedatur Andree Alanson pro xxiij s. iiij d. Qui mortuus est Nunc autem assedatur Roberto Alanson filio primogenito dicti Andree soluendo vt supra cum alio seruitiis debitis et consuetis factum apud edinburgh xviij septembris anno 1553.

Alia pars assedatur bartolomeo flemyn pro xxiij s. iiij d. et mortuus est. Et nunc eadem pars assedatur Joanni hammylton pro xxiij s. iiij d. factum penultimo Januarii anno etc. xxxviij et mortuus est et nunc eadem pars assedatur Roberto hammyltoune fratri Joannis defuncti soluendo vt supra factum xv nouembris anno Domini m° v° xl°.

*Wester cochnay* vj lib. xiij s. iiij d. v s. in bonsiluer v. cariage.

Vna pars assedatur gylberto boill pro xvj s. viij d. et nunc assedatur Jacobo boill filio eius primogenito soluendo vt supra cum seruicio consueto et debito plegio Johnnne hog Et nunc cum consensu dicti Jacobi assedatur Andree hammylton capitanes de Dumberten Et Joanni hammylton eius filio soluendo vt supra factum apud Edinburcht xxv augusti anno 1550.

Alia pars assedatur roberto sclater pro viij s. iiij d. Et cum consensu dicti.

Alia pars assedatur agnete bawquhennan pro viij s. iiij d. cum consensu ipsius agnetis assedatur patricio forsyth pro viij s. iiij d. ut supra cum seruicio debito et consueto Nunc cum consensu dicti patricii assedatur valtero forsyth filio dicti patricii soluendo vt supra Et vsufructu reseruato patri factum apud hammylton xij maii anno 1554.

Alia pars assedatur Jhoanni le pro xvj s. viij d. Et nunc cum consensu dicti Joannis assedatur Jacobo le filio primogenito dicti Joannis soluendo vt supra cum alio seruicio debito et consueto factum apud lythgw xviij Junii anno 1554.

Alia pars assedatur Wilelmo nevyn pro xiij s. x d. Et nunc cum consensu dicti villielmi nevin assedatur andree hammylton et Joanni hammylton eius filio primogenito soluendo vt supra factum apud paslay xvj decembris anno 1551.

dimedia pars roberti paterson viz. vj s. viij d. cum consensu dicti roberti assedatur andree hammylton de cochnay et Joanni hamilton eius filio primogenito soluendo vt supra factum apud paslay xvj decembris anno 1551.

Alia pars assedatur Jhoanni paterson pro xiij s. iiij d. Et nunc assedatur roberto paterson eius filio sed tamen pater eius eadem gaudebit terra quoad vixerit soluendo vt supra anno Domini M° v° xxxj xviij° Julii.

Alia pars assedatur Jacobo brisone pro xvj s. viij d. Et nunc assedatur gilberto porterfeild post mortem ipsius Jacobi brison soluendo vt supra factum xj nouembris anno Domini m° v° xxxviij°. Et mortuus est nunc assedatur Joanni porterfeld eius filio primogenito soluendo vt supra factum apud paslay penultimo maii anno 1553.

Illa pars assedatur Jacobo thomeson pro xv s. Nunc cum consensu dicti Jacobis assedatur Andree hammylton capitaneo de Dumberton Et Joanni hammylton eius filio soluendo vt supra factum apud edinburcht xxv augusti anno 1550.

Alia pars assedatur Willelmi hog pro xxv s. cum consensu ipsius Wilelmi assedatur Johanni hog pro xxv s. ut supra cum alio seruicio debito et consueto.

*The chapelland* xiij s iiij d.

Assedatur Wilelmo Alanson pro xiij s. iiij d.

*Cochnay ester* vj lib. xiij s. iiij d. v s. in bonsiluer v lang cariage.

Assedatur Joanni howston domino eiusdem secundum tenorem et formam assedacionis sue de eisdem terris ei facto anno Domini m° v° xxix° die xiij mensis decembris.

In few. To andro hamylton his airis.

*Drumtoquhyr* iiij lib. vj s. viij d. iiij s. in bonsiluer iij lang cariage t. ij c. bere.

Vna pars assedatur Jhoanni Sprewill pro xliij s. iiij d. et mortuus est Et nunc assedatur thome Sprowll filio Joannis Sprowll soluendo vt supra cum alio seruitio debito et consueto.

Alia pars assedatur Jacobo Dowglas pro xx s. xx d. Et post mortem huius Jacobi Jacobus eius senior filius gaudebit eadem terra quam nunc pater eius possedit anno Domini 1 M. v° xxix° xij° Januarii.

Pars Roberti donald cum consensu dicti Roberti assedatur Roberto hammylton In Dunterclunan soluendo vt

Alia pars assedatur Jacobo fynneson xx s. xx d. et reliquit terram Et nunc media pars eius viz. x s. x d. land assedatur roberto Donaldi soluendo x s. x d.

Et altera pars eius assedatur Willelmo soluendo x s. x d. cum alio seruicio debito et consueto factum xj Julii anno Domini m° v° xxxviij°. Et

supra factum apud lythgw xix novembris anno 1552.

nunc cum consensu Willelmi assedatur Jacobo Dowglas seniori soluendo x s. x d. cum alio seruicio debito et consueto factum xxij octobris anno Domini m v° xxxix.

*The myll croft of Drumthochyr* xiij s. iiij d. assedatur thome Sprewll soluendo xiij s. iiij d. cum alio seruicio debito et consueto factum xxix° aprilis anno &c. xlj°.

*Edynbernan* iiij lib. vj s. viij d. iiij s. in bonsiluer t. iij lang cariage.

Vna pars assedatur Jonete houston pro xliij s. iiij d. t. mortua est Et nunc assedatur Stephano Sprewyll pro xliij s. iiij d. cum aliis seruiciis debitis et consuetis xviij° augusti anno etc. quingentesimo xxvij°.

Alia pars assedatur Alexandro houston pro xxj s. viij d. cum aliis seruiciis debitis et consuetis Et nunc assedatur fynlao howstone eius filio soluendo vt supra xij novembris anno Domini m. v° xxxviij°.

Alia pars assedatur Jhoanni Edmeston pro xxj s. viij d. cum aliis seruiciis debitis et consuetis Et nunc cum consensu dicti Joannis assedatur Stephano Spreull et katarine hall eius sponse soluendo in omnibus vt supra factum apud glasgu quarto augusti anno etc. 1549.

*Cragbanzoch* xiij s. iiij d. set to ye tenandis of Edynbernan.

*Auchynlek* v lib. iiij s. in bonsiluer t. iij lang cariages.

Vna pars assedatur fynlao m'gregor pro xxv s. cuius pars media viz. xij s. vj d. land cum consensu dicti fynlay assedatur Willielmo Jhoneson juniori soluendo in omnibus vt supra cum aliis seruiciis debitis et consuetis Reservato vsufructu dicto fynlayo factum apud paslay xxvj may anno 1553.

Alia pars Willelmo Jonson pro xij s. vj d. et nunc assedatur cum consensu huius Wilelmi Willelmo Jonson juniori filio suprascripti Wilelmi soluendo vt supra vj° martii anno Domini m° v° xl°.*

* Et nunc eadem pars cum consensu dicti villelmi assedatur georgio Johnson filio dicti villelmi soluendo ut supra xxiij februarii 1544.

Alia pars assedatur Johanni bryson pro xxv s. cuius media pars assedatur patricio bryson filio eiusdem Joannis brison pro xij s. vj d. cum le bonis siluer t. cariage.

Alia medietas assedatur Jacobo brison primogenito dicti Johannis soluendo xij s. vj d. cum le bwnesiluer et caragio debitis et consuetis apud paslay xx octobris 1545.

Alia pars assedatur Johanni edmeston pro xij s. vj d. Et nunc cum consensu dicti Joannis assedatur patricio Jhonson filio georgii Jhonson soluendo vt supra factum apud glasgw quarto augusti anno etc. 1549.

Alia pars assedatur Johanni flemyn pro xxv s. et vj b. ordei Et mortuus est et nunc assedatur Joanni flemyng et roberto flemyng vnicuique xij s. vj d. land soluendo vt supra factum apud Edinburcht xxiij aprilis anno 1548.

*Culbuy ester* v lib. land iiij s. in bonsyluer iij lang cariage t. xxx bere.

Vna pars assedatur patricio mores pro xxxiij s. iiij d. viij b. ordei.

Alia pars assedatur Willelmo henderson pro xxv s. v b. 1 f. ordei Et nunc assedatur archibaldo henderson filio primogenito dicti quondam Willelmi soluendo ut supra

xxij maij 1543. factum apud hamylton xxij may anno Domini 1 m. v° xliij°

Pars Joannis henderson assedatur cum consensu Roberto hamylton In Dunterclunan soluendo vt supra in omnibus factum apud lynlythgw xix nouembris anno 1552.

Alia pars assedatur Johanni henderson pro xij s. vj d. et mortuus est t. ij b. ij f. ij p. ordei pars quondam Johannis hendersoun prefati decendentis nunc assedatur Johanni hendersoun suo filio primogenito soluendo annuatim vt supra cum aliis seruiciis debitis et consuetis factum apud hammilton xxvij° aprilis anno Domini etc. 1551.

Alia pars assedatur Johanni fynne pro xvj s. viij d. et nunc cum consensu dicti Joannis senioris patris sui assedatur Joanni fynneson filio suo primogenito soluendo annuatim xvj s. viij d. iij b. ij f. ordei Et nunc ob non solutione firmarum cœnobio assedatur sub hac conditione per equales partes archibaldo henderson et roberto fynny donec Joannes fynne persoluerit dictis archibaldo et roberto firmam per eos solutam granatario et loco factum apud ix octobris anno 1555.

Alia pars assedatur ade henderson pro xij s. vj d. ij b. ij f. ij p. ordei.

Pars olim ade hendersoun nunc assedatur cum consensu dicti ade, Jacobo henderson eiusdem fratri germano soluendo vt supra cum aliis seruiciis debitis et consuetis factum apud hamilton xxvij° aprilis 1551.

*Maquhanray* x merkland vj s. in bonsyluer v lang cariages iij c. xij b. farine et ij c. ordei.

anno xxix° Assedatur Willelmo edmeston secundum formam et tenorem assedationis sue per Joannem commendatario eidem factum anno Domini 1 M. v° xxix° que assedatio sine sigillo communi data erat per xix annos duratura.

In few.

In few. *Auchyngu* xxvj s. viij d. occupeit be ye tenandis of maquhanran.

*Chapelland of Maquhanran* xiij s. iiij d.

Assedatur Roberto hamylton officiario.

Assedatur Willelmo atzyn pro xiij s. iiij d. et nunc cum consensu eius Willelmi assedatur Donaldo atkyne soluendo xiij s. iiij d. cum alio seruitio debito et consueto Et nunc cum eius viz. Donaldi atkyne soluendo xiij s. iiij d. cum alio seruitio debito et consueto factum apud paslay 3° mertii 1545.

*The bernys* ij c. v. b. farine 1 c. ordei.

Assedatur roberto knok et thome knok equaliter pro ij c. v b. farine 1 c. ordei.

Item, ye medow of ye bernys won mawyn t. stakit fre be ye said tenandis of ye bernys. Item, at ye tenandis pay zerly xiij s. iiij d. for ye quheit syluer.

dimedia pars eius quam possedebat thomas knok qui nunc mortuus est assedatur mariote hammylton vidue olim sponse suprascripti thome soluendo pro illa dimedia parte proportionabiliter ad alias partes factum penultimo Januarii anno etc. xxxviij°.

Media pars de bernis viz. tota illa pars quam possedebat thomas knok nunc assedatur — knok eius filio.

The half of ye bernis yat thomas knok occupeit of befor now set to Robert knok his sone payand zeirly [of his awyn expens ye half] 1 c. ij b. ij f. farine viij b. ordei and wynnand zeirly of his awyn expens ye half of ye medowis of ye bernis and als payand zeirly vj s. viij d. for his part of ye quheit siluer and marrion hammylton ye relict of thomas knok sal bruik for his lyftim ye half heir of conform to hir rental maid to hir of befor at paslay ye xxvj day of Aprill ye zeir of god 1 M. v° t. xlj zeir.

Pars roberti knok qui mortuus est nunc assedatur Joanni knok eius filio cum consensu Domini patricii eius fratris seniori soluendo In omnibus vt supra factum apud glasgw primo Januarii anno Domini 1547 Qui mortuus est Nunc autem assedatur Joanni knok eius filio primogenito soluendo in omnibus vt supra factum apud lynlythgw ix Januarii anno etc. 1553.

The fischyng of linbrane set to my lord of Ergill for fyff zeris payand xxxvj salmondis souerte donald campbell of . . . .

The fyschyng of Cruktshot set to George bronsyd for . . . .

The fyschin of ye watter of paslay.

The fyschin of ye watter of blaxton wyth ye crewis.

The fyschin of ye locht of lochtwynnock wyte our boit set to James glen of ye bar Indurand our will alanerly payand.

The xx s land of ye kyrk of auchynlek set til Schir Wilzam hwme curat of the sammyn allowand yerfor v lib. in his fee as he was rentallit in it be Robert abbot and as his letter proportis maid anno xxiij° be ye said Robert abbot etc. die xxiiij° Nouembris anno 1525.

---

### *Rentale de Monktoun et Dalmulyn.*

Memorandum of ye statut of ye do seruice yat ilk capon is viij d. ilk pultre iiij d. ilk chykin ij d. ye laid of colis iiij d. ye plewch ij s. ye day scheryn iij d. Item, ij pultre for a capon ij chykyns for a pultre. Item, ilk laid of colis iij crelis of huch to be laid in ye abbotis place betuex witsonday t. mychelmess or ellis ye price of ye laid vj d. The entray of ye fowlis begynnis at pais caponis t. chykynis quhill mychelmes and fra mychelmes pultre quhill fastrynnis ewyn The penny maill to be payt at witsonday and mertymes The doseruice as cariagis pluwyn harrowyn t. scheryn to be payt at mertymes wyth ye rest of ye colis and fowlis And ye sergiand to ansuer herefor as he dois for ye penny maill of yaim yat are wnspecifeit Item, efter ilk pleuch vj d. for harroyng ilk merk land iij caponis Ilk lang cariage x s.

*Monktone hyll* v lib. xviij s. land.

Vna pars assedatur patricio Rese pro xv s. iiij d. ij capon ij pultre ij pulle ij laid colis ½ bed ½ plewcht a lang cariage t. v dais scheryng et mortuus est Et nunc eadem pars assedatur Willelmo cwnyngham filio Alexandri cwnyngham soluendo vt supra factum apud paslay xxviij Januarii m. v° xl.

Alia pars assedatur Alexandro Conynghame pro xv s. iiij d. ij capon ij pultre ij pulli ij laid colis ½ bed ½ plewcht a lang cariage t. v dais scheryng Et nunc eadem pars assedatur Willelmo Cwnyngham filio Alexandri cum consensu eiusdem sed tamen et Alexandri gauderit eadem parte ad vitam xxviij° Januarii anno domini m. v° xl.

Vxor thome dormond xxvij s. iiij d. iij capon iij pultre vj pulli iiij laid colis a plewcht a bed a lang cariage a Ridand man viij dais scheryng ye entra siluer nocht pait cuius medietas nunc assedatur Joanni barclay soluendo pro illa medietate proportionabiliter ad supradicta Et nunc altera pars eidem Joanni assedatur soluendo pro tota illa terra etc. vxor thome dormond prius soluit.

Jhon osbern xxxvj s. iiij capon iiij pultre viij pulle iiij laid of colis a ridand man a lang cariage a bed a plewcht viij dais scheryng Et nunc eadem pars assedatur Joanni osberne filio quondam Joannis osberne soluendo in omnibus vt supra.

Relicta alani greiff xxiiij s. ij capon ij pultre vj pulle ij laid colis a bed a pleucht a lang cariage v dais scheryng Et nunc assedatur Roberto boyd qui nupsit Relicte alani greif pro xxiiij s. ij capon ij pultre vj pulle ij laid collis a bed a plewcht a lang cariage v dais scheryng vt supra Et nunc hec eadem pars cum consensu tam eiusdem Roberti boid quam vxoris eius assedatur Joanni hammyltone de Camskeytht soluendo annuatim vt supra factum xxix anno Domini millesimo v<sup>c</sup> xlj° Et nunc hec eadem pars assedatur Joanni hamtoun alias vocato Johanni ye monk filio Joannis hamiltoun de Camskeyth soluendo vt supra factum anno Domini m° v° xlj° xxviij aprilis Nunc assedatur margrete hamiltoun filio domini de Camskeyth soluendo vt supra factum xj° februarii anno Domini 1 m. v° fyfti tway.

*The myll of monktone* wyth ye mylland of ye sammyn set to margret dicksone for all ye dayis of hir lyif payand zeirly yarfor at candelmas t. lammas twenty pundis alanerly and now wyth hir consent sett to Dauid hamtoun in ye vther manis of monktone payand zeirly yarfor as is abun writtin at paslay ye xxviij day of aprill ye zeir of god 1 m. v° t. xlj zeir t. wyth consent of ye said Dauid christen schaw his spous is rentellit wyth him in ye said myll for hir liftyme factum xvj maii anno 1544.

The ouer manys of monktone extendand to fowr pundis land wyth ye pertenent set to Dauid hammyltone t. cristyne schaw his spows t. thai ar rentalit in ye sammyn payand zeirly four lotis of mail t. xx s. for al vther dewiteis t. dewseruice at termys vsit t. wont siclik as Adam Wallace t. Jonet maxwell his spous t. vtheris of befor payit for ye sammyn and this rentilyng maid t. subscrivit wyth our hand at paslay ye xxj day of april ye zeir of god 1 m. v° xxxix zeiris befor thir witnes master James forster domino Johne sandelandis t. peter algeo noter publict.

Jhone abbot
of paslay.

The town of monkton xlj lib. iij s. viij d. land.

Vna pars assedatur Mariote brown pro liij s. iiij d. iiij capon iiij pultre viij pulli iij laid colis 1 rydand man 1 lang cariage 1 plewcht 1 bed v days scheryng.

v f. corn.

Et nunc assedatur Joanni neill filio suprascripti mariote brown soluendo in omnibus vt supra.

Alia pars viz. ye kyrkbank vocata continens vnam dimediam acram terre assedatur patricio smyth soluendo tres solidos annuatim factum ix mertii anno lij.

Alia pars assedatur Katrine neill pro liij s. iiij d. iiij capon iiij pultre viij pulli iij laid colis j rydand man 1 lang cariage 1 pleucht 1 bed v dais scheryng.

v f. corn.

Et nunc assedatur Jhoanni Adamsone filio eiusdem Katrine neil soluendo in omnibus vt supra Qui mortuus est Et nunc assedatur Joanni Adamson filio primogenito dicti Joannis reseruando tamen vidue vsum et consuetudinem domini soluendo vt supra factum apud air primo Aprilis anno 1552.

Alia pars assedatur Dauid gothra pro xxxvj s. viij d. iiij capon iiij pultre viij pulli iiij lade colis j rydand man j lang cariage j pleucht j bed x dais scheryng cuius vna pars.

vj f. corn.

Et nunc assedatur Joanni gottra soluendo xij s. vj d. proportionabiliter ad supradicta et altera eius pars viz. xj s. land assedatur Joanni gottray filio mergarete Jonston soluendo xj s. proportionabiliter ad supradicta.

Et altera pars viz. xij s. vj d. land assedatur ade gottray ij pultre & al dew seruice to be delt amangis yaim al thre efferand to euery man's part.

xxiiij° aprilis anno etc. xlj°.

Alia pars assedatur Johanni osborne pro xxviij s. iij capon vj pulli iij laid colis j rydand man j lang cariage j plewcht j bed v dais scheryng et mortuus est et nunc assedatur alexandro osborne filio Joannis cui reliquit beneuolentiam suam de eadem terra pater eius soluendo in omnibus vt pater eius prius soluit factum xxv Januarii anno etc. xxxviij°.

Alia pars assedatur Johanni Wile pro xxviij s. iij capon iij pultre vj pulli iij laid colis j rydand man j plewcht j bed j lang cariage v dais scheryng Qui mortuus est Nunc assedatur Andree Vilie filio dicti Joannis soluendo vt supra factum apud lynlythgw xv mertii anno 1552.

vj f. corn.

Alia pars assedatur Johanni fynlaw pro xxx s. iij capones iiij pultre vj pulli iij laid colis j rydand man j plewcht j bed j lang cariage v dais scheryng Et nunc consensu dicti Joannis assedatur Joanni fynlay filio primogenito soluendo vt supra ac etiam reseruando vsufructum patri factum apud paslay xxiiij anno 1552.

iij f. ij p. corn.

v p. corn. Alia pars assedatur thome lowre pro viij s. j capon j pultre ij pulli j laid colis ½ cariage ij ½ dais scheryng Et mortuus est et Nunc autem assedatur Jacobo neill filio Joannis neill soluendo vt supra nouissimum cum consensu dicti Jacobi neill assedatur dauidi hamilton de ouer manis et Jacobo hamilton eius filio soluendo vt supra factum apud edinburcht xxj maii anno domini etc. xlvij.

v p. corn. Alia pars assedatur Jacobo clerk pro viij s. j capon j pultre ij pulli j laid of colis ½ cariage ij ½ dais scheryng et mortuus est et nunc assedatur willelmo clerk vt supra excepto prato lato in manu domini ix Januarii anno m. v° xl°.

Alia pars assedatur ade huntar pro xxxvj s. iiij capon iiij pultre viij schykynis iiij colis j rydand man j lang cariage j plewcht j bed v dais scheryng Et nunc assedatur patricio huntar filio dicti ade soluendo in omnibus vt supra xxiij die Junii anno Domini m. v° xxxj.

vj f. corn.
Pars patricii hunter viz. xxxvj s. land

assedatur cum consensu patricii dicti Willelmo hunter eius primogenito et eo deficiente Alexandro hunter secundo genito soluendo vt supra factum apud lythgw x martii anno 1552 Reseruando vsufructum patri.

Alia pars assedatur allexandro neill pro xxix s. iij capon iij pultre vj pulli iij laid colis a ridand man j lang cariage j plewcht j bed v dais scheryng of ye quhilk part yis Allexander neill hais gyffyne his kyndness of ye tane half part of yis malyng extendand to xiiij s. vj d. land to Jekyne osborne t. is tane tenand to ye sam be our master ye abbot payand effeirandly for his part in al thingis ye vther half assedatur Joanni osborne filio Jonete caldwell payand siclik as ye vther part payis.

Alia pars assedatur Johanni cristell pro xiij s. iiij d. of ye browster land Et nunc cum consensu dicti Joannis assedatur colin cristell filio soluendo vt supra factum apud lynlythqu xv° Junii anno etc. xlvij.

Pars alexandri neil assedatur Joanni osborne filio Jonete caldwell soluendo xxix s. iij capon iij pultre vj pulli iij laid colis j rydand man j lang cariage j plewcht j bed . . dayis scheryng factum xxvij Septembris anno etc. xxxj.

*Ouer manis of ye monktone* iiij lib. land.

*Nethir manis of monktone* xx[ti] lib. iiij dd. capon.

Vna pars eius quam occupabat Joannes hunter in carrik nunc assedatur wilelmo hunter pro l s. vj capon cum alio seruitio debito et consueto factum xx februarii anno Domini m. v° xxxviij° et mortuus est et nunc assedatur Joanni huntar filio dicti willelmi huntar pro l s. vj capon cum alio seruitio debito et consueto factum apud monkton xv anno etc. xl°.

Alia pars assedatur georgio nycholl qui mortuus est et nunc cum consensu sponse dicti quondam georgii assedatur domino cudberto gottray soluendo l s. vj capon cum alio seruicio xxj maii anno Domini m° v° xlij.

Alia pars assedatur Jacobo hunter filio roberti hunter pro l s. vj capones cum alio seruitio debito et consueto factum xx februarii anno domini m. v° xxxviij.

Alia pars assedatur Ade huntar pro l s. vj capon Qui mortuus est Nunc assedatur Joanni hamilton de cunnok soluendo vt supra factum apud Stirlyng 5° Januarii anno Domini 1547 Reseruato vidue ritum cenobie de vsufructu.

Et nunc cum consensu dicti Joannis assedatur patricio hunter et Joanni hunter eius filio primogenito factum apud paslay viij Januarii anno 1552.

Alia pars assedatur carolo Wilson et mortuus est et nunc assedatur Willelmo osborne pro supra xxv februarii anno Domini etc. xxxiiij[to].

ane half. Alia pars assedatur alexandro bell Et nunc assedatur dauid Wallace soluendo annuatim lv s. vj d. vj capon ad terminos consuetos cum seruicio debito et consueto factum apud Edinburcht v nouembris 1544.

Qui mortuus est Et assedatur Willielmo vallace eius fratri soluendo vt supra factum apud hamilton xxix aprilis anno 1551.

Alia pars assedatur matheo mure Et nunc assedatur dauid mwer primogenito dicti mathei soluendo annuatim ad terminos consuetos lv s. vj d. vj capones cum seruitio debito et consueto factum Edinburcht iiij° nouembris 1544.

Alia pars assedatur Ade gylcrist pro xxxiij s. iiij d. iiij capones cum seruicio debito et consueto Et nunc assedatur Johanni gilcrist primogenito dicti Ade et Johanni huntar nepote dicti andree soluendo vt supra. Memorandum yat w. osborne dauid wallace & dauid mure suld pay ye ij pennys t. ye ij caponis reserued of ye haill rentall of yis towne becaus yai haif oder land yarfor. factum apud paslay vltimo augusti 1545.

*Brorat* xl s. land.

Vna pars assedatur roberto wilsone pro xx s. ij capon iij pultre iiij chekynis 1 lang cariage ij laid colis ½ plewcht ½ bed v dais scheryng Et nunc assedatur patricio vilsown filio dicti roberti soluendo ut supra factum apud Edinburcht iiij° nouembris 1544. v f. corn.

Alia pars assedatur Johanni conegame pro xx s. ij capon iij pultre iiij pulli ij laid colis j lang cariage ½ plewcht ½ bed v dais scheryng. v f. corn.

Pars olim domini Cudberti gottray capellani assedatur Joanni hammylton alias vocatus de blaxton soluendo l s. vj capon cum auenis et aliis seruiciis debitis et consuetis factum apud Edinburcht secundo octobris anno 1553.

*Cowquhit mur* xxxvj s. viij d. land iiij capon iiij pultre iiij pulli ij laid of colis a Ridand man ane lang cariage a plewyche ane bed v dayis scheryng.

*Bronsyde* vj s. viij d. land.

Tota pars assedatur Jonete rig vj s. viij d. iiij capon casting of ye mill laid.

*Wardhouse* xiij s. iiij d.

Assedatur Emeote smyth pro xiij s. iiij d. allanerly.

*Dalmulyn.*

*Kyrkland holme* liij s. iiij d.

Vna pars assedatur Wilelmo fergushyll pro xxvj s. viij d. vj. capon iij laid colis ½ a rydand man a lang cariage j plewcht j bed v dais scheryng Et cum consensu dicti Wilelmi assedatur Roberto fergushill eius filio soluendo vt supra.

Alia pars assedatur Jacobo galloway pro xxvj s. viij d. vj capon iij laid colis ½ a ryand man a lang cariage j plewcht j bed v dais scheryng Et nunc cum consensu huius Jacobi assedatur Jacobi galloway filio eius soluendo vt supra factum xxj decembris anno etc. xxx viij°.

*Kyrkhyll* iij lib. xiij s. iiij d. land.

Vna pars assedatur roberto fergushill pro ij lib. ix s. x capon iiij laid colis j rydand man j lang cariage j plewcht j bed v dais scheryng Et nunc assedatur Joanni fergushill filio suprascripti roberti fergushil soluendo vt supra factum xviij septembris anno domini m° v° xxxv Et cum consensu dicti Joannis assedatur archibaldo fergushill eius filio primogenito soluendo vt supra factum apud paslay xx Januarii anno 1551.

Alia pars assedatur relicte henrici huntar pro xxiiij s. iiij d. v capon ij laid colis j lang cariage ½ plewcht ½ bed v dais scheryng et nunc assedatur henrico huntar juniori soluendo vt supra in omnibus factum xxij octobris anno Domini m° v° xxxix°.

Pars henrici hunter assedatur cum consensu dicti henrici Wilielmo hunter eius filio seniori soluendo vt supra factum apud Edinburcht x die Januarii anno etc. xlvj.

*blakhowse* assedatur Joanni Wallace filio helene chalmer cui prius assedabatur cum consensu eiusdem helene soluendo Idem Joannes annuatim xxvj s. viij d. vj capon iiij laid colis ane plewcht ane furneist bed j lang cariage j rydand man v dayis scheryng cum alio seruitio debito et consueto Et quod seruet stilos et statuta curie nostre seu predecessorum nostrorum sub pena amissionis et perditionis huius rentalis seu assedacionis etiam amissionis pecunie pro eadem assedatione date factum apud pasletum vj Junii anno domini m. v° xxxviij° Et nunc cum consensu suprascripti Joannis Wallace eadem terra de blakhowse assedatur Joanni bannatyne domino de Corus soluendo vt supra in omnibus factum xviij mertii anno Domini m. v° xxxviij° Et nunc cum consensu dicti Johannis bannatyne domini de eadem pars assedatur dicto Johanni wallace soluendo vt supra.

factum apud Edinburcht xxix° die Januarii 1545.

*Damylling* mylquarter iiij lib. xiij s. iiij d.

Vna pars assedatur relicte quondam Willelmi Wallace pro xxvj s. viij d. vj capon iiij laid coillis j plewcht j bed furnist j lang cariage j ridand man v dais scheryng.

The Chapelland Adam Wallace xiij s. iiij d.

Et nunc assedatur Willielmo hammylton de sanquhar militi Et Willielmo hammylton eius filio et eorum diutius viuenti soluendo vt supra factum apud Edinburcht xxvij aprilis anno etc. xlvj.

Alexander Galloway xiij s. iiij d. iij capon ij laid colis ½ plewcht ½ bed a lang cariage v dais scheryng Et nunc cum consensu dicti Alexandri assedatur matheo eius filio primogenito soluendo vt supra factum apud air sexto aprilis 1552.

*Blakhous.*

Blakhous cum consensu Joannis bannatyne Domini de Corrons assedatur Johanni filio helene chalmer soluendo annuatim ad terminos consuetos xxvj s.

laidis of colis ane plewcht ane fwrnist bed j lang cariage j ridand man v dayis scheryng cum alio seruicio debito et consueto.

Edinburcht xxix Januarii 1545.

Matho rodman xl s. ix capon iiij laid colis a Rydand man j lang cariage j plewcht a furnist bed v dais scheryng mortuus est.

Set to ye lord of cambuskeyth for maill t. dewtes ut supra vj$^{e}$ mertii anno etc. xxviij$^{e}$ xvj s. land yat maryone Rankyn occupeit Set to Jame Reid ye sone of vmquhill andro Reid for xvj s. avarage t. cariage dewteis et dewseruis vsit t. wont and ye said maryone Rankyn sal browk ye tane halff of ye land for hyr tym.

The miltone alias vocata rodmanis malying assedatur Joanni rodman filio suprascripti mathei soluendo xl s. ix capon iiij laid colis ane rydand man j lang cariage j plewcht ane furneist bed v dayis scheryng cum alio seruicio debito et consueto factum anno Domini m$^{o}$ v$^{c}$ xxxv xiij mensis octobris.

Mylland in ye myllaris hand vj capon t. a fed bar.

*The Maritoun* quarter iiij lib. xiij s. iiij d. land.

Assedatur roberto schaw pro iiij lib. xiij s. iiij d. xxj capon vj laid colis j rydand man j lang cariage j plewcht j furneist bed v dais scheryng Et mortuus est Et nunc assedatur Willielmo schaw filio et heredi dicti roberti soluendo vt supra factum anno Domini m$^{o}$ v$^{e}$ xxxix$^{o}$ vj mensis augusti.

*Tatis quarter* iiij lib. xiij s. iiij d. land.

Vna pars assedatur roberto schaw pro xx s. iiij capon iij laid colis j lang cariage.½ plewcht ½ bed v dais scheryng Et nunc assedatur Willelmo schaw filio et heredi dicti roberti soluendo vt supra factum vj augusti anno Domini m$^{o}$ v$^{c}$ xxxix$^{o}$.

Thom galloway xl s. ix capon iiij laid colis a rydand man a lang cariage a plewcht a bed v dais scheryng.

Et nunc assedatur mergrete dickson t. post mortem eius assedatur Andree hammiltone soluendo vt supra factum vij augusti anno domini m$^{o}$ v$^{c}$ xxxviij$^{o}$ Et nunc assedatur Dauid hammylton in ye manys of munkton soluendo ut supra ij may anno m. v$^{c}$ xliiij zeris.

Jasper Steyn xvj s. viij d. iii capon ij laid colis ½ plewcht ½ bed a lang cariage v dais scheryng et mortuus est et nunc assedatur Andree hammylton soluendo vt supra factum tertio septembris anno domini m$^{o}$ v$^{c}$ xxxviij$^{o}$ Et nunc assedatur Dauid hammylton in ye manys of munkton soluendo ut supra ij$^{o}$ maii anno 1544.

Jhon Steynson xvj s. viiij d. iij capon ij laid colis ½ plewcht ½ bed a lang cariage v dais scheryng Et nunc assedatur roberto cristall soluendo vt supra in omnibus factum xij Junii anno domini m$^{o}$ v$^{c}$ xxxvj$^{o}$.

*Rentale of ye akyrdalis* in anno etc. xxvij$^{e}$.

*Pawitland.*

vj acris. Dauid Inglis ane akyr v f. bere.
Megge Lowcheid ane akyr v f. bere.
Peter neyll ane akyr v f. bere.
Jok foster ane akyr v f. bere.
Dauid Inglis t. Jok cowchie a akyr v f. bere.
Deme Sandelandis a akyr v f. bere.

*Tayts flat.*

xij akyris. Rob. hendersone elder ane akyr a b. bere.
thom morton ane akyr ——— a b. bere.
Jhon tynnegam t. male mychell a akyr j b. bere.
Rob. henderson zonger a akyr a b. bere.
Jhon bowe ane akyr j b. bere.
Wylle brown ane akyr j b. bere.

gylbert Alexanderson ane akyr j b. bere.
Jhon Abyrnethe a akyr j b. bere.
Jhon ves ane akyr j b. bere.
Jok vre ane akyr j b. bere.
Deme Sandelandis ij akyris ij b. bere.
*blo syd.* Jhon Alexander elder ane akyr j b. bere.
xiiij acris. Jame quaroor ane akyr j b. bere.
Jhon abernethe ane akyr j b. bere.
Jhon modervell ane akyr j b. bere.
W. Rankyn ane akyr j b. bere.
Patrik mosman ane akyr j b. bere.
Jok bowe talzor ane akyr j b. bere.
Jok bowe talzear ij akyrris ij b. bere.
Thom bowe ij akyrris ij b. bere.
Joh brownsyd iij acris iij b. bere.
Steyn Ves iij acris iij b. bere.
Jame quareor ane akyr j b. bere.
Jok Wylson ane akyr j b. bire.
Arche howme v. Rud j b. j f. bere.

*Wod quarter* vj lib. ij d. land.

Vna pars assedatur roberto galloway pro xxiij s. viij d. v capones iij laid colis j lang cariage ½ plewcht ½ bed vij dais scheryng Et nunc eadem pars assedatur cuthberto galloway filio ipsius roberti galloway cum consensu eiusdem roberti soluendo in omnibus vt supra Et nunc cum consensu eiusdem cuthberti assedatur petro algeo soluendo ut supra apud paslay xxiiij Julii 1545. (anno xxx.)

Wille Richmontis wiff xxiij s. viij d. iiijȝ capon ij laid colis a lang cariage ½ plewcht ½ bed vij dais schering Et nunc assedatur richardo bannatyne burgensi de ayr soluendo in omnibus vt supra factum anno Domini m° v° xxxiiij x may Qui mortuus est Et nunc assedatur nycolayo bannatyne eius filio cum consensu fratris primogeniti soluendo vt supra.

Jhone cambell xliij s. ix capones iiij laid colis a lang cariage a rydand man j plewcht j bed x dais scheryng Et nunc cum consensu dicti Johannis assedatur alexandro cambell eius filio soluendo vt supra factum apud edinburcht xx augusti anno xlvj reseruando patri vsufructum quoad vixerit.

Pate thomson xxiij s. x d. vj½ capon iij laid colis a lang cariage a rydand man j plewcht j bed vij dais scheryng Et nunc assedatur antonio thomson filio dicti patricii soluendo vt supra factum apud paslay ij aprilis 1547.

Grais tak vj s. viij d. ij capon j laid colis v dais scheryng assedatur roberto schaw Et nunc assedatur Willelmo Schaw filio t. heredi dicti roberti schaw soluendo vt supra vj augusti anno Domini m° v° xxxix°.

*The fyschyne of Wolschot t. Wlquhar.*

Assedatur Willielmo hammylton de Sanquhar militi Et Willielmo hammilton eius filio et eorum diutius viuenti soluendo annuatim tres duodenas salmonum In loco nostro de monkton factum apud Edinburcht xxviij anno Domini etc. xlvj.

*fyschyn of ye Langcraig.* Assedatur dauidi hammylton de ouer manis de monkton soluendo duodecim salmones factum xij may anno 1551.

---

*Zerly anwellis.*

Ye anwell of adamtone in ye zer xl s.
Ye anwell of awchynlek xx s.
Ye anwell of corsbe viij s.

The myll of Dalmalyng wyth ye mylland set to mergret Dicksone for al ye dayis of hir lyif payand zeirly yarfor xiij lib. vj s. viij d. alanerly at candelmes t. lammes And efter hir deceis set to Androw hammyltone her sister sone payand trettene pundis vj s. viij d. zeirly siclik as ye said mergret payis xvj day of merche ye zeir of god j m. v$^{c}$ xl zeris And now ye said myll sett to Dauid hammilton in ye manys of monkton payand as is abone factum ij$^{a}$ may 1544 Et nunc cum consensu dicti dauidis Assedatur willielmo hammylton eius filio et eorum diutius viuenti cum omnibus proficuis vtilitatibus commoditatibus et cum le suckyn thyrll multuris et aliis servitiis dicto molendino spectantibus soluendo annuatim vt supra factum apud Edinburgum xvj maii anno Domini j m. v$^{c}$ xlvj.

*Corsflat.*

xvij acris. Jok vre ane akyr j b. bere.
Jhone allexander ane akyr j b. bere.
Rob. henderson zonger ij acris ij b. bere.
Rankyn pacok ane akyr j. b. bere.
Anne lowre ane akyr j b. bere.
Jok flemyn ane akyr j b. bere.
Besse lowre ane akyr j b. bere.
Jhone moderwell t. megge sandelandis vij rudis vij f. bere.
Jok Vre ij acris ij b. bere.
Male Cuyk ane akyr j b. bere.
Jane fynne ane akyr j b. bere.
Besse horne ane akyr j b. bere.
Rob Symson ane akyr j b. bere.
Patrik mosman ane akyr j b. bere.

*West syd of grenlaw.*

xiiij acris. Watte bowe iij acris iij b. bere.
xv½ acris. Jane Pantor ij acris ij b. bere.
Besse horne 1 akyr j b. bere.
Jok paslay ij akyris ij b. bere.
Jok Smyth ane akyr j b. bere.
Anne lowre ij akyrris ij b. bere.
hendre neyll ane akyr j b. bere.
Jhone moderwell ane akyr j b. bere.
Wylle crag ane akyr j b. bere.
Andro paull twa rudis ij f. bere.
Jhon flemyng ane akyr j b. bere.

*The Mwr.*

Watte bowe j b. beyr.

Jok brownsyd j b. beyr.

*Est syd of grenlaw.*

Set to Watte bowe for vij b. beyr.

*Brownes.* akyr. Set to male cuyk for v f. beyr.

*Clayfauld* x *rud.*

Set to wylle quhyt for iij b. beyr.

*Ouer ward* quhen it is sawyn xxviij b. beyr.

Vna eius pars viz. fowr acris assedatur Joanni quhit lapicidario pro qualibet acra vnam bollam ordei Et pro eius seruitio vt cum eo conuentum est In dicto seruicio lap . . . xviij Julii anno 1554 . . . Inde extendentes ad . . bollas . . . ordei.

*Nether ward* quhen it is sawyn xxij b. bere t. xx b. corne.

Vna pars eiusdem viz. quinque acre vocate brown holme cum duabus acris contigue jacens versus brunis akyr assedatur petro algeo soluendo quinque bollas ordei Reseruando nobis cuniculos et cuniculararios factos aut fiendos in dicta terra factum xxviij Julii anno 1554.

*The abbottis ij croftis.*

*The landis.* Casualites standis t. consistis in gersumes of landis change of tenandis eschettis vardis t. mariage forfaltyng of tenandis for brekyn of ye statutis.

*The kyrkis.* Casualites of ye kyrkis set for moeny consistis in gersumes of xix zeris takis or in rasayving ane taxt man for ane wyn sic as ye

Gersum for xix zeir tak of Innerwik v[c] merkis t. may pay mair.

Gersum of lydgerwod iij[c] merkis for xix zeir tak t. may pay mekill mair.

Gersum for largis t. Innerkeip for xix zeir ix[c] merkis t. may pay mair.

Gersum for xix zeiris tak of Rossneyth iiij[c] merkis t. may pay mair.

Gersum of Dundonald for xix zeris tak iij[c] lib. at ye lest or v[c] merkis.

Rentale R. P. Joannis Archiepiscopi Sanctiandree P. N. L. Monasterii que de Pasleto Abbatis factum vigesimo Junii anno domini millesimo quingentesimo quinquagesimo vbi nomina continentur tenentium et Inhabitantium de presenti qui occupant terram pro toto tempore vite Ipsorum seruando acta et stilos nostre curie.

*Dominium de pasleto.*

*The Inche.*

*Inche* xviij merk land assedatur tenentibus suprascriptibus pro xviij celdris antique mensure viz. xij peckis pro qualibus bolla xij dosane pultre viij[c] xl crelis pettis vone t. stakit on ye vatter syd ye abbot payand ten s. for euery hundretht creillis to ye tenandis cum aliis seruitiis.

*hillynton* ix merk land ix c. auenarum ij dd. capon.

*Grenlaw* ij merk land.

*Corsflat* xl s. land.

*Brablo* xxviij s. iiij d. assedatur pro ij c. j boll j f. ordei.

*Gallohillis over* iiij lib. land cum bonis mona.

*Gallohillis neder* ij merk land ij dd. pul.

*lylisland* xx boll auenarum.
*Toddisholme* ij s land.
*Cariagehyll* iiij merk land iiij dd. pul. ij lang cariagis.
*Rycardbar* xl s. land iij c. auenarum xij pultre ij s. bonsiluer.
*Mekylryggis* viij lib. iiij lang cariagis viij dd. pullorum.
*fergusly* vj lib. land In few to Jhone hammylton.
*Bradyland* xx s. land xviij pultre xij d. in bonsiluer j lang cariage wyth seruice.
*Corsbar* and *Thomasbar* v merk land.
*Berschawen* iiij merk land iiij c. auenarum xxxij pultre ij s. iiij c. creillis pettis for tene s. euery hundrethe creillis.
*Nevton* iiij merk land iiij c. auenarum xxxij pultre.
*Duskayth* In few to William Stewart.
*Candren t. quhitcruk* iij lib. xvj s. viij d.
*lyncleiff.*
*Ruthbank* v. merkland.
*Neder thornle* v merkland.
*knaiffisland* v s. land.
*Drumgrane* cum molendino xiij lib. xiij s. iiij d. ix lang cariage xviij dd. pultre ix s. in bonsiluer.
*fowlton* cum molendino xxxvij lib. xvj s. viij d. iiij lang cariage xv dosane vj pultre cum alio seruitio debito et consueto.

*Dominium de Glene.*

*Bar* and *Brygend* ten merkland In feudefirma Jacobo glene pro x lib. xij s. vij dosane pultre ij lang cariage or xx s.

*Mylbank.*

*Wester kers* xliij s. iiij d. land ij s. in bone iij dosan pultre ij lang cariagis.
*Ester kers* xliij s. iiij d. land iij dosan pultre ij s. in bon ij lang cariage.
*Joffra tak* xxiij s. iiij d. xviij pultre ane lang cariage ane schort.
*Bermoklo* x s. land xij d. in bone ix pultre ane cariage.
*Mavisbank* x s. land xij d. in bone ix pultre ane cariage.
*Langstainle* xv s. land xij d. in bon xij pultre ane cariage.
*Caimhill* xx s. land xviij d. in bone ij dosane iij pultre ane cariage.
*Lorenbank.*
*Auldzard.*

*Dominium de Glen.*

*Langzard.*
*ffairhillis.*
*Gavilmoss.*
*hyllizzard.*
*Littil Clook.*
*Langcroft.*
*Qwinsyd mur.*
*Monyabrocht.*
*Barnatht ouer.*
*Authynhame.*

*Lynthillis.*
*Candilmur.*
*Barnatht nedder.*
*Clook.*
*Came.*
Molendinum xxiiij boll farine cum edificatione et sustentatione molendinarum.

## M.

### THE BLACK BOOK OF PAISLEY.

The Black Book of Paisley, now in the Royal Collection in the British Museum, is a transcript of the Scotichronicon, and is one of the oldest, if not the oldest manuscript of that work which is extant. It was known as the "Magnus et niger liber Passleti" as early as 1501, and there is reason to believe that it was in the possession of the Monastery from shortly after Bower's death in 1449. It is a large heavy volume of 271 folios, written in double columns, and is in beautiful preservation. The Scotichronicon occupies from folio 28 to folio 266 inclusive. The earlier folios are devoted to an Alphabetical Index, a Table of Monasteries, &c., Lists of Popes and Emperors and of Metropolitancies, Cardinalates and Bishoprics, an extract from the "Chronicon Rythmicum," and a short chronology, the "Scotichronicon Compendium Metricum," Extracts "de Pestilentia" from Isidore Hispalensis and others, St. Bernard's letter to Ranuldus, and two genealogical trees. A considerable number of these pieces likewise occur in the Schevez MS., in the Harleian Collection, in the Brechin Castle MS., and in the late transcript in the Edinburgh University Library; and Goodall has printed some of them from the latter MS. in his edition of the Scotichronicon.

After the text of Scotichronicon in the Black Book come an Extract from Henry of Huntingdon, an extract from Seneca, a tract "De Fide Christiana," which has only recently been printed, and is ascribed to Boethius, St. Bernard's "Tractatus de Formula Honeste Vite," Prester John's letter to the Greek Emperor, a list of Councils, a selection of moral and religious precepts, and, lastly, a number of quotations from one of Bower's favourite authors, St. Brigitta of Sweden.

At the top of folio 16, on the upper margin, in a plain hand, but evidently from its position posterior in date to the text, is

**Iste liber est de Conventu Pasleti.**

Similar inscriptions occur at various other places throughout the volume, and at the top of folio 28, and as a colophon, we have

**Iste liber est Sancti Jacobi et Sancti Mirini de Pasleto.**

A copy of this Manuscript was made about 1500 by John Gibson, Canon of Glasgow and Rector of Renfrew, which is now in the Library of Corpus Christi College, Cambridge, and is remarkable for its coloured illustrations of incidents in the text. These were most probably executed in the Abbey of Paisley.

In 1501 the Black Book was abridged by John Gibson, junior, Notary Public and Chaplain of Canon Gibson, the Rector of Renfrew. The abridgement belonged to the latter, and afterwards to Henry Sinclair, Dean of Glasgow, to Sir William Sinclair of Roslin, Lord Justice General of Scotland, and to Sir Robert Sibbald, and is now in the Advocates' Library.

At the dissolution of the Abbey the Black Book itself passed into the hands of Sir William Sinclair of Roslin, and was subsequently the property of Archbishop Spottiswood, and of his son, Sir Robert Spottiswood, the Lord President of the Court of Session, on whose death General Lambert obtained possession of it. He made a gift of it to his patron, Lord Fairfax, who, in his turn, presented it to Charles II. It thus found its way into the Royal Library at St. James, and was, with the rest of that collection, incorporated in the British Museum in 1759.

Lord Fairfax has read it carefully, as his notes upon almost every page bear witness. The words, "ne reo credas," on the margin of the facsimile page, are his. There are also notes in two other hands, one of which is believed to be that of the transcriber of Hector Boece's Manuscript of Fordun's own work, now in the Library of Trinity College, Cambridge.

The Black Book of Paisley is quoted by the author of the "Extracta e Variis Chronicis Scocie," by Bishop Lesley, George Buchanan, and Archbishop Spottiswood. In 1685 it formed the subject of a lively controversy between Sir George Mackenzie and Stillingfleet, Bishop of Worcester, then Dean of St. Paul's, in the course of which the Lord Advocate propounded that charge of lese majesty against those who question the existence of the early kings who figure in the pages of our annalists, which is so humorously reproduced by Sir Walter Scott in the passage at arms betwixt Sir Arthur Wardour and Mr. Jonathan Oldbuck.

---

The Facsimile Page of the Black Book.

The facsimile page of the Black Book of Paisley given in Chapter X. of the present work is from the latter part of Chapter 13 and the beginning of Chapter 14 of Book XII., and is the *verso* of folio 199, which is the first sheet of quire 22.

The title of Chapter 13 is "Concerning the defeat at Slenach and the Death of Edward." After mentioning that, in the year 1307, John Comyn, Earl of Buchan, hearing that King Robert Bruce and his army were at Slenach*, started with a number of the nobility, both English and Scotch, whom he had along with him to intercept the King and offer battle, the narrative goes on to say that when they saw that Bruce was prepared to meet them they paused, and at last, overcome with shame, sent to him on Christmas-day proposing a truce, which was graciously granted. After the truce, the King boldly remained in the same place for eight days, but, says the historian:

*[Ubi magnam in]currebat infirmitatem ita quod in grabato vehebatur quocunque eum contingit removeri.* De hac fuga dicitur

M. semel et ter C. septem cum† his superadde
Natalique die pars Anglica victa pudore
De Slenach rediit Trengas de rege petiuit
Quas rex concessit clementer et inde recessit
Attamen intrepidus ibi persistit octo diebus.

Anno precedente circa festum Annunciacionis nostre domine Dominus Symon Frasar, Dominus Walterus Logan, milites et plures valentes armigeri et mediocres‡ capti fuerunt per quosdam § Scotos || regi Anglie adhaerentes. Qui¶ Symon ductus est Londoniis et diversis penis interemptus. Ceteri in Dunelmia in praesencia Eadwardi de Carnarwan filii regis Anglie tunc princeps** Wallie suspendentur.

Parti tunc†† regis Anglie prae ceteris et potenciores Scoti fuerunt Domini Johannes Comyn comes de Buchan‡‡ Willelmus Comyn et Johannes de Mowbre milites, qui adjunctis sibi Anglie

* Barbour calls it Slevach (The Bruce, Ed. Innes, lxvii, 15, page 196—Spalding Club), and it is identified by Dr. Joseph Robertson as Slioch, in the parish of Drumblate, in the Garrioch (Collections for the Shires of Aberdeen and Banff, p. 476).

† Goodall, tamen. ‡ G. adds. vernaculi. § G. adds, perfidos. || G. adds, tunc.

¶ The Black Book here corresponds with the Edinburgh MS. The Perth and Cupar MS., as Goodall points out, add a clause, which is also to be found in the "Extracta e Variis Chronicis," p. 133.

** G. gives principis, the correct word. †† G. places tunc *after* Anglie.

‡‡ The Black Book here agrees with the Edinburgh MS., and omits a clause given in the Cupar and Perth MSS.

post haec regem R. acriter invaserunt et in maximo prelio usque obitum regis Anglie constituerunt Qui anno Domini M° ccc° vij° in vigilia Sancte Johannis Baptiste de Lanercost ubi tactus fuit infirmitate in expedicione sua ad humiliandum regem nostrum Robertum et regnum Scocie ut* finaliter proposuit subjugandum versus Helme cultont† tendens pro aura puriore sanitate consequenda pridie ante festum translacionis Sancte Thome martiris in vehiculo suo recumbens apud Burgum Sabuli $^{\text{sine}}_{\text{sis}}$ nota penitencie miserabiliter expirauit. In eadem itineracione infirmabatur secum quidem miles Anglice nacionis Willelmus Banister nomine qui in‡ eadem nocte qua rex obiit in extasi raptus vidit Dominum suum Regem in spiritu uncatum a magna multitudine demonum circumseptum eidem cum maximo cachinno insultantium et dicentium. De morte Eadwi. primi post conquestum Anglie regis.

Qlr rex tyrans. a demonibus cruciatur.

En rex Edwardus debacchans ut leopardus.
Olim dum vixit populum Domini maleflixit.
Nobis vie talis comes ibis care sodalis.
Quo condempneris ut demonibus socieris.
Te sequimur voto prorsus tempore remoto.

Cum hoc flagellis et scorpionibus cedentes eum abigebant. Cantemus aliquantulum inquiunt huic misere anime debitum mortis canticum: quia filia est mortis et cibus ignis inextinguibilis, amica tenebrarum et inimica lucis, dicentes, En rex Eadwardus, &c.§ Ecce misera|| populus quem elegisti cum quibus arsura es sine fine, nutrix scandali, amatrix discordie pacis emula, caritatis inscia. Quare nunc non superbis? Quare non letaris? Ubi nunc est vanitas tua? Ubi vana letitia? Quid profuit tibi inanis gloria, brevis leticia, mundi potencia, carnis voluptas, false divicie, conquestus terre, magna familia et mala concupiscentia? Ubi iocus, ubi risus, ubi iactancia ubi arrogancia? De tanta leticia quanta tristicia, post tantam voluptatem tam gravis miseria, post tantam exaltacionem tam magna ruina, post tantas victorias tam immania tormenta: cito ¶ ignominia sit superbi gloria. Reo ne credas.

Cumque hujusmodi exprobacionibus et verberibus sibi spiritus maligni insultassent, aciem oculorum suorum ad me inquit miles trementem et exsanguem direxit innuens ut conjecturavi me sibi velle sicut solito in bellis opem ferre. Sed quia mecum neque vox neque sensus remansit terribilis oculis intuitus est me: ita ut dum vixero et illius recordavero nunquam letari potero. Cum hoc absorptus est in momento** infernali puteo voce lugubri eiulans et exclamans,

Heu cur peccavi, fallor, quare non bene cavi.
Heu cur peccavi, perit, et nihil est quod amavi.
Heu cur peccavi, video, quia littus araui.
Cum sudore gravi, mihimet tormenta paraui.

Ad se igitur miles de extasi reversus misit pro regis cubiculario, suo caro cognato, petens ab eo quomodo se habuit rex. Bene, ait iuvenis, incipit convalescere: haec sibi propterea insinuans ne si sibi infirmanti veritatem annunciaret nimiam tristiciam avunculo suo inferret. Non sic inquit miles, quia mortuus est, duplici heu morte preventus, et non est qui ei opem ferat ex omnibus caris eius.††

QUALITER WILLELMUS BANESTER TERRITUS VISIONE DESPEXIT MUNDUM C. XIIIJ.

Missum est‡‡ pro regis filio principe tunc Vallie. Quo protinus veniente exsequiis§§ patris sepulture dispositis Londonias corpus perducitur ubi nunc humatum requiescit; extales tunc||| et

* G. places ut after finaliter. † G. cultir. ‡ G. omits, in.
§ G. adds, ut supra. || G. adds, anima.
¶ G. inserts quam before cito. ** G. adds, in. †† G.—suis.
‡‡ G. adds interim. §§ G. adds que. ||| G. omits tunc.

intestina sua in Holmio subterrantur. *Hic in principio milicie sue bella movens Anglicos diris flagellis verberauit et suis nequiciis totum orbem perturbauit et crudelitate commovit. Passagiam terrae sanctae suo dolo impedivit; Scociam invasit et Scotos cum regno fraudulenter subegit: Valliam perfligavit, Johannem de Balliolo regem cum filio carceri mancipavit: ecclesias stravit, prelatos vinculavit et carcerali squalare quosdam extinxit: populum occidit et alia infinita mala perpetravit. Huic successit filius eius de Carnarvan Eadwardus ijs post conquestionem alias quintus.*

Versus de morti Patris.
M semel et ter C. septem numerabis in orbe,
Martire translato Thome sine fine beato.
In burgo Sabuli quo fixit marchia regal.
Eadwardus cecidit qui Scotos male cadit.
Viscera cum cerebro cujus tumulantur in Holmo.
Iste monens bella cedit Anglis dira flagella.
Colla superborum pede conculcavit eorum.
Orbem corrupit. Terram Sanctamque fefellit.
Scotos invasit regnum cum fraude subegit.
Ecclesias stravit, prelatos carcere clausit.
Occidit populum Christi, decime tulit aurum.
Cujus peccata toto sunt orbe notata.
Anglica* deflebit quando vastata iacebit.
Socia plaude manu pro funere regis avari.
Grates redde Deo, Roberto rege creato.
Quem vi virtutis castigat virga salutis.
Suis in orbe statum faciet Deus esse beatum.

Ho anno vij Angli combusserunt de Pasl.

Hoc† anno scis M° ccc° vij° Anglici combusserunt monasterium de Pasleto.

Dictus dominus Willelmus Banester de infirmitate convalescens quanto prius fervencius circa actus militares estuabat, tanto in virum alterum mutatus vehemencius animum ejus desiderio milicie spiritualis Christi attendebat. Territus enim in tantum fuit horrifica visione demonum, calamitosis exacerbacionibus et flagellacionibus in dominum suum regem fremencium, quod ruinosum mundum cum flore ejus omnino despexit, et ad emendacionis conversacionis solitariam vitam se contulit. Qui ut dicitur tanquam propheta ventura predixit et presentibus absencia annunciare promeruit.

Hic rex Eadwardus dictus xiij ab illo‡ comite Andegauie qui desponsavit sibi diabolam humana carne velatam.

The corresponding passage in Fordun's own work is in chapters 122 and 123 of Book V. of Dr. Skene's edition. In the foregoing transcript this is printed in italics so as to distinguish it from Bower's additions, which form the great bulk of the narrative.

The variations between Goodall's text and that of the Black Book are pointed out in the notes. The collation has been made with the printed text, and not with the Edinburgh College MS. itself, which does not seem to have been accurately transcribed in all cases.

Fordun and Bower relate the battle of Slevach prior to their account of Edward I.'s death, while Barbour places it after this event. See Kerr's History of Robert the Bruce, Vol. I., p. 331, et seq.

David Murray.

* G. Anglia. † G. adds in. ‡ G. adds, Galfrido.

## N.

### BULL OF POPE JULIUS III. CONFERRING THE ABBEY *IN COMMENDAM* ON LORD CLAUD HAMILTON.—DATED 5TH DECEMBER, 1553.

*(Now published for the first time.)*

"Julius Episcopus servus Servorum Dei Dilecto filio Claudio Hamyltoun clerico Glasguensis dioceseos Salutem et apostolicam benedictionem Romani Pontificis providentia circumspecta ecclesiis et monasteriis singulis que vacationis incommoda deplorare noscuntur ut Gubernatorum utilium fulciantur presidio prospicit diligenter ac personis ecclesiasticis quibuslibet ut in suis opportunitatibus aliquod suscipiant relevamen de subventionis auxilio prout decens est providet opportuno Dudum siquidem provisiones ecclesiarum et monasteriorum omnium apud Sedem apostolicam tunc vacantium et inantea vacaturorum ordinationi et dispositioni nostræ reservavimus Decernentes ex tunc irritum et inane si secus super hiis per quoscunque quavis auctoritate scienter vel ignoranter contingeret attemptari Postmodum vero Monasterio de Pasleto Cluniacensis ordinis Glasguensis dioceseos ex eo quod venerabilis frater noster Johannes Archiepiscopus Sanctiandree Regimini et administrationi illius cui tunc ex dispensatione apostolica preerat per dilectum filium Andream Oliphant clericum Sanctiandree dioceseos procuratorem suum ad hoc ab eo specialiter constitutum in manibus nostris sponte et libere cessit Nosque cessionem ipsam duximus admittendam apud sedem predictam vacante Nos tam eidem monasterio de cuius provisione nullus preter nos hac vice se intromittere potuit aut potest reservatione et decreto obsistentibus supradictis de Gubernatore utili et idoneo per quem circumspecte regi et salubriter dirigi valeat quam tibi asserenti te dilecti filii Nobilis viri Jacobi Ducis a Chastellerault qui et Comes Aranie et Charissime in Christo filie nostre Marie Scotorum Regine Illustris minorannis Tutor et Regni Scotie generalis Gubernator existit Natum et in Quartodecimo tue etatis Anno constitutum existere pro quo prefata Maria Regina seu dictus Jacobus Dux et Tutor ac Gubernator nobis super hoc per suas literas humiliter supplicavit apud nos de vite ac morum honestate aliisque probitatis et virtutum meritis multipliciter commendato ut commodius sustentari valeas de alicujus subventionis auxilio providere volentes Teque a quibusvis excommunicationis suspensionis et interdicti aliisque ecclesiasticis sententiis censuris et poenis a iure vel ab homine quavis occasione vel causa latis si quibus quomodolibet innodatus existis ad effectum presentium dumtaxat consequendum hac serie absolventes et absolutum fore censentes Necnon omnia et singula beneficia ecclesiastica cum cura et sine cura Secularia et quorumvis ordinum Regularia que et ex quibusvis concessionibus et dispensationibus apostolicis in titulum et commendam ac alias obtines et expectas necnon in quibus et ad que ius tibi quomodolibet competit quecumque quotcumque et qualiacumque sint eorumque fructuum reddituum et proventuum veros annuos valores ac concessionum et dispensationum huiusmodi tenores necnon quorumcumque fructuum reddituum et proventuum ecclesiasticorum loco pensionum annuarum ac quarumcumque pensionum annuarum super similibus fructibus redditibus et proventibus tibi reservatorum et assignatarum quantitates presentibus pro expressis habentes Monasterium predictum cuius et illi forsan annexorum fructus redditus et proventus ad Sexcentos Florenos auri in libris Camere apostolice taxati reperiuntur Sive premisso sive alio quovismodo quem etsi ex illo quevis generalis reservatio et in corpore iuris clausa resultet presentibus haberi volumus pro expresso aut ex alterius cuiuscumque persona seu per similem cessionem dicti Johannis Archiepiscopi vel cuiusvis alterius de illius regimine et administratione in Romana curia vel extra eam et coram notario publico et testibus sponte factam vacet etsi tanto tempore vacaverit quod eius provisio iuxta Lateranensis Statuta Concilii aut alias canonicas Sanctiones ad sedem predictam legitime devoluta et illa ex quavis causa ad sedem eandem specialiter vel generaliter pertineat ac de illo consistorialiter disponi consueverit seu debeat Et super illius regimine et administratione inter aliquos lis seu super illorum possessorio vel quasi molestia cuius statum presentibus haberi volumus pro expresso pendeat indecisa Dummodo tempore dationis presentium eidem Monasterio de Abbate provisum aut illud alteri commendatum canonice non existat cum annexis huiusmodi ac omnibus iuribus et pertinentiis suis tibi per te quoad vixeris et unacum omnibus et singulis compatibilibus beneficiis ecclesiasticis cum cura et sine cura Secularibus et Regularibus que in titulum et commendam ac alias obtines ut prefertur et in posterum obtinebis ac quibusvis fructibus redditibus et proventibus ecclesiasticis loco pensionum annuarum nec non quibusvis pensionibus annuis super similibus fructibus redditibus et proventibus tibi reservatis et assignatis ac in posterum reservandis et assignandis quos et quas percipis et percipies in futurum tenendum regendum et gubernandum Ita quod liceat tibi debitis et consuetis ipsius Monasterii et dilectorum filiorum Conventus ejusdem supportatis oneribus ac quarta si Abbatialis separata et seorsum a conventuali Si vero communis inibi mensa fuerit tertia parte omnium et singulorum fructuum redditưum et proventuum ipsius Monasterii in restaurationem illius fabrice seu ornamentorum emptionem vel fulcimentum aut pauperum alimoniam prout maior exigerit et suaserit necessitas omnibus aliis deductis oneribus annis singulis impartita de residuis illius fructibus redditibus et proventibus disponere et ordinare sicuti ipsius Monasterii Abbates qui pro tempore fuerunt de illis disponere et ordinare potuerunt seu et debuerunt Alienatione tamen quorumcumque bonorum immobilium et preciosorum mobilium ipsius Monasterii tibi penitus interdicta apostolica auctoritate commendamus Decernentes cum commenda huiusmodi cessare contigerit de ipso monasterio tamque de vacante per cessionem regiminis et administrationis huiusmodi in specie et non eo quo ante commendam ipsam vacabat modo in genere disponi debere ad effectum ut inde commendari nequeat Ac tecum ut Monasterium predictum vigore presentium recipere et in huiusmodi commendam quoad vixeris retinere libere et licite valeas auctoritate predicta tenore presentium de specialis dono gratie dispensamus Et ne in eventu in que prefatus Johannes Archiepiscopus cui et hodie omnimodam administrationem dicti Monasterii tam in spiritualibus quam in temporalibus prefata auctoritate reservavimus seu reservari concessimus antequam tu vigesimumtertium dicte etatis annum attingas ab humanis decedat dictum monasterium propter etatem tuam aliquibus in eisdem spiritualibus et temporalibus subjaceat detrimentis dilectum filium Priorem Claustralem ipsius Monasterii in illius administratorem in eisdem spiritualibus et temporalibus donec tu eundem Vigesimumtertium annum attigeris cum salario sibi per Ordinarium Loci constituendo auctoritate et tenore predictis constituimus et deputamus Curam regimen et administrationem ipsius Monasterii tibi et Administratione huiusmodi durante eidem priori in spiritualibus et temporalibus plenarie committendo Quocirca Venerabilibus Fratribus nostris Balneoregiensi et Dumblanensi ac Orchadensi Episcopis per apostolica scripta mandamus quantocius ipsi vel duo aut unus eorum per se vel alium seu alios tibi in adipiscenda possessione vel quasi regiminis et administrationis predictorum ac bonorum ipsius Monasterii auctoritate nostra assistentes faciat tibi a Conventualibus prefatis obedientia et reverentia congruentes necnon a dilectis filiis Vassallis et aliis subditis ipsius Monasterii consueta servitia et iura tibi ab eis integre exhiberi Contradictores per censuram ecclesiasticam appellatione postposita compressendo Non obstantibus defectu etatis premisse que ad hoc pateris in dicto Quartodecimo anno constitutus ut prefertur et Lateranensis Concilii ac felicis recordationis Bonifacii pp VIII predecessoris nostri et aliis apostolicis constitutionibus necnon Monasterii et ordinis predictorum et iuramento confirmatione apostolica vel quavis firmitate alia roboratis statutis et consuetudinibus privilegiis quoque indultis et literis apostolicis Monasterio et ordini predictis sub quibuscumque tenoribus et formis ac cum quibusvis et derogatorarum derogatoriis aliisque efficatioribus et insolitis clausis necnon irritantibus et aliis decretis per quoscumque

Romanos Pontifices predecessores nostros ac nos et sedem eandem ad quorumcumque et Regum vel aliorum principum instantia seu eorum contemplatione vel intuitu et motu proprio et ex certa scientia ac ex quibusvis causis et iteratis vicibus in genere vel in specie concessis approbatis et innovatis etsi in eis ac statutis predictis caveatur expresse quod predictum et alia eiusdem ordinis Monasteria quovismodo pro tempore Vacantia nullatenus aut non nisi ordinem ipsum expresse professis ac iuxta illius regularia instituta et forsan alias certo modo in illis expresso qualificatis personis ac de consensu Superiorum et Conventuum Monasteriorum eorundem commendari penitus et alias de illis et per sedem prefatam et cum statutorum ac privilegiorum et indultorum huiusmodi expressa derogatione quomodolibet pro tempore facte commende nullius sint roboris vel momenti Quodque eisdem statutis privilegiis et indultis nullatenus aut non nisi modis et formis ac cum expressionibus in eis contentis derogari possit et si illis derogari aliter contingat derogationes hujusmodi nemini suffragentur Quibus omnibus et si pro illorum sufficienti derogatione de illis eorumque totis tenoribus specialis specifica expressa et individua ac de verbo ad verbum non autem per clausas generales idem importantes mentio seu quevis alia expressio habenda aut aliqua exquisita forma servanda foret tenores huiusmodi ac si de verbo ad verbum nihil penitus omisso et forma in illis tradita observata inserti forent presentibus pro sufficienter expressis habentes illis alias in suo robore permansuris hac vice dumtaxat specialiter et expresse derogamus Quodque tu iuxta statuta ac privilegia et indulta predicta qualificatus non sis contrariis quibuscumque Aut si Conventui Vassallis et subditis prefatis vel quibusvis aliis communiter vel divisim ab eadem sit sede indultum quod interdici suspendi vel excommunicari non penitus per literas apostolicas non facientes plenam et expressam ac de verbo ad verbum de indulto huiusmodi mentionem Volumus autem quod propterea in dicto Monasterio divinus cultus ac solitus monachorum et ministrorum numerus nullatenus minuatur sed illius ac Conventus predictorum congrue supportentur onera antedicta Et quod antequam regimini et administrationi dicti Monasterii te in aliquo immisceas in manibus Episcoporum predictorum vel alicuius eorum nostro et Romane ecclesie nomine fidelitatis debite solitum prestes juramentum iuxta formam quam sub bulla nostra mittimus introclusam Ac formam iuramenti huiusmodi quod prestabis nobis de verbo ad verbum per tuas patentes literas tuo sigillo munitas per proprium Amicum quantocius destinare procures Et insuper ex nunc irritum decernimus et inane si secus super hiis a quoquam quavis auctoritate scienter vel ignoranter contigerit attemptari Datum Rome apud Sanctumpetrum anno Incarnationis dominice Millesimo quingentesimo quinquagesimotertio nonis Decembris Pontificatus nostri anno quarto.

# THE NEW CLUB SERIES.

Instituted, June, M.dccc.lxxvii.

PUBLISHER: ALEX. GARDNER, PAISLEY.

# REGULATIONS.

I. The Series shall be called the New Club Series.

II. The express object and design shall be to print in a uniform and handsome manner a Series of Works illustrative of the Antiquities, History, Literature, Poetry, Bibliography and Topography of Scotland in former times.

III. The number printed of each work shall be strictly limited to 100 copies, 86 in Post 4to, and 14 in Royal 4to.

IV. Two volumes shall be issued in each year.

V. When works printed are of very special importance or magnitude, and of general interest, in order to lessen the cost, which otherwise would fall upon the subscribers to the Series, the publisher reserves the liberty to throw off an impression for sale, but on paper inferior in size and quality to that used for the Series.

VI. A list of the works most suitable for publication shall be submitted to the subscribers from time to time, that they may have an opportunity of regulating the order in which such works shall be printed. Subscribers and others are invited to transmit to the publisher notices of ancient manuscripts, works, or tracts connected with the objects of the Series. All such communications shall be carefully entered in an Album to be kept for the purpose, together with the names of the senders. The contents of this Album shall, from time to time, be submitted to the subscribers.

VII. If any subscriber or private individual shall undertake to print any work of interest connected with the objects of the Series at his own expense, he shall receive the necessary supply of paper (to serve as a distinguishing mark of the origin and destination of such work) *free of charge*, it being understood that every subscriber shall receive a copy of such work. In order further to preserve uniformity, such work shall be printed at the same press as the regular issues of the Series.

VIII. That, unless in such special cases as are referred to in Rule V. no copies of any work printed in the Series shall, on any account whatever, be offered for sale by the publisher.

# THE NEW CLUB SERIES.

M.DCCC.LXXVIII.

---

LARGE PAPER.

1. **Her Most Gracious Majesty Queen Victoria.**
2. ROBERT BROWN, ESQ.
3. R. T. HAMILTON BRUCE, ESQ.
4. J. CLELAND BURNS, ESQ.
5. JAMES CALDWELL, ESQ.
6. THOMAS COATS, ESQ.
7. JAMES DICKIE, ESQ.
8. THE REV. JAMES DODDS.
9. WILLIAM GARDNER, ESQ.
10. J. GRAHAM GIRVAN, ESQ.
11. J. WYLLIE GUILD, ESQ.
12. ALEX. B. M'GRIGOR, ESQ., LL.D.
13. G. S. VEITCH, ESQ.
14. WILLIAM WILSON, ESQ.

---

ORDINARY COPIES.

1. **Her Most Gracious Majesty Queen Victoria.**
2. EDWARD ADAMSON, ESQ., M.D.
3. WALTER ALEXANDER, ESQ.
4. MAJOR-GENERAL A. STEWART ALLAN.
5. R. VANS-AGNEW, ESQ., M.P.
6. THOMAS BROOKE, ESQ., F.S.A.
7. JOHN BROWN, ESQ.
8. ROBERT BROWN, ESQ.
9. THE MARQUESS OF BUTE, K.T.
10. A. DUNCOMBE CAMPBELL, ESQ.
11. D. C. R. CARRICK-BUCHANAN, ESQ.
12. THE CHISHOLM.
13. JAMES COPLAND, ESQ., F.S.A. SCOT.
14. THOMAS CHORLTON, ESQ.
15. JAMES CLARK, ESQ.

16. JOHN CLARK, ESQ.
17. STEWART CLARK, ESQ.
18. WILLIAM CLARK, ESQ.
19. ARCHIBALD COATS, ESQ.
20. SIR PETER COATS, KNIGHT.
21. THOMAS COATS, ESQ.
22. ALEXANDER O. COWAN, ESQ.
23. JAMES COWAN, ESQ.
24. ROBERT CRAWFORD, ESQ.
25. LORD CURRIEHILL.
26. WILLIAM DOWNING, ESQ.
27. WALTER EASTON, ESQ.
28. THOMAS FALCONER, ESQ.
29. D. FISHER, ESQ.
30. JAMES GARDNER, ESQ.
31. WILLIAM GARDNER, ESQ.
32. WILLIAM GEMMILL, ESQ.
33. ROBERT GIBSON, ESQ.
34. THE EARL OF GLASGOW.
35. THE REV. ALEX. THOMSON GRANT.
36. GEORGE GRAY, ESQ.
37. ROBERT GUY, ESQ.
38. GEORGE GUTHRIE, ESQ., M.B.
39. THE REV. DUNBAR STEWART HALKETT, M.A.
40. WILLIAM HOLMS, ESQ., M.P.
41. ROBERT HOLT, ESQ.
42. HUGH HOPKINS, ESQ.
43. THE REV. WILLIAM A. KEITH.
44. WALTER KING, ESQ.
45. JAMES W. KNOX, ESQ.
46. JOHN KNOX, ESQ.
47. JAMES BARR LAMB, ESQ.
48. JOHN LOGAN, ESQ.
49. D. LYELL, ESQ.
50. ALEXANDER M'ALISTER, ESQ.
51. JAMES MACDONALD, ESQ.
52. H. MACFARLANE, ESQ.
53. WILLIAM S. MACKEAN, ESQ.
54. ALEXANDER MACKENZIE, ESQ.
55. MACMILLAN & Co., CAMBRIDGE.

56. JAMES D. MARWICK, ESQ.
57. JAMES MUIR, ESQ.
58. THE REV. WILLIAM M'INDOE.
59. JOHN M'INNES, ESQ.
60. JOHN MILLAR, ESQ.
61. JOHN MORISON, ESQ.
62. JAMES BARCLAY MURDOCH, ESQ.
63. DAVID MURRAY, ESQ.
64. DAVID MURRAY, ESQ., PAISLEY.
65. WILLIAM MURRAY, ESQ.
66. WILLIAM PATERSON, ESQ.
67. R. W. COCHRAN-PATRICK, ESQ., F.S.A. SCOT.
68. HUGH PENFOLD, ESQ., M.A.
69. A. RUSSELL POLLOCK, ESQ.
70. JOHN POLSON, ESQ.
71. REEVES & TURNER.
72. WILLIAM REID, JUN., ESQ.
73. DAVID SEMPLE, ESQ., F.S.A. SCOT.
74. HUGH H. SMILEY, ESQ.
75. JOHN GUTHRIE SMITH, ESQ.
76. JOHN STEWART, ESQ.
77. WILLIAM THOMSON, ESQ.
78. ROBERT THOMSON, ESQ.
79. WILLIAM WOTHERSPOON, ESQ.
80. ALEX. YOUNG, ESQ.
81. THE BODLEIAN LIBRARY, OXFORD, PER REV. H. O. COXE.
82. THE PAISLEY PHILOSOPHICAL INSTITUTION.
83. THE BOSTON PUBLIC LIBRARY, U.S.A., PER MESSRS. LOW & CO., LONDON.
84. THE LIBRARY OF CONGRESS, WASHINGTON, U.S.A., PER E. G. ALLEN, ESQ., LONDON.
85. THE MITCHELL LIBRARY, GLASGOW.
86. THE LIBRARY OF THE FACULTY OF PROCURATORS, GLASGOW.

Printed in the United Kingdom
by Lightning Source UK Ltd.
130980UK00001BA/6/A